Panama

Scott Doggett

Panama

1st edition

Published by
Lonely Planet Publications
Head Office: PO Box 617, Hawthorn, Vic 3122, Australia
Branches: 150 Linden St, Oakland, CA 94607, USA
10A Spring Place, London NW5 3BH, UK
1 rue du Dahomey, 75011 Paris, France

Printed by
Colorcraft Ltd, Hong Kong

Photographs by
Front cover: Tom Boyden, leaf-footed bug *(coreidae)*

Amado Araúz	Library of Congress
Tom Boyden	Alfredo Maiquez
Scott Doggett	James C Simmons / Dave G
Dave G Houser	Houser Stock Photo
Instituto Panameño de Turismo	Joe Viesti - The Viesti
Daniel Komer / D Donne	Collection, Inc.
Bryant Stock	Stuart GR Warner W

Published
January 1999

Although the author and publisher have tried to make the information as accurate as possible, they accept no responsibility for any loss, injury or inconvenience sustained by any person using this book.

National Library of Australia Cataloguing in Publication Data

Doggett, Scott.
Panama.

1st ed.
Includes index.
ISBN 0 86442 566 X

1. Panama – Guidebooks. I. Title.

917.287

text & maps © Lonely Planet 1999
photos © photographers as indicated 1999
climate charts compiled from information supplied by Patrick J Tyson, © Patrick J Tyson, 1999

Scott Doggett

Scott's interest in Latin America became personal when, in 1983, as a recent graduate of the University of California at Berkeley, he moved to El Salvador to work as a photojournalist. His initial career was followed by postgraduate study at Stanford University; reporting assignments for United Press International in Los Angeles, Pakistan and Afghanistan; and, most recently, seven years as an editor for the *Los Angeles Times* (he and his wife, Annette, currently cowrite a weekly business column for the newspaper). During his free time, Scott travels and writes about his adventures for newspapers and magazines. He is coauthor of Lonely Planet's *Mexico* and an author and coeditor of *Travelers' Tales Brazil*. He has also written guidebooks on Los Angeles and Las Vegas. At the time this book went to press, Scott was finishing work on Lonely Planet's *Dominican Republic & Haiti* and was preparing to write Lonely Planet's *Nicaragua*. If you have just returned from Panama and would like to apprise him of a new attraction or service that he may be unaware of, Scott would like to hear from you. His email address is sdoggett@aol.com.

From the Author

This book is dedicated to my parents, and to Wendy, Victoria and Annette.

Quite a number of people assisted me with this labor of love. To you all, a heartfelt thank you. In Panama, Ricardo de la Espriella III offered me invaluable insight into his country, and on many occasions he took me to wonderful places I might otherwise have missed. Ricardo's better half, Joanne, and photographer and historian Stuart GR Warner W read early drafts of the introductory chapters and offered many valuable suggestions on how I might improve them. Adrienne Samos, the director of *Talingo,* the Sunday arts supplement of *La Prensa,* Panama's premier newspaper, likewise offered excellent suggestions concerning the general-information chapters. Adrienne also introduced me to Panama's rich art scene and deserves credit for much of the information appearing in the Arts section of the Facts about Panama chapter. Roberto Sarmiento, administrative librarian of the Panama Canal Commission's Technical Resources Center, was of tremendous help to me in locating historical documents I was unable to find elsewhere. Professor Vladimir Berrío-Lemm, the country's foremost expert on Panamá La Vieja, taught me a great deal about the early history of Panama City. Despite my criticisms of Panama's department of tourism, several of its employees went well beyond the call of duty in assisting me with many and varied requests. Chief among these folks is the incomparable Ingunn Méndez, to whom I am extremely grateful. Many thanks also to Omar Dubos and David Urriola, who never steered me wrong.

At the US office of Lonely Planet Publications, there is a team of highly skilled professionals who, by the nature of their jobs, don't receive a fraction of the credit they deserve. They are going to receive some here. Over the years I've had the good fortune of seeing my work adroitly edited by staffers at the *Los Angeles Times, The Washington Post, The Miami Herald* and other leading US newspapers. I can sincerely say that few have demonstrated the talent I've seen in Laura Harger, the editor of this book. In the publishing business a really terrific editor is said to have the eyes of a hawk; Laura seems to have the eyes of 10 hawks, catching discrepancies and removing ambiguities with remarkable skill. *And* she's as amiable as she is talented. My sombrero is also off to Eric Kettunen, who does a superlative job of managing the company's editorial and business operations for the Americas; senior editor Carolyn Hubbard, whose humor and voice of reason have been a godsend to me on more than one occasion; production manager Scott Summers; cartographers Tracey Croom and Patrick Huerta; illustrators Hayden Foell, Jim Swanson and Hugh D'Andrade; and designers Hugh D'Andrade and Rini Keagy – the talented people who created, selected and/or shaped everything in this book except the text. To Joslyn Leve and Erica Pelino, who answer the phones at LP Central and who have every right to tell me to stop calling so much but instead are friendly every time – thank you, thank you and thank you. Of course, none of us would be doing what we're doing if our books weren't reaching our esteemed readers; I raise my margarita glass in salute to everyone in the marketing and sales departments.

From the Publisher

This book was edited and indexed by Laura Harger, with oversight from Carolyn Hubbard and Kate Hoffman, and proofed by Carolyn Keating, Kim Zetter and Carolyn Hubbard. Tracey Croom and Patrick Huerta drew and corrected the maps and designed the book with guidance from Richard Wilson and with oversight from Alex Guilbert and Scott Summers. Joslyn Leve helped with map proofing and reviewed layout. Rini Keagy designed the cover, and Hayden Foell, Jim Swanson and Hugh D'Andrade drew the illustrations.

This Book

Scott Doggett researched and wrote this 1st edition of *Panama*. Nancy Keller researched and wrote the information on Panama that appeared in Lonely Planet's *Central America on a shoestring* (3rd edition), and some of her observations and comments were used in these pages. In addition, some general information was drawn from Rob Rachowiecki's *Costa Rica* (3rd edition).

The Panamá La Vieja map appearing in the Panama City chapter was prepared from a map provided by Professor Vladimir Berrío-Lemm.

Warning & Request

Things change – prices go up, schedules change, good places go bad and bad places go bankrupt – nothing stays the same. So, if you find things better or worse, recently opened or long since closed, please tell us and help make the next edition even more accurate and useful.

We value all the feedback we receive from travelers. A small team reads and acknowledges every letter, postcard and email, and ensures that every morsel of information finds its way to the appropriate authors, editors and publishers. Everyone who writes to us will find his or her name in the next edition of the appropriate guide and will also receive a free subscription to our quarterly newsletter, *Planet Talk*. The very best contributions will be rewarded with a free Lonely Planet guide.

Excerpts from your correspondence may appear in new editions of this guide, in *Planet Talk* or in the Postcards section of our website – so please let us know if you don't want your letter published or your name acknowledged.

Contents

Map Legend

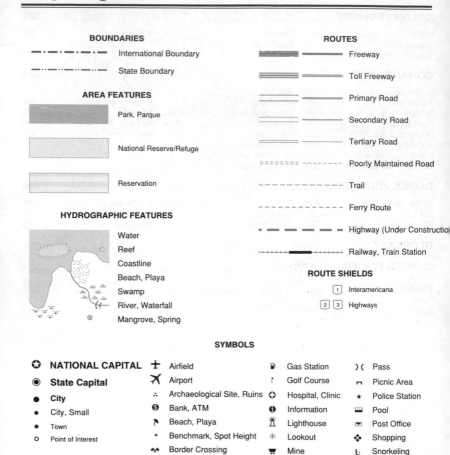

BOUNDARIES

- International Boundary
- State Boundary

AREA FEATURES

- Park, Parque
- National Reserve/Refuge
- Reservation

HYDROGRAPHIC FEATURES

- Water
- Reef
- Coastline
- Beach, Playa
- Swamp
- River, Waterfall
- Mangrove, Spring

ROUTES

- Freeway
- Toll Freeway
- Primary Road
- Secondary Road
- Tertiary Road
- Poorly Maintained Road
- Trail
- Ferry Route
- Highway (Under Construction)
- Railway, Train Station

ROUTE SHIELDS

- ⬡1 Interamericana
- ⬡2 ⬡3 Highways

SYMBOLS

✪ NATIONAL CAPITAL	✚ Airfield	Gas Station	)(Pass
◉ State Capital	✈ Airport	Golf Course	Picnic Area
● City	∴ Archaeological Site, Ruins	☉ Hospital, Clinic	★ Police Station
● City, Small	⑤ Bank, ATM	➊ Information	Pool
● Town	Beach, Playa	🎍 Lighthouse	Post Office
○ Point of Interest	× Benchmark, Spot Height	※ Lookout	❖ Shopping
	✦ Border Crossing	Mine	♭ Snorkeling
	Cathedral, Catedral	▲ Mission	Stately Home
■ Hotel, B&B	Cave	▲ Monument	Surfing
▲ Campground	† Church, Iglesia	▲ Mountain	☎ Telephone
RV Park	Dive Site	Museum	Tomb, Mausoleum
Shelter, Refugio	Embassy, Consulate	Observatory	Trailhead
▼ Restaurant	Fishing	← One-Way Street	Transportation
Bar (Place to Drink)	Footbridge	▲ Park, Parque	Volcano
Cafe	Garden	Parking	Zoo

Note: Not all symbols displayed above appear in this book.

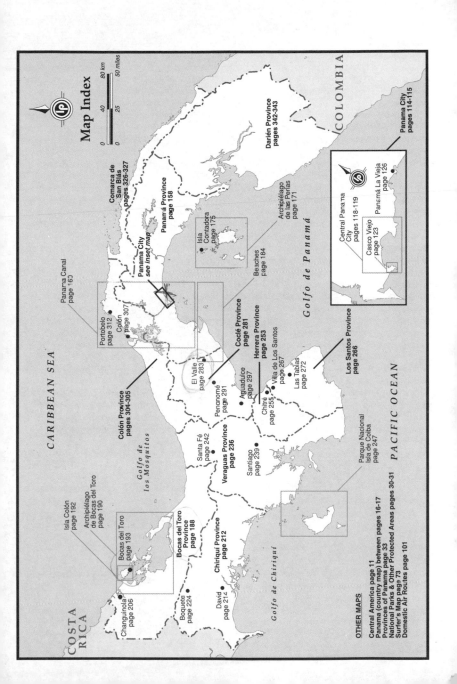

Map Index

Central America page 11
Panama (country map) between pages 16-17
Provinces of Panama page 33
National Parks & Other Protected Areas pages 30-31
Surfer's Map page 73
Domestic Air Routes page 101

OTHER MAPS

CARIBBEAN SEA

COSTA RICA

COLOMBIA

PACIFIC OCEAN

Golfo de los Mosquitos

Golfo de Chiriquí

Golfo de Panamá

Comarca de San Blás pages 326-327

Darién Province pages 342-343

Panama Canal page 160

Panamá Province page 158

Portobelo page 312

Colón page 307

Colón Province pages 304-305

Panama City *see inset map*

El Valle page 283

Penonomé page 291

Aguadulce page 297

Coclé Province page 281

Chitré page 255

Villa de Los Santos page 267

Las Tablas page 272

Herrera Province page 253

Los Santos Province page 266

Santa Fé page 242

Santiago page 239

Veraguas Province page 236

Parque Nacional Isla de Coiba page 247

Isla Contadora page 175

Beaches page 184

Archipiélago de las Perlas page 171

Isla Colón page 192

Archipiélago de Bocas del Toro page 190

Bocas del Toro page 193

Bocas del Toro Province page 188

Chiriquí Province page 212

Changuinola page 206

Boquete page 224

David page 214

Central Panama City pages 118-119

Casco Viejo page 123

Panamá La Vieja page 126

Panama City pages 114-115

80 km
50 miles
40
25
0
0

Introduction

Panama offers some of the finest birding, snorkeling and deep-sea fishing in the Americas, but few foreigners know the country for more than its canal or the scandalous regime of General Manuel Noriega during the late 1980s. Today's Panama, however, is a proud nation that respects its seven Indian tribes and its Spanish heritage and embraces visitors so fervently that it's difficult to leave without feeling that you're in on a secret the rest of the traveling world has yet to discover.

At the southern end of Central America, Panama is an 800km land bridge where the wildlife of North and South America meets and intermingles. It is largely because of this geographical position that Panama is home to a recorded 940 bird species – more than in all of North America. Panama is the only country where jaguars and pumas prowl a short drive from the capital, and yet the country also has vast jungles containing not a single road. Panama has some of the most remote and some of the most accessible rainforest in the world.

This country, whose Indian name means 'abundance of fish,' has somehow evaded the tourist's radar screen despite having much more to offer than its wildly popular western neighbor, Costa Rica. Tour guides in Panama are fond of saying that in Costa Rica 20 birders would be lucky to see one resplendent quetzal, while in Panama one birder might see 20 quetzals. There's truth in what they say: The crush of tourists who pass through Costa Rica's national parks tends to scare off wildlife, while in Panama tourists are as scarce as harpy eagles and wildlife abounds.

There are rivers in Panama where rafters can ride 20 sets of rapids in a single afternoon. There are scores of picturesque palm-lined beaches with hardly a human on them. There are several peaks from which travelers can see the Pacific Ocean over one shoulder and the Caribbean Sea over the other. There are mangroves on both Panamanian coasts that transport imaginative souls to times when dinosaurs roamed the earth. In fact, the dinosaurs' closest living relative – the

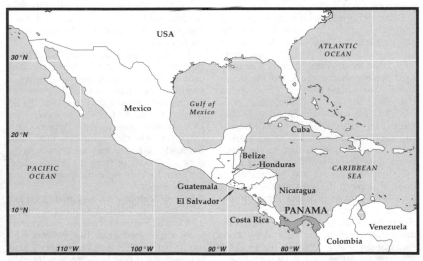

crocodile – still lurks in many Panamanian mangroves.

Unfortunately, deforestation is continuing outside and within Panama's 12 national parks. The governmental agency tasked with protecting the country's natural resources as often as not does little to defend them. Many are the stories of logging concessions awarded in environmentally sensitive areas. Many are the stories of park rangers doing nothing while encroachment on 'protected' lands goes on about them. Despite the size of Panama's national parks, such actions threaten their long-term survival. But at least for now, Panama's jungles are as biologically rich as any in Central America and can thrill even the most jaded naturalist.

There are 1518 islands off the coasts of Panama and, because the coasts are less than an hour's drive apart, you can easily spend the morning snorkeling in the Caribbean and the afternoon swimming in the Pacific. Some of the best snorkeling and scuba diving in Central America can be found near Panama's Isla de Coiba, which is both a national park and home to a penal colony. If you stay on Coiba, your boatman will likely be a tough-looking policeman and your cook a soft-spoken prisoner.

Divers who are looking for something completely different ought to consider plunging into the Panama Canal, home to a submerged train and dredging equipment abandoned by the French nearly a century ago. Surfers should check out the occasional world-class surf at Playa Santa Catalina in Veraguas Province, which periodically hosts waves with 5m faces. Orchid lovers can see some of the world's largest and smallest in Santa Fé, an easygoing town set amid spectacular jungle three hours' drive from Playa Santa Catalina.

Fishing enthusiasts will be pleased to know that more deep-sea fishing records have been broken in Bahía Piña, off the Pacific coast of Panama, than anywhere else in the world. You can see sea turtles by the dozen much of the year along both Panamanian coasts, although the Indians' penchant for eating them is taking a heavy toll. Cana, at the heart of Parque Nacional Darién, is birding nirvana, where four species of macaw – including great greens and blue-and-yellows – shriek across the sky with astonishing frequency.

As for culture, Panama beams with it. The Península de Azuero in central Panama is like a slice of Spain dropped into the Americas, with traditional Spanish festivals celebrated often and with great gusto. And unlike some places where locals put on a show for tourists, on the Azuero the people perform for themselves. The country's Indian tribes are scattered across the country and vary considerably, but they all share one thing – a desire to maintain their traditions. They are a pleasure to encounter on an island or in a jungle, as long as you don't hound them with cameras or otherwise behave badly.

Historically, Panama is a story of riches – of Peruvian gold carried by Spaniards across the isthmus from Panama City on the Pacific coast to Nombre de Dios and (later) to nearby Portobelo on the Caribbean coast, where the precious metal was stored until it could be shipped to Spain. Huge forts were built from blocks of rock and coral to protect the gold from marauders, but the bastions failed to deter pirates. Ruins from those days of yore, complete with cannons and moats, make for fascinating touring.

And then there's the canal. Its construction by the USA during the early 20th century is, like the pyramids of Egypt, a stunning testament to what humans can accomplish. Almost 90 years after the SS *Ancon* became the first ship to traverse the lock-and-lake waterway, the Panama Canal remains one of the engineering marvels of the world. Whether they are seen from the deck of a boat or from a viewing stand, the great locks of the canal leave no visitor unimpressed.

It is difficult to write an introduction to a guidebook on Panama without sounding a bit like a tourism official; the country truly is an unpolished gem. But Panama isn't tourist-perfect. Because the country's tourism industry is now in its infancy, travelers expecting to find five-star accommodations a stone's throw from a pristine rainforest will be disappointed. And reaching destinations can be a pain; for starters, the country could do with a few thousand more road signs. Speaking of roads, driving in Panama City is not for the faint of heart; it's never easy due to dense traffic, undisciplined drivers and a shortage of traffic signals.

But if you have ever found yourself saying, 'Oh, you should have seen this place 10 years ago, before it was overrun with tourists,' chances are you would leave Panama today feeling you'd visited at just the right time. As John le Carré writes in his novel *The Tailor of Panama,* 'We've got everything God needed to make paradise. Great farming, beaches, mountains, wildlife you wouldn't believe, put a stick in the ground you get a fruit tree, people so beautiful you could cry.' It's the voice of a fictional character, but it's also the attitude of most Panamanians, who take great pride in their country. As well they should.

Facts about Panama

HISTORY
Pre-Columbian History

Archaeological evidence shows that people have been living in Panama for at least 11,000 years and that agriculture arose here as early as 1500 BC. Panama's first peoples lived beside the Pacific and fished in mangroves and estuaries, just as many of the country's Indians do today. Archaeological sites dating from 5000 BC contain remains of large fish, but they lack obvious fishing artifacts, such as hooks and sinkers. This suggests the people probably caught fish using traps near shore.

Fishing was still the main occupation of the Indians as late as 1500 BC. By this time the Pacific communities were taking larger numbers of very small fish that swim farther from shore. Instead of using shore traps, they were probably using gill nets tossed from boats. By 400 BC villagers living 10 to 20km inland were using marine fish from a wide variety of habitats, suggesting that the coastal villages were each catching particular types of fish and trading them. Evidence also shows that the fishermen were going farther out than before.

By 1600 AD European colonists had introduced new methods of fishing, but the ancient techniques used by the region's first inhabitants have continued to be used to the present day. Given the tremendous importance fish have had in the lives of isthmians since humans arrived 13 millenniums ago, it seems only fitting that the country's name is an Indian one meaning 'abundance of fish.'

Archaeologists divide pre-Columbian Panama into three distinct cultural zones – western, central and eastern – based on the types of pottery and other artifacts found at various archaeological sites. None of these zones was culturally isolated; evidence of trading shows ties not only among the zones but between them and Colombia, other parts of Central America and even Mexico and Peru. In addition to commercial trade and fishing, the economies of all of Panama's early societies were based on extensive agriculture and hunting. It is believed that these societies were hierarchical and headed by chiefs, and that war played a significant role.

In western Panama on the slopes of the Barú volcano, Barriles is an important archaeological center where finds have included unusual life-size stone statues of human figures, some with one figure sitting astride another's shoulders. Giant *metates* – flat stone platforms that were used for grinding corn – have also been found here.

Archaeologists estimate that the early civilization represented at Barriles was established around the 4th or 5th century BC when settlers arrived from the west (now Costa Rica). This culture came to an abrupt end when Volcán Barú erupted violently in the 5th century AD. Later, the region was inhabited again, this time by two different groups whose archaeological remnants include a great variety of distinctive types of pottery.

Between Penonomé and Natá in the central region, Sitio Conte is an important archaeological zone and ancient ceremonial center where thousands of pieces of pottery, as well as tombs and many other items of interest, have been unearthed.

Another central archaeological zone, Cerro Juan Díaz, near Villa de Los Santos on the Península de Azuero, is believed to have been inhabited from about 300 BC until the time of the Spanish conquest. Presently being excavated by the Smithsonian Institution, it is yielding many items of interest, such as evidence that pottery made here was traded for pre-Columbian goods, including gold. Pre-Columbian pottery and other artifacts have also been found at sites in Parque Nacional Sarigua on the Península de Azuero.

Not as much is known about the early peoples of the eastern region of Panama, because archaeologists have yet to conduct extensive studies there. Most knowledge of the area's history and its peoples' hierarchical, tribal social structure has been gleaned from accounts by the first Spanish explorers, who arrived in the Darién region of present-day eastern Panama and western Colombia during the 16th century.

Gold objects appeared in Panama suddenly, with a sophisticated and completely developed technology. Metallurgy was practiced in Peru as early as the 2nd century BC; by the 1st century AD it had arrived in Panama. Archaeologists believe it probably arrived from the Sinú, Quimbaya and Tairona regions of Colombia, with the Urabá area as the point of contact and interchange.

Colombia, Panama and Costa Rica all became metallurgic provinces, and objects of gold and other metals were exchanged all the way from Mesoamerica to the Andes. Gold was made into ornaments (necklaces, nose rings and so on) and animal, human and other figures, and it was also used for ceremonial purposes; it probably did not connote wealth to the Indians in the same way that it did to the Spaniards.

Spanish Colonization

When Spaniards first arrived on the isthmus of Panama in the early 16th century, they found it inhabited by various indigenous peoples. The population may have been as large then as it is now, but it was rapidly decimated by European diseases and Spanish swords. Several dozen Indian tribes lived in the region at the time of the Spaniards' arrival, but only seven of these exist today: the Kuna, the Ngöbe-Buglé (also known as the Guaymís), the Emberá, the Wounaan, the Bokatá, the Bribri and the Teribe (also known as the Naso).

The first Europeans in the area were led by the Spanish explorer Rodrigo de Bastidas, who sailed along Panama's Caribbean coast in 1501 with Vasco Núñez de Balboa and Juan de la Cosa as his first mates. The following year, Christopher Columbus sailed along the coast on his fourth and final New World voyage. An attempt by him to establish a colony at the mouth of the Río Belén in 1503 ended when he fled an imminent Indian attack.

In 1510 Diego de Nicuesa, attempting to do what Columbus couldn't, was also driven by Indians and hunger from the Río Belén. Leading a small fleet with 280 starving men aboard, the weary explorer looked upon a protected bay 23km east of what is now Portobelo and exclaimed: '¡Paremos aqui, en nombre de Dios!' ('Let us stop here, in the name of God!') Thus was named in advance the town of Nombre de Dios, one of the first Spanish settlements on the continental New World. It was soon abandoned, then was resettled in 1519, and it was for many decades thereafter the main Caribbean port for commerce along the isthmus, as well as the beginning of the trail leading to the city of Panamá on the Pacific side. Nombre de Dios was finally abandoned in 1597 by order of King Félipe II of Spain.

Nearly 300km southeast of Nombre de Dios, on the eastern side of the Golfo de Urabá in what is now Colombia, Spanish explorer Alonso de Ojeda founded San Sebastian de Urabá in 1510. Ojeda named the settlement in honor of the arrow-martyred saint whose protection the harried captain craved against the venomous darts of the natives. But the saint's protection was ineffective, and all the colonists could do was await reinforcements, which Ojeda had requested from Hispaniola.

When the rescue ship eventually reached San Sebastian, the fort and 30 houses that Ojeda had erected were in ashes and his men slain. Several of the rescue party came across Indians while foraging and were themselves struck with envenomed arrows. They died tortuous deaths that terrified the remaining would-be rescuers, who included Balboa.

Balboa had sailed with Bastidas and told the frightened men around him that the western shore of the Golfo de Urabá was fertile and rich with gold, and though the Indians there were warlike, they did not use poisoned arrows. This was great news to their ears, and the conquistadors eagerly sailed to the western side of the gulf, to the mouth of the Río Atrato. The new settlement, within present-day Colombia, was named Santa María la Antigua del Darién.

In time Indians told Balboa of a large sea and a wealthy, gold-producing civilization – almost certainly referring to the Inca empire of Peru – across the mountains of the isthmus. Balboa subsequently scaled the mountains and on September 26, 1513, became the first European to set eyes upon the Pacific, claiming it and the lands it touched for the king of Spain. He named the ocean the Mar del Sur (South Sea) because he had crossed Panama from north to south. The Caribbean was likewise known as the Mar del Norte (North Sea) for many years.

In 1519 a cruel and vindictive man named Pedro Arias de Ávila (or Pedrarias, as many of his contemporaries called him) founded the city of Panamá on the Pacific side, near where Panama City stands today. The governor is also remembered for ordering the beheading of Balboa in 1517 on a trumped-up charge of treason and for ordering murderous attacks against Indians, whom he roasted alive or fed to dogs when opportunity permitted. Panamá became an important Spanish settlement, commercial center and the springboard for further explorations, including the conquest of Peru and expeditions north into Central America. The ruins of this old settlement, now known as Panamá La Vieja, can still be seen today.

Goods from Panamá and Peru were transported across the isthmus by foot to the town of Venta de Cruces, and then by boat from there to Nombre de Dios via the Río Chagres. This route was called the Sendero Las Cruces (Las Cruces Trail, also known as the Camino de Cruces), vestiges of which can still be found. Goods moved between the two ports until late in the 16th century, when Nombre de Dios was destroyed by the English pirate Sir Francis Drake. The small nearby bay of Portobelo then became the chief Caribbean connection. The Sendero Las Cruces continued to be used until the mid-19th century, when the Panama Railroad was completed.

Also used to transport goods across the isthmus during the early Spanish days was El Camino Real (King's Highway), a series of trails that linked Panamá with Portobelo. Indeed, from the late 16th century until the advent of the Americans in 1904, El Camino Real was the only semblance of a roadway across the isthmus. Peruvian gold and other natural products were brought to Portobelo along El Camino Real by mule train from Panamá. The products were then held for an annual trading fair that lured Spanish galleons laden with European goods.

All this wealth concentrated in one small bay naturally attracted English, French, Dutch and other pirates who were plying the Caribbean at the time. The Spaniards built large stone fortresses to try to ward off attack; the ones at Portobelo and at Fuerte San Lorenzo, at the mouth of the Río Chagres, can still be visited today.

These fortifications weren't enough, however. In 1671 the Welsh buccaneer Sir Henry Morgan overpowered Fuerte San Lorenzo, sailed up the Río Chagres and crossed the isthmus. His forces sacked the city of Panamá, making off with its entire treasure and arriving back on the Caribbean coast with 200 mules loaded with loot. The city burned during Morgan's stay there, but no one knows for certain whether it was his men or fleeing Spaniards who put it to the torch. The town was rebuilt a few years later on a cape several kilometers west of its original site, on the spot where the Casco Viejo district of Panama City is today.

In 1739 Portobelo was destroyed by British Admiral Edward Vernon, finally forcing Spain to abandon the Panamanian crossing in favor of sailing the long way around Cape Horn to the western coast of South America. Panama declined in importance and it eventually became part of the Viceroyalty of Nueva Andalucía, later called Nueva Granada and thereafter Colombia.

Top Left: Chief of the Teribe Indians
Bottom Left: Península de Azuero girl in traditional
dress

Top Right: Shredding coconut, Isla Grande
Bottom Right: Campesino in Panama hat near Villa de
Los Santos

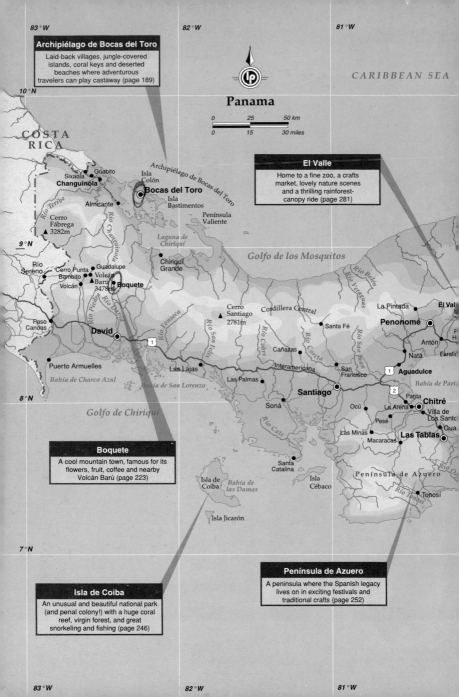

Archipiélago de Bocas del Toro

Laid-back villages, jungle-covered islands, coral keys and deserted beaches where adventurous travelers can play castaway (page 189)

El Valle

Home to a fine zoo, a crafts market, lovely nature scenes and a thrilling rainforest-canopy ride (page 281)

Boquete

A cool mountain town, famous for its flowers, fruit, coffee and nearby Volcán Barú (page 223)

Isla de Coiba

An unusual and beautiful national park (and penal colony!) with a huge coral reef, virgin forest, and great snorkeling and fishing (page 246)

Península de Azuero

A peninsula where the Spanish legacy lives on in exciting festivals and traditional crafts (page 252)

Panama

0   25   50 km
0   15   30 miles

CARIBBEAN SEA

COSTA RICA

Guabito
Sixaola
Changuinola
Archipiélago de Bocas del Toro
Isla Colón
Bocas del Toro
Almirante
Isla Bastimentos
Península Valiente

Río Teribe
Cerro Fábrega 3282m
Río Changuinola

Laguna de Chiriquí

Golfo de los Mosquitos

Chiriquí Grande

Río Belén
Río Veraguas

Río Sereno
Cerro Punta   Guadalupe
Bambito   Volcán   Barú 3478m
Volcán   Boquete

Paso Canoas

David

Río Piedra   Río Chiriquí

Río Fonseca

Cerro Santiago 2781m

Cordillera Central

La Pintada   El Val

Penonomé

Santa Fé
Río San Juan
Antón
Natá   Faralló
F H

Puerto Armuelles

Bahía de Charco Azul

Las Lajas

Río San Félix

Las Palmas

Interamericana

Cañazas

Río Cobre

Río Cobre

San Francisco

Aguadulce

Bahía de Pari

Bahía de San Lorenzo

Golfo de Chiriquí

Soná

Santiago

Ocú   La Arena
Pesé   Parita
Chitré
Villa de Los Santo
Gua

Río Cate

Río San

Las Minas
Macaracas

Las Tablas

Santa Catalina

Isla de Coiba   Bahía de las Damas

Isla Cébaco

Península de Azuero

Río O

Tonosí

Isla Jicarón

Río Tonosí

Isla Barro Colorado

A world-renowned biological reserve with lush rainforest in the midst of the Panama Canal (page 164)

Archipiélago de San Blás

An off-the-beaten-track chain of lovely Caribbean isles ruled by Kuna Indians (page 324)

Panama City

The country's lively capital, with vibrant nightlife, fascinating historic sites, myriad restaurants and splendid shopping (page 113)

Panama Canal

One of the world's engineering marvels, bordered by beautiful parklands (page 157)

Parque Nacional Darién

Panama's most spectacular park, offering sandy beaches, rocky coasts, mangroves, marshes, mountains and fantastic bird watching (page 347)

80°W · 79°W · 78°W · 10°N · 9°N · 8°N · 7°N

Isla Grande · Nombre de Dios · El Porvenir · Wichub-Walá · Archipiélago de San Blás
Portobelo · Cartí · Río Sidra · Corazón de Jesús
Bahía de Portobelo · Nusatupo · Isla Tupile
Colón · Río Gatún · Río Chagres · Serranía de San Blás
Cerro Azul · El Llano
Chepo · Río Chepo · Río Cañazas
PANAMA CITY · Serranía de Majé · Ipetí · Higuéronal · Caledonia
a Chorrera · Tortí · Serranía del Darién · Puerto Obaldía
Interamericana · Isla Taboga · Las Aguas Frías · Río Chucunaque · Capurganá
Bahía de Chame · Punta Chame · Santa Fé · R Membrillo
Bahía de Panamá · Isla Contadora · Meteti
San Miguel · Isla del Rey · La Palma · Río Tuira
Isla San Telmo · El Real · Río Pucuro
Archipiélago de las Perlas · Ensenada de Garachiné · Sambú · Yaviza · Río Yape
Golfo de Panamá · Garachiné · Serranía del Sapo · Río Mogué · Río Sambú · Cana
Parque Nacional Darién · Río Balsas
Bahía Piña · Jaqué
Pedasí
COLOMBIA

PACIFIC OCEAN

Elevation

1800m
1350m
900m
360m
180m
Sea Level

SCOTT DOGGETT

TOM BOYDEN

TOM BOYDEN

TOM BOYDEN

Top: Abandoned mine train in the jungle at Cana, Darién Province

Bottom Left: The resplendent quetzal, a spectacular find for bird watchers in Panama

Middle Right: Blooming bromeliad

Bottom Right: Well-camouflaged praying mantis, Isla Barro Colorado

Independence

In 1821 Colombia, including Panama, gained its independence from Spain. Panama joined Gran Colombia, which included Bolivia, Colombia, Ecuador, Peru and Venezuela, forming the united Latin American nation that had long been the dream of Simón Bolívar. Later Gran Colombia split up, but Panama remained a province of Colombia.

Panama Railroad

From the moment that the world's major powers learned that the isthmus of Panama was the narrowest point between the Atlantic and Pacific Oceans, they focused attention on the region.

In 1846 Colombia signed a treaty permitting the USA to construct a railway across the isthmus. The treaty guaranteed the USA the right of free transit across the isthmus and the right to protect the line with military force. This was a time of great political turbulence in Panama. Construction of the railroad began in 1850 and concluded in 1855; during that time Panama had 20 governors.

The California gold rush of 1848, which resulted in thousands of people traveling from the East Coast of the USA to the West Coast via Panama (to avoid hostile Indians living in the central states), helped to make the railway a profitable venture, and it also spurred efforts to construct an interoceanic canal across Central America.

Panama Canal & the French

The idea of a canal across the isthmus was first broached in 1524, when King Charles V of Spain ordered that a survey be undertaken to determine the feasibility of constructing such a waterway. In 1878 the Colombian government awarded a contract to build a canal to Lucien NB Wyse, who sold the concession to the French diplomat Ferdinand de Lesseps, who was then basking in his success as the contractor-builder of the Suez Canal.

Lesseps' Compagnie Universelle du Canal Interocéanique began work in 1881. Lesseps was determined to build a sea-level canal alongside the interoceanic railway, but the project proved more difficult than anyone had expected. Yellow fever and malaria killed some 22,000 workers, there were insurmountable construction problems and financial mismanagement drove the company bankrupt by 1889.

One of Lesseps' chief engineers, Philippe Bunau-Varilla, formed a new canal company, but at the same time the USA was seriously considering putting its own canal somewhere through Central America. Nicaragua seemed the most likely site, but taking over the canal in Panama was also a possibility. The French, unable to complete the canal, finally agreed to sell the concession to the USA. In 1903 Bunau-Varilla asked the Colombian government for permission to conclude the sale. Colombia refused.

Panama Becomes a Nation

Revolutionary sentiments had been brewing in Panama for many years, but repeated attempts to break away from Colombia had met with no success. In 1903 a civil war in Colombia created fresh discontent as

PANAMA RAILROAD.

Panamanians were drafted to fight and Panamanians' property was seized by the Colombian government for the war effort.

When the Colombian government refused to allow the transfer of the canal treaty to the USA, it thwarted US and French interests as well as Panama's own. Bunau-Varilla, who had a lot to gain financially if the sale went through, approached the US government to back Panama if it declared its independence from Colombia.

A revolutionary junta declared Panama independent on November 3, 1903, with the support of the USA, which immediately recognized the new government. Colombia sent troops by sea to try to regain control of the province, but US battleships prevented their reaching land.

The First Canal Treaty

Bunau-Varilla, now Panamanian ambassador to the USA, moved quickly to pre-empt the arrival in Washington, DC, of an official delegation from Panama that was slated to negotiate the terms of the canal treaty. On November 18, before the delegation arrived, he signed the Hay-Bunau-Varilla Treaty with US Secretary of State John Hay. It gave the USA far more than had been offered in the original treaty rejected by the Colombian government. The treaty's 26 articles awarded the USA 'sovereign rights in perpetuity over the Canal Zone,' an area extending 8km on either side of the canal, and a broad right of intervention in Panamanian affairs. The treaty was ratified over the Panamanian delegation's protests.

The treaty led to friction between the USA and Panama for decades, partly because it was overly favorable to the USA at the expense of Panama and partly due to lingering questions about its legality. Colombia did not recognize Panama as a legitimately separate nation until 1921, when the USA paid Colombia US$25 million in 'compensation.'

The USA Builds the Canal

Construction began again on the canal in 1904. The project remains one of the greatest engineering achievements of the 20th century, completed despite disease, landslides and many other difficulties. More than 75,000 workers were employed on it. Canal heroes included Colonel William Crawford Gorgas, who managed a massive campaign to eliminate yellow fever and malaria, and two chief engineers, John F Stevens and Colonel George Washington Goethals. Construction took 10 years. The first ship sailed through the canal on August 15, 1914.

See the Panamá Province chapter for more details on the canal.

Rise of the Military

The US military intervened repeatedly in Panama's political affairs until 1936, when the Hay-Bunau-Varilla Treaty was replaced by the Hull-Alfaro Treaty. The USA relinquished its rights to use its troops outside the Canal Zone and to seize land for canal purposes, and the annual sum paid to Panama for use of the Canal Zone was increased.

With the new restrictions on US military activity, the Panamanian army grew more powerful. In 1968 the Guardia Nacional deposed the elected president and took control of the government; the constitution was suspended, the national assembly was dissolved and the press censored. The Guardia's General Omar Torrijos Herrera emerged as the new leader.

Torrijos conducted public-works programs on a grand scale, including a massive modernization of Panama City, which won him the support of much of the populace but also plunged Panama into huge debt.

1977 Canal Treaty

US dominion over the Canal Zone, and the canal itself, were continuing sources of conflict between Panama and the USA. After years of negotiation that foundered in a series of stalemates, a new treaty was finally accepted by both sides in 1977. It was signed by Torrijos and US President Jimmy Carter.

The new treaty provides that US control of the canal will be gradually phased out, with Panama assuming complete ownership and control on December 31, 1999. It also provides for the phasing out of US military bases in Panama. A separate treaty ensures that the canal shall remain open and neutral for all nations, during both peace and war. In 1978 the US Senate attached extenuating conditions that grant the USA the right of limited intervention and rights to defend the canal beyond the 1999 date. The treaty finally went into effect on October 1, 1979.

Manuel Noriega

Torrijos was killed in a plane crash in 1981. In September 1983, after a brief period of leadership by Colonel Rubén Darío Paredes, Colonel Manuel Antonio Noriega took control of the Guardia Nacional and then of the country itself.

Noriega, a former head of Panama's secret police and a former CIA operative, quickly consolidated his power. He enlarged the Guardia Nacional, expanded its authority and renamed it the Panama Defense Forces. He also closed down all media that criticized him, and created a paramilitary 'Dignity Battalion' in every city, town and village, its members armed and ready to inform on any of their neighbors showing less than complete loyalty to the Noriega regime.

The first presidential election in 16 years was held in 1984. Although the count was challenged, Noriega's candidate, respected economist Nicolás Ardito Barletta, was declared the winner. A year later Barletta was removed by Noriega for insisting on a top-level investigation into the murder of a popular Panamanian political leader, Dr Hugo Spadafora.

In early 1987 Noriega became the center of an international scandal. He was publicly accused of involvement in drug trafficking with Colombian drug cartels, murdering his opponents and rigging elections. According to a *New York Times* article published in June 1986, he was also involved in clandestine arms trading and the sale of high-technology equipment to Cuba. Many Panamanians demanded Nori-

Noriega, nicknamed 'The Pineapple' (for his bad skin), is now serving time in a Florida jail.

ega's dismissal, protesting with general strikes and street demonstrations that resulted in violent clashes with the Panama Defense Forces.

Relations with the USA went from bad to worse. By February 1988 the USA had indicted Noriega for drug trafficking and involvement in organized crime. In the same month, Barletta's successor as president, Eric Arturo Delvalle, attempted to dismiss Noriega, but Noriega still held the reins of power, and Delvalle ended up fleeing Panama after being deposed himself. Noriega appointed a substitute president.

Noriega's regime was now an international embarrassment. In March 1988 the USA imposed economic sanctions against Panama, ending a preferential trade agreement, freezing Panamanian assets in US banks and refusing to pay canal fees. Panama's international offshore banking industry, which the USA had asserted was deeply involved with international drug cartels and with laundering money for organized crime, buckled under the strain of the American sanctions.

A few days after the sanctions were imposed, there was an unsuccessful military coup. Noriega responded by stepping up violent repression of his critics, including the increasing numbers of anti-government demonstrators.

Presidential elections were held once again in May 1989. When Noriega's candidate failed to win, Noriega declared the entire election null and void. Guillermo Endara, the winning candidate, and his two vice-presidential running mates were assaulted by Noriega's forces, a scene captured live on national TV and broadcast to a furious nation. An attempted coup in October 1989 was followed by even more repressive measures.

On December 15, 1989, Noriega's legislature declared him president. At the same time Noriega announced that Panama was at war with the USA. The following day, an unarmed US Marine dressed in civilian clothes was killed by Panamanian soldiers.

Operation Just Cause
US reaction was swift. In the first hour of December 20, 1989, Panama City was attacked by aircraft, tanks and 26,000 US troops in a mission called 'Operation Just Cause.' US President George Bush said the invasion had four objectives: to protect US lives, to maintain the security of the Panama Canal, to restore democracy to Panama and to capture Noriega and bring him to justice.

Shortly before the invasion, there had been an attempt to kidnap Noriega, but he had gone into hiding. On Christmas Day, the fifth day of the invasion, he went to the Vatican nuncio to request asylum. He remained in the Vatican Embassy for 10 days. Outside, US soldiers reinforced diplomatic pressure on the Vatican to expel him by setting up loudspeakers in front of the embassy and blaring rock music to unnerve those inside. Meanwhile, angry crowds near the blocked-off embassy urged Noriega's ousting.

The chief of the Vatican Embassy finally persuaded Noriega to give himself up by threatening to cancel his asylum. Noriega surrendered to US forces on January 3, 1990. He was flown immediately to Miami, where he was tried on numerous criminal charges and convicted in April 1992 on eight charges of conspiracy to manufacture and distribute cocaine. In July 1992 he was sentenced to 40 years in prison. Today he is serving his sentence in a Florida jail.

Post-Invasion Panama
After Noriega's ouster, Guillermo Endara, the legitimate winner of the 1989 election, was sworn in as president, and Panama City attempted to put itself back together. It had suffered damage not only from the invasion itself but from widespread looting. Many residential blocks of the district of Chorrillo, near the Panama Defense Forces headquarters, burned to the ground during the invasion.

The death toll from the invasion was a subject of great controversy. The official toll was put at 540; a human-rights commission later determined that at least 4000 Panamanians had been killed, and other sources gave estimates as high as 7000, asserting that unknown numbers of bodies were buried in mass graves.

The Endara government did not turn out to be a panacea. There was public concern over what many considered Endara's excessive involvement with the USA, his handling of the military and his inability to create economic well-being for the country following Noriega's ouster (in fairness to Endara, the US invasion left the country financially crippled for five years). The public was also concerned with the future of the canal.

In the next presidential election, held on May 8, 1994, Ernesto Pérez Balladares, candidate of a political alliance including the Partido Revolucionario Democrático (PRD) and Partido Laborista (PALA) parties, won by a narrow margin, with 33% of the vote. Rubén Blades, an internationally renowned Panamanian salsa music star, represented the Movimiento Papa Egoró

Musician and politician Rubén Blades

country in the shape of an S, bordered on the west by Costa Rica, on the east by Colombia, on the north by a 1160km Caribbean coastline and on the south by a 1690km Pacific coastline. The total land area is 78,046 sq km. By comparison, Panama is slightly bigger than Ireland or Austria, one-fifth the size of Japan or California, more than three times the size of Belize or Israel, one-hundredth the size of Australia, and 2½ times bigger than Belgium or Vancouver Island, Canada.

While traveling about Panama, one must remember that the isthmus of the Western Hemisphere runs west to east; that Colón, on the Caribbean Sea, is not only north but also west of Panama City; and that in the latter city the sun appears to rise out of the Pacific Ocean. Most visitors (myself included), cognizant that Panama's land boundaries are *North* and *South* America, find it difficult to grasp that Panama runs west to east. As historian Tracy Robinson once said, 'There is a suspicion of something crooked about this.'

The isthmus of Panama is the narrowest land mass between the Atlantic and Pacific Oceans. At its narrowest point it is less than 50km wide. The Panama Canal, which is about 80km long, effectively divides the country into eastern and western regions. The provinces of Herrera, Los Santos and Veraguas are often referred to as the 'central provinces' or as 'the interior' – as in the interior of the country.

Two mountain chains run along Panama's spine, one in the east and one in the west. The highest point in the country is 3478m Volcán Barú, in western Chiriquí Province. Panama's only volcano, it is dormant, although hot springs around its flanks testify to continuing activity under the ground.

Like all the Central American countries, Panama has large, flat coastal lowlands. In some places these lowlands are covered in huge banana plantations, particularly in the area of Changuinola in Bocas del Toro Province and around Puerto Armuelles in Chiriquí Province. These plantations are owned by the Chiriquí Land Company,

(MPE) party and took third place, receiving 17% of the vote.

In 1998, four years into his five-year term, Pérez Balladares appeared headed for another five years in office, although his party first needed to amend the constitution to permit reelection. Under his leadership, the government has allocated unprecedented levels of funding for education, health, farming assistance, housing projects and infrastructure improvements. Many citizens, however, privately wonder if government corruption and involvement with illegal activities such as money laundering have really changed much.

Panamanian opinion of the USA remains divided. On the one hand, many people are glad that the USA got rid of Noriega, admitting that the Panamanians themselves had been unable to do it. Others resent the continuing involvement of the USA in Panamanian affairs – a situation that will continue, however, at least until the final transfer of ownership and control of the canal from the USA to Panama. This is occurring in scheduled stages, with the final transfer scheduled for December 31, 1999.

GEOGRAPHY

Panama is the southernmost of the Central American countries. It is a long, narrow

which is a subsidiary of the Chiquita Brands International corporation.

There are about 480 rivers in Panama that drain into the Pacific Ocean or Caribbean Sea, and 1518 islands off its coasts. The two main island groups, both in the Caribbean, are the San Blás and Bocas del Toro Archipelagos, but most of Panama's islands are in fact on the Pacific side, small and often unmapped. Even the Panama Canal has islands, including Isla Barro Colorado, which has a world-renowned tropical rainforest research station operated by the Smithsonian Tropical Research Institute.

GEOLOGY

The surface of the Earth is covered with 13 tectonic plates which, over many millions of years, have moved to create the planet's surface as we know it. Central America began to be formed only 20 million years ago, when the Cocos Plate began its northeastern shift and collided with the Antilles Plate. This collision forced the edge of the Cocos Plate up and the edge of the Antilles Plate underneath it. Gradually the edge of the Cocos Plate rose from the ocean to form most of Central America.

From a geological perspective, Panama is a youngster. The country began to emerge from the sea only 3 million to 4 million years ago, and the Cocos Plate is continuing to slide over the Antilles Plate at a rate of about 10cm every year – quite fast by geological standards. The movement of one huge land mass shoving another huge land mass out of its way creates a tremendous amount of friction, which we observe in the form of earthquakes and volcanic activity throughout Central America.

The emergence of Panama created a land bridge between the American continents, which until then were separated. That bridge remained intact for at least 200,000 human generations until a wee nine decades ago, when people cut a canal across the isthmus. Before humans intervened, some species in South America wandered into North America and vice versa. It is because of this wandering that such origi-nally South American creatures as armadillos, anteaters and sloths can be found in North America, and North American natives such as tapirs, jaguars and deer can be found in South America (see Flora & Fauna, later in this chapter, for further details).

CLIMATE

Like the rest of Central America, Panama has two seasons: the dry and the rainy. The dry season (summer, or *verano*) lasts from around mid-December to mid-April; the rainy season (winter, or *invierno*) lasts from mid-April to mid-December. Even at the height of the rainy season, all-day rains are rare in Panama. Typically rain arrives in downpours lasting less than an hour. It should also be noted that Panama lies below the hurricane track, though occasionally a weak tropical depression skirts the Caribbean coast.

Rain patterns differ markedly from one side of the country to the other, with the Caribbean side receiving much more rain than the Pacific side. The mountains that extend almost all the way along the spine of the country form a barrier against the warm, moist trade winds blowing from the Caribbean. As the warm air rises against the mountains, the moisture it holds falls, frequently and heavily, as rain. The Caribbean coast receives around 1500 to 3500mm a year; downpours are possible at any time of year. There are lush rainforests on much of the Caribbean side, along the Panama Canal and in Darién Province.

Most people live on the Pacific side of the mountains, which until the past 100 years were covered with deciduous forest; today that forest has all but disappeared, felled to make way for pasture and crops. Here, with the exception of the rainy Darién, the annual rainfall is 1140 to 2290mm. This is still no small amount, but the rains are confined almost entirely to the period from mid-April to mid-December. This seasonal weather pattern never did support tropical rainforest; the Pacific side, with the exception of the Darién, is lined

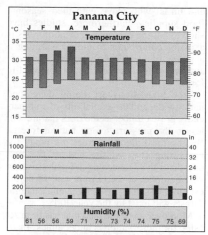

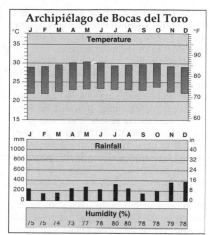

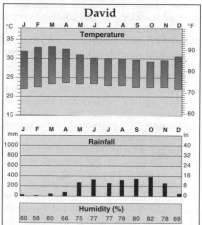

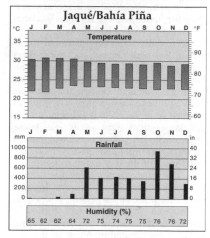

with broad grasslands, savanna and what remains of the deciduous forests. Longtime residents say the Pacific side used to receive a lot more rain – back in the days when their now-denuded hills were blanketed with forests.

Temperatures are typically hot in the lowlands (day/night temperatures are around 32°/21°C) and cool in the mountains (around 18°/10°C). These temperatures remain about the same all year. In Panama City the heat is usually tempered by fresh sea breezes, although periods of high humidity are not uncommon.

ECOLOGY & ENVIRONMENT

With about 30% of its total land placed in areas set aside for conservation, Panama *is* making an effort to protect some of its remaining natural resources. In fact, Panama has set aside more land for habitat protection than any other Central American country, and Panama's forests contain the greatest number of species of all the New

World countries north of Colombia. But it's doubtful whether Panamanians will be able to live in harmony with their wilderness areas in the years to come.

For one thing, a significant sector of Panamanian society believes it's manly to cut down trees. If you listen in on conversations among common folk in Los Santos Province, for example, it won't be long before you overhear talk about the good old days – when you could cut down trees as wide as cars. The urge to log goes well beyond economic welfare. In this province women compete with trees for men's hearts. As a result, there's hardly a patch of forest remaining there, and the *hombres* are so anxious to fell more trees that they're moving to the Darién, where big trees still abound. This is one reason that Los Santos' population has been falling in recent years, while the populations of all eight of Panama's other provinces have grown.

Additionally, Panama's national parks contain few park rangers, and the rangers aren't given patrol vehicles or radios, although their areas of coverage are colossal. In Parque Nacional Darién, for instance, there are never more than six rangers assigned to protect 576,000 hectares – an area larger than some countries. These rangers, who live in two small, windowless outposts, are unarmed, poorly paid and spend most of the day trying to figure out what they are going to eat for dinner. Meanwhile hunting, settling and logging are taking place in their park. Unless the Panamanian government gets serious, it may not be long before the country's 'protected' areas are nothing more than paper parks.

Environmental Problems
Deforestation & Soil Erosion The major problem facing the nation's environment is deforestation. Panama's natural vegetation was originally almost all forest, but most of this has been cleared, mainly for pasture and agriculture. The destruction of a rainforest not only wipes out the animals that had inhabited it but also kills many migratory animals (among them bats, butterflies and birds) who move with their seasonal food supplies. Furthermore, studies have shown that the destruction of rainforests is a major contributor to global warming – a series of events with potentially catastrophic consequences for all known life forms.

Tree plantations are being developed nationwide, and the availability of commercially grown timber as the trees mature will lessen the pressure to log natural forests. But by the time these trees are ready for harvesting (toward the end of the first decade of the 21st century), the destruction will be done; at the current rate of deforestation, less than 20% of Panama's natural forests will exist by the year 2005.

Moreover, even the land that has been set aside for preservation is under attack. Inadequate funding, indifference and corruption have allowed logging and hunting to occur virtually unabated in supposedly protected areas. Also, laws prohibiting the killing of endangered animals are not enforced and are widely ignored; *tortuga* (sea turtle) often appears on Panamanian menus, for example, and some restaurants and hotels display jaguars, ocelots and margays in tiny cages, knowing that the agency responsible for preventing such crimes likely won't intervene.

Deforestation has resulted in yet another serious problem for Panama: soil erosion. Huge, exposed tree roots prevent heavy rains from washing away the thin layer of nutrient-rich topsoil found in tropical forests. Take out the trees and the next big storm to hit the denuded area will carry the topsoil into rivers and out to sea, leaving only the nutrient-deficient lower soil where the vibrant jungle once stood. When you consider that 50% of the country's soil is of poor quality to begin with and that 75% of it is located on hillsides, the seriousness of the problem becomes apparent. And yet ranchers, who have deforested most of the Pacific slope from the Costa Rican border to Yaviza, are still allowed to clear-cut forest to create pasture for their cattle.

The government has occasionally made a modest attempt to curb the destructive practices of the ranchers, but those attempts have failed every time. In 1987, for instance, the government announced a five-year suspension of tree-felling; no primary or secondary forest more than five years old was to be cut. In response, cattle ranchers encouraged peasants to move into frontier lands and chop down tracts of rainforest. Fearing negative publicity, no action was taken against the peasants to stop the deforestation. The ranchers later moved their cattle onto the land cleared by the peasants. Today both sides of the Carretera Interamericana (Pan-American Hwy) from Chepo to Yaviza are barren as far as the eye can see, the end product of the specious suspension of tree-felling.

Mangrove Destruction Another major environmental problem in Panama today is the destruction of mangroves, which play an important role in stemming beach erosion and in maintaining balance in delicate marine ecosystems. Mangrove destruction also takes a heavy toll on the country's important seafood industry, because many species of fish need mangroves to survive. Regardless, mangroves throughout Panama are being cut down to make room for shrimp farms, resorts and urban development. Red-mangrove bark, which is used by the tanning industry, is being exported to Costa Rica, where harvesting of the bark is prohibited.

Water Pollution Panama is also starting to encounter some serious water-pollution problems, alleviated only by the fact that the country remains sparsely populated. Water pollution is most apparent in and around Panama City and Colón – areas where 90% of Panamanians live. Most of the sewage from these cities is discharged untreated directly into coastal waters or canals that flow through the cities. Skin afflictions among children who swim in the Bahía de Panamá are common.

The water-pollution crisis is also evident in the Darién and central provinces, where rivers are widely used as garbage dumps; only the rains that frequent these areas keep the rivers from becoming toxic. Likewise, throughout the Archipiélago de San Blás, the resident Kuna Indians use the ocean around them as a natural toilet, building their outhouses directly over the sea, and they think nothing of tossing refuse into the water.

Conservation Organizations
The Panamanian government has limited or forbidden development on about one-third of the country's land, which is good, and it has given responsibility for protection of that land to the Instituto Nacional de Recursos Naturales Renovables (National Institute of Renewable Natural Resources, or INRENARE), which is bad. As manager of Panama's national park system, INRENARE has proved impotent at curbing encroachment on the parks by squatters and at preventing logging and hunting within them.

In its defense, INRENARE faces some major obstacles in its role as protector of lands set aside for conservation. For one thing, many of these lands were inhabited at the time they were designated national parks or protected areas, and those inhabitants were permitted to stay where they were despite the many inherent problems associated with allowing people to live in environmentally sensitive regions. Also, INRENARE park rangers are not outfitted with weapons, vehicles or radios, although they are tasked with patrolling vast wilderness areas. The unmanned INRENARE ranger station is an all too common sight.

One of INRENARE's functions is the allocation of unprotected state lands for private uses, and in this capacity the agency's record is indefensible. The agency is still allowing loggers, ranchers and settlers to fell rainforest, despite the now widely known environmental damage that results. Furthermore, Panamanian law states that logging companies must plant trees to replace the ones they cut down, but in reality this is seldom done; it is a law that INRENARE is supposed to enforce.

As impotent as INRENARE is today, it is better than it would be if not for the private Asociación Nacional para la Conservación de la Naturaleza (National Association for the Conservation of Nature, or Ancon; ☎ 264-8100, fax 264-1836, ancon@pty.com, www.ancon.org), Apartado 1387, Panamá 1, República de Panamá. Founded in 1985 by academic and business leaders, Ancon has played a major role in the creation of national parks and on many occasions has spurred INRENARE into action. Whenever the government is under attack for permitting logging where it shouldn't, invariably it is Ancon's directors who are spearheading the assault.

In addition, with money donated primarily by US conservation groups and wealthy Panamanians, Ancon has purchased several large tracts of rainforest for preservation. Through a subsidiary, Ancon Expeditions of Panama, it is making these and other biologically rich areas more accessible to tourists; without question, the country's finest nature guides work for Ancon Expeditions. Ancon also organizes nationwide litter-removal campaigns and sponsors programs that show farmers how they can utilize their land in an efficient, sustainable and environmentally sensitive manner.

Ancon's potentially greatest contribution has yet to be realized. In 1990 the nonprofit organization cleared 64 hectares of land covered with invasive elephant grass and replaced the nonnative plant with 100,000 rapid-growing seedlings that will produce teak, cedar, mahogany and a variety of other trees. These trees will in turn produce seeds for reforestation projects nationwide, which will relieve pressure on natural forests. Many species of fruit trees were also planted, to create a generic bank of native Panamanian fruit species; such trees are critical to Panama's native wildlife.

Panama's many less significant conservation organizations include the Student Association for the Conservation of the Environment (ACECAP) and the Project for the Study and Management of Wild Areas of the Kuna Yala (PEMASKY). The student group's main achievement has been successfully pressuring the government to protect two endangered areas along the Caribbean coast. PEMASKY is a grassroots movement led by the Kuna, and its primary aim is to prevent outsiders from settling on their land.

FLORA & FAUNA

Panama's position as a narrow land bridge between two huge continents has given it a remarkable variety of plant and animal life. Its great biodiversity is directly attributable to the fact that it is home to North and Central American species at their southernmost range and South American species at their northernmost range.

Panama's geographical position also makes it a crossroads for migratory birds. Out of the country's 940 recorded bird species, 122 occur only as long-distance migrants – they don't breed in Panama. These migrants can be amazing to watch. As I write this in a hotel room in Panama City in November, literally millions of hawks are passing overhead en route to South America. There are so many hawks that they've made a black streak across an otherwise blue sky.

The migration of turkey vultures over the islands of Bocas del Toro in early March and October is another almost unbelievable spectacle. These big, black-bodied, red-necked birds can streak the sky and are able to soar for long periods without a single flap as they migrate between southern Canada and Tierra del Fuego.

Panama's biodiversity is also a product of the size of its wilderness regions. Jaguars and cougars, for example, need large tracts of forest to survive. Without them, the big cats eventually exhaust their food supply and perish. In Panama there are no fewer than five protected areas large enough to sustain jaguar and cougar populations. The size of these regions has the added advantage of minimizing the adverse effects of human encroachment. Just how big are these areas? In the Darién and La Amistad parks, for instance, you can hike in one direction for more than a week and never cross a road.

Additionally, Panama has no fewer than 125 animal species found nowhere else in the world; these endemic species include 56 types of freshwater fish, 25 types of amphibian, 22 types of reptile, 12 types of mammal and 10 types of bird.

Panama's offshore waters host a fascinating assortment of creatures. Reefs are found off both coasts, and aquatic species in Panamanian waters include jack, snappers, jewfish, eel, sailfish, corvina, puffer fish, rays, lobsters, caimans and octopi. Visitors to the national marine parks might spot humpback whales, reef sharks, bottlenosed dolphins, or killer or sperm whales. Sea turtles, whale sharks and white-tip sharks also visit.

Tropical rainforest is the dominant vegetation in the canal area, along the Caribbean coast and in most of the eastern half of the country. Parque Nacional Darién protects much of Panama's largest tropical rainforest region. Other vegetation zones include grassland on the Pacific coast, mountain forest in the highlands, alpine vegetation on the highest peaks and mangrove forest on both coasts and around many islands.

Endangered Species

According to the World Conservation Monitoring Centre, a respected UK-based conservation organization, there are at least 105 species threatened with extinction within Panama. Among the animals appearing on its 'red list' for Panama are the jaguar, the spectacled bear, the Central American tapir, the American crocodile, all five species of sea turtle that nest on Panamanian beaches, and dozens of birds, including several eagle species and the military and scarlet macaws.

The Panamanian legislature has passed legislation to curb illegal hunting and logging, but the laws are widely ignored due to an absence of enforcement. For example, keeping a parrot, toucan or macaw in a cage is a fineable offense in Panama. Yet not only can you see them in cages outside many residences, but many hotel managers apparently are under the

The harpy eagle, a Panama native, is the world's most powerful bird of prey.

impression that tourists enjoy seeing large tropical birds in itty-bitty cages. Unfortunately, most captive animals cannot be returned to the wild because they were separated from their mothers before they learned how to fend for themselves.

You can help reduce the threat to Panama's endangered species. If you see caged animals at a hotel, complain to the manager and take your business elsewhere. Report the crime to INRENARE (☎ 232-7228/7223) and to Ancon (☎ 264-8100). And please don't eat *tortuga* (sea turtle), *huevos de tortuga* (turtle eggs), *cazón* (shark), *conejo pintado* (paca), *ñeque* (agouti), *venado* (deer) or iguana if you see them on a menu or if they are offered to you.

Obviously, buying jaguar teeth, ocelot skins and objects made from turtle shells directly contributes to these animals' extinction. If a sense of moral outrage doesn't stop you from considering such a purchase, you might like to know that the penalty for trying to leave Panama with any of these products is a fine typically accompanied by jail time.

NATIONAL PARKS

The development of wildlife sanctuaries in Panama began in 1966 with the establishment of the Parque Nacional Altos de Campana. It was not until 1975 that a second park was created. Today Panama has 12 national parks and 19 other protected areas (see details below in the Other Protected Areas section).

To enter any national park, travelers must pay US$3 (or US$10 if it's a national marine park) at INRENARE headquarters or at any of the agency's many regional offices. INRENARE has its headquarters (☎ 232-7228/7223) near Panama City's Terminal de Buses al Interior, on Avenida Ascañio Villalaz in the Curundu district; Spanish and English are spoken. The agency's mailing address is Depto de Parques Nacionales y de Vida Silvestre, Apartado 2016, Paraíso, Corregimiento de Ancón, Panamá, República de Panamá.

Permits to stay at an INRENARE ranger station or to camp in a national park can be obtained at the headquarters or regional offices. If you believe you'll be visiting more than one national park, you would be wise to obtain permits for them all at once at INRENARE's headquarters; this can save you headaches later, as the regional offices are often closed when you visit them.

The cost of the permits varies. A permit for camping in an INRENARE-protected area is US$5 per night. A permit to stay at an INRENARE ranger station is also US$5 per night. INRENARE also maintains four scientific stations – at Boca Chica (Chiriquí Province), Cayo Zapatilla Sur (Bocas del Toro Province), Isla de Coiba (Veraguas Province) and Pirre (Darién Province) – and the cost of a permit to stay at them is US$10 per night.

Generally, food is not available for visitors at the ranger stations; if you intend to eat, you should bring food with you. If the food requires cooking, most rangers are happy to cook for you for a tip (US$2 per person per meal is most appreciated). I always bring extra food and a six-pack of beer for the rangers. It's been my experience that when I've been generous with them, they have done what they could to make my stay enjoyable.

Panama's national parks, from west to east, are as follows:

Parque Nacional Volcán Barú – This park contains the giant Barú volcano, which soars to the highest elevation in Panama (3478m above sea level). From its usually cloud-shrouded summit, it is occasionally possible to glimpse the Pacific Ocean and the Caribbean Sea. The resplendent quetzal, a world-class find, is here. Endemic bird species include the volcano junco and the baru burbit. Access is from Boquete and Volcán. (14,300 hectares, Chiriquí Province)

Parque Nacional Isla de Coiba – This remote park protects marine and coastal ecosystems in an almost virgin setting. It is the last refuge in Panama for the scarlet macaw, and the waters around the island are breeding grounds for several species of whale. Visitors' movements are restricted due to the presence of a penal colony on the island. (270,000 hectares, of which 216,543 are oceanic; Veraguas Province)

Parque Nacional Cerro Hoya – This park, on the southwestern side of the Península de Azuero, protects the headwaters of three rivers. It also protects many endemic plant species and animals like the carato parakeet. Within the confines of the park is some of the last remaining forest on the peninsula. (32,577 hectares, Veraguas and Los Santos Provinces)

Parque Nacional El Copé – Near the center of the isthmus, this park includes cloud forest, rubber trees and the watersheds of the Ríos Bermejo, Marta, Blanco, Guabal and Lajas. It's of particular interest to ecotourists for its foothill birds and golden frogs. There are some fine hiking opportunities near the summit. Access is from the town of El Copé. (6000 hectares, Coclé and Colón Provinces)

Parque Nacional Sarigua – On the northeastern side of the Península de Azuero, this park contains some dry forest, salt marsh and mangroves, and an archaeological zone. With its salt pans, wind-blown sand and cacti, most of the park resembles desert, but it's not; Sarigua receives more than a meter of rain each year. Instead, what you see here is environmental devastation – the product of overgrazing, loss of topsoil and erosion. Access is from Chitré. (8000 hectares, Herrera Province)

Parque Nacional Altos de Campana – This park protects two watersheds, the Río Sajalices, which empties into the Pacific, and the Ríos Cirí and Trinidad, which flow into the Río Chagres basin, the water catchment system for the Panama Canal. Endemic species include Panama's famous golden frogs, the common vampire bat and the colored rabbit. There's also a great variety of native conifers. Picturesque cliffs abound. (4816 hectares, Panamá Province)

Parque Nacional Interoceánico de las Américas – Established in 1993, Panama's newest national park protects the watershed along the western side of the Panama Canal. Access is from Panama City or Colón. (62,159 hectares, Colón Province)

Parque Nacional Soberanía – Also protecting the watershed of the Panama Canal, this park contains excellent hiking trails, including the famous Camino del Oleoducto (Pipeline Road), one of the world's top birding sites, and the short Sendero El Charco nature trail. At last count 525 species of bird and 105 species of mammal, including the jaguar, resided here. Morpho butterflies are common in this park. Access is from Panama City. (22,104 hectares, Panamá Province)

Parque Nacional Camino de Cruces – On the old Camino Real – the cobblestone road by which stolen Peruvian gold was taken on its way to Spain – this park forms an ecological corridor connecting Parque Nacional Soberanía and Parque Natural Metropolitano. There are waterfalls and a great variety of flora and fauna, including marmosets, armadillos, green iguanas and three-toed sloths. Access is from Panama City. (4000 hectares, Panamá Province)

Parque Nacional Portobelo – East of Colón, this World Heritage Site protects 70km of coastal areas with rich coral reefs, and the ruins of the historic Spanish forts and settlement at Portobelo. In colonial times it was the site of storehouses for gold and silver stolen from the Inca empire. It was here that Spanish galleons loaded on treasure for their voyage back to Europe. Access is from Panama City or Colón. (35,929 hectares, Colón Province)

Parque Nacional Chagres – This park preserves the main watershed of the Panama Canal. About 80% of the water needed for the canal's operation and all of the drinking water for Panama City comes from this watershed. The park includes the Río Chagres, Lago Alajuela, much of El Camino Real and traditional settlements of the Emberá. This park is also the site of elfin forests. Access is from Panama City. (129,000 hectares, Panamá Province)

Parque Nacional Darién – A World Heritage Site and a Biosphere Reserve, Panama's largest national park contains the greatest tropical rainforest wilderness in Central America and forms an effective barrier between Panama and Colombia. At its heart is Cana, a former mining valley that is the top birding site in Central America. Access to the park is by air or trail from El Real, Yaviza and other places; no roads lead into or out of Cana. (576,000 hectares, Darién Province)

Additional details on many of these parks can be found in the regional chapters.

OTHER PROTECTED AREAS

In addition to the 12 national parks, there are 18 more areas under INRENARE's administration. These include two national marine parks, four forest reserves, two protected forests, four wildlife refuges, two protected forests that border reservoirs, one natural monument, one nature park, one recreational area and one municipal park. Additionally, Panama shares an international park with Costa Rica, and commercial fishing is not allowed in the vicinity of Bahía Piña.

Parque Nacional Marino Golfo de Chiriquí – On and around Isla Parida, the Golfo de Chiriquí marine park protects insular, marine and coastal areas. It is used as a nesting site by five species of sea turtle and the scarlet macaw. Several species of monkey inhabit Isla Boca Brava, which borders the park. Snorkeling and diving here can be excellent. Access is from Boca Chica. (14,740 hectares, Chiriquí Province)

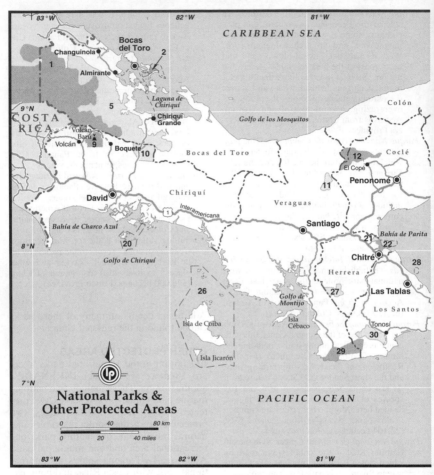

National Parks & Other Protected Areas

Parque Nacional Marino Isla Bastimentos – On the Caribbean coast of western Panama, the Isla Bastimentos marine park conserves marine and coastal ecosystems, including wetlands, mangroves, coral reefs, white-sand beaches and more than 200 species of tropical fish. The diving and snorkeling here are quite OK when the visibility is good – about half the time. Access is from Bocas del Toro town on Isla Colón. (13,266 hectares, Bocas del Toro Province)

Parque Natural Metropolitano – This park, 15 minutes' drive from central Panama City, has nature trails and is the site of scientific tropical rainforest research. Although close to the city, it is home to more than 250 species of bird and 40 species of mammal. The view from atop Cerro Mono Tití is spectacular, offering a panoramic vista of the city, the port of Balboa and neighboring Parque Nacional Camino de Cruces. (265 hectares, Panamá Province)

Parque Internacional La Amistad – Shared by Panama and Costa Rica, this park contains seven of the 12 classified life zones, with great biodiversity and numerous endemic

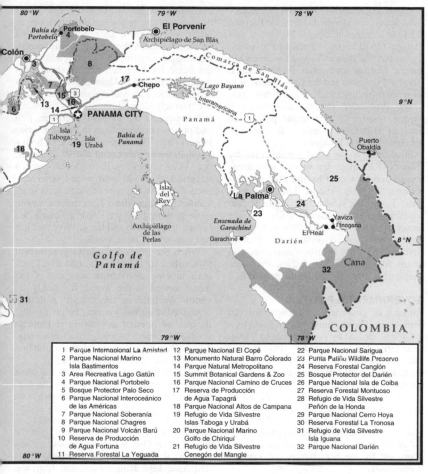

1 Parque Internacional La Amistad	12 Parque Nacional El Copé	22 Parque Nacional Sariguá
2 Parque Nacional Marino Isla Bastimentos	13 Monumento Natural Barro Colorado	23 Punta Patiño Wildlife Preserve
3 Area Recreativa Lago Gatún	14 Parque Natural Metropolitano	24 Reserva Forestal Canglón
4 Parque Nacional Portobelo	15 Summit Botanical Gardens & Zoo	25 Bosque Protector del Darién
5 Bosque Protector Palo Seco	16 Parque Nacional Camino de Cruces	26 Parque Nacional Isla de Coiba
6 Parque Nacional Interoceánico de las Américas	17 Reserva de Producción de Agua Tapagrá	27 Reserva Forestal Montuoso
7 Parque Nacional Soberanía	18 Parque Nacional Altos de Campana	28 Refugio de Vida Silvestre Peñón de la Honda
8 Parque Nacional Chagres	19 Refugio de Vida Silvestre Islas Taboga y Urabá	29 Parque Nacional Cerro Hoya
9 Parque Nacional Volcán Barú	20 Parque Nacional Marino Golfo de Chiriquí	30 Reserva Forestal La Tronosa
10 Reserva de Producción de Agua Fortuna	21 Refugio de Vida Silvestre Cenegón del Mangle	31 Refugio de Vida Silvestre Isla Iguana
11 Reserva Forestal La Yeguada		32 Parque Nacional Darién

species. Quetzals and harpy eagles reside here. It is also home to members of three Indian tribes and is a World Heritage Site. The park has entrances at Wetzo and Las Nubes. Access is from Cerro Punta and Changuinola. (407,000 hectares, Bocas del Toro and Chiriquí Provinces)

Panama's four *reservas forestales* (forest reserves) are La Yeguada (3000 hectares, Veraguas Province), Montuoso (10,000 hectares, Herrera Province), La Tronosa (20,579 hectares, Los Santos Province) and

Canglón (31,650 hectares, Darién Province). Panama also has the Bosque Protector Palo Seco (Bocas del Toro Province) and the Bosque Protector del Darién (Darién and San Blás Provinces).

The country's four *refugios de vida silvestre* (wildlife refuges) are Cenegón del Mangle (776 hectares, Herrera Province), Peñón de la Honda (2000 hectares, Los Santos Province), Isla Iguana (55 hectares, Los Santos Province) and Islas Taboga y Urabá (258 hectares, Panamá Province).

Panama also has two *reservas de producción de agua* (watershed reserves): Fortuna (15,000 hectares, Chiriquí Province) and Tapagrá (2520 hectares, Panamá Province). It also has the Barro Colorado *monumento natural* (natural monument; 5400 hectares, Panamá Province) and the Lago Gatún *area recreativa* (recreational area; 348 hectares, Colón Province). Panama also has one *parque municipal* (municipal park), the Summit Botanical Gardens & Zoo (46 hectares, Panamá Province).

In addition to the areas administered by INRENARE, there are several vast areas owned and protected by the private environmental group Ancon. The largest of these is the 26,315-hectare Punta Patiño wildlife preserve, Panama's first private nature preserve. In Darién Province, it harbors a variety of ecosystems: mangroves, beaches, dry land forests, rainforests and cloud forests. See the Darién Province chapter for more details on the preserve.

GOVERNMENT & POLITICS

Panama is governed as a constitutional democracy. The executive branch is led by a president, elected by popular vote to a five-year term. He is assisted by two elected vice presidents and an appointed cabinet. President Ernesto Pérez Balladares was elected to a five-year term in May 1994.

The legislative assembly has 72 members, also elected by popular vote to five-year terms. The judiciary consists of a nine-member supreme court, appointed to 10-year terms by the president and approved by the legislature and various lower courts.

Panama consists of nine provinces (see the Provinces of Panama map) and an autonomous region – the Kuna Yala, also known as the Comarca de San Blás – governed by Kuna tribal leaders, or *caciques*. Each province has a governor appointed by the president, and each is divided into municipal districts.

ECONOMY

Panama has the highest per-capita income of the Central American countries, but according to the World Bank half of its households are below the poverty level; in other words, they do not have enough income to meet their basic living needs. Critical poverty (income insufficient to buy the basic food basket) affects about one-third of households. Unemployment hovers around 20%. Panama's income distribution is extremely skewed.

Nowhere is the disparity between rich and poor so noticeable as in Panama's two largest cities. The capital is home to both a Manhattanesque financial district of gleaming skyscrapers and commuter-packed streets, and an old quarter and other districts that have the type of slums seen in all Latin American cities. The contrast is even more striking between Colón's Zona Libre (a free-trade zone) and the poverty that lies just outside the zone's walls.

When the Pérez Balladares government took office in 1994, it admitted that Panama's income distribution was one of the most skewed in the world. It quickly set about overhauling the country's deteriorated educational system, believing that its quality needed improving if Panama was to become a more egalitarian society. Today Panama's annual education budget accounts for 20% of public spending.

In 1995 Panama embarked on the most important change of direction in the predominantly service-based economy in more than 45 years. Reform of tax incentives and exemptions, labor market reforms, privatization and membership in the World Trade Organization represent a complete break with the interventionist policies that have kept Panama isolated from the free-market changes sweeping through Latin America. It remains to be seen whether these policies will greatly improve Panama's lopsided income distribution, but efforts are being made to correct the situation.

Finance and real estate account for about 15% of the country's gross national product, followed by commerce, restaurants and hotels (12%); government services (10%); agriculture (10%); manufacturing (9%); the Zona Libre (9%); the Panama

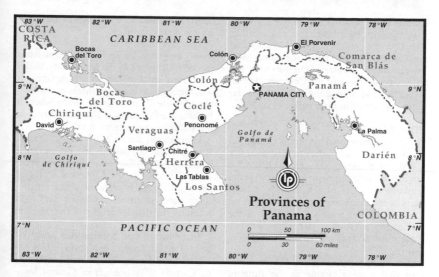

Provinces of Panama

Canal (8.5%); and utilities (3%). Other components make up the balance.

Agriculture, including fishing, livestock and forestry, employs 27% of the work force. The principal crops are bananas, plantains, sugar cane, rice, maize, coffee, beans and tobacco. Cattle, pigs and poultry are farmed; sea products include fish, shrimp and lobster. Industry and mining employ around 12% of the labor force; manufacturing employs about 9% of the labor force.

Bananas, produced primarily around the Changuinola and Puerto Armuelles areas, account for almost 40% of Panama's exports; other important exports include shrimp (19%), coffee (5%), sugar (5%) and clothing (5%). The USA is Panama's main trading partner, taking 45% of its exports and providing 40% of its imports. Other important trading partners include Japan, Germany, Costa Rica, Ecuador and Venezuela.

Despite the hopes of nearly everyone in Panama, tourism remains a sluggish industry, due at least in part to poor promotion by the Instituto Panameño de Turismo (IPAT), the government tourism board. (See the Facts for the Visitor chapter for more information on IPAT.)

POPULATION & PEOPLE

Panama's population was estimated to be 2.7 million in 1998, based on a 1990 census and an annual growth rate of 1.6%. The majority of the population (65%) are *mestizos* of mixed indigenous and Spanish descent, but there are also a number of other sizable groups. Blacks make up 14% of the population, whites comprise 10% and Indians 10%.

The blacks are mostly descendants of English-speaking West Indians, such as Jamaicans and Trinidadians, who were brought to Panama as cheap labor on various projects. West Indians worked on banana plantations in Bocas del Toro Province, the transisthmian railway in the 1850s, the French canal project in the 1880s and the US construction of the canal in the early 20th century. Many Panamanian blacks speak English and Spanish; on the islands of Bocas del Toro many also speak Patois, a blend of English, Spanish and Gali-Gali (a local dialect).

Of the several dozen Indian tribes that inhabited Panama when the Spanish arrived, seven now remain: the Kuna, the Guaymís, the Emberá, the Wounaan, the Bokatá, the Bribri and the Teribe (also known as the Naso). Each of these groups maintains its own language and culture. The Guaymís number about 125,000 and are Panama's largest tribe; the Kuna, who govern their ancestral territory as the autonomous region of the Comarca de San Blás and send representatives to the legislature, are the most politically organized.

EDUCATION

Panama's educational system is composed of elementary, secondary and university levels, each lasting six years. Officially, education is compulsory for six years between the ages of six and 15. Actual enrollment in elementary school is high (over 90%), but there's a drop-off at the secondary level (about 50% enrollment). Education is free up to the university level.

According to 1990 figures, the most current that were available at the time of writing, the median number of years spent in school by the typical adult Panamanian was 6.7. The illiteracy rate was said to be 3.6% in urban areas and 19.7% in rural areas, and over 50% among the country's indigenous populations.

Education for students with disabilities is the responsibility of the Panamanian Institute of Special Rehabilitation. Among the many schools under its authority are the National School for the Deaf, the Special Education School, the Helen Keller School for the Blind, the School for Premature Growth and the Vocational School.

Panama has three primary universities: the Universidad de Panamá, the Technological University and the Universidad Santa María la Antigua. All three offer programs in the arts and sciences and offer bachelor's and master's degrees, with total enrollment ranging from approximately 32,000 students at the Universidad de Panamá to 6100 students at Universidad Santa María la Antigua.

The Universidad de Panamá, founded in 1935, is the largest university in the country as well as the official university of the republic. Its main campus is in Panama City's El Cangrejo residential sector, and it operates six smaller campuses in the country's central provinces.

The Technological University, commonly known as La Technológica, also has its central campus in the capital city, and it has seven smaller regional campuses. It was the engineering department of the Universidad de Panamá until 1975, when it became the Polytechnic Institute. It rose to the status of a university in 1984.

Universidad Santa María la Antigua is Roman Catholic, private and nonprofit. It began in 1965 in the compound of the archbishop's palace in the Cathedral sector of Panama City and is proud of producing distinguished scientists and scholars and teaching 'Christian morals for the creation of a fairer society.'

In addition, two foreign-run universities – La Universidad del Istmo of Colombia and the Universidad Latinoamericana de Ciencia y Tecnología of Costa Rica – have campuses in Panama. Two Florida-based universities also teach courses in Panama, though on a much more limited basis: Florida State University and Nova University.

Despite the abundance of universities in Panama and their affordability (tuition at the Universidad de Panamá, for example, is a mere US$30 per semester), most Panamanians who can afford to and have good grades attend universities in the USA.

Besides the universities, higher education is offered in educational centers such as the International Banking Institute, the Institute of Management, the Center for Higher Management Studies, the Hotel and Tourism College, the Nautical School of Panama and the National Agriculture Institute.

ARTS

Panama's arts scene reflects its ethnic mix. A slow spin on the radio dial or a hard look at Panamanian nightclubs will reveal salsa, Latin and American jazz, traditional Panamanian music from the central provinces, reggae, and Latin, British and American rock 'n' roll.

Traditional Panamanian products include wood carvings, textiles, ceramics, masks, straw goods and other handicrafts. Some of the more famous include *molas* (colorful hand-stitched appliqué textiles made by Kuna women) and the *pollera* (the intricately stitched, lacy, Spanish-influenced dress of the Península de Azuero, which is the national dress of Panama for festive occasions).

The country has quite a few impressive painters and writers, some of whom are internationally recognized and have won major competitions. There is also fair representation in dance, theater and other performance arts, which are managed by the Instituto Nacional de Cultura (the National Institute of Culture, or INAC). INAC also manages the country's museums, exhibition halls and schools of fine art.

Music

Salsa is the most popular music in Panama, and live salsa is easy to find, particularly in Panama City (see the Panama City chapter for details). The country's most renowned salsa singer, Rubén Blades, is something of a national hero. A kid from the barrio, Blades has had several international hits and has appeared in *Fatal Beauty, Dead Man Out, The Milagro Beanfield War* and other motion pictures. He ran for president in 1994, finishing third.

Jazz, which was brought to Panama by Americans, and calypso music from the West Indies can also be heard in clubs in Panama. Rock 'n' roll, in both English and Spanish, is played on most Panamanian FM radio stations, and some very decent bands play it in Panama City clubs. Venues for jazz and rock bands appear in the Panama City chapter.

The jazz composer and pianist Danilo Pérez, trained at the prestigious Berklee College of Music in Boston, is widely acclaimed by serious American and European jazz critics. His CD *Panamonk,* on which he puts a Latin spin on many Thelonius Monk compositions, makes for some very pleasurable listening.

Los Rabanes is the most talented rock 'n' roll group in the country. They have come up with innovative and original

Jazz virtuoso Danilo Pérez

music that fuses diverse Panamanian musical folklore. They too have won international recognition, and perform throughout Latin America. Calypso favorites are singers Lord Cobra and Lord Panama.

Panamanian folkloric music (called *típico*), in which the accordion dominates, is well represented by Dorindo Cárdenas, Victorio Vergara, Osvaldo Ayala, and Sammy and Sandra Sandoval. There are several popular locales to hear this type of music in Panama City; see that chapter for details.

Panama's classical music scene is dismal. Only one of Panama's 90 or so radio stations plays any classical music, and the Panama National Orchestra, created in 1941, gives only irregular and infrequent performances. However, a private organization, the Asociación Nacional de Conciertos, periodically organizes excellent concerts by local and foreign artists.

Handicrafts

Panama's handicrafts are varied and often of excellent quality. The Wounaan and Emberá in Darién Province produce some beautiful woven baskets, most of which are exported to the USA and Europe, although many of high quality can be found in Panama. These tribes also sell life-size images of snakes, parrots, toucans and other jungle wildlife carved from cocobolo, a handsome tropical hardwood, and they carve tiny figurines (typically of iguanas, turtles, crocodiles and birds) from the ivory-colored tagua nut. Both tribes also make, and to a lesser degree sell, silver jewelry.

The Kuna of the Comarca de San Blás are known worldwide for their molas – the blouse panels used by women in their traditional dress and sold as crafts. Molas symbolize the identity of the Kuna people to outsiders, and their designs may be very elaborate; they are always colorful and typically depict sea turtles, birds and fish. If you visit an inhabited San Blás island, you will likely see at least a few women making molas.

A variety of handicrafts and curios are available on the Península de Azuero as well. The towns of Ocú and Penonomé produce superior Panama hats, the finest of which are so tightly woven they can hold water. Polleras – elaborate outfits of Spanish origin that consist of an intricately embroidered white skirt with an off-the-shoulder flounced blouse, contrasting petticoats edged with lace, and many pairs of shimmering filigree ornaments worn in the hair with a large comb – are handmade in Guararé and in villages around Las Tablas. Also found on the Azuero are festival masks (in Parita) and pottery (in La Arena).

Many of the handicrafts mentioned here can be purchased in Panama City. See the Shopping sections in the Facts for the Visitor and Panama City chapters for additional information.

Painting

Trained in France, Roberto Lewis (1874-1949) became the first prominent figure on Panama's art scene. He painted portraits of the nation's leaders and allegorical images to decorate public buildings; among his most notable works are those in the Palacio de las Garzas in Panama City.

In 1913 Lewis became director of Panama's first art academy, where he and his successor, Humberto Ivaldi (1909-47), educated a generation of artists. Among the school's students were Juan Manuel Cedeño and Isaac Benítez, as well as the painters who would come to the fore in the 1950s and 1960s. This group includes Alfredo Sinclair, Guillermo Trujillo, Ciro Oduber, Eudoro Silvera and others. Most of these artists are still active today, and their works are occasionally shown in local galleries.

Of this group, Trujillo is the most celebrated. His personal iconography is rooted in Panama's pre-Columbian history and Indian mythology, its landscapes and flora. With a rich and versatile oeuvre ranging from social satires to imagined landscapes and delicate semiabstractions, Trujillo has achieved international success as a painter. As a professor, he promoted a lasting interest in watercolor painting, ceramics and printmaking in Panama.

Although there are some exceptions, most contemporary Panamanian artists have not concentrated on political subjects. However, during the 1980s many artists turned to figuration and a focus on the human condition. Among them is Brooke Alfaro, whose nightmarish images and disturbing visions of common people and authority figures have achieved international recognition.

Other valuable contemporary painters are Antonio Alvarado (abstract), Isabel de Obaldía, Raúl Vásquez, Roosevelt Díaz, Tabo Toral, Guillermo Mezza, Ana Elena Garuz (abstract), Teresa Icaza, Vicky Suescum (abstract) and Julio Zachrisson (a winner of Spain's prestigious Goya Award). The work of these and other fine artists can be seen and bought in the best galleries in Panama City; see that chapter for details.

The largest Panamanian art exposition – the Bienal de Arte – is held every two years at the Museo de Arte Contemporáneo, on Avenida San Blás at Avenida de los Mártires in the Ancón district of Panama City. The paintings and sculptures on exhibit are selected by a reputable international jury. The monthlong exposition will be held in

October 2000 and October 2002, and it is very worthwhile.

Sculpture

Sculpture is not a strong tradition in Panama, but there are a few extraordinary artists in the trade: Guillermo Trujillo is doing beautiful, elegant bronze sculptures; Isabel de Obaldía is an internationally acclaimed glass sculptor; Raúl Vásquez creates totemlike wooden pieces; and Susie Arias has done several public sculptures in California, where she resides (but some of her small pieces can be bought in Panama). Other fine sculptors are Donna Conlon (working in marble), Emily Zhukov (cast aluminum) and Lezlie Milson (a hybrid between painting and sculpture). Coincidentally, these last three are Americans who have lived in Panama for many years. Sculpture can be seen at galleries in Panama City. See details in that chapter.

Literature

Unfortunately, many of Panama's greatest written works, such as those of Roque Javier Laurenza and José de Jesus Martínez, are no longer available in most of the country's bookstores. However, there are still good things in stock at some stores, mainly at Librería Cultural Panameña (☎ 223-6267), near the western end of Vía España, near Colejio Javier (a well-known school) in Panama City. Here you can find what many consider to be five of Panama's best novels:

El ahogado – The drowned man, a 1937 novel by Tristán Solarte (pen name for Guillermo Sánchez Borbón, a poet, novelist and journalist of international recognition), ingeniously blends elements of the detective, gothic and psychological genres, along with a famous local myth, into the narration of the events that lead to the tragic death of Rafael, an attractive but demonic young man.

El desván – In *The garret,* a 1954 novel with a surprise ending, Ramón H Jurado explores the emotional limits of the human condition through the delirious monologue of a man whose sickness is slowly paralyzing him.

Panama's Super Stamps

In the world of stamp collecting, Panama is a top producer. The teams of engravers and painters, lithographic artists and graphic designers who create the nation's postal issues are widely regarded as among the world's best. Panamanian stamps not only capture the country's history, places, people and nature but also honor world events and figures. Among Panama's 1997 releases were a set of stamps that pays homage to Mahatma Gandhi and a set that celebrates the birth of Jerusalem, 3000 years ago. ∎

Gamboa Road Gang – This 1960 novel by Joaquín Beleño is the best work of fiction about the political and social events surrounding the Panama Canal. It's in English.

Loma ardiente y vestida de sol – Burning and sun-drenched hill, a 1974 novel by Rafael Pernett y Morales, is a bold look at Panama City's poor, mainly the squatters, in which the author, armed with considerable wit and imagination, tries to rescue popular urban customs and lingo.

Semana sin viernes – In his 1996 novel *A week without Friday,* Justo Arroyo writes about a young man whose obsession with mastering the game of pool leads him to the verge of murder.

Some of these works are available in English translations, but they can only be found in Panama.

An excellent short-story writer is José María Sanchez, whose work was first published in the 1940s but has recently been re-released in an anthology titled *Cuentos de Bocas del Toro (Tales of Bocas del Toro).* Set in the beautiful province of Bocas del Toro (where the author was born and raised), these fun stories, whose protagonists are driven by the sensuous, baroque excesses of the tropical jungle and sea, possess a language charged with powerful imagery.

Another superb collection of short stories is *Inauguración de La Fe (Inauguration of La Fe,* 1995), by writer and poet Consuelo Tomás; the tales are full of her characteristically playful but biting humor and her innate ability to depict the idiosyncrasies of the popular neighborhoods of Panama City. Both collections are available at Panamanian bookstores.

Panama can boast of its poets of extraordinary quality, such as Ricardo Miró, Rogelio Sinán (also a fiction writer, perhaps the best known outside Panama), Demetrio Herrera Sevillano, Demetrio Korsi, Tristán Solarte, César Young Núñez, Bertalicia Peralta, Manuel Orestes Nieto and Edison Simmons.

Theater

The theater scene in Panama is limited to the capital city, and even there it's weak. There are no professional theater companies in the country, although there are groups of amateurs who stage various low-budget productions. The Teatro En Circulo (Circular Theater) operates as an organized amateur troupe with its own theater, as does the Ancon Theater Guild. Check *Talingo,* the arts supplement in the Sunday edition of *La Prensa,* for a list of cultural events scheduled for the upcoming week.

An experimental theater troupe, Oveja Negra (Black Sheep), periodically puts on productions. When they do, their performances are always excellent and are usually held at the Alianza Francesa Panameña in Panama City. Panama City has several other venues for theater; see that chapter for details.

Photography

Panama has several gifted photographers, including Iraida Icaza, Stuart GR Warner W and Sandra Eleta. Icaza, who lived for many years in Tokyo and now resides in New York, makes abstract art using photographic equipment. Her work is very bold and innovative.

Warner, who has spent much of his life in Asia, the Middle East, Europe and the USA, captures the human spirit in beautiful landscapes and portraits. Unlike many professionals, Warner never relies on artificial lighting or lens filters.

Sandra Eleta's portraits of black inhabitants of Panama's Caribbean coast (particularly of Portobelo, where she resides part of the year) have made her one of the most important photographers in Latin America. A book of her work can be found at Librería Argosy in Panama City (see Bookstores in the Panama City chapter).

SOCIETY & CONDUCT
Racial Issues

Panama is home to many ethnic groups. The Indian tribes; the various peoples of the West Indies; the Spanish-Indian mestizos; the Chinese, Middle Eastern, Swiss and Croatian immigrants; the North and South Americans; and others all maintain their own cultures, yet some elements of their cultures have mixed to form new combinations. It is partly because of the mixing that the various groups are able to live together. As one Panamanian friend of mine put it, 'That man there is black, but next to you I am black. I must have some black or Indian in me. So, you see, we're just talking about different shades of the same color.'

But class distinctions *do* exist in Panama. While politicians from the president on down take pride in mingling with the public and maintaining some semblance of a classless society, the whites (who make up only 10% of the population) control the majority of the wealth and nearly all the power. And within that group are several dozen wealthy families who are above the law – people able to escape arrest by mentioning the names of others who could complicate life for a lowly police officer.

This same group can get hard-to-come-by reservations with a phone call. They generally are able to go right to the front of lines because of who they are and because they ask to speak directly with managers, who are keen to attend to the rich and powerful (and the offspring of the rich and powerful) out of respect, envy and fear. In Panama members of a certain class marry only members of that certain class. And at the almighty Union Club, *the* social club of Panama City, memberships are not given to people of color, to Jews (with a few exceptions) or to other 'minorities.'

As a white person traveling around Panama, I was always a little surprised and somewhat saddened to find that the color of my skin gave me immediate access to places dark-skinned people would have had trouble entering. For example, one night I went bar-hopping without an ID, which is illegal. Every time a doorman asked for my ID and I said I didn't have it, I was let into the club anyway; blacks would not have been admitted. Some nights I'd try entering places with restricted access, such as gated residential areas, and as soon as a guard could see that I was white I was waved through. Strangely

enough, the doormen and guards who let me pass were always people of color.

All this racism might sound terrible, and certainly it is, but it is much less terrible than situations found in most countries. There's no counterpart to the Ku Klux Klan here; there are no skinheads committing hate crimes. For all its inequities, Panama is closer to the ideal in this respect than most developed nations.

Dos & Don'ts

Because Panama is so diverse, what's acceptable in one part of the country may be totally unacceptable in another part. For example, it's quite OK to get a full-body tan on Playa de las Suecas (Swedish Women Beach) on Isla Contadora – in fact, it's Panama's only government-approved nude beach – but lie naked on a beach in the Archipiélago de San Blás and you can expect a good scolding. Indeed, although the Kuna tolerate sunbathing on their beaches, they are very offended when foreign women enter their villages in bikini tops or short shorts.

Panama City is a dressy town. The men typically wear business shirts and slacks and the women dresses even when they're just tooting about. At work and when club-hopping, they typically dress to the nines. Many dance clubs in the city won't let in men who are wearing collarless shirts or tennis shoes. A halter top and shorts are OK during the daytime when it's hot, but Panamanians look down upon people who don't dress better after dark. Strategically ripped jeans, tank tops and the like are very frowned upon.

Panama is a conservative country where people generally have a great deal of respect for one another. If, for example, you have a business meeting with a Panamanian, you can expect the Panamanian to be well dressed out of respect for you. Conversely, out of respect for the Panamanian, you should dress well. Foreign women who are trying to win the respect of Panamanian men will dress smartly, and foreign men trying to win the respect of Panamanian women will do likewise. Even on very hot days in Panama, you'll rarely see a man working with his shirt off or a woman wearing shorts hemmed above the knee. Leave the grunge behind.

In Panama you are considered guilty until proven innocent. For this reason it's wise to avoid placing yourself in situations where a crime is occurring or is likely to occur. For example, if people near you light up a joint or snort cocaine, get away from them; if police see those people doing drugs, they might presume that you're doing drugs too. Public drinking is illegal in Panama. (See Legal Matters in the Facts for the Visitor chapter for more information on drugs and alcohol.)

You should have a photographic ID on you at all times; it's the law. Preferably this should be a passport, and it should contain a tourist card if applicable (see the Facts for the Visitor chapter for details on tourist cards).

The Kuna Indians are a most attractive people. It may be tempting to take photographs of them. If you wish to do so, be polite and ask their permission beforehand. Note that there is usually a US$1 fee attached to every photo you take of a Kuna, payable to the subject. This fee was arrived at after a Kuna chief saw a postcard of a Kuna woman, learned that it was selling for US$1 and grew incensed when he realized that the subject was not benefiting from the sale of the postcard.

In common with most Latin American countries, greetings are very important to Panamanians. In all situations, politeness is a valued habit. A certain degree of formality and floweriness is often used in conversation. Expect total strangers to say, *'Buenas días,' 'Buenas tardes'* and *'Buenas noches'* to you, and be prepared to do likewise. Male friends and casual acquaintances meeting one another in the street shake hands at the beginning and end of even a short meeting; women kiss one another on the cheek in greeting and farewell. Men often kiss women decorously on the cheek, and vice versa.

The well-documented fact that smoking is hazardous to one's health is widely known and respected in Panama. There are nonsmoking sections in restaurants, and many hotels have nonsmoking rooms. In keeping with Panamanians' respect for one another (their driving practices notwithstanding), nonsmoking signs are universally obeyed in Panama.

Punctuality in Panama is very different from punctuality in the USA, Canada, Japan and elsewhere. In Panama people expected to attend a business meeting scheduled for 3 pm may not arrive until 3:30 pm or later – and that's acceptable. If you are short on time and are scheduling a meeting, emphasize the designated time. If you're speaking Spanish, follow the designated time with an *'en punto'* – 'on the dot' – as in, *'Vamos a las dos en punto'* ('Let's go at two on the dot').

Other things to remember include the following:

- If you're found in possession of pre-Columbian art, you will go to jail.
- The use of flash equipment in churches and museums is prohibited.
- Shorts, halter tops and tank tops are not permitted in churches.
- Shorts are not permitted in any governmental building.
- It is unlawful to drive without wearing a shirt.
- Drinking on All Souls' Day (November 2) is considered disrespectful.

RELIGION

Freedom of religion is constitutionally guaranteed in Panama, although the preeminence of Roman Catholicism is also officially recognized. The major faiths are Roman Catholicism (85%), Protestant denominations (5%), Islam (5%) and Baha'i (1%). There are also small numbers of Hindus, Jews and other believers. In addition, the various Indian tribes have their own belief systems, although these are fading quickly due to the influence of missionaries preaching Christianity.

Religion is especially mixed in Panama City, home to immigrants from all over the world. The city has many Catholic and Protestant churches, three Jewish synagogues and two Moslem mosques, and the Hindu and Baha'i religions each have a temple.

LANGUAGE

Spanish is the official language of Panama, but no fewer than 14 other languages can also be heard on the isthmus. Eight languages are spoken by Panama's seven Indian tribes (the Kuna living in the villages of Paya and Pucuro, in southeastern Panama, speak a language that's quite different from that of Kuna residing elsewhere). Two Chinese languages, Arabic, Hebrew, San Miguel Creole French and Western Caribbean Creole English are also spoken in Panama.

San Miguel Creole French is spoken by scattered groups whose ancestors came from St Lucia during the mid-19th century as laborers. Western Caribbean Creole English is spoken by an estimated 14% of the population, whose ancestors came from Barbados and Jamaica in the 19th century to work in fruit plantations and later to build the Panama Railroad and Canal. Creole English is commonly heard in Bocas del Toro Province and in Colón. Other Panamanians have learned English at school or from US soldiers and Panama Canal workers.

Many Chinese also came to Panama to work on the railway and the canal, and their descendants speak Cantonese or Hakka. During the 20th century, Chinese immigrants arrived as merchants. There is a hearty Chinatown in Panama City and a substantial Chinese community in Colón. Likewise, many Arabs and Jews came to these two cities to conduct business. Today Arabs from several Middle Eastern countries and Jews from Israel and the USA comprise two of the most powerful groups in Panama.

Just as most Panamanian immigrants have learned to speak Spanish as a second language, any traveler to Panama would be wise to learn at least a little Spanish as a matter of courtesy and convenience. If you don't already speak some Spanish, please look at the Spanish for Travelers section at the back of this book, and at the very least learn how to say 'good morning,' 'good afternoon,' 'good evening,' 'goodbye,' 'thank you' and 'glad to meet you' in Spanish. Generally, if you try speaking Spanish in Panama and the person you are talking to speaks English, that person will respond in English.

Facts for the Visitor

PLANNING
When to Go
Panama's tourist season is the dry season – from mid-December to mid-April. During the rainy season, the weather is typically hot and steamy in the lowlands, and the humidity can reach saunalike levels. But even during the rainy season, days-long rains are rare. Rain in Panama, as elsewhere in the Tropics, tends to come in short downpours that freshen the air, clean the streets and precede wonderful sunshine.

If you'll be doing any serious hiking, the dry season is the most comfortable time to do it – and the least arduous, because you'll have better traction, no sucking mud to contend with and fewer creeks to cross. For planning purposes, be aware that the mountains in western Panama are much cooler than the lowlands; if you're considering camping, be sure to bring warm clothing.

If you like to party, try to be in Panama City or on the Península de Azuero for Carnaval (Mardi Gras), held each year during the four days leading up to Ash Wednesday. Panama City's Carnaval celebration is one of the world's largest. On the Península de Azuero it's great fun, too, but the crowds are not as huge. Hotel reservations during Carnaval are a must and need to be made well in advance. Panama has a number of other festivals worth catching, especially on the Azuero; see the Herrera Province and Los Santos Province chapters for details.

Maps
International Travel Maps (☎ 604-687-3320, fax 604-687-5925), 736A Granville St, Vancouver, BC V6Z 1G3, Canada, publishes an excellent 1:800,000 color map showing the geographical features, cities, towns, national parks, airports and roads of Panama (US$7.95). It also publishes an excellent 1:800,000 color map of Central America (US$8.95).

The Instituto Geográfico Nacional (☎ 236-2444), just off Avenida Simón Bolívar in Panama City, sells a tourist map (US$1.50) with a good street map of Panama City on one side and a country map on the other. It also sells 1:50,000 topographical maps, nautical maps, provincial maps, city maps and other kinds of maps. Taxi drivers know the institute as simply 'Tommy Guardia' in honor of the man who founded it.

Free tourist publications, including *Focus on Panama* and *Panama 2000* – available at some Instituto Panameño de Turismo (IPAT) offices and at the country's finer hotels – contain fold-out maps showing Panama on one side and Panama City, David and Colón on the other. These maps, though occasionally helpful, don't warrant a special trip to an IPAT office.

What to Bring
You can buy anything you are likely to need in Panama and probably more cheaply than you can back home, but if you're short on time, try to bring everything you think you'll need with you. And although the risk of contracting malaria is quite remote, if you intend to be on antimalaria medication during your trip, you'll want to start taking it before you leave as it takes a couple of weeks to kick in (see the Health section, later in this chapter).

If you'll be camping, bring a sweater or jacket for chilly nights. If you're planning on scuba diving or snorkeling while you're in Panama, check the Activities section in this chapter for tips on items to bring.

City & Beach Clothing Panamanians place a lot of importance on appearances. If you want to be treated with respect, don't dress like a bum. Only the poorest Panamanian would wear cut-offs, and no locals

Floss It

For the cost of a crummy cigar, you can buy a vacation-saving item. It's called dental floss, and its uses are innumerable. Got a fishhook but no line? Four words: green waxed dental floss. Need to secure a mosquito net? Reach for dental floss. Forgot to pack a clothesline? You're in luck if you've packed dental floss. Tear in your jeans, rip in your pack? A little dental floss and a sewing needle and life goes on.

Dental floss comes in 50m and 100m lengths and is sold in nifty little cases complete with built-in cutters. It's cheap, it's light, it's strong and it's outrageously useful. Some say dental floss can even remove decay-causing material from between teeth and under gums. Now in cinnamon, mint and grape flavors. No kidding. ■

strut around in bikini tops except at the beach. Due to the heat, the most appropriate clothing for Panamanian cities is made of 100% cotton fiber or (even better, but pricier) material designed to wick moisture away from the skin; such high-tech wear usually can be found in stores specializing in outdoor apparel.

If the club scene is your scene, keep in mind that casual-to-dressy officewear is the norm here, and collared shirts are preferred to T-shirts. Most clubs, even in the run-down Casco Viejo district of Panama City, deny entry to people in shorts. Entry to government buildings, too, is often denied to people in shorts. Shoewise, Panamanians seem to stop wearing sneakers at about age 16 in favor of leather shoes.

The beach scene ranges from the Brazilian (brief briefs and thong bikinis) to the US (baggy shorts and enveloping one-pieces). Nudity will attract unwanted attention or detention, except at the country's only official nude beach, on Isla Contadora. Remember, every day of the year a sunburn spoils someone's vacation. Regardless of your other beach apparel,

wear sunscreen if you are susceptible to burning. You'll be glad you did.

Jungle Gear If you'll be spending a significant amount of time in the jungle, consider bringing the following items along with you:

- lightweight hiking boots with good traction if your jaunts will be short
- military boots with drainage holes and ankle support for long treks
- strong (95% Deet) insect repellent for skin and clothes
- a heavy-duty rain poncho
- an extralight blanket
- an air-inflated sleeping pad (Thermarest is best)
- washable tennis, running or walking shoes
- a pair of sandals (strap-on sports-style sandals recommended)
- six pairs of cotton-polypropylene/nylon socks
- a pair of wool-blend socks
- two pairs of lightweight, quick-dry field pants
- two pairs of quick-dry shorts
- five changes of underwear
- two long-sleeved cotton shirts (big enough to layer for extra warmth)
- a lightweight jacket or windbreaker
- a sun hat or cap
- a swimsuit
- a first-aid kit (see Predeparture Preparations, later in this chapter)

Of all the items listed above, the three most important are the boots, the insect repellent and the poncho. I've worn all kinds of boots in all kinds of places and have determined that – for my feet, anyway – nothing beats US Army boots. They were perfected for jungle wear during the Vietnam War of the 1960s, and no one's improved upon them in all the years since. As for bug repellent, even if you're the sort of person who enjoys inhaling a mosquito every now and then, you ought to apply repellent to protect yourself against insect-transmitted diseases. A heavy-duty poncho is very important, and not only for keeping the rain off you – it'll help prevent ticks and other bugs from clinging to you when you brush against branches. The best places to buy jungle boots, bug spray and heavy-duty ponchos are Army/Navy surplus stores.

TOURIST OFFICES
Local Tourist Offices
At the time this book went to press, the Instituto Panameño de Turismo (IPAT), the national tourism agency, had its headquarters (☎ 226-3483, fax 226-4849) in the Centro Atlapa on Vía Israel in the San Francisco neighborhood of Panama City. IPAT was planning to relocate its office to the Casco Viejo district of the capital city; an exact site had not been chosen. If you need to speak with someone at IPAT when you're in Panama City, call directory assistance (☎ 102) and ask for IPAT's current location and telephone number.

IPAT has information counters at the ruins of Panamá La Vieja and at Tocumen International Airport. The agency also has tourist centers in Bocas del Toro town, Boquete, Colón, David, Penonomé, Portobelo and Santiago, and new ones are planned in Chitré and El Valle and near Villa de Los Santos. There is also a center in Paso Canoas, the principal border crossing between Panama and Costa Rica. Be forewarned: IPAT's maps and brochures are usually unhelpful, and IPAT offices tend to be staffed by people who speak only Spanish and probably won't have answers to your questions.

Tourist Offices Abroad
Panama has no tourist offices in other countries, but IPAT literature and other information is sometimes available at Panamanian consulates and embassies (see the Embassies & Consulates section in this chapter). Again, IPAT publications tend to be unhelpful and rich with inaccuracies. If you have access to the Internet, it may be worth your while to do a keyword search for *Panama* and see what appears; Panamanian businesses and international tour operators were creating websites like crazy at the time of writing, and some contained useful information – even maps.

VISAS & DOCUMENTS
Passports, Tourist Cards & Visas
Everyone needs a valid passport and an onward ticket to enter Panama, but further requirements vary from country to country and change frequently. Anyone who is planning a trip to Panama would be well advised to first contact the Panamanian embassy or consulate in his or her home country to obtain the latest information on entry requirements.

At the time of writing, people holding passports from the following countries needed only to show their passports to enter Panama: Austria, Chile, Costa Rica, Denmark, El Salvador, France, Germany, Guatemala, Honduras, Italy, the Netherlands, Portugal, Switzerland, the UK (including Britain, Northern Ireland, Scotland and Wales) and Uruguay.

People holding passports from the following countries needed to show a passport and a tourist card (see details below) to enter: Australia, Brazil, Canada, China, Finland, Greece, Ireland, Japan, Mexico, New Zealand, South Korea and the USA. Several dozen other countries were on this list.

People holding passports from the following countries needed to show a passport and a Panamanian visa (see details below): Cuba, Indonesia, Kuwait, Nepal, Pakistan, Russia, Saudi Arabia, Turkey and Vietnam. Many other countries, including all those on the African continent, appeared on this list.

A tourist card costs US$5 and is available from Panamanian embassies and consulates, and also from most airlines serving Panama, from the Tica Bus company and at the airport or border post upon entry. (See contact information for airlines and Tica in the Getting There & Away chapter.) Visas are issued at Panamanian embassies and consulates and typically cost US$20.

No matter where you are coming from, you will be given a 30-day stamp in your passport when you enter Panama. This means you are allowed to remain in Panama for 30 days without having to obtain further permission from the authorities. After 30 days, visas and tourist cards can be extended an additional 60 days at Migración y Naturalización (Immigration and Naturalization) offices. See details on how to get extensions under Extending Your Stay, below.

Those planning to enter Panama overland would be wise to obtain visas before showing up at the border, even if visas are not required of them; the border post may run out of tourist cards, which has happened more than once. If it is out of tourist cards, you can't get in (the border post at Guabito in northwestern Panama is the exception). You may need to show an onward ticket, and sometimes a show of cash is also required to cross land borders – US$500 per month of your planned stay is generally sufficient. Panamanians are sensitive to appearances; wearing decent clothes and avoiding unusual fashions will make entrance procedures easier.

Extending Your Stay Staying in the country once your tourist card or visa has expired is not risk free. If, for example, a police officer checks your ID (as often happens on some of the San Blás islands and in remote areas) and your tourist card or visa has expired, you may be detained until you can convince the person in charge that you'll remedy the situation as soon as possible. An on-the-spot fine may be levied as well, depending on the mood of the person in charge. It's a bit of a hassle to get a visa or tourist card extended, but you won't risk such run-ins if you do.

If you intend to stay more than 30 days and want to do things by the book, you'll need to obtain a Panamanian ID card, which will allow you to remain in Panama another 60 days. You can obtain one at a Migración y Naturalización office; there's one in Panama City (☎ 225-1373, 227-1077) on Avenida Cuba at Calle 29 Este, and there are also offices in Chitré, Changuinola, David and Santiago. You'll need your passport, US$10, a photocopy of the passport page containing your personal information, a photocopy of the passport page showing the stamp of your most recent entry into Panama, two passport-size

photos, an onward air or bus ticket and a completed form called a *prórroga de turista* (tourist extension), which you can get at the immigration offices.

The prórroga de turista is written in Spanish, but you can fill it out in English. It requests the following information:

nombre	name
fecha de nacimiento	date of birth
lugar de nacimiento	place of birth
estado civil	civil status
profesión u oficio	profession or work
pasaporte no	passport number
validez	date validated
fecha de llegada a Panama	date of arrival in Panama
procedente de	where you arrived from
en calidad de	the purpose of your visit
con visa o tarjeta turismo no	enter visa or tourist card number
con que objeto solicita la prórroga	state your reason for seeking an extension
dirección en Panama	address in Panama
pasaje de regreso	airline ticket number
nombre de la madre	mother's name
nacionalidad	mother's nationality
nombre del padre	father's name
nacionalidad	father's nationality
nombre de la esposa(o)	spouse's name
nacionalidad	spouse's nationality
firma del solicitante	your signature
fecha de la solicitud	date of request

Exit Permits
If you are in Panama for more than 30 days, you must obtain a *permiso de salida* (permit to leave) to be able to exit the country. This is necessary even if you have obtained a Panamanian ID card as described above. To obtain this permit, you must first obtain a *paz y salvo* – a stamped piece of paper indicating that you don't owe the Panamanian government any money (the paz y salvo is intended to catch tax cheats).

A paz y salvo can be obtained for US$1 from the Ministerios de Hacienda y Tesoro (Ministries of House and Tax) on the ground floor of the Edificio Hatillo (Hatillo Building) in Panama City. When you enter the building, look for a counter with a sign marked 'paz y salvo.' At the counter you'll be given a form to complete that asks for your name, your passport number, home address, telephone number, employer's name, number of years you've worked for that employer, the date of your arrival and the date of your departure.

When you've completed the form, submit it and US$1 to an official at the counter. That person will go to a computer and see if you owe taxes to the Panamanian government. If you don't, you'll then be given a paz y salvo – a small but official-looking slip of paper that you should place in your passport.

The next step in the process is to take the paz y salvo and your passport to a Migración y Naturalización office (see locales under Extending Your Stay, above). There you'll need only to submit the paz y salvo and pay a fine for staying in the country more than 30 days. (Officially, the fine ranges from up to US$25 for staying one month past deadline to US$40 for staying three months over, but often it isn't levied.) Your passport will then get a permiso de salida stamp, which you'll present to an immigration agent at the airport or border when you leave the country.

It is imperative that you obtain a permiso de salida to leave the country if you have overstayed your 30 days. No amount of pleading, no repeating to immigration agents that your pricey airplane ticket is nonrefundable, etc, will substitute for a permiso de salida if you arrive at the airport or border without one and your tourist card or visa has lapsed.

At the time of writing, there was talk of making this entire process more tourist friendly; it's possible there will be fewer requirements during your visit. Obtaining a permiso de salida as described above generally takes about two hours.

Onward Tickets

Travelers officially need onward tickets out of Panama before they are allowed to enter. This requirement is not often checked at Tocumen International Airport because most airlines will not let you board their planes in your home country unless you have an onward or roundtrip ticket. Those travelers arriving by land may need to show an onward ticket as well.

If you're heading to Colombia, Venezuela or another South American country from Panama, you may need an onward or roundtrip ticket before you will be allowed entry into that country or even allowed to board the plane if you're flying. A quick check with the appropriate embassy – easy to do by phone in Panama City – will tell you whether the country that you're heading to has an onward-ticket requirement.

Travel Insurance

No matter how you're traveling, make sure you take out travel insurance. This should cover you not only for medical expenses and luggage theft, but also for unavoidable cancellation or delays in your travel arrangements, and everyone should be protected against worst-case scenarios, such as an accident that requires hospital treatment and a flight home.

Coverage depends on your insurance and type of ticket, so ask both your insurer and your ticket-issuing agency to explain the finer points. Council Travel and STA Travel, with offices in many countries (see the Getting There & Away chapter for contact information), offer a variety of travel insurance options at reasonable prices. Ticket loss is also covered by travel insurance. Make sure you have a photocopy of your ticket and your policy tucked away in case one or both are lost.

Buy travel insurance as early as possible. If you buy it the week before you fly, you may find, for instance, that you're not covered for delays to your flight caused by strikes or other labor actions that may have been in force before you took out the insurance.

Driver's License & Permits

You can drive on a foreign license in Panama for up to 30 days. Drivers should carry their passports in addition to their licenses. To rent a car, your passport, driver's license and credit card are generally required. Also, you must be at least 25 years old to rent a car, or 23 if you have an American Express card.

If you plan on driving down to Panama from points north, you will need all the usual insurance and ownership papers. If you are bringing a vehicle into the country, you must pay US$6 for a vehicle control certificate *(tarjeta de circulación)* and to have your vehicle fumigated. With extensions, you and your vehicle can stay in the country for up to 90 days. However, after 30 days you'll need to get a Panamanian driver's license.

You can sell your car in Panama, but you must take it to a customs broker *(corredor de aduana)* for inspection, valuation and taxation. You'll find some customs brokers listed under *aduanas, corredores de* in the yellow pages of the phone book. Used-car lots can do all the paperwork for you. Be advised that it's common to negotiate payment of the taxes with the prospective buyer.

It's possible to drive into Panama from the three border posts it shares with Costa Rica. At this time it is not possible to drive into Panama from Colombia, as no roads connect the two countries. See the Getting There & Away and Getting Around chapters for more driving information.

Hostel & Student Cards
Sorry, there aren't any youth hostels in Panama, and student cards generally won't save their carriers any significant amount of money.

EMBASSIES & CONSULATES
Panamanian Embassies & Consulates
If you need a visa, you can obtain one from a Panamanian embassy or consulate in another country. Some countries have several Panamanian consulates; in the USA, for example, Panama maintains consulates in Atlanta, Chicago, Honolulu, Houston, Miami, New Orleans, New York, Philadelphia, San Diego and San Francisco, in addition to its embassy in Washington, DC.

Unless otherwise noted, the Panamanian diplomatic missions listed below are embassies.

Brazil
  Rua Figueredo Magalhaes 122,
  Copacbana, Rio de Janeiro
  (☎ 21-255-8512, fax 21-255-9085)
Canada
  130 Albert St, Suite 300, Ottawa, ON K1P
  5G4 (☎ 613-236-7177, fax 613-236-5775)
Colombia
  Calle 92, No 7-70, Bogotá
  (☎ 1-257-5067, fax 1-257-5068)
Costa Rica
  Calle 38, Avenidas 5 and 7, 275m from the
  center of Colon, north of San José
  (☎ 257-3241, fax 257-4864)
El Salvador
  Alameda Roosevelt, No 2838, and
  55 Avenida Norte, above Compañía
  Panameña de Aviación, San Salvador
  (☎ 260-5452, fax 298-0884)
France
  145 Avenue de Suffren, 75015 Paris
  (☎ 01 47 83 23 32, fax 01 45 67 99 43)
Germany
  Lutzowstrasse 1, 53173 Bonn
  (☎ 228-36-10-36, fax 228-36-35-58)
Guatemala
  5 Avenida 15-45, Zona 10, Centro
  Empresarial Torre II, Guatemala City
  (☎ 2-337-2445, fax 2-337-2446)
Honduras
  Colonia Palmira, Palmira Building, 2nd
  floor (in front of the Hotel Honduras Maya),
  Tegucigalpa (☎ /fax 31-5441)
Israel
  Hei Be'Iyar, No 2 10, 3rd floor, Kikar
  Hamedina, Tel Aviv 62093
  (☎ 3-696-0849, fax 3-691-0045)
Italy
  Viale Regina Margherita, No 239, 4th floor,
  Interno 11, 00198 Rome
  (☎ 6-4425-2173, fax 6-4426-5443)
Japan
  Kowa International Building, Room 902,
  Nishi Azabu, 12-26, 4-Chome, Minato-Hu,
  Tokyo 106
  (☎ 3-3499-3741, fax 3-5485-3548)
Mexico
  Schiller 326, 8th floor, Colonia Chapultepec-
  Morales, CP 11570, México DF
  (☎ 5-250-4229, fax 5-250-4045)
Nicaragua
  Pancasán No 61; from the Hotel Colon, one
  block from the lake and 25 flights up, Casa
  No 73, Managua (☎ 278-1619)
Singapore
  16 Raffles Quay, No 41-06, Hong Leong
  Building, Singapore 048581
  (☎ 221-8677, fax 224-0892)

Spain
    Claudio Coello 86, 28996 Madrid
    (☎ 91-576-50-01, fax 91-576-71-61)
UK
    48 Park St, London W1Y 3PD
    (☎ 0171-493-4646, fax 0171-493-4499)
USA
    2862 McGill Terrace NW, Washington, DC
    20008 (☎ 202-483-1407, fax 202-483-8413)
    Consulates:
    California – 870 Market St, San Francisco
    94102 (☎ 415-391-4268)
    Florida – 444 Brickell Ave, Suite 729,
    Miami 33131 (☎ 305-371-7031)
    New York – 1212 Ave of the Americas, 10th
    floor, New York 10036 (☎ 212-840-2450)

There is no Panamanian mission in Australia. Australians are encouraged to contact the Panamanian mission in Singapore (see the Singapore listing, above).

Embassies & Consulates in Panama
Foreign embassies and consulates are in Panama City; see the Panama City chapter for contact information for many of them. Costa Rica has a consulate in David, too; see the Chiriquí Province chapter.

CUSTOMS
You may bring up to 200 cigarettes and three bottles of liquor into Panama tax free. If you try to leave Panama with products made from endangered species – like jaguar teeth, ocelot skins and items made out of turtle shell – you'll face a fine that is usually accompanied by jail time.

MONEY
Currency & Exchange Rates
The US dollar has been Panama's currency since 1904, although it is called the *balboa* here for nationalistic reasons; prices appear with either a '$' or a 'B/.' out front. US$1 is equal to B/.1. Panamanian coins are of the same value, size and metal as US coins; both are used. Coins include one, five, 10, 25 and 50 *centesimos;* 100 centesimos equal US$1 (or B/.1, if you prefer).

With the exception of a Banco Nacional de Panamá counter at Tocumen International Airport, not one Panamanian bank will exchange currency (although some foreign banks may exchange US dollars for their home currencies). Not even the country's five-star hotels change money. Once you've left the airport, the only place willing to swap your marks, yen or other major currency for US dollars is a *casa de cambio* (exchange house). There are several in Panama City but few outside the capital.

Exchange rates vary daily. At the time of writing, the US dollar was strong and the sample rates shown below reflect that. However, the actual exchange rates you will encounter could be considerably higher or lower than these figures. Daily exchange rates can often be found in the financial pages of major newspapers and at larger banks.

Australia	A$1	=	B/.0.60
Canada	C$1	=	B/.0.63
France	1FF	=	B/.0.15
Germany	DM1	=	B/.0.50
Italy	L1000	=	B/.0.51
Japan	¥100	=	B/.0.69
New Zealand	NZ$1	=	B/.0.53
UK	UK£1	=	B/.1.45
USA	US$1	=	B/.1

Cash
Panama has no paper money of its own, but it does issue an impressive array of coins, the most common of which are on par with US coinage in size, shape, content and denomination. The only paper currency accepted in Panama is the US 'greenback,' and the only coinage accepted is either US or Panamanian.

Large bills can be troublesome in Panama, particularly outside the capital city. Only the priciest hotels and restaurants in Panama City are accustomed to breaking US$50 and US$100 bills. Even US$10 bills can pose problems for small vendors in the country's central provinces. Unless you will be staying at upscale hotels or don't mind changing bills at banks, bring plenty of US$10 and US$20 bills; anything larger will likely prove inconvenient.

Traveler's Checks
Traveler's checks in currencies other than US dollars are not accepted anywhere in

The Rich History of Panama's Coins

From the time Europeans first laid eyes upon the isthmus until Panama's national coinage was issued in 1904, coins of many nations were used in the country. Initially Spanish money was used, introduced by the conquistadors. Those coins were supplemented from the 17th century until the early 19th century by coinage produced by colonial Spanish-American mints. Colombian coinage was introduced and circulated from 1821 until shortly after Panama issued its own coins as an independent republic.

Panama's independence from Colombia occurred just one year before the USA began work on the Panama Canal. The USA and Panama agreed that the two countries' currencies would be interchangeable to facilitate the buying power of canal workers and to stabilize the new Panamanian currency by linking it to the reliable US dollar. Panama minted its coins in the USA and adopted the US greenback as its paper currency (but it called the US greenback a *balboa*). Although Panama often alters the images on its coinage, the coins are equal in metallic content, denomination, size and weight to US coins.

Two images that have not changed over the years are those of Indian chieftain Urraca, a warrior who resisted the conquistadors, and Vasco Núñez de Balboa, the first European to view the Pacific Ocean. The image of Urraca has appeared on the Panamanian one-*centesimo* coin since 1935, and that of Balboa is on several coins of different denominations (the one shown here is a one-balboa coin). Although Panama has had a great many talented artists over the years, the designer who created the images of Urraca and Balboa was William Clark Noble, an American from Newport, Rhode Island. ■

Panama. Because of the appearance of high-quality counterfeits, some banks will only accept American Express traveler's checks or traveler's checks issued by one of their branches or presented by their account holders. The banks that do accept traveler's checks typically charge an exchange fee equal to 1% of the amount of the check. Also, traveler's checks are rarely accepted by Panamanian businesses. In short, traveler's checks are inconvenient to use in Panama.

You are well advised to carry only cash or cash and credit cards and to withdraw funds via an automated teller machine (ATM) when needed. If you choose to use traveler's checks, those issued by American Express are the most widely accepted.

Credit Cards

Credit cards are widely accepted at travel agencies, upscale hotels and pricey restaurants nationwide, but they can be problematic almost everywhere else in Panama. Panama remains very much a cash society; if you intend to travel outside the capital city for a significant period, don't count on being able to use a credit card to pay your bills.

Receiving cash advances against a credit card can be a headache in Panama. For example, if you have a Citicorp Visa card and you want to get a cash advance against it, you have to go to a Citicorp bank to do it; Banco Nacional de Panamá branches will not honor your Visa card except at their ATMs (where the amount of a cash withdrawal is limited and you must know your personal identification number).

Remember, a cash advance against a credit card is typically accompanied by a high interest rate from the moment you make the withdrawal. However, you can avoid high interest charges by leaving a positive balance in your account before you travel – in other words, pay off your entire bill and add however much money you think you might need to receive in Panama.

Because mistakes happen, a credit-card user should ask the company that issued his or her card for the non-toll-free telephone number to use in case the card is lost while in Panama. Remember to obtain non-toll-free telephone numbers, as toll-free numbers are limited to domestic calls.

ATMs

ATM cards are widely used throughout Panama. Many Panamanian banks are linked to the worldwide Plus and Cirrus automated teller systems, so even if your home bank does not have a branch in Panama, you will likely be able to use your ATM card here. (Check the back of your credit and debit cards for the Plus and Cirrus symbols; cards that do not show one or the other likely will not be accepted by ATMs in Panama. Also, to be able to use them you must have a personal identification number. If you don't have one, contact the company that issued your card and obtain one.) Credit cards linked to Plus and Cirrus can also be used at many ATMs in Panama, but as noted above, cash withdrawn against credit cards usually carries a hefty interest rate.

Most Panamanian banks charge a US$3 fee for every ATM transaction, and the amount that can be withdrawn at one time varies from bank to bank and even from machine to machine at the same bank. For example, at Banco Nacional de Panamá, which has the largest number of branches, most ATMs will allow the cardholder to withdraw up to US$500 per transaction, but some ATMs stop dispensing cash at US$200. Just why that is is a bit of a mystery.

Also, if your home bank has placed a maximum limit on the amount its clients can withdraw, that limit will be honored by Panama's ATMs. Bank of America, for example, limits ATM withdrawals to US$300 per day. That limit applies to Bank of America debit cards used at ATMs in Panama.

International Transfers

If you need money sent to you from home, you'll find that many banks in Panama will accept cash transfers, but you'll also find that you must first open an account with them; they will charge a commission, and the size of the cash transfer is often limited to avoid the appearance of money laundering.

At Banco Nacional de Panamá, for example, in addition to opening an account you must state why you are seeking the money, provide your address in Panama and show your passport and a valid tourist card or visa. The transfer requires two days, and the bank charges a transfer fee; the sender also has to pay a fee.

You can reduce the inconvenience by transferring the money via Western Union, but its transfer fees are very steep. For example, the fee for transferring US$50 by Western Union is US$13; for transferring US$5000 it's US$200. However, there's lots less paperwork involved and the transfer can take as little as 15 minutes. There are more than 20 Western Union offices in Panama City, and others can be found in Aguadulce, Changuinola, Chitré, Colón, Coronado, David, La Chorrera, Las Tablas, Paso Canoas, Penonomé and Santiago.

Security

Pickpockets prey on easy targets, and unsuspecting tourists fit that bill. Avoid losing your money by following a few precautions: Carry money in inside pockets, money belts or pouches beneath your clothes. Don't carry a wallet in a back pocket or an outside jacket pocket. Don't put all your money in one place. Reports of people having their pockets picked are rare in Panama, but it's best to assume pickpockets are around and act accordingly.

Costs

Budget accommodations tend to be slightly more expensive in Panama than in other parts of Central America; a hotel room that might cost US$6 in Nicaragua or Guatemala might cost US$10 here. In Panama City you can get a very basic room for US$8 a night; a modern room in a better area costs around US$15 to US$20. Away from Panama City, accommodations are less expensive; a modern room may cost around US$12. Die-hard shoestring travelers can still find a room almost anywhere in the country for around US$6. Prices for everything else – food, transportation, places to visit – are very reasonable.

Tipping & Bargaining

You can tip some small change, or around 10% of the bill if you're feeling affluent, in fancier restaurants; in small cafés and other casual places, tipping is not necessary and is seldom done. It is not necessary to tip taxi drivers; however, bellhops are usually tipped.

Haggling over prices is not the custom in Panama. However, if you really want an item at a store where you suspect there are steep price markups – at a watch or camera store, for example – prices may be flexible. It never hurts to make an offer.

Taxes

A tax of 10% is added to the price of hotel rooms in Panama; when you inquire about a hotel price, be sure to determine whether the quoted price includes the tax. Hotel prices given in this book include the 10% tax, and they are high-season rates. There's also a 5% sales tax.

POST & COMMUNICATIONS
Sending Mail

An airmail letter from Panama to the USA weighing 20g or less requires 35¢ postage (25¢ for a postcard) and takes five to 10 days to arrive; an airmail letter to Europe or Australia requires 45¢ postage (40¢ for a postcard) and takes 10 days to arrive; to Japan the letter requires 60¢ postage (45¢

for a postcard) and takes 10 to 14 days to arrive. Parcels can also be mailed; they tend to be rather expensive and always take longer to reach a foreign destination.

The better hotels sell stamps; otherwise you'll need to buy them at a post office. Unfortunately, vending machines selling stamps have yet to appear in Panama. If you're near an upscale hotel, see if you can stamp and mail your correspondence at the hotel to avoid having to wait in line at a post office. US stamps are not accepted.

Most post offices in Panama are open 7 am to 6 pm weekdays and 7 am to 5 pm Saturday. In addresses, *Apartado* means 'PO Box'; it is not a street or apartment address.

Receiving Mail

Poste restante mail can be addressed to '(name), Entrega General, (town and province), República de Panamá.' Be sure the sender writes the country's name as 'República de Panamá' rather than simply 'Panamá,' or the mail may be sent back. Post offices in Panama will hold mail for 30 days before returning it. There is no fee for this service. You will need to show an ID to receive your mail, and it's not possible to pick up other people's mail.

If you have mail sent to the post office, remember that the mail is filed alphabetically; if it's addressed to John Gillis Payson, it could well be filed under 'G' or 'J' instead of 'P.' Ask your correspondents to clearly print your last name and to avoid appending witticisms such as 'World Traveler Extraordinaire' to your name.

Poste restante parcels can also be sent to you. If the parcel weighs less than 2kg and isn't particularly large, it will generally arrive at the post office. If it's heavy or large, it will likely be held at the post office in the El Dorado district of Panama City, where it will have to clear customs. You'll be notified that it's there by personnel at the post office addressed by the sender.

Telephone

Panama's longtime state-run telephone company, Intel, was purchased by a British consortium in 1997 for US$625 million and renamed Cable & Wireless. At the time of the buyout, the country's phone system was horrible, due to the fact that it had far fewer cables installed than could accommodate the number of calls being placed. Also, pay phones were in short supply, and most of those that did exist had been vandalized.

At the start of 1998, Cable & Wireless announced a five-year, US$572 million modernization plan. The plan called for 10,000 new pay phones, a US$110 million cellular phone network and an ambitious employee retraining program. To cut down on vandalism to pay phones, which was generally done by thieves seeking coins, Cable & Wireless was planning to issue telephone calling cards.

Cable & Wireless offices throughout Panama offer international telephone, telegraph, fax and sometimes email and modem services.

Local Calls Telephone calls to anywhere within Panama can be made from pay phones. Local calls cost 15¢ for three minutes. Five-cent, 10¢ and 25¢ coins are accepted (both Panamanian and US coins are OK). Follow the directions given on the phone; some phones require you to insert the coin first, and others instruct you to first wait for the tone and then dial the number. For the latter type, don't deposit the coin until the call has been answered at the other end. To speak with a national operator, dial ☎ 101. For directory assistance, dial ☎ 102.

International Calls When placing international calls, you can connect directly to an operator of that country from any public or private phone. However, most hotels require that you go through a switchboard so that they can charge an outrageous connection fee; in the pricier hotels this fee can be US$4 or more – even if you are simply asking to be connected to an international operator.

Furthermore, many hotels in Panama charge a per-minute fee for international calls that is far in excess of what the telephone company charges them. And on top of that, there is often a three-minute minimum; a 20-second call to Tokyo, for example, might cost US$15 because the cost was US$5 per minute and a three-minute minimum applied. In short, avoid placing international calls from hotels or at least ask what the connection fee and per-minute rate are before calling, so that you won't receive a surprisingly high telephone bill at the time you check out.

Connecting to an international operator from a residential, business or pay phone is easy. To connect with a local international operator, simply dial ☎ 106. For an international operator in the USA, dial ☎ 108 (MCI), 109 (AT&T), 115 (Sprint) or 117 (TRT). For a Costa Rican operator, dial ☎ 107; for a Colombian operator, dial ☎ 116.

At the time of writing, a phone call from a public phone to the USA cost about US$1 per minute, to Europe US$3 per minute, to Australia US$4 per minute and to Japan US$5 per minute. As these prices tend to change every six months or so, you would be wise to call an international operator and learn current rates before calling anyone else.

To call Panama from abroad, use the international code (507) before the seven-digit Panamanian telephone number. There are no city codes in Panama.

Fax & Email
Fax services are offered by Cable & Wireless offices throughout the country; email and modem services are sometimes also available at these offices. Many upscale hotels also offer fax service, and some were planning to offer email service on a per-minute basis at the time this book was written (the Hotel Costa Inn in Panama City was one such place).

Internet cafés were springing up around Panama at the time of writing – and they were going out of business nearly as quickly. In Panama City one that seemed to have a bright future was the Internet Café, charging US$4 per hour before 5 pm and US$5 thereafter. See the Information section in the Panama City chapter for details.

INTERNET RESOURCES

Travel Agencies
Council Travel
www.counciltravel.com

Cruises Inc
www.cruisesinc.com

STA Travel
www.statravel.com

Travel CUTS
www.travelcuts.com

Travel Organizations
The Latin American Travel Advisor
www.amerispan.com/latc

South American Explorers Club
www.samexplo.org

Tour & Activity Operators
Adventure Associates
www.adventureassociates.com

Ancon Expeditions of Panama
www.ecopanama.com

Bocas Water Sports
www.bocasdeltoro.com/watersport.htm

Canopy Adventure
canopy.mit.edu

Chiriquí River Rafting
www.panama-rafting.com

Coiba Explorer Panama
www.coibaexplorer.com

Ecotours
www.pty.com/ecotours

Journey Latin America
www.journeylatinamerica.co.uk

Lost World Adventures
www.gorp.com/lostworld.htm

Mountain Travel-Sobek
www.MTSobek.com

Wildland Adventures
www.wildland.com

Environmental &
Scientific Organizations
Asociación Nacional para la
Conservación de la Naturaleza (Ancon)
www.ancon.org

Audubon Society of Panama
www.pananet.com/audubon

Smithsonian Tropical Research
Institute (STRI)
www.stri.org

Places to Stay
The Bristol
www.rosewood-hotels.com/bristol.htm

Caesar Park Hotel
www.caesarpark.com

Canopy Tower
canopy.mit.edu

Hotel Suites Central Park
www.suitescentralpark.com

La Montaña y el Valle
www.ncal.verio.com/~ptpub/montana

Mangrove Inn Eco-Dive Resort
www.bocas.com

Miramar Inter-Continental
www.interconti.com

Tropic Star Lodge
www.tropicstar.com

Other
Chiquita Brands International
www.chiquita.com

Language & International Relations
Institute (ILERI)
www.panamacanal.com/ileri.htm

If you're staying in Panama for a while and want a local email address, you can get one from Sinfonet (☎ 265-6000) at Centro Comercial Balboa on Vía Italia in Panama City. At the time of writing, Sinfonet charged US$49 a month for unlimited use.

Please realize that given the speed with which the cyberworld changes, it's possible that Sinfonet, Panama's largest Internet provider at the time of writing, won't exist by the time you read this. Your best bet is to speak with local users (you'll find some at the Internet cafés) before signing up with an Internet provider.

See the Internet Resources sidebar for a list of useful websites about Panama.

BOOKS

Many of the books listed below are available outside Panama. A few bookstores in Panama City carry some of the titles; they are listed in the Panama City chapter.

Lonely Planet

Lonely Planet's *Central America on a shoestring* is useful for travelers on a tight budget who are visiting several Central American countries. Lonely Planet's *Costa Rica* and *Colombia* are the finest guidebooks on those countries. Its *Latin American Spanish phrasebook* contains practical, up-to-date words and expressions in Latin-American Spanish.

Guidebooks

When choosing travel guidebooks, try get a recent edition. The older the guidebook, the greater the likelihood that it contains inaccuracies.

The Panama Guide (Seaworthy Publications, 1996), by Nancy Schwalbe Zydler and Tom Zydler, is *the* cruising guide to the isthmus of Panama. It offers piloting directions, charts, anchorages, history, even instructions for transiting the Panama Canal. My experience with ocean-going vessels can be summed up in two words – motion sickness – and yet I found this book a captivating read. You might, too. Copies are available in Panama City.

History

The Sack of Panamá: Sir Henry Morgan's Adventures on the Spanish Main, by Peter Earle, is a vivid though not particularly well-sourced account of the Welsh pirate's looting of Panamá in 1671.

Old Panama and Castilla Del Oro (The Page Company, 1911), by CLG Anderson, is a narrative history of the discovery, conquest and settlement of Panama by the Spaniards. This hard-to-find but impressive tome also reports on the search for a strait

through the New World and early efforts to build a canal.

Panama: Resumen Histórico Ilustrado del Istmo 1501-1994 (Antigua Films, 1996), by Ricardo de la Espriella III, is a well-written and beautifully illustrated history of Panama from the arrival of Rodrigo de Bastidas through the US invasion. It is only available in Spanish.

Panama: Four Hundred Years of Dreams and Cruelty, by David A Howarth, is a readable history of the isthmus from Balboa's 1513 exploration through 1964. This book was titled *The Golden Isthmus* for one printing.

Panama Canal

The Path Between the Seas: The Creation of the Panama Canal is an exciting account of the building of the canal, written by the award-winning historian David McCullough. It is 700 pages long and reads like a suspense novel from cover to cover. It is the best book written about the construction of the canal.

And the Mountains Will Move, by Miles P Du Val, is a scholarly account of the digging of the canal from the start of the unsuccessful French effort through the US achievement.

Other books describing the building of the unnatural waterway include *The Impossible Dream: The Building of the Panama Canal,* by Ian Cameron; *The Panama Canal: The Crisis in Historical Perspective,* by Walter LaFeber; and *Portrait of the Panama Canal* (Graphic Arts Center Publishing Company, 1996), by William Friar.

An American Legacy in Panama (US Department of Defense, 1995), by Suzanne P Johnson, was prepared for the US Army to provide an overview of US military installations in the Canal Area, and it does indeed give a very thorough report on current and former US installations near the canal.

Politics & the Noriega Era

Inside Panama (Interhemispheric Resource Center, 1995), by Tom Barry and John Lindsay-Poland, is a look at the political, economic and human-rights scenes in

Panama, with special emphasis on Panamanian society since the 1960s and on US-Panama relations from that time through the mid-1990s.

The Noriega Mess: The Drugs, the Canal, and Why America Invaded, a 1000-page tome by Luis E Murillo, is quite interesting and very readable. It's based on a variety of sources and information that have come to light in the years since 1989.

Panama: The Whole Story, by Kevin Buckley, is another fine book about Noriega and the events that led to the 1989 US invasion; 'as readable as a spy thriller,' the book's jacket proclaims, and it nearly lives up to its billing.

For yet another perspective on the Noriega story, look for his memoir, *America's Prisoner: The Memoirs of Manuel Noriega*, cowritten with Peter Eisner, who has researched Noriega's claims and footnoted the text.

Nature & Wildlife

The 2nd edition of *A Guide to the Birds of Panama*, by Robert S Ridgley and John A Gwynne, Jr, is the foremost field guide to Panama's birds. It's an expensive but very comprehensive volume that also includes a list of the avifauna of Costa Rica, Honduras and Nicaragua.

Birds of Tropical America (Chapters Publications, 1994), by Steven Hilty, is subtitled *A Watcher's Introduction to Behavior, Breeding and Diversity* and provides plenty of interesting background on the birds that you'll see on your trip. The author is a professional ornithologist.

The Botany and Natural History of Panama (Missouri Botanical Gardens, 1985), edited by William G D'Arcy and Mireya D Correa, is a collection of research papers that covers a wide body of work, including the results of aviary experiments and instructions on how to construct aerial walkways in rainforest canopies.

A Panama Forest and Shore: Natural History and Amerindian Culture in Bocas del Toro (Boxwood Press, 1983), by Burton L Gordon, is an academic's look at western

Panama based on the author's observations of Bocas del Toro during seven field trips.

A Field Guide to the Orchids of Costa Rica and Panama, by Robert Dressler, has 240 photos and almost as many drawings of orchids within its 274 pages.

Indians

Secrets of the Cuna Earth Mother: A Contemporary Study of Ancient Religions, by Clyde E Keeler, is a collection of notes on the religion and lives of the Kuna and a comparison of their religion with some in the Far East.

Ancient Arts of the Andes, by Wendell C Bennett, discusses the Indian art of Panama, which is related to the pre-Columbian art of the Andes.

NEWSPAPERS & MAGAZINES

La Prensa (independent centrist) is the most widely circulated daily newspaper in Panama. Other major Spanish-language dailies include *El Siglo* (sensationalist), *El Periódico* (pro-Partido Revolucionaro Democrático), *La Estrella de Panamá* (center-right), and *El Panamá América*, *Crítica* and *Primera Plana* (all right wing).

The *Star and Herald*, the oldest English-language newspaper in Panama, was originally founded to serve the US citizens making their way from the East Coast of the USA to California during the mid-19th century.

The Panama News is published in English twice monthly; it is distributed widely and is often found in hotels and restaurants in Panama City. It's free. *The Visitor*, published in English and Spanish and written for foreigners, is another free publication, broadly distributed in tourist haunts.

The *Miami Herald International Edition* is widely available. English-language magazines and newspapers, including the *International Herald Tribune*, are available at Farmacias Arrocha and Gran Morrison stores in Panama City.

RADIO & TV

There are three commercial TV stations in Panama (channels 2, 4 and 13) and two devoted to public broadcasting (channels 5 and 11). Sports programming, including NBA and NFL games, is generally shown on channel 2, while channels 4 and 13 favor national productions, situation comedies and movies. Most hotel rooms are equipped with cable TV.

There are about 90 radio stations in Panama, mostly FM and mostly operated on a commercial basis. Popular FM stations and the music they play include 97.1 and 102.1 for salsa, 94.5 for traditional Panamanian, 88.9 for Latin jazz, 88.1 for reggae, 105.7 for classical, 107.3 for disco, 101.1 and 104.7 for easy listening, 106.7 for Latin rock and 93.9 and 98.9 for US rock. The US military runs a station at 91.5 on the dial.

If you have a portable short-wave radio, you can hear the BBC World Service, Voice of America and Radio Moscow.

PHOTOGRAPHY
Film & Equipment
The price of high-end camera equipment in Panama is quite competitive, particularly in the Zona Libre in Colón, although the savings are not terribly impressive. The inventory, however, can be excellent; I found two 20 to 35mm Nikon lenses in the zone less than a month after I was unable to locate even one in Los Angeles.

Filmwise, Panama City has everything, but outside the capital city you'll be hard-pressed to find Kodachrome 64 or Fuji Velvia slide films – the really good stuff. At the many Supercolor stores in Panama City (check the phone book for addresses and phone numbers), not only can you find Fuji Velvia, but it's well priced.

A total paranoid when it comes to film, I always have mine processed by a Fuji processing center in the USA. But I've been told by many people – and I have no reason to believe otherwise – that you can trust the film processors in Panama to do good work. If you're going to be in Panama a while and are anxious to see your photos, consider having one roll developed in Panama and examining the results before submitting additional rolls.

Technique
Tropical shadows are very strong and come out almost black on photographs. Often a bright but hazy day makes for better photographs than a very sunny one. Photography in open shade or using fill-in flash will help. Polarizing filters reduce glare and accentuate colors.

You will need high-speed (400 ASA or faster) film or flash equipment and/or a tripod if you want to take photographs within a rainforest. I prefer high-quality but super-slow (50 ASA) Fuji Velvia slide film and a tripod to the convenience of high-speed film that produces grainy images. The amount of light penetrating the layers of vegetation is remarkably low.

As a general rule, the best time for shooting is when the sun is low – the first and last two hours of the day. Remember too that flash equipment is forbidden in Panama's churches and museums.

Photographing People
Panamanians make wonderful subjects for photos. However, most people resent having cameras thrust in their faces, and some attach price tags to their mugs (see Dos & Don'ts in the Facts about Panama chapter). As a rule, you should ask for permission if you have an inkling your subject would not approve.

And please be sensitive of people's feelings; remember, you're not simply a tourist but a representative of your country when you leave its borders. A 50-something British deviant trying to get a photo of an elderly Kuna woman's private parts in 1994 nearly closed the Archipiélago de San Blás to all travelers once word of his actions reached Kuna leaders.

Airport Security
The security folks at Panama's Tocumen International Airport have told me perhaps a dozen times that their x-ray machines are film safe and computer friendly, but I've never sent my film or laptop through one of them and I recommend that you don't either. Airport security personnel the world over are generally amenable to inspecting

film and computers by hand, and those at Tocumen are friendly enough.

TIME
Panama time is in line with New York and Miami, five hours behind Greenwich Mean Time (GMT) and one hour ahead of the rest of Central America. If you're coming from Costa Rica, be sure to reset your watch.

ELECTRICITY
Beware of variations in electrical currents in Panama. Almost everywhere, voltage will be 110 volts, but there are exceptions – an ordinary socket may be either 110 or 220 volts. Find out which it is before you plug in your appliance. Many travel gadgets can be adjusted for different voltages. Sockets are two-prong.

Also, be aware that power surges and brief outages are fairly common in Panama, particularly in Panama City. If you're planning on using a laptop computer in Panama, you'd be wise to hook it up to a surge protector; these are fairly inexpensive (under US$20) and widely available in Panama City, David and other major cities.

WEIGHTS & MEASURES
The metric system is the official system for weights and measures, but the US system of pounds, gallons and miles is also used. This book uses the metric system; conversion information is given inside the book's back cover.

LAUNDRY
Laundromats (lavamáticos) are abundant and cheap in Panama; usually you drop off your laundry, they wash and dry it, and you pick it up a few hours later. Cost per load is 75¢ to wash, 75¢ to dry and another 25¢ for detergent unless you bring your own.

Dry cleaners (lavanderías) are also widely available but considerably more expensive. Many dry cleaners will not wash undergarments.

If you stay at a luxury hotel, note the price of the laundry service before you use it. It will be outrageous. For example, the cost of having one old pair of blue jeans washed at

the Radisson in Panama City is US$7.70 – and you won't get them back the same day!

TOILETS
Panamanian plumbing generally is of high quality, although on some San Blás islands and elsewhere you'll find signs beside the toilets asking you to place your used paper in the trash bins provided instead of flushing it away. That's because narrow piping was used during construction and the owners fear clogging. Putting used toilet paper into a trash bin may not seem sanitary, but it is much better than clogged bowls and overflowing toilet water.

Public toilets are limited mainly to bus terminals, airports and restaurants. Restrooms are called baños and are often marked caballeros (gentlemen) and damas (ladies). Outside the cities, toilet paper is not always provided, so you may want to consider carrying a personal supply.

HEALTH
It's true that most people traveling for any length of time in Latin America are likely to have an occasional upset stomach. It's also true that if you take certain precautions before, during and after your trip, it's unlikely that you will become seriously ill.

Dengue fever, a mosquito-spread disease, is on the rise in Panama, as is leishmaniasis, a disease spread by sand flies, and malaria can be found in five of the country's nine provinces. Despite this, few Panamanians are ever afflicted with these diseases, and by taking steps to reduce insect bites you can make the risk of contracting these diseases negligible.

Predeparture Preparations
Vaccinations The Panamanian authorities generally do not require anyone to have an up-to-date international vaccination card to enter the country. However, travelers coming from a country experiencing a cholera epidemic may be asked to show proof that they have received vaccinations against the disease. Likewise, travelers coming from areas with a high incidence of malaria may be

asked by the authorities if they are using antimalaria medication.

Regardless of the entry requirements, you should take steps to protect yourself against these diseases if you know you will be spending time in an area where they pose a real health hazard. Pregnant women should consult with their doctors before receiving any vaccinations.

Travel Insurance Regardless of how fit and healthy you are, *do* take out travel insurance, preferably one with provisions for flying you home in the event of a medical emergency. Even if you don't get sick, you might be involved in an accident. Many are the stories of poor souls who thought they'd save some money by passing on travel insurance only to face enormous medical bills when disaster struck.

Travel Health Guides If you are planning to be away for a long period of time or to travel in remote areas, you should consider taking a more detailed health guide. These usually can be found in the Health section of a general bookstore. There are also a number of excellent travel health websites on the Internet. From the Lonely Planet website (www.lonelyplanet.com), there are links to the World Health Organization (WHO) and to the Centers for Disease Control & Prevention.

First-Aid Kit How well stocked your first-aid kit should be depends on your knowledge of first-aid procedures, where you will be going, how long you will need the kit and how many people will be sharing it. The following is a suggested checklist, which you should amend as needed:

- your prescription medications
- antiseptic cream
- antihistamine or other anti-itch cream for insect bites
- Tylenol or a similar painkiller, but preferably not aspirin
- Lomotil or a nonprescription medicine such as Pepto-Bismol for diarrhea
- antibiotics (be aware that some people are very allergic to them)
- throat lozenges
- ear and eye drops
- antacid tablets
- anti-motion-sickness medication
- alcohol swabs
- water purification tablets
- powdered rehydration mixture for severe diarrhea
- lip salve and sunscreen
- sunburn salve (aloe vera gel works well)
- antifungus powder (for foot and groin)
- thermometer in a case
- surgical tape, gauze and bandages
- moleskin for blistered feet
- scissors, tweezers and earplugs
- first-aid booklet

A convenient way to carry your first-aid kit so that it doesn't get crushed is in a small plastic container with a sealing lid, such as Tupperware.

Don't use medications indiscriminately, and be aware of their side effects: Some people are allergic to drugs as common as aspirin. Antibiotics such as tetracycline make your skin more susceptible to sunburn. Antibiotics are not recommended unless needed – they destroy the body's natural resistance to diarrhea and other diseases. Lomotil counteracts the symptoms of diarrhea, but it doesn't cure the problem. Anti-motion-sickness or antihistamine medications can make you very drowsy.

Other Preparations Smart travel begins with preparation, and nothing is more important than your health. Don't belittle this fact. If you wear prescription glasses, make sure you take a spare pair and a copy of the prescription with you to Panama. The tropical sun is strong, so you may want to have a prescription pair of sunglasses made before you leave home. If you are going on a long trip, make sure your teeth are OK.

Regardless of your natural skin color, play it safe and take sunscreen with you. Sunscreen is readily available in pharmacies throughout Panama, but why wait to buy something you'll likely need? A minimum sun protection factor of 15 is good; 35 is even better.

Water & Food

Tap water is safe to drink throughout Panama. The government agency in charge of water treatment regularly checks the drinking water to ensure compliance with the WHO's standards. As a rule, you should never drink unfiltered or untreated water from streams, rivers or lakes because of the parasites that lurk within them.

If you're one of those people who always seem to get bitten or get a tummy ache when no one else does, play it super-safe and drink bottled water, soft drinks or Gatorade instead of tap water in areas where you suspect the water might be hazardous to your health; canned and bottled beverages are readily available alternatives in Panama.

Use common sense when it comes to food. Roadside stands are never as clean as restaurants, so avoid them; if it's midday and there's no one inside the restaurant you've just entered, assume the locals know something about the place that you don't and back out; and if a restaurant smells or otherwise seems unhealthy, suppose it is and move along.

The beef in Panama is grass fed and tends to be lean and tough. Inspections are spotty and Panamanian meats are not up to US, European and Canadian standards. To avoid problems, don't eat locally raised meat, poultry and seafood that is undercooked. Eat raw fish only at sushi restaurants.

Medical Problems & Treatment

Cholera Cholera is an acute diarrheal illness caused by infection of the intestine by the bacterium *Vibrio cholerae*. It's transmitted directly through food or water contaminated with fecal material from infected people. The symptoms are severe watery diarrhea and vomiting, which cause massive fluid and electrolyte loss, leading to severe dehydration. The only treatment for cholera is prevention. Get vaccinated against cholera before you travel into Central America, where the disease periodically appears.

Dengue Fever This viral disease is carried by the same mosquito that carries yellow fever. There are several hundred known cases each year in Panama. There is no prophylactic available for dengue. The main preventative measure is to avoid getting mosquito bites by using insect repellent (see the Insect Repellent sidebar on the next page for some good advice), mosquito netting and bug jackets when appropriate (such as in the jungle or at the beach at sunset). The areas of highest risk are Darién, Los Santos and Coclé Provinces, but cases have been reported even in Panama City. Symptoms include any of the following: fever, chills, severe back and joint aches, pain behind the eyes, rash. There is no treatment except for rest and painkillers. Do not take aspirin; drink plenty of liquids. Dengue sometimes kills. If you think you've got it, go to a hospital.

Diarrhea Most diarrhea is noninfectious and self-limited and may arise from changes in food, water or altitude, combined with fatigue and emotional stresses. This type of diarrhea often clears up on a bland diet, with particular avoidance of fats and alcohol. The important factor in treating any diarrhea is to replace lost fluids by drinking water, tea, broth or carbonated beverages. Gatorade, diluted half and half with water, is good for replacing lost fluids and electrolytes. A useful drug to relieve excessive diarrhea and cramps is Pepto-Bismol, available throughout Panama.

Dysentery If your diarrhea continues for several days and it is accompanied by nausea, severe abdominal pain and fever, and you find blood in your stools, it's likely that you have contracted dysentery. Fortunately, dysentery is not common in Panama. There are two types: amoebic and bacillary. It is not always obvious which kind you have. Although bacillary responds

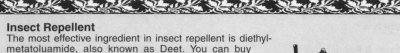

Insect Repellent

The most effective ingredient in insect repellent is diethyl-metatoluamide, also known as Deet. You can buy repellent with 90% or more of this ingredient; many brands contain less than 15%, however. I find that the rub-on lotions are the most effective, and pump sprays are good for spraying clothes, especially at the neck, wrist, waist and ankle openings.

Some people find that Deet is irritating to the skin – they should use lower strengths. Everyone should avoid getting Deet in their eyes, on their lips and on other sensitive regions. This stuff can dissolve plastic, so keep it off plastic lenses, etc. I know of someone who put plenty of Deet onto his face and forehead, then began sweating and got Deet-laden sweat in his eyes, resulting not only in eye irritation but also in clouding his plastic contact lenses!

Deet is toxic to children and shouldn't be used on their skin. Instead, try Avon's Skin So Soft, which has insect-repellent properties and is not toxic – get the oil, not the lotion. Camping stores sometimes sell insect repellents with names such as 'Green Ban' – these are made with natural products and are not toxic, but I find them less effective than repellents with Deet.

You can also sometimes find mosquito spirals (coils). They work like incense sticks and are fairly effective at keeping insects away. – *Rob Rachowiecki*

well to antibiotics, amoebic – which is rarer – involves more complex treatment. If you suspect you have dysentery, you should seek medical advice.

Hepatitis Hepatitis A, the most predominant form in Panama, is caused by ingesting contaminated food or water. Salads, uncooked vegetables, unpeeled fruit and unboiled drinks are the worst offenders. Infection risks can be minimized by using bottled drinks, washing your own fruits and vegetables with purified water and paying scrupulous attention to your toilet habits. If you get the disease, you'll know it. Your skin and especially the whites of your eyes turn yellow, and you feel so tired that it literally takes all your effort to go to the toilet. There is no cure except rest.

Protection can be provided either with the antibody gamma globulin or with a relatively new vaccine named Havrix 1440, also known as hepatitis A vaccine. Havrix provides long-term immunity (possibly more than 10 years) after an initial course

of two injections and a booster at six to 12 months. It may be more expensive than gamma globulin, but it certainly has many advantages, including length of protection and ease of administration. It will take about three weeks to provide satisfactory protection, so plan carefully prior to travel.

Gamma globulin is an antibody that reduces the chances of hepatitis infection. Because it may interfere with the development of immunity, this vaccine should not be given until at least 10 days after administration of the last vaccine needed; it should also be given as close as possible to departure, because it is at its most effective in the first few weeks after administration and the effectiveness tapers off gradually between three and six months. The incidence of hepatitis A is low in Panama, so many travelers opt not to bother with these shots.

Leishmaniasis There are 76 known species of *chitra* (sand fly) in Panama, and five of them are known to carry the leishmaniasis parasite. Once a victim is bitten by an infected sand fly, the parasite enters the body, where it may remain for up to six months without making itself known. Then a sore can develop anywhere on the body, even on the corneas. At first the sore resembles a pimple, but instead of going away it swells and opens up. Leishmaniasis sores can grow to the size of a half-dollar or larger, and at this size they resemble festering wounds and can be crusty in places. A test for the presence of leishmaniasis exists. Treatment involves a series of injections.

Malaria A parasitic infection, malaria is transmitted to humans by mosquitoes. Signs of infection range from fever to flu-like symptoms, including chills, achiness and fatigue. If left untreated, malaria can cause anemia, kidney failure, coma and death. There is risk of malaria in the rural areas of Darién, Chiriquí and Bocas del Toro Provinces and around the Lago Bayano and Lago Gatún areas. There is no risk in or near Panama City. If you plan on spending a significant amount of time in the infected areas, you might want to consider taking antimalaria medication. It is supplied in the form of pills that must be taken from two weeks before until six weeks after your visit. Be advised that antimalaria medication makes you more susceptible to sunburn, which is something to factor into your decision if you burn easily anyway and if you plan to be taking precautions against mosquito bites (such as using repellent, bug jackets and so on).

Rabies Rabies is a fatal viral infection found in many countries, including Panama. Many animals can be infected (such as dogs, cats, bats and monkeys), and it is their saliva that is infectious. Any bite, scratch or even lick from a warm-blooded, furry animal should be cleaned immediately and thoroughly. Scrub with soap and running water, and then apply alcohol or iodine solution. Medical help should be sought promptly to receive a course of injections to prevent the onset of symptoms

and death. There are vampire bats in many parts of Panama; if you will be sleeping outside, be sure to keep your feet covered and use mosquito netting to keep them off your head. Typically people learn that they have been visited by a vampire bat when they wake up and find blood in their hair or around their toes.

Tetanus Tetanus occurs when a wound becomes infected by a germ that lives in soil and in the feces of various animals. It enters the body via breaks in the skin. All wounds should be cleaned promptly and an antiseptic cream or solution applied. Use antibiotics if the wound becomes hot or throbs or pus develops. The first symptom may be discomfort in swallowing or stiffening of the jaw and neck; this is followed by painful convulsions of the jaw and whole body. The disease can be fatal. A tetanus vaccine is available and is strongly recommended.

Yellow Fever Yellow fever is now the only vaccine that is a legal requirement for entry into many countries (it is not required for entrance into Panama). This rule is usually only enforced when visitors are coming from an infected area. Protection lasts 10 years. The Darién is the only area of risk in Panama, and even there the risk is minute. Be advised that the vaccination poses some risk during pregnancy. Also, people allergic to eggs may not be able to have this vaccine. Discuss it with your doctor.

Insect Problems Insect repellents go a long way in preventing bites, but if you do get bitten, avoid scratching. Unfortunately, this is easier said than done.

To alleviate itching, try applying hydrocortisone cream, calamine lotion or some other kind of anti-itch cream, or soaking in baking soda. Scratching will quickly open bites and cause them to become infected. Skin infections are slow to heal in the heat of the Tropics, and all infected bites as well as cuts and grazes should be kept scrupulously clean, treated with antiseptic creams and covered with dressings on a daily basis.

Another insect problem is infestation with lice (including crabs) and scabies. Lice crawl around in your body hair and make you itch. To get rid of them, wash with a shampoo containing benzene hexachloride or shave the affected area. To avoid being reinfected, wash your clothes and bedding in hot water and the shampoo. It's probably best to throw away your underwear if you had body lice or crabs. Lice thrive on body warmth; these beasties lurking in clothes will die in about 72 hours if the clothing isn't worn.

Chiggers are mites that burrow into your skin and cause it to become red and intensely itchy. These are also known as sand flies, or *chitras* in Spanish. They are common on Panama's beaches and in the jungle. Once you've got them, you just have to endure them for a few days. They do not pose any serious health threat unless they are leishmaniasis carriers; the chance that they are carrying leishmaniasis is slight, and even then the disease is treatable. I've had to endure hundreds of the little buggers over the years; as one friend of mine likes to say, 'Just enjoy them.' The best preventative is sprinkling sulfur powder on socks, shoes and lower legs before walking through grass. Liberal application of insect repellent works pretty well.

Scorpions and spiders can give severely painful – but rarely fatal – stings or bites. A common way to get bitten is to put on your clothes and shoes in the morning without checking them first. Develop the habit of shaking out your clothing before putting it on, especially in the lowlands. Check your bedding before going to sleep. Don't walk barefoot outdoors, and watch where you place your hands when you are reaching for a shelf or branch.

Snakebite This is extremely unlikely. Should you be bitten, the snake may be a nonvenomous one (try to identify the offending creature). And even venomous snakes withhold their poison most of the time when they bite. But if you are bitten, assume the worst and try to prevent the circulation of any venom already inside you by following the advice in the next paragraph. Do not try the slash-and-suck routine on the bite.

The venom of most dangerous snakes does its nasty work via the lymph system, not the bloodstream, so treatment aimed at reducing the flow of blood or removing venom from the bloodstream is likely to be futile. Aim to immobilize the bitten limb and bandage it tightly and completely (but do not make a tourniquet; this is now considered too dangerous and not particularly effective). Then, with a minimum of disturbance, particularly to the bound limb, get the victim to a hospital as soon as possible (most Panamanian hospitals stock antivenin). Keep calm, and reassure the victim.

One of the world's deadliest snakes is the fer-de-lance, which is found in most of Panama's national parks. It has an anticoagulating agent in its venom. If you're bitten by a fer-de-lance, your blood coagulates twice as slowly as the average hemophiliac's; slashing at the wound with a razor is a good way to help yourself bleed to death. The slash-and-suck method does work in some cases, but this should be done only by someone who knows what he/she is doing and only as a last resort. Even the fer-de-lance only succeeds in killing a small percentage of its human victims.

Sexually Transmitted Diseases Prostitution is legal in Panama, and female prostitutes are required to be registered and receive regular medical checkups. Nevertheless, the incidence of sexually transmitted diseases (STDs) is increasing among Panamanian prostitutes. In addition, some prostitutes are transvestites, who are unlikely to receive the required medical care because of social prejudice against them.

The use of condoms will reduce your chances of contracting an STD. Condoms (*preservativos*) are available in Panamanian pharmacies. However, I wouldn't feel right if I didn't mention that while condoms do reduce the risk of contracting HIV, they don't prevent the transmission of herpes, a disease that only requires skin-to-skin contact. Please remember that herpes is forever.

HIV/AIDS The human immunodeficiency virus (HIV) leads to acquired immune deficiency syndrome (AIDS, or SIDA in Spanish). Panama is ranked 19th in the world on a per-capita basis for HIV/AIDS cases, with an estimated 26,000 infected people in 1997; that number is expected to increase to 38,000 by the year 2000.

Transmission is predominantly through homosexual sexual activity, but the disease is spreading among heterosexuals as well. Apart from abstinence, the most effective preventative is to use condoms and avoid sex that involves an exchange of bodily fluids. It is impossible to detect the HIV-positive status of a healthy-looking person without a blood test.

HIV/AIDS can be spread via infected blood transfusions; if you need a transfusion, go to the best clinic available. It can also be spread by dirty needles – vaccinations, acupuncture, tattooing and ear or nose piercing can potentially be as dangerous as intravenous drug use if the equipment is not clean. If you need an injection, ask to see the syringe unwrapped in front of you, or buy a needle and syringe pack from a pharmacy if there is any doubt about the sterility of the needle.

Fear of HIV infection should never preclude treatment for serious medical conditions. Although there may be a risk of infection through an infected needle, it is very small indeed.

Environmental Hazards

Fungal Infections Fungal infections occur more commonly in hot weather and are usually found on the scalp, between the toes or fingers, in the groin and on the body (ringworm). You get ringworm (which is a fungal infection, not a worm) from infected animals or other people. Moisture encourages these infections.

To prevent fungal infections, wear loose, comfortable clothes, avoid artificial fibers, wash frequently and dry thoroughly. If you do get an infection, wash the infected area at least daily with a disinfectant or medicated soap and water, and rinse and dry well. Apply an antifungus cream or powder such as tolnifate (also known as Tinaderm). Try to expose the infected area to air or sunlight as much as possible, and wash all towels and underwear in hot water, change them often and let them dry in the sun.

Heat Exhaustion Dehydration and salt deficiency can cause heat exhaustion. Take time to acclimatize to high temperatures, drink sufficient amounts of liquids and do not do anything too physically demanding. Salt deficiency is characterized by fatigue, lethargy, headaches, giddiness and muscle cramps; salt tablets may help, but adding salt to your food is better.

Anhydrotic heat exhaustion, which is caused by an inability to sweat, is quite rare. It is likely to strike people who have been in a hot climate for some time rather than newcomers.

Heatstroke This serious, occasionally fatal condition can occur if the body's heat-regulating mechanism breaks down and body temperature rises to dangerous levels. Long, continuous periods of exposure to high temperatures and insufficient fluids can leave you vulnerable to heatstroke.

The symptoms are feeling unwell, little or no sweating and a high body temperature (39°C to 41°C or 102°F to 106°F). Where sweating has ceased, the skin becomes flushed and red. Throbbing headaches and lack of coordination will also occur, and victims may be confused or aggressive. Eventually victims will become delirious or convulse. Hospitalization is essential, but in the interim get victims out of the sun, remove their clothing, cover them with a wet sheet or towel and fan them continually. Give fluids if victims are conscious.

Prickly Heat Prickly heat is an itchy rash caused by excessive perspiration trapped under the skin. It usually strikes people who have just arrived in a hot climate. Keeping cool, bathing often, drying the skin and using a mild talcum or prickly heat powder, and resorting to air-conditioning may help.

Sunburn In the Tropics you can get sunburned surprisingly quickly, even through dense cloud cover. Use sunscreen liberally and put barrier cream on your nose and lips. Calamine lotion and aloe vera gel are good for mild sunburns. Protect your eyes with good-quality sunglasses, particularly if you will be near water. A hat can save you pain, and wrinkles.

Women's Health
Antibiotic use, wearing synthetic underwear, sweating and use of contraceptive pills can lead to vaginal infections when you're traveling in hot climates. Wearing loose-fitting clothes and cotton underwear will help to prevent these fungal infections, characterized by a rash, itch and discharge. Such infections can be treated with a vinegar or lemon-juice douche or with yogurt. Nystatin, miconazole or clotrimazole pessaries or vaginal cream are the usual treatments.

Medical Facilities
The best hospital in Panama is the Centro Medico Paitilla (☎ 263-6060), at Calle 53 Este and Avenida Balboa in Panama City, where many of the doctors speak English. See the Information section in the Panama City chapter for details.

WOMEN TRAVELERS
Women travelers find Panama safe and pleasant to visit. This is not to say that machismo is a thing of the past. On the contrary, it is very much alive and practiced. Panamanian men generally consider *gringas* to have looser morals and to be easier 'conquests' than local women. They will often make flirtatious comments or stare at single women, both local and foreign. Women traveling together are not exempt from this attention; women traveling with men are less likely to receive such attention.

Comments are rarely blatantly rude; the usual thing is a smiling *'Mi amor,'* an appreciative hiss or a honk of the horn. The best way to deal with this is to do what Panamanian women do – ignore the comments and don't look at the man making them.

Women travelers will meet friendly Panamanian men. It is worth remembering, though, that gentle seduction is a sport, even a way of life for many Panamanian men, particularly in Panama City. Men may conveniently forget to mention to you that they are married. Indeed, quite a few Panamanian men have both a wife and a girlfriend.

Women who firmly resist unwanted verbal advances from men are normally treated with respect. But there is always a small number of men who will insist on trying to hold hands or give a 'friendly' hug or kiss; if the feeling is not mutual, turn them down explicitly. Some women find that wearing a cheap 'wedding' ring helps – though, of course, you have to be ready to answer the inevitable 'Where is your husband?'

What to Wear
As stated elsewhere in this book, Panamanians are generally quite conservative in dress. Women travelers are advised to follow suit to avoid calling unnecessary attention to themselves. Neither women nor men wear shorts in the cities. On the beach, skimpy bathing costumes are acceptable, although topless bathing and nudity (with the exception of one beach) are not.

Some women travelers tend to think that what they do on the Mediterranean they can do in Panamanian beach areas, and parade around topless. This may be fine in other places, but it is generally unacceptable to Panamanians. On San Blás islands, which are under Kuna law, sunning in the buff is a jailable offense.

GAY & LESBIAN TRAVELERS
If you are a gay or lesbian traveler and looking to spend time in a country that generally respects people regardless of their sexual preference, Panama is not the country for you.

In Panama you can lose your job simply because you are gay. There are no gay lobbyists. There are no openly gay politicians (although there are quite a few 'in the closet'). Panama's gay community has no generally accepted leaders. There aren't any local gay newspapers, magazines or newsletters. Gay-pride parades? Unimaginable.

About the only openly gay anything one is likely to come across is Panama City's low-profile gay bars and the transvestite prostitutes who ply several street corners near the city's Casco Viejo district. And you won't find a list of gay bars in the phone book.

The situation may be changing. In 1997 Panama City Mayor Mayín Correa expressed her desire to create a 'pink zone' where gay and transvestite prostitutes would be allowed to operate openly. She even declared her general opposition to discrimination against homosexuals.

The pink-zone proposal immediately came under attack from the political right, Catholic priests and many others. But for months the proposal had the country arguing about the nature of love – and about what goes on in the shadows. The discussions, and Correa's declarations, were firsts in a country where even suggesting that gays and lesbians are entitled to basic human rights is viewed as an act of treason by most heterosexuals.

Meeting Places

Gay bars in Panama are well-kept secrets. The owners, fearing vandalism and worse, never advertise the sexual preference of their clienteles, don't list their establishments in phone directories and in some instances don't even post any signs in front of their bars.

Most of Panama City's gay and lesbian clubs are in the Casco Viejo district. Many of these places don't have much in the way of decor – they're just one room with tables, a bar and a jukebox – but they make up for it in atmosphere. There are other gay clubs scattered around the capital city, and they are likewise happening places. See the Entertainment section of the Panama City chapter for names and locations.

Outside Panama City, gay bars are few and far between. In most instances gays and lesbians just blend in with the straight crowd at the hipper places and avoid cantinas and other conventional lairs of homophobia.

DISABLED TRAVELERS

According to Law 1 of January 28, 1992, all Panamanians and foreigners with Panamanian residency status who have serious mental or physical impairments are entitled to the same employment and educational opportunities as everyone else and are granted public medical care for their disabilities. Another law specifies that retired disabled Panamanians and foreigners with Panamanian residency status are entitled to discounts such as a break on mortgage, medical and telephone bills.

Additionally, the Instituto Panameño de Habilitación Especial (Panamanian Institute for Special Rehabilitation, or IPHE; ☎ 261-0500), on the Camino Real in the Betania district of Panama City and open from 7 am to 4 pm weekdays, was created by the government to assist all disabled people in Panama, including foreign tourists. However, the law does not require – and Panamanian businesses do not provide – discounts to foreign tourists with disabilities.

Panama is not wheelchair friendly; with the exception of handicapped parking spaces, wheelchair ramps outside a few upscale hotels and perhaps a few dozen oversize bathroom stalls, accommodations for people with physical disabilities do not exist in Panama. Even at the best hotels, you won't find railings in showers or beside toilets.

SENIOR TRAVELERS

According to Law 15 of July 13, 1992, all Panamanians and foreigners with Panamanian residency status who are female and 55 years old or older, or are male and 60 years old or older, are entitled to a wide range of discounts, such as the following: 50% off tickets for movies, theater, sports and special events; 25% off tickets for domestic air travel; 25% off the price of restaurant meals; and 15% off medical bills. The list goes on. However, the law does not require – and Panamanian businesses do not offer – discounts to foreign tourists on the basis of age.

TRAVEL WITH CHILDREN

Children pay full fare on buses if they occupy a seat, but they often ride for free if they sit on a parent's knee. Children ages two to five pay 75% of the full fare on domestic airline flights and get a seat, while infants under two pay 10% of the fare but don't get a seat. Children's car seats are not always available from Panamanian car-rental agencies, so bring one if you plan on driving with a baby or toddler.

In hotels the general rule is simply to bargain. Children should never have to pay as much as an adult, but whether they stay for half-price or for free is open to discussion. A few hotels don't allow children under a certain age, in order to maintain a quiet atmosphere.

While 'kids' meals' (small portions at small prices) are not normally offered in restaurants, it is perfectly acceptable to order a meal to split between two children or an adult and a child.

Visitors traveling with children are still a curiosity in Panama and will meet with extra, generally friendly attention and interest. For more suggestions, see Lonely Planet's *Travel with Children,* by Maureen Wheeler.

USEFUL ORGANIZATIONS

If you haven't quite decided whether Panama is a smart destination for you, consider contacting the following organizations to see what they have to say about the country.

South American Explorers Club

The SAEC (☎ 607-277-0488, fax 607-277-6122, explorer@samexplo.org, www .samexplo.org) is at 126 Indian Creek Rd, Ithaca, NY 14850, USA. The club is an information center for travelers, adven-

turers, scientists, etc. The people who answer the phones and attend to email there are extremely well informed about Central and South America and are a pleasure to communicate with. They are always pleased to provide back issues of their excellent *South American Explorer* magazine for a reasonable fee. The people who write for the magazine include *National Geographic* photographers and hard-core adventurers – people who really know what they're talking about.

SAEC maintains clubhouses in Lima, Peru, and Quito, Ecuador, that have extensive libraries of books, maps and trip reports left by other travelers. Many maps and books are for sale.

The SAEC is an entirely membership-supported nonprofit organization. Individual membership costs US$40 and lasts for four quarterly issues of the magazine. Members can make use of the clubhouses (if heading on to Peru or Ecuador) as well as the extensive information facilities and books available by mail before they go. I've been a dues-paying member for years and expect to be for many more.

The Latin American Travel Advisor

You can get up-to-date information on safety, political and economic situations, health risks, costs, etc, for all the Latin American countries from *The Latin American Travel Advisor.* This is an impartial, 16-page, English-language quarterly newsletter published in Ecuador. Four issues are US$39, the most recent issue is US$15 and back issues are US$7.50, sent by airmail.

The Latin American Travel Advisor (fax 593-2-562-566, www.amerispan.com/latc) is reachable at PO Box 17-17-908, Quito, Ecuador.

DANGERS & ANNOYANCES

Crime is a problem in certain parts of Panama City. However, the city's better districts are much safer than similar areas in many other capitals; witness the all-night restaurants and activity on the streets at night. On the other hand, it is dangerous to walk around at night in the Casco Viejo district, where the cheapest accommodations are found. In general, use common sense; stay where it's well lit and there are plenty of people.

Colón has some upscale residential areas, but most of the city is a sad slum widely known for street crime. If you walk around there, even in the middle of the day, well-meaning residents will inform you that you are in danger. Unless you've just got to visit Colón's Zona Libre, it's best to avoid the city altogether.

Parts of Darién Province are extremely dangerous. There are numerous stories of people – including tourists and missionaries – being kidnapped and/or murdered there. The area of the Darién all along the Colombian border contains Colombian bandits and paramilitary units and Panamanian special forces. Particularly dangerous is the area between Yaviza and the border; to go there is foolhardy.

Plying the waters of the Archipiélago de San Blás are numerous Colombian boats that run back and forth between the Zona Libre in Colón and Cartagena, Colombia. It has been well documented that some of these boats carry cocaine on their northbound voyages. If you decide to ride on one of these slow cargo boats, be forewarned that your crew may be drug traffickers, and Colombian drug traffickers aren't known for being nice guys.

Thefts & Muggings

Tourist-oriented crime is uncommon in Panama. Although rip-offs are a fact of life when you're traveling in any country, you'll find Panama is still less plagued by theft than many countries. You should nevertheless avoid carrying all your money in one place, avoid entering areas that appear unsafe and adhere to the rule 'if a deal seems too good to be true, it probably is.' This last rule is a reference to Panama's confidence men, of which there are many.

If you elect to go bar-hopping in Casco Viejo at night or to do some equally risky thing, play it smart and follow this advice: Leave your watch, jewelry and expensive clothing at the hotel; take only the amount of money you think you'll need, and then a little extra tucked away in a shoe; and be sure to carry photographic ID (it's the law). If you look like you don't have anything of value on you, you won't likely interest a mugger.

It is a good idea to carry an emergency packet somewhere separate from all your other valuables. It should contain a photocopy of the important pages of your passport. On the back of the photocopy you should list important numbers, such as your traveler's checks' serial numbers, airline ticket numbers, and credit card and bank account numbers. Also keep one high-denomination bill with this emergency stash.

If you are robbed, you should get a police report as soon as possible. This is a requirement for any insurance claims, although it is unlikely that the police will be able to recover the property. If you don't speak Spanish and are having a hard time making a police report, your embassy can often advise and help.

Panama has a long history of business-related crimes – real estate and investment scams have occurred frequently over the years. If you want to sink money into any kind of Panamanian business, make sure you know what you are doing and check out the business thoroughly. Selling the same piece of property to more than one party is quite common, with greedy lawyers in on the deal. Whatever you do, don't invest more in Panama than you can afford to lose.

Police

Police corruption is not a big problem in Panama. However, it's not unheard of for a Panamanian police officer to stop a motorist for no obvious reason, accuse him or her of violating a law, and levy a fine to be paid on the spot. If there are people around, making a big scene will sometimes fluster the officer into letting you go. Most of the time, however, you become an unwilling participant in a waiting game.

Your best option, unless you want to try to wait out the officer, is to negotiate the fine down. If the officer says the fine is US$50, insist it is US$20. If he says that it's US$20, insist it's US$10. Failure to pay anything can result in your being led to jail with the officer insisting you really did break some law.

Fighting

If you are the sort of person who tends to pick fights or otherwise cause trouble, it may interest you to know that many law enforcement officers in Panama do not wear uniforms. Additionally, because the only requirement for a concealed-weapon permit in Panama is a clean criminal record, more than 70,000 Panamanians legally pack pistols. Panamanians are not a violent people, but if you pick a fight with a local, there's a very good chance you'll find yourself looking down the barrel of a gun.

Swimming Safety

The tourist brochures, with their enticing photographs of tropical paradises, do not mention the drownings that occur every year in Panamanian waters. Of these, about 80% are caused by rip currents. A rip current is a strong current that pulls the swimmer out to sea. It is caused when two currents that move parallel to the shore meet. When they meet, the opposing waters choose the path of least resistance, which is a path out to sea. It is most important to remember that rip currents will pull you *out but not under.*

If you find yourself caught in a rip current, stay calm and let the current take you away from shore. Rip currents dissipate fairly quickly, and you must simply wait them out before you begin to swim back to shore. When the current dissipates, swim back in at a diagonal angle – in other words, swim at a 45° angle to the shore to avoid being caught by the current again. Do not try to swim directly back in, as you will be swimming against the rip current and you will only exhaust yourself. Do not fear that the rip current will take you far out to sea.

If you feel a rip current while you are wading, try to come back in sideways, thus

Why Muddy Beaches Are Best

Odd as it sounds, muddy beaches are more popular with most Panamanians than their country's lovely white-sand beauties. That's because most Panamanians have a real fear of being swept out to sea. Rip currents, which can carry a swimmer away from shore, are usually found in front of beaches covered with fine sand; in fact, currents are needed to create the granular silica that sunbathers love. It's the motion in the ocean that gives sand its size and texture.

Beaches with a lot of mud in their sand are nearly always found beside the mouths of rivers, which dump silt from terra firma into the sea. As silt builds up near a river's mouth, the offshore Panamanian ocean becomes increasingly shallow. Shallow water prevents hazardous currents from forming, which swimmers really do appreciate, but it also means that the beach is dirty rather than sandy. ■

offering less body surface to the current. If you cannot make headway, remember to walk parallel to the beach so that you can get out of the rip current.

Hiking Safety

Many visitors like to hike in the national parks and wilderness areas. You should be adequately prepared for such trips. Always carry plenty of water, even on short journeys, and always bring adequate clothing; jungles *do* cool down a lot at night, particularly at higher elevations. Hikers have been known to get lost in rainforests – even seemingly user-friendly ones such as Parque Nacional Volcán Barú. A Panamanian hiker who entered that park in 1995 was never seen again; it's assumed that he got lost, died of hypothermia and was fed upon by various creatures.

Never walk in unmarked rainforest; if there's no trail going in, you can assume that there won't be one when you decide to turn around and come back out. Always let someone know where you are going, in order to narrow the search area in the event of an emergency.

EMERGENCY

Throughout Panama, the police emergency number is ☎ 104; for fire emergencies, call ☎ 103. Telephone numbers for hospitals and ambulances are found on the first page of the national phone directory. In the blue pages of the directory, you'll find a list of service providers that appear under English headings ('attorneys,' 'physicians,' etc).

LEGAL MATTERS

In Panama you are presumed guilty until found innocent. If you are accused of a serious crime, you will be taken to jail, where you will likely spend several years before your case goes before a judge. Some valuable advice: Stay away from people who commit crimes. For example, you can expect to go to jail if the car you are in is stopped and found to contain illegal drugs, even if they aren't yours and you don't do illegal drugs.

More valuable advice: Ignore locals who say these warnings are exaggerated. The fact is that punitive actions taken against a local and a foreigner often vary. It is assumed that if you can afford to travel to Panama, you must have a lot of money and therefore can afford to pay a steep fine. Stories of *gringos* paying much larger fines than Panamanians for the same offense are well known.

If you are jailed, your embassy will offer only limited assistance. This may include a visit from an embassy staff member to make sure that your human rights have not been violated, letting your family know where you are and putting you in contact with a lawyer (whom you must pay yourself). Embassy officials will not bail you out. Remember, while in Panama you are subject to Panamanian laws, not the laws of your home country.

Remember that you are legally required to carry ID at all times. This should be a photographic ID, preferably a passport with (if applicable) a tourist card.

Drugs

In Panama penalties for possession of even small amounts of illegal drugs are much stricter than in the USA, Europe, Australia and most everywhere else. Defendants often spend years in prison before they are brought to trial and, if convicted (as is usually the case), can expect sentences of several more years in prison. Most lawyers won't even accept drug cases because the outcome is certain: conviction.

Furthermore, if you are convicted, it is the practice of most embassies to notify your country's federal narcotics agency, which can have long-term repercussions. For example, if you are a US citizen convicted of possession of even just one marijuana cigarette, your name will be sent to the US Department of Justice, the US Drug Enforcement Administration and the US Customs Service. Their computers will show only that you were convicted of a drug offense in a foreign country; they do not differentiate between someone who is caught with a single joint and someone who is caught with 1000kg of heroin. At the very least, you and your baggage will be *thoroughly* searched every time you enter the USA.

Alcohol

Public drinking is not tolerated in Panama. If a police officer sees you staggering down the street with a beer in hand, at the very least you will be lectured; most likely you will be handcuffed, searched and led to a jail to sober up. Strange as it may sound to some people, in Panama it's OK to drink and drive, but driving while legally intoxicated (with a blood alcohol level of .1% or above) is a serious offense. If you're drunk and you run over someone and are apprehended, you will be sent to prison for a very long time. The legal drinking age is 18.

BUSINESS HOURS

Business hours are normally 8 am to noon and 1:30 to 5 pm weekdays and 8 am to noon Saturday. Government offices are open 8 am to 4 or 4:30 pm weekdays and don't close for lunch. Most banks are open from 8:30 am to 1 pm Monday to Thursday and 8:30 am to 3 pm Friday; some are open 8:30 am to noon or 1 pm Saturday as well. Stores are generally open 9 or 10 am to 6 or 7 pm Monday to Saturday.

PUBLIC HOLIDAYS & SPECIAL EVENTS

National holidays *(días feriados)* are taken seriously in Panama, and banks, public offices and many stores close. Public transportation tends to be tight on all holidays and the days immediately preceding or following them, so book tickets ahead.

There is no bus service at all on the Thursday afternoon and Friday before Easter, and many businesses are closed for the entire Semana Santa (Holy Week, the week before Easter). From Thursday to Easter Sunday, all bars are closed and alcohol sales are prohibited. Beach hotels are usually booked weeks ahead for the Semana Santa, though a limited choice of rooms is often available.

The week between Christmas and New Year's, along with the first week of the year, tend to be unofficial holidays. In addition, various towns have celebrations for their own particular days. These other holidays and special events are not official holidays, and businesses remain open.

All the official national holidays are listed below, and most are celebrated on Monday to create long weekends: When holidays fall on a Thursday or Friday, they are celebrated on the following Monday; holidays that fall on Tuesday or Wednesday are celebrated the prior Monday.

January 1	*New Year's Day*
January 9	*Martyrs' Day*
March/April	*Good Friday, Easter Sunday*
May 1	*Worker's Day*
August 15	*Founding of Old Panama* (celebrated in Panama City only)
October 12	*Hispanic Day*
November 1	*National Anthem Day*
November 2	*All Souls' Day*
November 3	*Independence Day*
November 10	*First Call for Independence*
November 28	*Independence from Spain*
December 8	*Mothers' Day*
December 25	*Christmas Day*

Carnaval, the Panamanian version of Mardi Gras, is celebrated during the four days leading up to Ash Wednesday. A major holiday in Panama City, it involves costumes, music, dancing, general festivities and a big parade on Shrove Tuesday. Carnaval is also celebrated on the Península de Azuero in Las Tablas, Chitré, Villa de Los Santos and Parita. The celebrations in Panama City and Las Tablas are famous and well worth attending, but hotel reservations must be made well in advance. Upcoming Ash Wednesdays will fall on the following dates:

1999	February 17
2000	March 8
2001	February 28
2002	February 13

Semana Santa is another occasion for special events throughout the country, including the reenactment of the events surrounding the crucifixion and resurrection of Christ; on Good Friday religious processions are held all over the country.

The famous Corpus Christi celebrations in Villa de Los Santos take place 40 days after Easter. Masked and costumed dancers representing angels, devils, imps and other figures enact dances, acrobatics and dramas.

The Península de Azuero also has a number of other notable festivals; patron saint festivals are held in Ocú (January 20 to 23), Soná (May 15), Chitré (June 24), Las Tablas (July 21) and Guararé (September 23 to 27).

The Black Christ celebration held in Portobelo on October 21 attracts tens of thousands of pilgrims from near and far; the celebration for Nuestra Señora del Carmen, which takes place on Isla Taboga on July 16, also attracts large crowds. In western Panama, Boquete's Feria de las Flores y del Café (Fair of Flowers and Coffee), held for 10 days in January, attracts visitors from all over Panama.

Panama's many ethnic groups each have their own cultural events; the Kuna and the descendants of West Indians and Spaniards all have their own special music and dance. If you get a chance to attend any of these occasions, don't miss it. Be aware that while the Kuna allow foreigners to observe their cultural events, they generally do not permit them to be photographed.

ACTIVITIES

Because Panama's tourism industry is still in its infancy, many of the activities available in well-trampled countries such as Costa Rica are not yet available in Panama. Unless you bring a sailboard with you, with two exceptions you won't be able to go windsurfing here. Same goes for river kayaking, although several places now rent sea kayaks. Bungee jumpers, bring your own cord. Hot-air balloons, maybe in 2005. On the other hand, it's specifically because tourists aren't tripping over one another in Panama that someone isn't filling the sky with hot-air balloons and someone else isn't trying to make money offering bungee jumps off the Puente de las Américas (Bridge of the Americas).

Details on activity sites and operators can be found in the regional chapters.

Diving & Snorkeling

There are many decent dive spots – and several very good ones – off both coasts of Panama. Panama's three best dive sites are the Archipiélago de San Blás on the Caribbean side and Isla de Coiba and the Archipiélago de las Perlas on the Pacific side. On the Pacific side you'd be looking for reef sharks, groupers and sea turtles near shore,

and sailfish, amberjacks and dog-toothed snappers farther out. In the Caribbean the fish tend to be smaller but more colorful, the coral is much more appealing and the visibility is better.

The Kuna, who control the San Blás islands, have prevented dive operators from opening shops there since a diving mishap in the 1980s left one Kuna dead. Presently no one is taking divers to the islands. However, if you have your own boat, it is quite OK to dive there as long as you don't disturb anything and enter the water without gloves or boots. The closest tank facilities are at Portobelo. The best diving and snorkeling in this island chain can be found near Cayos Holandéses, Cayos Ordupuquip and Puenta Cocoye (see the Comarca de San Blás chapter for information on these sites).

There's an unfenced penal colony on Isla de Coiba and, for obvious reasons, tourists can't just show up there. All trips to the island and all diving nearby must be arranged through a tour or dive operator. Because the island is far from land and the cost of fuel high, a cheap dive trip to Coiba and vicinity is not possible. However, one dive operator does make the trip (see the Veraguas Province chapter for details).

The Archipiélago de las Perlas is lovely, ringed by lots of appealing beaches that offer excellent snorkeling and scuba diving possibilities. Scuba gear is not really necessary here: Sea turtles, white-tipped reef sharks and numerous other intriguing creatures ply the shallow water just off the beach of the Hotel Contadora Resort, a mediocre hotel on Isla Contadora where most island visitors stay (see the Panamá Province chapter for more details). A snorkel, mask and pair of fins are all that are needed to take in the marine life here.

Panama offers some unique dives. For example, it's possible to dive to a 32-car train, complete with locomotive, abandoned by the French 100 years ago and now at the bottom of the Panama Canal. It's also possible to dive both the Pacific Ocean and the Caribbean in one day.

Scubapanama (☎ 261-4064/3841, fax 261-9586, 0003866445@mcimail.com), at Apartado 666, Balboa, República de Panamá, the country's oldest and most respected dive operator, offers these bicoastal dives for about US$110 per person (the price varies with the size of the group).

There's also good diving to be had near Bahía Piña, Punta Mariato and Punta Burica on the Pacific side (none of which is served by dive operators) and Isla Escudo de Veraguas, Cayos Zapatillas and Portobelo on the Caribbean side (the latter two are served by dive operators). If you've dived some of the world's top spots, these sites won't wow you, but for most divers they're quite OK and they can surprise. At Portobelo, for example, it's possible to dive a 110-foot cargo ship and a C-45 twin-engine plane.

When you're making travel plans, bear in mind that the Caribbean Sea is calm during the dry season (mid-December to mid-April). During the rainy season (mid-April to mid-December), the Caribbean is treacherous due to high winds and strong currents. On the Pacific side strong winds are common during February and March.

Decompression Chambers A warning: Divers, as there are only four decompression chambers in the entire country – one in Colón, one at Lago Gatún and two in Panama City – don't take unnecessary risks. If you stay down too long or come up too fast, you'll be in serious trouble.

Snorkel Gear It's sometimes possible to rent face masks, snorkels and fins, but if snorkeling is an important part of your trip to Panama, you should bring your own gear to ensure comfort and fit. Also, many travelers seem to forget to bring sunscreen, dark glasses and nondrowsy motion-sickness suppressants. If you're fair-skinned, a hat, long-sleeved shirt and baggy lightweight pants are a good idea when you're riding in a boat. Flashlights are not rentable in Panama; if you think you might be doing some night snorkeling, bring an underwater flashlight with you.

Dive Gear Consider bringing all the items listed under Snorkel Gear plus the following: an equipment bag, a regulator and BCD, gloves, boots and a 3 to 5mm wetsuit if you'll be diving the Pacific or a Lycra suit if you'll only be diving the Caribbean. It's also a good idea to mark all your equipment if you'll be diving with others, to avoid mistaking your equipment for someone else's or vice versa; this is particularly true with regard to charcoal-colored fins, which are so popular among divers.

Good dive equipment is available for rent or purchase at the Scubapanama store (see Scubapanama's phone number above) on Calle 6 C Norte, near the Vía Transístmica in the El Carmen neighborhood of Panama City.

Surfing

The best surfing beaches in Panama are Playa Santa Catalina, Playa Teta and Playa Río Mar (all on the Pacific side near the center of the country). All three are reef beaches and all three break both ways, but the right break at Santa Catalina has no equal in all of Central America when the southern swells appear. (See the Surfer's Map for additional sites.)

The best months for Santa Catalina are February to mid-August, but the surf breaks here year-round. The face of a typical wave at Santa Catalina is 2 to 3m; it's not uncommon, especially during April, July and August, to see waves with 5m faces. On a good day during medium to high tide, rides approaching 150m are quite possible. The waves here are at their best during medium to low tide. Surf booties are a must at Santa Catalina due to the volcanic rock beneath the surf and the long walk to the waves during low tide. The water here is never cold, but a Lycra vest is recommended during February and March, when strong offshore winds are common. (See the Veraguas Province chapter for details on facilities at Santa Catalina.)

Playa Teta is very popular with Panamanian surfers due to its beauty and its proximity to Panama City, but its ride is nowhere near as sweet as Santa Catalina's.

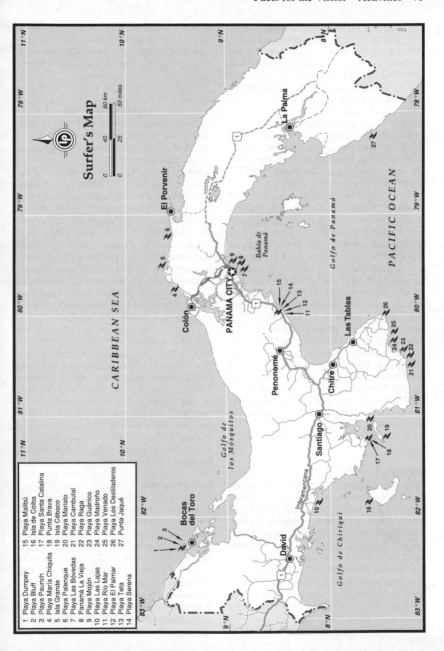

Surfer's Map

1 Playa Dumpey
2 Playa Bluff
3 Playa Paunch
4 Playa María Chiquita
5 Isla Grande
6 Playa Palenque
7 Playa Las Bóvedas
8 Panamá La Vieja
9 Playa Mojón
10 Playa Las Lajas
11 Playa Río Mar
12 Playa El Palmar
13 Playa Teta
14 Playa Serena
15 Playa Malibú
16 Isla de Coiba
17 Playa Santa Catalina
18 Punta Brava
19 Isla Cébaco
20 Playa Mariato
21 Playa Cambutal
22 Playa Raga
23 Playa Guánico
24 Playa Madroño
25 Playa Venado
26 Playa Los Destilladeros
27 Punta Jaqué

The face of a typical wave at Teta is only 2m, and there are often long stretches between big waves. But when there are big southern swells coming all the way from New Zealand, Teta is a fantastic place for getting barrel. Faces on waves here during this time can reach 4m. The bottom is both rocky and sandy; booties aren't really needed. The best months for Teta are May, June, July and August, but even during these months the waves can be disappointing. Also, there are a lot of people in the water here because the beach is only a 45-minute drive from Panama City.

Playa Río Mar, near Teta in Panamá Province, is only really surfable during medium to low tide, because during high tide the waves generally don't break. What is special about this place is the length of the ride, which can last 100m, and the waves here are really easy to ride. The bottom is primarily rocky and there are lots of broken oyster shells in the sand that are as dangerous as broken bottles. Booties are a good idea at low tide. Like Teta, this beach is very accessible and popular. The best months to surf Río Mar are May, June, July and August. Beware: If there's little swell, you'll be waiting a long time for a good wave. (See the Panamá Province chapter for more details on this beach.)

Boards are not rentable in Panama; you'll need to bring your own. See Swimming Safety, earlier in this chapter, for advice about rip currents at Panamanian beaches.

Hiking

Hiking opportunities abound in Panama. From Boquete, you can hike to the top of Volcán Barú, Panama's highest peak, from which you can see both oceans on a clear day. There are also plenty of other walks around Boquete, where the narrow roads wind up and down slopes among coffee plantations. The Sendero Los Quetzales is a trail that leads from Boquete over Volcán Barú to Guadalupe on the other side; it's a six-hour hike through deep jungle, and since it's almost inevitable that you will lose the trail if you go on your own, it's best

to hire a guide in Boquete (through hotels such as the Hotel Panamonte and La Montaña y el Valle) or Panama City (through tour operators). See the Chiriquí Province chapter for more information.

The little town of El Valle, nestled into the Valle de Antón about a two-hour drive west of Panama City, is a fine place for walking. Many trails lead into the hills around the valley; they are well defined, as the local *campesinos* (peasants) frequently use them.

Near Panama City on the shores of the canal, Parque Nacional Soberanía contains a section of the old Sendero Las Cruces (Las Cruces Trail), used by the Spaniards to cross between the coasts. Here, too, is a short and easy but interesting nature trail, the Sendero El Charco, which is signed from the highway (see the Panamá Province chapter for details). Parque Natural Metropolitano, on the outskirts of Panama City, also has some good walks, including a nature trail and a 'monkey trail' (see the Panama City chapter for details).

The most famous walk in Panama is the trek of a week or more across the Darién Gap, where the Carretera Interamericana (Pan-American Hwy) comes to a dead end and a jungle wilderness stands between Panama and Colombia. This route can only be undertaken during the dry season and is extremely dangerous, to the point of being suicidal. Safer Darién treks are described in detail in the Darién Province chapter.

See Hiking Safety, earlier in this chapter, for advice on what to bring on your hike.

Bird Watching

Panama offers magnificent bird watching. The Panama Audubon Society, which does an annual bird count, consistently counts more species of bird in Panama than are recorded anywhere else in Central America. This is due to a couple of factors: Panama's location relative to two continents and its narrow girth. Birds migrating between North and South America tend to be funneled into a small area. Many North and South American species are represented, both native and

Panama's macaws are a bird watcher's delight.

migratory. Panama also has many endemic species of bird.

The famous resplendent quetzal, symbol of Central America, is more abundant in western Panama than anywhere else in the region. It can be seen around Volcán Barú, notably in the hills around Boquete and Cerro Punta, where it is common much of the year.

Other birds of particular interest include the three-wattled bellbird, the harpy eagle, the great green macaw and the king vulture – the list goes on and on. All told, 940 species (native, migratory and endemic) have been identified in Panama.

To see birds in Panama, just get a good set of binoculars and get out on a trail. The Camino del Oleoducto (Pipeline Road) trail near Panama City is a favorite with birders; more than 500 species were sighted there in a single day during a Christmas bird count. Most birds are seen around dawn and just afterward, so avid birders will want to arrive just before daylight. (See the Panamá Province chapter for more details.)

A Guide to the Birds of Panama is extremely helpful (see the Books section in this chapter). Helpful organizations include the Panama Audubon Society (☎ 224-4740, audupan@pananet.com, www.pananet.com/audubon) in Panama City, which organizes birding expeditions. Commercial companies offering birding expeditions include Ancon Expeditions of Panama, Pesantez Tours and Iguana Tours, which are all based in Panama City (see the Tour Companies in Panama section in the Getting Around chapter).

Fishing

Panama has 1518 islands, 2988km of coast and 480 rivers that empty into the oceans (plus an unknown number that don't), so there's no problem finding a fishing spot.

For deep-sea fishing, Panama offers three world-class areas: Bahía Piña and the Pearl and Coiba archipelagos. All three sites are served by fishing outfits. Piña is served by Tropic Star Lodge, which boasts more than 50 current world records (see the Darién Province chapter for further details). The Archipiélago de las Perlas is served by Salvatore Fishing, which features full and half-day trips (see the Panamá Province chapter). The Coiba group is served by Coiba Explorer Panama, which offers shipboard and beachfront lodging (see the Parque Nacional Isla de Coiba section in the Veraguas Province chapter).

Other angling possibilities include bass fishing in Lago Gatún and trout fishing in the rivers running down Volcán Barú near the towns of Boquete, Volcán, Bambito and Cerro Punta. See the Chiriquí Province chapter for information on trout fishing.

River Running

There are two kinds of river running in Panama, both of which I highly recommend. You can go white-water rafting on the Ríos Chiriquí and Chiriquí Viejo, where trips are offered by the country's only white-water outfit, Chiriquí River Rafting (☎ 236-5218, ☎/fax 236-5217, hsanchez@panama.c-com.net, www.panama-rafting.com), Apartado 1686, Balboa, Ancón,

Panamá, República de Panamá. See the Chiriquí Province chapter for details.

The second variety relies on dugouts instead of rafts; it affords many of the same thrills as rafting but with less emphasis on rapids. In Bocas del Toro and Darién Provinces, many locals rely on these somewhat unstable boats as their main mode of transportation. I've used dugouts in both provinces on a number of occasions and found the jungle-flanked rides quite thrilling – and to my surprise I've yet to tip a dugout.

Cycling

Cycling is an excellent way to see most of Panama (although riding in Panama City is not recommended due to heavy traffic). The roads here, while rougher than those found in most First World countries, are the best in Central America. The Interamericana is in good condition from the Costa Rican border to Panama City and beyond, and most of the roads intersecting it have been or are being improved to increase tourism. The major factor when considering a lengthy bike ride is the weather. No matter what bike you're on, it's not safe to ride in the rain, and it rains quite a lot here – particularly on the Caribbean side.

It is possible to bring your own bike by air and, due to the dearth of bicycle-rental places, this is definitely the thing to do if you plan on seeing the country by bike. Most airlines will fly a bike as one of your pieces of checked baggage if you box it. However, boxing a bike gives baggage handlers little clue to the contents, and the box is liable to be roughly handled, possibly damaging the bike. An alternative is wrapping it in heavy plastic or bubble wrap – baggage handlers are less likely to drop or throw the bike in this case. Airlines' bicycle carrying policies vary a lot, so ask around.

It is possible to rent bicycles for a day, a week or a month, though as I've said few rental places exist in Panama. There are occasional and very popular group rides you can join in on; they're a great way to meet people and see some of the countryside at the same time. See the Bicycle section in the Panama City chapter for more details on these events.

Sea Kayaking

It's possible to rent sea kayaks from Tropic Star Lodge at Bahía Piña, Hotel Las Brisas in Bocas del Toro town and several other places. At the time of writing, only one tour operator was offering sea kayaking trips (see below), but given the great number of islands on both sides of Panama and its thousands of kilometers of beautiful coastline, it's a sure bet that more operators will offer kayaking tours as time passes.

Mountain Travel-Sobek (☎ 510-527-8100, 888-687-6235, fax 510-525-7710, www.MTSobek.com), at 6420 Fairmont Ave, El Cerrito, CA 94530, USA, offers 'Kayaking with the Kuna Indians: Paddling the San Blás Islands in Panama.' Land costs (which don't include airfare) for the guided 15-day adventure range from US$2200 to US$2700 per person, depending on the size of the group.

LANGUAGE COURSES

There are two reputable Spanish-language programs in Panama; both are in Panama City. See the Panama City chapter for details.

WORK

It's difficult for foreigners to find work in Panama. The government doesn't want them to take jobs away from Panamanians, and the labor laws reflect that sentiment. Basically, the only foreigners legally employed in Panama work for their own businesses, possess skills not found in Panama or work for companies that have special agreements with the Panamanian government (for example, if a French company builds a US$50 million hotel in Panama City, its owners will likely be permitted to fill the general manager's position with a French citizen).

Volunteer Work

The Asociación Nacional para la Conservación de la Naturaleza (National Association for the Conservation of Nature, or Ancon; ☎ 264-8100, fax 264-1836, ancon@pty.com, www.ancon.org), Apartado 1387, Panamá 1, República de Panamá, offers opportunities for volunteering on projects in national parks and other beautiful natural areas. Volunteers might protect nesting sea turtles near Bocas del Toro town, do environmental-education work in the Darién or assist national park rangers. You can volunteer for any length of time, from a week up to several months; you won't get paid, but Ancon will supply your basic necessities, such as food and shelter. Contact Ancon for details.

ACCOMMODATIONS

Accommodations prices cited in this book are 1998 high-season rates, and they include Panama's 10% tax on hotel rooms.

Hotels

There usually is no shortage of places to stay in Panama, although getting a hotel room during Carnaval, Easter week and other holiday times can be difficult in some places. Finding a room on a popular island (Isla Contadora or Isla Grande, for example) can be tough on a lovely weekend during the dry season. Hotel accommodations also can be tight if there is a special event going on in a particular town.

Some travelers prefer to make advance reservations everywhere; this is generally possible and recommended in the better places. Faxes are increasingly used to make reservations, as they are cheaper than telephone calls and solve the problem of language difficulties (if written in English, they can be translated readily enough). In some of the top-end hotels, email is beginning to be used as a way of making reservations and providing information. Air mail is slow. In the Places to Stay sections in this book, I've given telephone and fax numbers, street addresses, and email addresses for those hotels that have them.

Before accepting a room, ask to see several. The same prices are often charged for rooms of widely differing quality. Even in

the US$5-a-night cheapies it's worth looking around. If you are shown a horrible airless box with just a bed and a bare light bulb, you can ask to see a better room without giving offense. You'll often be amazed at the results. Naturally, hotels want you to rent their most expensive rooms; if you're on a tight budget, make a habit of asking if hotels have economical rooms (many do but don't post their lowest prices).

Hotel Categories Those hotels listed as 'budget' are certainly the cheapest but not necessarily the worst. Although they are usually very basic, with just a bed, a light and four walls, they can nevertheless be well maintained, very clean and an amazing value for the money. They are often good places to meet other travelers, both Panamanian and foreign.

The difference between a bad budget place and a decent economical hotel often cannot be detected from the street. A place may look just fine from roadside, but its rooms might have horrible stains or strong odors. Other places may look like fleabags from the outside, but to your pleasant surprise you'll discover that the rooms are spacious and clean, the beds firm and the shower water perfectly hot.

Keep in mind too that some lower-end lodgings in Panama may be used by locals only as temporary crashpads or as spots for romantic rendezvous. In addition, some budget places do double duty as brothels – the presence of prostitutes and their clients may mean that your room is more likely to be robbed and that you might be mistaken for a prostitute (if you're a woman) or a client (if you're a man). Check carefully before you take a room. Listings in this book generally focus upon the places that offer acceptable lodgings.

Prices in the budget category begin at about US$5 per person and go up to US$20 for a double room. Almost every town has hotels in this price range. Although you'll usually have to use communal bathrooms in the cheapest hotels, you can sometimes find rooms with a private bathroom for as little as US$10 double.

Hotels in the 'middle' category usually charge about US$20 to US$40 for a double room, but the cheaper ones are not always better than the best hotels in the budget range. On the whole, you can find some very decent hotels. Even if you're traveling on a tight budget, there may be occasions when you feel like indulging in comparative luxury for a while.

The top-end hotels charge over US$40 double, and rates can go to five times that in Panama City and in the beach resorts. The prices and services in the best places compare favorably with international standards.

Hotel Tax A 10% tax is added to hotel prices. Some hotels give prices including the tax, others give prices without the tax, so always clarify this point when asking about room rates. As noted above, I have given full prices including taxes for the 1998 high season. As the number of tourists rises, the prices will surely rise as well. If you're buying this book toward the end of its shelf life – around 2001 – add another 15% to the hotel prices given here to avoid sticker shock.

Bathrooms Bathroom facilities in the cheaper hotels are rarely what you may be used to at home. The cheapest hotels don't always have hot water. Even when they do, its availability may be limited to certain hours of the day.

An intriguing device you should know about is the 'electric shower.' This consists of a single cold-water showerhead hooked up to an electric heating element that is switched on when you want a hot (more likely tepid) shower. Don't touch anything metal while you're in the shower or you may discover what an electric shock feels like. The power is never high enough to actually throw you across the room, but it's unpleasant nevertheless.

Flushing a toilet in some of the cheaper hotels can create another hazard – overflow. See the Toilets section in this chapter for details.

Security Most hotels will give you a key to lock your room, and theft from hotel rooms is not as common as it is in some other countries. Once in a while you'll find that a room doesn't look very secure – perhaps there's a window that doesn't close, or the wall doesn't come to the ceiling and can be climbed over. It's worth finding another room. This is another reason why it's always good to look at a room before you rent it.

You should never leave valuables lying around the room; the person cleaning it likely makes less than US$10 a day. Money and passports should be in a secure body pouch; other valuables can usually be kept in the hotel strongbox. Beware of local 'fishermen' – people who poke sticks with hooks on them through openable windows to fish out whatever they can get.

B&Bs

Almost unknown in Panama until the mid-1990s, the B&B phenomenon is sweeping the country. Rates at B&Bs range from middle to top end. B&Bs are mentioned throughout the book.

Camping & Hostels

There are no youth hostels in Panama; student IDs and 25¢ will get you only a coffee. Cheap camping facilities *are* available in many of the national parks but in only a few of the towns. At the time of writing, there was only one campground equipped for motor homes (in Santa Clara, Coclé Province).

FOOD

You don't have to eat at a fancy restaurant to enjoy good food in Panama. A good indication of the quality of food a restaurant serves is the number of locals you see eating there – a restaurant generally isn't empty if its food is delicious and reasonably priced. If you're on a tight budget, eat the set meal offered in most restaurants at lunchtime; it's usually filling and cheap.

You'll find a good range of restaurants at all price levels throughout this book.

Remember that tips are rarely included in the check. If you are happy with the service you've received and want to leave a generous tip, leave an amount equal to 10% of the bill. Your tips won't likely do much damage to your budget, as service in Panamanian restaurants usually needs improving.

What to Order

Most restaurants serve *bistec* (beef), *pollo* (chicken) and *pescado* (fish) dishes. Vegetarians should note that *carne* literally means 'meat,' but in Panama it tends to refer to beef. Chicken, *puerco* (pork) and *chivo* (goat) aren't necessarily included in a dish's description, so be specific if you want something without any meat. Generally, Panamanian food is tasty rather than spicy hot.

In keeping with its international and multiethnic character, Panama offers a variety of food. The national dish is *sancocho,* a fairly spicy chicken and vegetable stew. *Ropa vieja* ('old clothes'), a spicy shredded beef combination served over rice, is another common and tasty dish. Other typical Panamanian dishes include the following:

carimañola – a roll made from ground and boiled yucca that is filled with chopped meat and then deep-fried.

casado – a set meal that is often filling and always economical. It normally contains *arroz* (rice), *frijoles* (black beans), *plátano* (fried plantain), beef, chopped *repollo* (cabbage) and maybe an egg or an avocado.

ceviche – the classic Panamanian ceviche includes *corvina* or *conchas* (shellfish), chopped onion and *ají chombo* (which is one of the hottest chili peppers in the world), marinated in lemon juice. Increasingly, ceviche in Panama is offered with *langostinos* (shrimp) or *pulpo* (octopus) in lieu of corvina or shellfish.

empanadas – corn turnovers filled with ground meat and fried.

gallo pinto – literally, 'spotted rooster'; a soupy mixture of rice and black beans, often with a pig's tail thrown in for flavor. Gallo pinto is traditionally served at breakfast, sometimes with *natilla* (something like a cross between sour cream and custard) or *huevos fritos/*

revueltos (fried/scrambled eggs). This dish is lightly spiced with herbs and is filling and tasty.

patacones – fried green plantains cut crossways in thin pieces, covered in salt and then pressed and fried.

plátano maduro – also called *plátanos en tentación;* ripe plantains cut in slices lengthwise and baked or broiled with butter, brown sugar and cinnamon; served hot.

tajadas – ripe plantains sliced lengthwise and fried.

tamales – made from boiled ground corn with spices and chicken or pork; the tamale is wrapped in banana leaves and boiled.

tasajo – dried meat cooked with vegetables.

tortilla de maíz – a thick, fried cornmeal tortilla.

Seafood is excellent and abundant in Panama. On the Caribbean coast and islands, common everyday foods include lobster, shrimp, Caribbean king crab, octopus and fish such as corvina. Often the seafood is mixed with coconut milk; coconut rice and coconut bread are other Caribbean treats.

The area around Volcán Barú is known for its mountain rainbow trout, coffee, Boquete navel oranges and many other fruits and vegetables.

In Panama City you'll often see men pushing carts and selling *raspados,* cones made of shaved ice topped with fruit syrup and sweetened condensed milk. This is no gourmet dish, but on a hot day nothing is more satisfying.

Many bars serve *bocas.* These are little savory side dishes such as black beans, ceviche, chicken stew, potato chips and sausages, and they are designed to make your drink more pleasurable – maybe you'll have another one! If you have several rounds, you might eat enough bocas to make a light meal.

DRINKS
Nonalcoholic Drinks

Fresh fruit drinks, sweetened with heaping tablespoons of sugar and mixed with water or milk, are called *chichas* and are very common. These drinks originated in Chiriquí Province and are now popular throughout Panama. At Niko's Cafe in

Panama City, for example, more than a dozen chichas are sold. Fruit drinks to try include *piña* (pineapple), *sandía* (watermelon), *melón* (cantaloupe), *mora* (blackberry), *zanahoria* (carrot), *cebada* (barley) and *tamarindo* (a slightly tart but refreshing drink made from the fruit of the tamarind tree).

A nonalcoholic drink found in Panama and nowhere else is the *chicheme*. This delicious concoction consists of milk, sweet corn, cinnamon and vanilla. Many Panamanians believe chicheme has certain health-giving properties and think nothing of driving many kilometers to buy it in La Chorrera, a city in Panamá Province that produces the best chicheme. (See the Panamá Province chapter for more details.)

Perhaps the healthiest drink available in Panama is the one served in its natural container: coconut juice. On certain stretches of the Carretera Nacional (National Hwy) on the Península de Azuero and on some San Blás islands, you'll see people selling coconut juice from little stands. You'll recognize the stands by the piles of coconuts beside them. For 25¢, the vendor will hack a hole in a coconut and serve it to you. The juice is sweet and pure; you needn't worry about bugs. When you're through with the juice, ask the vendor to split the coconut in half. If you're lucky, the meat that it contains will be delicious. Some coconuts have tasty meat, some don't. I hope that you luck out.

Coffee is traditionally served very strong and offered with cream or condensed milk. Café Durán is the most popular of the local brands, and it's quite good. Cappuccinos are increasingly available in Panama City. Tea (including herb tea) is available in the cities but difficult to find in towns. Milk is pasteurized and safe to drink. The usual brands of soft drinks are available.

Alcoholic Drinks

The national alcoholic drink is made of *seco,* milk and ice. Seco, like rum, is distilled from sugar cane, but it doesn't taste anything like the rum you know. This is the drink of campesinos. Order a *seco con leche* in sophisticated Panama City and you'll likely receive some odd looks, but a true world traveler wouldn't leave the country without trying one.

By far the most popular alcoholic beverage in Panama is *cerveza* (beer), and the most popular local brands are Soberana, Panamá, Balboa, Cristal and Atlas. None of these is rich in taste, but served ice cold they're hard to beat on a hot day. A large Atlas at a typical cantina can cost as little as 50¢; the same beer can cost you US$2 at an upscale restaurant.

Just behind cerveza on the popularity index are the hard liquors, often referred to by both sexes as *baja panties* (panty lowerers). Of these, rum, scotch and vodka are the big sellers. The Panamanian label Old Parr scotch tastes a lot like old shoe. Wines are not terribly popular. Those that are offered in most restaurants generally come from Chile, France or the USA and are of mediocre quality. However, quite good wines from California, France, Spain, Italy and Argentina can be found in fine restaurants and wine stores, although the variety is not huge.

There's a drink that peasants in the central provinces particularly like: *vino de palma,* which is sap extracted from the trunk of an odd variety of palm tree called *palma de corozo.* This collected sap can be drunk immediately (it's delicious and sweet) or fermented (which is kind of hard to take for someone not used to its harsh flavor).

Most bars in Panama have a happy hour – drinks are half-price during certain late-afternoon hours, typically 4 to 6 pm or 5 to 7 pm. Many nightclubs offer 'open bars,' which means you pay a certain amount to enter the establishment and thereafter the drinks are free. Generally only local brands, which are far less expensive than imported ones, are served at open bars.

ENTERTAINMENT

Panama City has the best selection of entertainment in Central America. On a typical weekend night visitors have the

Green Is Good

Many of Panama's beaches are lined with coconut trees, and their fruit is delicious to eat and drink. The coconut has a thick husk, beneath which is a hard shell. Lining the interior of the shell is the fruit's white meat, which may be soft or hard depending on the coconut's age. Filling most of the shell is the fruit's sweet juice, which chiefly consists of mineral-rich, naturally filtered water that's said to be very good for the kidneys. Coconut juice and coconut meat are best consumed when the fruit is green; when the fruit is brown, the meat has hardened and the juice has begun to sour. Naturally fallen coconuts are decomposing and should not be eaten.

Tapping the juice and exposing the meat is a tricky matter best attempted with a machete. Machetes can be found throughout Panama and usually cost US$5; a small machete is a wise buy if you intend to spend a lot of time at secluded beaches, where purified water isn't readily available to you.

Stand the coconut on end so that its stem faces the ground. Hack the pointy top of the coconut at a 45° angle, rotate the fruit one-fifth and repeat. Do this until a portion of the shell about the length of your thumb is exposed; the husk will peel out and away from the exposed shell as you hack. Carefully strike the bared shell until you've made a hole in it. Tilt your head back and enjoy the refreshing juice. Once it's gone, place the coconut on the ground and split it in two to get at the meat. The meat is best scooped out of the shell with a spoon, but fingers work fine too.

Getting your hands on a coconut can be a problem. The easiest way is to pay someone to climb a tree and pick a few nuts; where there are coconut trees, there is usually a kid around who's happy to liberate a few nuts for 50¢ or so. If you're on your own, pick up a fallen coconut and heave it, bowling-ball style, at the lowest bunch on the tree. You can drop several coconuts with a well-aimed throw. My personal best: four with one toss – enough to last me an entire day of lounging under the hot sun of the Tropics. ■

Luck of the Draw

Panamanians *love* lotteries, and there are two national lotteries in the country. One allows you to pick your numbers, and the other offers tickets with numbers already on them. As in lotteries everywhere, the goal is to possess those numbers that are randomly selected as winners by the government. No tax is levied on lottery prizes in Panama. Profits from ticket sales go to hospitals and other charitable institutions.

Where can you buy a lottery ticket? Seemingly everywhere. Sellers get a tiny commission for every ticket they sell, so many retired people sell tickets to pick up a little extra money to supplement their pensions. Tickets are also available at most liquor and convenience stores. Winning numbers appear in local newspapers and are often found scribbled on pieces of paper posted in stores that sell tickets. ■

community that doesn't have at least one watering hole at which to pass the time with some friendly people. Details on local entertainment alternatives are found throughout the regional chapters of this book.

SPECTATOR SPORTS

Panamanians are enthusiastic sports fans. As in all of Latin America, soccer is a favorite; in Panama baseball, softball and basketball are also all the rage. Boxing is another popular spectator sport; it has been a source of pride to Panamanians (and to Latin Americans in general) ever since Roberto Durán, a Panama City native and boxing legend, won the world championship lightweight title in 1972. He went on to become the world champion in the welterweight (1980), light middleweight (1983) and super middleweight (1989) categories.

SHOPPING

A remarkable variety of imported goods, including cameras, electronic equipment and clothing, is sold in Panama, both in Colón's tax-free Zona Libre and in Panama City. The giant stores in the Zona Libre cater mostly to mass buyers, and most of them will not sell individual items (see the Colón Province chapter for details). Panama City's Avenida Central, however, is a mecca for bargain hunters. Shop around and bargain, as there's a lot of competition.

It's possible to purchase high-quality replicas of *huacas* – golden objects made on the isthmus centuries before the Spanish conquest and placed with Indians at the time of burial. These range in price from US$5 to more than US$1000. See the Panama City chapter for details.

The favorite handicraft souvenir from Panama is the *mola,* a colorful, intricate, multilayered appliqué textile sewn by Kuna women of the Archipiélago de San Blás. Small, simple souvenir molas can be bought for as little as US$5, but the best ones are sold on the islands and can fetch several hundred dollars.

options of hearing live jazz, rock, salsa or Panamanian music; seeing the newest Hollywood movies in English at any of a number of cinemas; dancing at no fewer than five classy, high-tech dance clubs; drinking in fancy bars, neighborhood pubs or traditional cantinas; gambling at casinos; shooting pool; and/or checking out the strip clubs.

The best place to obtain information about upcoming cultural events in Panama City is *Talingo,* a supplement that appears in the newspaper *La Prensa* every Sunday. On the last inside page of *Talingo,* under the heading 'Nacional,' are lists (in Spanish only) of the art events, concerts, conferences, classes, gallery openings and recommended TV movies for the coming week.

The number of entertainment options drops off dramatically outside the capital city, although it's odd to come across a

Other handicrafts include wood carvings, masks, ceramics and clothing. *Polleras,* the lacy, frilly, intricately sewn dresses that are considered Panama's national dress, are made in Guararé on the Península de Azuero. You can buy one, but they're not cheap; some cost more than US$1000. See the Veraguas, Herrera and Los Santos chap-

ters for details on traditional handicrafts particular to certain villages.

All the Gran Morrison chain department stores have handicraft and traditional art sections. Other stores and galleries where visitors can shop for handicrafts in the capital city are mentioned in the Panama City chapter.

Getting There & Away

Panama's geographic location between two large continents and two great oceans makes it a true crossroads of the world. Each year more than 300 cruise ships transit the Panama Canal. Airlines serving Panama on a regular basis include not only major North and South American carriers but also Taiwanese, Israeli, Russian and Spanish airlines. Overland travelers are entering the country in increasing numbers, and international tour operators have begun offering Panamanian tours.

AIR

Airlines connect Panama with all the other Central American countries, the Caribbean, and North and South America. If you're traveling a long distance, you can usually arrange a ticket with one or more free stopovers.

The main air connection points in North America for flights to and from Panama are Miami; Houston; Newark, NJ; New York; Washington, DC; Dallas; and Los Angeles. Miami is the principal one. Fares from the USA are competitive but generally change seasonally, with higher fares during the peak travel periods of mid-December to mid-January and mid-June to mid-August.

Panama has two international airports (one in Panama City and one in David), and travel agencies can be found in the major cities. There's a US$20 departure tax on international flights. See the Visas & Documents section in the Facts for the Visitor chapter for entry and exit requirements.

Airports & Airlines

Tocumen International Airport, 35km from downtown Panama City, is where most international flights to Panama arrive. Aeropuerto Enrique Malek, in David, 75km southeast of the Costa Rican border, also handles flights to and from San José.

Going through immigration, baggage pickup and customs at Tocumen airport is

Remember, Before You Fly . . .
- Always reconfirm airline reservations, even for short flights.
- Arrive at the airport an hour before departure for domestic flights.
- Arrive at the airport two hours before departure for international flights.

easy and usually takes about 30 minutes. If you don't have a tourist card when you reach the immigration booth, you'll likely be directed to an airline counter 20m away where you can get one for the regular fee of US$5. After you've completed the short form, return to the immigration booth and submit it. You'll then receive an entry stamp valid for 30 days. (Note that not everyone needs a tourist card to enter Panama; see Visas & Documents in the Facts for the Visitor chapter for details on requirements.)

Just beyond immigration is an Instituto Panameño de Turismo (IPAT) counter. If you have any questions or want help securing a taxi ride into town, don't hesitate to approach the counter; the people behind it are there to help you. Unfortunately, unless you speak Spanish they likely won't be able to help you. IPAT, an agency with a big budget and a work force of hundreds, rarely staffs its tourist centers with people who speak English, French or German. Many people in Panama speak English, but IPAT almost without exception hires people who don't.

Around a corner, you'll come to a conveyor belt where your baggage will appear. After claiming your bags, proceed to customs. There you will be asked to press a large red button that will randomly illuminate one of two lights. If you get a green light, you can proceed without having your bags checked. If you get a red light instead, you must present your bags to a customs inspector.

The main airlines flying to Panama come from the USA. These include American Airlines, Aviateca, Continental Airlines, Delta Air Lines, EVA Airways, Lacsa, Mexicana, TACA and United Airlines. From Europe, most airlines connect with flights from Miami. Iberia from Spain and LTU International Airways charters from Germany may avoid Miami, but they usually stop somewhere in the Caribbean instead. COPA is Panama's national airline, offering flights to and from the USA, numerous Latin and South American countries, and the Caribbean. See the Panama City chapter for airline telephone numbers in Panama.

Panama also has four domestic carriers, and several charter airlines operate out of Panama City. It's even possible to charter helicopters, although they are very expensive. See the Getting Around chapter for details on domestic air travel.

Buying Tickets

The ordinary economy-class fare is not the most economical way to go. It is convenient, however, because it usually enables you to fly on the next plane out and your ticket is valid for 12 months. In my experience, contacting the airlines directly is a waste of money. A good travel agent is more likely to find the airline with the best deal for you. If you want to economize further, there are several options, which are discussed below.

Youth & Student Fares People with international student ID cards can get discounts with most airlines. Student fares are not only cheap but also often include free stopovers, don't require advance purchase and may be valid for up to a year. Although youth and student fares can be arranged through most travel agents and airlines, it is a good idea to go through agents that specialize in student travel.

There are two agencies with worldwide offices that provide excellent service

to student travelers: STA Travel (www.statravel.com) and Council Travel (www.counciltravel.com). STA Travel is the world's largest travel organization specializing in low-cost travel for students. It has more than 100 offices worldwide, several of which are listed in this chapter. It can get competitive airfares for nonstudents too.

Council Travel is affiliated with the Council on International Educational Exchange and is a well-recommended company for budget travel. It has sales offices in 60 US cities and in France, Germany and the UK. Like STA Travel, Council Travel can also offer competitive airfares for nonstudents. Several of its offices are listed in this chapter.

Airline Deals Whatever your age, if you can purchase your ticket well in advance and stay a minimum length of time, you can find a fare usually about 30% to 40% cheaper than the full economy fare. These are often called 'APEX,' 'excursion' or 'promotional' fares, depending on the country you are flying from and the rules and fare structures that apply there.

Often the following restrictions apply: You must purchase your ticket at least 21 days (sometimes more or fewer days) in advance; you must stay for a minimum period (about 14 days on average); and you must return within 180 days (sometimes sooner; for example, passengers from the USA must return within 30 days to qualify for the lowest APEX fares). Individual airlines have different requirements, which change from time to time. Most of these tickets do not allow stopovers, and there are extra charges if you change your destination or dates of travel. These tickets are often sold out well in advance of departure, so try to book early.

Standby fares are another possibility from some countries, such as the USA. Some airlines will let you travel at the last minute if they have available seats just before the flight. Standby tickets cost less than an economy fare but are usually not as cheap as other discounted tickets.

Discounted Tickets A cheap way to go is via ticket consolidators, or 'bucket shops,' which are allowed to sell discounted tickets to help airlines fill their flights. These tickets are often the cheapest of all, particularly in the low season, but they may sell out fast and you may be limited to only a few available dates.

Discounted, economy and student tickets are available directly from the airlines or from travel agencies (there is no extra charge for any of these tickets if you buy them from an agent rather than directly from the airline), but consolidated discount tickets can be purchased only from the discount-ticket agencies themselves. Most of them are good, reputable, bonded companies, but once in a while a fly-by-night operator comes along. Carefully check what you are buying before handing over your money.

Discount-ticket agencies often advertise in the travel sections of newspapers and in travel-oriented magazines. Note that STA Travel and Council Travel, which specialize in procuring inexpensive airline tickets for students, can also obtain competitive airfares for nonstudents.

Courier Flights If you are flexible with dates and can travel with minimal baggage, you can fly to Panama as a courier. (This is most practical from the USA; see the USA section, below.) Couriers are hired by companies that need to have packages delivered to Panama (and many other international destinations). They will give the courier an exceptionally cheap ticket in return for using his or her baggage allowance. You can bring carry-on baggage only. These are legitimate operations; all baggage that you are to deliver is completely legal. And it is amazing how much you can bring in your carry-on baggage! Remember, you can buy things like T-shirts, a towel and soap after you have arrived at your destination, so traveling with just carry-on baggage is certainly feasible.

Other Considerations Roundtrip fares are always much cheaper than two one-way tickets. They are also cheaper than 'open-jaws' tickets, which enable you to fly into one city (such as Panama City) and leave from another (such as Guatemala City). However, a few agencies can get some good fares on open-jaws tickets, which are suitable for someone wanting to do a little overland traveling in Central America, so it's a good idea for you to shop around.

If a late flight (but not a rescheduled one) causes you to miss a connection or forces you to stay overnight, the carrier is responsible for providing you with help in making the earliest possible connection and paying for a room in a hotel of its choice. It should also provide you with meal vouchers. If you are seriously delayed on an international flight, ask for these services.

Travelers are sometimes confused about the meaning of a 'direct flight.' A direct flight goes from your departure point to your destination and does not require that you get off the plane. However, unless it is specifically called a *nonstop* direct flight, the flight can stop in several cities en route to its final destination.

Nonstop direct flights will often cost more than other flights, but money isn't everything. If your trip to Panama is short and meant to be an escape from the frustrations of your day-to-day life, try to avoid starting your vacation with a headache. I've flown on TACA's relatively cheap – but never nonstop – direct flights from Los Angeles to Panama and other Central American countries perhaps two dozen times, and have concluded that for me it makes better sense to pay somewhat more and take a nonstop flight. For example, at the time of writing, TACA's Los Angeles-Panama City flight was actually a Los Angeles-Guatemala City-San Salvador-Managua-San José-Panama City flight, with a long stopover in San Salvador. By the time you reach Panama on this flight, you're ready to kill a TACA representative. However, for US$100 more the Taiwanese carrier EVA Airways offered a nonstop from Los Angeles to Panama City. Additionally, TACA was using cramped Boeing

737s, while EVA was using spacious 747s. It really pays to shop around.

Baggage & Other Restrictions

These vary depending on the airline and the class of service you have chosen. The airline or your travel agent will be able to explain restrictions to you. As a minimum, you will be allowed two pieces of baggage totaling 20kg, plus a carry-on bag that fits under the seat in front of you. On some airlines or in business and 1st classes, you will be allowed more.

Restrictions on cheaper tickets usually mean that you cannot get a refund, and if you change your dates of travel, you must pay an additional charge.

Travelers with Special Needs

If you have special needs of any variety – a broken leg, dietary restrictions, dependence on a wheelchair, responsibility for a baby, fear of flying – you should let the airline know as soon as possible so that they can make arrangements accordingly. You should remind them when you reconfirm your reservation (at least 72 hours before departure) and again when you check in at the airport. It may also be worth calling around the airlines before you make your reservation to find out how they can handle your needs.

Airports and airlines can be surprisingly helpful, but they do need advance warning. Most international airports can provide escorts from check-in desk to plane when needed, and there should be ramps, lifts, accessible toilets and reachable phones. Aircraft toilets, on the other hand, are likely to present some problems; travelers should discuss this with the airline at an early stage and, if necessary, with their doctors.

Guide dogs for the blind often have to travel in a specially pressurized baggage compartment with other animals, away from their owners, though smaller dogs may be admitted to the cabin. Guide dogs are not subject to quarantine as long as they have proof of being vaccinated against rabies.

Award Yourself Some Space

Gone are the days when you could receive a free trip to an exotic locale as a valued frequent flyer after flying to only a few, albeit distant, destinations. That's because many airlines realized several years ago that the generous frequent-flyer programs they created during the booming '80s were costing them a fortune. Today you've practically got to fly to another solar system to accrue enough kilometers to qualify for one free airline ticket.

Regardless of the award requirements, there's a very good reason for you to enroll in the frequent-flyer program offered by the airline (or airlines) you'll use for your upcoming trip to Panama: Most carriers allow their frequent-flyer members to board early. Sure, disabled people, 1st-class passengers and families with small children are always allowed to board first. But increasingly frequent flyers are called immediately afterward, before row-by-row announcements begin. Boarding early is important because it virtually assures you plenty of overhead cargo space for your carry-on baggage. This may not seem important to you when you're at home selecting your luggage with great care and planning baggage space with utmost efficiency. But you'll be glad to be in front of the herd when you're returning from Panama with newly bought goodies that you'd rather not place in the care of airport baggage handlers.

Joining a frequent-flyer program is easy. You can do it at the time you purchase your ticket, if you obtain the ticket directly from an airline. If you obtain it from a ticket consolidator or travel agent, call the airline and ask to join its program. There's never any charge to join, and most applications can be made simply by calling the airline's toll-free reservations number. Once the application is completed, you'll be mailed a membership card to present at the time you check in. *Bon voyage!* ∎

Deaf travelers can ask that airport and in-flight announcements be written down for them.

Children younger than two travel for 10% of the standard fare (or for free on some airlines) as long as they don't occupy a seat. (They do not receive a baggage allowance, either.) 'Skycots' should be provided by the airline if requested in advance; these will take a child weighing up to about 22lbs. Children between two and 12 can usually occupy a seat for one-half to two-thirds of the full fare and do get a baggage allowance. Strollers can often be taken on as hand baggage.

The USA
The following airlines (and their domestic toll-free telephone numbers) serve Panama from the USA:

American Airlines	☎ 800-433-7300
Aviateca	☎ 800-327-9832
Continental Airlines	☎ 800-231-0856
COPA	☎ 800-359-2672
Delta Air Lines	☎ 800-221-1212
EVA Airways	☎ 800-695-1188
Lacsa	☎ 800-225-2272
Mexicana	☎ 800-531-7921
TACA	☎ 800-535-8780
United Airlines	☎ 800-241-6522

As noted earlier in this chapter, the principal US gateways to and from Panama are Miami; Houston; Newark, NJ; New York; Washington, DC; Dallas; and Los Angeles. At the time of writing, sample roundtrip economy fares for direct flights from Miami to Panama City ranged between US$413 and US$481. Similar fares from Los Angeles ranged between US$615 and US$675.

Advertisements for ticket consolidators may be found in the Sunday travel sections of the *Los Angeles Times* and *The New York Times*. I've used ticket consolidators many times, including for multistop round-the-world jaunts, and I've never had a problem with them.

Students and/or people under 26 years of age should try Council Travel and STA Travel. Council Travel has 60 offices in the USA; its head office (☎ 212-822-2600, 800-226-8624, fax 212-822-2699, www .counciltravel.com) is at 205 E 42nd St, New York, NY 10017. Call it for the office nearest you. STA Travel (☎ 310-394-5126, 800-777-0112, fax 310-394-4041, www.statravel.com), at 411 Santa Monica Blvd, Santa Monica, CA 90401, also maintains offices in Boston; Chicago; Miami; New York; Philadelphia; San Francisco; Seattle; Washington, DC; and other cities. Call its toll-free 800 number for office locations.

For cheap fares from gateway towns, an excellent contact for travelers is Tico Travel (☎ 800-493-8426, fax 954-493-8466, tico@gate.net, www.ticotravel.com), at 161 E Commercial Blvd, Fort Lauderdale, FL 33334, which has deeply discounted fares to anywhere in Central America.

Another excellent travel agency that can provide deeply discounted tickets is Worldwide Holidays Inc (☎ 305-665-0841, 800-327-9854, fax 305-661-1457, wwhgps@ icanect.net), 7800 Red Rd, Suite 112, South Miami, FL 33143.

Courier travel is another possibility. Most courier flights to Panama originate in Miami, though some are available from New York and Los Angeles as well. *Travel Unlimited,* PO Box 1058, Allston, MA 02134, is a monthly listing of courier and cheap flights to Panama and many other countries. A one-year subscription costs US$25 (US$35 foreign); a single issue costs US$5. For a general overview, there are several books available, including the *Courier Air Travel Handbook,* by Mark Field.

For details on tours to Panama from the USA, see the Organized Tours section at the end of this chapter. Note that 'tours' doesn't necessarily mean a tour group; many tour companies will customize a tour for just one person or a couple.

Canada
There were no direct flights from Canada to Panama at the time of writing. Travelers needed to connect through one of the gateway cities in the USA. United Airlines,

Continental Airlines and American Airlines all have good connections from major Canadian cities. You can also fly with Air Canada and connect to another airline, but it's usually best to try to fly all the way with one airline to reduce the risk of your baggage missing its connection.

A recommended Canadian travel agency is Travel CUTS (☎ 416-977-3703, fax 416-977-4796, www.travelcuts.com), 171 College St, Toronto, ON M5T 1P7, with more than 50 other offices across Canada. It has good deals for students, and it works with the general public as well.

STA Travel (☎ 416-977-5228, fax 416-977-7112, www.statravel.com), 187 College St, Toronto, ON M5T 1P7, also has offices in Montreal, Calgary, Edmonton and Vancouver.

Canadians will find that several companies arrange cheap winter getaway charters to Panama. Often these include several days of hotel accommodations in Panama City and/or a beach resort, and they usually represent good value for the money if the hotels prove to your liking. It is usually best to go through a travel agent, as charter companies don't always sell directly to the public. Two that do are Fiesta Holidays (☎ 416-498-5566) out of Toronto and Fiesta West (☎ 604-688-1102) out of Vancouver.

Latin America & the Caribbean

The Central American airlines – Aviateca, Lacsa, Mexicana and TACA – mentioned in the USA section of this chapter also provide services between all the Central American capitals and Panama City. In addition, COPA (the Panamanian airline) offers flights between Panama City and Colombia, Costa Rica, Cuba, the Dominican Republic, Ecuador, El Salvador, Guatemala, Haiti, Jamaica, Mexico and Peru; Aeronica (the Nicaraguan airline) also provides services to and from Panama City.

In South America you'll find that service to and from Panama is offered by AeroPeru in Peru; Avianca in Colombia; Lacsa in Ecuador, Peru and Venezuela; and Varig in Brazil. American Airlines, Continental Airlines, Delta Air Lines and United Airlines all have connections from Panama City to several Latin American countries.

These flights tend to be expensive because most Latin American countries tax airfares heavily (usually over 10%) and the number of APEX fares is limited. Ticket consolidators aren't found easily, if at all. If you plan on traveling from outside the region to several Latin American countries by air, it is better to book tickets in advance at home rather than paying as you go.

Students considering a trip to Panama should get in touch with STA Travel (www.statravel.com), which has offices in Buenos Aires, Argentina; Sao Paulo and Rio de Janeiro, Brazil; Santiago, Chile; Bogotá, Colombia; and also Caracas, Venezuela.

The UK

At the time of writing, there were no direct flights between the UK and Panama; travelers needed to connect through US or Latin American gateways.

Ticket consolidators generally provide the cheapest fares from Europe to Latin America. Fares from London, where competition is fiercest, are often cheaper than from other European cities; thus some Europeans find it cheaper to fly via London than directly from their home countries.

Agencies advertise in the classifieds of newspapers ranging from *The Times* to *Time Out*. Journey Latin America (☎ 0181-747-3108, fax 0181-742-1312), 16 Devonshire Rd, Chiswick, London W4 2HD, has a healthy reputation. It specializes in cheap fares to Latin American countries as well as arranging itineraries for independent and escorted travel. It also has an office in Manchester.

Another reputable budget travel agency is Trailfinders (☎ 0171-937-5400), 194 Kensington High St, London W8 7RG. It also maintains branches in Birmingham; Bristol; Manchester; and Glasgow, Scotland. Voyages Jules Verne (☎ 0171-723-5066), 21 Dorset Square, London NW1 6QG, reportedly has cheap weekly charters out of Gatwick.

Agencies specializing in student fares and youth discounts include the following:

Campus Travel, 52 Grosvenor Gardens,
   London SW1W 0AG (☎ 0171-730-8111)
Council Travel, 28a Poland St, Oxford Circus,
   London W1V 3DB (☎ 0171-437-7767,
   www.counciltravel.com)
STA Travel, 86 Old Brompton Rd,
   London SW7 3LQ (☎ 0171-581-4132,
   fax 0171-938-4755, www.statravel.com)
   Additional offices in London and
   Manchester

Continental Europe

Some flights from Europe will take you to Miami, where you can connect with other airlines for flights to Panama. The Spanish airline Iberia has a direct flight to Panama City (with stops in the Caribbean). LTU International Airways has charter flights from Germany. Fares, routes and low/high seasons change frequently; the best information is to be had from travel professionals.

Companies dealing with cheap fares and charters to Central America include the following:

Uniclam, 63 rue Monsieur Le Prince,
   75006 Paris, France (☎ 01 43 29 12 36)
Voyages Découvertes, 21 rue Cambon,
   Paris, France (☎ 01 42 61 00 01)
Globetrotter Travel, Remweg 35,
   8001 Zurich, Switzerland (☎ 1-211-7780)

There's also Nouvelles Frontières (☎ 01 41 41 58 58) in Paris and all over France.

Students should contact STA Travel (www.statravel.com) for cheap airfares. Below are the addresses of several of its European offices:

France
   Voyage Wasteels, 2 rue Michel Chasles,
   75012 Paris
   (☎ 01 43 43 46 10, fax 01 43 45 75 40)
   Additional office in Nice
Germany
   STA Travel, Berger Strasse 118,
   60316 Frankfurt 1
   (☎ 69-43-01-91, fax 69-43-98-58)
   Additional offices in Berlin, Cologne,
   Hamburg and Heidelberg
Italy
   Viaggi Wasteels, TES – Train Europe

Service, Via Barberini 87-89,
   1-0D187 Rome
   (☎ 6-474-55-52, fax 6-488-16-47)
   Additional office in Milan
Spain
   Barcelo Viajes, Princesa 3, Madrid 28008
   (☎ 91-569-18-19, fax 91-569-13-25)
   Additional offices in Barcelona, Bilbao,
   Malaga and Palma de Mallorca
Switzerland
   SSR Reisen, Ankerstasse 112, 8026 Zurich
   (☎ 1-297-1111, fax 1-297-1112)
   Additional office in Lausanne

STA also maintains offices in the Czech Republic, Denmark, Greece, Hungary, Malta, the Netherlands, Russia, Sweden and Turkey.

Courier flights are possible from Europe, although they are not yet as well known or popular as they are in the USA. Look in the classifieds of Sunday newspapers or read a book on the subject (check with a local bookstore).

Australia & New Zealand

Travelers coming from Australia's east coast will usually fly to Panama via the USA or Mexico. Qantas Airways, Air New Zealand and other trans-Pacific carriers fly to Los Angeles via Auckland; Nadi, Fiji; or Honolulu, usually with one stopover allowed on the roundtrip, and connect with various carriers onward to Panama.

Fares from New Zealand via the Pacific will be somewhat lower than those from the east coast of Australia. Routes via Asia are impractical.

Students would do well to contact STA Travel (STA actually stands for 'Student Travel Australia,' and the company has many offices there):

Australia
   224 Faraday St, PO Box 75, Carlton South,
   Melbourne, VIC 3053 (☎ 1300-360-960,
   03-9347-6911, fax 03-9347-0608)

   855 George St, Ultimo, Sydney, NSW 2007
   (☎ 02-2212-1255, 800-637-444)

   Student Union Building, ground floor,
   Tasmania University, Sandy Bay, Hobart,
   TAS 7005 (☎ 02-243-496)

Additional offices in Adelaide, Brisbane, Cairns, Canberra, Crawley, Darwin, Kings Cross and Perth

New Zealand
10 High St, Auckland (☎ 0800-100-677, 9-309-0458, fax 9-309-9829)

233 Cuba St, Wellington (☎ 4-385-0561, fax 4-385-6170)

Additional offices in Christchurch, Dunedin and Palmerston North

Asia

There are few direct flights and no nonstop flights between Asia and Latin America, and usually no bargains. Generally the cheapest route is to fly to the West Coast of the USA and connect from there.

Some offices for STA Travel in Asia are as follows:

Japan
Star Plaza Aoyama Building, 1st floor, 1-10-3 Shibuya-Ku, Tokyo 102 (☎ 3-5485-8380)
Toko Building, 2nd floor, 1-5 Yotsuya, Shinjuka-ku, Tokyo 160 (☎ 3-5269-0751)
Nukariya Building, 7th floor, 1-16-20 Minami-Ikebukuro, Toshima-Ku, Tokyo 171 (☎ 3-5391-2922, fax 3-5391-2923)
Honmachi Meidai Building, 6th floor, 2-5-5 Azuchi-machi, Chuo-Ku, Osaka 541 (☎ 6-262-7066, fax 6-262-7065)
Malaysia
Lot 506, 5th floor, Plaza Magnum, Letter Box 506, 128 Jalan Pudu, 55100 Kuala Lumpur (☎ 3-248-9800)
Singapore
No 01-01 Science Hub, 87 Science Park Rd, Singapore 118256 (☎ 773-9188)
Singapore Polytechnic, Canteen No 5 500 Dover Rd, Singapore 139651 (☎ 774-2270)
Thailand
Wall St Tower Building, 14th floor, Room 1406, 33 Surawong Rd, Bangrak, Bangkok 10500 (☎ 2-233-2582)

LAND

If you live in North or Central America, it is possible to travel to Panama overland. The US town nearest to Panama is Brownsville, TX, on the Mexican border. From there, it is about 5000km by road to Panama City; nearly half of this distance is through Mexico and the rest through Guatemala, Honduras, Nicaragua, Costa Rica and western Panama. It is possible, though not necessary, to travel through El Salvador and Belize as well. Panama has land borders with Costa Rica to the west and Colombia to the east. It is not possible to travel overland by car or bus from Colombia.

You can drive your own car, but the costs of insurance, fuel, border permits, food and accommodations will be much higher than the cost of an airline ticket. Many people opt for flying down and renting cars when they arrive in Panama City.

If you do drive down, think about the following: Driving Central American roads at night is not recommended – they are narrow, rarely painted with a center stripe (forget about lights), often potholed and subject to hazards such as cattle and pedestrians in rural areas. Traveling by day from the USA or Canada, allowing for time-consuming and bureaucratic border crossings, will take about a week – definitely more if you want to enjoy some of the fantastic sights (ruins, villages, markets, volcanoes, etc) en route.

But the trip can certainly be done. My main advice here is to get good insurance, be prepared for border bureaucracy, have your papers in impeccable order and never leave your car unattended except in safely guarded parking areas. Don't leave anything of value in the car unless you are with it, and your car shouldn't have fancy hubcaps, mirrors, etc, which are liable to be stolen. US license plates are very attractive to thieves, so you should display these inside the car. Unleaded gas is not always available in some parts of Central America. (It should go without saying that you need a reliable vehicle in excellent mechanical shape.)

If you are bringing a car into Panama, you must pay US$5 for a vehicle control certificate (tarjeta de circulación) and another US$1 to have the car fumigated. You will also need to show a driver's license, proof of ownership and all the usual insurance papers. Your passport will be stamped to show that you paid the US$6 and followed procedures when you brought the vehicle into the country.

The American Automobile Association (AAA) publishes a map of Mexico and Central America (free to AAA members) that highlights the Carretera Interamericana (Pan-American Hwy) and major side roads. Another excellent map of the region is the *Traveller's Reference Map* of Central America, published by International Travel Maps (☎ 604-687-3320, fax 604-687-5925), 736A Granville St, Vancouver, BC V6Z 1G3, Canada.

The AAA sells insurance for driving in Mexico but not in Central America. For insurance in Mexico and Central America, call Sanborn's, which has offices in several cities close to the US-Mexican border, including McAllen (☎ 956-686-0711), 2009 South 10th, McAllen, TX 78501. Alternately, talk to your insurance agent.

A series of public buses will take you all the way from the USA to Panama City. Bus travel is slow and cramped, but cheap. See Lonely Planet's *Central America on a shoestring* or *Mexico* for details on bus travel and places to stay en route. Be forewarned that when you add up all the costs of bus tickets plus food and hotels, you'll pay at least as much as the airfare.

A passport is required to enter Panama. Some people will need tourist cards or visas as well (see Visas & Documents in the Facts for the Visitor chapter for details on entrance requirements). If you plan to enter Panama overland, it's a good idea to get a visa before showing up at the border, even if a visa is not required of you; border posts occasionally run out of tourist cards. If a post is out of tourist cards, you can't get in (the border post at Guabito in northwestern Panama is the exception). You may need to show an onward ticket, and sometimes a show of cash is also required to cross land borders (US$500 per month of your planned stay is generally sufficient). Panamanians are sensitive to appearances; wearing decent clothes and avoiding unusual fashions will make entrance procedures easier.

Costa Rican Border Crossings

There are three road border crossings between Costa Rica and Panama. Border-crossers should note that Panama's time is always one hour ahead of Costa Rica's.

Paso Canoas This crossing is on the Interamericana and is by far the most frequently used entry and exit point on the border with Costa Rica. Half of the dusty, transient city is in Costa Rica, half in Panama. The border posts are located about the city's waist. For no good reason, the border hours here change frequently; when last I checked the border was open 6 am to 11 pm daily. Beware: There are many hotels on the Costa Rican side but none on the Panamanian side.

To enter Panama from Costa Rica, you'll need a passport. Some people will also need visas or tourist cards (see requirements in the Facts for the Visitor chapter). Visas are not obtainable at the border; tourist cards are officially available, but the immigration office on the border has been known to run out of them (if possible, get your visa or tourist card in advance). The cost of a tourist card is US$5.

Once you have entered Panama, you will see taxis and buses stationed just past the border, on your left. The nearest Panamanian city with a hotel is David, 1½ hours away by bus. (See the Chiriquí Province chapter for more information on David.) Buses depart Paso Canoas for David every 10 minutes between 5 am and 8:40 pm (US$1.50); look for a bus with 'Frontera – David' on its windshield. There are four buses daily from Paso Canoas to Panama City, and they depart at 8:30 and 11 am and 4 and 10 pm. The first three buses make numerous stops along the way; travel time is about 10 hours (US$12). The 10 pm bus makes only a couple of brief food stops and takes about eight hours (US$17).

There is a taxi stand near the bus station. Taxis are available 24 hours a day. A taxi ride from the border to David will cost US$25 to US$30, depending on the driver.

If you are entering Costa Rica, you may be required to show a ticket out of the country, although this is rarely requested. If you don't have one, buy a Tracopa bus ticket in David for David to Paso Canoas and the return trip; this is acceptable to the Costa Rican authorities. Buying just the Paso Canoas-to-David section at the border is not acceptable to the authorities.

There is a Costa Rican consulate in David, as well as in Panama City. IPAT, the Panamanian tourism agency, has a tourist center in Paso Canoas.

Sixaola/Guabito This crossing is on the Caribbean coast. Sixaola is the last town on the Costa Rican side; Guabito is its Panamanian counterpart. There are no hotels or banks in Guabito, but stores there will accept your Costa Rican *colones,* Panamanian *balboas* or US dollars. After Guabito colones are no longer accepted.

The border is officially open from 7 am to 11 pm daily. However, immigration and customs officers don't work past 7 pm, which is when bus service on both sides also grinds to a halt. During the day, there are frequent minibuses from Guabito to Changuinola, 17km away; the fare is 75¢. The minibuses can be found on the southern side of the elevated entrance road, just past the immigration office. Taxis are found on the northern side of the road; the fare to Changuinola is US$5.

To enter, you'll need a passport. Some people will also need visas or tourist cards. A tourist card can be obtained for US$5 at the Panamanian Embassy in San José (see its address in the Facts for the Visitor chapter). Or, in lieu of a tourist card, you can go to the Banco Nacional de Panamá, near the airport in Changuinola, and for US$10 obtain a stamp, which you should then take to Changuinola's immigration office. The office will put the stamp in your passport along with an official signature; this will serve as your tourist card.

The border officials reside in nearby houses, and if it is hot (as it usually is in Guabito), they sometimes go home to sleep when they're supposed to be working. If you arrive at the border and you have a passport that needs stamping or otherwise need their services, feel free to look around for them. Even if you don't speak Spanish, if you're wandering around with a passport

in your hand and looking confused, it'll only be a matter of minutes before someone takes pity on you and leads you to an official's home. If awakened, he'll return to his post with you and stamp your passport.

In Changuinola there is a bank, some decent restaurants, several bars and dance clubs and an airstrip (with a hangar beside it that serves as an airport) with daily flights to David and Panama City. There are several fairly cheap hotels; see the Bocas del Toro Province chapter for more information on Changuinola.

From Changuinola, several buses travel the 21km to Almirante. From Almirante, cheap but exceedingly slow passenger/vehicle ferries (US$3) and speedy water taxis (US$10) depart to the town of Bocas del Toro on Isla Colón, which offers a variety of lodging and dining possibilities. The surrounding water features decent surfing and some fine diving and snorkeling opportunities. Alternately, you can bypass the Bocas del Toro islands and travel by water taxi or ferry from Almirante to Chiriquí Grande. (A road between the two towns was under construction at the time of writing.) From Chiriquí Grande, a road goes to David and the rest of Panama.

Río Sereno This little town at the eastern terminus of the scenic Concepción-Volcán road sees so few *gringos* that locals stare at the few who pass through. If you arrive here from Costa Rica by small bus (as most people do), you'll be hard pressed to figure out where one country ends and the other begins. There's no fence, not even a 'Now Leaving Costa Rica – Welcome to Panama' sign. The closest thing to that is a sign announcing that Panama is free of pig disease, which is kind of a mean sign to post when your neighbor is not free of pig disease. The Río Sereno crossing is open from 8 am to 6 pm daily.

The immigration officials here are sticklers on formalities: To enter Panama you must show them a return ticket to your country of origin and show that you are economically solvent (you must have at least US$500 in cash or the equivalent on you), and you must possess a passport with a visa or tourist card (whichever applies; see the Facts for the Visitor chapter). The poorly signed immigration station is beside the well-signed police station.

There's one hotel in this sleepy town nestled amid coffee plantations and patches of forest. *Pensión Los Andes* (no phone), above the pharmacy at the southeastern corner of the town plaza, has 14 rooms with shared bathroom (US$9/14 for one/two people) and two rooms with private bathrooms (US$15 per room). There's hot water. The place is quite OK.

There is a Banco Nacional de Panamá in town, but it's not possible to cash traveler's checks, get cash advances against a credit card or even withdraw money from an ATM there. Exchange foreign currency? Forget it. About the only thing this bank is good for – from the traveler's perspective – is changing large bills into smaller ones.

Buses from Río Sereno travel to Concepción and David; the last bus leaves the crossing at 5 pm daily.

Bus At all three of these border crossings, you can take a local bus up to the border on either side, cross over, board another local bus and continue on your way. Be aware that, as previously mentioned, the last buses leave the border crossings at Guabito and Río Sereno at 7 pm and 5 pm, respectively; the last bus leaves Paso Canoas for Panama City at 10 pm.

Two companies, Panaline (☎ 262-1618) and Tica Bus (☎ 262-2084/6275), operate daily direct buses between San José, Costa Rica, and Panama City, traveling by way of the Carretera Interamericana. Both recommend that you make reservations a few days in advance to ensure that you've got a seat.

In Panama City, Panaline buses arrive at and depart from the Hotel Internacional on Plaza Cinco de Mayo. They depart Panama City at 1 pm daily, arriving in San José the following morning around 5 am. These are good buses, equipped with air-con, bathrooms and video; riders get free sodas. The

fare is US$25/50 one-way/roundtrip.

Tica Bus arrives at and departs from the Hotel Ideal, Calle 17 Oeste, No 15-55, a block west of Avenida Central in Panama City. These buses depart at noon daily, arriving in San José the following morning around 4 or 5 am. The fare is US$20/40 one-way/roundtrip. You must bring your passport when you reserve your ticket. Tica Bus also has buses continuing up through Central America as far as Guatemala.

Colombian Border Crossing

No roads link Panama and Colombia. The Interamericana does not go all the way from Panama into Colombia, but terminates at the grimy, muggy town of Yaviza, in the Darién, and reappears some 150km farther on – far beyond the Colombian border. This break in the highway between Central and South America is known as the Darién Gap. If you wish to take a vehicle into South America from Panama, you must ship it around the Darién Gap.

There is only one place to cross along the entire length of the Panama-Colombia border – a rugged point on the Caribbean coast between rustic Puerto Obaldía (on the Panamanian side) and the resort of Capurganá (on the Colombian side). From either direction, you can reach the other country by boat or by hiking across the point to it. But before you board a boat or put on your walking shoes, you must first obtain the proper passport stamps (see details below).

If you're heading into South America by land or by sea, you must first get to Puerto Obaldía, Panama's official border town (which is actually a few kilometers from the border). The simplest way to do this is to fly from Panama City. Aereo Taxi (☎ 264-8644) and Ansa (☎ 226-7891) fly between Panama City and Puerto Obaldía thrice weekly. The one-way/roundtrip fare on both airlines is US$44/88.

The alternative is to arrive by boat, usually as the last stop on an island-hopping excursion through the Archipiélago de San Blás. You have three boating options: Pay a Kuna Indian to take you from the San Blás islands to the border in a long, narrow boat – the only kind the Indians use. Or catch a ride on one of the slow-moving coconut boats heading for Puerto Obaldía from El Porvenir in the San Blás islands; these boats stop at many islands, picking up coconuts, and for US$30 or so you can often negotiate a ride (you'll want to bring a hammock to sleep in). The third option is to negotiate a ride on a Colombian merchant boat, which I don't advise – these boats, which travel between Colón and Cartagena, Colombia, are notorious for running drugs and contraband.

Puerto Obaldía is a nine-square-block tropical way station. Its beaches are strewn with litter and there's little to do in the town itself. There are no services, just a police station (you must check in with the police immediately upon arrival), a couple of immigration offices, one basic hotel and a black community that lives in simple wooden houses. There's one main road, with a soccer field at one end and the police station at the other. In between are the Panamanian and Colombian immigration offices and the *Pensión Conde* (no phone), which offers 15 basic rooms with private bathrooms for US$12 per room.

If you're heading into Colombia, you need to check with the Panamanian immigration office for an exit stamp or, if you're heading into Panama, an entry stamp. Make sure you have all the necessary documents (passport and tourist card or visa if required) and onward tickets, as well as sufficient funds; US$500 per month of your planned stay is usually enough. Although you may not be asked for these, it's a long backtrack if you show up short. The office is open 9 am to 5 pm weekdays; it closes at noon on Saturday and is closed all day Sunday. An entry stamp is supposed to cost US$5, but officers have been known to ask for US$10, US$15 or US$20, depending on their moods.

Once you have your exit stamp, you must then go to the Colombian immigration office and obtain a Colombian entry stamp. There's a US$5 charge. Check with the Colombian Embassy or Consulate in

Driving to the Darién Gap

The Carretera Interamericana (Pan-American Hwy) stops near the Colombian border at the Darién Gap, a stretch of unbroken wilderness that divides the continents of North and South America and bisects the otherwise continuous hemispheric highway that winds from Alaska to the tip of Chile. The Panamanian and Colombian governments are planning to build the highway across the gap, but for the moment it's impossible for you to drive across or to the Panamanian-Colombian border.

It is possible, however, to drive from the capital to Yaviza, the Darién town at which the Interamericana finally peters out. The drive – along 266km of mostly bad road – presently takes about nine hours during the dry season, but efforts to pave the Interamericana all the way to Yaviza began in early 1998, and thereafter the trip should be quicker.

Along the way you'll pass a variety of small towns: Chepo, El Llano, Cañita, Ipetí, Tortí, Las Aguas Frías, Santa Fé and Metetí. For details on facilities in these towns, see the Panamá Province and Darién Province chapters. ∎

your home country to find out what the entrance requirements are for you (requirements vary from country to country).

There are two transportation options between Puerto Obaldía and Capurganá: traveling by boat or by foot. Boats depart for Sapzurro (the first community on the Colombian side, it's a lovely fishing village) when they collect enough people. The ride costs US$10 and lasts 15 minutes. The boats then continue to Capurganá, an additional 10-minute ride; the Puerto Obaldía-Capurganá fare is US$20. The boatmen often try to make foreign travelers pay more by claiming it's an 'international route' or saying that your backpack is heavy. A good laugh often lets them know you're not falling for it. Present what others are paying, and no more.

The alternative is to walk. This option, given problems along the first portion of the path, is not a prudent one, but it does exist. The journey by foot from Puerto Obaldía to Sapzurro takes about 2½ hours. The first part of the trail goes from Puerto Obaldía to La Miel, the last Panamanian village; it's a two-hour walk. This part of the track is unsafe for walking due to bandits and smugglers in the area. Also, the trails are so indistinct that you can easily become lost in the jungle. It may be wisest to travel to La Miel by boat; rides can be negotiated in Puerto Obaldía.

Once you reach La Miel, there are no further problems. From the village, you climb a small hill, pass the border marker on the top and descend to Sapzurro – all that in half an hour. Small and pleasant Sapzurro is beautifully set on the shore of a deep horseshoe-shaped bay. There are a couple of *hospedajes* (guesthouses), several restaurants and a narrow but clean white-sand beach that's shaded by coconut palms.

From Sapzurro, the footpath (there is no road) climbs again and then drops to the next coastal village, Capurganá. This portion can be easily walked in 1½ to two hours – go at a leisurely pace to take in the splendid scenery.

Capurganá, with a strip of fine hotels lining a wide sweep of beach, is the most touristy place in the whole area and gets pretty crowded from mid-December to the end of January (the Colombian holiday season), but at other times it's quiet and easygoing. Hotel rates during the low season range from US$15 to US$90. The best of the budget hotels is the *Hostal Marlin* (no phone), which is near the beach and offers good beds, fans, screened windows and shared bathroom for US$15/20 single/double. Capurganá is a pleasant place to spend a day or two. A few businesses in the village change US dollars, though at a poor rate.

SEA

Every year some 300 cruise ships transit the Panama Canal. Some carry as many as 2000 passengers and are so large that there's scarcely a meter to spare between the ships and the walls of the locks. Most of the cruise ships make the transit during the months of January, February and March, often while returning to the Caribbean from cruises off the Alaskan coast. A few passenger ships trickle in during April, but by May and June hardly a cruise liner can be found there; it's just too hot and humid to be aboard a ship in the canal. The transcanal cruises pick up again in October and November. December's generally a slow month. Then the cycle repeats itself.

Odd as it may seem, not a single one of the cruise ships offers a Panama shore excursion. There's simply no dock for them, although there has been talk of building one for years. So about a half-million tourists a year visit Panama without actually setting foot in the country. If you're anxious to see the canal and all the other attractions Panama has to offer, you'd be wise to leave the cruise-ship trip for another time.

If staying aboard the ship is OK with you, you might like to know that the best cruise lines with regular canal transits are Princess Cruises (in the USA ☎ 310-553-1770), Crystal Cruises (☎ 310-785-9300), Celebrity Cruises (☎ 305-262-6677, 800-437-3111) and Holland America Line (☎ 800-426-0327). They are also the most expensive, with rates ranging from US$250 to US$350 per person per day, excluding airfare and taxes. Down a step in both price and luxury are Costa Cruises (☎ 305-358-7325) and Royal Caribbean Cruise Lines (☎ 305-539-6000), charging about US$200 per person per day. The most-bang-for-the-buck award would go to the Carnival (☎ 305-599-2600) or Norwegian (☎ 305-436-4000) cruise lines, charging about US$125 per person per day. Among the sailing ships making the transit, Windstar Cruises (☎ 206-281-3535) in Seattle, WA, enjoys a strong reputation.

An excellent resource if you're considering a cruise and have questions is Cruises Inc (☎ 315-463-9695, 800-854-0500, info@cruisesinc.com, www.cruisesinc.com), at

5000 Campuswood Drive, E Syracuse, NY 13057, a US-based travel agency specializing in cruises. The company represents all the major cruise lines, and I've found their representatives helpful and extremely knowledgeable.

If you're planning on sailing a private vessel to or around Panama, consider reading *The Panama Guide,* a cruising guide to the isthmus by Nancy Schwalbe Zydler and Tom Zydler (see Books in the Facts for the Visitor chapter for more details).

DEPARTURE TAXES

There is a US$20 departure tax on international flights from Panama City and David. If you overstay the 30-day limit, you'll need to get an exit stamp before leaving the country (see the Visas & Documents section in the Facts for the Visitor chapter). Travelers departing overland usually are not charged the full US$20, and often they are charged nothing at all. The amount seems to vary with the person on duty.

ORGANIZED TOURS

Compared to such beaten-path Latin American countries as Costa Rica and Guatemala, Panama is not served by many tour operators. Those that do send people here typically combine nature and adventure offerings. One or more national parks are usually visited, with overnight lodging in rustic but comfortable hotels. Apart from guided rainforest hikes, other activities may include transiting the Panama Canal, river rafting, snorkeling and visiting ruins.

Costs for the best arranged tours can exceed US$200 per person daily, plus airfare to and from Panama City. These tours usually provide an experienced bilingual guide, the best lodging available, all in-country transportation and most meals.

If you are shopping for a tour, you'll obviously be interested in the itinerary. In addition, you should check out what kind of guide is provided. Is the guide fluent in English? What are the guide's particular qualifications? Will he/she accompany you throughout the trip or will there be different guides for different portions? Other questions to consider are: How many people will be in the tour group? How many meals are included? What kinds of accommodations are used? Can you speak with past clients?

The advantage of a tour is that everything is taken care of from the time you arrive until the time you leave. You don't have to worry about speaking Spanish, figuring out itineraries, finding bus stations, haggling with taxi drivers, locating hotels with available rooms or translating restaurant menus. People on tours have activities scheduled for every day of their trips and don't need to spend time figuring out what to do and how to do it once they get to Panama City. Tours are often preferred by people who have a short vacation period and enough money to afford this kind of care.

Even if you don't want a tour, there's a good reason to contact a tour operator: savings. If you simply walk into a hotel, you will be given what the tourism industry refers to as the 'rack rate,' which is the posted rate. However, if a tour operator makes the hotel reservation for you, the amount you pay for the room will be less than the rack rate. For example, a hotel with a rack rate of US$150 per night might sell a room to a tour operator for US$90. The operator might offer you the room for US$120, saving you US$30. The tour operator makes US$30. The hotel has an occupied room. Everyone's happy. It never hurts to see what a tour operator can do for you, particularly if it has a toll-free telephone number.

Travelers who would like the advantages of a tour but can't stand the idea of traveling with a tour group are served by several companies that can arrange custom itineraries. These are never cheap, but they aren't necessarily terribly expensive. You can ask for the more economical hotels and often you'll get a choice of places that the company recommends. Guides can be arranged, but if you go with the custom itinerary route, these can be fairly expensive for just one or two people. If you are traveling with a small group of friends or family members, a guide will be afford-able, as the cost will be split among several people.

The tour operators described below have strong reputations. Most have sliding price scales (a group of four on a two-week trip might pay about US$300 per person more than a group of 14, for example). Prices are based on double occupancy, and people sleeping in single rooms may pay consider-ably more, depending on the hotels used. Prices can be a little lower in the low season.

The tour operators listed here are based outside Panama. For information on tours around Panama operated by Panamanian companies (some of which also have a US address or contact phone), see the Getting Around chapter.

Tour Companies
The USA There are many companies in the USA offering package tours to Panama, but only a few I can highly recommend.

Wildland Adventures (☎ 206-365-0686, 800-345-4453, fax 206-363-6615, www .wildland.com), 3516 NE 155th St, Seattle, WA 98155, is a company that does things the right way. Its friendly staff can arrange specialty trips, particularly birding, family travel, honeymoon adventures, trekking adventures and student/teacher study trips. It offers many high-quality, personalized natural history trips. It offers cushy accom-modations for cushy people, hard-core adventures for hard-bodied rugged types and lots of in-between. I've reviewed all the tours offered by Wildland Adventures, and not one is weak or hyped. In-country costs for 10 to 14-day tours from Panama City range from US$1700 to US$2400.

Preferred Adventures Ltd (☎ 612-222-8131, 800-840-8687, fax 612-222-4221, paltours@aol.com), One W Water St, Suite 300, St Paul, MN 55107, is another top-notch tour operator with many years in the business and excellent Panama offerings. In addition to birding, horticultural, natural history, cultural and special-interest study trips, this company can arrange customized itineraries. In my opinion, Preferred Adventures and Wildland Adventures are the top US-based tour operators serving Panama. Both rely heavily upon the very reputable Ancon Expeditions of Panama for ground transportation and guides. In-country costs for Preferred's two to 14-day tours from Panama City range from US$184 to US$2400.

Lost World Adventures (☎ 404-373-5820, 800-999-0558, fax 404-377-1902, www.gorp.com/lostworld.htm), 220 2nd Ave, Decatur, GA 30030, offers only two package tours to Panama, but both are excellent. Lost World's 14-day 'Panama Trans-Darién Expedition' – which Wild-land Adventures and Preferred Adventures also offer – is a heavy-duty, porter-assisted trek across some of the world's most impenetrable forest; in-country cost from Panama City is US$2700. Its 10-day 'Panama Explorer' tour features a boat trip in the Panama Canal, birding on famous Camino del Oleoducto (Pipeline Road), more birding at Finca Lérida and around Volcán Barú, and visits to several San Blás islands. The in-country cost from Panama City is US$1700.

Canada At the time of writing, only one Canadian tour operator offered a package trip to Panama: Quest Nature Tours (☎ 416-221-3000, 800-387-1483, fax 416-221-5730, travel@worldwidequest.com), 36 Finch Ave W, Toronto, ON M2N 2G9. This is a first-class operation. It offers only one package tour to Panama each year, but it's a good one, emphasizing Panama's nat-ural beauty. Destinations include Parque Internacional La Amistad, Lagunas de Volcán, Finca Lérida, Boquete, Parque Nacional Marino Isla Bastimentos, Camino del Oleoducto, Cerro Azul and the Monu-mento Natural Barro Colorado. The cost of the 12-day trip from Panama City is US$2600.

The UK At the time of writing, only one tour operator in the UK offered a package trip to Panama, and even it was part of a multicountry tour: Journey Latin America

(JLA; ☎ 0181-747-8315, fax 0181-742-1312, www.journeylatinamerica.co.uk), at 16 Devonshire Rd, Chiswick, London W4 2HD. JLA features Panama in its 'Alcion Escorted Economy' tour, which begins in Panama City and finishes in Antigua, Guatemala. Panama stops include the Casco Viejo district of Panama City, the Panama Canal, David, Boquete and Paso Canoas. Costs for the 30-day journey begin at UK£1425 per person and include airfare from London to Panama City and the return flight to London from Guatemala City, a JLA tour leader, all surface transportation, and some excursions. Accommodations are not included. JLA can arrange 'open-jaws' tickets and air passes for you, too.

Australia At the time of writing, only one tour operator in Australia was offering a package trip to Panama: Adventure Associates (☎ 02-9389-7466, fax 02-9369-1853, www.adventureassociates.com), at 197 Oxford St, Bondi Junction, Sydney, NSW 2000. In 1998 this company offered two tours. The six-day 'Highlights of Panama' tour includes a tour of Panama City, a Panama Canal transit and one day each on Isla Contadora and Isla Taboga. Its three-day 'Isla Iguana' tour includes snorkeling at Isla Iguana and a visit to a rather unimpressive archaeological site. The cost of these tours is A$1450 and A$400, respectively. Airfare to and from Panama is extra.

WARNING

The information in this chapter is particularly vulnerable to change. Prices for international travel are volatile, routes are introduced and canceled, special deals come and go, and rules and visa requirements are amended. Airlines and governments seem to take a perverse pleasure in making price structures and regulations as complicated as possible.

The upshot of this is that you should get opinions, quotes and advice from several airlines and travel agents before you part with your hard-earned cash. The details given in this chapter should be regarded as pointers and are not a substitute for your own up-to-date research.

Getting Around

Local transportation in Panama is very good. There are airstrips throughout the country, and most receive commercial flights. The domestic airlines are relatively inexpensive, and they are safe; their pilots are accustomed to inclement weather, and if they feel that a storm prevents them from making a safe landing at a particular airstrip, they'll fly to another one, wait for the storm to pass and then fly to the primary airstrip. They won't compromise your welfare just to adhere to a schedule.

Because so many Panamanians depend on buses, there's also an excellent bus system serving all the road-accessible parts of the country. Intercity fares are typically in the US$2 to US$5 range, except for long-distance routes, which can run up to US$25 for nonstop rides on very comfortable Mercedes-Benz buses. Bus fares within cities are typically 15¢.

Taxis are one of the best deals going in Panama. Despite the relatively high cost of gasoline in the country (double what you'd pay in the USA, although slightly less than in Europe), the most you have to pay to take a taxi from one part of a city to another part of the same city is US$2 – except in Panama City, where you might have to pay US$4. For this reason, taxis are very popular in Panama, and they are usually easy to find.

There are no subways in Panama, and train service is almost nonexistent. Boats are the best way to get around in some parts of the country, and this option is discussed in detail in pertinent sections of the regional chapters.

AIR
Domestic Airports & Airlines
Panama is well served by its domestic airlines: Aeroperlas, Aereo Taxi, Ansa and Aviatur. All four airlines have their headquarters at the country's chief domestic air-port, Aeropuerto Marcos Gelabert in the Paitilla district of Panama City. Most people – including taxi drivers – know the airport only as Aeropuerto Paitilla (Paitilla Airport).

It is important to note that in 1998 there were plans to relocate this airport from Paitilla to the site of the former Albrook Air Force Station, which the USA handed over to Panama in late 1997. Albrook is on the edge of Panama City, while Aeropuerto Paitilla is on prime real estate near the center of town. By early or mid-1999, it is quite possible that a new domestic airport will be open and that the site of Aeropuerto Paitilla – now slated for high-rise development – will be undergoing a major transformation.

When you're taking domestic flights, be aware that you will be asked to present your passport and that your carry-on luggage will be inspected. Your total luggage is limited to 25kg. If your luggage exceeds this limit, you may incur an overweight charge and, if the flight is full, you may be told that your luggage will be placed on a later flight. You will also be asked to specify your body weight.

As a general rule, it is a good idea to book as far in advance as possible. Be sure to reconfirm your reservation 72 hours ahead of the scheduled departure time, even for short flights. Furthermore, always arrive at the airport at least an hour early; domestic airline representatives, as a practice, release reserved seats to standby passengers as early as 45 minutes prior to departure in their quest to fill planes.

Keep in mind too that air passes are not available in Panama, and student fares don't exist.

The table on the following page lists flights from Aeropuerto Paitilla on the country's largest domestic carrier, Aeroperlas (☎ 269-4555 in Panama City).

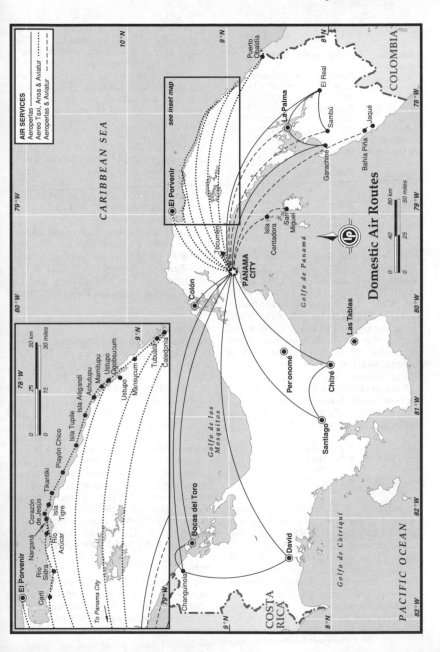

AIR SERVICES
Aeroperlas ———
Aereo Taxi, Ansa & Aviatur ··········
Aeroperlas & Aviatur — — —

CARIBBEAN SEA

see inset map

El Porvenir

Puerto
Obaldía

La Palma
El Real
Sambú
Jaqué
Bahía Piña
Garachiné

COLOMBIA

Colón

Tocumén

PANAMA CITY

Isla
Contadora

San
Miguel

Golfo de Panamá

Peronomé

Chitré

Las Tablas

Santiago

Golfo de los Mosquitos

Bocas del Toro

David

Golfo de Chiriquí

Changuinola

PACIFIC OCEAN

COSTA
RICA

Domestic Air Routes

0   40   80 km
0   25   50 miles

Inset map:

El Porvenir

Cartí
Río
Sidra
Narganá
Corazón
de Jesús
Río
Azúcar
Isla
Tigre
Tikantiki
Playón Chico
Isla Tupile
Isla Ailigandí
Achutupu
Mamitupu
Ustupo
Ogobsucum
Ustupo
Mansucum
Tubuala
Caledonia

To Panama City

0   15   30 miles
0   25   50 km

Destination	Frequency	Fare (one-way/ roundtrip)
Bahía Piña	Thrice weekly	US$42/84
Bocas del Toro town	Daily	US$48/96
Changuinola	Daily	US$56/112
Chitré	Daily	US$29/58
Colón	Weekdays only	US$26/52
David	Daily	US$55/110
El Real	Daily	US$37/74
Garachiné	Thrice weekly	US$34/68
Isla Contadora	Daily	US$79 (roundtrip)
Jaqué	Thrice weekly	US$42/84
La Palma	Daily	US$75 (roundtrip)
Sambú	Thrice weekly	US$35/70
San Miguel	Thrice weekly	US$22/44
Santiago	Daily	US$33/66

Other Aeroperlas routes include David-Changuinola (thrice daily, US$24/48), Changuinola-Bocas del Toro town (daily, US$10/20), Santiago-Chitré (twice daily, US$18/36), La Palma-El Real (thrice weekly, US$21/42), La Palma-Garachiné (thrice weekly) and El Real-Sambú (thrice weekly). For people short on time, Aeroperlas also offers its 10-minute 'Flight Express,' which flies from Aeropuerto Paitilla to Tocumen International Airport at 8:25 am weekdays for US$20; the drive at that hour usually takes 30 minutes.

Three airlines fly between Aeropuerto Paitilla and the Comarca de San Blás:

Airline	In Panama City
Aereo Taxi	☎ 264-8644
Ansa	☎ 226-7891
Aviatur	☎ 270-1748

The airlines fly to 20 San Blás destinations: Cartí and El Porvenir (the towns nearest to Panama City), Río Sidra, Río Azúcar, Narganá, Corazón de Jesús, Isla Tigre, Tikantiki, Playón Chico, Isla Tupile, Isla Ailigandí, Achutupu, Mamitupu, Ustupo Ogobsucum, Ustupo, Mansucum, Lulatupu, Tubualá, Caledonia and Puerto Obaldía (near the Colombian border).

Reservations are a must, as the Comarca de San Blás is served by small aircraft and the seats fill up quickly. Be aware that an airplane flying from Panama City to the district may stop at several islands before reaching your destination; be sure to ask the name of the island you're on before leaving the plane. Likewise, it's quite possible that the aircraft you board in the Comarca de San Blás to return to Panama City will make several stops before it arrives in the capital.

Aereo Taxi and Ansa serve all the destinations daily except Puerto Obaldía, which is served three days a week. Sample fares include US$28/56 one-way/roundtrip to El Porvenir and US$44/88 to Puerto Obaldía. Fares to other San Blás destinations fall somewhere in between.

Aviatur has morning flights to all 20 San Blás destinations, but it does not offer any flights to the district on Sunday. Aviatur also flies from Aeropuerto Paitilla to Isla Contadora and San Miguel daily, and La Palma, Sambú, Jaqué and Bahía Piña thrice weekly.

Charters

Aeropuerto Paitilla also caters to single and twin-engine aircraft, which can be chartered to just about any locale in the country that has an airstrip. Aero Facilidades (☎ 269-6970, fax 269-6886), which has an office at the airport, charters three-passenger Cessna 182s for US$200 per hour. Sample roundtrip prices include Cartí, US$189; Colón, US$200; Isla Contadora, US$189; and Santiago, US$390.

Even if your trip is one-way, you also have to pay for the return flight, unless you can arrange for the company to fly you out on a day when it is picking somebody up. Night flights are prohibited. Aero Facilidades also charters four-passenger Bell helicopters for US$575 per hour and six-passenger Bells for US$900 per hour.

BUS

You can take a bus to just about any community in Panama that is reachable by road. Some of the buses are huge, new Mercedes-Benzes equipped with air-con, feature films and reclining seats. These top-of-the-line buses generally cruise long stretches of highway; for example, they are used to transport passengers from Chiriquí Grande to Panama City and from Paso Canoas, on the Costa Rican border, to the capital city.

More frequently used – and often seen on the Carretera Interamericana (Pan-American Hwy) – are Toyota Coaster buses that can seat 28 people. These are not as comfortable as the Mercedes-Benzes, but they are quite OK and are less expensive. They are an excellent way to visit towns on the Península de Azuero and along the Interamericana.

Also seen on Panamanian roads – particularly within cities – are converted school buses. They are neither comfortable (they were designed for children) nor convenient (they stop every 10m, or so it seems), and they are always crowded. Still, they are an extremely cheap way to get around and they beat hoofing it – particularly when the rain starts coming down.

See the Getting There & Away section of the Panama City chapter for details on the country's main bus station and services to and from the capital city.

TRAIN

The famous old passenger train that once ran along the canal between Panama City and Colón was allowed to fall into ruin during the 1980s. Efforts to get the train up and running again began in 1997, but a dispute soon arose regarding the ownership of property under the tracks. It's unlikely that the dispute will be settled, the repairs completed and service restored before 2000. If you're interested, check with a tour operator or the Instituto Panameño de Turismo in Panama City (see that chapter for contact information).

The trains connecting the Costa Rican border and the port of Almirante in Bocas del Toro Province are running again after a hiatus caused by an earthquake in 1991, but only the most fanatical train buff would ride them. They are used to move bananas from the steamy fields around Changuinola to the docks at Almirante, but for public

relations reasons their owner, the Chiriquí Land Company (the CLC; ☎ 758-8414 in Changuinola), includes a few old passenger cars. The passengers, mostly banana workers' children who are going to or returning from school, must wait while the banana cars are loaded. If you choose to ride the banana trains (note that the company doesn't encourage you to do so), bring lots of mosquito repellent. You'll need it.

Panama's other banana trains – the ones serving Puerto Armuelles in Chiriquí Province and the banana plantations near it – likewise carry schoolchildren along with fruit. Tourists wanting to ride the trains need permission from the CLC beforehand; call the company in Puerto Armuelles at ☎ 770-7245.

CAR & MOTORCYCLE

Few tourists drive to Panama in their own vehicles, though it is certainly possible to do so. Renting a car after arrival, on the other hand, is something many travelers do during parts of their trips. A smaller number rent motorcycles.

Road Rules

The universal road signs apply – about half the time. For example, often motorists can only tell which streets are one-way from past experience; one-way signs are as rare as harpy eagles in Panama. Also, during commuter hours some two-way streets suddenly become one-way streets. This is especially true in Panama City. No signs indicate when this changeover occurs. The locals know about such trick streets, but tourists are occasionally spotted taking a wrong turn and confronting several lanes of oncoming traffic.

Another thing to consider before driving in Panama is local disrespect for stop signs. Generally Panamanians will only come to complete stops at stop signs if they feel there's a good chance they'll collide with an oncoming vehicle. When two vehicles approach an intersection without a traffic signal and are on a collision course, generally the driver of the bigger vehicle blasts through the intersection and the driver of the smaller vehicle brakes.

A really good thing to do before renting a vehicle in Panama is to stand near a busy intersection for a while so you'll know what you'll be getting yourself into. If you do rent a car, be aware that Panamanians almost *never* slow to allow pedestrians to cross the street in front of them. When people do slow down, their kind act is often followed by bewildered motorists rear-ending them. This is also something to keep in mind if you're walking around the city.

Driving in Panama is on the right, and passing is allowed only on the left. Beware: You can get a traffic ticket for not wearing a seat belt. It is illegal to enter an intersection unless you can also leave it (in other words, don't block intersections), and it is illegal to make a right turn on a red light unless a sign indicates that a turn is permitted. At unmarked intersections you're supposed to yield to the car on your right.

Because of difficult driving conditions, there are speed limits of 80kph on all primary roads and 60kph or less on secondary roads. Drivers should carry their passports as well as driver's licenses.

Road Safety

In addition to the concerns expressed in the preceding section, you should be aware of two often overlooked facts about Panama's roads: Animals seem to use them as much as people, and places you can't go by bus are usually inaccessible by other kinds of vehicles (a fact many motorists learn the hard way).

In Panama the immortal question 'Why does the chicken cross the road?' is answered: 'So that its owners can collect US\$4.' That's what a driver is expected to pay to the owner of the chicken he or she has just flattened. On the Península de Azuero and throughout Chiriquí Province, chickens often wander onto busy roads – as do dogs, cats, pigs, goats, cows and horses. In Darién Province more sloths are killed by cars than die of natural causes.

Many people rent 4WD vehicles so that they can get to places not served by buses (such as Volcán Barú), but underestimate the dangers that they may encounter. I once tried to drive a Toyota Land Cruiser to the top of the volcano, only to discover that the road was so rutted that the truck couldn't make it on its own. I happened to luck out; someone with a much stronger engine and better tires chained my truck to his and all but dragged my 4WD up the hill. I could have easily gotten stuck on the little-used road, where nighttime temperatures can drop close to freezing. I was dressed in shorts and a T-shirt, like most people who visit the volcano.

A month later in Darién Province, my truck hit a rut so hard that the spare tire that was chained to the bottom of the vehicle exploded. I immediately turned around and headed back to the city. Had I continued on and had one of my working tires then gone out, I'd have had to hike at least 25km to reach a main road to summon help.

If you are involved in an accident, you should not move the vehicles until after the police have arrived and made a report. This is essential for all insurance claims. Injured people should not be taken from the scene except by the paramedics. Try to make a sketch of what happened, and don't make statements except to police. If you're driving a rental, call the rental company to find out what it wants you to do with the vehicle. If the accident results in injury or death, you may be prevented from leaving the country until all legalities are handled. Drive defensively.

If you see oncoming cars with headlights flashing, it often means that there is some kind of road problem ahead. Slow down immediately. Also be on the lookout for branches placed on the side of the road;

this often means that a vehicle is broken down just ahead.

Rental

Due to the low cost and availability of buses and taxis, it really isn't necessary to rent a vehicle in Panama unless you intend to go to places far off the beaten track. Should you choose to rent, however, you'll find plenty of car-rental agencies in Panama City, but few in other cities. Several agencies also have offices at Tocumen International Airport in the capital. It's also possible to rent vehicles from rental counters at several of Panama City's top hotels, including the Hotel Caesar Park and the Hotel El Panamá. See the Panama City chapter for rental companies' contact information in the capital city.

Many of the major car-rental companies in Panama, such as Avis, Budget, Dollar, Hertz and National, have offices worldwide, so you can reserve a car in advance from home. Making reservations from home is a very good idea. Normally you need to book a car at least 14 days in advance, and the rate when you book one at home is often a little cheaper than the rate when booked in Panama. The major companies' toll-free reservation numbers in the USA are as follows:

Avis	☎ 800-831-2847
Budget	☎ 800-527-0700
Dollar	☎ 800-800-4000
Hertz	☎ 800-654-3131
National	☎ 800-227-7368

Car rental in Panama is not cheap. Expect to pay US$45 per day for a car or US$100 per day for a 4WD vehicle; in Panama such a vehicle is called a '4 by 4' or a 'cuatro por cuatro.' Rates include mandatory insurance and unlimited mileage (or kilometraje, as they call it). From October to April – the high tourist season for rental-car companies – discounts are often available, as the agencies are competing for your business.

To rent a vehicle in Panama, you must be 25 or older and present a passport and driver's license (if you rent the vehicle using an American Express card, you need be only 23). In most cases you need to have a credit card; however, some companies, including Hertz, will allow people without credit cards to rent cars if they put down a big deposit (US$250 for one day, US$400 for one week). You must have a credit card to rent a 4WD vehicle.

If you rent a car, carefully inspect it for minor dents and scratches, missing radio antennae or hubcaps and anything else that makes the car look less than brand-new. These damages *must* be noted on your rental agreement; otherwise you may be charged for them when you return the car.

There have been many reports of theft from rental cars. You should never leave valuables in an unattended car, and you should remove luggage from the trunk when you're checking into a hotel overnight. Many hotels provide parking areas for cars. It is safer to park a car in a guarded parking lot than on the street.

Bringing Your Own

There is a fair amount of paperwork involved in bringing a car into the country, but not so much that it should dissuade you (see the Land section in the Getting There & Away chapter for details). However, unless you plan to be in the country a good while or unless you're just passing through, I recommend that you use buses and taxis instead. They are quite all right – and they are cheaper, all things considered. Alternately, if you're traveling far afield, rent a vehicle in Panama.

Remember that if you want to take a vehicle between Central and South America, you will have to ship it around the Darién Gap, as the Carretera Interamericana stops short of the Colombian border.

Motorcycle

I've owned a motorcycle and I've loved the experience of riding one, so I can relate to a biker's desire to ride around Panama. But because of the number of animals on the roads and the inclement weather, it isn't a good idea.

A small number of tourists do rent motorcycles in Panama, however. They are somewhat cheaper than cars, but not by very much. One business in Panama City rents 125cc motorcycles. See the Getting Around section in the Panama City chapter for details.

TAXI

It may come as a surprise to most people that taxis are considered a form of public transportation outside urban areas. Taxis can be hired by the hour, the half-day or the day. Taxi meters are not used in Panama, although there are fixed prices for certain destinations. On long trips you'll want to arrange fares with drivers beforehand.

Set fares for one passenger on standard routes from Tocumen International Airport, as determined by the government, include the following:

Destination	Fare
Balboa	US$22
Amador, Corozal, Diablo, Los Ríos or the former Albrook Air Force Station	US$24
Paraíso	US$30
La Chorrera or Gamboa	US$40
Colón	US$60

The price for each additional passenger ranges from US$8 to US$15.

Additionally, taxi drivers are supposed to adhere to set fares for the following trips: Panama City to the Canal Area, with a two-hour stay and return (US$20 for one or two people); two hours of sightseeing within Panama City (US$20 for one or two people); a combination of sightseeing in the Canal Area and touring in the city (US$30 for one or two people); a coast-to-coast trip from Panama City to Colón and back, leaving at 8 am and returning at 6 pm (US$100 for one to four people).

Outside these set routes, the price of a ride is negotiable. Usually, if you're not leaving the city limits – even Panama City's wide limits – you'll never pay more than US$4 for a ride (for one, two or three people). You are, however, expected to pay more late at night because the driver is working after hours; a ride that costs US$2 during the day might cost twice that at night.

BICYCLE

You can bicycle through Panama easily enough, but using a bicycle to travel within larger Panamanian cities – particularly Panama City – is not wise. The roads tend to be narrow, there are no bike lanes, the motorists drive aggressively and it rains a lot, reducing motorists' visibility and your tires' ability to grip the road.

Outside the cities, a bicycle permits you to soak up the lovely countryside while getting good exercise. Roads outside cities tend to be in fine shape, and there are few places where lodging is more than a day's bike ride away. If you have enough time in the country to sit out rainy days and if you're in good health, seeing Panama by bike might be worth considering.

In Panama City bicycles are available for long and short-term rental; see the Panama City chapter for details. Bicycles are sold in most Panamanian cities, and they are reasonably priced. A good mountain bike will cost between US$200 and US$300. Bike repair shops can be found in the country, but you should arrive prepared to do your own repairs.

See the Activities section in the Facts for the Visitor chapter for more advice about cycling in the country. See the Bicycle section in the Panama City chapter for information on cycling events.

HITCHHIKING

Hitchhiking is not as widespread in Panama as elsewhere in Central America; most people travel by bus, and visitors would do best to follow suit. The exception is holiday weekends, when buses are full to overflowing and hitchhiking may be the only way out of a place. If you get a ride, offer to pay for it when you arrive; '¿Cuánto le debo?' ('How much do I owe you?') is the standard way of doing this.

Hitchhiking is never entirely safe in any country, and Lonely Planet doesn't recommend it. Travelers who decide to hitchhike should understand that they are taking a small but serious risk. You may not be able to identify the local rapist/murderer before you get into his vehicle. However, if you do choose to hitchhike, the following advice should help to make your journey as fast and safe as possible: Try to talk to the occupants of the car to get an idea about them before getting in; if you get bad vibes from them, don't get in. Always try to hitchhike from somewhere (a gas station, store, restaurant or police post) that you can retreat to if you don't like the look of your prospective ride. Hitchhiking with a companion is safer than hitchhiking alone.

BOAT

Boats are the chief means of transportation in several areas of Panama, particularly in Darién Province, the Archipiélago de las Perlas and the San Blás and Bocas del Toro islands. Some of Panama's most fascinating destinations, such as Isla de Coiba, are only reachable by boat. And while at least one eccentric soul has swum the entire length of the Panama Canal, most people find that a boat simplifies the transit enormously.

There aren't many roads in eastern Darién Province, and especially during the rainy season boat travel is often the most feasible way to get from one town to another. The boat of choice here is a long canoe, or *piragua,* carved from the trunk of a giant ceba tree. Piraguas' shallow hulls allow them to ride the many rivers that comprise the traditional transport network of eastern Panama. Many such boats – including the ones travelers usually hire – are motorized. See the Darién Province chapter for more information.

Piraguas are also widely used on the open sea on both sides of Panama. About the only people not using them are sport and commercial fishermen, tour operators serving divers and snorkelers, and vessels used to ferry goods and people.

Colombian merchant boats carry cargo and passengers all along the Caribbean coast between Colón and Puerto Obaldía,

stopping at up to 48 of the San Blás islands to load and unload people and goods. Occasionally these boats are used to traffic narcotics. Travel by these often dangerously overloaded boats is neither comfortable nor safe. Hiring a local boatman is a safer option for getting around these islands; see the Comarca de San Blás chapter for further details.

The popular town of Bocas del Toro, on Isla Colón, is accessible from Almirante and Chiriquí Grande by speedy and inexpensive water taxis, or if pain is your pleasure, you can take the all-day ferries that move cars and other big items between the mainland and the island. See the Bocas del Toro Province chapter for details.

Many boat trips are offered from Panama City, including ferry trips to offshore Isla Taboga and full and partial transits of the Panama Canal. Trips are also offered to Isla Barro Colorado in the canal's Lago Gatún. See the Panamá Province chapter for details. *Bon voyage!*

LOCAL TRANSPORTATION
Bus

Local buses serve the urban and suburban areas, but services can be difficult to figure out. There are no signs indicating local buses' destinations. Panamanians are usually friendly, and this includes bus drivers; they'll often be able to tell you where to wait for a particular bus, provided you speak Spanish (few bus drivers speak any English).

In general, unless you've come to Panama specifically for its urban-bus experience, leave that for another life and take taxis. They're cheap, and you've got better things to do with your time than ride a slow, crowded, frequently stopping bus.

Taxi

As mentioned earlier in this chapter, Panamanian taxis don't have meters, but there are some set fares. Taxis are cheap and, most of the time, they are plentiful. But they can be difficult to hail late at night and just before and during holidays. During times like these, it's best to call for a radio taxi. Listings for reliable radio taxis can be found in the yellow pages of phone directories throughout Panama. They are conveniently listed under the heading *Taxis* (who'd have thought of that?).

In Panama City several companies offer 24-hour radio taxi service (see the Getting Around section in the Panama City chapter for a list). Just call and give your location (preferably mentioning cross streets, a landmark or a well-known building or business), and you can expect your taxi to arrive in 10 minutes or sooner. Radio taxi fares are no higher than any other taxi's fares. They're a real bargain!

There is one group of taxis that do charge more than others. These taxis operate from particular upscale hotels (the Hotel Caesar Park and the El Ejecutivo Hotel in Panama City are among these). The taxi drivers generally mill about the front doors of the hotels and ask every exiting individual if he or she would like a cab. The drivers have a minimum rate that is usually twice what you'd pay a hailed cab. If you're staying at one of these hotels and don't want to pay more than you have to for a taxi, simply leave the hotel's premises and hail a cab.

Walking

Panama has several options for adventurous walks in the mountains and rainforests (see Hiking in the Facts for the Visitor chapter). Walking around cities is generally safe, even at night, if you stick to the well-lit areas. As always, there are parts of towns that can be dangerous; these are mentioned where appropriate throughout the book.

If you intend to do a lot of walking, bring comfortable walking shoes with you. A mistake many people make is buying these shoes just before they leave – they don't allow time to break in the shoes. Then while they are on vacation, they get terrible blisters because the shoes haven't had enough time to conform to their feet. The experienced traveler never takes brand-new walking or hiking shoes on a trip.

ORGANIZED TOURS

Although Panama has so much to offer the tourist, the country's tourism industry is young and the number of local tour operators quite small. In fact, Panama's tourism industry is so small that I've included a list of the country's top guides farther on in this section.

Most Panamanian tour companies specialize in nature tours, offering visits to the national parks and wilderness lodges. They can provide entire guided itineraries (with English-speaking guides) and private transportation to any part of the country. Most of these companies also specialize in adventure tourism, such as river running or trekking. Almost all of them also provide services such as day trips to the Panama Canal, Panama City tours, hotel reservations and airport transfers.

Prices vary depending on the services you require. Two people wishing to travel with a private English-speaking guide and a private vehicle will obviously pay more than two people who are prepared to join a group or who can understand a Spanish-speaking guide. If you can afford it, consider hiring a guide for at least a portion of your travels. In my opinion, good guides are like flying 1st class; they make the trip so much more enjoyable.

Tour Companies in Panama

All the tour operators in Panama have their headquarters in Panama City. While none are particularly cheap, they do offer the easiest way to explore Panama's natural wonders. If you can afford it and want to get the most out of your time in Panama, I recommend that you use the services of one of the reputable outfits mentioned below. This list is by no means complete; it includes only the tour operators that impress me.

In my opinion, the best company of the bunch is Ancon Expeditions of Panama (☎ 269-9414/9415, fax 264-3713, sales@ecopanama.com, www.ecopanama.com; in the USA ☎ 847-392-7865, 888-888-4106), in the El Dorado Building on Calle Elvira Méndez at Calle 49 A Este. Its mailing address is Apartado 0852-1509, Panamá, República de Panamá. Created by Panama's top conservation organization, Ancon Expeditions employs four of the country's finest nature guides and offers a variety of interesting tours, and the level of service it provides is superlative. All four guides are avid birders, speak flawless English, are enthusiastic about their work and have playful dispositions.

Pesantez Tours (☎ 263-8771, fax 263-7860, pesantez@sinfo.net), on Avenida Balboa near the Centro Medico Paitilla, is a major player in Panama's fledgling tourism industry and has been providing quality service for a long time. Pesantez Tours offers the greatest number and variety of one-day tours in the Panama City area, although all the companies mentioned here are pleased to create custom itineraries for their clients.

Iguana Tours (☎ 226-8738, fax 226-4736, iguana@sinfo.net), which is on Avenida Belisario Porras between Calles 72 Este and 73 Este, offers a number of competitive tours, including 'The Gold Route,' which includes a visit to Panamá La Vieja, Sendero Las Cruces and Portobelo; a visit to Isla Barro Colorado, home to one of the world's most prestigious tropical research centers; and bird watching at Parque Nacional Soberanía, which offers some of the finest birding anywhere.

Many tour operators in Panama offer white-water rafting adventures. Four out of five times, they subcontract such trips to Chiriquí River Rafting (☎ 236-5218, ☎/fax 236-5217, hsanchez@panama.c-com .net, www.panama-rafting.com), Apartado 1686, Balboa, Ancón, Panamá, República de Panamá, an extremely professional and safety-conscious outfit owned and managed by Hector Sanchez. Sanchez is one of Panama's top guides and an extremely pleasant man. You'll find a brief description of him in the Guides section, below.

For specific information on tours offered by Ancon Expeditions, Iguana and Pesantez, including prices, see the Organized Tours section of the Panama City chapter. For details on Chiriquí River Rafting's trips, see the Chiriquí Province chapter.

Guides

Many people in Panama refer to themselves as guides, but most couldn't distinguish a heron from an ibis or tell you which famous pirate's body lies at the bottom of the Bahía de Portobelo. While the following list is not all-inclusive, those whose names appear on it are true guides.

Hernán 'Howler' Araúz A master naturalist, Hernán specializes in bird watching, natural history, Panamanian history and jungle expeditions. He has vast experience in all of Panama's life zones and historical areas. He's also the foremost guide for the Darién region and the Panama Canal area, with eight trans-Darién expeditions to his credit, as well as 350-plus tours to the Monumento Natural Barro Colorado and countless tours around the rest of Panama. Hernán is the official guide for several top US birding and natural history tour operators. He is widely regarded as the best guide in Panama, a bit of a wild man who really knows his stuff. There's never a dull moment when this guy's around. He speaks English and Spanish and works at Ancon Expeditions (☎ 268-0438, beeper 194-6903, fax 264-1533, birder@sinfo.net; in the USA ☎ 888-888-4106).

Vladimir Berrío-Lemm A brilliant young man who knows much about Panama's history, Vladimir makes his living as a part-time university professor and director of philately for Panama; as part of his many duties, he decides on the art that appears on Panama's highly respected postage stamps. Because he is a perfectionist at heart, the work suits him to a tee. Vladimir, whose formal education is in law and history, specializes in historical tours of colonial areas and excels in historical data and interpretation. Anyone interested in stamp collecting and Panama City's history is in excellent hands with him. He speaks English and Spanish. Contact him at ☎ 221-9793, fax 221-9793, or write to him at Apartado 810-348, Panamá 10, República de Panamá.

Richard 'Porkrinds' Cahill One of Panama's top naturalists and expedition guides, Richard specializes in the former Panama

Canal Zone, the Monumento Natural Barro Colorado, Isla de Coiba and trans-Darién expeditions (which he has led four times). I've called upon Richard's expertise on numerous occasions – in the Darién, on the Península de Azuero, throughout the Archipiélago de las Perlas and Archipiélago de San Blás – and I've always found him to be an extremely hard-working, thoughtful and humorous guide. He's got a can-do spirit and, as you might have guessed from his nickname, a sense of humor. Richard speaks English and Spanish and works for Ancon Expeditions (☎ 264-8086, fax 264-1533, cahill2000@hotmail.com; in the USA ☎ 888-888-4106).

Anayansi 'Ana' Castillo A master naturalist and longtime Panama Canal guide, Ana is a full-time guide for the Panama Canal Commission. Within the field of natural history, she specializes in entomology and birds. Ana's vast knowledge of the canal and her gracious interpretive skills make her one of the best canal guides and allowed her to graduate as the top student at the respected Ecotours Naturalist Guide Course, the only formal nature-guide training program in Panama (it is taught by Hernán Araúz). She speaks English and Spanish. Contact her at ☎ 213-0049 or write her at Apartado 87-0875, Panamá 7, República de Panamá.

Marisin Granados Marisin works as a staff guide for the Smithsonian Tropical Research Institute at Isla Barro Colorado, specializing in natural history and bird watching. Her area of expertise is the Panama Canal watershed. A graduate of the Ecotours Naturalist Guide Course, she is an active member of the Panama Audubon Society and speaks English and Spanish. Contact her at ☎ 233-1451, beeper 270-0000, pelly@sinfo.net, or write her at Apartado 6874, El Dorado, Panamá, República de Panamá.

Mario Bernal Greco Mario, who was a park ranger for the Smithsonian Tropical Research Institute for many years, special-

izes in natural history. His areas of expertise are the Monumento Natural Barro Colorado and his native town of El Valle, where he and his wife own and manage Cabañas Potosi (four very well-priced cabins in a parklike setting; see the Coclé Province chapter for details). Always ready with a smile or joke, Mario is very involved in conservation activities with local youth groups in El Valle. He speaks English and Spanish, and he works for himself (☎ 983-6181, beeper 231-3811).

Ivan Hoyos An extremely enthusiastic and well-traveled individual, Ivan specializes in natural history and bird watching. Born and raised on the Península de Azuero, Ivan spent much of the mid-1990s living in Changuinola, and he became the foremost wildlife expert in western Panama before moving to Panama City to work for Ancon Expeditions. His experience also includes many tours to the Monumento Natural Barro Colorado and the national parks protecting the Panama Canal watershed. Ivan is fluent in English, Spanish and German and is an enormously pleasant person to be around. Contact him at ☎ 269-9414, fax 264-3713.

Archibald 'Archie' Kirchman Archie is a veteran of the Panama tourism scene and has worked for several of the top local tour operators as a freelance nature guide. In this capacity he has acquired great experience in both natural history and Panama City tours. His specialties, not surprisingly, are tours of the capital city and the Panama Canal watershed. He speaks English and Spanish; contact him at ☎ 226-4828, beeper 263-5044.

Wilberto 'Willy' Martinez Willy is one of Panama's best birding guides, with many years of experience in this field. He leads tours for several US birding operators in all of Panama's life zones. He was the chief birding instructor at the Ecotours Naturalist Guide Course before Hernán Araúz assumed that role. His areas of expertise include the Panama Canal watershed, the

Darién and the Chiriquí highlands. Willy's sparkling personality and natural ability to spot birds like few others make him an extremely sought-after guide. He owns and manages the Rancho Ecológico, on the Chiriquí Grande-David road; see the Bocas del Toro Province chapter for details. He speaks English and Spanish. Contact him at ☎/fax 442-1340, beeper 872-0481, panabird@sinfo.net.

Hector Sanchez Hector is Panama's most experienced white-water guide and outfitter. He owns and manages Chiriquí River Rafting, which runs the Río Chiriquí and the Río Chiriquí Viejo (see the Chiriquí Province chapter for details). For many years Hector was the head tour coordinator for the US Armed Forces recreational activities department in the Canal Area. He emphasizes safety like no one I've ever

met. Although the rivers contain lots of rapids, you always feel safe in Hector's hands. His team of river guides are equally safety conscious. He speaks English and Spanish. See contact information under Tour Companies in Panama, above.

Vicky Turner If your idea of a good time is shopping, and if you'd like to be accompanied by a knowledgeable Canadian-born Panama resident with an eye for quality and bargains, this is the woman to call. Vicky has more than 25 years of experience in Latin America and specializes in Panama City's shopping and dining scenes. However, she can also custom-design programs to fit your other desires, such as a visit to the canal, Panamá La Vieja or El Valle. She speaks English and Spanish; contact her at ☎/fax 264-8855, cellular 613-5653.

Panama City

Panama's capital is a modern, thriving center of international banking and trade, with a wildly diverse population and a cosmopolitan flair. The variety of restaurants in this city of 700,000 rivals that in Los Angeles, and the nightlife doesn't rest before sunrise. Most anything that you can buy in Tokyo, Frankfurt or Montreal you can find in Panama City. Because the taxis are inexpensive, it's easy to get around on the cheap. Decent accommodations cost as little as US$10.

HISTORY

The city was founded on the site of an Indian fishing village by the Spanish governor Pedro Arias de Ávila (or Pedrarias, as his Spanish contemporaries called him) in 1519, not long after explorer Vasco Núñez de Balboa first looked upon the Pacific and claimed it and everything it touched as the property of Spain.

The Spanish settlement, known as Panamá, quickly became an important center of government and church authority. It was from Panamá, too, that gold and other plunder from the Pacific Spanish colonies were taken along the Camino Real (King's Highway) and the Sendero Las Cruces (Las Cruces Trail) across the isthmus to the Caribbean.

This treasure made Panamá the target of many attacks over the years. In 1671 the city was ransacked by the Welsh buccaneer Sir Henry Morgan and 1200 of his men. A terrible fire ensued – no one knows for certain whether it was set by the pirates or by fleeing landowners – leaving only stone ruins. Now known as Panamá La Vieja (Old Panama), these ruins can still be seen today.

Three years later, the city was reestablished about 8km to the southwest, down the coast at what is now the San Felipe district (or Casco Viejo, as it is popularly known). The Spaniards believed that the

PANAMA CITY

new site, on a small peninsula, would be easier to defend: A shallow sea flanked the city on three sides and a moat was constructed on the fourth side, separating the city from the mainland. Indeed, the new city, known as Nueva Panamá (New Panama), was never successfully attacked. Unlike Panamá La Vieja, the new site was protected by a massive stone-and-brick wall 7 to 14m high and more than 3m wide, with bastions or watchtowers every 75m. Access was gained through three massive gateways. So expensive were the fortifications of Nueva Panamá that the council of Spain, auditing the accounts, wrote to inquire whether the wall was constructed of silver or gold.

The streets of the new city were laid out at right angles about a central plaza. A cathedral, governor's house and bishop's palace would eventually face the plaza, and many churches and convents were gradually constructed throughout the town. The famous Arco Chato (Flat Arch) of the ruined church of Santo Domingo was built in the 1670s and is one of the wonders of

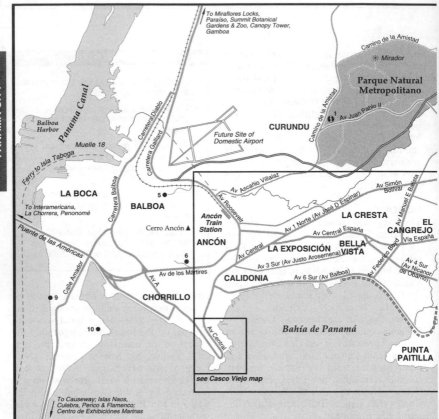

architecture, and it continues to stand in apparent defiance of the laws of gravity. The cathedral, with its two imposing towers, was completed in 1760. The palace of the president, leading businesses, and municipal offices and those of foreign legations were constructed within a short distance of Parque Catedral.

Unlike Nueva Panamá, the Camino Real overland trade route was attacked repeatedly, and the principal Caribbean port at Portobelo was destroyed. In 1746 the Spaniards stopped using the route altogether; Panama City subsequently declined in importance. It was not until the 1850s

that the city returned to prominence. It was then that the Panama Railroad was completed, and it was used by gold rushers from the US East Coast who made their way to the West Coast via Panama to avoid hostile Indians in the central USA.

Panama was declared independent of Colombia on November 3, 1903, in Panama City's Parque Catedral; the city then became the capital of the new nation. Since the Panama Canal was completed in 1914, the city has grown in importance as a center for international business and trade.

In 1989 Panama City was invaded by the USA in Operation Just Cause, which

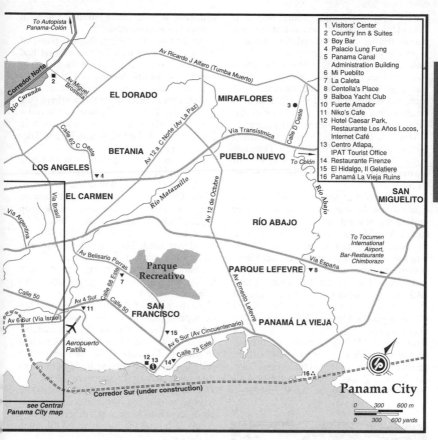

1 Visitors' Center
2 Country Inn & Suites
3 Boy Bar
4 Palacio Lung Fung
5 Panama Canal
   Administration Building
6 Mi Pueblito
7 La Caleta
8 Centolla's Place
9 Balboa Yacht Club
10 Fuerte Amador
11 Niko's Cafe
12 Hotel Caesar Park,
   Restaurante Los Años Locos,
   Internet Café
13 Centro Atlapa,
   IPAT Tourist Office
14 Restaurante Firenze
15 El Hidalgo, Il Gelatiere
16 Panamá La Vieja Ruins

ousted Manuel Noriega from power. The
capital suffered damage both from the
invasion itself and from looting; many residential blocks of the Chorrillo district were
lost to fire. For details on the invasion and
the city's modern history, see the History
section in the Facts about Panama chapter.

ORIENTATION

Panama City stretches about 10km along
the Pacific coast, with the Bahía de Panamá
to the south, the Panama Canal to the west,
protected forest to the north and the stone
ruins of Panamá La Vieja (the city's original site) to the east. Buses to most other

parts of the country arrive at and depart
from the Terminal de Buses al Interior, on
Avenida Ascañio Villalaz about 2km from
the financial district. (Residents of Panama
City refer to the rest of mainland Panama
as 'the interior.')

On the western side of town near the
Canal Area is the neighborhood of Casco
Viejo. At the foot of Cerro Ancón (Ancón
Hill), it was the site of Nueva Panamá, built
after Henry Morgan sacked the original
settlement of Panamá.

From Casco Viejo, two major roads
head east through the city. The main road,
Avenida Central, runs past the cathedral in

Casco Viejo to Parque Santa Ana and Plaza Cinco de Mayo; between these two plazas, traffic is diverted and the avenue is a pedestrian-only shopping street. At a fork farther east, the avenue becomes Avenida Central España; the section that traverses El Cangrejo, the financial district, and heads eastward toward Tocumen International Airport is called Vía España. The other part of the fork becomes Avenida 1 Norte (Avenida José D Espinar), Avenida Simón Bolívar and finally Vía Transístmica (Transisthmian Hwy) as it heads out of town and across the isthmus toward Colón.

Avenida 6 Sur branches off Avenida Central not far out of Casco Viejo and undergoes several name changes. It is called Avenida Balboa as it curves around the edge of the bay to Punta Paitilla, the bay's eastern point, opposite Casco Viejo; it then continues under various names past Aeropuerto Paitilla and the Centro Atlapa (Atlapa Convention Center) to the ruins of Panamá La Vieja. Comprising the remains of the original settlement, Panamá La Vieja was established by the Spanish governor Pedrarias in 1519 and abandoned in favor of the Casco Viejo site in 1674 – three years after Morgan looted the original city. At the time it was set aflame, Panamá La Vieja comprised about 5200 homes, a cathedral, a government building and eight convents and churches.

At the time of writing, the first phase of an expressway named Corredor Norte had just been completed, linking the Curundu area to the Autopista Panama-Colón (a toll road that is now under construction) via a loop highway that circles the northern side of the city. The second phase of Corredor Norte, which is slated for completion in 2002, will link the San Miguelito and Tocumen areas.

Two other major highways were being built at the time of writing, and both were scheduled for completion in the summer of 1999: Corredor Sur will connect Panama City and the Tocumen area via a loop expressway ringing the southern side of the capital city; its precise route was still being determined. The second highway, the Autopista Panama-Colón toll road, will significantly reduce the driving time between Colón and Panama City, to about 40 minutes.

To the north of the city is forest that has been designated for conservation because it is part of the watershed for the Panama Canal. Protecting the watershed is critical to the canal's survival. If the forest were felled, the water needed to fill the locks that raise and lower transiting ships into and out of Lago Gatún (Gatún Lake) would have to be pumped from the ocean at enormous expense. Moreover, soil erosion as a result of felling the forest would fill much of the canal.

Maps

For highly detailed maps, go to the Instituto Geográfico Nacional 'Tommy Guardia' (☎ 236-2444), just off Avenida Simón Bolívar opposite the Universidad de Panamá; it is open 8 am to 4 pm weekdays. It has an excellent map collection for sale, including topographical maps, city maps, tourist maps and more. Several free tourist magazines available at tourist offices and hotels contain small fold-out country and city maps.

The maps appearing in this book were made from more than 60 large maps provided upon special request from Panama's

Buccaneer Henry Morgan, destroyer of the first Panama City

census bureau, which produces the most accurate maps. These are not available to the general public, however.

INFORMATION
Tourist Offices
At the start of 1998 the Instituto Panameño de Turismo (IPAT; ☎ 226-3483, fax 226-4849) had its headquarters in the Centro Atlapa on Vía Israel in the San Francisco neighborhood, but its directors were looking to relocate the agency by year's end. A site had not been chosen, although Casco Viejo was under consideration. If you need to speak with someone at IPAT, call directory assistance (☎ 102) and ask for IPAT's current location and telephone number. IPAT's business hours are 8 am to 6 pm daily. The agency also maintains information counters at Panamá La Vieja and Tocumen International Airport.

At the time of writing, IPAT had little to offer the tourist in the way of helpful literature or good recommendations. Its maps were unhelpful, and only a smattering of English was spoken among the staff greeting tourists. It's possible that IPAT may have made improvements since the time this book was written.

The Instituto Nacional de Recursos Naturales Renovables (INRENARE; ☎ 232-7228/7223), supposed guardian of Panama's national parks, has its headquarters near Panama City's Terminal de Buses al Interior, on Avenida Ascañio Villalaz in the Curundu district; it's a fair distance from the city center. INRENARE can occasionally provide maps and information on the national parks. It's open 8 am to 4 pm weekdays. Spanish and some English are spoken. To write to INRENARE before you travel to Panama, address correspondence to INRENARE, Depto de Parques Nacionales y de Vida Silvestre, Apartado 2016, Paraíso, Corregimiento de Ancón, Panamá, República de Panamá.

Embassies & Consulates
More than 50 countries have embassies or consulates in Panama City, including the following:

Belize
  Calle Quinta, Colonias del Prado, Casa 592 (☎ 266-8939)
Canada
  Avenida Samuel Lewis and Calle Gerardo Ortega, Banco Central Hispano Building, 4th floor, in front of the Comosa Building (☎ 264-9731)
Colombia
  Calle Manuel María Icaza, Grobman Building, 6th floor, in front of the Comosa Building (☎ 223-3535)
Costa Rica
  Calle Gerardo Ortega and Vía España, Miraflores Building, ground floor, beside Niko's Cafe (☎ 264-2937, fax 264-6348)
El Salvador
  Avenida Manuel E Batista, Metropolis Building, 4th floor, behind the Iglesia del Carmen (☎ 223-3020)
France
  Plaza de Francia, Las Bóvedas, Casco Viejo (☎ 228-7824/7835)
Germany
  Calle 50 and Calle 53 Este, Bancomer Building, 6th floor (☎ 263-7733)
Guatemala
  Avenida Federico Boyd, Bella Vista district, over the Colossal store (☎ 269-3475)
Honduras
  Calle 31 Este, Tapia Building, 2nd floor, Oficina 2-01, between Avenidas Justo Arosemena and México (☎ 225-8200, ☎ /fax 225-3283)
Mexico
  Calle 50 and Calle 53 Este, Bancomer Building, 5th floor (☎ 263-5021)
Nicaragua
  Avenidas 4 Sur and Federico Boyd, Zona 1, Bella Vista district (☎ 223-0981, 269-6721)
UK
  Calle 53 Este, Swissbank Building, 4th floor, Marbella district (☎ 269-0866)
USA
  Avenida Balboa and Calle 37 Este (☎ 227-1777)

Immigration
The Migración y Naturalización (Immigration and Naturalization) office in Panama City (☎ 225-1373, 227-1077) is on Avenida Cuba at Calle 29 Este in La Exposición neighborhood. Visas and tourist cards can be extended here.

PANAMA CITY

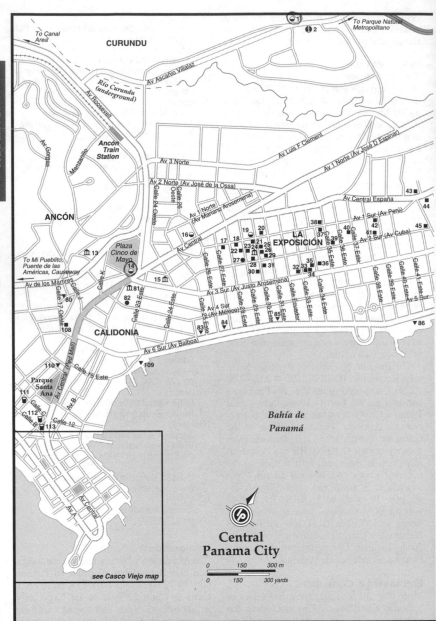

Central Panama City

| 0 | 150 | 300 m |
| 0 | 150 | 300 yards |

see Casco Viejo map

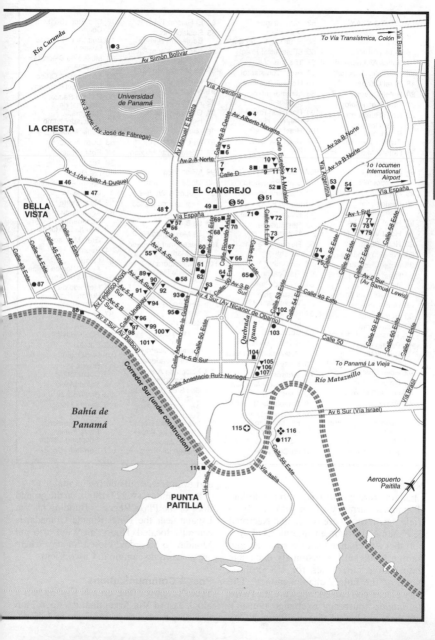

PANAMA CITY

PLACES TO STAY
6　Las Vegas Suites Hotel
8　Hotel Marbella
9　Suites Ambassador
17　Hotel Río de Janeiro
18　Hotel Caribe
20　Hotel Veracruz
21　Gran Hotel Soloy
22　Hotel Benidorm
23　Hotel Covadonga, Residencial Turístico Volcán
25　Hotel 2 Mares
26　Hotel Acapulco
28　Residencial Compostela
29　Hotel Lisboa
30　Residencial Alemeda
31　Hotel Arenteiro
32　Hotel Villa del Mar
33　Hotel Roma
34　Pensión América
35　Hotel Discovery
36　Hotel Centro-americano
37　Pensión Las Torres
38　Hotel Venecia
39　Hotel Latino
40　Residencial Turístico El Dorado
41　Pensión Las Palmeras, Residencial Jamaica
42　Hotel Costa Inn
43　Hotel Europa
44　Hotel California
45　Residencial Primavera
46　Hotel Suites Central Park
47　Hotel Montreal
49　Hotel El Panamá

52　Hotel Riande Granada
56　Hotel Costa Del Sol
59　El Ejecutivo Hotel
61　The Bristol
69　Hotel Continental
70　Hotel Suites Alfa
88　Miramar Inter-Continental
104　Radisson Royal Panama Hotel
108　Hotel Ideal
114　Hotel Plaza Paitilla Inn

PLACES TO EAT
5　Caffé Pomodoro
7　Cafeteria Manolo
10　Martín Fierro
11　Ginza Teppanyaki
12　Restaurante Matsuei
55　Restaurante-Bar Tinajas
57　Calcutta
63　Tre Scalini
64　El Pavo Real
66　Restaurante Vegetariano Mireya
67　Restaurante y Pizzeria Sorrento
68　Costa Azul
72　Niko's Cafe No 1
73　Restaurante Furama
75　Sushi Itto
76　Athen's
77　Trattoria D'America Takeout
78　Trattoria D'America
79　Restaurante y Pizzeria Napoli No 2
80　Restaurante y Pizzeria Napoli No 1
83　La Cascada

84　El Rincón Tableño
85　Restaurante Boulevard Balboa
86　Panama Yacht Club, La Marina
89　La Mexicanita No 1
90　La Toja
91　Nobu
92　Athen's
94　Gaucho's Steak House
96　Mangos
97　La Cocotte
98　Restaurante Mexico Lindo
99　Millennium
100　Madame Chang
101　Crepes & Waffles
102　Restaurante Casco Viejo
105　Le Bistrot
106　La Mexicanita No 2
109　Restaurant Mercado del Marisco
110　Panificadora y Dulceria Reina

OTHER
1　Terminal de Buses al Interior
2　INRENARE
3　Instituto Geográfico Nacional 'Tommy Guardia'
4　Ancon Headquarters
13　Museo de Arte Contemporáneo
14　Bus Stop (Buses to Balboa & Ancón Areas, Canal Area, Tocumen International Airport, Panamá La Vieja)
15　Museo Afro-Antilleano

16　Bus Stop (Buses to Colón)
19　Bus Stop (Express Buses to Colón)
24　Museo de Ciencias Naturales
27　Immigration Office
48　Iglesia del Carmen
50　Edificio Banco Nacional de Panamá, Banco del Istmo
51　Panacambios
53　Librería Argosy
54　Post Office
58　Tabou
60　Bacchus
62　Ancon Expeditions of Panama
65　Mezzanotte
69　Agencia de Viajes Continental, Joyeria La Huaca
71　Gran Morrison
74　Reprosa
81　Museo Antropológico Reina Torres de Araúz
82　Mercado de Buhonerías y Artesanías
87　La Faraona
93　Sahara
95　TGI Friday's
103　Patatús
107　Rock Café
111　Boite La Cosmopolita
112　Salon Madrid
113　Bar Tropical
115　Centro Medico Paitilla
116　Gran Morrison, Plaza Paitilla Shopping Center
117　Carretero Sports

Money

Changing foreign currency into US dollars (Panama's currency of choice) can be a tricky business. There is a Banco Nacional de Panamá at Tocumen International Airport that will change major currencies, and foreign banks will occasionally exchange their native currencies for US dollars. None of the hotels change money. The only places you can count on are the *casas de cambio* (currency exchange houses), and there are few of these in Panama City and even fewer outside the capital.

Panacambios (☎ 223-1800), on the ground floor of the Plaza Regency Building on Vía España near the Hotel Riande Granada, is centrally located. Hours are 9 am to 6 pm Monday to Saturday; closed Sunday. There are no casas de cambio in Casco Viejo.

Post & Communications

There's a post office on Vía España half a block east of Vía Argentina; it's open 7 am to 5:45 pm weekdays and 7 am to 4:45 pm

Saturday. Another is on Avenida Balboa near Calle 31 Este. There are others around town. Many hotels sell stamps, and some will accept guests' letters for mailing. See the Facts for the Visitor chapter for details on Panama's postal service.

International telephone and fax services are available at the Cable & Wireless office (☎ 264-6200) in the Di Lido Building on Calle Manuel María Icaza, half a block from Vía España; it's open 7:30 am to 9:30 pm daily. Nearby on Vía España, email and modem services are available at Cable & Wireless' Ventas (Sales) office (☎ 263-8696), in the Banco Nacional Building, Torre 2, 6th floor; it's open 8 am to 4:30 pm weekdays. Another Cable & Wircless office with international telephone and fax services is on Calle Gavilán in the Balboa district.

Internet cafés were just beginning to appear in Panama City at the time of writing. No doubt more will exist by the time you read this book. The Internet Café (☎ 270-1052/1053) is on the corner of Calle 76 Este and Avenida 5 B Sur, near the Hotel Caesar Park; it's open 11:30 am to 11 pm Tuesday to Saturday and 1 to 11 pm Sunday. The café charges US$4 per hour before 5 pm and US$5 thereafter. Discounts are available, English is spoken, and liquor, sandwiches and burgers are offered.

Travel Agencies

As befits the 'crossroads of the world,' Panama City has a great many travel agencies. One that enjoys a sterling reputation is Agencia de Viajes Continental (☎ 263-6162/5531, fax 263-6493), at the Hotel Continental on Vía España. English and Spanish are spoken. Student discounts on international airfares, so widely available in Europe, the USA and elsewhere, are unheard of in Panama.

Bookstores

Librería Argosy (☎ 223-5344), on Vía Argentina near the corner of Vía España in El Cangrejo neighborhood, is a bookstore and cultural institution. Argosy's owner,

the interesting and ebullient Greek-born Gerasimos 'Gerry' Kanelopulos, offers a fine selection of books in English, Spanish and French.

Other good places to look for books are Legends (☎ 270-0096), on Calle 50 near Calle 71 Este, and Librería El Campus (☎ 223-6598), on Avenida José de Fábrega in front of the Universidad de Panamá. Also try the Librería Universitaria, located on the university's campus, and Allegro, on Calle 73 Este near Calle 50, which is a good place for books in English (as well as CDs). Librería Cultural Panameña (☎ 223-6267), near the western end of Vía España, has a good literature selection.

There are several Gran Morrison department stores around town (see the Central Panama City map); they carry a selection of books, magazines and postcards in English and Spanish. Farmacia Arrocha, which also has branches around the city, carries a smaller selection of books and magazines, also in English and Spanish.

Laundry

Laundromats (lavamáticos) are easy to find in Panama City. They're also inexpensive: Normally you drop off laundry, the laundromat washes and dries it and you pick it up in a few hours. The usual cost per laundry load is 75¢ to wash, 75¢ to dry and 25¢ for detergent unless you bring your own. In Casco Viejo try the Lavamático Tanita, beside Parque Herrera; it's open 7 am to 9 pm daily.

You'll also find plenty of dry cleaners (lavanderías) in the capital, but these are significantly more expensive. Many of them won't wash undergarments. Luxury hotels may offer laundry service, but check the price before you use it. It can be very expensive.

Medical Services

In Panama, as in most countries, there are some excellent doctors and some mediocre ones. Centro Medico Paitilla (☎ 263-6060), at Calle 53 Este and Avenida Balboa, has the lion's share of well-trained physicians. The doctors listed below all work at Paitilla and speak English and Spanish; most received their medical training in the USA, and all enjoy healthy reputations within their fields:

Name & Specialty	Telephone
Alberto Arrocha	
Cardiology	☎ 269-0566
Doris Estella Lau Villarreal	
Dermatology	☎ 263-7977
Jacobo S Cohen	
Ear, nose & throat	☎ 269-5222
Daniel Abouganem	
Endocrinology	☎ 263-8220
Jose M Fabrega	
Family practice	☎ 263-7977
Rosendo Gonzales Gomis	
Gastroenterology	☎ 269-3178
Jorge Motta	
Internal medicine	☎ 263-7977
Cesar A Pinilla	
Neurology	☎ 264-3148
Rosa C de Britton	
Obstetrics/gynecology	☎ 269-0928

The cost of a consultation with any physician in Panama will rarely exceed US$40 and, of course, you can always inquire about the charge before you are seen by a doctor.

Emergency
The emergency phone numbers in Panama City are as follows:

Ambulance	☎ 225-1436
Drug overdose	☎ 226-0000
Fire	☎ 103
Police	☎ 104

Dangers & Annoyances
Casco Viejo is a very interesting place, but if you enter it looking like a million bucks, there's a fair chance that you'll leave it without any. Muggers look for wealthy, easy prey: an elderly man with a thick bulge in a rear pocket where the wallet belongs; a slightly built person sporting a Rolex watch or flashy jewelry; a single *gringa* with a fancy purse dangling from an arm. Rule of the Road No 64: Look like

slim pickings and the predators will leave you alone.

The bar scene in Casco Viejo at night also needs to be approached with caution. These streets contain many unemployed or underemployed people. When I go barhopping in this neighborhood, I never dress better than I have to (a T-shirt, blue jeans and sneakers are just fine), and I always leave my wallet at the hotel and wear my cheap watch instead of my Seiko. I take only my passport and enough money to get me through the night, plus a folded US$20 in each shoe.

Use common sense when you're in any poor neighborhood: Never leave your vehicle unlocked; never leave valuables or packages in your vehicle in easy view of passersby; avoid vacant, dimly lit streets; don't use big bills in places where a thug is likely to be watching you.

As for annoyances, there's nothing more annoying than settling into a hotel only to discover at bedtime that your room's above a noisy bar, that the bed sags horribly or that your hotel is a true fleabag. Always ask to see a room before you check in. Carry earplugs with you, and consider eyeshades. Panama City has few street signs, so try to leave the driving to others.

There are few antismoking laws in Panama City, but many hotels and restaurants here accommodate nonsmokers. If cigarette smoke bothers you, request a nonsmoking room; if enough people request them, eventually all hotels and restaurants will offer nonsmoking rooms.

WALKING TOUR
One of the more interesting parts of the city is **Casco Viejo**, with its mix of colonial architecture, cobblestone streets and ethnic diversity. Some, though only a few, of the buildings have been pridefully restored, and in those buildings you can sense how magnificent the area must have looked in past years. Sadly, nowadays it isn't one of the more affluent districts and, as mentioned earlier, it's unsafe to walk here at night. Even in the daytime, you must take care when walking down side

streets. If you stick to the main streets and don't flaunt your wealth, you should be fine.

The capture and plunder of Panamá (the original Panama City) by the pirate Sir Henry Morgan in 1671 convinced the king of Spain that the city was unsafe from buccaneers, and he ordered that it be rebuilt on another site. Three years later, efforts to create a new city began on a rocky peninsula at the foot of Cerro Ancón, 8km southwest of the original city. The new location was easier to defend, and reefs prevented ships from coming up to the city except at high tide. Casco Viejo was surrounded by a massive wall, which is how it got its name (Casco Viejo means 'Old Compound'). Some of the old stone-and-brick wall and original Spanish cannons can still be seen today.

In 1904, at the time construction began on the Panama Canal, all of Panama City existed where Casco Viejo stands today. The city's population was around 30,000 (about the same population as the original city of Panamá when Morgan sacked it). Since that time, the population of Panama City has increased more than twentyfold, and the city has spread so far to the east that Casco Viejo is now merely a district

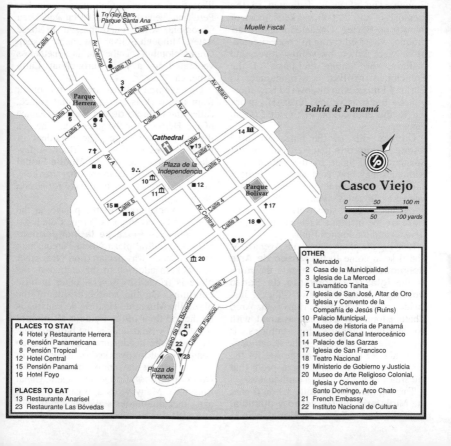

Casco Viejo

Bahía de Panamá

PLACES TO STAY
4   Hotel y Restaurante Herrera
6   Pensión Panamericana
8   Pensión Tropical
12 Hotel Central
15 Pensión Panamá
16 Hotel Foyo

PLACES TO EAT
13 Restaurante Anarisel
23 Restaurante Las Bóvedas

OTHER
1   Mercado
2   Casa de la Municipalidad
3   Iglesia de La Merced
5   Lavamático Tanita
7   Iglesia de San José, Altar de Oro
9   Iglesia y Convento de la
    Compañía de Jesús (Ruins)
10 Palacio Municipal,
    Museo de Historia de Panamá
11 Museo del Canal Interoceánico
14 Palacio de las Garzas
17 Iglesia de San Francisco
18 Teatro Nacional
19 Ministerio de Gobierno y Justicia
20 Museo de Arte Religioso Colonial,
    Iglesia y Convento de
    Santo Domingo, Arco Chato
21 French Embassy
22 Instituto Nacional de Cultura

in the southwestern corner of the modern capital city.

You could start a walking tour in Casco Viejo at the **Paseo de las Bóvedas** (Promenade of Vaults), on the southern tip of the peninsula. A walkway runs along the top of the sea wall built by the Spaniards to protect the city. From here you can see ships lining up to enter the canal and the Puente de las Américas (Bridge of the Americas), which arches over the southern entrance to the path between the seas.

Below the wall, on the tip of the peninsula, is **Plaza de Francia**, where large stone tablets tell the story (in Spanish) of the canal's construction and the role of the French. The plaza is dedicated to the memory of the 22,000 workers, most of them from France, Guadeloupe and Martinique, who died trying to create a canal. Most were killed by yellow fever and malaria, and among the busts of the Frenchmen involved is a monument to Carlos J Finlay, who discovered how mosquitoes transmit yellow fever. His work led to the eradication of the disease in Panama.

On one side of the plaza are nine restored **dungeons** that were used by the Spaniards and, later, by the Colombians. Although they now contain an art gallery and a classy restaurant/piano bar (Restaurante Las Bóvedas), you can still see the dungeons' original stonework. Also on the plaza are the Instituto Nacional de Cultura (INAC) and the French Embassy.

Leaving the plaza to walk up Avenida A, you'll soon come to the **Museo de Arte Religioso Colonial**, alongside the ruins of the **Iglesia y Convento de Santo Domingo** on the corner of Calle 3. Just inside the doorway of the ruins is the Arco Chato, a long, flat arch that has stood, with no internal supports, for centuries. It reportedly played a part in the selection of Panama over Nicaragua as the site for the canal; its survival was taken as proof that the area was not subject to earthquakes.

Turning north along Calle 3, you'll pass the **Ministerio de Gobierno y Justicia**, and behind it the **Teatro Nacional**, built in 1907. The ornate interior has been restored, and it boasts red and gold decorations, a ceiling mural by Roberto Lewis (one of Panama's finest painters), an impressive crystal chandelier and several tiers of seats. Performances are still held here; to find out about them or just to have a look at the theater, go around to the office door at the side of the building.

Opposite the theater is the **Iglesia de San Francisco**, facing onto **Parque Bolívar**. In 1826 in a schoolroom opposite this park, Simón Bolívar held a meeting urging the union of the Latin American countries. After many struggles against Spanish domination, Bolívar succeeded in liberating Bolivia, Colombia, Ecuador, Peru and Venezuela, and he created Gran Colombia, which encompassed all these states. Although Bolívar was unable to keep Gran Colombia together, he is nonetheless venerated as a hero throughout Latin America.

On Avenida Alfaro around the block from this park is the presidential palace, called the **Palacio de las Garzas** (Palace of the Herons) for the great white herons that strut about here. The president of Panama lives on the upper floor. A few blocks farther west are the **Muelle Fiscal** (the port) and the **mercado** (market), major activity centers that make for strong photographs.

Two blocks south of the palace, at the center of Casco Viejo, is Parque Catedral – later renamed **Plaza de la Independencia** – the central plaza where Panamanian independence was declared on November 3, 1903. In addition to the cathedral, the plaza is fringed by several other historic buildings. On the southern side of the plaza, the Museo de Historia de Panamá is on the top floor of the **Palacio Municipal** (City Hall). Next door is the building that was once the headquarters of the French company that first worked on the canal; in 1997 it became the site of the **Museo del Canal Interoceánico** (Interoceanic Canal Museum). Many years ago canal officials and other dignitaries stayed at the nearby and still functioning (though rundown)

Hotel Central, which was a very luxurious place back in those days.

On Calle 7 a half-block south of the plaza are the ruins of another church, the **Iglesia y Convento de la Compañía de Jesús**. Walk to the end of the block to rejoin Avenida A and then walk a block west to arrive at the **Iglesia de San José**. Its famous Altar de Oro (Golden Altar) is the only thing of value salvaged after Henry Morgan sacked Panamá in 1671. When word came of the pirate's impending attack, according to local tales, a priest painted the altar black to disguise it. The priest told Morgan that the famous altar had been stolen by another pirate and even convinced Morgan to donate handsomely for its replacement. Morgan is said to have told the priest, 'I don't know why, but I think you are more of a pirate than I am.' Regardless of the accuracy of this story, the baroque-style altar, made of carved mahogany painted and veneered with gold, escaped the pirates' attention and was eventually moved to its present site.

A block farther west is another park, **Parque Herrera**. A block north of that, on Avenida Central two blocks west of the cathedral, is the **Iglesia de La Merced**.

Walk out of Casco Viejo along Avenida Central, past the Casa de la Municipalidad, and after a couple of blocks you'll come to **Parque Santa Ana**, with its Iglesia de Santa Ana. Parque Santa Ana marks the beginning of the Avenida Central shopping district; it is surrounded by restaurants and there are buses to the financial district.

About five blocks farther north along Avenida Central, past all the big air-conditioned stores with hawkers outside, is the large **Plaza Cinco de Mayo**. Avenida Central between Parque Santa Ana and Plaza Cinco de Mayo is a pedestrian-only shopping street. On Avenida Central opposite Plaza Cinco de Mayo is the excellent **Museo Antropológico Reina Torres de Araúz**, which focuses on the anthropology and archaeology of Panama; behind it is the handicrafts market, the **Mercado de Buhonerías y Artesanías**.

Plaza Cinco de Mayo is a major bus stop. Buses leave here for the Canal Area (including the Miraflores and Pedro Miguel Locks, Paraíso, Gamboa and other locales), the Ancón area (including the causeway and the Balboa Yacht Club), Tocumen International Airport and other destinations. Any Vía España bus will take you into the banking district of El Cangrejo but not along Avenida Central (later Vía España) itself, which is a one-way street as it heads westward toward Casco Viejo; the buses mostly run along Avenida Perú, one block to the south. In El Cangrejo the white French-Gothic style **Iglesia del Carmen**, on the corner of Vía España and Avenida Federico Boyd, is one of the city's most distinctive buildings.

PANAMÁ LA VIEJA

At the eastern edge of the city are the ruins of Panamá La Vieja. Founded on August 15, 1519, by Spanish conquistador Pedro Arias de Ávila, the city of Panamá was the first European settlement along the Pacific. For the next 150 years it profited mainly from Spain's famed bullion pipeline, which

TOM BOYDEN
Ruins of the original Panama City

ran from Peru's gold and silver mines to Europe via Panamá. Because of the amount of wealth that passed through the city, the Spaniards kept many soldiers here, and their presence kept the buccaneers away.

For many years Panamá was the metropolis of the Pacific. In addition to being a gateway for the bullion of Peru, it was the entrepôt for the silks and spices of the Orient. From Panamá, these riches were carried across the isthmus to be loaded onto the Spanish galleons at Nombre de Dios or Portobelo. The towns of Venta de Cruces and Chagres (where the road crossed the Río Chagres) were halfway sta-

tions on the road to the northern coast. The Spaniards used to pack bars of silver and gold over this road (which came to be called Sendero Las Cruces) like cordwood. Also used to transport goods was El Camino Real, a land route running from Panamá to Portobelo. It was near Venta de Cruces that the English pirate Sir Francis Drake held up a train of 190 pack mules on the night of February 14, 1573, and made off with tons of gold and silver.

Nearly a century later, in 1671, 1200 pirates led by Henry Morgan ascended the Río Chagres as far as Venta de Cruces and then proceeded overland to Panamá. The

Panamá La Vieja

Not to Scale

1 Puente del Rey (Bridge of the King)
2 Bread Oven (Possible)
3 Iglesia de San José (Church of St Joseph)
4 Ermita de San Cristóbal (Hermitage of St Christopher)
5 Iglesia y Convento de Santo Domingo (Church and Convent of St Dominic)
6 Antigua Casa del Obispo (Old Bishop's House)
7 Casa Alarcón
8 Casa de los Genoveses (Slave Market)
9 Iglesia y Convento de La Merced
10 Mal Llameda Piedra del Sacrificio (so-called sacrifice stone; actually part of windmill ruins)
11 Iglesia y Convento de San Francisco
12 Hospital de San Juan de Dios (Hospital of St John of God)
13 Iglesia y Convento de la Concepción
14 Iglesia y Convento de la Compañía de Jesús
15 Casas de Terrín
16 Catedral de Nuestra Señora de la Asunción (Our Lady of the Assumption Cathedral)
17 El Camino Real (King's Highway)
18 Puente del Matadero (Bridge of the Slaughterhouse)
19 Fortín de la Natividad (Nativity Fort)
20 Aguadero Salubre (Public Water Receptacle)
21 Mercado (Market)
22 Museo de Sitio Panamá Viejo
23 Hostal (Inn)
24 Mercado Nacional de Artesanías, El Trapiche
25 Plaza Mayor (Grand Plaza)
26 Cabildo de la Ciudad (City Hall)
27 Wall Protecting the Casas Reales
28 Casas Reales (Royal Houses)

city was not fortified, but it was protected on three sides by the sea and marshes. On the land side was a causeway, and a bridge in its middle permitted tidal water to pass underneath. But to the bewilderment of historians, when Morgan and his men neared the city, the Spanish soldiers left this natural stronghold and confronted the buccaneers in a hilly area outside town.

It was the first of their many mistakes. When the two forces met in battle, the Spanish infantry left their ranks after mistaking a repositioning of some of Morgan's men for a retreat. The Spanish soldiers ran after the pirates, leaving a high position for a gully. French sharpshooters within Morgan's band were delighted by the development and opened fire on the Spaniards from nearby knolls. The first volley of musket fire dropped about 100 soldiers, and the Spanish force fell to pieces.

'Hardly did our men see some fall dead and others wounded,' reported the Spanish president at the time, Don Juan Perez, 'but they turned their backs and fled and it was not possible to stop them.' Morgan had control of the town within hours.

At the time Panamá fell, the city contained a magnificent cathedral, several beautiful churches and eight convents. There were more than 200 warehouses stocked with foreign goods, 200 residences of European elegance and 5000 houses of the common sort. The city also possessed a mint, a large hospital, the king's stables and a slave market. When Morgan left, little more than building material remained. Nearly everything of value was plundered by the pirates and divvied up later.

For the next three centuries, the city's remains – mostly beams and stone blocks – served as a convenient source of building materials. Yet most of the remnants of the one-time metropolis were still intact as recently as 1950, when the limits of modern Panama City reached the ruins in the form of a squatter settlement. But by the time the government declared the ruins a protected historic site, 26 years later, most of the old city had been dismantled and overrun.

Today much of Panamá La Vieja lies buried under a poor residential neighborhood. So little of the original city remains that its size, layout and appearance are the subjects of much conjecture. What follows are details agreed upon by experts.

The city was founded on a coastal bar alongside a shallow cove. The primary government buildings were at the mouth of the cove, which was rather spacious at the time and could be used as a port; today it is largely mangroves. The cathedral was erected nearby. The major Catholic religious orders – the Franciscans, Dominicans, Jesuits and Augustines – had churches and convents in town. The best houses and most of the convents were built on the narrow strip of land along the beachfront.

The colonial city seems to have followed a grid plan, with blocks of various sizes and a main square; the visible remains of Panamá La Vieja are certainly laid out that way. The lots tended to be narrow, and the houses often consisted of two or three stories. The suburbs that developed to the north and northwest appear to have lacked much planning; common houses and hovels were scattered along crooked lanes.

It requires a good imagination to visualize the city before the arrival of Captain Morgan and his men. The churches, some of which faced the sea, were the most outstanding buildings. All were rectangular, with stone outer walls, timber roofs and internal wooden supports. Few had towers. The adjoining convents had inner courts surrounded by wooden galleries. It appears that the larger ones had enclosed gardens and orchards.

Most of the better houses were built of timber and placed wall to wall, with small inner courts, open-air kitchens and separate wings for the servants. Some had ground-floor galleries and balconies; most had plain exterior walls. A few of the fancier homes were built of stone, and their ruins remain. The poor had far simpler dwellings, usually thatched huts built with inexpensive materials like reeds.

The center of power resided at the **Casas Reales** (Royal Houses), a complex ringed by timber ramparts and separated from the city proper by a moat. Within the complex were the customs house, the royal treasury, a prison and the governor's house. Despite the obvious historical importance of the site, past governments have allowed sections of the property to be used as a landfill and for horse stables. Only scattered walls remain of the once-impressive structures.

The **Catedral de Nuestra Señora de la Asunción**, built between 1619 and 1626, is the best-preserved building of them all. In traditional fashion, it was designed so that its two side chapels gave the cathedral a crosslike shape as viewed from the heavens. The bell tower was at the back of the church and may have served double duty as a watchtower for the Casas Reales. The main façade, which faced the Plaza Mayor (Grand Plaza), is gone. Only the walls remain.

Also facing the Plaza Mayor were the **Cabildo de la Ciudad** (City Hall) and the **Casas de Terrín**, houses built by one of the city's wealthiest citizens, Francisco Terrín.

Immediately north of the cathedral are the massive ruins of **Casa Alarcón**, the town's best-preserved and largest known private residence. It dates from the 1640s. Just north of the former residence is the **Iglesia y Convento de Santo Domingo** (Church and Convent of St Dominic), the best-preserved church. The convent dates from the 1570s and the church was built 20 or more years later.

Arriving a decade or so after the Dominican friars were the Jesuits, and they built a stone church, the **Iglesia y Convento de la Compañía de Jesús**, whose ruins are likewise visible today. Just west of the Jesuits' facilities are the spacious ruins of a church and convent, the **Iglesia y Convento de la Concepción**, which were erected by the nuns of Nuestra Señora de la Concepción (Our Lady of the Conception). Most of the ruins, which cover the better part of two blocks, were part of the church; little remains of the convent.

Between the nuns' church and the sea was the city's sole hospital, the **Hospital de San Juan de Dios**. Unfortunately, much of the hospital's remains were scattered when Avenida Cincuentenario and a side road were put in not long ago. Also bordering the avenue, two blocks west of the hospital's ruins, are the remains of the **Iglesia y Convento de San Francisco**, the facilities erected by the Franciscans. The church faced the sea and stood on a massive base.

Continuing two blocks west along Avenida Cincuentenario, you'll arrive at the ruins of the **Iglesia y Convento de La Merced**. Erected by the Mercedarian friars in the early 17th century, the buildings actually survived the fire that swept the city following Morgan's assault. The church's façade is missing because the friars dismantled it and moved it to Casco Viejo, where it can be seen today.

Farther west (beyond the Bohío Turístico Restaurant) and paralleling the modern bridge is the **Puente del Matadero** (Bridge of the Slaughterhouse), a horribly over-restored stone bridge that took its name from a nearby slaughterhouse. It marked the beginning of the Camino Real to Portobelo. A much more significant bridge is visible from Avenida Cincuentenario near the northern edge of town. It is called **Puente del Rey** (Bridge of the King); built in 1617, it may be the oldest bridge in the Americas.

About halfway between that bridge and the Iglesia y Convento de Santo Domingo lies the **Iglesia de San José**, which belonged to the Augustine order. Marking this building as special were its vaulted side chapels – an architectural feature seldom seen in Panama. The ruins of the separate adjacent chapel are gone today.

The city's ruins are not fenced and you can visit them any time; Panamá La Vieja buses coming from Plaza Cinco de Mayo will bring you here. There's the fine **Mercado Nacional de Artesanías** (National Artisans Market) beside the ruins; it is open 9 am to 6 pm daily. Sharing a building with the market is the restaurant

Panama City

Top Left: Casco Viejo, the modern capital's oldest district and home to museums and fine old colonial buildings

Middle Left: Vía España, one of the capital's bustling commercial boulevards

Top Right: The ruins of Panamá La Vieja, the first capital, sacked by pirates in 1671

Bottom: The skyline of modern Panama City, seen from the Bahía de Panamá

STUART GR WARNER W

STUART GR WARNER W

ALFREDO MAIQUEZ

STUART GR WARNER W

Panamá Province

Top Left: Ships snaking through the Panama Canal's Gaillard Cut

Middle Left: The *Queen Elizabeth 2* luxury liner passing beneath the Puente de las Américas

Top Right: Locomotives pull ships through Miraflores Locks.

Bottom: Emberá Indian family poling down the Río Chagres

El Trapiche (see the Places to Eat section of this chapter for details).

Adjacent to the artisans market is the **Museo de Sitio Panamá Viejo**, which contains a rather impressive scale model of Panamá La Vieja prior to 1671. As you gaze upon it, a tape recording in Spanish or English recounts the history of the site. The museum also contains many colonial artifacts, most of which were brought from Spain. Unfortunately, all the signs are in Spanish and all the guides (every tour is guided for security reasons) speak only Spanish. It is customary to tip the guides US$1 or US$2. Hours are 9 am to 4 pm Monday to Saturday, 9 am to 1 pm Sunday. Museum admission is a bargain at US$1.

CAUSEWAY

At the Pacific entrance to the Panama Canal, a 2km long *calzada* (causeway) connects the four small islands of Naos, Culebra, Perico and Flamenco to the southern tip of La Boca district. Solidaridad, the beach on Naos, is one of the most popular in the area. The **Centro de Exhibiciones Marinas** (Marine Exhibitions Center) is on Culebra, and it includes a museum housed in a building that Noriega often used for entertaining. Nearby are two lovely aquariums. And near the aquariums is a patch of forest containing sloths and iguanas. The causeway, the islands and the Centro de Exhibiciones Marinas make for some fascinating touring.

The causeway, which was constructed from rock that was removed to make the Panama Canal, is a very enjoyable place. Many people arrive in the early morning and the late afternoon to walk, jog, skate, bicycle or drive along it. There's generally a pleasant breeze on the causeway, and it always offers sweeping views of the financial district, some 8km away. Bicycles Moses operates a booth at the causeway entrance where you can rent a bicycle or in-line skates; see the Bicycle section, later in this chapter, for details.

If you don't have a vehicle, it's most convenient to take a taxi to the causeway (US$3) and to hail another when you're ready to return to town. There's a 25¢ fee to enter the causeway.

All four of the causeway islands used to comprise Fort Grant, which was established in 1913 to guard the southern entrance to the canal. Between 1913 and WWII, the USA made Fort Grant into the most powerful defense complex in the world.

In 1928 two 14-inch guns with ranges up to 44km were brought to Panama. Mounted on railway carriages, they could be moved across the isthmus via the Panama Railroad to defend either entrance to the canal. The Pacific-side emplacement for the railroad guns was on Culebra. You can still see the tracks today on the driveway leading up to the Centro de Exhibiciones Marinas. The concrete rooms nearby, now used by marine-center staff, once housed the guns' ammunition. In 1941 the Japanese assault on Pearl Harbor showed that carrier-based aircraft could attack successfully far beyond the range of artillery. Suddenly obsolete, many of the big guns were retired from service even before the end of WWII.

The Centro de Exhibiciones Marinas is run by the Smithsonian Tropical Research Institute. There are many exhibits at the center, including a small six-sided building with sweeping views of the Bahía de Panamá that was built by Noriega for intimate gatherings. Today it houses a museum containing exhibits with signs in Spanish and English that mention how Panama's first peoples gradually developed a variety of strategies to harvest fish from the sea.

At the museum you can also learn about the role that Panama's marine resources play in the country's economy, and the destructive and wasteful effects of harvesting fish and shrimp by net. All of the text is beautifully illustrated with high-quality photos.

Outside the museum is something that will thrill ship enthusiasts: large, intelligent illustrations of vessels that allow visitors to glance out at the ocean and identify the types of ships waiting to transit the canal. It's a lot of fun. And there's a telescope here that you can use free of charge. Ever wonder if the crews aboard tankers fish from the bridges of their ships? See if you can spot any doing that. For me, a person who has spent little time at the ocean, studying the anchored ships with the telescope was like looking upon another world.

Two large aquariums, also part of the marine center, are 50m from the museum. One contains fish from the Pacific, the other fish from the Caribbean, allowing you to compare the two sets. You'll be struck by how much more colorful, and how much smaller, are the fish from the Caribbean. Staff on hand can tell you why that is so. The Centro de Exhibiciones Marinas is open 9 am to 5 pm daily; admission costs 50¢.

Dry forests once lined Central America's Pacific coast. Relatively easy to clear and burn for agriculture, these forests have now all but disappeared. The forest that you can see from the center, which lines the shore just south of the Puente de las Américas, is one of the largest remaining dry forests in Central America. There's even some dry forest near the aquariums. Be sure to take a stroll into it. The last time I was there I saw a three-toed sloth asleep in the crook of a tree, two huge green iguanas soaking up the sun and a brown pelican that seemed deep in bird thought.

BALBOA YACHT CLUB

On your way to or from the causeway, you might want to pay the yacht club (☎ 228-5794) a visit. Only about a 15-minute walk from the entrance to the causeway, the club has a pleasant open-air canalside bar/restaurant where you can sit and watch the ships glide under the Puente de las Américas while the waters of the canal lap at your feet. Sandwiches with fries are around US$3, complete dinners from US$7.50 to US$10. Of course, no one will say anything if all you really want to do is sip a drink.

This is the place to meet yachties on the canal's Pacific side; a bulletin board has notes from those offering and seeking rides across the canal, jobs line-handling, crew positions or sailing trips to faraway lands.

PANAMA CANAL MURALS

The story of the monumental effort to build the Panama Canal is powerfully depicted in murals mounted in the rotunda of the Panama Canal Administration Building (☎ 272-3202) in Balboa Heights.

The murals tell the story of the canal's construction through four main scenes: the digging of Gaillard Cut at Gold Hill, where the canal passes through the Continental Divide; the building of the spillway of the Gatún Dam, which dammed the Río Chagres and created Lago Gatún; construction of one of the giant lock gates (the canal uses some 80 of these gates); and the construction of the Miraflores Locks near the Pacific entrance to the canal. A frieze located immediately below the murals presents a panorama of the excavation of Gaillard Cut.

The murals were created by William B Van Ingen of New York, an outstanding artist who had achieved considerable fame for his murals in the Library of Congress in Washington, DC, and those in the US Mint in Philadelphia. Van Ingen agreed to produce the murals for US$25 per square foot; the finished murals cover about 1000 sq feet.

According to a leaflet at the administration building, Van Ingen and two assistants first made charcoal sketches of canal construction activities during two visits to Panama in 1914. Van Ingen then painted the murals on separate panels in his New York studio. The panels were shipped to Panama and installed during a three-day period in January 1915 under the artist's personal supervision. The paintings have the distinction of being the largest group of murals by an American artist on display outside the USA.

The administration building is open from 7:30 am to 4:15 pm weekdays. It's closed weekends, but guards will usually let you in between 10 am and 2:30 pm if you ask them.

MI PUEBLITO

At the foot of Cerro Ancón, on the western side of town near the intersection of Avenida de los Mártires and Calle Jeronimo de la Ossa, is a life-size replica of a rural village like those found on the Península de Azuero. There's a central square, a colonial church, a grocery store, a barber shop and a fine little restaurant that serves Panamanian specialties.

Created in 1994, Mi Pueblito (My Little Village) is quite a lovely place, even if it isn't authentic. One of its strengths is its numerous craft shops, where you'll find handicrafts from throughout the country. The quality is usually very good to excellent, but the prices are much higher than you'd find in their cities of origin.

Mi Pueblito is open from 11:30 am to 11:30 pm Tuesday to Saturday and 10 am to 10 pm Sunday.

MUSEUMS

Sadly, the establishment and preservation of museums is not a governmental priority in Panama City. Those that do exist are mostly the products of extraordinary efforts by individuals who took it upon themselves to move a bureaucratic mountain and create institutions in which Panama's human and natural histories could be preserved.

Foremost among this select group of individuals was the late Reina Torres de Araúz, one of the country's distinguished anthropologists. Before she passed away in 1982 at age 49, she successfully battled for the creation of seven museums – including the country's finest museum, the anthropology museum that bears her name.

The strength of Panama City's museums lies not in a single institution or two but in their variety. In the capital city there are museums devoted to religious colonial art, natural science, Panamanian history, Afro-Antilleans, contemporary art, the Panama Railroad and the canal. Unfortunately, signs at all the museums are in Spanish only, and literature in other languages is not available.

A list of city museums follows:

Museo Antropológico Reina Torres de Araúz – Housed in the imposing former main railway

station, built in 1913 and closed in the 1940s, this fascinating museum conveys the rich cultural heritage of Panama. It emphasizes, naturally, pre-Columbian artifacts and culture to give the visitor an appreciation for life on the isthmus before the arrival of the Spaniards. However, a number of exhibits also show how people live in different parts of Panama today, with the various ethnic groups well represented. Hours are 9:30 am to 4 pm Tuesday to Friday and 9 am to 3 pm Saturday. Admission costs US$1.50/50¢ adults/kids. Plaza Cinco de Mayo, Avenida Central (☎ 262-8338)

Museo de Arte Religioso Colonial – This museum is in a chapel of the Iglesia y Convento de Santo Domingo, which was built in 1756. With the exception of the museum, the church and convent now stand in ruins. This museum contains sacred artifacts from the colonial era, including sacred paintings and sculptures from various parts of the country, dating from the 16th, 17th and 18th centuries. Among the exhibits is a golden altar from the former chapel of the monastery that dates from the 18th century. Within the adjacent ruins is the famous Arco Chato (see the Walking Tour section). Hours are 9 am to 4:15 pm Tuesday to Saturday; 75¢/25¢ adults/kids. Avenida A at Calle 3 in Casco Viejo (☎ 228-2897)

Museo del Canal Interoceánico – Widely known only as the Panama Canal Museum, this museum is housed in an elegant building built by the French in French colonial style in the mid-1870s. It opened as a hotel and later became the headquarters of the French and (later) US canal commissions. The museum, which opened in 1997, contains such varied displays as Spanish armor and weapons, rifles from California's gold-rush days (many US prospectors passed through the city on their way to California), the desk at which Panama's declaration of independence was signed in 1903 and many Panama Railroad and Canal exhibits. The museum presents a detailed history of the railroad and canal through the use of panels covered with well-presented text, paintings and photos. There are many artifacts from the two eras. English-speaking guides are available. Hours are 9:30 am to 5:30 pm Tuesday to Sunday; US$2/1 adults/kids. Beside Plaza de la Independencia in Casco Viejo (☎ 211-1650)

Museo de Historia de Panamá – This not terribly impressive museum contains exhibits on the history of Panama from Spanish colonial times until 1977, the year the USA agreed to turn over control of the canal to Panama. Hours are 8:30 am to 3:30 pm weekdays; US$1/25¢ adults/kids. Palacio Municipal, 3rd floor, beside Plaza de la Independencia in Casco Viejo (☎ 228-6231)

Museo Afro-Antilleano – This small museum is dedicated to Panama's West Indies community, with special emphasis placed on Afro-Antillean participation in the construction of the canal. Its hours are 9 am to 4 pm Tuesday to Saturday; US$1/25¢ adults/kids. Avenida Justo Arosemena at Calle 24 Este (☎ 262-5348)

Museo de Arte Contemporáneo – This privately owned museum has an excellent collection of works on paper by Latin American artists. The rest is usually not so hot, except for an occasional temporary exhibition by a national or foreign artist and the monthlong Bienal de Arte, the country's largest art exhibition. Hours are 9 am to 4 pm weekdays and 9 am to noon Saturday. Admission is free. Avenida San Blás at Avenida de los Mártires in the Ancón district (☎ 262-8012)

Museo de Ciencias Naturales – This museum has sections on geology, paleontology, entomology and marine biology. What I found most impressive were the quantity of stuffed animals and the quality of the taxidermy. Numerous examples of Panama's wildlife can be found here, as well as stuffed lions, tigers, rhinos and buffalo. Its hours are 9 am to 4 pm Tuesday to Saturday and 9 am to 1 pm Sunday; US$1/25¢ adults/kids. Avenida Cuba between Calles 29 Este and 30 Este (☎ 225-0645)

Casa-Museo del Banco Nacional – This bank museum displays coins and bills circulated in Panama from the 16th century to the present, as well as stamps and other objects related to the history of the Panamanian postal service. Hours are 8 am to 12:30 pm and 1:30 to 4 pm Tuesday to Friday, 7:30 am to noon Saturday. Admission is free. Calle 34 Este at Avenida Cuba (☎ 225-0640)

PARQUE NATURAL METROPOLITANO

Upon a hill to the north of downtown, this 265-hectare park protects a wild area of tropical forest within the city limits. It has two main walking trails – the Nature Trail and the Tití Monkey Trail – that join to form one long loop, and a 150m high *mirador* (lookout point) offering a view over Panama City, the bay and the canal all the way to the Miraflores Locks. It is the only city park in Latin America that contains tropical semideciduous forest.

Mammals in the park include marmosets, anteaters, sloths and white-tailed deer; reptiles are represented by iguanas, turtles and tortoises. There are more than 250 known species of bird here, including the lance-tailed manakin. Fish, shrimp and turtles live in the Río Curundu, which runs along the eastern side of the park.

An international team of scientists from the Smithsonian Tropical Research Institute has set up a crane in the park to study the forest canopy; there is a complete ecosystem 30 to 50m up, including many animals that could never be studied from the ground. Unfortunately, the crane is off-limits to the general public.

The park is bordered on the west and north by Camino de la Amistad and on the south and east by Corredor Norte; Avenida Juan Pablo II runs right through the park. Admission costs 50¢/25¢ adults/children. There's a visitors' center (☎ 232-5516/5552) on Avenida Juan Pablo II, 40m north of the park entrance; it's open 8 am to 4 pm daily. A pamphlet for a self-guided tour is available in Spanish and English. Rangers offer one-hour tours with a slide show for groups of five or more; the cost is US$5.

Additionally, the Panama Audubon Society (☎ 224-4740, audupan@pananet .com, www.pananet.com/audubon) holds its monthly meeting at the visitors' center from 7:30 to 9:30 pm on the second Thursday of every month. The meetings are open to the public and often feature interesting speakers. Both English and Spanish are spoken here, and the group's website is bilingual as well. These meetings provide an excellent opportunity to get to know some Panamanians, to meet other birders and to learn more about birds.

The park was the supposed site of an important battle during the US invasion to oust Noriega (see The 'Battle' in the Park sidebar). Also of historical significance are

PANAMA CITY

The 'Battle' in the Park
A key battle was supposedly fought in Parque Natural Metropolitano during the US invasion of Panama in 1989. Here, it was reported, an American service-woman led troops into battle for the first time in US military history. According to a press report widely circulated during the invasion, Army Captain Linda Bray led a force of 30 military police in a fierce three-hour firefight at a Panama Defense Forces guard-dog kennel that left three Panamanian soldiers dead.

The US Army later acknowledged that the gunfire lasted only 10 minutes and was 'sporadic,' that no one was killed and that 29-year-old Captain Bray was not at the kennel at the time of the shooting but was in fact 1km away at a command post. However, the inaccurate press report led to heated debate in the USA about the role of US servicewomen in combat and eventually led to ground-breaking legislation that allowed them access to various combat jobs previously denied them. ■

the concrete structures just past the park entrance. They were used by the US military during WWII as a testing and assembly plant for aircraft engines. Today one of the buildings is an environmental education center. The other structure is vacant.

LANGUAGE COURSES
There are only two Spanish-language schools in Panama City. The Language & International Relations Institute (ILERI; ☎ /fax 260-4424, www.panamacanal.com/ileri.htm), at Altos de Chase, Casa 42-G, Vía la Amistad, El Dorado, enjoys the stronger reputation. ILERI offers two plans: The first option includes instruction, an exercise book, canal tour, field trips, lectures, and lodging, food and laundry service with a host family; the second option consists of instruction, a canal tour, field trips and lectures. Costs for the first option range from US$300 for a week to US$1065 for four weeks; the second option costs US$200 for one week to US$640 for four weeks. Both options include four hours of classwork per day. ILERI, which has schools in Panama and Costa Rica, also offers a two-weeks-in-each-country course.

The US Embassy sends members of its staff to Centro PanUsa (☎ 232-6718, fax 232-7292, panusa@sinfo.net), next to the train station on Avenida Roosevelt in the Balboa district, which periodically offers six-week courses for US$205, with slightly more than five hours of instruction per week. PanUsa's per-hour price is lower than ILERI's, but with so few hours of instruction (about one hour per day) it's highly unlikely that you'll be fluent in Spanish at the end of the PanUsa course. However, after six weeks of ILERI instruction you would definitely be able to communicate in Spanish, although you'd still have a lot of work to do before you'd be able to qualify for that UN translating job you've always dreamed about.

ORGANIZED TOURS
There are numerous tours available in and around the city, offered by companies with widely varying reputations. The companies listed here are well respected within Panama and enjoy solid reputations among international tour operators. All the tours mentioned here commence in the capital city. Please note that these are 1998 prices; add another 10% for 1999 prices, 20% for 2000 prices and 30% for 2001 prices. See the Organized Tours section in the Getting Around chapter for additional information.

Ancon Expeditions of Panama (☎ 269-9414/9415, fax 264-3713; in the USA ☎ 847-392-7865, 888-888-410; sales@ecopanama.com, www.ecopanama.com), in the El Dorado Building on Calle Elvira Méndez at Calle 49 A Este, is the country's leading tour operator because it hires only top-notch guides and offers only well-tested tours. Among its offerings are the tours listed on the following page.

Panama City Tour (US$55 for a full day of sightseeing, US$25 for a half-day of touring)
Pipeline Road in Soberanía National Park (US$65 for a full day of birding along one of the world's top bird-watching trails)
Fort San Lorenzo (US$69 for a full-day visit to this historic fort and other impressive sites)
Barro Colorado Nature Monument (US$85 for a full-day natural history tour)
Panama Canal Transit (US$109 for a full transit, US$49 for partial transit)

Ancon Expeditions also offers day tours of Sendero Las Cruces (US$65), the Miraflores Locks (US$69) and Fuerte Portobelo (US$69).

Pesantez Tours (☎ 263-8771, fax 263-7860, pesantez@sinfo.net), on Avenida Balboa near the Centro Medico Paitilla, has provided quality service for many years. Prices shown here are for one/two people:

Three-Hour Evening Party in Open Bus (US$20 per person)
Folkloric Show with Dinner (US$38/32)
Half-Day Shopping in Panama City (US$40/35)
Panamá La Vieja and Other Colonial Sites (US$44/24)
Half-Day City Tour (US$45/24)
All-Day Taboga Island (US$45/36)
Half-Day City and Canal (US$46/24)
Partial Canal Transit (US$63/56)
All-Day Shopping in Colón Free Zone (US$70/35)
All-Day Canopy Cable-Ride Adventure in El Valle (US$95/95)
All-Day Canal Locks and Docks (US$98/58)
All-Day Barro Colorado Nature Monument (US$118/118, two-person minimum)
All-Day Diving in Portobelo (US$135/135, two-person minimum)
All-Day Portobelo and Lunch (US$150/85)

Other tours are available.

Iguana Tours (☎ 226-8738, fax 226-4736, iguana@sinfo.net), on Avenida Belisario Porras between Calles 72 Este and 73 Este, offers a number of competitive tours, including 'The Gold Route,' which includes a visit to Panamá La Vieja, Sendero Las Cruces and Portobelo (US$85). It also offers the following tours:

Panama City Tour (US$35, with a two-person minimum)
Panama City Tour and Miraflores Locks (US$40, two-person minimum)
Canal Locks and Gatún Lake Boat Trip (US$55, two-person minimum)
Bird Watching at Soberanía National Park (US$65, two-person minimum)
Barro Colorado Nature Monument Hike (US$85, four-person minimum)
Visit to El Valle (US$95, two-person minimum; add US$15 each for optional Canopy Cable-Ride Adventure)
Panama Canal Full Transit (US$106)

Chiriquí River Rafting (☎ 236-5218, ☎ /fax 236-5217, hsanchez@panama.c-com.net, www.panama-rafting.com), Apartado 1686, Balboa, Ancón, Panamá, República de Panamá, the outfit that pioneered whitewater rafting in Panama, offers trips on the beautiful Río Chiriquí and Río Chiriquí Viejo. See the Chiriquí Province chapter for details.

SPECIAL EVENTS

Although not as famous as the celebrations in Rio de Janeiro or New Orleans, Carnaval in Panama City is celebrated with the same level of unrestrained merriment and wild abandon during the four days preceding Ash Wednesday. From Saturday until the following Tuesday, work is put away and masks, costumes and confetti are brought to the fore. For 96 hours, almost anything goes.

The festivities formally begin with the coronation ceremony on Friday, during which a Carnaval queen and her attendants are chosen from candidates representing a variety of social clubs, volunteer organizations, neighborhoods and private groups. Throughout her reign, the queen presides at all official receptions and is the center of attention in the daily parades scheduled each afternoon.

Officially, the craziness starts slowly, with a small parade on Saturday that consists of little more than the queen and her court. Unofficially, the cork is way out of the bottle by then. Vía España fills with people, and everyone is in high spirits and partying in an atmosphere that is sexually charged and free of class distinctions. Music pours from all directions and spontaneous dancing is everywhere. Masquerade characters cavort among the crowd. Street vendors weave through the throngs of people. Improvised entertainment abounds. The party moves indoors at night – into cantinas, private clubs and hotels – where combos play Afro-Cuban and typical Panamanian music and the dancing and drinking continue till dawn.

The celebration, the origins of which have been obscured with the passage of time, kicks into a higher gear on Sunday, when folk dance groups decked out in Panama's national costumes join the queen and her attendants in the afternoon parade down Vía España, traveling from near Vía Brasil to near Avenida Federico Boyd (the exact beginning and ending points vary from year to year). To cool the sunbaked masses, fire and garden hoses are turned on the crowd at every opportunity. It's said that four months of water are spent in four days of Carnaval.

The madness peaks on Shrove Tuesday with the biggest parade of all. Floats of all sizes rule the avenue, separated by bands of gaily dressed people walking slowly in themed formations – not the least conspicuous of which is the traditional formation of transvestites. Most of them carry a razor in each hand as a warning to macho types that a punch thrown at them will not go unanswered.

Carnaval officially closes with the first rays of sunlight on Wednesday morning, when the hardiest celebrants appear on the beach of the Bahía de Panamá to bury a sardine in the sand – a symbolic gesture intended to convey the end of worldly pleasures for the Lenten season.

PLACES TO STAY

There are many dozens of hotels in Panama City, and guestrooms range from cell-like (small, dirty and hot, with shared bathroom, cold water, etc) to opulent (tastefully appointed with just the right mix of mahogany and marble, with to-die-for views, acres

ALFREDO MAIQUEZ
Carnaval queen greets the masses.

of space, art on the walls, a butler, computer, executive desk, minibar, satellite TV, Olympic-size bathtub with separate shower, etc). Prices for a standard room in this town range from US$5 to US$250.

Budget accommodations run up to US$20, midrange lodgings from US$21 to US$50 and top-end places from US$51 on up. Prices cited here include Panama's 10% hotel tax. There are no youth hostels, campgrounds or RV centers in Panama City.

While conducting research for this book, I inspected at least two rooms at every hotel in the city. Most of the hotels open for business at that time appear on the following pages. I've excluded those that were either rat-plagued, roach-ridden or flea-infested; or located in unsafe areas without any redeeming qualities; or rude to a polite stranger and prospective patron who simply asked if he could see a couple of rooms. New hotels may have opened since this book was researched, and those are not included in these listings.

Places to Stay – budget
Casco Viejo The Casco Viejo (San Felipe) area is home to the city's lowest-priced lodgings; in fact, only low-priced lodgings are available here, and none of the hotels have hot water. The places mentioned here

are, in my opinion, quite OK for streetwise people who can do without all the amenities for a little while. If you're on a tight budget, if you prefer risky and adventurous to safe and predictable, this area's for you. If you take a few precautions, you likely won't have any problems, and you'll leave Casco Viejo thinking about it as I do – it's a fascinating place with a great cast of characters and a fabulous history. (See Dangers & Annoyances in this chapter for some good advice.)

The architecturally attractive *Hotel y Restaurante Herrera* (☎ 228-8994), beside Parque Herrera on Calle 9, has rooms with fan for US$7/9 single/double with shared bathroom, or US$12 with private bathroom. A room with two beds and private bathroom, fan, fridge and TV goes for US$13. Rooms with private bathrooms, air-con, fridges and TVs cost US$18. This is the best of the budget places in Casco Viejo, and there's a good, cheap restaurant and a laundromat just a few paces away.

The *Pensión Panamá* (☎ 262-8053), on Calle 6 a block and a half from the cathedral, has rooms with shared bathroom for US$5/7 single/double. For two beds, the price soars to US$8. At the bottom of the barrel in the budget category is the *Pensión Tropical* (☎ 228-8889), on Calle 8 near Avenida A. Rooms go for US$7.50/10 with shared/private bathroom. There's only a bed and a fan in each room.

Hotel Foyo (☎ 262-8023), opposite the Pensión Panamá at Calle 6, No 8-25, is basic but clean, with rooms for US$7/12 with shared/private bathroom; a few smaller rooms adequate for one person cost US$6. Some of the rooms of the same price are better than others; ask to see several.

The *Pensión Panamericana* (☎ 228-8759), at Avenida A and Calle 10, offers worn rooms for one or two people for US$8.50/10 with shared/private bathroom. There's a ceiling fan, a dresser and a decent bed in each room.

Hotel Central (☎ 262-8044), on Calle 5 facing Plaza de la Independencia, was very grand at the start of the 20th century; illustrious figures from the canal's history lodged here in its early days. The hotel has been allowed to deteriorate, but the bare-essentials rooms still have high ceilings and arched French doors opening onto private balconies overlooking the Plaza de la Independencia. Singles/doubles cost US$9/10 with shared bathroom, US$10/12 with private bathroom.

La Exposición This bustling, centrally located area contains quite a few budget hotels and many midrange ones. It's a good area for people who value inexpensive but decent lodgings and who would prefer to see Casco Viejo only by day.

The best budget hotel among a slew of good values in this neighborhood is the *Residencial Turístico Volcán* (☎ 225-5275), on Calle 29 Este between Avenidas Perú and Cuba. All rooms have private bathrooms and TVs, and they're comfortable, well maintained and clean. Doubles cost US$13/15 with ceiling fan/air-con. Doubles with air-con and two beds cost US$18. If you stay a week or more and pay in advance, the rates are even lower – plus, you can use the lovely 24-hour rooftop pool at the Hotel Covadonga, next door. (The owner's daughter owns and operates the Covadonga.)

Residencial Primavera (☎ 225-1195), simple but clean and well kept, is in a good location on Avenida Cuba near Calle 43 Este, in a residential neighborhood just a block from Avenida Central España. All the rooms have private bathrooms and ceiling fans, and at US$11 a night this place is an excellent value.

Pensión Las Palmeras (☎ 225-0811), Avenida Cuba, No 38-29, near Calle 38 Este, is also simple but clean, with rooms for US$11 with a shower in the room and toilet down the hall, or US$13 with private bathroom.

The *Residencial Turístico El Dorado* (☎ 227-5767), on Calle 37 Este between Avenidas Cuba and Perú, has rooms with private bathrooms for US$11 with fan, US$13 with air-con or US$17 with air-con and color TV.

The *Pensión América* (☎ 225-1140), on Avenida 3 Sur near Calle 33 Este, offers rooms with fan/air-con for US$11/17. Overall, this place is not very pretty, but some of its rooms are better than others.

Pensión Las Torres (☎ 225-0172), on the corner of Calle 35 Este and Avenida Perú, offers rooms with private bathrooms for US$15/18 with fan/air-con. This place has lots of character and is quite popular with college students. I'd be extremely high on Las Torres if it were not for the fact that none of its bathrooms have doors; it's part of the design, but it's also a major drawback for people who don't like to share everything.

The *Residencial Compostela* (☎ 227-6396) is on Avenida Cuba between Calles 29 Este and 30 Este. The rooms of this charming hotel are equipped with air-con, phones and TVs. At US$17/20 a single/double, it's a good value.

Hotel Ideal (☎ 262-2400), Calle 17 Oeste, No 15-55, a block from the Avenida Central pedestrian street, isn't in the best part of town, but it's where all the Peace Corps volunteers stay. It's a large hotel where all the rooms have air-con and color cable TVs. Singles/doubles with shared bathrooms cost US$18/20; those with private bathrooms cost US$20/22. Downstairs is a 24-hour restaurant. Local buses stop nearby, and the Tica bus to Costa Rica comes and goes from here.

The *Hotel Villa del Mar* (☎ 225-8111), at Calle 33 Este and Avenida 3 Sur, has rooms with air-con, TVs, phones and private bathrooms, but it's a bit rundown and lacks any semblance of charm. It's the kind of place that couples might use for an hour, if you catch my drift. Rates are US$17/22. The *Hotel Discovery* (☎ 225-3568), on Calle 34 Este near Avenida 3 Sur, is the same kind of place.

A good value can be found at the *Hotel Acapulco* (☎ 225-3832, fax 227-2033), at Avenida Cuba and Calle 30 Este. There's a writing desk in each room, as well as air-con, TV and a telephone. The rooms (US$20/22) are spacious and some have small balconies.

The *Residencial Alemeda* (☎ 225-1758, fax 225-7806), on Calle 30 Este near Avenida Cuba, offers tiny cubicles that its staff generously calls guestrooms. Rates are US$20/22. Rooms have air-con and TVs, and parking and fax service are available.

The worst of the budget places that I'm willing to mention is the *Hotel Río de Janeiro* (☎ 227-2145), on Avenida Perú near Calle 28 Este. Rates are US$17/24. This place has more security bars than most mints. Its clientele is mainly professional – working ladies and men who pay for sex. I mention this hotel only because I have fond memories of Rio – the real one.

Places to Stay – middle

Of the hotels in this price range, the *Hotel Covadonga* (☎ 225-3998, fax 225-4011), on Calle 29 Este between Avenidas Perú and Cuba, is tough to top. This well-maintained establishment offers comfortable rooms with air-con, TVs, phones, room service and excellent beds for US$22/27 single/double. There's a very appealing 24-hour swimming pool on the hotel's roof and a 24-hour restaurant on the ground floor.

The *Hotel 2 Mares* (☎ 227-6149, fax 227-3906), on Calle 30 Este between Avenidas Perú and Cuba, has so-so rooms with air-con for a very reasonable US$17/22. A room with a view and a king-size bed costs US$28. Adding a large bathtub to the features of the US$28 package costs US$33. This place is quite OK.

The *Hotel California* (☎ 263-7736), on Avenida Central España near Calle 43 Este, has good, clean rooms with private bathrooms, phones and color TVs for US$22. There's a restaurant/bar downstairs and free coffee in the lobby.

The *Hotel Lisboa* (☎ 227-5916, fax 227-5919), on Avenida Cuba between Calles 30 Este and 31 Este, offers rooms for a flat US$22 rate for one or two people. It's a newer place, with spacious rooms with air-con, writing tables, TVs and phones. It's very nice.

Next door to the Pensión Las Palmeras (see above) on Avenida Cuba, the *Residencial Jamaica* (☎ 225-9870) has clean and pleasant rooms with private bathrooms, hot water, private phones, air-con and color TVs for US$23 apiece.

The *Hotel Arenteiro* (☎ 227-5883), opposite the Residencial Alemeda on Calle 30 Este near Avenida Cuba, is a new place with rooms with TVs, air-con, hot water and phones, but they're small and rather stuffy. Rates are US$20/24 single/double.

The *Hotel Centroamericano* (☎ 227-4555, fax 225-2505), at Calle 34 Este and Avenida 3 Sur, is an excellent value, with very clean rooms with air-con, TVs, private bathrooms, hot water and firm mattresses for US$21/24.

The *Hotel Venecia* (☎ 227-7881, fax 227-5642), on Avenida Perú near Calle 35 Este, is a new, small but pleasant place offering rooms with good beds, cable TVs, air-con and private bathrooms. At US$22/27, this is another excellent value.

The *Hotel Benidorm* (☎ 225-3035), on Calle 29 Este near Avenida Perú, offers air-con rooms with TVs and telephones for US$22/27. This place is a bit barren and could really use a good paint job.

The *Hotel Latino* (☎ 227-3395), on Avenida Cuba near Calle 35 Este, is a newer place but appeared to be wearing badly. Its rooms come with air-con and TVs and cost US$17 for a single and US$30 for a room with two beds. The hotel has a very decent restaurant on the ground floor.

The *Hotel Montreal* (☎ 263-4422), on Vía España at the corner of Avenida Justo Arosemena, has the usual amenities, plus a rooftop swimming pool and secure parking. Rates are a very reasonable US$24/31 for rooms with a single/double bed.

The 11-story *Hotel Caribe* (☎ /fax 227-2525), on the corner of Calle 28 Este and Avenida Perú, offers spacious rooms, each with air-con, phone, cable TV and a refrigerator if you request one. There's a pool on the roof and an ice machine on every floor. There's even laundry service. Rates are US$27/33.

Well situated but in need of updating is the *Las Vegas Suites Hotel* (☎ 269-0722, fax 223-0047), at Calle 49 B Oeste and Avenida 2 A Norte in El Cangrejo. All rooms have small kitchens, refrigerators,

TVs, air-con and phones. The hotel's court-yard restaurant, Caffé Pomodoro, is the highlight of the hotel (see Places to Eat). And even if your travel isn't business-related, you can request the hotel's corporate rate, which is US$33/38.

The *Hotel Veracruz* (☎ 227-3022, fax 227-3789), on Avenida Perú near Calle 31 Este, offers clean but worn rooms with TVs and air-con for US$37/46. All of the rooms ending with the numbers '08' have balconies.

A good value and a popular place, the *Hotel Marbella* (☎ 263-2220, fax 263-3622) is on Calle D between Calles 49 B Oeste and Eusebio A Morales. Every room has a writing/dining table, air-con, cable TV and good beds. Laundry service is available. Rates are US$43/49.

The *Gran Hotel Soloy* (☎ 227-1133, fax 227-3948), on Avenida Perú at Calle 30 Este, has fairly cheerful rooms, but they are showing signs of wear and lack of maintenance. The highlight of this place is a popular bar and dance club on the 12th floor (it's open Thursday, Friday and Saturday after 5 pm). Rates are US$43/49.

On Avenida Central España is the *Hotel Europa* (☎ 263-6911), which is not as nice as the Hotel California, across the street; its drab rooms go for US$44/49.

Taking a step up in quality, we arrive at the *Hotel Costa Inn* (☎ 227-1522, 225-1281, costainn@panama.phoenix.net), on Avenida Perú near Calle 39 Este. The 130 rooms come with air-con and satellite TVs, and there's a gym, a pool, a restaurant and a person who will send email for you at US$2 per message. Rates are US$44/50. Discounts are available for longer stays.

Hotel Roma (☎ 227-3844, fax 227-3711), on Calle 33 Este at Avenida 3 Sur, has a pool on its roof and cheerful rooms with air-con, TVs, phones and good beds. However, it's a bit on the expensive side at US$48/51.

Places to Stay – top end
There's no shortage of top-end accommodations in Panama City, but few offer the level of service that most international trav-

elers expect from purportedly four and five-star hotels. This is due to the fact that most of the capital city's pricey hotels have not been around very long and their staffs are still in training.

On a positive note, the rates quoted here are considerably less than you would pay for similar lodgings in most other modern capital cities. And if you rely on a tour operator or travel agency to book your hotel reservation, you can expect to pay at least 10% less than the rates quoted below. The rack rate – the rate you pay if you simply walk into a hotel and ask for a room – is nearly always more than the rate that a tour operator or travel agent can obtain for you.

The best of the top-end bunch is the five-star *Hotel Caesar Park* (☎ 270-0477, 800-228-3000, fax 226-2693, www.caesarpark .com), opposite the Centro Atlapa on Calle 77 Este near Vía Israel. Part of the Westin chain, this is where heads of state stay when they visit Panama. Facilities include a health club, tennis courts, swimming pool, three executive floors, a casino, dance club, stores and five restaurants (ranging from a pizzeria to a fancy all-you-can-eat place to an elegant dining room 16 floors up). Rates range from US$145 to US$245 per room.

The *Hotel Suites Alfa* (☎ 263-4022, fax 223-0724), on Calle Ricardo Arias at Vía España, is nothing special, but its central location and relatively low prices of US$55/62 make it a fairly popular choice. Each room is spacious and equipped with a kitchenette.

The *Hotel Riande Granada* (☎ 264-4900, fax 263-7179), on Calle Eusebio A Morales near Vía España in El Cangrejo, has attractive rooms, a pool, casino, bar and restaurant. If the pool and casino are important to you, then at US$80/90 (20% less if you ask for the corporate rate) the Riande Granada is reasonably priced. If you're really only looking for a decent room in El Cangrejo, stay at the less expensive but otherwise comparable Hotel Marbella (see Places to Stay – middle) and save some money.

El Ejecutivo Hotel (☎ 264-3333, fax 269-1944), at Avenida 3 Sur and Calle Aquilino de la Guardia, is a longtime favorite with the business crowd because of its central location, modern rooms and nightly open bar for guests. There's also a pool, restaurant and business center. The rates of US$85/95 single/double are competitive, as the hotel's longtime popularity attests.

The new *Country Inn & Suites* (☎ 236-9321, 800-456-4000, fax 264-6082) is on Avenida Miguel Brostella west of Avenida Ricardo J Alfaro, 5km from the city center but near the road to Colón. The entire lodge has a country-inn feel to it, and it also has a swimming pool and a TGI Friday's restaurant on its premises. The hotel isn't conveniently close to anything except the road to Colón, nor is it inexpensive (US$90/100). Most tourists would be much better off closer to downtown.

Centrally located and offering large, handsome rooms, the *Suites Ambassador* (☎ 263-7274, fax 264-7872, ambassad@ sinfo.net) is on Calle D between Calle Eusebio A Morales and Calle 49 B Oeste in El Cangrejo. The smallest room at this very smart hotel would be a junior suite anywhere else. Each room comes with a true sitting area and an attractive kitchenette. Use of a conference room is offered at no extra charge. Service here is the best in town. A state-of-the-art security system monitors every floor, and the rooftop pool is quite inviting – two more reasons that this hotel is favored by visiting diplomats and executives. Rooms cost US$110, less if you say you're here on business. Weekly and monthly discounts are available.

The *Hotel Continental* (☎ 263-9999, fax 269-4559), at Calle Ricardo Arias and Vía España, is the only hotel in the country with a glass elevator. The hotel was recently remodeled and it is now quite nice. Each guestroom is furnished with a handsome four-poster bed and a bathtub that has handrails – rare features in Panama. Ask for a room in the new wing. Standard rates are US$122/134; ask for the corporate rate, however, and you'll get 20% off the currently posted room prices. Not bad at all.

A former Holiday Inn, the *Hotel Plaza Paitilla Inn* (☎ 269-1122, fax 223-1470), on Vía Italia at Avenida Churchill, is very well maintained, with tasteful if cheap furniture in its guestrooms. All of its rooms have bathtubs and balconies, and the hotel is on the water. There's a handsome pool and a very popular bar. Rack rates are US$122/134; the corporate rates, however, are US$86/96.

The *Hotel Costa Del Sol* (☎ 223-7111, fax 223-6636), on the corner of Vía España and Avenida Federico Boyd, has some pleasant surprises. For one thing, each room has a kitchenette. The roof of the multistory hotel is home to a swimming pool, restaurant and bar, and has sweeping views of the city; it's a good place to enjoy a drink even if you're not a guest. The food isn't exceptional. There's also a tennis court and spa. Rates are US$95/105.

A wise choice for working visitors, particularly ones traveling with children, is the *Hotel Suites Central Park* (☎ 223-3100, 800-528-1234, fax 223-9630, www.suitescentralpark.com), on Vía España at Avenida 4 Sur. Each guestroom is designed so that the TV-equipped sleeping quarters can be closed off from the sitting area and work desk. There's a computer with free Internet access and printer on most of these desks, as well as fax and answering machines – and even a portable phone with a 2km range. This Best Western hotel has a pool, bar and restaurant. Room rates, which include a poolside buffet breakfast, start at US$140/150 single/double.

The *Radisson Royal Panama Hotel* (☎ 265-3636, fax 265-3550, www.radisson.com), on Calle 53 Este at Avenida 5 B Sur, is trying to compete with the Hotel Caesar Park, and failing. Charging US$150 per room and up, it does have lovely rooms and a pool, coffee shop, specialty restaurant, piano bar, exercise room and tennis court, but the facilities are generally not as well done as those at the Caesar Park, and there aren't nearly as many of them.

The landmark *Hotel El Panamá* (☎ 269-5000, 800-457-4000, fax 269-5990), on Calle 49 B Oeste near Vía España, gets the lion's share of foreign tourists due to long-established relations with travel agencies and tour operators. Its chief strengths are its central location and, for some lucky guests, its older, spacious poolside rooms. But service at this so-called 'five-star hotel' is terrible, and the new wing (where most of the guests are placed) is nothing special. There's a pool, casino, bar and restaurants. For the money – US$170 per room – you're much better off at the Hotel Caesar Park.

One of Panama's least successful hotel stories to date has got to be the *Miramar Inter-Continental* (☎ 214-1000, fax 223-4891, www.interconti.com), on Avenida Balboa near Avenida Federico Boyd, the second of Panama's true five-star hotels (the Caesar Park is the other). The Miramar's guestrooms face either the Bahía de Panamá or the gleaming financial district. The 206-room hotel features two gourmet restaurants, a piano lounge, a bar and dance club, a private dining salon, an inviting pool with an island in the middle, a gym, ballrooms, tennis, etc. But with room prices starting at US$235/255, hardly anybody stays here. Perhaps it's a hotel before its time.

The newest member of the Rosewood Hotels & Resorts chain, *The Bristol* (☎ 265-7844, fax 265-7829, www.rosewood-hotels.com/bristol.htm; in the USA and Canada ☎ 888-767-3966), is half a block south of El Ejecutivo Hotel on Calle Aquilino de la Guardia. The Rosewood group prides itself on personal service, and The Bristol is overflowing with it: Each guest is attended by a butler. Personal business cards and stationery are produced for the guest upon arrival. Guests can use the hotel's cars, when available, for free. The list goes on and on. The lovely rooms are equipped with fax machines and separate Internet and telephone lines in addition to all the usual amenities. Rates start at US$245.

If you love nature and have never spent the night in a former military radar installation deep inside a national rainforest park, you'll want to know about the *Canopy*

Tower. It's a very cool place. See the Canal Area section of the Panamá Province chapter for details.

PLACES TO EAT

There's no shortage of restaurants in Panama City. You won't have trouble finding cuisine from Italy, Spain, Mexico, Japan, Argentina, China, France, India, Britain and Greece. Of course, Panamanian specialties and seafood abound.

The international fast-food giants – *McDonald's, Burger King* and *KFC*, to name a few – are well represented. At the other end of the cholesterol spectrum, there are also a couple of vegetarian restaurants. The sections that follow lead with the best restaurant in each category in terms of quality of food, and (unless otherwise stated) I can recommend all the businesses mentioned here.

Panamanian

Between the Panamá La Vieja ruins and the ocean is *El Trapiche.* It's known for tamal de olla (tamale casserole; US$3.75), corvina Capitán Morgan (corvina with white sauce containing chunks of jumbo shrimp and lobster; US$12.50) and cazuela de mariscos Panamá Viejo, which contains lots of seafood (US$11.50). The restaurant, which is in the Mercado Nacional de Artesanías building, is open 8 am to 11 pm daily.

Restaurante-Bar Tinajas (☎ 263-7890, fax 264-4858), on Avenida 3 A Sur near Avenida Federico Boyd, is a large, multi-level restaurant decorated to resemble a traditional Península de Azuero village. Typical dishes include pastel de yuca (country pie made with yucca, chicken, corn, capers and raisins; US$7.50), chuletas ahumadas (smoked pork chops with honey-pineapple sauce; US$8.50) and gaucho de mariscos (fresh seafood stew, served with coconut rice; US$8.50). Tinajas is well known for its popular folkloric dance shows, offered at 9 pm on Tuesday, Thursday and weekend nights; there's a US$5 entertainment fee on those nights. Tinajas is open 11:30 am to 11 pm Monday to Saturday.

Far less costly than Tinajas but popular with both the working class and the pin-striped crowd is *Restaurante Boulevard Balboa,* on Avenida Balboa at Calle 31 Este. This place specializes in grilled sandwiches and burgers, few of them over US$3. Burgers are US$1.50. Very popular is the milanesa a caballo, which consists of a breaded steak topped with two eggs served sunny-side up (US$4.50). If you're traveling on a tight budget and looking for a cheap but filling meal, this is a good place to visit. It's open 7 am to midnight daily.

The menu changes daily at *El Rincón Tableño,* on the corner of Calle 27 Este and Avenida Balboa. The items rotate at this open-air eatery, but the type of food never does: it's always 100% working-class Panamanian. Typical items include sopa de carne (meat soup; 90¢), camarones guisados (shrimp in tomato sauce; US$2.50), and ropa vieja (literally, 'old clothes'; marinated shredded beef with a mild red sauce; US$2.10). There are a half-dozen or so natural fruit juices to choose among, each priced less than US$1.

Restaurante Anarisel, beside Plaza de la Independencia in Casco Viejo, isn't the kind of place you'd likely write home about, but it is a good place to fill up inexpensively and may be the cleanest of the budget restaurants in this district. Anarisel excels at encebollado de bistec (beef with onions), pollo asado (baked chicken) and the fish of the day; each sells for US$2. It's open from breakfast-time to dinnertime daily.

Seafood

The *Restaurant Mercado del Marisco,* on Avenida Balboa at Calle 15 Este, is – as its name says – the 'seafood market restaurant.' On the 2nd floor of Panama's new two-story seafood market, this very casual place boasts 'the best and freshest fish and seafood in Panama' – and it delivers. The open-sided, fan-cooled diner has been popular since the day it opened in 1997, offering shrimp (US$4.95), squid (US$5.95), mussels (US$6.25), octopus (US$6.95), jumbo shrimp (US$7.95), lobster (from US$10 to

US$19) and tropical king crab (US$19.95). Corvina, guabina and red snapper all cost around US$6. It's open 6 am to 10 pm daily except Sunday.

Elegant and dressy *La Toja,* at Calle Uruguay and Avenida 4 A Sur, excels at corvina gratinada en salsa de cangrejo (corvina au gratin in crab sauce; US$14), parrillada de mariscos (grilled seafood, specifically lobster, shrimp, jumbo shrimp, octopus, squid and mussels; US$14.50) and paella a la Valenciana (Valencian-style paella; US$18 for two people). Its hours are noon to 11 pm daily.

Centolla's Place, on Vía España near Calle 94 Este, serves seafood Bocas del Toro-style 11 am to midnight daily. Popular dishes at this fun and casual place are pescado relleno (mackerel stuffed with onions, cilantro and garlic; US$3.50), cambombia (conch with wine or garlic sauce; US$5.50) and pulpo al ajillo (octopus in garlic sauce; US$7.95). Be sure to order an 'ice glass' (US$1) before your dinner; it consists of marine algae, dark beer, nutmeg, milk and rum. Blended, of course.

The Panama Yacht Club, on Avenida Balboa near Calle 40 Este, has an excellent bar/restaurant called *La Marina.* This cozy 2nd-floor landmark is popular with the business crowd during lunch hours and with yuppies at night. Appetizers include soups (from US$2.75 to US$4), ceviche (US$4.50), clams in red sauce (US$4.50) and shrimp cocktail (US$6.75). Main dishes include corvina (from US$8.50 to US$12), jumbo shrimp (US$15), paella (US$18) and lobster (US$25). It's open noon to 1 am daily.

The *Costa Azul,* on Calle Ricardo Arias about 100m south of Vía España, serves corvina a dozen different ways (US$5.50 to US$9.50) and the light white fish guabina. The restaurant's long menu also includes more than three dozen sandwiches (US$1.50 to US$4) and a wide variety of pasta, chicken and beef dishes.

Although occasionally recommended by people who likely haven't eaten there, *La Casa del Marisco,* on Avenida Balboa, is very expensive and has a stuffy ambiance.

Steaks

For beef, the name is *Martín Fierro,* on Calle Eusebio A Morales in El Cangrejo. The quality of meat here has no equal in the country. The top selections are US-imported 16oz New York rib steak (US$16), US-imported rib eye (US$22) and bife chorizo (US$9.50). Bife chorizo is the same cut as the New York steak, but it's local and grass fed. It's chewier but also tastier. Prices include salad bar and a choice of French fries, baked potato or rice. It's open noon to 3 pm and 6 to 11 pm Monday to Saturday and noon to 9:30 pm Sunday.

Gaucho's Steak House, at the corner of Calle Uruguay and Avenida 5 A Sur, is very popular and nicely decorated, but in my opinion the meat isn't quite as good as the meat at Martín Fierro. Selections include bife chorizo (US$11.50), colita de cuadril (beef tri tip; US$11.50) and asado de tira (beef short ribs; US$12.75). All the meat is imported from the USA. Hours are noon to 3 pm and 6 to 10:30 pm daily.

South American

Restaurante Los Años Locos, on Calle 76 Este behind the Hotel Caesar Park, specializes in grilled Argentinean food. Its most popular dish is the parrillada Los Años Locos (mixed grilled meats; US$24 for two people). Its corvina dishes (all are US$9.50) are also often ordered. People looking for traditional Argentinean dishes order milanesa Napolitana (breaded tenderloin with red sauce and mozzarella au gratin; US$12) or the milanesa Los Años Locos (breaded tenderloin with two eggs on top and a side of fries; US$12). A typical portion of meat served at this upscale, intimate, tastefully appointed restaurant weighs 1lb. There's a salad bar, too. Come with an appetite. Los Años Locos' hours are noon to 3 pm and 6 to 11 pm weekdays, noon to 9:30 pm weekends.

The *Bar-Restaurante Chimborazo,* on Vía Jose Agustin Arango east of downtown, is both a lively bar on weekend nights and a traditional Peruvian restaurant with dozens of tables out back, each with its own thatched roof. There are 110 items on the menu of this family business, which opened in the early 1970s. Among the more popular items are sopa de levantamuertos ('soup to wake you from the dead,' a green soup of seafood, rice and cilantro; US$2.50), sopa parihuela (a spicy soup with chunks of seafood, crayfish and root; US$5.50), filete de corvina a lo macho (corvina served with shrimp, octopus and garlic; US$7) and langostinos (jumbo shrimp, prepared in 10 different ways; US$8). It's open 10 am to midnight daily.

French

La Cocotte, on Calle Uruguay a few paces from Avenida Balboa, has brought fine Parisian cuisine to Panama. Its chef, Fabien Migny, studied at the Ecole Hotelliére Belliard from 1984 to 1987 and simultaneously underwent his training at the renowned Restaurant Jamin de Joel Robouchon of Paris. Appetizers include pâté de canard and sautéed mushrooms. Entrées include confit de canard and fresh salmon in a red wine sauce. Desserts include chocolate truffles, apple tarts and crêpes soufflées au chocolat. Dinners average US$30 to US$40. It's open for lunch and dinner weekdays, dinner only on Saturday; it's closed Sunday.

The best restaurant in Casco Viejo is *Restaurante Las Bóvedas,* on Plaza de Francia. This lovely French restaurant is situated in the vaults of a 300-year-old fort. What is now the dining room was used for years during the 19th century to house political prisoners. The menu varies daily, subject to the catch of the day, but typical prices are US$15 for filet of fish, US$17 for mixed meats and US$18 for a New York steak. This place is particularly well known for its mero (grouper). You can hear jazz in the last vault, beginning at 9 pm weekend nights.

Another fine French restaurant is the *Restaurante Casco Viejo,* on Calle 53 Este at Calle 50. Some of the better offerings include French onion soup (US$6), escargots au gratin (US$8), veal tongue with passion-fruit sauce (US$16.50) and corvina filet stuffed with lobster (US$19). Every Friday the popular bar swings into life with live bands, typically playing salsa or merengue. Hours are noon to 3 pm and 7 pm until the last patron decides to move on, Monday to Friday. There's no lunch on Saturday, when the Restaurante Casco Viejo opens at 7 pm.

Crepes & Waffles, on Avenida 5 B Sur just west of Calle Aquilino de la Guardia, has been a hit since it opened in 1997. The most popular of the restaurant's many crepes are espinaca, queso ricotta y tomate Napolitano (spinach, ricotta cheese and tomatoes; US$3.75); mozzarella y tomate (mozzarella and tomatoes; US$3.75); and lomito a la pimienta (strips of roast beef with pepper sauce; US$5.75). There's also a fine selection of sandwiches and desserts. Crepes & Waffles is open noon to 11 pm daily.

Asian

Top honors in the Chinese-food category are a toss-up; both *Madame Chang* and *Palacio Lung Fung* are excellent restaurants. Madame Chang, on Avenida 5 A Sur just west of Calle Aquilino de la Guardia, is known for its pato al estilo Pekin (Peking duck), priced at US$20/40 for a half/whole duck. This elegant and dressy restaurant is also known for filete 'tit pang' (sizzling sliced beef with oyster sauce; US$10.75) and its pichón en pétalos de lechuga (a combination of duck, chicken and pigeon, served on a bed of crispy rice noodles; US$15). Hours are noon to 3 pm and 6 to 11 pm Monday to Saturday and noon to 11 pm Sunday.

Palacio Lung Fung, a huge restaurant on Calle 62 C Oeste at the entrance to the Los Angeles neighborhood, is considerably less expensive than the Madame Chang. One popular combination, for example, consists of soup, pork with almonds and vegetables, beef chop suey, shrimp rolls, chicken fried rice and jasmine tea or coffee, and costs US$9 per person. This restaurant serves dim sum until 11 am every day. It's open 6:30 am to 11 pm daily.

Nobu, at Calles Uruguay and 4 A Sur, which is owned by a Chinese man and his Japanese wife, specializes in Chinese food but also has a sushi bar. This fairly elegant and popular restaurant with a lovely full bar is known for its arroz frito Nobu (fried rice, vegetables, pork and shrimp; US$6.75 for two people or US$8.75 for four), tempura (US$2 to US$12), filete Nobu (chopped filet of beef served with oyster sauce; US$12.75) and its combination sushi plate that consists of 10 pieces (US$20). Hours are noon to 3 pm and 6 to 11 pm Tuesday to Sunday; closed Monday.

Dropping down in price but not quality is the *Restaurante Furama,* on the corner of Avenida 2 Sur and Calle 51 Este, serving excellent food at low prices. This very understated restaurant offers rollo de primavera (spring rolls; US$3), singapur main fun (yellow curry with noodles; US$4), puerco asado agridulce con piña (sweet and sour pork with pineapple; US$5) and an entire pato al estilo Pekin (US$32). While certainly not as fancy as Madame Chang, Lung Fung or Nobu, Furama is definitely No 1 in value. It's open 11 am to 11:30 pm daily.

When in Barrio Chino (Chinatown), do what the Chinese do: Eat at *Panificadora y Dulceria Reina,* on Calle H about a half-block west of Avenida Central. This is the best restaurant in the area, and very cheap. Dim sum is served all day; regardless of the contents, each tray of four items costs just US$1. A standard plate – sweet and sour pork, stir-fried chicken, etc – typically costs US$4.50 for a huge serving. This place is also known for its delicious sweetbreads. Hours are 6:30 am to 5:30 pm daily.

At all teppan-style Japanese restaurants, including *Ginza Teppanyaki,* on Calle D at Calle Eusebio A Morales, a chef prepares your food on a scalding skillet directly in front of you. These places always tend to be expensive, and this one is no exception: the special dinner combination, which includes fish, prawns, chicken, steak, vegetables and rice, costs US$22. Most items, such as squid (US$6) and scallops (US$8), are cheaper, but you wouldn't order only one. Ginza Teppanyaki's hours are noon to 3 pm and 6 to 10:30 pm daily.

Across the street from Ginza Teppanyaki is *Restaurante Matsuei,* which is known for its sukiyaki (US$12) and tempura (US$13 for a filling combination plate), and for its long sushi bar, Panama's finest. Sushi here ranges from US$15 for eight local pieces plus four rolls to US$30 for a seven-piece, four-roll combination with fish imported from Miami. Matsuei is open from noon to 11:30 pm Monday to Saturday and 6 to 11:30 pm Sunday.

Modern and stylish without being fancy, *Sushi Itto,* on Avenida 2 Sur just east of Calle 54 Este, offers traditional sushi and some combinations you'd never find in Japan (such as a maki roll with chicken inside). The combination plates are the best deals here, with an eight-piece plate going for US$9 and a 13-piece plate going for US$13.50. Some of the fish is purchased locally, but most comes from the USA and Chile. Hours are noon to 10 pm weekdays and 12:30 pm to midnight weekends.

Mediterranean

Established in 1963 and generally regarded as one of the country's top restaurants, *Trattoria D'America* is on Calle 57 Este just south of Avenida 1 Sur. The specialty of the house is raviolis verdes rellenos de salmón ahumado con salsa de puré (green raviolis stuffed with smoked salmon, covered with a heavy sauce of tomato and cream; US$13.75). The capellini importados a la marichelle (imported capellini with cream, tomato and prosciutto; US$13) is also excellent. Some people say the sopa de pata (hoof soup; US$5) is the best in Panama. It's open noon to 10 pm Tuesday to Sunday.

The same award-winning food that's available at Trattoria D'America for big money can be had for a fraction of the cost at the restaurant's takeout kiosk around the corner, on Avenida 1 Sur near Calle 56 Este. The restaurant and takeout stand share a kitchen, and the same fuss is given to the bagged goods as is given to the servings placed on elegant plates. And you don't even need to get dressed up to visit the trattoria's kiosk. What a deal!

Not quite up to Trattoria D'America standards but very good, *Tre Scalini,* on Calle 49 A Este just north of Avenida 4 Sur, is most noted for its pasta primavera especial (eggplant in white wine sauce, served with spaghetti or fettuccine; US$8.75), filete Tre Scalini (filet of beef in red wine, onions, peppers and mushrooms; US$12.75) and spaguettini o fetuccini a la pepperonccino con langostinos o langosta (spaghetti or fettuccine prepared with peppers and butter, with jumbo shrimp or lobster; US$15). This casual-to-dressy business is open noon to 3 pm and 6 to 11 pm daily.

La Caleta, on Calle 68 Este near Avenida 3 Sur, specializes in 'new Italian' cuisine. Favorites include ravioli rellenos de calabaze (ravioli stuffed with pumpkin; US$9), filete de res al vino Chianti y hongos (filet of beef with Chianti and mushroom sauce; US$12), filete de puerco al romero (pork filet with rosemary and garlic; US$12) and spaguettini al cenollo (spaghetti with tropical crab; US$15). The tiramisu and the panna cotta (both US$4) are divine. Hours are noon to 2:30 pm and 6:30 to 10:30 pm Tuesday to Sunday.

Much less expensive and extremely popular is *Caffé Pomodoro,* at Calle 49 B Oeste and Avenida 2 A Norte. There's seating inside and outside in this casual but classy restaurant. The antipasti run from US$2 for grilled Italian bread topped with fresh tomato and basil up to US$9 for smoked salmon. The main course consists of a noodle and sauce selection, with no combination over US$9 (and most nearly half that). There's a takeout service next door. Remember this place for breakfasts, too: yogurt with fruit (US$2.75), pancakes (US$3) or a plate of fresh fruit (US$4). It's open 7 am to midnight daily.

A very popular restaurant with a varied menu and a specialty in pasta is *Cafeteria Manolo,* on the corner of Calle 49 B Oeste and Calle D. Gut-busting dinners here will run you about US$7. If you don't want to spend that much, there are 25 sandwiches to choose among, none over US$4. Break-

fasts run about US$3.50. Manolo features a full bar and indoor and outdoor seating. Hours are 6 am to 1 am daily.

Panama's oldest pizzeria, *Restaurante y Pizzeria Napoli No 1,* on Calle Estudiante at Lado del Instituto Nacional, just south of Avenida de los Mártires, serves tasty and cheap pizzas fast. A 10-inch combo costs only US$3 and a 15-incher only US$7.50; most small pizzas cost less than US$3, and most large ones about US$6.50. Its clam pizza (US$3.50/7.50 small/large) is quite popular. Also popular are the pastas, particularly the raviolis (US$2.50 to US$4) and the fettuccines (US$2.50 to US$5). The same man who opened this Napoli in 1962 has opened several others around town (there's another on Calle 56 Este south of Avenida 1 Sur); more are planned. Hours are 11 am to 11 pm daily except Tuesday.

Restaurante y Pizzeria Sorrento, on Calle Ricardo Arias near Avenida 3 Sur, is known throughout the city for serving a large plate of clams in a delicious tomato or garlic sauce for only US$3. Its lasagna cardinale (US$3.50) and fettuccine carbonara (US$4) are also divine. Its pizzas are cooked in a wood-burning oven and are greaseless, except for the ones with pepperoni or sausage. Still going strong since it opened in 1968, Sorrento charges US$2.50 to US$5 for its 10-inch pizzas. This is an excellent find. Hours are 11:30 am to 11:30 pm Tuesday to Saturday; closed Monday.

Restaurante Firenze, at Avenida 4 C Sur and Calle 79 Este, offers 20 pasta, seafood and meat dishes, but it's best known for its pizzas, which range from US$2.75 for a small cheese to US$13 for a large with the works. Pasta dishes go for US$6.50 to US$9.59, meat US$5 to US$12 and seafood US$8.50 to US$17.50. There's indoor and outdoor seating at the popular, very casual diner.

One of the best values in town is *Niko's Cafe.* The original Niko's opened years ago, the dream of a Greek immigrant who initially sold food from a cart, then from a stand and then at the Niko's Cafe No 1 on Calle 51 Este near Vía España. Today there are four Niko's, each owned and managed by a son. The three newer ones are very 'in' these days, and all offer burgers (US$1), breakfasts (US$2), excellent gyros (US$3), pasta (from US$1.25 to US$3.50) and filet mignon (US$3.50). OK, so the food's not very Greek. But it sure is a bargain. And all four restaurants are open 24 hours a day.

Athen's, on the corner of Calle Uruguay and Avenida 4 Sur, serves excellent Greek food and pizza, including a delicious roast-beef pizza. Prices are very reasonable, and there are tables inside (where there's air-con) or outside on the covered verandah. It's open 11 am to 10 pm daily except Tuesday. There's a second Athen's on Calle 56 Este.

Mexican

Very popular due to its location, its party atmosphere and its nightly live music is *Restaurante Mexico Lindo,* on Avenida Balboa at Calle Uruguay, specializing in 18th-century Mexican cuisine. Its best dishes are the fajitas de filete de res con queso gratinado (fajitas with a filet of beef smothered in cheese, served with refried beans, guacamole and tortillas; US$10.50), el filete Mexico Lindo (beef medallions covered in a mild red salsa; US$10) and el pollo en mole poblano (boned chicken bathed in mole sauce, served with rice and beans; US$8.50). Hours are 5 pm to whenever, Monday to Saturday.

The very casual and low-priced *La Mexicanita* has two locations: on Avenida 4 Sur near Calle Uruguay and on Calle 53 Este close to Calle Anastacio Ruíz Noriega. Typical and tasty items on the long menu include an order of three tacos of your choice (from US$2.75 to US$3), a burrito especial (US$3.60) and an enchilada con salsa roja (US$4.85).

British

El Pavo Real, on Avenida 3 B Sur near Calle Ricardo Arias, attracts yuppies on the prowl for business and social partners. It also attracts quite a few *gringos* who read about the place in John le Carré's thriller *The Tailor of Panama.* (The British Foreign Service employee turned best-selling novelist spent a lot of time here while he was conducting research for his book. The pub/restaurant's owner, Sarah Simpson, is also an ex-BFS employee. Coincidence?) The food here is delicious and filling. The offerings include a burger with fries (US$3.50), chicken breast sandwich served on a French roll (US$4.75) and fish 'n' chips (US$6.50). Popular local rock bands play here most Wednesday, Thursday and weekend nights after 9:30 pm; there's never a cover charge. There are dart boards and pool tables to boot. It's open from noon to midnight daily except Sunday.

Indian

At *Calcutta,* on Avenida Federico Boyd near Vía España, the food is authentic and the decor is tasteful, but the prices are rather steep. Curries, for example, range from US$5 up to US$13, and the side dishes are extra. But Calcutta's specialties (curries and vegetarian dishes from northern India) are cooked as they should be – in the traditional rounded clay oven known as the tandoor – and you can taste the difference. Expect to pay US$20 to US$25 per person with beverage. Calcutta is open for lunch and dinner daily except Monday.

Vegetarian

Restaurante Vegetariano Mireya, at Calle Ricardo Arias and Avenida 3 Sur, is a budget traveler's delight, with scarcely any item over US$1.25. Typical offerings at this very low-key establishment include eggplant with vegetables (US$1.25), a soy burger (US$1.25), cauliflower and potatoes (US$1.25), yogurt (75¢) and many juices to choose among (US$1). Hours are 6 am to 8 pm daily except Sunday.

International

Mangos, on Calle Uruguay one block north of Avenida Balboa, is very popular with the 'in' crowd for its food and as a meat market for the city's young, rich and beautiful. While the crowd is often dressed for success, the decor is informal and cozy. Large works of illuminated stained glass, many tables angled for visibility and yet allowing privacy, and a long, handsome bar create an intimate setting even when the place is packed. And there's not a weakness on the menu. Among my favorites are the house burger (US$4.25), the Greek salad (US$5.50) and the fettuccine carbonara (US$6.75). It's open daily from noon until the last customer decides to leave. Live bands play on Thursday, Friday and Saturday nights (US$5 cover).

The semiformal *Le Bistrot,* on Calle 53 Este near Calle Anastacio Ruíz Noriega, is well known for its appetizer of calamar relleno de cangrejo (squid stuffed with crabmeat and cooked in its own ink), which goes for US$12 for a half order and US$4 more for a full order. Other specialties include callos con garbanzos (tripe with chickpeas; US$10.50) and langostinos Le Bistrot (jumbo shrimp and crabmeat covered in mushroom sauce; US$18). It's open 11:30 am to 11:30 pm daily.

Classy and semiformal *Millennium,* on Avenida 5 B Sur just east of Calle Uruguay, bills itself as specializing in 'world and new American cuisines.' I'm not exactly sure what that means, but the food here is delicious and interesting although a bit overpriced. Some examples: pave de corvina al horno (oven-baked corvina pavé served over bok choy sautéed in cilantro oil; US$12), chuleta de cerdo a la parrilla (grilled pork chop served over sweet and sour cabbage with gorgonzola and cheddar polenta and shiitake sherry reduction sauce; US$14) and filete de salmon asado (baked salmon filet with horseradish aioli and yellow pepper sauce; US$15). There's jazz here on Wednesday night, and there's a lovely piano bar as well. Millennium is open noon to 3 pm and 7 to 11 pm weekdays and 7 to 11 pm Saturday; it's closed Sunday.

La Cascada, on the corner of Avenida Balboa and Calle 25 Este, is a good place for a pleasant evening out. It has a large garden dining patio and a bilingual menu with many choices. The meals are gigantic and very reasonably priced; for US$5.25 you can get an excellent steak or corvina, or try the giant seafood platter (US$9.25). It's open 3 to 11 pm Monday to Saturday.

Ice Cream
The best ice cream in town is sold at *Il Gelatiere,* on Avenida Belisario Porras at Avenida 3 L Sur, a six-block walk from the Hotel Caesar Park. As you may have guessed, Il Gelatiere specializes in Italian ice cream. This cheerful little restaurant also offers tasty but cheap pizzas, a dozen sandwiches, delicious cookies and many desserts. Its hours are from 11 am to 11 pm Monday to Thursday and from 11 am to midnight Friday and Saturday; it's closed Sunday.

ENTERTAINMENT
Panama City has *mucho* to offer in this area, especially to party animals. The club scene ignites about 11 pm and its embers are still glowing at sunrise. The cinemas throughout town show the latest Hollywood releases, always in English, with or without Spanish subtitles. If you like to gamble, I'll bet you'll be glad to know that there's no shortage of casinos in town. And there's a sleazy element as well.

For information about cultural events in the capital city, check *Talingo,* a supplement that appears in the newspaper *La Prensa* every Sunday and lists happenings for the coming week.

Clubs
Rock Ladies born to be wild, *Mezzanotte* has tables for you – tables made of steel, bolted to the floor. Every weekend night, usually around midnight, the otherwise refined women patrons of this 2nd-floor club, on Calle 51 Este at Avenida 3 Sur, kick off their inhibitions and dance on the tables. Yes, this place exists for the wild at heart, and they for it. Admission is free on Tuesday and costs US$5 or more other nights. Women drink for free on Thursday, and they get in free on Saturday.

The hottest dance club in town is *Bacchus,* on Calle 49 A Este south of Vía España. Decorated in an elaborate Roman theme, this place has state-of-the-art sound

PANAMA CITY

and light systems, a big-screen TV and strategically placed monitors for rock videos, occasional live bands and the requisite liquid-smoke machine. All that's missing is Travolta. It's very, very popular. Cover charge is typically US$10; the club is closed Monday.

Also up there in popularity is the long-time favorite *Sahara,* on Avenida 4 Sur near Calle Aquilino de la Guardia. Just how wild is this place? Often there's a rock band and a reggae band playing at the same time, less than 50m apart. The club has two huge bars, lots of little tables, a dance floor and pool tables. It's open nightly, but bands play only on Thursday, Friday and Saturday, starting around midnight. Women never pay a cover charge, but the lesser sex usually pays US$5 and sometimes has to ante up US$10. Across the street, *Tabou* is also a hopping place, for straights and gays.

What do you get when you mix together lots of tequila, live rock 'n' roll and a roomful of Tom Petty fans? You get *Restaurante Mexico Lindo,* at the corner of Avenida Balboa and Calle Uruguay, at 2 am on a Saturday or Sunday. Those are the firefightin' nights, although there's music every night except Sunday. Bring your party sombrero. There's an occasional cover charge.

'Meat market' accurately describes *TGI Friday's,* on Calle Aquilino de la Guardia at Avenida 4 A Sur, just around midnight on its namesake night. This slice of the USA dropped into Panama comes complete with rock music, generally of the canned variety. There's no cover.

A mango is a tropical fruit with a smooth rind and sweet, juicy, yellow-orange flesh. *Mangos* is a beautiful-people restaurant by day and a heavy-duty rock scene with live bands on Thursday, Friday and Saturday nights. It's on Calle Uruguay, one block from Restaurante Mexico Lindo. (If you're standing in the bay, you really meant to go one block the *other* way.)

Without the same level of zaniness of some of the above clubs, but also never charging an entrance fee, is *El Pavo Real,* on Avenida 3 B Sur. Home to strong rock 'n' roll bands on Friday and Saturday nights, the Peacock (its English name) is very popular with locals and visitors alike. It's an easy place to meet people because its two pool tables lend themselves nicely to newcomers asking to join in. I've shot many a game and made many a friend here. It's open until midnight every night but Sunday.

At all the aforementioned places, you can enter with a receding hairline or support stockings and not feel out of place. But *Rock Café,* on the corner of Calles 53 Este and Anastacio Ruíz Noriega, isn't that kind of place. You practically have to be under 25 to get in, and once you're inside it's wall-to-wall youth, very dark and best enjoyed by people who love secondhand smoke. The music's live most nights. The cover is usually US$10.

The same crowd that patronizes Rock Café also frequents *Patatús,* up the block on Calle 50. The US$15 cover on Thursday, Friday and Saturday nights covers your bar bill as well as your entrance fee, but the hard stuff is limited to vodka, seco and rum. This place resembles bad Mexican art, but in a good way: lots of black lights, Day-Glo paints, neon and a wall of video monitors. The place is quite popular, but I find it boring. Too old, I guess.

If you're going nightclubbing, remember to bring an ID with you, as you will likely be asked for one.

Jazz *Restaurante Las Bóvedas,* on Plaza de Francia in Casco Viejo, is a lovely place to listen to live jazz. The bands set up at one end of this former dungeon with 4m thick brick walls, and play to a fairly small audience tucked into intimate cushioned niches along the walls. The acoustics are superb, and the atmosphere is something special. Jazz is offered on Friday and Saturday nights only, from 9 pm to 1 am. There's never a cover charge. Las Bóvedas is known for its caipirinhas, Brazilian drinks made from cachaça, lemon juice, sugar and ice.

Within the classy restaurant *Millennium,* on Avenida 5 B Sur slightly east of Calle

Uruguay, is a lovely piano bar that features jazz every Wednesday night and piano accompanied by a singer on Friday night. The bar, open to nondiners, does not have a cover charge. Appetizers are served in the bar, such as a popular ripe plantain shrimpcake (US$6) and duck salad (US$8.50).

Yet another elegant place to hear jazz is the lobby-level *Mi Rincón* lounge of the Hotel Caesar Park, on Calle 77 Este one block from the bay. Jazz is featured every Wednesday night with the Jimmy Maxwell Quartet. There's no cover, and talented guests are welcome to join the band.

Salsa & Merengue The elegant French *Restaurante Casco Viejo,* on the corner of Calle 53 Este and Calle 50, has a very popular bar that features live music, usually salsa or merengue, every Friday night. The cover charge is typically US$10 but can be more.

Cuban Five nights a week at the *Hotel Plaza Paitilla Inn,* on Vía Italia at Avenida Churchill, a group of talented Cuban musicians and dancers performs. The singing and dancing is thrilling. The price of the show is US$12 Tuesday, Wednesday and Thursday, and US$15 Friday and Saturday.

Folk/Traditional Music Panamanian folkloric music, or típico, in which the accordion dominates, can be heard at *Magnum Eventos,* behind the Farmacia Arrocha on Vía Brasil near Vía España, and *Cosita Buena,* on Avenida Fernández de Córdoba near the Sears store and Vía Transístmica.

The *Restaurante-Bar Tinajas,* on Avenida 3 A Sur near Avenida Federico Boyd, presents Panamanian folkloric dancing at 9 pm on Tuesday, Thursday, Friday and Saturday nights. There's a US$5 charge. Most guests have dinner during the show; meals run about US$15 per person. These shows are very popular. Reservations are recommended.

The *Hotel Plaza Paitilla Inn* (see above) presents a folkloric show every Wednesday night that's quite popular. The US$15 charge includes a buffet dinner.

Gay & Lesbian As mentioned in the Gay & Lesbian Travelers section of the Facts for the Visitor chapter, gay clubs aren't easy to find. They're never advertised, their façades are never suggestive and even their names aren't always posted, so eager are the establishments' owners to avoid problems with gay-bashers and other intolerant people.

That said, the country's largest and wildest gay dance club, *Boy Bar,* is in Panama City next to an ice factory on an unnamed street in an industrial area north of downtown. There is no sign in front of the club, which occupies a former autopainting shop and looks like every other structure in the neighborhood, but its entire façade is painted black. There's no cover charge on Thursday, when all drinks are US$1.25 apiece. On Friday and Saturday you pay US$7 at the door and drinks are free. On Sunday there's no cover and all drinks are US$1 each. The music is mostly recorded. There's a show with live music monthly, usually for charity; the date varies. Call ☎ 230-3128 for further details (English-speakers should ask to speak with Minerva, Spanish-speakers with Irving). Boy Bar, open 10 pm to 7 am Thursday to Sunday, is best reached by taxi; drivers know the place as El Garage.

A little closer to downtown is another popular dance club, *El Hidalgo,* on Avenida Belisario Porras near the ice-cream store Il Gelatiere. Known to taxi drivers as Pasos (its name for many years), El Hidalgo is very popular late on weekend nights, when it usually features a male strip show (and a US$10 cover charge). But unlike Boy Bar, there's never live music here.

In the downtown area is *La Faraona,* on Calle 43 Este near Avenida Balboa. With its many cozy tables, a pool table in the back and a close-knit clientele, this gay and lesbian bar has the warm feel of a neighborhood pub where everyone knows everyone. It opens at 5:30 pm daily and closes when the last customer wanders out, usually just before sunrise.

Most of Panama City's gay and lesbian clubs, however, are in the Casco Viejo district. Typically the clubs consist of one long, narrow room with a dozen or so couples' tables scattered about, a bar to one side and a jukebox in the back. What they lack in decor they make up for in atmosphere.

Among the most popular of the Casco Viejo bunch are *Boite La Cosmopolita,* at Calles C and 13 Oeste; *Salon Madrid,* on Calle 12 Oeste between Calles B and C; and *Bar Tropical,* on Calle B near Calle 12 Oeste. There are a good many others in the area.

Cinemas

There's no shortage of movie theaters in town; many are on the main boulevard, Vía España. Check the yellow pages under *Cines* for a list of cinemas, with addresses. Check the daily entertainment pages of *La Prensa* for listings and show times.

Casinos

None of the casinos are on the verge of stealing business away from the cavernous entertainment centers/megacasinos of Las Vegas, but there are three attractive and popular houses of chance in the capital city and three others that simply serve their purpose. All are located inside top hotels.

The three most attractive casinos can be found in the *Hotel Caesar Park,* the *Miramar Inter-Continental* and the *Hotel El Panamá.* The three others are in the *Hotel Plaza Paitilla Inn,* the *Gran Hotel Soloy* and the *Hotel Riande Granada.* See the Places to Stay section for telephone numbers and addresses.

Theater

Performances by the experimental theater troupe Oveja Negra (Black Sheep) are periodically held at the *Alianza Francesa Panameña* (☎ 223-5792), on Avenida 4 Sur at Avenida Federico Boyd. Check *Talingo* for upcoming performances.

Productions are also held at other venues, including the following:

Teatro Anayansi, in the Centro Atlapa
 (☎ 226-7000)

Teatro Balboa, across from the Avenida Balboa
 post office (☎ 272-0372)
Teatro En Circulo, Avenida 6 C Norte near Vía
 Transístmica in El Carmen neighborhood
 (☎ 261-5375)
Teatro La Cúpula, Calle F near Vía España in
 El Cangrejo district (☎ 233-7516)
Teatro La Huaca, in the Centro Atlapa
 (☎ 267-4313)
Teatro Nacional, Avenida B at Calle 3 in Casco
 Viejo (☎ 262-3582)

Strip Clubs & Brothels

Prostitution in Panama is legal and, despite the moral issues and sexual diseases at play, business is booming on the isthmus. If you're a young man far from home, you may be tempted to enter one of these places. The information given here is intended only to inform, not to promote.

In Panama City there are two kinds of sex parlors, both geared for men but not closed to women: There are fancy strip clubs, and there are rooms-in-the-back brothels; there's no shortage of either type. The strip parlors have fancy names: *Josephine's Gold, Elite, Le Palace* and so on. There are many of them. They open in the evening on most days, and they close around 4 am. There's never a cover charge, but what they don't get out of you at the door they'll get out of you in drinks; a beer usually costs US$3, and well drinks US$4 and up.

These places are swarming with young women in lingerie, and about every 30 minutes one of them appears on stage and removes her clothes, usually to French music. All the women are available for lap dances (usually US$15 per dance), and all are available for 'servicing,' as they call it here; typically, you pay the establishment US$50 and negotiate a price with the woman. The servicing that's provided by these women is expected to take place at a hotel.

The brothels – *La Gruta Azul, La Gloria, Club Fenix, Club Costa Brava* – follow the same basic design: a large room, well-stocked bar, lots of little tables and dim lighting. Some have strip stages. Most have a half-dozen rooms in the back;

the price charged varies with the services that the women perform.

Regardless of the club, these women are justly terrified of AIDS and insist on using condoms. If you're considering a visit to any of these places, I strongly advise you to read the Sexually Transmitted Diseases section in the Facts for the Visitor chapter first.

SHOPPING

Most anything that you can buy in other modern capital cities you can find in Panama City. This is so because many of the stores in Colón's Zona Libre have outlets in the capital. Often these outlets can arrange to have an item from a Colón store – a particular Rolex watch or Nikon camera, for example – sent from Colón to Tocumen airport, where you can pick it up just prior to leaving the country; you can avoid the sales tax by doing business this way.

Because of their proximity to mineral-rich Colombia and Brazil, the jewelry stores here often have high-quality gems at excellent prices. Beware: There are many fake gems on the world market, as well as many flawed gems that have been altered to appear more valuable than they really are. The only jewelry store here with which I have done business is the very reputable Joyeria La Huaca, in front of the Hotel Continental at Calle Ricardo Arias and Vía España. A high-quality sapphire ring made for me there cost one-third less than I would have paid for it in Los Angeles or New York.

The most authentically Panamanian items to take home are described below. The handicrafts mentioned here can often be found at the Mercado de Buhonerías y Artesanías, behind the Reina Torres de Araúz anthropological museum; at Mi Pueblito, a life-size replica of a rural village at the foot of Cerro

The National Hat

The classic woven-straw hat that many people associate with Panama was made internationally famous in the late 19th century by Ferdinand de Lesseps, builder of the Suez Canal and the brains behind the failed French attempt to build a canal in Panama.

The much-photographed Lesseps was balding when he arrived in Panama, and he found that the light but durable hat provided excellent protection against the sun. Most newspaper photographs taken of him here showed the larger-than-life figure looking even more worldly in his exotic headgear. Soon men around the globe began placing orders for the 'Panama hat.'

Oddly, most Panama hats are made in Ecuador, just as they always have been. Some hats of this style are made in Panama, however, and the best-quality ones can be found in the towns of Ocú (Herrera Province) and Penonomé (Coclé Province). The Ocú hats are always white; the hats from everywhere else are black-and-white. The finest Panama hats are so tightly woven that they can hold water.

A man and his hat: Ferdinand de Lesseps and the headgear he made famous

The best places to buy these hats in Panama City are the Flory Salzman Shop, on Vía Venetto near the Hotel El Panamá, and at stores inside that hotel and the Hotel Caesar Park. ■

Ancón near the intersection of Avenida de los Mártires and Calle Jeronimo de la Ossa; and at the Mercado Nacional de Artesanías, beside the ruins of Panamá La Vieja.

Additionally, Colecciones, the well-priced, high-quality crafts and furniture store facing the Hotel Plaza Paitilla Inn on Vía Italia, often has tagua carvings and baskets made by the Emberá and Wounaan peoples. The store's owner, Irene De Vengoechea, also stocks top-quality ceramics and beautifully painted serving trays from Mexico, hammocks from Colombia, Filipino handicrafts of a quality one rarely sees, and a whole lot more.

Huacas

It's possible to purchase high-quality replicas of *huacas* – golden objects made on the isthmus centuries before the Spanish conquest and placed with Indians at the time of burial. The Indians believed in an afterlife, and the huacas were intended to accompany and protect their souls on the voyage to the other world.

The huacas were mainly items of adornment, the most fascinating being three-dimensional figure pendants. Most took the form of a warrior, crocodile, jaguar, frog or condor. Little else is known about the exact purpose of these golden figures, but probably each held mystical, spiritual or religious meaning.

You can purchase exact (solid gold) and near-exact (gold-plated) reproductions of these palm-size objects. They are available at reasonable cost at Reprosa (☎ 269-0457), at Avenida 2 Sur and Calle 54 Este. If you're looking for something special to bring back for a loved one, this is the place to come.

Baskets

The Wounaan and Emberá in Darién Province produce some beautiful woven baskets, most of which are exported to the USA and Europe, although many can be found in Panama. The Guaymís in Chiriquí and Veraguas Provinces also produce baskets, but they are of an inferior quality and in little demand.

The baskets of the Wounaan and Emberá are of two types: the utilitarian and the decorative. The utilitarian baskets are made primarily from the chunga palm but can contain bits of other plants, vines, bark and leaves. They are usually woven, using various plaiting techniques, from single plant strips of coarse texture and great strength. They are rarely dyed. These baskets are often used for carrying seeds or harvesting crops.

The decorative baskets are much more refined, usually feature many different colors and are created from palm materials of the nahuala bush and the chunga tree. The dyes are 100% natural and are extracted from fruits, leaves, roots and bark. Typical motifs are of butterflies, frogs, toucans, trees and parrots. The baskets are similar in quality to the renowned early 20th-century Chemehuevi Indian baskets of California.

You can buy baskets at Colecciones (see above).

Wood & Tagua Carvings

In addition to producing fine baskets, the Wounaan and Emberá also carve animal figures from the wood of the cocobolo tree and the ivory-colored tagua nut (variously known as the palm seed, ivory nut and vegetable ivory). The figures made from the tropical hardwood are often near-life-size; popular subjects are boas, toucans and parrots. From the egg-size tagua nut come miniature iguanas, crocodiles and birds.

The quality of both the cocobolo and tagua carvings can be very fine. A superior cocobolo boa, for example, is a meter or more in length, with its back polished shiny-smooth and its underside a field of perfectly carved scales. Its eyes and mouth are delicately formed and its head perfectly proportioned. The highly honed skills of a true craftsperson are readily apparent in the finest of these carvings.

A high-quality tagua carving is also finely carved, well proportioned and realistic, if miniature. While the natural color of cocobolo figures is left unchanged, the tagua nut – after it is carved with hand tools and polished with fine abrasives – is beautifully painted with vibrant colors, using India inks and natural plant extracts.

The best place to shop for tagua carvings is Galería Bernheim, in the Tronlap Building on Avenida 4 Sur near Calle Aquilino de la Guardia. Cocobolo carvings can be found at Gran Morrison department stores; there's one on Vía España near Calle 51 Este and another in the Plaza Paitilla shopping center.

Molas

A popular handicraft souvenir from Panama is the *mola,* a colorful, intricate, multi-layered appliqué textile sewn by Kuna women. Small, simple souvenir molas are widely available in Panama City and can be bought for as little as US$5, but the best ones are sold on the San Blás islands and can fetch several hundred dollars.

The Flory Salzman Shop, on Vía Venetto near the Hotel El Panamá, has a large selection and perhaps the best quality you'll find outside the islands. Molas are also on sale in stores inside the Hotel El Panamá, the Hotel Caesar Park and other grand hotels. Gran Morrison stores also stock molas (see locales under Wood & Tagua Carvings, above).

Artworks

The works of some of Panama's best contemporary painters and sculptors can be viewed and purchased at a number of galleries around the city. Try Galería y Enmarcado Habitante, on Calle Uruguay; Mvsevm, on Vía Italia near the Hotel Plaza Paitilla Inn; Galería Bernheim (see Wood & Tagua Carvings, above); Legacy Fine Art, in the Centro Comercial Balboa on Avenida Balboa near Calle Aquilino de la Guardia; and Galería Arteconsult, on Avenida 2 Sur between Calles 55 Este and 56 Este, near the Reprosa jewelry store.

GETTING THERE & AWAY
Air

International flights arrive at and depart from Tocumen International Airport, 35km northeast of the city center. See the Getting There & Away chapter for more information about the airport and services to Panama.

International airlines serving Panama City from the USA include the following:

Airline	In Panama
American Airlines	☎ 269-6022
Aviateca	☎ 223-2991/2992/2994
Continental Airlines	☎ 263-9177
COPA	☎ 227-5000/5232
EVA Airways	☎ 263-7731
Lacsa	☎ 265-7814
Mexicana	☎ 264-9855
TACA	☎ 269-6066

Delta Air Lines and United Airlines also offer service from the USA. Airlines serving Panama City from Europe include Iberia from Spain and LTU International Airways charters from Germany. Numerous Central and South American airlines serve the city from Latin America and the Caribbean; see the Getting There & Away chapter for details.

Several airlines provide service between Panama City and other parts of the country. See the Getting Around chapter for details. Domestic flights and charter services arrive at and depart from Aeropuerto Paitilla, in the city. At the time this book went to press, there were plans to relocate the airport to the site of the former Albrook Air Force Station. It is quite possible that a new domestic airport will be open by early or mid-1999.

Bus

Buses to most other parts of the country arrive at and depart from the Terminal de Buses al Interior, on Avenida Ascaño Villalaz in the Curundu district. Below is a listing of most of the major bus routes and schedules. Fares cited are one-way; a roundtrip ticket costs double.

Aguadulce – 185km, 4½ hours, US$6.50; every 1½ hours, 6 am to 6 pm
Antón – 126km, two hours, US$3; every 25 minutes, 6 am to 6 pm
Cañita – 80km, 2½ hours, US$2.50; every 40 minutes, 8:30 am to 5:10 pm

Chame – 77km, 1½ hours, US$2; every 30 minutes, 5 am to 9 pm

Chepo – 52km, 75 minutes, US$1.20; take the Cañita bus, departing every 40 minutes, from 8:30 am to 5:10 pm

Chitré – 241km, four hours, US$6; hourly, 6 am to 11 pm

David – 438km; regular bus every 45 minutes, 7 to 11:30 am; then every 1¼ hours until 8 pm (6½ to seven hours, US$11); express bus departs at midnight (5½ to six hours, US$15)

El Copé – 188km, 4½ hours, US$5; every 1½ hours, 6 am to 5 pm

El Valle – 123km, 2½ hours, US$3.50; hourly, 7 am to 6 pm

Las Aguas Frías – 160km, three hours, US$4.75; every 30 minutes, 5 am to 8:30 pm

Las Minas – 126km, five hours, US$6.50; take the Ocú bus, departing every 1½ hours, 7 am to 4:30 pm

Las Tablas – 282km, 4½ hours, US$6.50; every 1½ hours, 6 am to 6 pm

Macaracas – 244km, five hours, US$7; every two hours, 8:30 am to 2:30 pm

Ocú – 228km, five hours, US$6; every 1½ hours, 7 am to 4:30 pm

Penonomé – 144km, 2½ hours, US$3.75; every 20 minutes, 4:50 am to 9 pm

Pesé – 272km, four hours, US$6; every two hours, 9:30 am to 3:30 pm

San Carlos – 92km, 1½ hours, US$2.75; every 20 minutes, 6:30 am to 7 pm

Santiago – 250km, four hours, US$6; at 1, 3 and 4 am; then half-hourly to 7 pm; then at 8, 9 and 11 pm and midnight

Soná – 288km, 4½ hours, US$7; every two hours, 6 am to 4 pm

Villa de Los Santos – 245km, four hours, US$6; take the Chitré bus, departing hourly, 6 am to 11 pm

Yaviza – 266km, 10 hours, US$14; hourly, 5 to 10 am

To get more information about routes and schedules, it's best to go to the terminal and talk with drivers or station personnel.

Buses to the Canal Area (Miraflores and Pedro Miguel Locks, Paraíso, Gamboa and other locales), Tocumen International Airport, Panamá La Vieja and the Balboa and Ancón areas depart from the bus stop at Plaza Cinco de Mayo on Avenida Central. A ride usually costs no more than US$2.

Bus service from Panama City to other locales includes the following:

Colón – 76km, 1¾ hours; regular bus service departs from Calle P (opposite Calle 26 Este) at the corner of Avenida Central every 20 minutes from around 5 am to 9 pm; the last bus departs at 1 am. Express buses, which depart on the same schedule from a stop on Avenida Perú between Calles 29 Este and 30 Este, are air-conditioned and cost a bit more but don't get there much faster.

Costa Rica – Panaline (☎ 262-1618) and Tica Bus (☎ 262-2084/6275) both offer direct bus services between Panama City and San José, Costa Rica. See the Land section in the Getting There & Away chapter for details.

Train

The historic train that used to take the famously scenic route alongside the Panama Canal and through the canal's lush watershed from Panama City to Colón was allowed to fall into disrepair during the 1980s, and it has yet to be repaired. To learn its current status, check with IPAT (see Information) or, better yet, any of the local tour operators mentioned in the Organized Tours section.

Boat

Passenger ferries between Panama City and Isla Taboga depart from Muelle (Pier) 18 in the Balboa district, west of downtown. Tour boats go along the Panama Canal. See the Panamá Province chapter for details.

Cargo boats to Colombia depart from the docks near Casco Viejo. See Dangers & Annoyances in the Facts for the Visitor chapter for a warning about cargo boats plying between Panama and Colombia.

GETTING AROUND
To/From the Airport

Tocumen International Airport is 35km northeast of the city center. Buses to Tocumen depart every 15 minutes from the bus stop on Plaza Cinco de Mayo; they cost 50¢ and take an hour to reach the airport. A taxi ride from downtown to the airport costs US$20.

When you arrive at Tocumen from abroad, look for the *'Transportes Turísticos'* desk at the airport exit. Beside it is a taxi stand, with posted prices. Taxi drivers will assail you, offering rides into town for US$20, but the staff at the desk will inform you that you can take a *colectivo,* or shuttle van, for US$8 per person (for three or more passengers) or US$12 per person (for two passengers). For two or more people traveling together, a taxi can be cheaper.

Aeropuerto Paitilla, in the city, handles domestic flights. City bus No 2, which runs along Avenida Balboa, stops there; the very slow ride costs 15¢. A taxi is a better option.

Bus

Panama City has a good network of local buses, which run from 5 am to 10 pm daily and charge just 15¢ a ride. However, they are always crowded and take forever to get from one side of the city to the other due to frequent stops. A taxi, for a little more money, is the only sensible way to get around town if you value your time and don't have your own wheels.

Car & Motorcycle

For details on renting a car or truck in Panama, see the Car & Motorcycle section of the Getting Around chapter. Rental-car companies in Panama City include the following (airport numbers listed are at Tocumen International Airport):

Avis	☎ 264-0722; airport 238-40567
Barriga	☎ 269-0221; airport 238-4495
Budget	☎ 263-8777; airport 238-4069
Central	airport ☎ 230-0447
Dollar	☎ 269-7542; airport 238-4032
Hertz	☎ 264-1111; airport 238-4081
International	☎ 264-4540; airport 238-4404
National	☎ 264-8277; airport 238-4144
Thrifty	☎ 264-2613; airport 238-4955
Toyota	☎ 223-6085
Vantage	☎ 226-8122; airport 238-4500

As always, it pays to shop around to compare rates and special promotions. At the time of writing, rates ranged from US$30 to US$45 per day for the most economical

cars, with insurance and unlimited mileage *(kilometraje)* included.

It is also possible to rent vehicles from rental counters at several of the city's top hotels. Contact the Hotel Caesar Park or the Hotel El Panamá (see Places to Stay).

Motos Minsk (☎ 213-0618), at Vía Brasil, Final No 53, rents 125cc motorcycles for US$20 per day, plus US$3 for a helmet; a US$100 deposit is refunded when you return the bike in good condition. A special motorcycle driver's license is not required; your ordinary driver's license will do.

Taxi

Taxis in Panama City are plentiful and cheap. They are not metered, but there is a list of standard fares that drivers are supposed to charge, measured by zones. The fare for one zone is a minimum of 75¢; the maximum fare within the city is US$4. An average ride, crossing a couple of zones, costs US$1 or US$2, plus 25¢ for each additional passenger.

Watch out for unmarked, large-model US cars serving hotels as cabs. Their prices are up to four times that of regular street taxis. If it's late at night, if you're in a hurry or if you're in an area not frequented by cabs, call for a radio taxi. These taxis are dispatched moments after you call and usually arrive within minutes. Larger radio-taxi companies include the following:

Ama	☎ 221-1865
America	☎ 223-7694
El Parador	☎ 238-9111
Latino	☎ 226-7313
San Cristóbal	☎ 221-8704
Setsa	☎ 221-8594
Union Servicio Unico	☎ 221-4074

Bicycle

Cycling within the capital city is not a great idea, due to narrow roads and aggressive drivers. Cycling outside the city, however, is safer and can be quite enjoyable.

There's only one place in town to rent a bicycle: Bicycles Moses (☎ 228-0116), out at the entrance to the causeway, operates a booth where you can rent a mountain bike for US$2.25 per hour (more around the Christmas and Easter holidays) or in-line skates for US$1 per hour. It also has economical daily and weekly rates. The booth is open 10 am to 7 pm weekdays, 7 am to 7 pm weekends. The owner speaks English.

The leading bike store in town, Carretero Sports (☎ 223-8053, fax 223-8054, comrali@sinfo.net), on Avenida Balboa near Vía Italia, does not rent bicycles, but it does arrange popular bike rides. For years now, groups as large as 200 people have gathered at the store's invitation for these trips, which are usually held every other weekend. A recent trip included touring El Valle. More than 100 people showed up, and they and their bikes were transported free of charge to El Valle, 123km away, where the groups investigated the beautiful valley. The store even arranged lodgings for the riders, who bore the cost of the accommodations. These rides are a great way to meet people and see some of Panama's countryside; for information on upcoming trips, contact the store (English and Spanish are spoken) or drop by when you're in town.

The bike shop's sign is not easy to find; it's a couple of doors south of a Gran Morrison department store. Look for the hard-to-miss ad for Rali bikes: 'Bicicletas Rali.' If you've found that sign, you've found the store.

Panamá Province

Panamá Province has a little bit of everything and most of the canal. It's got *two* island groups that have been great escapes since the days of the pirates. It's got more history than any one place has a right to. It offers lots of wild jungle for exploring, scores of lovely beaches and road trips that'll knock your socks off. And in its capital of Panama City, this province has an ample array of cultural attractions and nocturnal distractions.

Statistically, the province contains the largest population of Panama's nine provinces – 1,072,000 people, according to the most recent census. It also has a population density of 90 people per square kilometer – three times the national average. There are slightly more women than men here, but the figure of four women to every man often heard in Panama City bars is only so much wishful thinking. The province has a surface area of 11,887 sq km, making it the second largest behind Darién Province (16,671 sq km).

As might be expected, Panamá Province also boasts the highest ratio of urbanites to rural folk 79.6% to 20.4%, respectively. Yet the province also claims highly developed agriculture in Chepo and La Chorrera, shrimp farming in Chame and large fruit farms in Capira. Perhaps its success in those fields has something to do with the fact that the province also contains the country's best-educated people: Its illiteracy rate of 4.3% is by far the lowest in the country, which has an overall rate of 10.7%.

Around Panama City

PANAMA CANAL

The USA's construction of the Panama Canal during the early 20th century is a larger-than-life true story of adventure, ordeal and accomplishment. It followed on the heels of the catastrophic French attempt to cut a path between the seas, which claimed 22,000 lives. Despite all the technological advances that have taken place since the completion of the canal almost 90 years ago, the lock-and-lake waterway remains one of the great engineering marvels of all time.

The canal extends 80km from Colón on the Caribbean side to Panama City on the Pacific. Each year more than 12,000 ocean-going vessels transit it – well over 30 a day. So significant is the canal to international shipping that ships the world over are built to fit within the dimensions of its locks: 305m long and 33.5m wide. At times a huge ship will squeeze through the locks with less than a meter to spare on each side. It's a sight onlookers never forget.

HIGHLIGHTS

- The awesome Panama Canal, a must-see for Panama visitors
- Camino del Oleoducto in Parque Nacional Soberanía, one of the world's premier bird-watching sites
- Isla Barro Colorado, a world-famous jungle research center at the heart of Lago Gatún
- Archipiélago de las Perlas, the islands named for their pearls and known for their pirate past
- Surfing beaches and romantic hideaways on the Pacific coast southwest of the capital

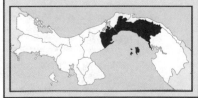

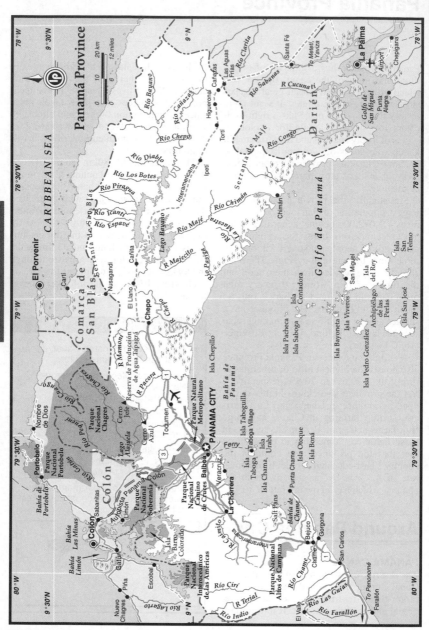

The principal physical features of the Panama Canal are as follows:

Lago Gatún (Gatún Lake) – This artificial lake stretches nearly all the way across the isthmus. Its creation submerged 29 villages and huge swaths of forest and displaced 50,000 people. Gatún remained the largest artificial lake in the world for 22 years, until the 1936 completion of the USA's Hoover Dam and the resulting creation of Lake Mead.

Gaillard Cut – This colossal excavation through the Continental Divide extends Lago Gatún to locks on the divide's Pacific slope. Originally excavated to a width of more than 90m and later widened, the cut was carved through solid rock and shale for most of its 14km. It is currently being widened again to allow a greater number of ships to transit the Panama Canal.

Locks – The locks on both sides of the isthmus raise and lower ships between sea level and lake level; some of the locks' enormous doors weigh upward of 800 tons apiece, yet so precise were the design and follow-through on their construction that only a 40-horsepower motor is needed to move them.

Balboa & Cristóbal – The ports of Balboa and Cristóbal are on the Pacific and Caribbean coasts, respectively. It is at these ports that canal pilots board and disembark from vessels passing through the canal. The port of Balboa borders the safe and attractive Balboa suburb of Panama City, and the port of Cristóbal borders the unsafe city of Colón.

Gamboa – At the northern end of the Gaillard Cut, this small port is home to two of the largest cranes in the world, confiscated from Nazi Germany at the end of WWII. Resembling giant insects, the cranes are so intriguing to mechanical engineers that many travel thousands of miles just to see them with their own eyes.

The approach to the canal from the Caribbean is along 7.2km of dredged channel. The canal then proceeds for 11.1km, veering slightly westward before reaching the Gatún Locks. Ships are lifted 25.9m by these three locks, to the level of Lago Gatún. The locks open directly into one another and are paired, as are the other locks, so that one ship can be raised while another is lowered. All the lock chambers have the same dimensions.

From the Gatún Locks, the canal passes through Lago Gatún in a southern and then southeastern direction to the mouth of the Gaillard Cut. At the end of the cut are the Pedro Miguel Locks, which have a drop of 9.4m. The locks border Lago Miraflores, which is 16.8m above the level of the Pacific. The canal continues 2.1km through Lago Miraflores and reaches the two Miraflores Locks, which lower ships to Pacific tidewater level. From the locks, the canal runs 4km to Balboa, and from there a dredged channel extends 8km out into the Bahía de Panamá.

Auxiliary facilities include the Madden Dam on the Río Chagres, which provides a reservoir to maintain the level of Lago Gatún during the dry season; breakwaters that protect channels at both ends of the canal; hydroelectric plants at the Gatún and Madden Dams; and the presently incapacitated Panama Railroad, which extends 76.6km from Colón to Panama City.

Speaking of railroads, to lessen the risk of a mishap, ships are cabled to locomotives at the approach to each series of locks and are pulled through them. There are 80 such locomotives in use, all made by Mitsubishi. Their cost? A mere US$1 million apiece! In 1998 another 100 locomotives were ordered from Mitsubishi at a cost of US$2 million each, to be delivered over several years. They're pricey, but then transit fees earn Panama hundreds of millions of dollars every year.

Ships pay according to their weights; the average fee for commercial ships is around US$30,000. The highest fee ever assessed was US$141,344.97, paid on May 2, 1993, by *Crown Princess,* the largest passenger ship that ever transited the canal; the lowest was 36¢, paid by Richard Halliburton, who swam through in 1928.

The more that you learn about the Panama Canal – both the monumental construction project itself and the associated political intrigues – the more interesting it gets. Many books have been written on the subject, the best of which is surely *The Path Between the Seas,* penned by award-winning historian David McCullough.

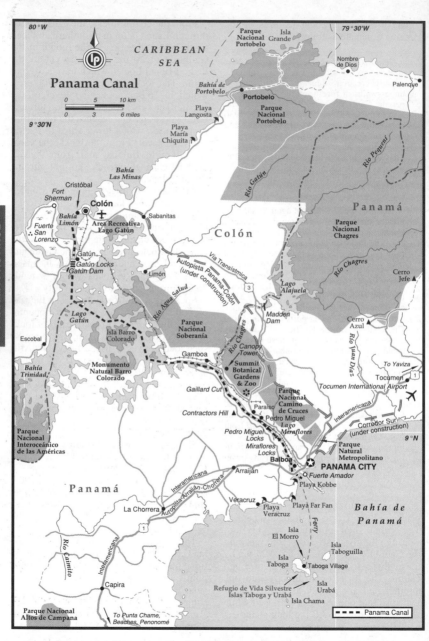

Bocas del Toro Province

Top Left: Hiking the boardwalk at the San-San Pond Sak Wetlands, home to monkeys, sloths, snakes and iguanas

Bottom Left: Green turtle searching for lunch off Isla Colón

Top Right: Ruins of Pana-Jungla, the Noriega-era jungle-survival training school in Parque Internacional La Amistad

Bottom Right: Family on steps of their home, Isla Colón

SCOTT DOGGETT

STUART GR WARNER W

STUART GR WARNER W

STUART GR WARNER W

Chiriquí Province

Top Left: Hikers on the graffiti-sprayed summit of Volcán Barú, Panama's highest peak

Bottom: The mountain town of Boquete, beloved for its fruit, coffee and cool weather

Top Right: Groom and thoroughbred stallion on stud farm near Cerro Punta

Middle Right: Mist descends on flock on the slopes of Volcán Barú

Canal Facts
- Each lock chamber holds about 2,675,200 cubic meters of water, equivalent to a one-day supply for a city of approximately 100,000 people.
- During WWII, more than 5300 combat vessels and about 8500 other craft serving the US military passed through the canal.
- The lock gates are composed of watertight compartments that make them buoyant, largely relieving stress on the bearings upon which they rest.

Keys to your battleship, please.

- The Panama Canal is the only place in the world where military commanders must turn over navigational control of their ships. An elite group of 200 pilots guide all ships that pass through the waterway.
- Even after the USA relinquishes control of the canal on December 31, 1999, it will by treaty retain the right to defend the waterway in the interest of its national security.

PANAMÁ PROVINCE

Miraflores Locks

The easiest and best way to see the canal is to go to the Miraflores Locks, the set closest to Panama City, where a viewing platform gives you a good look at canal locks in operation. A bilingual guide and bilingual illustrated pamphlets offer information on the canal, and there's a museum with a model and film about the famous waterway.

Hours are 9 am to 5 pm daily; admission is free. To get to the locks, take any Paraíso or Gamboa bus from the Plaza Cinco de Mayo bus stop in Panama City. These buses, which pass along the canalside highway that runs from the capital to Gamboa, will let you off at the 'Miraflores Locks' sign on the highway, about 8km from the city center. It's about a 15-minute walk to the locks from the sign.

Other Locks

Farther north, past the Miraflores Locks, are the **Pedro Miguel Locks**. You will pass them if you take the highway to Gamboa. You can see the locks from the road, but they have no provisions for visitors.

On the Caribbean side, the **Gatún Locks** have a viewing stand for visitors and a small replica of the entire canal that lets you place

the locks in context. You can also get a good look at the locks if you cross the canal to visit Fuerte San Lorenzo. See the Colón Province chapter for more details on these locks and the nearby Gatún Dam.

Canal Tours

Argo Tours (☎ 228-6069, fax 228-1234), the leader in canal tours for many years, operates partial canal transits on Saturday morning. These boat tours depart from Balboa, a western suburb of Panama City, travel through the Miraflores Locks to Lago Miraflores and back, and then cruise out into the bay for scenic views of the city and the Pacific approach to the canal. These fine tours last about 4½ hours and cost US$45/25 adults/children.

Six times a year, Argo Tours offers full transits of the canal, from Balboa to Cristóbal, passing through all three sets of locks, the Gaillard Cut, Lago Gatún and so on. The transit takes all day, from about 7:30 am to 5:30 pm; the cost is US$90/69 adults/children. Most people find the full transit a bit much due to the relentless heat and humidity.

If you take a trip to the Isla Barro Colorado area, you will travel by boat along part of the canal, from Gamboa to Isla Barro Colorado, but you won't go through any locks. (See the Isla Barro Colorado section in this chapter for details on these trips.)

CANAL AREA

On a day trip from Panama City, you could first visit the Miraflores Locks, then the Summit Botanical Gardens & Zoo and then cross into Colón Province to visit the Sendero El Charco nature trail in Parque Nacional Soberanía, which is 25km from the center of Panama City but seems like a different world.

All these places are along the highway that runs from Panama City to Gamboa, the small tropical town where the Río Chagres enters Lago Gatún. They can all be reached by taking the Gamboa bus from the bus stop at Plaza Cinco de Mayo in Panama City.

Summit Botanical Gardens & Zoo

On the highway to Gamboa, 10km past the Miraflores Locks, are the Summit Botanical Gardens & Zoo (☎ 232-4854). The botanical gardens were founded in 1923 to introduce, propagate and disseminate tropical plants from around the world into Panama. They contain more than 15,000 plant species, and 50 of these are marked along a trail.

Also at the park is an expanding zoo that contains animals native to Central America. Its greatest attraction is its enormous harpy eagle compound, which opened in 1998 in hopes that conditions would prove conducive to breeding. The harpy eagle is the national bird, and many ornithologists consider it the most powerful bird of prey on earth. Beside the compound is a state-of-the-art harpy eagle educational center with an impressive array of high-tech audio-visual equipment.

The park is open 8 am to 4 pm every day. Admission is a great bargain at 25¢/10¢ adults/children, and the fee includes some information and a trail map of the park. The Gamboa bus (see information above) stops here.

TOM BOYDEN

Locomotives haul ships through the Panama Canal's locks.

Contractors Hill

On the western side of the canal, Contractors Hill was originally 123m above sea level. It was one of the highest points along the Gaillard Cut. There were landslides along the cut, however, and in 1954 Contractors Hill was reduced to its present height of 111m in an effort to stabilize it.

Contractors Hill is one of the most accessible points from which you can see the Gaillard Cut, but only if you have a private vehicle; the hill is pretty remote and it is not served by public transportation. To get here from Panama City, just drive over the Puente de las Américas (Bridge of the Americas), take the Carretera Interamericana (Pan-American Hwy) and then take the first exit on the right (northern) side at the signs 'Soloy's Balseria' and 'Cocolí.' Continue on past the Horoko Club and turn at the first road on your left. You'll reach the hill in another 10 minutes.

Parque Nacional Soberanía

A few kilometers past Summit, across the border into Colón Province, 22,104-hectare Parque Nacional Soberanía is one of the most accessible tropical rainforest areas in Panama. It extends much of the way across the isthmus, from Limón on Lago Gatún to just north of Paraíso. It features hiking trails, the Río Chagres, part of Lago Gatún and a remarkable variety of wildlife – its known residents include 105 species of mammal, 525 species of bird, 55 species of amphibian, 79 species of reptile and 36 species of freshwater fish.

Hiking trails in the park include a section of the old **Sendero Las Cruces** (Las Cruces Trail), used by the Spaniards to transport gold and minerals by mule train between Panama City and Nombre de Dios, and the 17km **Camino del Oleoducto** (Pipeline Road), providing access (by driving or hiking) to Río Agua Salud, where you can walk upriver for a swim under a waterfall.

Camino del Olcoducto is a favorite with bird watchers. A healthy cluster of golden-collared manakins, colorful birds that produce a variety of sounds – including a firecrackerlike snap – is usually readily found at the end of the first 100m of the road, on the left side. Other typical sounds on the first 2km of the road come from white-bellied antbirds, black-bellied wrens, collared aracaris, keel-billed toucans and buff-throated woodcreepers. You'll likely hear a few howler monkeys as well. In addition, you may be treated to such rarities as the tiny hawk, the hook-billed kite, the great jacamar and the black-tailed trogon. And that's only the beginning. The jungle and wildlife on both sides of the road get increasingly thick as you proceed.

Unless you have a keen eye and are well versed in Panama's avifauna, I strongly recommend that you hire a guide to fully appreciate Camino del Oleoducto. This is one of the world's premier birding sites; it would be a minor tragedy to give it short shrift. See the Guides section in the Getting Around chapter for a list of the country's top naturalist guides. Most of the guides listed there charge about US$35 to guide a group of four for an entire morning on Camino del Olcoducto, if you provide the transportation; they charge more if you don't.

A shorter, very easy nature trail is the **Sendero El Charco**. The trail is sign-posted from the highway, about 3km past the Summit Botanical Gardens & Zoo.

Fishing (but not hunting) is permitted on the Río Chagres and Lago Gatún. Leaflets and information about the park, including a self-guiding brochure on the nature trail, are available from Parque Nacional Soberanía headquarters (☎ 276-6370) in Gamboa or from the Panama City office of the Instituto Nacional de Recursos Naturales Renovables (INRENARE; ☎ 232-7228/7223), near the Terminal de Buses al Interior on Avenida Ascañio Villalaz in the Curundu district. They're also available from the Asociación Nacional para la Conservación de la Naturaleza (Ancon; ☎ 264-8100, fax 264-1836, ancon@pty.com, www.ancon.org), Apartado 1387, Panamá 1, República de Panamá. If you want to camp in the park, you must first get permission from INRENARE or park headquarters.

Canopy Tower

In the 1960s the US Air Force built a radar installation atop a hill in what is now Parque Nacional Soberanía as an essential part of the USA's intercontinental defense. The site was later taken over by the US Federal Aviation Administration to control air traffic in the area. Most recently, it was used by the Panama Canal Commission as a communications tower.

The installation – its major feature is a three-story, cylindrical, enclosed tower with a viewing platform on top – was transferred to Panama in November 1996 in compliance with the Carter-Torrijos Treaties. Raúl Arias de Para, a friendly, forward-thinking man with a love of nature, saw its tourism potential and obtained a 20-year concession to develop the site.

Today Canopy Tower (☎ 264-5720, fax 263-2784, arba@pananet.com, canopy.mit.edu) contains a small ground-floor museum devoted to the history of the former military site and the local wildlife, and guest quarters with a shared bathroom on the 2nd floor. The rooms are dormitory-style, and beds are hammocks or cots – nothing fancy but quite all right. A restaurant is housed in a separate structure. There's also a 500-foot-long elevated walkway that takes you from the jungle's floor to its canopy.

What's really fun about this place, besides the childish thrill of staying in a building that feels like an enormous back-yard fort, is the surrounding forest. From the upper levels of the tower, you have a 360° view over some magnificent rain-forest, and you can even see ships passing through the canal, 2km away. The bird watching in the area is excellent. And a study conducted by Ancon has found that the hill upon which the tower was built hosts the greatest variety of mammals and reptiles along the eastern bank of the Panama Canal.

The per-person nightly rate of US$99 plus tax includes dinner, breakfast and transportation to and from Panama City. Three tours are available for people stay-ing in the city: a 6 to 11 am rainforest tour with continental breakfast (this is the best time for birding, and the howler monkeys are most active at this time); an 11 am to 3 pm top-of-the-hill tour with lunch (this is the best time to see birds of prey and ships in the canal); and a 5 to 9 pm tour with bar-becue dinner with wine and salad (you can listen to the jungle and watch the stars come out). Each tour costs US$50 and includes a stop at the Miraflores Locks and the Summit Botanical Gardens & Zoo. Contact the Canopy Tower for reservations and information.

Isla Barro Colorado

This lush island in the middle of Lago Gatún was formed by the damming of the Río Chagres and the creation of the lake. It is managed by the Smithsonian Tropical Research Institute (STRI), which adminis-ters a world-renowned research facility here. Although the 1500-hectare island was once restricted only to scientists, a limited number of tourists are now allowed onto it, and a visit to the island – known to STRI staff as BCI – makes an interesting day trip from Panama City. The trip includes a boat ride down an attractive part of the canal, from Gamboa across the lake to the island.

The institute traces its 75-year history in Panama from the construction of the Pana-ma Canal, when scientific surveys of the area's flora and fauna were undertaken with the goal of controlling insect-borne diseases such as yellow fever and malaria. After the canal opened, entomologists and biologists involved in these studies sought to establish a permanent biological reserve on an island created by the canal's con-struction. In 1923 Isla Barro Colorado became one of the first biological reserves in the New World. Since that time, the island has become one of the most inten-sively studied areas in the Tropics.

Home to 1316 recorded plant species, 381 bird species and 102 mammal species, the island also contains a 59km network of marked and protected trails. Visitors are only allowed on one designated nature trail to prevent them from inadvertently dam-aging anyone's valuable research. This 2.5km trail winds through some spectac-ular rainforest and ends at one of STRI's earliest structures, a headquarters-turned-visitors' center. It has a jungly and time-forgotten look and contains a gift shop and a small museum with vintage photos of researchers at work, a case containing tools used by the researchers and lots of other neat stuff. Frankly, in some ways this museum is more interesting than the on-island STRI laboratories, which you can't visit anyway.

STRI offers tours of the island, but the number of tourists is strictly limited: 10 visitors on Tuesday and 30 on each week-end day. Children under 10 are not allowed on BCI. A STRI-led visit takes a full day and it costs US$28 per person, which includes a guide, roundtrip boat transporta-tion between the island and Gamboa Pier, and lunch at the research station cafeteria. The island has many ticks, so you should wear long pants, high socks and closed shoes, and use insect repellent.

For reservations, contact STRI personnel on the island (☎ 227-6022, fax 232-6278, arosemo@tivoli.si.edu, www.stri.org) or stop by STRI's Panama City offices in the Tupper Research and Conference Center on Avenida Roosevelt, opposite the Leg-islative Palace in the Ancón district. The Tupper Center is open 8 am to 5 pm week-days, and it has a research library that's open to the public. There's also a fine bookstore and gift shop in the center. Be sure to bring ID; you will not be allowed into the center without it.

Make a reservation as far in advance as possible; to have a real chance of getting onto the island, you'll need to book at least one year in advance. However, if you happen to be in Panama and would like to visit the island, give STRI a call to see if there have been any last-minute cancellations; there had been such a cancellation when I called, and I was able to see the island the very next day.

At the time of writing, two tour operators had STRI permission to take tourists to the visitors' center on BCI, but not into the island's rainforest. These operators were Iguana Tours (☎ 226-8738, fax 226-4736, iguana@sinfo.net), on Avenida Belisario Porras between Calles 72 Este and 73 Este in Panama City, and Ecotours (☎ 263-3077/3078, fax 263-3089, ecotours @pty.com, www.pty.com/ecotours), on Calle Ricardo Arias just south of Vía España in the capital's El Cangrejo area. Ecotours charges US$91 per person for two people, US$85 per person for three and US$75 per person for four or more. Its trips visit the island and onshore rainforest across from the island. (Due to concerns I have about the quality of its tours, Ecotours is not mentioned elsewhere in this book.)

A number of tour operators (see the Organized Tours section in the Panama City chapter) offer Monumento Natural Barro Colorado tours. However, these should not be mistaken for tours of Isla Barro Colorado itself; most of the 5400-hectare monument consists of rainforest bordering the canal, and the island comprises only 1500 hectares of this area. That rainforest is quite spectacular and well worth seeing. It's entirely possible that STRI will eventually make the island's visitors' center available to tour companies besides Iguana Tours and Ecotours. When you're discussing a nature monument tour with any operator, be sure to inquire if its tour includes a stop on Isla Barro Colorado.

CERROS AZUL & JEFE

About an hour's drive northeast of Panama City is Cerro Azul, a 950m peak just south of Parque Nacional Chagres, a mountainous area of natural forest and streams. Several kilometers northeast of Cerro Azul is Cerro Jefe, a windy, cool ridge with rare elfin forest. Both peaks are popular with birders, who come looking for foothill species, including some from the Darién. Because of the difficulty of the terrain, particularly in the vicinity of Cerro Jefe, a 4WD vehicle is highly recommended. Buses do not go to this rugged area.

To reach the hills from Panama City, take the Interamericana eastward toward Tocumen. The highway passes the huge Hotel Riande (the hotel and its sign are visible 100m before you reach them). Just before the hotel, you'll come to an intersection. Take the wide, paved road to the left and drive 6.8km. You'll then come to a police station, on your left. Beside the station is the old paved road to Chepo; turn onto it and drive 2km. You'll reach a large Chinese pavilion, where you should turn left onto another paved road. This road, which ascends Cerro Azul, is fairly steep at times. After 11.5km, you will see the residential development of Monte Fresco; continue along the same road for 1km. You'll pass Goofy Lake on your left, and soon afterward you will come to Avenida de los Nimbos, where you should turn left. At this point you'll have reached a fairly undeveloped area of Cerro Azul. You can begin hiking here or go on 6km farther to Cerro Jefe, which is better for bird watching. Cerro Jefe can be discerned from a distance; there's a microwave tower atop it.

Unfortunately, no signs mark the way from Panama City to the hills, and the appearance of new buildings or the leveling of the Chinese pavilion could render these directions useless. Don't hesitate to ask for directions if you feel lost. If you don't speak Spanish, don't despair. Simply ask, '¿Cerro Azul (or Jefe), derecho?' (day-RAY-cho; straight ahead?); '¿derecha?' (day-RAY-cha; to the right?); '¿izquierda?'

PANAMÁ PROVINCE

(eez-key-AIR-da; to the left?) For clarity's sake, point in the relevant direction, and your listener will probably provide some helpful finger-pointing in return. If you hear the word *regreso* in the reply, it means you missed a turnoff and need to double back some distance.

BAHA'I & HINDU TEMPLES
On the crest of a hill on the outskirts of Panama City, 11km from the city center on the Vía Transístmica (Transisthmian Hwy), is the white-domed Baha'i Temple (☎ 231-1137/1191). It looks much like an egg from the outside, but inside it is surprisingly beautiful, with a fresh breeze always blowing through. This is the Baha'i House of Worship for all of Latin America. Information about the faith is available in English and Spanish at the temple; readings from the Baha'i writings (also in English and Spanish) are held at 10 am Sunday. The temple is open 10 am to 6 pm daily. Any bus from Panama City to Colón can let you off on the highway, but it's a long walk up the hill. A taxi ride from Panama City costs around US$10.

The magnificent Hindu Temple, which is also atop a hill, is on the way to the Baha'i Temple. It's open 7:30 to 11 am and 4:30 to 7:30 pm daily.

BEACHES
A popular beach, **Playa Kobbe**, is just across the canal from Panama City. Part of it is the Kobbe Beach Club (☎ 263-6885); at the entrance you pay US$7 for coupons good for food and drinks at the club's restaurant/bar. (You must pay this fee to use the beach.) The beach is safe and protected, and it has lifeguards; there are sailboards, boats for hire and other recreation options. Buses to Playa Kobbe leave the stop at Plaza Cinco de Mayo in the city. If you're driving, cross the Puente de las Américas, take the first exit and follow the signs to the beach.

About 1km beyond the Playa Kobbe entrance is the signposted entrance to **Playa Veracruz**, a free public beach. Food is available, and the beach is popular, especially on the weekends.

Islas Tabogas

This group consists of 10 main islands and dozens of smaller ones 20km south of Panama City. The largest – **Isla Taboga** – is a mere 571 hectares. Yet the size of the small island belies its rich history.

Taboga was inhabited until 1515 by Indians who resided in thatch huts and made their living from the sea. In that year Spanish soldiers reached the island, killed or enslaved the Indians and took their substantial pieces of gold. This occurred just two years after Balboa first sighted the Pacific and before the city of Panamá was constructed. A small Spanish colony was developed on the island, and the Spaniards had the place to themselves until 1549, when Panama freed its Indian slaves and a good number chose to make Taboga their home.

Peace did not reign. Pirates, including the infamous Henry Morgan and Francis Drake, frequented the island, using it as a base from which to attack Spanish ships and towns – or simply as a place to catch their breaths between raids. On August 22, 1686, Captain Townley, in command of English and French buccaneers, was lying in front of Taboga when he was attacked by three Spanish ships armed with cannons. During the ensuing battle, one of the Spanish ships blew up, and Townley's men were able to take the other two vessels as well as a fourth ship that had arrived as reinforcement.

The pirates' loss was only one man killed and 22 wounded, including Townley himself. The buccaneer commander sent a messenger to the president of Panama demanding supplies, the release of five pirates being held prisoner and ransom for Townley's many captives. When the president instead sent only some medicine, Townley said that heads would roll if his demands weren't met. When the president ignored that threat, Townley sent him a canoe that contained the heads of 20 Spaniards.

The heads got the president's attention, and he hastily released the five prisoners and paid out a ransom. Townley had won another battle, but he died of his wounds on September 9. For years afterward peace continued to escape the little island. As late as 1819, the pirate Captain Illingsworth and his party of Chileans landed on Taboga and sacked and burnt its village.

Around 1840, tiny Isla El Morro, which can be reached from Taboga by a sandbar at low tide, became the headquarters of the Pacific Steamship Navigation Company (PSNC). The PSNC consisted of a fleet of 12 vessels used to transport passengers and cargo between Valparaiso, Chile, and Taboga. The completion of the Panama Railroad in the mid-1850s put the PSNC out of business. Today you can still see remnants of the PSNC building and pier, and hand-blown bottles bearing the company's crest can be found among the islet's vegetation. Also on Isla El Morro is a tiny cemetery containing the remains of some PSNC workers.

During the 1880s, when the French took a stab at digging a canal across the isthmus, Taboga became the site of an enormous sanitarium for workers who had contracted malaria or yellow fever. The 'Island of Flowers,' as it is called, might well have earned its name from all the flowers placed on graves here. Sadly, Taboga's centuries-old cemetery has been looted so many times that it looks like it was hit by artillery fire.

Real artillery fire, in fact, also took a toll on Taboga. The US Navy used the broad hill facing the town for artillery practice during WWII. At that time the US military also installed searchlights, antiaircraft guns and bunkers atop the island. The bunkers, abandoned in 1960, can be visited today.

Today, after hundreds of years, peace has finally come to Taboga. Now the island is only assailed by weekend vacationers from Panama City and the occasional foreign tourist. There are two hotels, a few restaurants and bars on Taboga, but primarily people come just to stroll the town's quaint streets and to hike

about the island. More adventurous types come to scuba dive in waters once rich with plunder. (Many divers no doubt hope they'll come across some of this treasure.) Taboga also offers its visitors a chance to take it easy, to maybe do a little bird watching, exploring and snorkeling, and to watch ships lining up in the Bahía de Panamá and storm fronts moving in from the south.

Orientation

A ferry serves Isla Taboga from Muelle (Pier) 18 in the Balboa district of Panama City twice daily, tying up at a pier near the north end of the sole town on the island. As you exit the pier, you'll see the entrance of the Hotel Taboga to your right. To your left, you'll see a narrow street that is the island's main road. From this point, the street meanders 5.2km before ending at the old US military installation atop the island's highest hill, Cerro El Vigia.

Information

There's no tourist office, no bank, no post office and no store of any kind on Taboga, but there are scattered public phones.

INRENARE has an office (☎ 250-2082) on Taboga east of the ferry dock; it's supposedly open 8 am to 4 pm weekdays, but its staff seem to view its posted hours as a suggestion rather than a rule. It has information on the island's natural features and snorkeling spots.

Walking Tour

One of the pleasant ways to pass time on Taboga is walking to the top of the island. Walk left from the pier and you will first pass a beach (unless the tide's in) on a road that's barely wide enough for a car and is mainly used by pedestrians. The road forks after 75m or so; you will want to take the high way. After a few more paces you will come to a modest **church**, in front of which is a simple square. This unassuming church was founded in 1550. It is the second-oldest church in the Western Hemisphere. Inside it is a handsome altar and lovely artwork.

Continuing on, you'll come to a beautiful public garden filled with flowers. At its center is a statue of the island's patroness, **Nuestra Señora del Carmen** (Our Lady of Carmel). Every July 16 she is honored with a procession – the statue is carried upon the shoulders of followers to the oceanside, placed on a boat and ferried around the island. Upon her return she is carried around the island, while crowds follow and everyone else watches at their windows. The Virgin is returned to her garden shrine and the rest of the day is one of rejoicing, and seemingly everyone partakes in games, fire-breathing or dancing.

Continuing along the same road, you'll pass the Hotel Chu and, 400m farther, a **cemetery** that dates from the 16th century but is so overgrown with weeds and so picked over by looters that there's hardly anything worth seeing. Nearly all the mausoleums have been broken into and there are open graves everywhere. It seems that all the old headstones are gone; I could not find any dating from before 1900.

Continuing on, you'll note a cross upon Cerro de la Cruz, the large hill just ahead of you. It was placed here by the Spaniards during the 16th century. The US Navy used the hillside just below it for target practice during WWII. The road leaves the residential area and the incline increases as it passes some of the plants that earned Taboga the nickname 'Island of Flowers.' The wild hibiscus, bougainvillea, oleander and jasmine on the island explode in a riot of colors in April and May. During a morning stroll, you can hear and see the many birds that nest and feed among the flowers.

After 2km of this now-strenuous and woodsy walk, the road forks one last time. To the left are abandoned **bunkers** used by US troops during WWII. The bunkers are large and you can enter them. When you stand amid the thick concrete walls, it doesn't seem like the war was so long ago. Climb atop the bunkers for grand views: of ships in the bay, each awaiting its turn to enter the canal; of the skyscrapers of Panama City; of the nearby islands, forested coastline and wide-open sea. As you look out over the ocean, recall the time of the great explorers, when mariners hugged the coasts, the Atlantic was called the 'Sea of Darkness,' and most Europeans believed that if you sailed out upon it, you would never return.

If you look below and to the right of the old cross, you'll see a white-and-brown pile of rubble amid thickening vegetation. It's the ruins of a Spanish cannon emplacement put here 300 years ago to protect the island from pirates. The green-blue water below the ruins offers decent diving. Not visible from land but tucked into the cliff below the bunkers are two caves where Indian artifacts have been found. Up the road from the bunkers, on the road's less-traveled branch, are a radar installation and the island's secondary electrical plant; they are off-limits to the public.

Beaches

Most people come to Taboga to go to the beach. There are fine beaches in either direction from the ferry dock. You can visit any of them for free.

Many visitors head straight for the Hotel Taboga, to your right as you walk off the ferry dock; the hotel faces onto the island's most popular beach, arcing between Taboga and tiny Isla El Morro. A day entrance fee of US$5 gives you access to dressing rooms and showers and use of the large garden grounds; the hotel also rents paddle boats, beach umbrellas, hammocks, mats, snorkel and dive gear and the like. There's no need to pay the hotel simply to use the beach, however; there's an easily overlooked walkway to the beach, beside the gate entrance to the hotel.

Forest

On the trip back from the island, look to the west of the Puente de las Américas and you will see one of the last tracts of Pacific dry forest remaining in Central America. Such forests used to line much of the Pacific coast of Central America. Because they are easy to clear for agriculture, however, these forests have now all but disappeared.

Along the edge and near the center of the otherwise forested stretch of coastline are several large structures. They comprised Panama's last leper colony, which closed during the late 1970s. Today the facilities serve as a retirement home.

Snorkeling

On the weekends, when most people visit Taboga, you can find fishermen at the island's pier who will take you around the island in their small boats, so that you can see it from all sides and reach some of its good snorkeling spots. There are some caves on the island's western side that are rumored (of course) to hold golden treasure left there by pirates. During the week, when the small boats are nowhere to be found, you can still snorkel around Isla El Morro, which hasn't any coral but attracts some large fish.

Diving

Taboga offers typical Pacific-style diving, with rocky formations and a wide variety of marine life. The beauty of the Pacific lies in the schools of fish that roam about: On a good dive you can expect to see jack, snapper, jewfish, eels, corvina, rays, lobsters and octopi. With a little luck, you may also come across old bottles, spent WWII-era shells and artifacts from pirate days.

Expert divers who are totally equipped and only need rides to particular dive spots can rent low-sitting *panga* boats for about US$20 per hour; look for captains around the ferry pier. Everyone else should contact Scubapanama (☎ 261-4064/3841, fax 261-9586, 0003866445@mcimail.com), Apartado 666, Balboa, República de Panamá, which is Panama's oldest and most respected dive operator. It has a small dive center at the Hotel Taboga (see contact information below), but its twin-engine 200-horsepower dive boat actually leaves from Panama City. Scubapanama offers a package that includes pick-up from a Panama City hotel, plus a divemaster, two tanks, weights, lunch and sodas. Per-person rates are US$100 (for five or more

people), US$125 (four people), US$160 (three people), US$220 (two people) and US$320 (one person).

Bird Watching

The islands of Taboga and nearby Urabá are home to one of the largest breeding colonies of brown pelicans in the world. The colony has contained up to 100,000 individual birds, or about half of the world population of this species. A wildlife refuge, the **Refugio de Vida Silvestre Islas Taboga y Urabá**, was established to protect their habitat. The refuge covers about a third of Taboga as well as the entire island of Urabá, just off Taboga's southeast coast. May is the height of nesting season, but pelicans can be seen from January to June.

Whale Watching

On your way to and from the island, keep an eye on the ocean. On rare occasions during August, September and October, migrating humpback and sei whales can be seen leaping from the water near Taboga in spectacular displays.

Places to Stay & Eat

There are only two places to stay on Isla Taboga, and by far the better value is the *Hotel Chu* (☎ 250-2035 on Taboga; 263-6933 in Panama City). This two-story wooden structure, built on the beach in the early 20th century, has 15 basic but comfortable and breezy rooms upstairs, each with its own private balcony. Guests share a spotlessly clean bathroom. Downstairs there's an open-air restaurant with decent and inexpensive food and a sweeping view of the bay. Rates are US$25/30 for one/two people. There's a public phone out front. This is a fine place to return to at day's end. At night guests sleep to the soothing sound of surf.

The *Hotel Taboga* (☎ 264-6090, fax 223-0116) is an example of the disparity that sometimes exists between price and value. Rates range from US$60 to US$75, and though the 54 rooms have air-con and hot water, they smell mildewy, they don't have private phones, you can't hear the ocean from them and the TVs get only three fuzzy stations. Still, the rooms are located amid a pleasant setting of gardens beside the beach, and there's a pool. There are also five small cages containing five large, unhappy birds. The food at the Hotel Taboga is good, particularly the fish; expect to pay from US$10 to US$15 per person.

Entertainment
There isn't much nightlife on Taboga. It's pretty much limited to the bar/restaurant at the *Hotel Taboga* and to the much livelier *Jardín El Galeón,* which serves the cheapest drinks in town and is located beneath the Hotel Chu. This place is easy to miss, but it's right on the ocean and very unpretentious, and there are two popular pool tables on the premises.

Getting There & Away
The one-hour boat trip to Taboga is part of the island's attraction. The *Calypso Queen* ferry (☎ 232-5736, 264-6096) departs from Muelle 18 in the Balboa district of Panama City, and it passes along the Balboa port, under the Puente de las Américas and along the last part of the Panama Canal channel on its journey out to sea. It also passes the causeway that links La Boca district to four small offshore islands.

Tuesday to Friday, the ferry leaves Balboa at 8:30 am and departs Taboga on the return trip at 4 pm (3:30 pm on Friday). On weekends and holidays, the ferry departs Balboa at 7:45 and 10:30 am and at 4:30 pm; the return trip leaves Taboga at 9 am and 3 and 5:45 pm. The roundtrip fare is US$7.50.

Argo Tours (☎ 232-5395, 228-4348, fax 228-1234) operates two ferries to the island: the 200-passenger MV *Isla Morada* and the 600-passenger MV *Fantasía del Mar.* Argo Tours ferries depart Muelle 18 at 8:30 am and 3:30 pm weekdays, returning from the island at 10 am and 4:30 pm. On weekends and holidays, the boats depart Muelle 18 at 8:30 and 11:30 am and 4 pm, returning from Isla Taboga at 10 am and 2:30 and 5:30 pm. The roundtrip fare between the capital and Taboga is US$7.50.

To get to Muelle 18, take one of the squat little Balboa buses leaving Plaza Cinco de Mayo. Because Taboga is a popular retreat, you'd be wise to reserve a seat on one of the ferries a few days in advance. You'll want to call to confirm departure times anyway.

Getting Around
Few people feel a need to hire a taxi on Taboga, but if you do or if you want to reach the island's highest point without getting the exercise, you can usually go to the ferry pier and find a flatbed truck with benches in the back. There are two of them on the island, and they are its sole taxis. A ride to the Hotel Chu, on the waterfront near the center of town, costs US$2 per person. A ride to the top of the island and back runs US$5 per person, more if there's only one passenger.

Archipiélago de las Perlas

In January 1979, after the followers of the Ayatollah Ruholla Khomeini had forced Shah Mohammed Reza Pahlavi to pack up his hundreds of millions of dollars and flee Iran, the shah looked the world over and moved to Isla Contadora. It's one of 90 named islands in the Archipiélago de las Perlas, or Pearl Islands, any one of which is fit for a king – or a shah.

These islands, plus 130 unnamed islets in the Pearl chain, lie between 64 and 113km southeast of Panama City and are the stuff of travel magazines: white-sand beaches, turquoise waters, swaying palms, colorful fish and sea turtles sharing lagoons with snorkelers. And out of the oysters that abound here come some of the world's finest pearls, including the 31-carat 'Peregrina' pearl, which has been worn by a Spanish king, an English queen and a French emperor and today belongs to actress Elizabeth Taylor. (When the pearl was found, more than 400 years ago, it was considered so magnificent that the slave who discovered it was given his freedom!)

In fact, it was pearls that initially brought the islands to the Old World's attention. Vasco Núñez de Balboa, within days of his discovery of the Pacific Ocean, learned from an Indian guide of nearby islands rich with pearls. Balboa was anxious to visit the islands, but he was told that a hostile chief ruled them, and the explorer decided to postpone the visit. He nonetheless named the archipelago 'Islas de las Perlas' and declared it Spanish property. The year was 1513, and Balboa vowed to return one day to kill the chief and claim his pearls for the king of Spain.

But before he could fulfill his vow, Spanish governor Pedro Arias de Ávila, who loathed the great explorer for his popularity with the king, dispatched Gaspar de Morales, the governor's cousin, to the islands to secure the pearls spoken of by Balboa. Once on the islands, Morales captured 20 chieftains and gave them to his dogs to tear to pieces. The purportedly hostile chief, a man named Dites, initially resisted Morales and his men, but after a battle in which many Indians died, the chief saw the futility of warring with Spaniards, and he presented Morales with a basket of large and lustrous pearls. Despite

the gift, all the Pearl Indians were dead within two years.

History books do not record the circumstances of Dites' death, but they do record Balboa's. In 1517, the same year that Morales raided Las Perlas, Pedrarias (as the governor was often called) falsely charged Balboa with treason and had the loyal public servant and four of his closest friends beheaded in the Caribbean coastal town of Aclá. See the Comarca de San Blás chapter for details.

In the years that followed Morales' arrival in the archipelago, the Spaniards harvested the islands' oyster beds like the greedy businessmen they were. Because they had slain all the Indians, they found it necessary to bring in slaves from Africa to collect oysters. The island that was used for counting the pearls before they were shipped to Panama City – and thence to Spain – was named Contadora, which is Spanish for 'counting house.' The island has retained its name, and the blacks who presently live in the Archipiélago de las Perlas are direct descendants of the first slaves.

Today people inhabit no more than a dozen of the 220 islands and islets that comprise the Archipiélago de las Perlas. The largest of the group is Isla del Rey at 240 sq km, followed by Isla San José (45.3 sq km), Isla Pedro González (14.9 sq km), Isla Viveros (6.6 sq km) and Isla Caña (3.2 sq km).

With few exceptions, tourists visit only five of Las Perlas: Isla Contadora (at 1.2 sq km), Isla Saboga (2.96 sq km), Isla Casaya (2.75 sq km), Isla Casayeta (0.46 sq km) and Isla San Telmo (1.73 sq km). Of these, Contadora is the most accessible, developed and visited; Saboga attracts the occasional explorer who must check out the colonial church, but it is pillaged, unattractive and poorly maintained. Casaya and neighboring Casayeta are frequented by pearl shoppers, and Isla San Telmo is the site of a new lodge that's run by the environmental group Ancon and a WWII-era Japanese submarine that was abandoned on a beach.

Unfortunately, coral fields throughout the archipelago were severely damaged during the 1982-83 El Niño. (El Niño is a change in ocean temperatures that, among a great many other horrible things, starves marine life along the entire eastern Pacific coast.) The coral, which is mostly of the mushroom and elkhorn variety (there's also lots of brain and soft corals such as fans and sponges), was making a strong comeback when the 1997-98 El Niño struck. At the time this was penned (in early 1998), the coral was doing well but was not out of danger.

If snorkeling (and/or diving) is a big part of your trip, you should contact a reputable dive operator to learn the current conditions of the eastern Pacific coral fields before you make any reservations. That said, under normal circumstances – and even in El Niño-ish early 1998 – these waters contain many lovely creatures, including leatherback, carey and hawksbill turtles; bull, nurse and white-tip reef sharks; shovelnose guitarfish; and a wide variety of rays.

There is no tourist office, bank or post office on any of the islands in the Archipiélago de las Perlas, and accommodations are limited to the islands of Contadora and San Telmo.

ISLA CONTADORA

This small island is one of the closest of Las Perlas to Panama City and is by far the most visited. There are convenient daily flights to and from the capital, several options for lodging, good snorkeling and beaches, a reputable dive center and a variety of restaurants.

Nearly all the tourist facilities are on the northern side of the island, within walking distance of the airstrip. The other side consists primarily of forest, beautiful homes and secluded beaches. Contadora is also home to the country's only official nude beach, Playa de las Suecas (Swedish Women Beach).

There are public phones near the airstrip and the police station, and at the Hotel Contadora Resort.

Pirates in the Bay

Beginning in the late 17th century, the Bahía de Panamá, home to the Pearl and Taboga island groups, was the scene of pirate exploits unsurpassed anywhere in the New World. Henry Morgan's successful 1671 sacking of the city of Panamá induced other buccaneers to enter the area and try their hands at plundering and pillaging Spanish territory and ships along the Pacific coast. Many are the stories of pirates using the Archipiélago de las Perlas as a hideout and springboard for attacks.

One of the era's most significant escapades occurred in May 1685 near Las Perlas, when the largest number of trained seamen and fighters ever assembled under a buccaneer flag in the Pacific played cat-and-mouse with a Spanish armada of 18 ships. The pirate fleet consisted of 10 French and English vessels united under the English captain Edward Blake. Because his fleet was deficient in cannons but sufficient in muskets, it was Blake's policy to avoid long-range fighting. Despite his fleet's inferior numbers, he itched for a close encounter with the Spaniards.

When the two great forces came within sight of each other on May 28, Blake ordered two of his principal ships (one led by a Frenchman, the second by an Englishman) to initiate an attack on the Spanish fleet. Fearing the Spaniards' cannons, both men refused to obey. Blake's crew exchanged shots with the Spanish vice-admiral, but Blake – seeing the imprudence of continuing battle with the odds stacked against him and some of his officers bowing out – ordered his slower ships to flee while his and another fast vessel delayed the conquistadors.

The Spaniards opened fire with their big guns, but the pirates managed some nifty and risky evasive maneuvers between rocky islets at the northern end of the archipelago, and their pursuers gave up the chase. Blake's ships anchored off the archipelago's Isla Pacheca that night, fully expecting the Spanish armada to engage them the next day. Instead, for reasons that mystify historians, the Spanish admiral ordered his fleet to return to Panamá. In the days that followed, dissent arose among the buccaneers, and the short-lived French-English pirate confederacy dissolved.

Today little evidence of the pirates and Spaniards remains in the Archipiélago de las Perlas besides the distant offspring of the Spaniards' slaves. Forests once felled to make ships have grown back. Storms, termites and wood worms have destroyed the old Spanish structures. Only a church and a stone dam on Isla Saboga and wells on Islas Pacheca and Chapera testify to the Spaniards' presence. ∎

Beaches

There are 12 beaches on this 1.2-sq-km island, all covered with white sand and most unoccupied except during major holidays. Five beaches are particularly lovely: Playa Larga, Playa de las Suecas, Playa Cacique, Playa Ejecutiva and Playa Galeón. Although spread around three sides of the island, all can be visited in as little as 20 minutes on a rented four-wheeler or moped.

Playa Larga is always the most crowded of the beaches, as it is in front of the expansive Hotel Contadora Resort. Around the corner to the south is Playa de las Suecas, where you can sunbathe in the buff without violating any laws. Continuing west 400m, you'll find Playa Cacique, a fairly large and generally unvisited beach. On the northern side of the island, Playa Ejecutiva is intimate except during holidays; the large house on the bluff to the east is where the shah of Iran once lived. Playa Galeón, to the northeast, is conveniently located in front of a popular bar.

Snorkeling

The snorkeling around Contadora can be fantastic. There are five coral fields near the island, and within them you can expect to see schools of angelfish, damselfish, moray eels, parrotfish, puffer fish, butterflyfish, white-tip reef sharks and a whole lot more. Even in the waters off Playa Larga, the most popular of Isla Contadora's beaches, you can often see sea turtles, manta rays and amberjack.

The coral fields are found offshore from the following places: the eastern end of Playa de las Suecas; Punta Verde, just south of Playa Larga; both ends of Playa Galeón; and the western end of Playa Ejecutiva. Also, although there is little coral at the southwestern end of the island, there is a lot of marine life among the rocks in front and east of Playa Roca.

Snorkeling trips can be arranged at the Hotel Contadora Resort (see Places to Stay, below) and at Captain Morgan's Diving Center (☎/fax 250-4029). Captain Morgan's is near the northern end of the airstrip, close to the Aeroperlas ticket office; its mailing address is Centro de Buceo Capitán Morgan, Apartado 55-0398, Paitilla, Panamá, República de Panamá.

Salvatore Fishing (see Fishing, below) offers an attractive snorkeling package: three hours, three islands, for US$30 per person. It also offers a seven-island, wholeday snorkeling tour that costs a very reasonable US$25 per person (minimum eight people).

Diving

All the coral fields mentioned under Snorkeling (above) are fine dive sites. Another good site, in water too deep for snorkeling, is a rock shelf directly in front of Playa

Roca that abounds with marine life. In this deeper water you'll want to keep an eye out for snapper, grunt and white-tip reef sharks.

Captain Morgan's Diving Center (see above) is a full-service dive operator that offers a variety of options, including the following:

- a two-tank boat dive (includes weight belt only); US$40
- a one-tank night boat dive (includes weights and dive light); US$55
- a one-tank night boat dive (includes nose-to-toes gear and dive light); US$60
- a two-tank boat dive (includes nose-to-toes gear); US$75
- three days of diving (includes daily two-tank boat and shore dives); US$200

The center also offers scuba classes. A week's worth of instruction leading to a YMCA open-water diving certificate costs US$370. Advanced and specialty classes are available for US$150. For people who want to try scuba diving but don't want to become certified, there's a US$50 class. English, German and Spanish are spoken.

Fishing

Salvatore Fishing (☎/fax 250-4109), operating out of the Hotel Contadora Resort, offers half and full-day fishing trips for US$45 and US$90, respectively. You can rent a boat for US$180 per half-day. The business is run by Salvatore Morello and his wife, both of whom speak English and Spanish. Their boats include two 32-foot cabin cruisers and one 26-foot open fisherman.

Four-Wheeling

Contadora lends itself very well to tooting around on a four-wheeler (also known as a funny bike), which is a small vehicle like a golf cart but a lot more rugged. There are few other vehicles on the island to collide with, and four-wheelers are pretty easy to operate. If you're short on time and tight with your money, you can rent a four-wheeler first thing in the morning for an hour, scout out your favorite beaches or

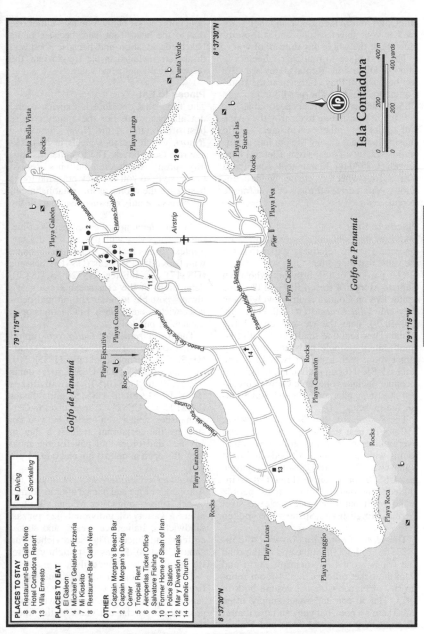

Isla Contadora

0	200	400 m
0	200	400 yards

PANAMÁ PROVINCE

PLACES TO STAY
8 Restaurant-Bar Gallo Nero
9 Hotel Contadora Resort
13 Villa Ernesto

PLACES TO EAT
3 El Galeón
4 Michael's Gelatiere-Pizzeria
7 Mi Kioskito
8 Restaurant-Bar Gallo Nero

OTHER
1 Captain Morgan's Beach Bar
2 Captain Morgan's Diving Center
5 Tropical Rent
6 Aeroperlas Ticket Office
9 Salvatore Fishing
10 Former Home of Shah of Iran
11 Police Station
12 Mar y Diversión Rentals
14 Catholic Church

⬕ Diving
ᵇ Snorkelling

Golfo de Panamá

Golfo de Panamá

Punta Verde
Punta Bella Vista
Playa Larga
Playa de las Suecas
Playa Fea
Playa Galeón
Playa Cacique
Playa Comoa
Playa Ejecutiva
Playa Camarón
Playa Caracol
Playa Lucas
Playa Dimaggio
Playa Roca

Paseo Balboa
Paseo Galeón
Paseo Rodrigo de Bastidas
Paseo de los Guaras
Paseo de los Cunas

Airstrip
Pier
Rocks

other sites, return the vehicle and then walk back to your selected spots and still pretty much have the whole day in front of you.

The best place to rent four-wheelers is Mar y Diversión Rentals, toward the southern end of Playa Larga near the Hotel Contadora Resort. The per-hour price is US$15; the per-day price is negotiable.

If it's in your nature to destroy the peace and quiet of other vacationers while chasing innocent marine life out into a dangerous sea, by all means rent a Jet Ski here as well (US$30 for 30 minutes). And if you rent a four-wheeler, please be ecoconscious – don't drive off roads or over fragile terrain.

Places to Stay

Lodgings on Contadora leave a lot to be desired: They're relatively expensive for the value that they offer.

The parents of the brothers who own Captain Morgan's Beach Bar and the dive center live on Contadora in a lovely home they call *Villa Ernesto* (☎ 250-4112, fax 250-4029), near the western end of the island. They rent one small room with two small, sinking single beds and a slightly larger room with a decent twin bed. The prices: US$30 for an individual, US$50 for a couple (includes one large German breakfast). German, plus some English and Spanish, are spoken.

The *Restaurante-Bar Gallo Nero* (☎/fax 250-4061), near the Aeroperlas office and overlooking the runway, rents three small rooms with air-con but soft beds and cold water only. Rates are US$40 for a single and US$50 for a couple (breakfast is included). The owners are the nicest people in the world, but these prices are excessive. German, English and Spanish are spoken here.

The *Hotel Contadora Resort* (☎ 250-4033, fax 250-4000), at the end of the road that winds around the airstrip's north end from the ticket office, is a 354-room monstrosity of French Colonial design, built in 1975. The air-con and water supply often fail. There's a pool, but you can't use it after 10 pm. There's a tennis court and a nine-

hole golf course, but no one uses either one due to the heat. That said, because of its beachside location and because food and drinks are included in the US$85 rate, the resort is really not a bad value.

Places to Eat

The food on Contadora is expensive and not all that good. For the money, you're best off staying at the *Hotel Contadora Resort,* which includes meals in its package rate (see above). The food here is usually pretty mediocre, but it's served buffet-style so you can pick out what looks best. Like the rooms at this establishment, the meals are only reasonable as part of the package.

At *El Galeon,* near the Aeroperlas office, the offerings vary with the catch of the day. Typical dishes include fish in garlic sauce with fries (US$15), steak (US$16), octopus (US$17) and lobster (US$20 to US$30, depending on the crustacean's size). It's always possible to order shrimp and octopus ceviche here (US$6). El Galeon is open noon to 11 pm daily.

The *Restaurante-Bar Gallo Nero,* uphill from the Aeroperlas office, offers salads (US$2.50), shrimp cocktails (US$8.50), fish plates (US$7.50 to US$9), meat items (US$7.50 to US$10.50), shrimp dishes (from US$13.50 to US$15) and lobster (US$19.50 to US$21). It specializes in German dishes, which aren't listed, but you can stop by the restaurant at least a day in advance and order and pay for the meal then. It's open noon to 3 pm and 6 to 11 pm daily.

Michael's Gelatiere-Pizzeria, near the Aeroperlas office and named after its former owner, singer-songwriter Michael Bolton, offers a variety of individual-size pizzas, sandwiches, Italian ice cream, and sodas, coffees and juices. The sandwiches run about US$4.50. Pizzas cost slightly more. It's open 8 am to 10 pm daily.

The small shop *Mi Kioskito,* just uphill from the Aeroperlas office, houses a tiny sandwich-and-beverage counter where it's possible to purchase a glass of the finest drink on earth: sangria made in the old-fashioned way (with fruit steeped in Burgundy for a night before serving). Mi Kioskito also sells ceviche, sandwiches, ice cream and cake.

Entertainment

Captain Morgan's Beach Bar, near the northern end of the airstrip, corners the market on after-dark fun on Contadora. Run by two wild German brothers, this is the place for party animals and firebugs. The 'Captain Morgan's Special' arrives in a glass the size of a Jacuzzi and consists of gin, rum, more rum and, I believe, more rum. When you're served a 'Fireball,' the lights are turned off and a flaming liquid is poured from a height of several feet into your glass.

Captain Morgan's becomes a dance club at 10 pm most nights and closes when the last patron waddles out. The bar opens at 5 pm daily and offers a happy hour between 5 and 7 pm and again between 11 pm and midnight. On the day of our Lord, happy hour goes from 9 pm till closing. Lordy! The Hotel Contadora Resort used to try to compete with the Captain but wisely gave up. Now it just provides transportation to the beach bar for its guests who live for the night.

A bit more staid is the restaurant-bar *El Galeon,* which has a lovely ocean view, tables inside and out and three pool tables. The *Restaurante-Bar Gallo Nero* has a full bar and overlooks the runway.

There's a bar at the *Hotel Contadora Resort,* and there are always people patronizing it because drinks are free to guests. There are tables inside and out, but for ambiance it does not compare favorably with Captain Morgan's, El Galeon or even the Mi Kioskito shop/restaurant.

Shopping

Pearls Oysters are still caught, and pearls are still found, around the Archipiélago de las Perlas. Although pearls are sometimes offered for sale on other islands, the best places to look for them are Isla Casaya and neighboring Isla Casayeta, about 12km to the south of Contadora; Captain Morgan's can take you there. Prices are generally

very reasonable, and there's always room for bargaining.

When you're looking at pearls, it's good to keep two things in mind. First, pearl sellers tend to keep their goods in oil, so that they'll have a lovely shine and sparkle; always dry the pearl that intrigues you and then see how it looks. Secondly, you can't add luster to a pearl – if the dry pearl in your hand looks dull, that's the way it's going to stay. No jeweler back home will be able to add luster to it, which is why a glistening pearl is worth so much more than a dull one.

Clothing Just uphill from the Aeroperlas office is the little shop Mi Kioskito, which is *the* place on Contadora to look for islandwear. The shop offers many all-cotton dresses of Balinese design made by local artist Carmen Andrés. The women's sun hats, also made by Carmen, are light, brightly colored and unique. There are lots of T-shirts, purses, dark glasses and knick-knacks as well. You can also buy food and great sangria here (see Places to Eat). Carmen is from Spain, which will become evident when you taste her sangria; only Spaniards know how to make memorable sangria.

Getting There & Away

Aeroperlas (☎ 250-4026 on Contadora; 269-4555 in Panama City) flies between Aeropuerto Paitilla in Panama City and Contadora twice daily on weekdays, three times on Saturday and four times on Sunday. The roundtrip fare is US$79. Flying time is 30 minutes each way. It also flies to San Miguel on Isla del Rey, southeast of Contadora, three times weekly (US$22/44 one-way/roundtrip).

Aviatur (☎ 270-1748 in Panama City) flies from Aeropuerto Paitilla to Contadora and San Miguel daily.

To get from one island to another, you must travel by boat, although some islands can be reached by chartered aircraft. Check with the Hotel Contadora Resort, Salvatore Fishing or Captain Morgan's Diving Center for boat rides to other islands.

Getting Around

Because the island is so small, there are no taxis on it. The Hotel Contadora Resort has a van that shuttles guests to and from the airstrip, and it will take guests to Captain Morgan's Beach Bar at night upon request. There are four-wheelers for rent (see the Four-Wheeling section).

ISLA SAN TELMO

One of the farthest of Las Perlas from Panama City, Isla San Telmo was donated to the environmental group Ancon during the mid-1990s and set aside for preservation. This heavily forested, 200-hectare island with numerous secluded beaches is perfect for someone in real need of an escape. There's no one on the island except Ancon personnel and guests of Ancon's 10 new, double-bedroom, air-con cabañas.

There's a lake on the island that's home to a big crocodile, and there are thousands of brown pelicans, frigatebirds and boobies in the area. The water around the island is clear and inviting, but the current is strong in places, so be careful. On one beach there's a rusting black Japanese submarine that was abandoned during WWII. During the war, many people wondered why the Japanese didn't attack the Panama Canal, which was of strategic importance to the USA. Perhaps the submarine was

part of an aborted mission. Also ripe for exploration are trails on the island, as well as trails on neighboring islands.

This place is really not for social animals, unless they're taking a break. But if your idea of a good time is having a beach to yourself, far from small talk, commuter traffic and telephones, this is a good getaway. The cabañas cost US$90 per night, including meals. For details and transportation to and from the island, contact Ancon Expeditions of Panama (☎ 269-9414/9415, fax 264-3713, sales@ecopanama.com, www.ecopanama.com; in the USA ☎ 847-392-7865, 888-888-4106), Apartado 0852-1509, Panamá, República de Panamá.

Eastern Panamá Province

Beyond the capital city, the Interamericana heads eastward through several small towns before arriving at the Darién Gap, that last defiant stretch of wilderness separating the continents of North and South America. The Darién Gap is the sole barrier in the way of an otherwise unbroken 30,600km highway winding from Circle, AK, to Puerto Montt, Chile.

Since the first Pan-American Highway Congress met in Buenos Aires in 1925, the nations of the Americas have devoted considerable money and engineering skills to the completion of a great hemispheric road system. Today only 150km of unfinished business prevent that system from being realized. Now the governments of Panama and Colombia stand poised to construct this missing bit of pavement. Barring an unexpected turn of events, the hemispheric highway will be completed during the first decade of the third millennium AD.

But until then, the highway on the Panamanian side of the divide will continue to end at the sweaty, ramshackle town of Yaviza, in Darién Province. Separating Yaviza and Panama City are 266km of mostly bad road and cattle country – the stuff of road trips. Efforts to pave the road all the way to Yaviza, perhaps a two-year project, were begun in early 1998.

The drive from the capital to Yaviza takes about nine hours during the dry season, longer during the rainy season, and will take much less time if the road becomes completely paved. For information on towns along the way beyond the Panamá-Darién border, see the Darién Province chapter.

CHEPO

Beyond the urban sprawl of eastern Panama City and past the turnoff for Tocumen International Airport, the landscape becomes increasingly barren on both sides of the Interamericana. Gas stations and accommodations become somewhat scarce and the views monotonous.

Not 40 years ago the highway ended at Chepo and a sign announced the start of the Darién Gap. (Today most Panamanians still consider all the country east of Chepo as the Darién, although much of it is actually within Panamá Province.) From Chepo to beyond the Colombian border, there was only roadless jungle. To go any farther by vehicle, one resorted to *piraguas* – needle-like canoes hollowed from logs. These were placed in the Río Mamoní and pushed deep into the Darién rainforest by outboard motors. The 'roads' from there on out were creeks, streams and rivers.

Today a main road swings out from the Interamericana and into Chepo. The town continues to exist mainly as a launching point into the Darién: there's a gas station, a place to buy ice and general stores with lots of canned goods. There's not a single *pensión* or hotel in town. People arrive, stock up and go.

There's a checkpoint 1km east of town where people coming from the Darién are stopped and asked to show their IDs and are sometimes searched. It's only 52km from Panama City, but it seems like another country and another time.

Buses leave the Terminal de Buses al Interior, on Avenida Ascañio Villalaz in the Curundu district of Panama City, for Chepo every 40 minutes from 8:30 am to 5:10 pm. The trip takes 75 minutes; the one-way fare is US$1.20. The bus continues on to Cañita.

NUSAGANDI

Just before you reach the town of El Llano, you'll see the turnoff for Nusagandi, a forest reserve on the El Llano-Cartí road just inside the Comarca de San Blás. The 40,000-hectare park was created by the Kuna, primarily to try to keep squatters from settling on their land. But the park consists mostly of species-rich primary forest and was a perfect choice for conservation.

If you're driving a 4WD vehicle with a strong engine and plenty of clearance, I highly recommend working this 20km detour into your hell-and-back road trip to the Darién Gap. The road is really bad and rarely traveled, but the reward is fantastic, especially for birders. This is the best spot in Panama to look for the speckled antshrike, the black-headed antthrush and the black-crowned antpitta. Various tanagers, including the rufous-winged, are numerous. There are some gorgeous waterfalls in this jungle as well.

There's the very basic *Nusagandi Nature Lodge* at about the 20km mark. However, you can't just show up there. The Kuna created an agency – the Project for the Study and Management of Wild Areas of the Kuna Yala (PEMASKY) – to administer the park, and it must be notified in advance of your arrival. Write the PEMASKY office in Panama City at Apartado 2012, Paraíso, Ancón, República de Panamá. Or, better yet, contact Ancon Expeditions of Panama (see the Isla San Telmo section in this chapter for contact information) and have it make the arrangements; although it offers guided tours to Nusagandi, its staff would be pleased to assist you.

EL LLANO

Eighteen km separate Chepo and El Llano, a small community with a couple of simple restaurants, plus a tire repair service and a public phone. The highway is no longer paved; it's now packed gravel.

The town is surrounded by rice fields and, beyond these, rolling hills covered with cattle and teak trees. Teak farms now abound in Panama. A sapling costs only 35¢. Plant it in the ground, let it grow for 12 years, then sell the precious hardwood; at current prices you'll reap US$1000 per tree. Teak projects reduce the pressure to log the remaining natural forests, but local birds don't know what to do with them. The trees were introduced to Panama from Asia and the local wildlife hasn't adapted to them. If you stroll deep inside a teak farm, you won't hear a single bird chirp.

CAÑITA

Ten km beyond El Llano is another small town bisected by the Interamericana. From this point on, the highway is dirt – or mud if you're on it during the rainy season. There's a gas station and a public phone in town.

There are also three restaurants; at one of them, thatch-roofed, open-sided *El Descanso,* the nailed-up skins of jaguars, ocelots and other animals attest to the health of the rainforest that used to blanket the area. It was felled within the last 20 years, mainly to make room for cattle ranches (see the Logging the Darién sidebar for more information). El Descanso is decent and cheap, with few meals over US$2. It's typical of the restaurants between Chepo and Yaviza. It doesn't have menus, but a waitress will tell you what's available. Meals typically consist of chicken or beef or pork, with rice and beans. The selection is usually dependent upon which trucks have stopped by recently. If a chicken truck has stopped, chicken will be offered. There's a bar next door. Nearby are the *Flor de Cañita* and the *Interiorano* restaurants, which aren't so good.

Buses leave Panama City's Terminal de Buses al Interior for Cañita every 40 minutes from 8:30 am to 5:10 pm. The trip takes 2½ hours; the one-way fare is US$2.50.

LAGO BAYANO

As you continue east along the Interamericana, the only forest you'll see is the secondary forest around Lago Bayano that

Logging the Darién
Trees are still being felled in Darién Province, and many are transported by truck along the Interamericana to two huge mills: one is in Chepo, and the other is in 24 de Diciembre, a village near Tocumen. On a single day in the dry season, you can count dozens of lumber trucks passing by.

An even greater number of Darién trees, which are clear-cut, are moved to the mills by barge. Still others are sprayed with a chemical that prevents rot and floated down rivers to the mills. The chemical has killed most of the fish in the rivers used by loggers.

The deforestation has also resulted in severe water shortages from Chepo to Yaviza during the dry season. There are other environmental problems, but still Panamanian politicians speak of completing the Carretera Interamericana through pristine Parque Nacional Darién into Colombia. The loggers have a lot of influence. ∎

protects the lake's watershed. Lago Bayano, which supports a hydroelectric project, was created by the damming of the Río Bayano. Because the forest is owned by a utility company, it will likely remain intact.

IPETÍ

This town, 35km east of Lago Bayano, offers the visitor a couple of restaurants, a gas station and a public phone. Between here and Las Aguas Frías, on the Darién Province-Panamá Province border, the Serranía de Majé (Majé Range) runs along the southern side of the highway. The range contains some lovely forest, at a distance from the highway; you can see this forest best as you approach the town of Tortí. It's disappearing rapidly but should still be visible through the shelf life of this book.

TORTÍ

In Tortí, 148km into the 266km road trip, you'll come across the first pensión east of Panama City – the *Hospedaje Tortí* (no phone). It has 20 rooms, each with a firm mattress, a portable fan, a small table with a candle, towels and soap. The floors are bare concrete, the bathroom is shared and the electricity goes off at 10 pm. But for US$6 a night, especially after a long day, it's a great value. The four shared showers and two shared toilets *are* clean. Also in town are three public phones, a health clinic, police and gas stations and several restaurants.

HIGUERONAL

There's a gas station, two restaurants and a public phone here. Down the road a little, the town of Cañazas offers tourists only a pay phone.

TO THE DARIÉN GAP

Crossing the border from Panamá Province into Darién Province, you'll pass the towns of Las Aguas Frías, Santa Fé and Metetí before you arrive in Yaviza. For details on these towns, turn to the Darién Province chapter.

Western Panamá Province

There are many communities in the western section of Panamá Province, but the area is known primarily for its many lovely beaches. Every weekend thousands of stressed-out Panama City residents hop into their cars or board buses and head west on the Interamericana, determined to have some fun in the sun beside the lapping Pacific.

LA CHORRERA

With 51,000 residents, La Chorrera is the second-largest city in Panamá Province. Despite its size, the city has relatively little to offer visitors. It is bisected by the Interamericana and located in a fairly prosperous agricultural area, but as one tourism official put it: 'It's a city people pass by.' Still, La Chorrera is a place with a past, a culture, a waterfall and a unique local drink: the *chicheme* (see Places to Eat for details).

Orientation

The Interamericana runs from east to west through La Chorrera, slowing to one sluggish lane in each direction as vehicles enter and exit the highway from side streets. It was mainly to reduce the traffic on the highway, which becomes Avenida de las Américas as it passes through town, that a parallel, four-lane highway was built just south of town in the 1980s. This young stretch of highway – the Autopista Arraiján-Chorrera, which is only 28km long – diverges from the Interamericana just west of La Chorrera and at Arraiján, a town northeast of La Chorrera. The new road enables motorists to bypass La Chorrera altogether, saving 30 minutes of driving time. There's one catch, however: The Autopista Arraiján-Chorrera exacts a US$1 toll. There's no free lunch.

Information

There is no tourist office in La Chorrera, but people wanting to know more about the city and surrounding area can obtain reliable information from the office of the Instituto Nacional de Cultura (INAC; ☎ 253-2306) at the intersection of Calle Maria Leticia and the Interamericana. The office, appropriately located in an art school, is open 8 am to 5 pm weekdays and 10 am to 2 pm Saturday. Only Spanish is spoken here. Here you can learn about the town's culture and festivals (see Special Events, below, for details).

There is no shortage of banks in La Chorrera, and most of them are conveniently located on the Interamericana halfway through town. Among them are the Banco Nacional de Panamá and the Banco del Istmo, with normal business hours.

The post office is on Calle San Francisco two blocks south of the Interamericana. It's open 8 am to 5 pm weekdays and 8 am to noon Saturday. There are many pay phones in town.

Waterfalls

La Chorrera has only one true tourist attraction and, sadly, it isn't what it once was. It's a series of cascades on the Río Caimito, the last of which takes a 30m plunge into a broad swimming hole. Years ago the Caimito was a raging river and both of its banks were swathed in pristine jungle. Today much of the river has been siphoned off upstream and dozens of plastic bottles bob in the natural pool below the falls. Some of the jungle still remains, and with a little effort by INRENARE, Panamá's natural resources agency, the site's beauty could be restored. But until then only blind romantics can ignore the pollution. The falls might be considerably prettier during a period of heavy rains.

To get here from the Interamericana, turn north onto Calle Larga at the Banco del Istmo and drive 1km until you reach an intersection with a Super La Fortuna market on one side and a Mini Super Pacific market on the other. Turn right just before the mini-market and then stay to the left on the road. The falls are at the end of this road, 1km from the intersection. If you do not have a vehicle, you can hire a taxi to take you to the falls (US$1.50 each way) or hail a bus with 'Calle Larga' scrawled on its windshield; they run up and down that street all day and charge 25¢ a ride.

Special Events

The region is known for its beautiful folkloric dances, which can best be seen during its popular fair. La Feria de La Chorrera lasts 10 days and is held in late January or early February; dates vary from year to year. The festivities also include parades, a rodeo and cockfights. La Chorrera is also known for drum dances that have their origin in African music brought over by slaves. You can see these dances during the fair.

Places to Stay

The *Hospedaje Chorrera* (☎ 253-7887), on Avenida de las Américas, has 10 rooms with air-con for US$16 apiece and 12 rooms with fan only for US$14 apiece. All of the rooms have private bathrooms, firm beds, TVs, tiled floors and cold water only. It's a clean and secure place. Across the street from the Chorrera and 100m to the

east is the *Hospedaje Tropical* (no phone), which looked inviting from the outside, but I wasn't allowed past the barred front doors.

Places to Eat

Broster Pollo, on Avenida Libertador one block east of Calle 31 Sur, serves tasty and filling red meat soup (US$1), a very decent bistec picado (US$3) and several chicken dishes (US$3.50). For Chinese food, locals recommend *Shangri La,* which is on the Interamericana near the eastern end of town.

A popular activity in La Chorrera is drinking chicheme, a nonalcoholic beverage. This local drink is made of milk, mashed sweet corn, cinnamon and vanilla. People come from as far away as Panamá City just to drink the stuff, which many view as a life-extending concoction. An excellent place to try chicheme is the takeout restaurant *El Chichemito,* on the corner of Calles L Oeste and 26 Norte. As you're driving west on the Interamericana, turn right onto Calle 26 Norte (just beyond the 'bbb' shoe store sign) and look for the restaurant, 30m farther on the left.

While you're at El Chichemito, try another local specialty, the boyo chorrerano. It's a sweet-corn tamale containing marinated chicken, bell pepper, garlic, celery, onion and raisins. The women who make it and other boyos (fillings vary; five kinds are made) insist that they're the best boyos in town, and the number of people who flock to this corner food stand evidently agree. El Chichemito is open from 7:30 am to 10:30 pm daily.

Entertainment

About 3km east of La Chorrera on the Interamericana is the *Club La Herradura,* offering three popular public swimming pools and picnic facilities, which are open Sunday only from 10 am to 5 pm; the cost is US$3 for women and children, US$5 for men. The club is also a hopping bar/dance club late on Thursday, Friday and weekend nights. Admission is free for women and usually costs US$5 for men.

Getting There & Away

East- and westbound buses stop at the Delta station, opposite the Pribanco on the Interamericana. Buses for Panama City leave every eight minutes and cost US$1. The ride lasts one hour. Ask for the express bus or you'll be making frequent stops. There are plenty of taxis in town to take you around.

PARQUE NACIONAL ALTOS DE CAMPANA

The easy-to-miss turnoff for this national park is 25km southwest of La Chorrera, on the western side of the Interamericana. The rocky road winds 4.6km to an INRENARE ranger station at the entrance to the park, which is located on Cerro Campana. At the station you must pay a US$1 entry fee. Camping is allowed (US$5 per night); there are no facilities.

About 200m beyond the station, there's a lookout point from which you have a fantastic view of mostly deforested but completely uninhabited mountains and the Pacific Ocean. Here you're at 1007m and the breeze is very refreshing.

This park requires at least several hours to be appreciated because it's best viewed on foot. Starting at the road's end, beyond the microwave tower, trails will take you into some lovely forest, which is on the much greener Atlantic slope. The difference between the deforested Pacific and the lush Atlantic slopes is nowhere more evident.

Birders are almost certain to see scale-crested pygmy-tyrant, orange-bellied trogon and chestnut-capped brush-finch. The list of rare possibilities includes the slaty antwren, the white-tipped sicklebill and the purplish-backed quail-dove.

No buses go up the road leading to the park. You pretty much need to have your own vehicle, rely on the services of a guide company or do some rather serious hiking to get in. However, getting to the turnoff for the park is easy. Virtually any bus using that section of the Interamericana will drop you there. Getting picked up isn't a problem during the day.

PUNTA CHAME

The turnoff from the Interamericana for Punta Chame is at the tiny hamlet of Bejuco, 3km west of the turnoff for Parque Nacional Altos de Campana. The paved road that links the Interamericana to the point first winds past rolling hills, then passes flat land that consists mainly of shrimp farms and red and white mangroves, and then passes dry forest. Few people live along this 24km road because very little rain falls in the area and brackish water makes farming difficult.

Punta Chame is a one-road town on a long, 300m wide peninsula, with residences and vacant lots lining both sides. To the north is a muddy bay; to the east is the Pacific. The bay is popular with windsurfers, but there's no windsurfing equipment available for rent here. The beach on the Pacific side (Playa Chame) has lovely sand, but almost no one comes here due to its inconvenient location and its lack of facilities.

What's intriguing about Punta Chame is that it's slowly being developed, but not in the way that one might expect. The entire point consists of a very clean sand, which is very desirable for use in concrete. So desirable, in fact, that when the Americans began building the locks for the Panama Canal, they used barges to bring sand from the point. Today barges are still taking chunks of Punta Chame away for use in building Panama City skyscrapers. Unless the barges stop arriving, there won't be a Punta Chame in another 100 years.

Places to Stay & Eat

The *Motel Punta Chame* (☎ 264-7560, fax 263-6590) has six cabañas and one house for rent. I can't think of any reason that anyone would want to overnight on the point, but if you do, the rates are a whopping US$49 to US$85. Because the motel faces the muddy bay, the sand here sticks to you. Why the motel wasn't built on the other side of the point, where the fine sand is located, is one of those little mysteries of life. Decent food at decent prices is available here.

PANAMÁ PROVINCE

Getting There & Away

To get to Punta Chame from the Interamericana, catch a bus at the stop at the Punta Chame turnoff (at Bejuco). A bus to the point leaves every hour from 6:30 am to 5:30 pm daily. The fare is US$1.

BEACHES

Starting just south of the town of Chame and continuing along the Pacific coast for the next 40km are dozens of beautiful beaches that are very popular weekend retreats for Panama City residents. About half of these beaches are in Panamá Province, while the remainder are in Coclé Province; those in Coclé are discussed in that chapter.

The beaches are quite similar to one another: All are wide, covered with salt-and-pepper sand and fairly free of litter. The waves at five of the beaches (Malibú, Serena, Teta, El Palmar and Río Mar) attract surfers. See the Surfing section of the Facts for the Visitor chapter for specific information about surfing Teta and Río Mar.

The most popular of these beaches can be reached by local bus or taxi from the Interamericana. Taxis can be hailed at the turnoffs for the beaches and are inexpensive.

Gorgona

Five km southwest of the turnoff for Punta Chame is the turnoff for Gorgona, a small oceanside community offering a variety of accommodations.

The *Hotel Gorgona Jayes* (☎ 223-7775, fax 264-3487 in Gorgona; ☎ 240-6095 in Panama City), 2km down the road to Gorgona, has 40 rooms and two cabañas. All the rooms have air-con, hot water and firm mattresses, and they are clean and otherwise OK. TV is available upon request. Rooms cost US$38 per day weekdays and US$85 Friday, Saturday and Sunday nights. The grounds are unattractive. The beach is about 400m away, and the hotel's van will take you there for 50¢. It's very hot here because there's no breeze.

Continuing another 100m, you'll see the turnoffs for two other hotels, the *El Canadian* (☎ 240-6066) and *Cabañas de Playa Gorgona* (☎ 269-2241/2433, fax 223-1218). El Canadian has six concrete cabins, some with air-con. The place is fairly ugly and rundown, but it's also just a minute's walk from the beach. It is arguably a good value at US$23/30 per cabin weekdays/weekends. There are three beds per cabin. There's no pool and no real facilities to speak of; it's just cheap digs near the beach.

The Cabañas de Playa Gorgona offers 43 concrete cabins, and some rooms are able to accommodate big families. All have kitchenettes and air-con, and there's a pool. Prices for one room with one bed are US$34/45 per night on weekdays/weekends. The largest cabañas cost US$70/100, respectively. This place is a good value, especially if you are in a group. Credit cards are accepted. The hotel also has beach property, which is open to all its guests and contains two pools, lots of palapas and a bar. You can hang out there during the day and retire to the hotel in the evening. There are also two US$90 cabins on the beach property that are quite OK.

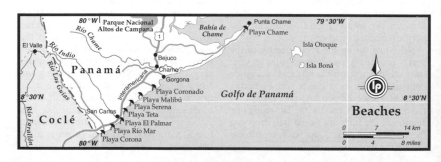

The *Restaurante Tucanes,* on the Inter-americana, looks lovely, but its food is not good. A few kilometers west along the highway is the *Restaurante Bar Mi Posada* in Las Lajas, 200m east of the turnoff for Playa Coronado. This place is very popular and has air-con and lots of cheap but tasty food.

Playa Coronado

The turnoff from the Interamericana for Playa Coronado, an affluent beachside community, is 4km southwest of the turnoff for Gorgona. There are two hotels here that I can recommend. The first is the *Club Gaviota* (☎ 227-4929/4969), adjacent to the beach and an extremely good value. There are only two cabañas here: a single for US$49/54 weekdays/weekends (or US$110 if you stay three nights), and a cabin with two beds for US$60/68 (US$135 for three nights). These are small but charming, with TVs and air-con. Breakfasts cost US$3.50, lunches about US$10 and dinners US$10 – but the club stops serving them at 5 pm, when the staff goes home! The place is a little odd in this way, but the grounds are lovely, the location is superb and there are two swimming pools. It's best to make a reservation; remember to call before 5 pm!

The second is the *Coronado Hotel & Resort* (☎ 240-4444, fax 240-4389), which is a true resort: 39 standard rooms, all gorgeous and spacious with every amenity; 12 grand suites and six with kitchenettes; the best beachside golf course in Central America; a good restaurant and an elegant one; tennis courts; a weekend casino; and other facilities like Jacuzzis, saunas, pools, an exercise room, bars and so on. The resort also shuttles guests to and from its beachside property, which features a lovely pool and bar, and guests can rent kayaks, Jet Skis and other water toys. Room rates range from US$135 to US$400.

Also in Playa Coronado is the *Shangri-La* (no phone), which consists of four two-story houses for rent. Even though this once-beautiful place is widely advertised in Panama City, it has been poorly maintained and I don't recommend it.

There are two very good restaurants in the area. Beside the turnoff for Playa Coronado is *Los Che's,* an attractive place with excellent but not inexpensive food, such as sandwiches (US$4), pasta (US$5), grilled corvina (US$7.50), filet mignon (US$9.50) and lobster thermidor (US$17). Los Che's is well known for its rotisserie-cooked meats and fish, its lobster and its clams. *Mi Posada* is 1km east on the highway, and here you can get a tasty and gut-busting meal for as little as US$4.

To get to Club Gaviota and the Coronado Hotel & Resort from the highway, hire one of the taxi vans that park from 6 am to 7 pm daily under the large tree beside the Texaco station at the Playa Coronado turnoff. They charge US$4 to take you to either hotel. Other taxis with longer hours are available in Bejuco, 9km northeast on the Interamericana. If you have your own vehicle, just head into Playa Coronado and ask the guard at the gate to point toward the hotel you want. To get a taxi back to the highway, just call ☎ 240-4960 and give your location; someone will come to pick you up.

San Carlos

Beside the Interamericana, 11km west of the Playa Coronado turnoff, are the *Cabañas Confortables,* which aren't comfortable and cost an outrageous US$67 per night. Across the street is *El Cevichito,* which sells pretty good ceviche cheap: US$2 for a mix of shrimp, corvina, octopus, onion, red pepper and lime juice.

The *Hospedaje San Carlos* (☎ 240-8185) is 200m to the west of the Cabañas Confortables and has 11 rooms with fans (US$13 per room) and four with air-con (US$19). There's no hot water, but the place is clean. The rooms are above a large but not-so-good Chinese restaurant.

Buses to San Carlos from Panama City depart from the Terminal de Buses al Interior every 20 minutes, from 6:30 am to 7 pm. The trip takes 1½ hours; the one-way fare is US$2.75.

Playa Río Mar

Only 1km west of San Carlos along the Interamericana is the turnoff for this small community, which has a nice surprise for the tourist: *Hotel Playa Río Mar* (☎ 240-8027, 223-0192, fax 264-2272), 2km from the highway on a bluff overlooking the ocean. Located 95km from Panama City, this place is a popular weekend retreat for residents of the capital. The hotel has an inviting pool, a bar and a restaurant. Below it is a favorite surfers' beach (see Surfing in the Facts for the Visitor chapter). There are 20 rooms, and each comes with a little table, a dresser and air-con. Five of the rooms have only one large bed; the rest have one big bed and two small beds. The couples' rooms cost US$60 on the weekends, half that during the week. Add US$5 for the larger rooms. Room Nos 15, 16 and 17 – all couples' rooms – are best. As with many of the hotels along this stretch of coast, there's a chance that you'll have the place to yourself on weekdays.

The restaurant here specializes in corvina: the corvina apanada (breaded corvina; US$9) is particularly good. The serving is generous, but if you're very hungry, you're better off with one of the rice dishes, such as the fried rice with chicken (US$6). The lobster thermidor (US$20) is excellent. The restaurant also serves four meat dishes (US$6 to US$13).

Playa Corona

Five km west along the Interamericana from the Playa Río Mar turnoff is a small sign announcing the turnoff for the *Hotel Playa Corona* (☎ 240-8037, fax 264-0872), which has an extremely exotic atmosphere. That's no fluke; its Russian owner planted hundreds of lush plants on the 1.5-hectare property when he bought it in the 1970s. The beach out front is lovely, wide and perhaps the safest in the area, because silt from a nearby river has tapered an otherwise quick drop-off.

There's a campground here with showers and bathrooms, charging US$11 per night. The rooms vary a lot, but all have air-con, refrigerators and private bathrooms. Ten rooms that can house four to six people go for US$55 per night. Other rooms cost US$75 to US$105. There are also eight little campers with fan but no air-con for US$22. There are washing machines and dryers here, a bar and a decent restaurant with food at reasonable prices. The owner was talking about selling the place when I visited it in 1998. If he does, I hope the new owner keeps it the way it is.

On the northern side of the highway, 4km west of the Hotel Playa Corona turnoff, is the *Río Gallal Lodge* (☎ 264-0910), which offers three clean rooms with air-con, firm mattresses, private bathrooms and hot water for US$34 apiece every night of the week. It's near a river I wouldn't go in, and it's not very close to the ocean. It's not a bad deal if you're just looking for a place to crash for the night. It would also make a good base camp if you have your own vehicle, and it's quite possible that the owner would reduce the nightly price if you were to stay three or more consecutive nights and pay in advance.

Bocas del Toro Province

Bocas del Toro Province is bordered by the Caribbean Sea to the north, Veraguas Province to the east, Chiriquí Province to the south and Costa Rica to the west. Most of the province is on the slopes of the Talamanca and Central mountain ranges, but the majority of its 93,000 inhabitants live in low-lying areas along the coast and on islands.

The province contains the large Archipiélago de Bocas del Toro at the mouth of the Laguna de Chiriquí, beginning 35km from the Costa Rican border. The chain consists of 68 islands and numerous mangrove keys. Around them are fields of coral, a titanic variety of marine life and water so emerald in color that Christopher Columbus named the region Veraguas – a contraction of *verdes aguas* (green waters).

When Columbus visited the territory in 1502, on his fourth and final New World voyage, it was inhabited by many nomadic tribes. He was so taken by the beauty of the area that he affixed his name to many sites: Isla Colón (Columbus Island), Isla Cristóbal (Christopher Island), Bahía de Almirante (Admiral's Bay), the major port of Almirante and other sites. Because little gold was found in Bocas del Toro, the Spaniards did not colonize the region, and the Indians were spared their wrath for a while.

During the 17th century, the archipelago became a haven for pirates, mainly because the Spaniards didn't have a presence here. The buccaneers repaired their ships on the islands, built others with wood from their forests and fed upon the many sea turtles that nested on the beaches. Even today most of the archipelago is flush with virgin rainforest, and four species of sea turtle continue to lay their eggs on its beaches, just as they have for thousands of years (see the Turtles' Tragic Troubles sidebar for more details). The pirates are said to have buried treasure on a number of the islands, but to date none of this loot has been found (or at least reported).

During the 17th and 18th centuries, most of the Indians were killed in battles among themselves, by Old World diseases brought by the Spaniards and by Spanish swords. Some Indians intermarried with French Huguenot settlers who arrived on the coast of Bocas del Toro around the end of the 17th century. By 1725 many of the Indians and Huguenots had been killed in fights with Spanish militiamen sent to dislodge the French settlers.

During the early 19th century, blacks from the USA and Colombia's San Andrés and Providencia Islands arrived as slaves of wealthy landowners looking to reestablish themselves in the province. When slavery was abolished, in 1850, the former slaves stayed and eked out a living as fishermen

HIGHLIGHTS

- Snorkeling, diving and sunbathing in the Archipiélago de Bocas del Toro
- Walking the San-San Pond Sak Wetlands, a swampy home to monkeys, sloths and iguanas
- Isla Bastimentos' lovely, seldom-visited beaches, nesting grounds for sea turtles
- Parque Internacional La Amistad, home to jaguars, Indian villages and spectacular jungle rivers
- Península Valiente, where forested slopes and postcard-perfect beaches meet a hammering surf

187

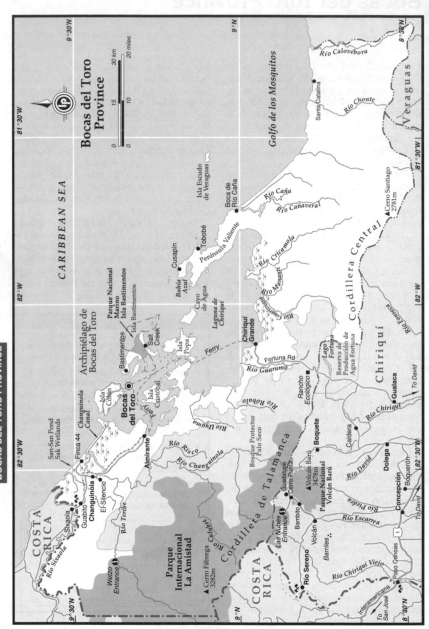

and subsistence farmers. Jamaican blacks joined them toward the end of the 19th century, as the province's banana industry began to develop.

Bocas del Toro's banana industry dates from 1890, when three American brothers arrived here and founded the Snyder Brothers Banana Company. They planted banana trees all along the shores of the Laguna de Chiriquí, at the mouth of which is Isla Colón. That island, because of its central location, quickly became the heart of this new activity. In 1899 the United Fruit Company planted itself in the town of Bocas del Toro on Isla Colón and bought the Snyder Brothers Banana Company.

In the years that followed, United Fruit and smaller growers established banana plantations over a vast area stretching from the archipelago to the Costa Rican border, all of which still exist. The company constructed bridges and roads and even dug a 15km canal to ease the transportation of bananas to the sea, where they were loaded onto ships for export (mainly to the USA). The company also built houses, restaurants, clinics and schools for its workers.

Today United Fruit, which was purchased and renamed several times, is part of the multinational Chiquita Brands International. Chiquita's workers in Bocas del Toro Province grow and export three-quarters of a million tons of bananas annually, and they comprise the largest work force in the province and the most diverse work force in the country. On the payroll are descendants of American, Colombian and Jamaican blacks; the descendants of blacks from the French Antilles who arrived in Panama to work on the railroad and, later, the canal; members of at least four of Panama's seven Indian groups; and many people of mixed indigenous and Spanish ancestry.

Except for a strange few, most tourists don't come to Bocas del Toro for the bananas. They come to enjoy the islands, to snorkel and scuba dive, and to hike in the rainforest. Most, I suspect, regret leaving. This little-visited province is an island-buff's delight and an explorer's treat, with

wide, jungle-flanked rivers, huge swaths of rainforest and long stretches of coastline largely devoid of human beings. Even the easily accessible islands remain relatively tourist-free and only sparsely inhabited.

A major coastal road on the mainland is slated for completion in the next couple of years, and rapid development is now underway on the islands, so progress of the variety not appreciated by naturalists *is* coming to the province. But for the near future, 8745-sq-km Bocas del Toro Province – home to both an enormous international rainforest park and a large group of picturesque islands – has a lot to offer travelers who prefer wild creatures to creature comforts.

Archipiélago de Bocas del Toro

The archipelago consists of six large, mostly forested islands and scores of smaller ones. The large islands are Isla Colón (61 sq km), Isla Popa (53 sq km), Isla Bastimentos (51 sq km), Isla Cristóbal (37 sq km), Cayo de Agua (16 sq km) and Cayo Nancy (8 sq km). Of these islands – four of which are among the country's 10 largest – only Isla Colón has roads, and only Colón and Bastimentos offer accommodations and food.

The archipelago is a biologist's fantasy. It and the adjacent shore represent an isolated pocket of lowlands, semicircled by the foothills of the Talamanca range and by marshes at the mouths of the Ríos Changuinola and Cricamola. Because of its biogeographical isolation, the wildlife in the lowlands of western Bocas del Toro Province includes many taxa not found outside the region. For example, there is a red frog on Isla Bastimentos that lives nowhere else.

A beautiful, coniferlike tree (*Myristicaceae*: prob *Iryanthera*) dominates the forest canopy of the larger islands, giving a unique look to their jungle. The jungle's

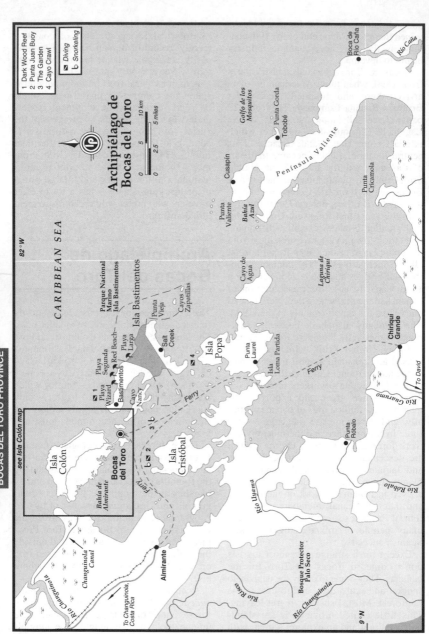

Archipiélago de
Bocas del Toro

Diving
1 Dark Wood Reef
2 Punta Juan Buoy
3 The Garden
4 Cayo Crawl

🄳 Diving
🅑 Snorkeling

0   5   10 km
0   2.5   5 miles

82°W

CARIBBEAN SEA

Boca de
Río Caña

Río Caña

Golfo de los
Mosquitos

Punta Gorda
Tobobé

Cusapín

Península Valiente

Punta
Valiente
Bahía
Azul

Punta
Cricamola

Cayo de
Agua

Laguna de
Chiriquí

Parque Nacional
Marino Bastimentos

Isla Bastimentos

Punta
Vieja
Cayos
Zapatillas

Playa
Segunda
Red Beach
Playa Larga

Salt
Creek

Isla
Popa

Chiriquí
Grande

Playa
Wizard
Bastimentos

Cayo Nancy

1

4

Punta
Laurel

Isla
Loma Partida

Ferry

To David

see Isla Colón map

Isla Colón

Bocas
del Toro

3 b

2
b

Isla
Cristóbal

Ferry

Río Uyama

Punta Róbalo

Río Róbalo

Río Guarumo

Bahía de
Almirante

Changuinola Canal

Río Changuinola

To Changuinola,
Costa Rica

Almirante

Río Risso

Bosque Protector
Palo Seco

Río Changuinola

9°N

interior has abundant lianas, vine tangles and forest palms. The rainy climate that maintains this rainforest is described locally as consisting of 'two seasons: wet and wetter.' A brief so-called dry season occurs in January and February, but even then afternoon showers that appear daily for up to a week are not unknown.

Culturally, the islands and the lowlands around them support a distinct group of Indians, the Guaymís. They still live by fishing and subsistence farming, they travel mostly by canoe and they reside in wooden, thatch-roofed huts without electricity or running water. While many of their canoes, or *cayucos,* are powered by outboard engines, most locals use sails made from rice sacks, or they simply paddle. Since this tribe usually does not live in groups but in widely scattered huts at water's edge, these canoes remain the Guaymís' chief mode of transportation.

The Guaymí language is still commonly spoken, although many Indians converse in Spanish or Gali-Gali, the distinct Creole language of Bocas del Toro Province that combines English, Spanish and Guaymí. This odd dialect had its origins among the Jamaicans brought over to harvest bananas. Descendants of these workers are a major segment of the population. They and a third group, the 'Latinos' of mixed Indian and Spanish ancestry, live in towns, unlike the Guaymís, who live along the forested coasts.

ISLA COLÓN

Isla Colón is by far the most visited and developed of the Bocas del Toro islands. On its southeastern tip is its major town and the provincial capital, the town of **Bocas del Toro**, which offers tourists a pleasant and convenient base from which to explore the Parque Nacional Marino Isla Bastimentos and other nearby sites. The town, the archipelago and the province as a whole all share the same name – Bocas del Toro. Isla Colón and Bocas del Toro town are often referred to as 'Bocas Isla.'

Bocas del Toro town is where most of the archipelago's accommodations and restaurants are found, as well as the chain's two dive operators. The town is a slow-paced community made up mostly of English-speaking black people of West Indian ancestry. There are many Spanish-speaking Latinos as well. The few Indians who live on the island often speak English, Spanish and Gali-Gali. Additionally, some blacks speak Patois, which is a mixture of Afro-Antillean English, Spanish and Gali-Gali. Patois is widely spoken on Isla Bastimentos, a 10-minute boat ride southeast of Isla Colón.

Bocas town is a great place to hang out for a few days. On the nearby islands and reefs are wonderful opportunities for swimming, snorkeling and diving, or lounging on white sandy beaches fringed by reeds and coconut palms. Water taxis (or *taxis marinos*), readily available in this small town of wooden houses built by the United Fruit Company, will take you to remote beaches and snorkeling sites. The town's relaxed, friendly atmosphere seems to rub off on everyone who visits; it's especially easy to meet locals and travelers here.

Relaxed as it is right now, Bocas town is experiencing a development boom; land prices have skyrocketed since 1994, with foreign investors buying up land like crazy and building hotels and restaurants. The town is undergoing a lot of changes.

Orientation
Bocas town is laid out in a grid pattern and has a main street (Calle 3), which is where you'll find most of the hotels, restaurants and bars. Perpendicular to the numbered streets are lettered avenues, from 'A' to 'H.' The only airport in the archipelago is on Avenida E, four blocks from the main street.

Water taxis to Almirante and Chiriquí Grande use two docks: One is near Calle 3 beside Le Pirate restaurant, while the other is near the intersection of Calle 1 and Avenida Central. Private boats can be hired at the dock beside Le Pirate restaurant. The ferry dock is at the southern end of town.

Information
The Instituto Panameño de Turismo office (IPAT; ☎/fax 757-9642), at water's edge on Calle 1, is a good source of information. It

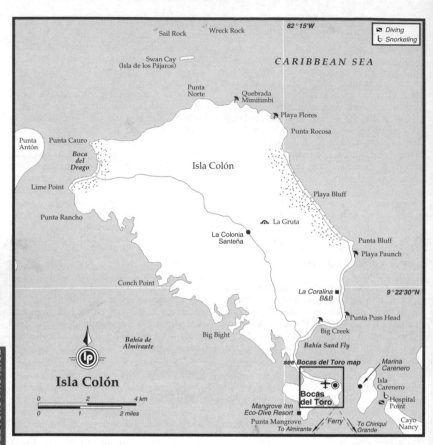

hands out the free magazine *Islas de Bocas,* available in both English and Spanish, which has maps of Bocas town and the islands and plenty of information about the area. The office is open 8:30 am to 4:30 pm weekdays, sometimes closing for an hour at lunchtime.

The Instituto Nacional de Recursos Naturales Renovables (INRENARE; ☎ 757-9244) has an office on Calle 1 at Avenida E, open 8 am to noon and 1 to 4 pm weekdays. It's not really set up as a tourist information office, though if you have questions about the Parque Nacional Marino Isla Bastimentos, staff can answer them; they

have information about all the protected areas in Bocas del Toro Province. If you want to camp out in any of the protected areas, you must first get a permit (US$5) from this or any other INRENARE office.

The Banco Nacional de Panamá, on Avenida E, changes traveler's checks; it's open 8 am to 3 pm weekdays, 9 am to noon Saturday. A post office is in the large government building on Calle 3, beside Parque Simón Bolívar. International telephone calls can be made from any of the pay phones around town and from the Cable & Wireless office on Calle 1, which is open 8 am to noon and 1 to 4 pm weekdays.

Dangers & Annoyances Tap water in the Bocas town area, unlike in most other places in Panama, is not safe for drinking. Bottled water is readily available, though expensive – almost US$2 for a 1.5 liter bottle. Sodas are readily available and much cheaper.

Beaches

Boca del Drago On the western side of Isla Colón, Boca del Drago is one of the best beaches on the island. Just offshore from the beach is a patchy coral-and-sand sea bottom that offers good snorkeling when the sea is calm and the water clear.

The water is shallow here; to avoid coral scrapes, watch where you place your feet. Keep your hands away from the coral when you're swimming, too.

Boca del Drago isn't nearly as nice as Red Beach or Playa Larga on Isla Bastimentos, where there's a good chance of seeing sea turtles if you camp out or make a night hike from one of that island's hotels. However, surf at those beaches makes swimming there unsafe.

A bus operates from Boca del Drago to Bocas town, ferrying workers who live at the beach to and from town. It leaves Boca del Drago around 7:30 am and returns in

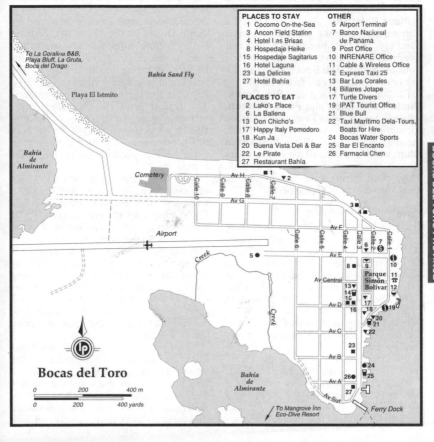

PLACES TO STAY	OTHER
1 Cocomo On-the-Sea	5 Airport Terminal
3 Ancon Field Station	7 Banco Nacional
4 Hotel Las Brisas	de Panama
8 Hospedaje Heike	9 Post Office
15 Hospedaje Sagitarius	10 INRENARE Office
16 Hotel Laguna	11 Cable & Wireless Office
23 Las Delicias	12 Expreso Taxi 25
27 Hotel Bahía	13 Bar Los Corales
	14 Billares Jotape
PLACES TO EAT	17 Turtle Divers
2 Lako's Place	19 IPAT Tourist Office
6 La Ballena	21 Blue Bull
13 Don Chicho's	22 Taxi Marítimo Dela-Tours,
17 Happy Italy Pomodoro	Boats for Hire
18 Kun Ja	24 Bocas Water Sports
20 Buena Vista Deli & Bar	25 Bar El Encanto
22 Le Pirate	26 Farmacia Chen
27 Restaurant Bahía	

Bocas del Toro

To La Coralina B&B,
Playa Bluff, La Gruta,
Boca del Drago

Bahía Sand Fly

Playa El Istmito

Bahía de Almirante

Cometery

Calle 10
Calle 9
Calle 8
Calle 7

Av H
Av G

Airport

Creek

Creek

Bahía de Almirante

To Mangrove Inn
Eco-Dive Resort

Ferry Dock

Av F
Av E
Av Central
Av D
Av C
Av B
Av A
Av Sur

Calle 6
Calle 5
Calle 4
Calle 3
Calle 2
Calle 1

Parque
Simón
Bolívar

0   200   400 m
0   200   400 yards

BOCAS DEL TORO PROVINCE

the late afternoon. In Bocas town the bus parks in front of the market between the Hotel Las Brisas and the fire station; at about 8:30 or 9 am, you can ask the driver if he'll take you out to the beach. The trip to Boca del Drago takes about 45 minutes; the roundtrip fare is about US$2.50. Or hire a taxi and have it return at a specified time. The roundtrip ride is about US$20.

Other Beaches There are plenty of other beaches around Isla Colón, reached by a road that skirts up the eastern coast from town. There's no public transportation to them, but a taxi will take you there, and you can arrange for the driver to come back for you at an appointed time.

Playa El Istmito, also called Playa La Cabaña, is the closest to town. It's on Bahía Sand Fly, and the *chitras* (sand flies) that live here have an itchy bite. Repellent is available in town. This is not the most attractive beach; better ones are farther north.

Farther up the coast are **Big Creek**, **Punta Puss Head** and **Playa Paunch**, which is dangerous for swimming but good for surfing. After you round Punta Bluff, the road takes you along the long **Playa Bluff**, which stretches all the way to Punta Rocosa. Endangered sea turtles nest on Playa Bluff during their nesting season, from around May to September.

Cave
Halfway to Boca del Drago, 8km from town, is a cave ingeniously named La Gruta (Cave). It's also called the 'Santuario Natural de Nuestra Señora de la Gruta' for the statue of the Virgen del Carmen at its entrance. It could also be called 'Bat Crap Cave,' because if you walk through it (there's an exit after 100m), you'll be ankle-deep in bat poop and be doused with it, too; and the smell – the smell! Besides the bats (and the fact that local villagers wash their clothes in the stream leaving the cave), there's nothing remarkable about La Gruta.

There's an interesting story about those bats. In 1974 a small village was born near the cave. The villagers had pigs, and soon the villagers noticed that the pigs' nipples

were red and sore. One night a villager heard a pig squeal and came out to find a bat biting the pig's nipples. The villagers were so upset with the nipple-biting bats that they went to the police. The police, being police, tear-gassed the Santuario Natural de Nuestra Señora de la Gruta, sending thousands of furious bats out of the cave in broad daylight, but the bats were back as soon as the smoke cleared.

In time the villagers learned that if they applied a substance similar to hot sauce to their pigs' nipples, the bats left them alone.

Diving & Snorkeling
Diving and snorkeling trips are offered by Bocas Water Sports (☎/fax 757-9541, www.bocasdeltoro.com/watersport.htm) and by Turtle Divers (☎/fax 757-9594), both on Calle 3. Both offer full-day snorkeling tours to the distant Cayos Zapatillas for US$40, including lunch, a laze on the beach and a jungle walkabout on Cayo Zapatilla Sur; these are very popular tours. The typical price for snorkeling trips, including gear, for a group of four is US$15 per person per day if a slow boat (40 horsepower) is used and more than twice that if a speedboat (200 horsepower) is used.

Most diving trips cost about US$30 for a one-tank, one-site dive (US$50 for two tanks and two sites). The farther from Isla Colón a trip goes, the more it costs. PADI open-water and advanced-diver courses are also available. Both dive shops rent gear.

If you have your own snorkel gear (or if you rent it), you can also get the local boatmen to take you to many good snorkeling spots around the area in their small motorized canoes *(botes)*. They know many good spots, and this option can be cheaper than the dive companies' trips; agree on a price before you go.

Be aware that although the Cayos Zapatillas are within the boundaries of the national marine park, they're not a particularly good place to dive – and the currents there upset many divers when they ought to be having fun. Better but not well-known sites include Cayo Crawl (a lovely reef with lots of fish, coral and lobster), south of Isla Bastimentos; Dark Wood Reef (with many nurse sharks and occasional hammerheads), northwest of Bastimentos; Hospital Point, a 50-foot wall off Cayo Nancy; and the base of the buoy near Punta Juan (with some beautiful coral), north of Isla Cristóbal. Of these, only the Punta Juan buoy and Hospital Point are also good for snorkeling. Another superior spot for snorkeling is The Garden, near Cayo Nancy; there's lots of coral there.

Be forewarned that the archipelago's waters are notorious for poor visibility. Sometimes you go under and find the visibility is very good; sometimes your visibility is limited to 3m. More than 40 rivers expire at bayside around the islands, and they unload a lot of silt into the sea after heavy rains in the mountains. If it's rained a lot in recent days, don't expect good visibility.

If you have your own boat, it may interest you to know that there's a marina near Bocas town; see the Getting There & Away section for details.

Bird Watching

While the birding on the islands isn't as good as that on the mainland, it can nonetheless be rewarding. Birds that have been recorded on the islands in recent years that are particularly rare or at least poorly known to Panama include the semiplumbeous hawk, white-tailed kite, zone-tailed hawk, uniform crake, olive-throated parakeet, red-fronted parrotlet, lesser nighthawk, green-breasted mango, chestnut-colored woodpecker, snowy cotinga, brown-capped tyrannulet, yellow-bellied elaenia, stub-tailed spadebill, purple martin, tree swallow and black-cowled oriole.

In early March and October many thousands of turkey vultures can often be seen gliding just above the forest canopy on the large islands. These are big black birds with featherless heads and reddish necks, and they are masterful fliers, soaring for long periods without a flap, tilting from side to side to take advantage of every favorable air current. These birds range from Canada to Chile. Many of the north-

ern birds winter in Central America and northwestern South America.

Organized Tours

Bocas Water Sports (see Diving & Snorkeling, above) offers trips upriver on the mainland to see manatees, jungle walks on Isla Bastimentos, beach picnics, and camping trips to lovely Red Beach on Isla Bastimentos. Turtle Divers (see Diving & Snorkeling) offers a historic tour to Hospital Point and Punta Mangrove, an 'Indian Tour' to a Guaymí village (both tours include snorkeling) and a 'Birds Tour' to Swan Cay (north of Isla Colón) and Boca del Drago.

Special Events

Bocas town observes all of Panama's holidays and a few enjoyable local ones besides. Annual events celebrated in Bocas town and on Isla Bastimentos include the following:

May
1st – *May Day*. While the rest of Panama is celebrating the Día del Trabajador (Worker's Day), the Palo de Mayo (a Maypole dance) is done by young girls in Bocas town and on Isla Bastimentos.

July
3rd Sunday – *Día de la Virgen del Carmen*. Everyone in Bocas town makes a pilgrimage to La Gruta, the cave in the middle of the island, for a mass in honor of the Virgen del Carmen.

September
28th – *Feria del Mar*. The 'fair of the sea' is a four-day festival held on Playa El Istmito, north of Bocas town; it begins on September 28 and ends on October 2.

November
16th – *Fundación de la Provincia de Bocas del Toro*. Celebrating the founding of the province in 1904, this day is celebrated with parades and other events; it's a big affair, attracting people from all over the province, and the Panamanian president also attends.

23rd – *Día de Bastimentos*. Bastimentos Day is celebrated with a parade and drums on Isla Bastimentos.

Places to Stay

When I last visited the island, there were 10 places to stay but more were under construction, including a 35-room hotel on the corner of Calle 3 and Avenida F. Still, you'd be wise to make a reservation and then reconfirm it once you arrive in the country. If Bocas town takes off as a tourist destination, as I suspect it will, it might be difficult finding a room – particularly during the height of the tourist season (December to April).

The IPAT tourist office (see Information) should have current information on lodging. There are a couple of places to stay on Isla Bastimentos as well, reachable by water taxi (see the Isla Bastimentos section, later in this chapter).

In Town *Hospedaje Heike* (no phone), on Calle 3 near the center of town, offers two charming rooms with two beds each, a fan, mosquito nets and shared bathroom (cold water only) for US$5 per person. There's also a small but nice restaurant here.

Las Delicias (☎ 757-9318), on Calle 3 near Avenida B, is a worn place with singles/doubles for US$7/11 with shared bathrooms or US$11/15 with private bathrooms. Larger rooms that have private bathrooms cost US$18; all the rooms have fans. Water isn't always available here.

Hospedaje Sagitarius (☎ 757-9578/ 9412), at the intersection of Calle 4 and Avenida D, is a fairly new place offering rooms with private bathrooms, color TVs and fans for US$16 for two, three or four people.

→The *Hotel Las Brisas* (☎/fax 757-9248), on the northern end of Calle 3, has worn and basic rooms, but all have private bathrooms with hot water; only some have windows. Singles/doubles cost US$18/20 with fan or US$21/22 with air-con. The hotel also rents kayaks for US$1.50 per hour.

The stately old wooden *Hotel Bahía* (☎/fax 757-9626), at the southern end of town, has an upstairs verandah overlooking the sea. Rooms for one to three people are US$18 with fan, US$22 with air-con; the newer rooms in the rear are quite pleasant. This building was once the headquarters of the United Fruit Company, and its huge safe is still here. Ask to see it.

Jumping up considerably in quality and price is the *Hotel Laguna* (☎ 757-9091, fax 757-9092, bcg@hotmail.com), on Calle 3 in the center of town. This new, two-story hotel offers 11 very lovely and spacious rooms with lots of pretty wood, good beds, air-con, hot water, private bathrooms and excellent lighting for US$39 for one or two people, US$65 for three. There's also one suite with a kitchen for US$65.

An even nicer place is *Cocomo On-the-Sea* (☎ /fax 757-9259), on the northern side of town. Two of its four breezy rooms are over the ocean, but all four have access to seaside terraces strung with hammocks. These rooms were built with close attention to detail, from the soundproof roofs that squelch the noise of driving rains to perfectly matching decor to pricey orthopedic mattresses (for bad backs) and slightly elevated beds (for bad knees). Rates for one or two people range from US$38 to US$45, one delicious breakfast included. Discounts are given for stays of more than three nights. No pets or children under six are allowed. The owners, Canadians Dorothy and Claus Claassen, are wonderful hosts.

The Asociación Nacional para la Conservación de la Naturaleza (National Association for the Conservation of Nature, or Ancon) operates a seaside *field station* on the northern side of town, next to Hotel Las Brisas. It has spacious guestrooms with air-con, firm mattresses and private bathrooms. The station is primarily used to house student groups on Ancon Expeditions tours, but the rooms are available to anyone. Rates are US$50 per person with meals, US$40 without. For details, check with Ancon Expeditions in Panama City (☎ 269-9414/9415, fax 264-3713, sales@ ecopanama.com, www.ecopanama.com; in the USA ☎ 847-392-7865, 888-888-4106), Apartado 0852-1509, Panamá, República de Panamá.

Just before this book went to press, a friend visiting Bocas town said that a new and cozy restaurant/*pensión,* the *Mondo Taitú* (no phone), near Cocomo On-the-Sea, had just opened. Rooms cost US$17 a night. The place is owned by Italians who, I'm told by my tasteful friend, 'really know how to cook seafood.' Meals cost about US$10 per person *(see notes for additions)*

Around the Island *La Coralina B&B* (☎/fax 757-9458) is on a hill overlooking the sea, 10km north of Bocas town and situated on 33 forested hectares in a former private estate. There are parrots and monkeys on the once-elegant property, but unfortunately it's not being maintained. Its rates of US$29 to US$70 are excessive, given the condition of the rooms.

The *Mangrove Inn Eco-Dive Resort* (☎/fax 757-9594, manginn@usa.net, www .bocas.com), a 10-minute boat ride from town, consists of five wooden cabins and a restaurant/bar, all built on stilts over the water and connected by walkways. A reef right out front offers good snorkeling. Each cabin has a private bathroom and holds four to six people. The rates – US$95/70 for divers/nondivers – include all meals, scheduled dives (or snorkeling tours for nondivers) and boat transportation to and from town. This place has occasional trouble with gnats.

Places to Eat
Bocas town is small but has several excellent places to eat. *La Ballena,* on Avenida E across from the government building, has excellent Italian food at affordable prices. Lobster with pasta is only US$8, and it's the most expensive item on the menu.

Le Pirate, on Calle 3, *had* served excellent Italian food, but just before this was written its chef quit. Its specialty was homemade pasta with crabmeat (US$6.50). Because the restaurant/bar is owned by finicky Italians, I have no doubt that another talented chef will be in the Pirate's kitchen by the time you read this. It's open from 10 am till the wee hours.

Happy Italy Pomodoro, upstairs over the Mangrove Roots shop on Calle 3, in the same building as Turtle Divers, serves good Italian food in a pleasant atmosphere and has a balcony overlooking the street. Pizza, pasta, seafood and lobster are the specialties. The open-air *Restaurant Bahía,* in front of the Hotel Bahía, also serves good Italian food.

The *Buena Vista Deli & Bar,* on the waterfront north of Le Pirate, makes a variety of excellent sandwiches and dinners consisting of a dish or two of meat or fish, but it's notorious for its margaritas – especially on game days (the American owners have DirecTV, always tuned to US sporting events). Another great thing about this place is that it provides you with coolers, sandwiches, drinks, desserts, breads or cookies to take on boat trips. It's closed Tuesday.

Lako's Place, on Avenida H, is another good spot for seafood, often recommended by locals. The locals' favorite spot to eat, however, is *Don Chicho's,* on Calle 3; it's actually named El Lorito, but no one ever calls it that. It's open from early in the morning till late at night.

Kun Ja, on Calle 3, serves very good and cheap Chinese food. A big plate of chop suey with chicken costs only US$3. It's open noon to 4 pm and 5:30 to 10 pm.

Entertainment
Bocas town has no shortage of bars. The most popular among *gringos* is the *Blue Bull,* on the waterfront, which is the only place in Bocas town where you can hear live calypso – played weekend nights starting around 8 pm.

The *Buena Vista Deli & Bar,* on account of its margaritas and DirecTV, is a hot spot every night except Tuesday, when it's closed.

Le Pirate has a bar that, because of its central location, is quite popular, but if you ask for a drink fancier than a rum and Coke, don't expect to receive anything familiar to you.

Bars that are particularly popular with the locals include *Bar El Encanto, Billares Jotape* and *Bar Los Corales.* All are on Calle 3, and all offer drinks for much less than you'd pay at any of the gringos' bars.

The little *cinema* on Calle 3 shows two different movies at 7 and 9 pm nightly for US$1.50 a pop (children pay half-price).

Getting There & Away

There are three ways to get to Isla Colón: You can travel by bus from David to Chiriquí Grande and take a water taxi or ferry to Bocas town from there; you can travel from the Costa Rican border to Almirante and travel by boat from there; or you can fly here from David, Changuinola or Panama City.

Air Bocas del Toro has a fine airport that's the pride of the town. Aeroperlas (☎ 757-8341 in Bocas town; 269-4555 in Panama City) offers daily flights connecting Bocas town with Panama City (US$48/96 one-way/roundtrip). A daily morning flight from David to Changuinola (US$24/48) takes on passengers in that city and then continues to Bocas town (US$10/20).

Boat Two companies, Taxi Marítimo Dela-Tours (☎ 757-9172) and Expreso Taxi 25 (☎ 757-9062), run frequent water taxis between Bocas town and Almirante and between Bocas town and Chiriquí Grande. Their offices/docks are near one another in all three towns; you can easily walk from one to the next to ask which has a taxi leaving soonest. Both companies' taxis leave on a more or less hourly schedule; the last taxi of the day leaves around 5 pm. The trip to Chiriquí Grande takes about 45 minutes and costs US$8 one way; the trip to Almirante takes about 35 minutes and costs US$10. Taxi Marítimo Dela-Tours boats leave Bocas town from the dock beside Le Pirate restaurant; Expreso Taxi 25 boats leave from the dock near the intersection of Calle 1 and Avenida Central.

Ferries (which carry both passengers and vehicles) run between Almirante and Chiriquí Grande, stopping at Bocas town as warranted. In Bocas town the ferry pier is at the southern end of Calle 3; you can call the ferry office at ☎ 757-9560. See the Almirante section, later in this chapter, for more information.

Marina Carenero (☎/fax 757-9242), on Isla Carenero directly east of Bocas town, has 20 slips that can accommodate boats up to 18m long. The marina has depth-marked moorings in addition to mail-drop and spare-parts ordering services out of Miami. Its power supply is 240 volts at 50 amps and 120 volts at 30 amps, using top-of-the-line marine electrical connections. Fresh water and a dinghy dock are also at hand.

Getting Around

Bicycles can be rented from the Farmacia Chen (☎ 757-9280), on Calle 3, for US$1.50/5/7.50 per hour/half-day/full day. Farmacia Chen also rents small motorcycles for US$5/15/25; Jet Skis are available as well. Kayaks can be rented from the Hotel Las Brisas for about US$1.50/10 per hour/day.

If you want to get to nearby islands, find one of the boatmen that operate motorized canoes (known as botes) from the dock beside Le Pirate restaurant on Calle 3. Because gasoline is expensive in Panama, their services are too (and some have been known to overcharge hapless tourists). I've hired Cesar Porta (☎ 757-9600), who owns the boat with 'Cesars Tours' painted on it, and was very pleased with his service. He has a speedy boat and he knows the good snorkeling and diving spots. Born and raised on the island, Cesar speaks English, Spanish and Patois.

ISLA BASTIMENTOS

Beautiful Isla Bastimentos is a 10-minute boat ride from Bocas del Toro town (see the Archipiélago de Bocas del Toro map). The small village of Bastimentos has no roads, only a wide, concrete footpath lined on both sides with wooden houses. Most are occupied by hard-working people who travel to Almirante daily to tend to banana fields. There are a couple of places to stay and eat here.

On the southeastern side of the island is the remote Guaymí village of Salt Creek. Tropical forest covers the interior of the island; you can explore it, but go only with a guide, as it's very easy to get lost. There's also a lake, Laguna Bastimentos.

The island has beautiful beaches. You can walk across the island from Bastimentos to **Playa Wizard** in about 15 minutes. Plenty of other beautiful beaches are also along the northern side of the island, including **Playa Segunda** and the long **Playa Larga**, where sea turtles nest from April to August. Playa Larga and much of the eastern side of the island are protected by Parque Nacional Marino Isla Bastimentos, a national marine park.

One particular beach – **Red Beach**, a 30-minute walk from town – has a small *rancho,* an open-sided thatch-roof shelter with two freshwater showers and a toilet. This beach also has a pier, so if you're short on time, you might want to boat directly here. The rancho is owned by Bocas Water Sports, which charges US$10 per person to use the facility; the fee includes roundtrip transportation between the beach and Bocas del Toro town. Be warned that surf at both Playa Larga and Red Beach makes going swimming here inadvisable.

Salt Creek

On the southeastern edge of Isla Bastimentos is the Guaymí village of Salt Creek, at the end of a long canal cut through a dense mangrove forest. The community consists of about 250 people, 60 thatch-and-bamboo houses, an elementary school, a handicrafts store, a general store and a soccer field.

Most of the people here eke out a living by fishing and subsistence farming. This settlement is typical of the many Guaymí villages scattered about the area (many Guaymí families, however, live on small, isolated plots of land rather than in towns). If you make it to Salt Creek, be sure to stop at the tiny store overlooking the soccer field and buy a ball of fresh chocolate. It's quite delicious.

Sea Turtle Protection Project

During sea turtle nesting season, which runs from around May to September, Ancon (☎/fax 757-9226 in Bocas del Toro town; ☎ 264-8100 in Panama City; ancon@pty.com, www.ancon.org), Apartado 1387, Panamá 1, República de Panamá, offers a volunteer program for the protection of the turtles on Isla Bastimentos' Playa Larga. Other year-round Ancon volunteer projects include patrolling the national marine park, reforestation around the island's Bahía Honda, a demonstration farming project at Boca del Drago on Isla Colón and environmental education around the local area. You don't get paid, but Ancon will take care of your basic needs. Contact either office listed above for details.

Places to Stay & Eat

Bastimentos town has two hotels, one on a hillside with a lovely view and the other on the water. The *Banana-View Restaurante and Rooms* (fax 757-9591) is perched atop a hill from which you can look out across treetops to the ocean. It rents two rustic but spacious rooms with lots of character. The bathroom is shared but quite OK. This is a great place to relax, and it's a short hike away from some lovely beaches. Rates are US$5/10 for one/two people.

The hotel on the water is the *Pensión y Restaurante Bastimentos* (no phone), which has five rooms. Each has a bunk bed, a large window for cross-ventilation, a light and a shared bathroom. Rates are US$8/11. There's a simple restaurant; the specialty is always the catch of the day. Meals typically cost US$5.

Getting There & Away

It's easy to get to Isla Bastimentos from Bocas del Toro town; just walk down to the pier next to Le Pirate restaurant and ask a boatman to take you over. The ride will cost US$5 to US$10 each way, depending on the size of the boat.

OTHER ISLANDS

The archipelago has many other beautiful islands, all with good snorkeling spots. Just across the water from Bocas town, **Isla Carenero** has a village with a couple of good though struggling restaurants.

Cayo Nancy, southeast of Isla Colón, has Hospital Point, named for the United Fruit Company hospital that was built here in 1900, when the company had its

Turtles' Tragic Troubles

Four of the world's eight sea turtle species nest on the beaches of the Archipiélago de Bocas del Toro, particularly the long beaches on the northern side of Isla Bastimentos. The loggerheads appear from April to September, the leatherbacks in May and June, the hawksbills in July and the greens in July and August.

Sea turtles leave the water only to lay their eggs. Two months after the eggs are laid, the hatchlings break loose from their shells, leave their sandy nests and enter the sea – if they are not first eaten by raccoons, birds or dogs. Many hatchlings, which are guided to the sea by moonlight, die because people using flashlights unintentionally steer the tiny turtles into the rainforest, where they are preyed upon or get lost and die of starvation or the heat.

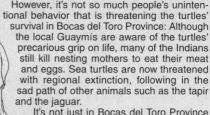

However, it's not so much people's unintentional behavior that is threatening the turtles' survival in Bocas del Toro Province: Although the local Guaymís are aware of the turtles' precarious grip on life, many of the Indians still kill nesting mothers to eat their meat and eggs. Sea turtles are now threatened with regional extinction, following in the sad path of other animals such as the tapir and the jaguar.

It's not just in Bocas del Toro Province that turtles are threatened, but all along both coasts of Panama. In the Archipiélago de San Blás, the Kuna Indians kill sea turtles that aren't even a year old. Fishermen in the Golfo de Chiriquí hack off the flippers of large sea turtles for meat and then throw the animals back into the water, where they drown because they cannot swim to the surface to breathe. ■

headquarters in Bocas del Toro town. The hospital was established to isolate victims of yellow fever and malaria; at the time it was not yet known that these diseases, then rampant in the area, were transmitted by mosquitoes. The hospital complex eventually included 16 buildings. It was here for only two decades, however; when a fungus killed the banana trees that United Fruit was growing on the islands, the company moved its banana operations to the mainland and dismantled the hospital buildings, and forest reclaimed the site. There's good snorkeling and diving in front of the point.

Swan Cay, also called Isla de los Pájaros, is off the northwestern shore of Isla

Colón, 20 minutes by boat from Boca del Drago. The island is home to a great many birds and, not surprisingly, popular with bird watchers. Most are hoping to see red-billed tropic birds and white-crowned pigeons. Nearby are **Wreck Rock** and **Sail Rock**, which have prematurely retired more than a few boats whose skippers mistakenly chose to sail at night in unfamiliar waters.

The **Cayos Zapatillas**, southeast of Isla Bastimentos, are one of the most popular destinations for snorkeling and diving trips, despite strong currents in the area. The two keys, Cayo Zapatilla Norte and Cayo Zapatilla Sur, have beautiful white-sand beaches surrounded by pristine reefs, plus forests for exploring. There is an INRENARE station on the south key, and it's often possible to stay at it. Check with INRENARE in Bocas del Toro town (see the Isla Colón section). Nearly every meter of this key, incidentally, was dug up in the early 20th century on the rumor that Captain Henry Morgan had buried treasure here. None was found.

On the way to the Cayos Zapatillas, **Cayo Crawl**, in the long, shallow channel between Isla Bastimentos and Isla Popa, is a popular stopover. The key has a meager market and a very unpretentious restaurant, *El Paso del Marisco,* both of which were built on stilts over part of the channel; they're linked to Cayo Crawl by a boardwalk. A beer or soda and a plate of fish with salsa and potatoes (about all that's available at El Paso) costs around US$3. The food's quite OK, and the location is perfect. From the restaurant, you can dive into the tranquil channel, which is home to several coral reefs that are fun to snorkel. Cayo Crawl is about a half-hour by fast boat from Bocas del Toro town.

PARQUE NACIONAL MARINO ISLA BASTIMENTOS

Established in 1988, this was Panama's first marine park. Protecting various areas of the Bocas archipelago, including parts of large Isla Bastimentos (especially Playa Larga) and the Cayos Zapatillas, the park is an important nature reserve for many species of Caribbean wildlife.

Its beaches are used as a nesting ground by four species of sea turtle. The abundant coral reefs, great for snorkeling and diving, support countless species of fish, lobster and other forms of sea life. The lagoons are home to other wildlife, including freshwater turtles and caimans, and there is still more wildlife in the forests. Unfortunately, hunting also occurs in the park.

You can get current park information from the IPAT office in Bocas del Toro town (see the Isla Colón section) or from any INRENARE office (there's one in Bocas town). The park entrance fee is US$10. The dive operators and boatmen in Bocas town are also good sources of infor-

mation about the park and its attractions. If you want to camp out anywhere in the park (or in any other Panamanian national park), you are required to first obtain a permit from INRENARE.

CHANGUINOLA CANAL

In 1903 a 15km canal connecting the Río Changuinola and Bahía de Almirante was dug parallel to the Caribbean shoreline, running within several hundred meters of it for most of its length. The work was begun a half-dozen years earlier by the Snyder Brothers Banana Company to facilitate the barging of bananas from the fields to ships. The 30m wide channel allowed transfer of the heavy fruit without interference from the open sea.

The canal, which sliced through dense rainforest, was abandoned years ago, and until the mid-1990s it was a bird watcher's dream. Today, sadly, this is no longer true; when I last cruised the length of the canal, in late 1997, I was shocked to see that nearly all the jungle on both sides of the waterway along its entire length had been cut down and burned to clear cattle pasture. Nonetheless, the historical interest of the canal makes a trip here worthwhile. Travelers can hire small boats in Bocas del Toro town to explore the canal.

PENÍNSULA VALIENTE

If you're an adventurous person looking to set up camp on an isolated stretch of beach, hire a boat in Bocas del Toro town to take you into Bahía Azul and then hike across the peninsula to the beaches facing the Golfo de los Mosquitos. This area is unreachable by car, and because the surf is always very rough along the coast, the only way to reach the beaches between Cusapín and Punta Gorda is on foot.

The bay itself is a bit disappointing: Most of the encompassing hills have been clear-cut to make way for cattle, and its innermost shore is mostly mud sprinkled with plastic refuse. Built on stilts above this mud is a miserable small store selling beer, soda, batteries and little else. Follow the trail from the store through increasingly lush vegetation, and 30 minutes later you will arrive upon a glorious tan-sand, palm-lined beach fit for framing. Walk in either direction for hours and you'll continue to see more of the same. It may interest you to know that most of the land is available for purchase from local homesteaders. The price: about US$4000 per hectare.

Mainland

The mainland of Bocas del Toro Province is awesome. Not as awesome as the Darién, which is world-class awesome, but wonderful all the same. As in the Darién, there is forest in parts of Bocas del Toro Province that is able to support jaguars and the world's most powerful bird of prey, the harpy eagle, both of which require enormous amounts of territory to survive.

The mainland is an explorer's dream. Its jungles are the stuff of Indiana Jones movies, complete with isolated Indians, snakes the size of fire hoses and insects that make your skin crawl. Its swamps, with their jet-black, anything-can-be-in-there waters, are as alluring as they are creepy. Some months of the year, in the dead of night, sea turtles lumber out of the choppy surf and onto the beaches north of the city of Changuinola to lay eggs, and then they're back in the water until the same time next year.

In Parque Internacional La Amistad, half of which is in Panama and half in Costa Rica, are 407,000 hectares of rainforest that contain seven of the 12 classified life zones. It's possible to ride some of its rivers for hours and only see a handful of human beings – Bribri Indians floating downstream on rafts consisting of three or four sections of trunk from a bolsa tree tied together with vines. These crude one-trip rafts have been used by the Bribri for generations.

CHIRIQUÍ GRANDE
This industrial-ugly town of 13,000 people is not the stuff of action-adventure movies (see Changuinola, later in this chapter, for

that). No, Chiriquí Grande is an oil town, the Caribbean terminus of the Trans-Panama Oil Pipeline, which has its Pacific terminus at Puerto Armuelles. The oil is brought by tankers from Valdez, AK, to Puerto Armuelles, and it is then pumped over the Continental Divide. The oil is initially stored in containers on a hill above Chiriquí Grande and then loaded onto tankers that dock in front of the town. The pipeline alleviates the need for these tankers to transit the Panama Canal and pay steep passage fees.

This humid, breezeless and dirty port town is also where you can catch a water taxi or slow ferry to Almirante or the Archipiélago de Bocas del Toro. Or, if you're coming from Costa Rica via Almirante and the islands, you can catch a bus here to take you over the mountains and down to the Carretera Interamericana (Pan-American Hwy). From the highway, most of Panama is but a drive away.

There was no road from Chiriquí Grande to Almirante at the time of writing, but one was being built and was scheduled to open in 2000 or 2001.

Places to Stay & Eat
If you must overnight in Chiriquí Grande, you'll find two places to stay in town. Both are beside the city's central intersection. The better of them is the *Hotel Emperador* (☎ 757-8678), which is a good deal, offering clean rooms with air-con, firm beds, TVs and private hot-water bathrooms for US$14/23 single/double. The *Hotel Restaurante Marysel* (☎ 757-9012) has not-so-nice rooms with soft beds for US$8/14. There's air-con in most rooms and private bathrooms in all.

The *Restaurante Steakmar,* in the center of town on the main road heading to David, and the restaurant on the 3rd floor of the Hotel Emperador both offer typical Panamanian food of decent quality at reasonable prices.

Getting There & Away
Bus There are two bus operators in town, both near the docks and difficult to miss.

At the well-signed Union de Buses Panamericanos office, you can buy tickets for a direct, comfortable ride in a Mercedes-Benz bus to Panama City. Just one bus daily makes the 10-hour trip, and it leaves at 9 am. The cost is US$26 each way for adults, US$9 for children under eight.

Across the street is the Cooperativa de Servicios Multiples, a company that operates smaller, 28-passenger Toyota buses between Chiriquí Grande and David. These indirect buses leave hourly from 6 am to 6 pm daily except Sunday, when they leave every two hours. The cost of the 106km journey is US$6 each way. Buses coming from David follow the same schedule.

Boat Two water-taxi services, Taxi Marítimo Dela-Tours (☎ 758-3117) and Expreso Taxi 25 (☎ 757-9691), both at the water's edge, shuttle passengers between Chiriquí Grande, Almirante and Bocas del Toro town. The first boat leaves at 7 am and the last at 4:30 pm. Most of the taxis' passengers are on their way to Almirante, but if at least five people want to get off in Bocas town, the captain will stop there en route to Almirante. The ride to Bocas town takes 45 minutes, and it's 35 minutes more to Almirante. The one-way fare is US$8 to Bocas town and US$10 to Almirante. If you arrive in Chiriquí Grande at night and want to get to an island or Almirante, you can usually find a boatman hanging out by the dock who's willing to make the trip for US$40 or US$50.

Ferries operate between Chiriquí Grande and Almirante, stopping at Bocas del Toro town as warranted. See the Almirante section, later in this chapter, for more information. You can reach the ferry office in Chiriquí Grande at ☎ 757-9767.

RANCHO ECOLÓGICO

Located 29km south of Chiriquí Grande on the road to David (also called the 'Fortuna Road' because the road passes by the Lago Fortuna reservoir), Rancho Ecológico (☎/fax 442-1340, beeper 872-0481, panabird@sinfo.net) is an upscale campground owned and managed by senior naturalist Wilberto Martinez. (See the Guides section of the Getting Around chapter for information on Willy.) In a lush gorge high in the Talamanca range, it consists mainly of a large, thatch-roof structure under which four four-person tents are pitched (bring your own sleeping bag and mat) and hammocks slung. There are toilets and showers, hot and cold water, and a kitchen and dining area.

I consider this place a very good find for campers, not only because of the new and well-kept facilities, but because of its location amid a cool cloud forest. In the immediate vicinity is a crystal-clear stream that feels great after a hike. There are several trails, one of which leads to a lovely set of waterfalls and their bathing pools. You can bring your own food or ask the staff to prepare your meals. There's a stand about 100m farther up the road that sells cucumbers and bananas and other delicious fruit.

Rancho Ecológico is only 16km from Lago Fortuna, a picturesque reservoir that serves a power plant. All around the reservoir is some of the finest forest in Panama, and it is strictly protected because it serves as the watershed for the Fortuna Dam. Because of Rancho Ecológico's proximity to this large forest and to the Bosque Protector Palo Seco, a forest reserve, the bird watching near the campground is excellent. Birders will want to keep an eye out for ashy-throated bush-tanagers; this is Panama's only known site for them.

Rancho Ecológico, which provides the only accommodations within 40km of Lago Fortuna, charges US$20 per person per night, or US$45 with three meals. The price with food, guide service and transportation to and from Panama City is US$90.

Getting There & Away

Almost any bus that travels Fortuna Road can drop you at Rancho Ecológico. You just need to tell the driver to let you out before you pass it; the campground is on the southern side of the road, where it makes a tight curve. Don't try to reach the campground at night, because it is set back from the road and easy to miss (there is a roadside sign).

Getting a ride out of the area basically requires catching one of the buses heading in the direction you wish to go. Any of the Toyota buses will stop, but the big Mercedes-Benzes won't unless the driver is in a great mood. As a courtesy to the bus driver and for safety reasons, walk a little way up the road so that you aren't encouraging the driver to pull over on a corner.

ALMIRANTE

From the traveler's perspective, this port town of 12,000 souls on the Bahía de Almirante is the jumping-off point for water taxis and ferries to Bocas del Toro town. Or, if the traveler is coming from

TOM BOYDEN

Almirante's gold

the islands, it's the first in the last series of stops on the journey to Costa Rica. But from the resident's perspective, Almirante means bananas, Chiquita bananas. Most Almirante residents are in the business, the vast majority of them poor folk who toil in the fields. These people inhabit the board-and-tin hovels you'll see throughout town.

Train tracks are seemingly everywhere in Almirante, because it's here that the banana trains from the huge plantations to the west bring their green fruit (the bananas ripen in transit and in markets). It's also in Almirante that the trains are repaired and housed when they're not in use. Judging from the bushes that have grown up around some locomotives, it appears that Almirante is also a train cemetery. The rusting hulks and most of the town are owned by the Chiriquí Land Company, a subsidiary of the multinational banana giant Chiquita Brands International, which exports the fruit to more than 40 countries.

The most important train tracks lead to the Muelle de Almirante (Admiral's Pier), which is used almost exclusively by ships bearing huge paintings of a banana sticker used by Chiquita Brands. For more information than you could ever want to know about the company, including 'The Story of Miss Chiquita' (no, she's not really a man) and details on how you can enter the Chiquita Banana Jingle Contest, see its bright-yellow website at www.chiquita.com.

Be advised that there are no accommodations in Almirante, not even one Pensión Banana. And what few restaurants there are seem to specialize in grease.

Getting There & Away

Buses to Changuinola are available near the canal used by Almirante's two water-taxi companies. The one-way fare is US$1; the ride takes 35 minutes. Taxis arrive in bunches in this city, to accommodate the hordes headed for Changuinola. The 20-minute ride there costs US$12. A taxi ride from the Costa Rican border to Almirante costs about US$15; it takes around 45 minutes and saves a lot of waiting for buses.

Train The Chiriquí Land Company (☎ 758-8414 in Changuinola) operates two trains between the border and Almirante, picking up bananas for shipping and offering free transportation for the workers on the plantations. Tourists can ride the trains but are not encouraged to do so; call the company for permission.

Boat Two companies, Taxi Marítimo Dela-Tours (☎ 758-3117) and Expreso Taxi 25 (☎ 758-3489), operate frequent water taxis between Almirante and Bocas del Toro town and between Almirante and Chiriquí Grande. Their offices/docks are near one another in all three towns; you can easily walk from one to the next to ask which has a taxi leaving soonest. Both companies' taxis usually leave Almirante hourly, beginning at 6:30 am. Dela-Tours operates the last taxi of the day, leaving at 5:30 pm. The trip to Bocas town takes 35 minutes and costs US$10 each way; the trip to Chiriquí Grande also costs US$10.

Painfully slow ferries operate between Almirante and Chiriquí Grande, carrying passengers as well as motor vehicles and other objects that are too heavy or large for water taxis. They stop at Bocas del Toro town as warranted. The Almirante Chiriquí Grande trip takes four hours; add another 1½ hours if the ferry makes a stop at Bocas town. Daily service is generally provided, but departure times frequently change. At ferry offices in Almirante (☎ 758-3731), Bocas town (☎ 757-9560) and Chiriquí Grande (☎ 757-9767), you can buy tickets and ask current schedules. At the time of writing, one-way fares were as follows:

Route	Per Person	Per Vehicle
Almirante- Chiriquí Grande	US$4	US$35
Almirante-Bocas del Toro town	US$3	US$20
Bocas del Toro town- Chiriquí Grande	US$4	US$35

CHANGUINOLA
Halfway between the Costa Rican border and the Archipiélago de Bocas del Toro, this city of 50,000 people has been transited by many tourists, but few ever overnight here. And that's a pity, because this always humid and variously dusty or muddy city makes an excellent base for forays into spectacular coastal and mountain wildernesses.

From Changuinola it's easy to get to the Río Teribe, from which you can make a dramatic entrance into the Parque Internacional La Amistad. If you head in the opposite direction (north, toward the coast), you can visit an extremely memorable boardwalk that passes through the San-San Pond Sak Wetlands and ends at a Caribbean beach where four species of sea turtle lay their eggs. Both the park and the wetlands are administered by INRENARE; to enter the park, you must obtain permission from the INRENARE office in town (see Information, below).

Orientation
The city can be described as very tall and slim; it runs considerably farther north-south than it does east-west. Its main street is Avenida 17 de Abril (also commonly called Avenida Central), which runs north to south. Most of the hotels and restaurants are along this long, two-lane avenue, from which the rest of the city stems. There's an airport near the northern end of town, and the bus station is near the city center – close to the INRENARE office, restaurants, bars, markets and hotels.

Vast banana plantations flank the city on all sides. Most of the in-city sites of interest to the traveler are easily reached on foot. Taxis are cheap and it's a good idea to use them after dark.

Information
There's no tourist office, but the cops at the police station are helpful and friendly; they speak only Spanish. The INRENARE office (☎ 758-8967), near the center of town, can provide information on transportation to Parque Internacional La Amistad; office hours are 8 am to 4 pm weekdays. Some English is spoken here. There's also an immigration office in the center of town.

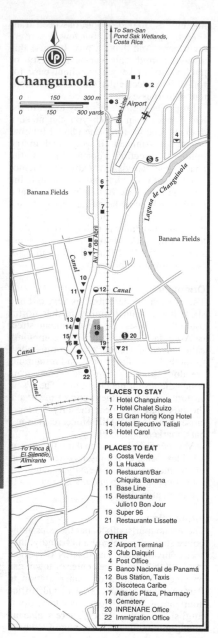

Changuinola

0   150   300 m
0   150   300 yards

To San-San
Pond Sak Wetlands,
Costa Rica

Banana Fields

Banana Fields

Laguna de Changuinola

Base Line

Airport

Av 17 de Abril

Canal

Canal

Canal

Canal

To Finca 8
El Silencio,
Almirante

PLACES TO STAY
1   Hotel Changuinola
7   Hotel Chalet Suizo
8   El Gran Hong Kong Hotel
14 Hotel Ejecutivo Taliali
16 Hotel Carol

PLACES TO EAT
6   Costa Verde
9   La Huaca
10 Restaurant/Bar
    Chiquita Banana
11 Base Line
15 Restaurante
    Julio10 Bon Jour
19 Super 96
21 Restaurante Lissette

OTHER
2   Airport Terminal
3   Club Daiquiri
4   Post Office
5   Banco Nacional de Panamá
12 Bus Station, Taxis
13 Discoteca Caribe
17 Atlantic Plaza, Pharmacy
18 Cemetery
20 INRENARE Office
22 Immigration Office

BOCAS DEL TORO PROVINCE

There's a Banco Nacional de Panamá and a post office near the airport. The pharmacy in the Atlantic Plaza, on Avenida 17 de Abril, is the best in town.

Places to Stay

The best deal in Changuinola is the *Hotel Changuinola* (☎ 758-8678, fax 758-8681), near the airport. The hotel offers 32 clean, basic rooms with air-con and private bathrooms, but has no hot water. Rates are US$17/21/23 single/double/triple. There's a good though somewhat expensive restaurant in the hotel. Taxis can easily be caught at the intersection in front of the airport, about 100m from the hotel.

The *Hotel Carol* (☎ 758-8731), on Avenida 17 de Abril, is less expensive than the Hotel Changuinola but quite drab. Its 40 fairly clean guestrooms with air-con and private bathrooms go for US$14/17/20. There's no hot water here, either.

The *El Gran Hong Kong Hotel* (☎ 758-5044), on Avenida 17 de Abril, offers six decent, basic rooms with private bathrooms for US$28 for one or two people.

Hotel Ejecutivo Taliali (☎ 758-6010, fax 758-8636), on Avenida 17 de Abril, is quite popular; unless you reserve one of the hotel's 15 rooms at least two weeks in advance, you won't likely get one. All of the rooms have air-con, TVs, telephones, fridges and private bathrooms and cost US$30/33 single/double. It's possible to rent a little economy car here for US$34 a day.

The fairly new *Hotel Chalet Suizo* (☎ 758-8242, fax 758-8165), also on Avenida 17 de Abril, is perhaps the Taliali's equal, but it's not as popular. Its six clean rooms come with cable TVs, fridges, air-con, hot water and private bathrooms, and there's a restaurant on the first of the hotel's two floors. Rates are US$31/37/46.

Places to Eat

The *Restaurant/Bar Chiquita Banana,* on Avenida 17 de Abril opposite the bus station, serves good food, but expect to wait a while to get it; the service is snail-slow. There are tables inside and outside on the patio.

The *Costa Verde,* on Avenida 17 de Abril on the way to the airport, feels more like a bar than a restaurant, with music always turned up a little too loud, but a lot of people like it. It's a bit of a gringo hangout. Ceviches cost US$2.50; grilled meats cost about US$3. There were plans to expand the menu. It's open from noon till late.

Another good late-night place is the *Restaurante Julio10 Bon Jour,* on Avenida 17 de Abril. The food's nothing to write home about, but this restaurant with a very strange name tends to attract gregarious patrons. The *Restaurante Lissette,* near the center of town, offers hearty, low-priced breakfasts and serves typical Panamanian dishes and seafood for lunch and dinner. Most meals cost around US$3.50.

Near the INRENARE office, the *Desuze* is well known for serving sea turtle meat, even though the turtles are endangered. I encourage you to not patronize places that serve sea turtle.

There are three markets: *Base Line,* which is the best stocked; *Super 96,* which is a hangout for old banana laborers; and *La Huaca,* which has a café. Beer is cheaper than soda at all three.

Entertainment

There are two dance clubs, a rough bar and a bar/brothel in town, and new places are planned. *Discoteca Caribe,* in the center of town on Avenida 17 de Abril, and *Club Daiquiri,* near the airport, are the dance clubs, and John Travolta won't be making an appearance at either real soon. But what the clubs lack in glitter they make up for in their bands; you can often hear some good salsa, merengue and reggae here.

If a fight breaks out and police are called, they're likely en route to *La Esquina Caliente.* Although the bar is full of local color, it also has an anything-goes atmosphere, and that anything ain't always a good thing. If you have an affinity for danger, this place is for you (women will probably want to steer clear, however). The taxi drivers know where it is.

Anyone can enter the *Montecarlo* bar/ brothel, a few kilometers north of Club Daiquiri, to have a drink and chat; the place is fine for that. But the Montecarlo also has rooms in the back, and the young women prancing about aren't as interested in the patrons as they are in their money. Anyone considering more than a drink here should first take a look at the Sexually Transmitted Diseases section in the Facts for the Visitor chapter.

Getting There & Away

Air Aeroperlas (☎ 758-7521/6097 in Changuinola; 269-4555 in Panama City) offers daily flights connecting Changuinola with Panama City (US$56/112 one-way/round-trip) and David (US$24/48).

The 45-minute flights between David and Changuinola operate three times daily. The morning flight from David to Changuinola continues to Bocas del Toro town for an extra US$10/20; this flight is a deal, since the same route by bus and boat takes several hours and costs more.

Bus The bus station is on Avenida 17 de Abril, right in the center of town. Below is a listing of most of the major bus routes and schedules. Fares cited are one-way; roundtrip ticket costs double.

Almirante – 21km, 35 minutes, US$1; every 20 or 25 minutes, 6:15 am to 9 pm.

El Silencio – 8km, 30 minutes, 50¢; frequent minibuses, 6 am to 8:30 pm.

Guabito – 17km, 25 minutes, 75¢; every 40 minutes, 6 am to 7 pm; buses go to the bridge at the border, where you can transfer to another bus on the Costa Rica side.

San José, Costa Rica – 281km, 5½ to 6½ hours, US$8. A direct express bus operates once a day between Changuinola and San José. In Changuinola it departs from the bus station at 10 am; in San José it departs from the Coca-Cola terminal, also at 10 am. The bus from San José arrives in Changuinola in time for you to continue on to Almirante and catch the water taxi for Bocas del Toro. Remember, there's a one-hour time change between Costa Rica and Panama.

Taxi Taxis can be found at the city bus station. A taxi ride from Changuinola to Almirante takes about 20 minutes and costs

US$12; if you're arriving in Changuinola by bus or plane, you can often find a few other passengers to share the ride and the cost. A taxi ride from Changuinola to the Costa Rican border at Guabito takes about 15 minutes and costs US$5.

AROUND CHANGUINOLA
Finca 8

If you feel a little stressed out or enjoy a good walk, I encourage you to take an afternoon stroll through Finca 8 (Farm 8), a neighborhood southwest of central Changuinola. Here you'll wander among older two-story wooden houses, plenty of trees and lots of tranquillity. There are no fewer than 50 bird species in the area.

Between 5 and 6:30 pm, the silence of Finca 8 is shattered by the screeching *keerr keerr* calls of hundreds of crimson-fronted parakeets. These birds, with their noticeable bare white eye-rings, range from Nicaragua to western Panama. You won't likely find these noisy creatures south of Changuinola.

San-San Pond Sak Wetlands

These wetlands, 5km north of central Changuinola (see the Bocas del Toro Province map), are fantastic, but they must be approached with a sense of humor and a spirit of adventure. Some luck is required as well, and jungle boots or other shoes that can get soaked are advisable. Sandals with straps will suffice.

Administered by INRENARE, the wetlands are on the edge of Finca 44, a huge banana farm reached by a road extending from the northern end of town. The best way to get here is to hire one of the 4WD taxis that hang out at the Changuinola bus station, have it take you as close to the wetlands as it can and arrange for the driver to pick you up two hours later. The ride will cost you about US$20.

Between Finca 44 and the designated wetlands is an undesignated wetlands that you must cross. Fortunately, the mud is only ankle-deep. If your driver only takes you to the edge of the banana fields, you'll have a 200m mud walk. To your right you

will see a barbwire fence. Follow it to its end and then turn right. After another 30m you'll see some elevated boards crossing a ditch. Welcome to the start of the San-San Pond Sak Wetlands boardwalk.

Almost immediately you'll enter rainforest rising from jet-black water. The boardwalk, which is less than a third of a meter wide in some places, is barely raised above the water and sometimes disappears into it. With the naked eye it's impossible to tell how deep the water is, but your instincts will encourage you to avoid it at all costs. Sometimes the boardwalk is as slippery as a banana peel placed on a slab of butter in an ice rink. Expect to slip at least once.

But the crazy boardwalk is a treat. It weaves through beautiful vegetation that's rich with howler and white-face monkeys, iguanas, sloths and toucans. Snakes for sure (it's better not to think about them). You can spot a variety of wrens, warblers and woodpeckers. And, 1.2km later, you'll arrive at the Caribbean.

The beach is strewn with driftwood and other stuff, but it's also a place where loggerhead, leatherback, green and hawksbill turtles lay their eggs. If you're in the area between April and August, I strongly encourage you to spend the night out at the beach and watch the turtles do their thing. And you'll never see so many stars.

There's a basic shelter right at the northern end of the boardwalk, always occupied by an INRENARE ranger, and for US$5 he'll let you stay there. If you want a friend for life, bring some food or at least some instant coffee with you. If you've got a hammock, bring it too. Same goes for a sleeping bag or blanket and bug spray. Dress warmly; it does cool off at night.

PARQUE INTERNACIONAL LA AMISTAD

This 407,000-hectare park, established jointly by Panama and Costa Rica in 1988, has territory in both countries – hence its name, La Amistad (Friendship). In Panama the park covers portions of Chiriquí and Bocas del Toro Provinces and is home to members of three Indian tribes: the Teribe, the Bribri and the Guaymís.

The park, slightly more than half of which is in Panama, contains some gorgeous rainforest that remains home to a recorded 90 mammal species (including jaguars and pumas) and more than 300 bird species (including resplendent quetzals and harpy eagles). Most of the park's area is rather remote, high up in the Talamanca mountain range. It's possible to enter the park from Changuinola, although it's much easier to enter it from Chiriquí Province. The two main Panamanian entrances to the park are Las Nubes (in Chiriquí Province) and Wetzo (in Bocas del Toro Province). Only the Wetzo entrance is discussed here; see the Parque Internacional La Amistad section in the Chiriquí Province chapter for details on the Las Nubes entrance and nearby facilities.

The Wetzo entrance is a 45-minute boat ride up the Río Teribe from the hamlet of El Silencio, which is reached via a 30-minute drive or bus ride from Changuinola (buses leave the Changuinola station about every 30 minutes). In El Silencio travelers can hire fishermen with boats at river's edge. Due to the high price of gasoline, river trips are expensive: about US$40 each way to Wetzo, or about US$100 should you go farther upriver to the Indian villages beyond Wetzo.

Once on the river, you'll pass hills blanketed with rainforest and intermittent waterfalls, and the backdrop is always the glorious Talamanca range. The jungle comes right to water's edge. There are a few sandbars, but the current's too swift for crocodiles. You're likely to see iguanas lounging in trees (though you'll have to look hard for them) and lots of birds; waterproof binoculars help a lot.

After about 45 minutes on the river, you'll come to a sign on the right bank that announces your arrival at the park's Wetzo entrance. All the property you will have passed until this point is privately owned.

Before the US invasion in 1989, Wetzo was named Pana-Jungla and was *the* jungle-survival training facility for Pana-manian soldiers. When I last visited the site, in late 1997, many of the old structures (barracks, mess hall, chapel, armory, serpentarium, etc) were still there, though dilapidated. Lovingly painted on many of the walls were poems (in Spanish, of course) such as this one:

Faithful Pana-Jungla, your life will always be immortal as long as there's a horizon and you always know how to reach the end.
While the jungle puts your mind in a stupor and your feet swell as you walk, there will be no jungle in the present that a Pana-Jungla cannot dominate.
My life will always be the green gold and the mountains of my heart. I am a Pana-Jungla that never gets lost in your trails of pure illusion.
When I look to the infinity and the green leaves of the immensity, the Pana-Junglas yell to God asking for your freedom.

I'm afraid the inscriptions, as well as the buildings, may be gone by the time you read this. By late 1997 INRENARE had turned the site over to Teribe rangers/guides to administer, and they didn't see any tourist appeal in the old structures. Instead the Indians had built a very rustic bamboo bungalow that contained the suffocating heat while allowing mosquitoes to come and go at will. More of these structures were planned, all for tourists.

Also at Wetzo is a 3.5km loop trail that cuts through recently disturbed, secondary and virgin rainforest. It's interesting to compare the three types, and the bird watching is excellent. (Hikers in search of more varied walks should consider the Las Nubes entrance, where there are additional trails; see the Chiriquí Province chapter.) You can also take a dip in the river, but be careful not to wade out very far into the water, or the current will carry you downstream. Keep in mind that the guides at Wetzo, all of whom are Indians raised in the area, speak only Spanish and Naso, their first language.

Anyone seeking to enter the park at Wetzo must first receive approval from Adventures & Marvels of the Naso World, a tourism organization owned and run by the Teribe; if you show up at Wetzo without the group's permission, you will be told to leave. At the time of writing, the group had just formed; interested readers should call INRENARE in Changuinola (☎ 758-8967) and ask for the phone number for Heliodoro Bonilla, the group's president.

The Teribe, who live farther up the river and who began calling themselves the Naso Nation in the early 1990s, don't want just anyone entering their world. Adventures & Marvels of the Naso World has boats and wants to benefit financially from all tourists heading into the park via the Río Teribe. With INRENARE's blessing, Adventures & Marvels was given control of Wetzo and authority over who can enter the park at this entrance. Admission to the park usually costs US$3; Adventures & Marvels clears entrance permission with INRENARE for you. If you wish to visit the Teribe and Bribri villages farther upstream, you must clear such trips with Adventures & Marvels ahead of time.

However, given the meager accommodations Adventures & Marvels was erecting for tourists, the fact that they had no English-speaking guides and no plans to find any, and the bureaucracy involved in gaining the group's permission prior to your visit, I suggest that you not visit Wetzo unless you use a local tour operator. (See the Tour Companies in Panama section in the Getting Around chapter for the names of reputable tour operators.) A tour operator

will make all the necessary arrangements for you and will go to bat for you if the Adventures & Marvels rangers at Wetzo say that they can't locate your reservation.

If you don't want to deal with Adventures & Marvels or a tour operator, there's another option: Arrange a river trip that doesn't go to Wetzo but explores the rainforest near the park's border. You can see a lot of beautiful rainforest long before you reach the border of the international park. To do this, take a taxi or bus to El Silencio, walk to the edge of the Río Teribe and hire a motorized canoe to take you up that river or the equally impressive Río Changuinola (the two merge just south of El Silencio).

All the people who operate motorized canoes on the rivers can take you to some wonderful places if you explain what you want to do (swim at the foot of a waterfall, bird watch at river's edge or on shore, explore a patch of forest with the boatman acting as guide, etc). On both rivers you'll be treated to some class II and class III rapids as well. This option really requires that you speak passable Spanish, so that you can tell the boatman what you want to see and do.

GUABITO

For information on entry requirements at the border crossing at Guabito (Sixaola on the Costa Rica side), see the Costa Rican Border Crossings section in the Getting There & Away chapter.

Chiriquí Province

Chiricanos claim to have it all, and there's an element of truth in what they say: The country's tallest mountains are in Chiriquí Province, as are some of its longest rivers. The province is home to spectacular rainforest, and yet it is also the country's top agricultural and cattle ranching region. Two of the country's largest islands and one of the world's biggest copper mines are in Chiriquí Province as well.

But it is the pleasant climate and beauty of several mountain towns that make the province a favorite vacation spot of Panamanians. Mention Boquete, Cerro Punta or Guadalupe to Panama City residents and they'll tell you how cool and lovely these towns are. It brightens their day just to hear *Boquete*. Nestled in a valley at the foot of Volcán Barú, the country's tallest mountain,

Boquete is also famous for its delicious oranges and coffee.

So proud are Chiricanos of their home province that talk of creating an independent República de Chiriquí is a popular topic. Indeed, the inhabitants of the region have been fiercely independent in spirit for a long time.

When the Spaniards first visited the area in the 1520s, they were astonished by what they found. Instead of one or two Indian tribes, they found many small groups living in relative isolation. Although often separated by only a few kilometers, these groups had distinct languages and religions. They fought among themselves and later against the conquistadors.

In the early 17th century Spanish missionaries led by Padre Cristóbal Cacho Santillana decided to make Christians out of the Indians and had 626 natives rounded up and placed in two towns he had founded. Santillana identified six distinct languages among this group, and he had started to record a vocabulary of the most common when measles brought by the colonists swept through the towns and killed half the Indians.

The survivors, having had enough of the Spaniards, took to the hills. The cleric was not discouraged, however. Santillana was determined to save the Indians' souls even if he had to kill all of them in the process. Of the many tribes that lived in the region at the time of the cleric's arrival – the Cotho, Borisque, Dorasque, Utelae, Bugabae, Zune, Dolega, Zariba, Dure and others – only the Guaymís survived. Today they are the most populous of Panama's seven Indian groups.

During the 17th century and into the 18th century, Chiriquí came under attack from pirates. It was just outside Remedios in 1680 that English buccaneer Richard Sawkins, attempting to lead an assault against the well-defended city, was fatally

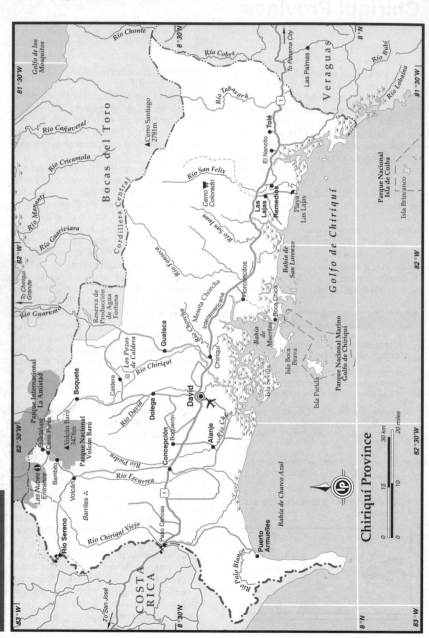

Chiriquí Province

wounded. Six years later, pirates coming down from Honduras sacked the towns of Alanje and San Lorenzo. And Miskito Indians behaving like pirates invaded the region in 1732, plundering and burning the city of David.

During the 19th century, another sort of foreigner moved in – farmers from the USA, Italy, Germany, England and Switzerland who viewed the climate and slopes of the Chiriquí highlands as prime for coffee, timber and other crops. Today their descendants are being joined by a new group of immigrants – *gringos* who look on the verdant hills and meadows and see a need for B&Bs.

And the Guaymís? They're living on a large reservation in the Chiriquí highlands and are seeking statehood. Their lives revolve around subsistence agriculture, just as they did when white people arrived nearly 500 years ago. But these days the Indians have representatives in the national government and their future is in their own hands.

Lowlands

DAVID

With 75,000 residents, David is Panama's third most populous city. It is the capital of Chiriquí Province and the center of a rich farming region. It has plenty of places to stay and eat, but few tourist attractions – and David is hot and sticky all year. Travelers stop here mainly on their way to or from the Costa Rican border at Paso Canoas, 54km away. David is also used as a base for visits to Boquete, Volcán and the Parque Nacional Volcán Barú, and islands in the Golfo de Chiriquí.

Orientation

David is approximately halfway between Panama City and San José, Costa Rica – it's about seven hours by road from either place. The Carretera Interamericana (Pan-American Hwy) does not enter the town but skirts around its northern and western sides. The city's heart is its fine central plaza, the Parque de Cervantes, about 1.5km southwest of the highway.

Information

Tourist Offices The Instituto Panameño de Turismo (IPAT; ☎/fax 775-4120) has a tourist information office upstairs in the Edificio Galherna, the building beside the church on the central plaza; a small sign is posted beside the stairway that leads upward. The office is open 8:30 am to 4:30 pm weekdays and has information on the whole of Chiriquí Province. English and Spanish are spoken.

The Instituto Nacional de Recursos Naturales Renovables (INRENARE; ☎ 775-7840/3163, fax 774-6671) has an office near the airport. Here you can get information on national parks and permits to camp in them. It's open 8 am to 4 pm weekdays.

Consulate The Costa Rican consulate (☎/fax 774-7725) is about 100m behind the Hospital Mae Lewis, which is on the Interamericana. The consulate is in a house; you'll recognize it by the flag out front. It is open 9 am to 2 pm weekdays.

Immigration The Migración y Naturalización office (☎ 775-4515), on Calle C Sur near the corner of Avenida Central, is the place to extend your Panamanian visa. The office is open 8 am to 4:30 pm weekdays. To get permission to leave Panama if you've been in the country for more than 30 days, you must first obtain a *paz y salvo* in Panama City (see the Facts for the Visitor chapter for details).

Money The Banco del Istmo, on Avenida 3 de Noviembre (on the way into town from the Interamericana), will let you withdraw cash 24 hours a day from an outside ATM. The ATM accepts Plus and Cirrus system cards. Inside the bank, you can cash American Express traveler's checks and get cash advances against your MasterCard or Visa card. The bank is open 8 am to 3 pm weekdays and 9 am to noon Saturday. There's another Banco del Istmo

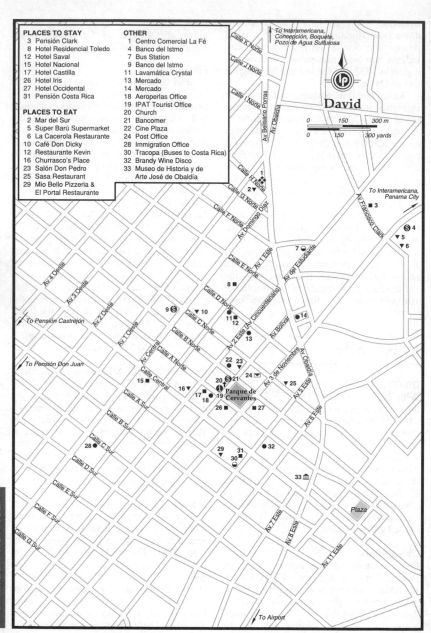

PLACES TO STAY
3 Pensión Clark
8 Hotel Residencial Toledo
12 Hotel Saval
15 Hotel Nacional
17 Hotel Castilla
26 Hotel Iris
27 Hotel Occidental
31 Pensión Costa Rica

PLACES TO EAT
2 Mar del Sur
5 Super Barú Supermarket
6 La Cacerola Restaurante
10 Café Don Dicky
12 Restaurante Kevin
16 Churrasco's Place
23 Salón Don Pedro
25 Sasa Restaurant
29 Mio Bello Pizzeria &
   El Portal Restaurante

OTHER
1 Centro Comercial La Fé
4 Banco del Istmo
7 Bus Station
9 Banco del Istmo
11 Lavamática Crystal
13 Mercado
14 Mercado
18 Aeroperlas Office
19 IPAT Tourist Office
20 Church
21 Bancomer
22 Cine Plaza
24 Post Office
28 Immigration Office
30 Tracopa (Buses to Costa Rica)
32 Brandy Wine Disco
33 Museo de Historia y de
   Arte José de Obaldía

To Interamericana,
Concepción, Boquete,
Pozo de Agua Sulfurosa

David

0   150   300 m
0   150   300 yards

To Interamericana,
Panama City

To Pensión Castrejón

To Pensión Don Juan

Parque de
Cervantes

Plaza

To Airport

CHIRIQUÍ PROVINCE

office with the same services and hours closer to downtown, on the corner of Avenida Domingo Diaz and Calle C Norte. There's also a Bancomer at the intersection of Calle B Norte and Avenida Bolívar, across the street from the Parque de Cervantes.

Post & Communications The post office is on Calle C Norte, a block northeast of the Parque de Cervantes. It's open 7 am to 5:30 pm weekdays and 7 am to 4:30 pm Saturday.

Domestic and international calls can be placed from any of the many pay phones around town. Remember that it's always cheaper to place a long-distance call from a pay phone than it is to place one from a hotel room.

Laundry The Lavamática Crystal (☎ 775-9339), on Calle D Norte between Avenidas 1 and 2 Este, will wash, dry and fold your laundry in a few hours (75¢ to wash, 75¢ to dry). It's open 7 am to 7 pm Monday to Saturday and 8 am to 1 pm Sunday.

Things to See & Do
Despite its size and role as a provincial capital, David doesn't offer much in the way of attractions. However, within an hour's drive are many good places to visit, including Boquete, Volcán, Cerro Punta, Playa Las Lajas and the Caldera hot springs. There's also the Hacienda Carta Vieja rum distillery (see the Around David section, later in this chapter).

David's small **Museo de Historia y de Arte José de Obaldía** is in a two-story house on Avenida 8 Este, near Calle A Norte. The museum contains many fine examples of colonial-era religious art, a wing devoted to Indian artifacts found in the vicinity of Volcán Barú, lots of photos from Chiriquí's past and many impressive photographs of the Panama Canal under construction.

The museum is in the former home of José de Obaldía Orejuela, founder of Chiriquí Province. The residence was built in 1880, and it is worth the admission price (US$1) just to get a good look at it. All the

furniture on the 2nd floor is original. A garden behind the museum is quite lovely, and beside it you'll find a representation of a traditional rural kitchen. The museum is open from 8:30 am to 4:30 pm every day except Sunday.

Incidentally, the museum is in the old section of town, which is known locally as Barrio del Peligro (Danger Zone) because the cemetery, the jail and the slaughterhouse are all located here. However, the neighborhood isn't as dangerous as its nickname suggests. Just don't stroll around it on a night when there's a full moon out!

There are two **mercados** (markets) in David that are worth a look if you've never seen a traditional Latin American market. The larger of the two faces the junction of Avenidas Bolívar and Obaldía, and the other is at the corner of Avenida 2 Este and Calle D Norte. Both sell produce for far less than you'd pay at a supermarket.

Ask at the IPAT tourist office whether the **Pozo de Agua Sulfurosa**, the medicinal sulfur springs on the outskirts of David, are open. The springs are off the road to the Universidad Santa María la Antigua. When I last checked, I was told that the springs were on private property and not open to the public, but that people were going there anyway.

Special Events
The Feria de San José de David, held for 10 days each March, is a big international fair. Concepción, half an hour's drive west of David, celebrates its saint's day every February 2.

Places to Stay – budget
Town Center *Pensión Costa Rica* (☎ 775-1241), on Avenida 5 Este between Calles Central and A Sur, offers singles/doubles with fans for US$4/9 with shared bathrooms or US$6/11 with private bathrooms. The 48 guestrooms tend to be clean, but even with the fans they are very hot. Buses to Costa Rica depart from the Tracopa office next door.

Hotel Saval (☎ 775-3543), on Calle D Norte between Avenidas Cincuentenario and 1 Este, has seen much better days. It has rooms with up to six beds, a sitting area under a covered patio and a little open-air restaurant in front. Singles/doubles, all with private bathrooms, cost US$8/10 with fan, US$12/16 with air-con.

The *Hotel Residencial Toledo* (☎ 774-6732, fax 774-6733), on Avenida 1 Este, an upstairs hotel built in 1995, has 28 clean rooms with air-con, private hot-water bathrooms, color TVs, firm mattresses and telephones for US$16.50 for one or two people. Ask for a room with windows. A restaurant and bar opened in 1997.

A Few Blocks Out *Pensión Don Juan* (☎ 775-1895), at Avenida 3 Oeste and Calle G Sur, a block from the Mercado San Mateo, near the fairgrounds, is an upstairs hotel with clean rooms for US$7/10 with fan/air-con.

Pensión Clark (☎ 774-3452) is on Avenida Francisco Clark about 1km northeast of the Parque de Cervantes, the fourth house from the corner of Avenida del Estudiante. It's a pleasant little family-run place, clean, quiet and respectable, with six rooms (four with private bathrooms), all priced at US$8. Ask for a room in the rear – each has a private balcony overlooking the lush green yard.

Pensión Castrejón (☎ 775-4447), beside the juncture of Calle F Sur and Avenida 4 Oeste, is another decent place. It's large, and its clean rooms with private bathrooms and ceiling fans encircle a shady interior garden courtyard, a separate space where you can wash and hang your clothes, and safe parking. Outdoor seats are provided for each room, or you can sit in the open-air, covered sitting area and watch TV. Singles/doubles cost US$10/15; larger rooms have up to five beds for US$25.

Places to Stay – middle

Three-story *Hotel Iris* (☎ 775-2251, fax 775-7233), beside the Parque de Cervantes, has 70 rooms with good beds and private bathrooms. Rates are US$17/19 single/double for a room with air-con and one bed, US$22 for air-con and two beds. A single with fan only goes for US$14. This place is quite OK, as is its restaurant.

Hotel Nacional (☎ 775-2222/2223), near the corner of Avenida Central and Calle Central, is a large hotel with a restaurant, pizzeria, casino, safe parking and a large swimming pool with diving board and slide. The 75 rooms, all with air-con, phones and private hot-water bathrooms, cost US$15/21 single/double; a few dollars extra gets you cable TV. There is also a cinema with four shows per day, in English with Spanish subtitles.

The *Hotel Occidental* (☎ 775-4695, fax 775-7424), on Avenida 3 de Noviembre beside the Parque de Cervantes, has 40 rooms with air-con and private bathrooms for US$17/21/25 single/double/triple. The rooms are a bit worn, but this place offers excellent value and it is quite popular. There's a casino on the hotel's premises and laundry service. The restaurant is cheap and popular.

By far the best place in town is the *Hotel Castilla* (☎ 774-5236, fax 774-5246), on Calle A Norte near the Parque de Cervantes. This three-story, 70-room hotel opened in 1996 and rooms here are often hard to come by. Every room is cheerful and equipped with air-con, phone, private bathroom and cable TV. Castilla's rates are US$25/30 single/double.

On the Interamericana about 1km east of the turnoff for Boquete is the *Hotel Fiesta* (☎ 774-4584), which has 60 rooms for US$25/33 and four suites for US$60. All the rooms have air-con, TVs, phones and private bathrooms, but the rooms at the Hotel Castilla are more pleasant.

Places to Eat

Town Center The restaurant at the *Hotel Occidental* is the best value in town. Typical items include scrambled eggs and toast (75¢), ham and eggs (US$1), sandwiches (under US$2) and even a banana split (US$1.50). A chocolate sundae costs 60¢. The restaurant is open every day, from 7 am to 10 pm.

Mio Bello Pizzeria and the adjacent *El Portal Restaurante,* on Calle A Sur near

Avenida 3 de Noviembre, share a menu and a kitchen but retain their original names. The biggest difference between them is that the pizzeria has air-con, while El Portal doesn't. These places are popular with the college crowd on weekend nights, mainly because El Portal has a cozy, cave-like, subterranean dining room that's quite hip. Pasta and seafood are the specialties of the house. A family-size pizza will set you back US$8. Fish and meat dishes run US$4 to US$7.

On Sunday the restaurant at the *Hotel Castilla* includes paella on its menu, and it is delicious. If you love paella and aren't in town on a Sunday, stop by the restaurant no later than noon or 1 pm and ask them to please prepare the dish for your dinner. Usually the chef will make it for two or more people, given four or five hours' notice. If there's just you, order enough for two and take some to go. A single order costs US$8.

The *Salón Don Pedro,* on Avenida Bolívar near the northern corner of the central plaza, offers Chinese as well as Panamanian food, an economical 'meal of the day' (US$2) and some of the coolest air-con in town. Most dishes cost about US$4 It's open 9:30 am to 10 pm every day.

Churrasco's Place, on Avenida 2 Este 1½ blocks from the Parque de Cervantes, is popular with locals for its good, inexpensive food. Its specialty is grilled meats. Downstairs is a covered, open-air restaurant; a slightly more expensive air-con bar/restaurant section is upstairs in the rear. Churrasco's Place is open 24 hours a day, every day.

Café Don Dicky, on Calle C Norte, is also open 24 hours a day. From the front it looks like a cheap open-air diner, but it makes good food and there's a more attractive dining area in the rear. Most dishes cost about US$3.

The *Sasa Restaurant,* on Calle C Norte 1½ blocks east of the Parque de Cervantes, is open-sided (and therefore hot), but it offers an excellent seafood soup – US$3.50 for a large portion – and a tasty guacho, which is like a thick soup and consists mainly of rice, peas and clams. Guacho is not found outside Chiriquí Province.

A pleasant little place for an inexpensive breakfast or lunch is the small open-air *Restaurante Kevin,* in the front of the Hotel Saval. Service is friendly here, and meals go for US$2.

A Few Blocks Out *Mar del Sur,* behind the large La Fé shopping center on Avenida Obaldía, is the best restaurant in town. I get excited just thinking about the place. It is quiet, romantic and upscale, and it specializes in Peruvian seafood and has a nice wine list. Main dishes range in price from US$7 to US$14. The ceviche is particularly good and served the Peruvian way – very spicy. Mar del Sur is open for lunch and dinner every day.

Among stores on the southern side of the Super Barú supermarket/shopping complex, near the corner of Avenidas Francisco Clark and 3 de Noviembre, is *La Cacerola Restaurante,* a popular buffet-style diner with plenty of air-con. Most dishes cost about US$2. Seafood soup costs US$2.50. The restaurant is open 7:30 am to 9 pm daily. The *Super Barú* supermarket has large deli and produce sections and a well-stocked pharmacy. There's even a small area where you can enjoy a dessert or cold beverage.

Mariscos y Steak House, on the Interamericana two buildings west of Avenida Obaldía, serves a superb seafood casserole, but it costs US$15, and the waiters tend to be unfriendly. Hours are 11 am to 11 pm daily.

Entertainment

The cinema, *Cine Plaza,* is half a block northwest of the Parque de Cervantes. *Jorón Zebede,* 1km from the Interamericana on the road to Boquete, is a traditional open-sided dance hall that only comes to life after 11 pm on Friday and Saturday, at which time it is *the* happening place in all of Chiriquí Province. There's a small cover charge, and the drinks are cheap.

There are numerous bars and dance clubs in town, none of them particularly memorable. The most popular of the bunch at the time of writing was the *Brandy Wine Disco,* a couple of blocks south of the main plaza.

Getting There & Away

Air David's airport, the Aeropuerto Enrique Malek, is about 5km from town. There are no buses to the airport; take a taxi.

Aeroperlas (☎ 721-1195 at the airport; 269-4555 in Panama City) offers daily flights connecting David with Panama City (US$55/110 one-way/roundtrip) and Changuinola (US$24/48). The Changuinola flight departs three times daily; the morning flight continues from Changuinola to Bocas del Toro town for US$10 more (total one-way fare US$34).

Aeroperlas also has flights between David and San José, Costa Rica, on Monday, Wednesday and Friday (US$83/147 one-way/roundtrip). The two-hour flight from David generally leaves around 8:15 am, while the David-bound flight from San José usually departs around 8:45 am.

There's an Aeroperlas office (☎ 775-7779, fax 774-2916) on Calle A Norte, next to the Hotel Castilla. It's open 8 am to 5 pm weekdays and 8 am to 3:30 pm Saturday.

Bus The bus station is on Avenida del Estudiante, about 600m northeast of the central plaza. It has a small office where you can leave luggage for 50¢ per day and a restaurant that's open 5 am to midnight.

David is the hub of bus transportation in western Panama and has buses to many places. Below is a listing of most of the major bus routes and schedules. Fares cited are one-way.

Boquete – 38km, one hour, US$1.20; every 30 minutes, 6 am to 9 pm

Caldera – 20km, 45 minutes, US$1.50; six buses daily, 10:15 am to 4:45 pm

Cerro Punta – 79km, 2¼ hours, US$2.65; take the Volcán bus, departing every 15 minutes, 5:30 am to 6 pm; bus continues from Volcán to Bambito (10 minutes from Volcán) and Cerro Punta (30 minutes more)

Chiriquí Grande – 106km, three hours, US$6; hourly, 6 am to 6 pm Monday to Saturday; every two hours on Sunday

Horconcitos – 45km, 45 minutes, US$1.50; two buses daily, 11:15 am and 5 pm

Las Lajas (town) – 100km, 1½ hours, US$2; six buses daily, 10 am to 5 pm

Panama City – 438km; regular bus runs every 45 minutes, 7 am to 8 pm (6½ to seven hours, US$10.60); four express buses, at 10 am, 2 pm, 10 pm and midnight (5½ to six hours, US$15)

Paso Canoas (Costa Rican border) – 54km, 1½ hours, US$1.50; every 10 minutes, 5 am to 8 pm

Puerto Armuelles – 88km, 2½ hours, US$3; every 15 minutes, 4:30 am to 8:30 pm

Río Sereno (Costa Rican border) – 104km, 2½ hours, US$4; every 45 minutes, 6 am to 6 pm, via Volcán

Volcán – 57km, 1¾ hours, US$2.30; every 15 minutes, 5:30 am to 6 pm

Bus service to David from Panama City departs the Terminal de Buses al Interior, on Avenida Ascañio Villalaz in the Curundu district, every 45 minutes from 7 to 11:30 am, then departs every 1¼ hour until 8 pm (6½ to seven hours, US$11). There's also an express bus that leaves the capital at midnight (5½ to six hours, US$15).

In addition to operating buses between David and the border crossings at Paso Canoas and Río Sereno, Tracopa (☎ 775-0585) also provides bus service between David and San José, Costa Rica. There's only one direct bus each day, and it departs at 8:30 am from the Tracopa office at the corner of Avenida 5 Este and Calle A Sur, beside the Pensión Costa Rica; it arrives in San José about eight hours later. From San José, buses depart on the return trip to David at 7:30 am. The one-way fare is US$12.50.

You can buy your ticket when you show up for the bus or up to two days in advance of your trip. The Tracopa office is open from 7:30 am to noon and 2 to 4 pm Monday to Saturday and from 7:30 to 8:30 am Sunday.

Getting Around

David has local buses and plenty of taxis. Taxi fares within the city are 65¢ to US$1; the fare to the airport is US$2.

Rental-car companies with offices in David include the following:

Avis   ☎ 774-7075
Budget   ☎ 775-1667
Chiriquí   ☎ 774-3464
Hertz   ☎ 775-6828
Hilary   ☎ 775-5459
Mike's   ☎ 775-4963

If you want to get off the beaten track, ask about renting a 4WD vehicle (known here as a *cuatro por cuatro*).

AROUND DAVID

The **Hacienda Carta Vieja**, the largest and oldest rum distillery in Panama (established in 1915), is just off the Interamericana, 20 minutes' drive west of David. Carta Vieja gives tours, but be warned that they are in Spanish only and are limited to parties of two or more. Phone the office in David (☎ 772-7083) for information or just stop at the distillery; it operates 7:30 am to noon and 12:30 to 4 pm weekdays. To get here, turn south (left if you're coming from David) at the intersection with the road to Boquerón, as if you're heading to Alanje; this turnoff is between David and the town of Concepción.

Also between David and Concepción is the *Hotel Centro Turístico Los Delfines* (☎ 722-4029), just north of the Interamericana in Boquerón. This is a pricey hotel (rooms cost US$65 a night) that was failing miserably at the time of writing. There are many facilities – a swimming pool, hot tub, sauna, gym, tennis courts, billiards, table tennis, a restaurant and a bar/dance club – but due to its cost and stark appearance (lots of blinding-white concrete), few people stay here and I can't recommend it.

Within an hour's drive of David are two rivers that, at the time of writing, were the only rivers used by any **white-water rafting** outfit in Panama. The Río Chiriquí and the Río Chiriquí Viejo both flow from the fertile hills of Volcán Barú and are flanked by forest for much of their lengths. At some places waterfalls can be seen at the edges of the rivers, and both pass through narrow canyons with awesome sheer rock walls.

Both rivers also offer lots of class II rapids and some class IIIs and IVs as well (there's a lot more of the latter during periods of heavy rain). The Río Chiriquí is most often run from May to December, and the Chiriquí Viejo is run the rest of the year; the rides tend to last four and five hours, respectively. Bring along plenty of sunscreen.

The country's sole white-water outfit, Chiriquí River Rafting (☎ 236-5218, ☎/fax 236-5217, hsanchez@panama.c-com .net, www.panama-rafting.com), Apartado 1686, Balboa, Ancón, Panamá, República de Panamá, goes back and forth between the rivers, depending on rainfall, the age and experience levels of its clients and other factors. The owner of the company, Hector Sanchez, speaks English and Spanish and is very safety conscious (see the Guides section in the Getting Around chapter for a profile of Hector). The company uses only first-class equipment and emphasizes safety – good moves on rivers with class III and IV rapids.

Chiriquí River Rafting offers a variety of options, including the following:

- One day of rafting and a box lunch; US$90
- Transportation to and from Panama City, one day of rafting, meals and lodging; US$150
- Transportation to and from Panama City, one day of rafting, one day of hiking across the central range, meals and lodging; US$210

For those short on time, US$200 will get you air transportation to and from Panama City, one day of rafting and a box lunch.

PASO CANOAS

See the Costa Rican Border Crossings section in the Getting There & Away chapter for information on this major border town.

PUERTO ARMUELLES

Located 34km from the Paso Canoas border crossing, Puerto Armuelles is a small, generally ugly and always muggy port town on Bahía de Charco Azul that

Loading bananas

grew around the banana production of the Chiriquí Land Company (CLC), which is owned by Chiquita Brands International.

The CLC plantations here were first established in the 1920s. The company still has 5000 hectares in production, operates trains to most of its 18 farms and has dock and loading facilities in town. There are independent banana farms in the area, too, covering another 2500 hectares. The area also has significant palm plantations and a cooperative that processes palm oil.

Puerto Armuelles may have the largest concentration of wooden buildings in the country, virtually all constructed when the plantations were established. Most are still occupied by some of CLC's 5000 workers.

Train buffs will be glad to learn that the company has 12 vintage General Electric locomotives, seven of which are still in operation. The youngest of the bunch was built around the end of WWII; the oldest was put together in the 1920s. These are worker trains. They are used year-round to transport pallets loaded with 40lb boxes of bananas from farms to a dock (the train tracks run onto a wharf, just as they do in Almirante, on the Caribbean coast), where the fruit is hoisted onto ships. A single ship will take on 1 million boxes of bananas before pushing off.

In addition, these old yellow locomotives haul trains that carry schoolchildren from the farms to classrooms in town. Tourists are not allowed to ride the trains without permission from the CLC (see Getting There & Away, below). However, it never hurts to ask, and the CLC also occasionally lets tourists visit the farms.

Because Puerto Armuelles is so incredibly hot and really has very little to offer except views of antique trains and old wooden houses, I recommend the town only as a day trip for people with a lot of time on their hands and an inclination to see the remains of a onetime banana republic.

Places to Stay & Eat
Puerto Armuelles has several hotels and restaurants. The best hotel, 1km outside town on the main road, is *Hotel Koco's Place* (☎ 770-7049), offering rooms for US$16.50/27.50 with fan/air-con. Koco's rooms are attractive, and there's a swimming pool, a restaurant and lots of large birds on the grounds. There's also a suite with air-con for US$44.

In town at the eastern end of the oceanfront road is the family-run *Pensión Balboa* (no phone), which offers clean, fan-cooled rooms with shared bathrooms for US$6/8 single/double and rooms with private bathrooms for US$12.

Also on the oceanfront road are two decent restaurants. Close to the Pensión Balboa is the *Restaurante y Pizzeria Don Carlos,* which specializes in seafood and pizza (a large combination costs about US$7.50). Farther in, the *Restaurante Enrique* specializes in Chinese food and has a large selection with no items over US$6. Its pork fried rice and rice with shrimp are quite OK.

Getting There & Away
Buses go to Puerto Armuelles from David every 15 minutes or so, from 4:30 am to 8:30 pm (88km, 2½ hours, US$3 each way). There are also the banana trains, run by the CLC, that serve the town and the farms around it. Travelers wishing to ride the trains require the company's permission; call the CLC at ☎ 770-7245.

GOLFO DE CHIRIQUÍ
South of David, the Golfo de Chiriquí is home to the **Parque Nacional Marino**

Golfo de Chiriquí, the 14,740-hectare national marine park that protects 25 islands, plus 19 coral reefs and abundant wildlife. Attractions include beaches, snorkeling, diving, surfing, bird watching and big-game fishing.

The 2000-hectare **Isla Parida** is at the heart of the marine park. A ferry once served the island from the port at Pedregal, a few kilometers south of David, but now the island is only reachable by water taxis and by boats belonging to a hotel on the island.

That hotel, *Las Paridas Island Resort* (☎ 774-8166 at the resort; ☎/fax 777-0032 in David, paridas@chiriqui.com), operated by Canadians Sharon and Dave Simpson, consists of four bungalows, a restaurant and a bar. The resort is nestled in jungle and faces a protected bay with water that's clear most of the time. Snorkeling and diving tours can be arranged. Its three-day, two-night package includes cabins, meals and roundtrip transportation to the island from David: US$220 (one person), US$150 per person double occupancy (two to four people), US$135 per person with shared accommodations (five to eight people). The hotel was for sale at the time this book went to print; readers considering a stay would be wise to contact the resort well in advance.

The 3000-hectare **Isla Boca Brava** is northeast of Isla Parida. To reach it, you must first drive or take a bus to the town of Horconcitos, south of the Interamericana and 45km east of David; two buses daily run to Horconcitos from David (45 minutes, US$1.50 each way). Then you must take a 20-minute taxi ride (US$10) from Horconcitos to Boca Chica, a small fishing village. The taxi ride will cost US$10. If you drive your own vehicle, you can safely leave it near the village's dock. At the dock you can hire a water taxi (US$2) to take you 200m to the island.

On Boca Brava, Frank Köhler and Elena Sanchez Gonzalez operate the *Restaurante y Cabañas Boca Brava* (☎/fax 774-3117). The lodgings consist of four modern, lovely and comfortable rooms with private bathrooms for US$15 to US$20 for two people and four rustic rooms with shared bathroom for US$8 for two people. If you want to sleep in a hammock between trees, the cost is US$2. Discounts are available for stays of a week or more.

The restaurant/bar features lobster for US$7; most other full meals are half as much. From the breezy restaurant, you're but a stone's throw from the boundary of the national marine park. And sharing the island with you are three species of monkey, four species of sea turtle and lots of parrots. This place is a great find, and at it you can catch water taxis to take you to some excellent snorkeling sites in the park. There are many coral reefs and picturesque beaches in the area; Frank and Elena would be happy to tell you all about them. They speak English, German and Spanish.

EAST TO VERAGUAS PROVINCE
Meseta Chorcha
On the northern side of the Interamericana, 24km east of David, is the enormous Meseta Chorcha (Chorcha Plateau), which photographers won't want to miss. As you approach the plateau from the west, you'll see a white streak running down its glistening granite face. As you come closer, you'll see that the streak is an extremely tall waterfall.

Unfortunately, the highway's as close to the falls as you can get without trespassing. The land between the highway and the foot of the falls belongs to a rancher who doesn't like strangers on his property.

Playa Las Lajas
Playa Las Lajas, 62km east of David and 13km south of the Interamericana via a paved road, is one of several long, palm-lined beaches along this stretch of the Pacific coast. With its broad expanse of white sand, Playa Las Lajas is quite popular on the weekends but often empty during the week. The waves are perfect for body surfing.

There's one place to stay at Playa Las Lajas, and it's really quite OK if you don't mind roughing it a little. If you turn left at the point where the road to the beach meets the coast, you'll soon come to a private club; if you turn right and proceed 1.5km, you'll come to *Las Lajas Beach Resort* (no phone), which uses the term 'resort' very loosely.

The place consists of six rustic bamboo cabañas. Each faces the beach and is a stone's throw from the surf. The floors are made of concrete, which is good because it means you'll take less sand with you to your sleeping quarters – the loft above. The 'beds' there are thin cotton pads, which are fine if you're one of those people who can sleep anywhere. There is no furniture; these cabañas are merely fancy palapas with lofts and pads. However, each cabaña does have electricity and an interior light.

The bathrooms are shared but quite decent, and there's a restaurant. At US$20 per cabaña, this place is a good find, given its seaside location. Backpackers might say it's a great find. There's no phone at the 'resort'; you just show up and take your chances. If you arrive during the week, you might have the place to yourself. Because the Playa Las Lajas turnoff is only 4km west of the turnoff for the Pozos de Galique hot springs (see below), you might want to consider combining the two.

Six buses a day run between the town of Las Lajas and David (1½ hours, US$2 each way); the first one leaves David at around 10 am, the last at around 5 pm. From Las Lajas, taxis are available to take you to the beach; the cost is US$3.

Cerro Colorado

One of the world's largest copper mines is an hour's drive north of the Interamericana via a private road that begins nearly opposite the Playa Las Lajas turnoff. Mineralogists estimate that there's approximately 1.4 million tons of copper in Cerro Colorado. The open-face mine is not open to tours; I mention it because some readers might be interested to know it's here.

Pozos de Galique

The Pozos de Galique (Springs of Galique) are three no-frills hot springs, each of which can accommodate several people, at the end of a badly rutted dirt road that stems north from the Interamericana. If you go nuts over hot springs like I do, you'll enjoy these – especially if you reach them in the early morning (before the day heats up) and bring lots of cold drinks. These hot springs have 'day trip' written all over them.

Beside the springs, which are nestled in a grassy hillside, are several really basic concrete-block *cabins* with a shared outhouse and an exposed bucket bath. If you dare to stay in one, expect lots of insect bites all night long. The price is right, anyway: US$2 per cabin (or US$7 with meals).

Bring lots of cold sodas, give the Indians who own the cabins a couple dollars as a friendly gesture when you arrive (they maintain these springs), and hand them another dollar or so to use their bucket to rinse off once you're finished with the hot springs. Be sure to take all your litter with you when you leave.

The easy-to-miss turnoff for the rutted 3.8km road to the springs, which basically requires a 4WD vehicle, is 27km east of the Interamericana turnoff for Horconcitos and 4km east of the turnoff for Playa Las Lajas. The springs turnoff is 30m west of a small bridge with 'Galique' written on it. There is no sign indicating the presence of hot springs.

Rock Carvings

About 5km west of the town of Tolé is a turnoff for El Nancito, a small community known for its carved boulders. Local people say the carvings were made more than 1000 years ago, but no one really knows; the rocks have yet to be studied. Few people even know about them.

From the Interamericana, turn north onto the road to El Nancito, and when you reach the 'Cantina Oriente' sign, turn west and drive 75m. You'll come across some rather large boulders with figures carved into them. The largest of the boulders is on the far side of a barbwire fence, behind a cattle chute. There are many other carved boulders in the area.

No buses stop in El Nancito. If you are relying on public transportation and your legs are in good shape, the best thing to do is to take any bus that passes by El Nancito, ask the driver to drop you at the turnoff on the Interamericana, and then hike the 1.5km to the boulders. Afterward, walk back to the highway and catch any bus heading in the direction you want to go. Be careful doing this in the late afternoon; you'll have difficulty catching a bus after sunset.

Kiosco Bar Criollo

A couple of kilometers west of Tolé (a hamlet near the Interamericana with no attractions and no hotels) is one of the most famous restaurants in western Panama, the Kiosco Bar Criollo. On the southern side of the highway, the restaurant is a favorite of truckers and is open 24 hours a day. If you're on a bus that passes through Tolé, chances are that your bus will make a quick stop here.

There's no menu, but chicken and beef dishes are always available. Ask for the carne guisada (beef stew) or the pollo guisado (chicken stew). The beef and chicken are slow-cooked and are as tender as can be. Rice and a hearty potato salad always accompany your choice of stew. The coffee, made from Chiriquí beans, is excellent. The service at Kiosco Bar Criollo is very quick. For soup, chicken or beef stew, a soda and coffee, you can expect to pay US$3.50.

Highlands

BOQUETE

This town of 3000 is only 38km north of the hot, bustling provincial capital of David, but it feels like it's in another country. Nestled in a craggy mountain valley at 1060m, with the sparkling Río Caldera running through it, Boquete is known throughout Panama for its cool, fresh climate and pristine natural environment. It's a fine place for walking, bird

watching and enjoying a respite from the heat of the lowlands. *Bajareque,* which roughly translates as 'slow drizzle,' is the name locals give to the light rainfall that comes to visit this pleasant town almost every afternoon.

Flowers, coffee, vegetables and citrus fruits are grown in and around Boquete. The navel-orange season, from November to February, is a popular time to visit. Boquete oranges, originally brought from Riverside, CA, are known for their sweetness, and the coffee is widely regarded as the country's finest.

On some nights temperatures can drop to near freezing. Visitors should pack some warm clothes if they plan to do any camping in the area.

Orientation

Boquete's central area comprises only a few square blocks. The main road, Avenida Central, comes north from David, passes along the western side of the town plaza and continues up the hill past the church.

Information

A IPAT tourist office is on the southern side of town, visible from the main road. Its staff have maps and can answer basic questions as long as they're in Spanish. There is a lovely view from the premises.

There's a Banco Nacional de Panamá on Avenida Central, and there's a post office on the eastern side of the plaza, open 7 am to 6 pm weekdays and 7 am to 5 pm Saturday. International calls can be made from the pay phone outside the post office and from phone booths elsewhere around town.

There's a laundry (Lavamática Diana) on Avenida Central, opposite and a little downhill from the church. It will wash, dry and fold your clothes for US$1.50 a load, and it's open from 7 am to 6 pm Monday to Saturday.

Two gas stations and a supermarket are on Avenida Central.

Things to See & Do

Boquete, with its flower-lined streets and nearby forest, is ideal for walking, hiking

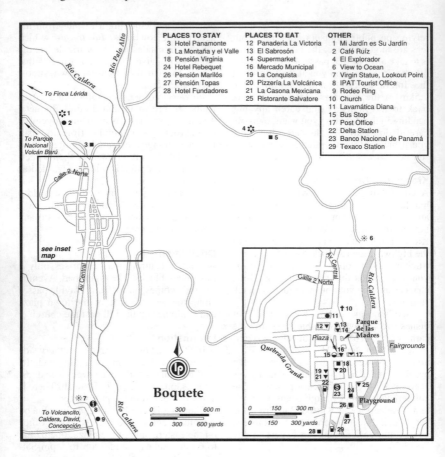

PLACES TO STAY
3 Hotel Panamonte
5 La Montaña y el Valle
18 Pensión Virginia
24 Hotel Rebequet
26 Pensión Marilós
27 Pensión Topas
28 Hotel Fundadores

PLACES TO EAT
12 Panaderia La Victoria
13 El Sabrosón
14 Supermarket
16 Mercado Municipal
19 La Conquista
20 Pizzería La Volcánica
21 La Casona Mexicana
25 Ristorante Salvatore

OTHER
1 Mi Jardín es Su Jardín
2 Café Ruíz
4 El Explorador
6 View to Ocean
7 Virgin Statue, Lookout Point
8 IPAT Tourist Office
9 Rodeo Ring
10 Church
11 Lavamática Diana
15 Bus Stop
17 Post Office
22 Delta Station
23 Banco Nacional de Panamá
29 Texaco Station

Boquete

and birding. The town lends itself to peaceful strolls and offers picturesque views. The more ambitious might fancy climbing the 3478m **Volcán Barú** in the nearby national park. There are several entrances to the park, but the easiest access is from Boquete (see the Pàrque Nacional Volcán Barú section, later in this chapter, for details).

A stroll around town will allow you to see the **Parque de las Madres**, with its flowers, fountain and children's playground; the fairgrounds; and the river. You'll also come across an old railway and

an exhibition wagon, leftovers from the days when a train linked Boquete with the coastal town of Puerto Armuelles.

At **Café Ruíz** (☎ 720-1392), on the main road about 600m north of the town center, you can get an up-close-and-personal look at the coffee business. The company offers free half-day tours that begin with picking coffee beans and end with watching bags of coffee being boxed.

There are other tours as well, including one that teaches you what to look for when tasting coffee. This 'tour,' which involves some classwork and much coffee sampling, is led by a professional coffee taster. If you wish to take a tour, Café Ruíz asks that you notify it at least one day in advance.

Mi Jardín es Su Jardín, just uphill from Café Ruíz, is a magnificent garden surrounding a luxurious private estate. The residence is off-limits to the public, but you are free to stroll about the garden as long as you like during daylight hours. There's no entrance fee. The grounds are open every day of the year.

In a hilly area a half-hour's walk northeast of the town center, **El Explorador** is a cafeteria and gardens. The cafeteria serves breads, hot chocolate, coffee drinks, chicken and fried bananas, and it's quite OK. Reached by a path behind the cafeteria, the gardens are like a page ripped from *Alice in Wonderland*. The path passes between tiny terraced gardens and over an itty-bitty bridge. On a small grassy slope beneath tall trees, big bunnies hop freely about.

There are TV sets everywhere in the gardens, and inside them are dioramas. Typical is a TV set that contains figurines comprising a choir. Elsewhere a shrub has been trimmed to resemble a beaver's face. In its mouth is a doll. A sign beside the artistic piece reads: 'If you're a pretty little doll, don't get close. I can eat you.' El Explorador is open only on weekends and holidays, from 9 am to 6 pm. Admission costs US$1.

Birders won't want to miss **Finca Lérida**, located above town. Most of the property is forested, and within the forest are resplendent quetzals, timberline wrens, black-and-yellow silky-flycatchers and more. Permission to enter the farm and directions to it can be obtained from the Collins family at the Hotel Panamonte (see Places to Stay, below).

Orchids are grown in nearby Volcancito on a farm owned by John Hackett (☎ 720-3284), a super-nice retired US military officer who enjoys showing his impressive collection. If you're unable to reach John, contact Frank Glavas at Pensión Marilós (see Places to Stay), who can arrange a visit. There's no charge.

Although Boquete is not known for having an extensive handicrafts market, as is El Valle in Coclé Province, every Sunday hundreds of Guaymís from outlying areas descend upon the central plaza to buy, sell and trade produce and manufactured goods at the **Mercado Municipal**.

Cockfights are held in the center of town on weekends. **Rodeos** are held from time to time in Boquete and neighboring towns, put together by a 'rodeo club' of local farmers and cattle ranchers. Boquete's rodeo ring is near the tourist office, on the southern side of town.

Other activities include **trout fishing** in the Río Caldera (bring your own tackle) and **horseback riding**. Plenty of people around Boquete have horses for hire; the

TOM BOYDEN

Picking coffee beans

Pensión Marilós or the Pensión Topas (see Places to Stay) can put you in touch with someone.

Special Events

The town's annual festival, the Feria de las Flores y del Café (Fair of Flowers and Coffee), held for 10 days each January, draws people from near and far.

Places to Stay

Because of the cool climate, all the places to stay in Boquete have hot showers.

Camping *La Montaña y el Valle* (☎/fax 720-2211, montana@chiriqui.com, www .ncal.verio.com/~ptpub/montana), a mountainside retreat 2.5km from town, has lovely 2.5-hectare grounds with nature trails and picturesque views. Three tent sites, each on a concrete platform for protection from dampness, cost US$7 per couple. Facilities for campers include hot showers, flush toilets, electricity, a covered cooking area, a library and – occasionally – gourmet food from the owners' kitchen. English and Spanish are spoken. This is a great find, but out of respect for the owners, campers *must* call ahead, and campers who show up after 4 pm will not be admitted. There are also cabins here; see details below.

Hotels *Pensión Marilós* (☎ 720-1380), on the corner of Avenida A Este and Calle 6 Sur, two blocks south of the plaza and two blocks east of Avenida Central, is a favorite of budget travelers. It's a great place to stay – family-run, clean and comfortable. You can cook in the kitchen, and morning coffee is free. Single/double rooms cost US$7/10 with shared bathrooms, US$10/16 with private bathrooms. Owner Frank Glavas speaks English and Spanish and can answer any questions you might have about Boquete. ✷

Pensión Virginia (☎ 720-1260), on the central plaza, is an older hotel with worn but clean singles/doubles for US$9/19 with shared bathrooms or US$13/24 with private bathrooms. There's an inexpensive restaurant downstairs and a piano and color TV in the upstairs sitting room. Spanish and English are spoken.

Pensión Topas (☎/fax 720-1005), on Avenida Belisario Porras three blocks south of the plaza and one block east of Avenida Central, has a swimming pool, an organic garden (help yourself) and just five rooms. Four rooms have private bathrooms and cost US$20 for one or two people from mid-May to November, and US$20/26 single/double from December to mid-May. One room, with an outside solar-heated bathroom, is cheaper. Breakfast is available for US$4. Children under 10 stay free. The gracious host, Alex Schöb, speaks English, Spanish and German. His two large dogs may intimidate you (they scared me).

The *Hotel Rebequet* (☎ 720-1365), opposite the Pensión Marilós, has nine attractive rooms with private bathrooms for US$20/30 single/double. Each room also has a TV and fridge; guests are welcome to cook in the kitchen, play billiards or use the TV room.

The *Hotel Fundadores* (☎ 720-1298, fax 720-1034), on Avenida Central, charges US$22 for fairly worn but OK rooms. The beds need replacing. The strength of this place is the lovely creek that runs through the property. Its restaurant is very good.

The *Hotel Panamonte* (☎ 720-1327), at the northern end of town, is a beautiful old hotel with dollhouselike charm that's in perfect harmony with its surroundings. The owners, the Collins family, have hosted many visiting naturalists over the years; rooms cost US$42 to US$55. Bicycle rentals are available.

La Montaña y el Valle (see Camping, above) is Boquete's best hotel. The guest quarters consist of three luxury cabins, new in 1997, each with a well-equipped kitchen, spacious living room/dining area, separate bedroom, hot-water bathroom and private terrace with valley views. The cabins, on a working coffee farm with trails into a lovely patch of forest, hold three to five people each; the cost is US$65 per couple, dropping to US$50 per night for stays of three or more nights.

Gourmet dinners, prepared by owners Barry Robbins and Jane Walker, two very likable expatriate Canadians, are available to guests only.

Places to Eat

Boquete has many inexpensive restaurants to choose among. *La Conquista,* on Avenida Central near the plaza, has typical food including trucha (local rainbow trout); no dishes are over US$5. Across the road, the *Pizzería La Volcánica* offers pizza and Italian dishes for around US$5.

Ristorante Salvatore, two blocks south and one block east of the plaza, has tables inside and out. It's slightly more expensive than the Volcánica, but the pizza's better. Other items include ceviche (US$3) and meat dishes (US$5 to US$8).

La Casona Mexicana, on Avenida Central near the center of town, serves good, cheap Mexican food. The restaurant is divided into a number of small, semiprivate rooms, and because of this it's popular with couples.

El Sabrosón, on Avenida Central uphill from the plaza, is a simple place that offers typical regional food at incredibly low prices. A meal consisting of pork, soup, rice, beans and fried plantains won't cost you more than US$2. It's open late.

If you're in town on Sunday, the buffet breakfast (US$6) at the *Hotel Fundadores* is an excellent value. Dinners range from chicken dishes (US$6) to lobster (US$12).

The area's fresh produce is sold at the weekly *Mercado Municipal,* on the northeastern corner of the plaza. Among the several bakeries in town, the *Panadería La Victoria,* on Avenida Central, is tops; it's worth a visit just to inhale the divine smells.

Getting There & Away

Buses to David, and local buses that will take you around the Boquete area, depart from the northern side of the plaza. Buses run between Boquete and David every 30 minutes. From David, the first bus leaves at 6 am; the last leaves at 9 pm. From Boquete, the first bus leaves at 5 am; the last leaves at 6:30 pm. The 38km trip on a good paved road takes an hour and costs US$1.20 each way.

Getting Around

Boquete is a small town and you can easily walk around the center in a short time. Walking is a great way to see the area, if you have plenty of time. The local *urbano* buses, winding through the hills among coffee plantations, farms and forest, cost just 50¢ and are a good way to get oriented. There are also taxis; US$2 fares are the norm.

Getting around on horseback is another option; the Pensión Marilós, the Pensión Topas and the Hotel Panamonte can all arrange for you to hire a horse.

LOS POZOS DE CALDERA

These natural hot springs are famous for their health-giving properties, especially for rheumatism sufferers. The springs are on private land near the town of **Caldera**, southeast of Boquete, and have not been developed for visitors. The owners, the Collins family (who also own the Hotel Panamonte in Boquete), don't mind if people visit the springs as long as they respect the property and take their rubbish out with them.

Caldera is 14km east of the David-Boquete road; a sign marks the turnoff. Six buses serve Caldera daily from David, leaving David from 10:15 am to 4:45 pm (45 minutes, US$1.50 each way). Alternately, you can take any bus between David and Boquete, get off at the turnoff and hitchhike the rest of the way (be warned, however, that the traffic is very light). Only one bus travels between Boquete and Caldera daily, and it follows no set schedule.

The springs are reached by a bad dirt road that stems from the paved road that passes through Caldera. The walk from the paved road to the springs will take you about 45 minutes. In a 4WD vehicle, you can drive to within about 10 minutes' walk from the springs. You'll need to ask the way, as there are numerous turnoffs and no signs.

PARQUE NACIONAL VOLCÁN BARÚ

Giant Volcán Barú is Panama's only volcano and the dominant geographical feature of western Panama. Its fertile volcanic soil and the temperate climate of its mid-altitude slopes support some of Panama's most productive agriculture, especially in the areas around Cerro Punta and Boquete. Large trees dominate the volcano's lower slopes, giving way on the upper slopes to smaller plants, bushes, scrub and abundant alpine wildflowers.

Volcán Barú is no longer active and there is no record of its most recent eruption. It has not one but seven craters. Its summit, at 3478m, is the highest point in Panama, and on a clear day it affords views of both the Pacific and Caribbean coasts.

The 14,300-hectare Parque Nacional Volcán Barú contains walking trails and provides ample possibilities for hiking, mountain climbing and camping. A climb to the top, though quite steep, is not technically difficult, and no special climbing equipment is required. However, even someone in great shape generally needs 10 hours to reach the top and eight more to descend. For this reason, it is best to plan on camping on the mountain at least one night, and you should be prepared for cold. In 1995 a Peruvian hiker who foolishly set out only in shorts and a T-shirt, without camping equipment, died of hypothermia on the mountain.

The park is home to abundant wildlife, including pumas, tapirs and the spotted *conejo pintado,* a raccoonlike animal. At lower elevations the mountain is good for bird watching; the famous resplendent quetzal is often seen in this park, especially during the dry season (November to April). Along the last 2km of the steep 14km road that winds without turnoffs to the top, the forest becomes elfin, and by the summit there's little more than scattered low bushes (Panama's only habitat of the volcano junco, a grayish-olive bird with a pink bill and bright-yellow or orange eyes).

There are entrances to the park on the eastern and western sides of the volcano.

The eastern access to the summit, from Boquete, is easiest, but it involves a strenuous (some say painful) uphill hike along a 14km dirt/mud road that goes from the park entrance – about 8km northwest of the center of Boquete – to the summit. The road from town to this entrance is paved, but if you plan on driving the unpaved road from the entrance to the summit, you'll need a 4WD vehicle and a winch. I needed to use a winch seven times to get my old Land Cruiser up the mountain.

To reach this entrance from central Boquete, turn west on Calle 2 Norte (see the Boquete map) and continue along this paved road for 7.5km, until it forks. Take the left fork, which forks again in 600m; here you'll want to take the gravel road to the right. There's a ranger station here, beside the entrance to the park, which is occasionally occupied. If it is, you'll likely need to show a permit from INRENARE to proceed; for current requirements, check with the INRENARE offices in David (see that section) or Panama City. There's no INRENARE office in Boquete. The park entrance fee is US$3, or US$5 if you intend to camp.

Hikers: When you've reached the 'Curva Ratón' sign, you've walked 10km of the 14km from the entrance to the top. And what can you expect to find at the top? A 3m tall concrete cross, once painted white but now covered in vandals' spray paint. There's more graffiti on the rocks all around the summit. But the vandalism can't spoil the ocean-to-ocean views – *if* your arrival is well timed. Because the summit is right at cloud level, that's a very big 'if.' The visibility from the mountain top is generally best just after sunrise. Soon afterward, clouds and fog rise in surrounding valleys, and views from the summit become scarce.

Another park entrance is just outside the town of Volcán, on the road to Bambito and Cerro Punta. The rugged road into the park here – which soon becomes too rough for anything but a 4WD vehicle – goes only a short way off the main road, to the foot of the volcano. The view of the summit and the nearby peaks from this entrance is impressive, and there's a lovely loop trail that winds through disturbed, secondary and virgin forest. The entrance fee is US$3.

AROUND PARQUE NACIONAL VOLCÁN BARÚ

A road branches off the Interamericana at Concepción (1200m) and climbs steadily through the towns of Volcán (1500m), Bambito (1600m) and Cerro Punta (1970m) until it stops at Guadalupe (2130m), on the western side of Volcán Barú. It's a good, paved road the entire way, frequently traversed by buses from David.

As in Boquete, the climate is cool and the air is brisk. The farmland around Cerro Punta has rich, black volcanic soil and is a great area for walking. As you near Cerro Punta everything starts to look European, with meticulously tended agricultural plots and European-style houses with steep-pitched tin roofs. A Swiss colony was founded here (one farm is named Nueva Suiza) many decades ago. Later immigrants included Croatians, and you can still hear their language spoken in the area.

This area produces not only abundant cool-climate crops, including vegetables, fruits, strawberries, flowers and coffee, but also trout, livestock and thoroughbred racehorses. You'll pass several *haras* (stables) where racehorses are bred along the Cerro Punta road.

As on the Boquete side of Volcán Barú, there are accommodations that range from budget to expensive. And you can camp in the national park – or in the more remote Parque Internacional La Amistad. Another option is to visit this area on a day trip from David; buses run frequently between David and Cerro Punta via Volcán and Bambito.

VOLCÁN

As you head north from Concepción, this little town of 9000 people (also called Hato del Volcán) is the first you'll encounter, 32km uphill from the Interamericana turn-off. Clinging to the flanks of the giant Volcán Barú, the town is dwarfed by its namesake. There isn't really much to do in Volcán itself, but the town does make a good base for excursions.

Orientation & Information

The road that links Concepción and Volcán forks in the center of town: one arrow points left toward Río Sereno, on the Costa Rican border (47km); the other points right toward Cerro Punta (16km).

Before you reach this fork, you'll see a small building marked 'Guias de Turismo' (☎ 771-4755); it's on the left side of the road if you're coming from Concepción. These friendly people, a cooperative of student guides, offer a number of inexpensive tours (in English and Spanish) around the area.

You're also welcome to stop here just to ask for information about the area; they offer a map and plenty of helpful information, including directions to places of interest, should you want to go on your own.

A similar tourism cooperative is based in a small office beside the Shell station at the road fork. It's marked 'Información al Turista' (☎ 771-4036). It too offers information, maps of the area, tours and guides.

Things to See & Do

On the western side of the Concepción-Volcán road, 3km south of Volcán, you'll see **Arte Cruz**, where artist José de la Cruz González makes wood carvings, sculptures, furniture and other wood products, and etchings on crystal and glass. His work is known throughout Panama. Visitors are welcome, and José is happy to demonstrate and explain his art. Small items are for sale, or he will make you a personal souvenir in just a few minutes.

The ruins of the pre-Columbian culture at **Barriles** are about a five-minute drive from the center of town. The ruins are on private land, but the family who lives on the land is very gracious, allowing visitors to see the ruins and answering any questions about them. Major artifacts from the archaeological site, including statues, *metates* (flat stone platforms used for grinding corn), pottery and jewelry are displayed in the Museo Antropológico Reina Torres de Araúz in Panama City.

CHIRIQUÍ PROVINCE

Just past Volcán, on the way to Bambito, is one of the entrances to Parque Nacional Volcán Barú; see the park's section, above, for details.

Other attractions around Volcán include springs, rivers, trout fishing, a botanical garden, coffee plantations (Cafetales Durán, with a million coffee bushes!), racehorse ranches and habitats of the quetzal and other exotic birds. Hiking trails in the area include one to the top of Cerro Punta; the Sendero Los Quetzales (the Quetzals Trail), which crosses the national park to Boquete (see the Guadalupe section, below); the Sendero del Tapir (Tapir Trail), which leads to a place where many tapirs live; and a number of others. Also nearby are the Lagunas de Volcán (see information below).

On weekends a **market** is held at the San Benito school in town; handicrafts are sold, as well as ordinary items at good prices. All proceeds benefit the school.

Places to Stay

You'll find most lodgings along the road that leads from Volcán to the border at Río Sereno. The ones listed below are the ones that I felt offered decent accommodations at the time this book was researched.

As you drive along the road to Río Sereno, the first good place you'll see is the *Motel California* (☎ 771-4272), which is run by José Zizic, a friendly old Croatian guy who speaks English and Spanish. His 15 clean, basic cabins with private hot-water bathrooms cost US$20, and there's a restaurant and bar.

Farther along on the same road, a sign points the way to the *Antojitos La Nona* (☎ 771-4284), 400m off the road. Behind the little restaurant are four clean cabins, each with a private hot-water bathroom. A two-room cabin with a kitchen, sleeping three people, costs US$35 a night; three three-room cabins without kitchen, each sleeping five, cost US$40.

A little closer to Río Sereno is the *Oasis* (☎/fax 771-4644), which has eight run-down rooms and lumpy beds and charges US$20/25 a single/double. The price includes breakfast and dinner. I don't recommend this place for lodging, but for the young and restless the dance club at the Oasis is *the* place to be on Friday and Saturday nights.

A much better value than the Oasis is the next place down the road, *Cabañas Mar y Sol* (☎ 771-4585), which has four basic rooms with decent beds, private hot-water bathrooms and even a dining table for US$10 to US$15. Two much larger cabins that have kitchenettes and many beds go for US$45.

Continuing, the *Hotel y Restaurante Don Tavo* (☎ 771-4258), built in 1996, has 17 very nice singles/doubles for US$25/33. Every room has a private bathroom with hot water. The hotel even has laundry service. There's a restaurant downstairs, but the food and service aren't good.

The next good place you'll come to is the very lovely *Cabañas Las Huacas* (☎ 771-4363), where five two-story A-frame cottages, each with a kitchen, six beds and hot-water bathroom, are set around attractive grounds that include a goose pond and gorgeous mountain vistas. Prices range from US$55 to US$65. One very large cabin with eight beds goes for US$85.

Farthest from town (2.5km from central Volcán), the *Hotel Dos Ríos* (☎ 771-4271) has the feel of a hunting lodge. The entire hotel is made of lightly stained oak, and all 16 guestrooms face a creek and the mountains. Rates at this attractive and peaceful place are US$28/33 single/double. The hotel was built in 1967 to replace the original Hotel Dos Ríos, which was built beside the Río Caldera in Boquete in 1961 and washed away during a terrible storm five years later.

Places to Eat

The restaurant at the beautiful yet rustic *Hotel Dos Ríos* serves very good food that's reasonably priced. It's open for breakfast, lunch and dinner, and items include sandwiches (US$1.50 to US$3), chicken (US$4.50) and fish or meat dishes (US$4.50 to US$7.50). In fact, it's the only restaurant in town with decent food.

Getting There & Away

Bus service to Volcán departs David every 15 minutes, 5:30 am to 6 pm (57km, 1¾ hours, US$2.30 each way). The bus continues to Bambito and Cerro Punta.

LAGUNAS DE VOLCÁN

At 1240m, the Area Silvestre Protegida Lagunas de Volcán, 4.5km from Volcán, is the highest lake system in Panama. There are two lakes here. Both swell after a big rain and are quite picturesque, with lush, virgin forest at their edges and Volcán Barú rising majestically in the background.

The lakes and the woodland around them are excellent sites for bird watching. On the lakes the birds of special interest are the masked duck and the northern jacana. At water's edge keep an eye out for the rose-throated becard (rare), pale-billed woodpecker, and mixed flocks of tanagers, flycatchers and antbirds.

To get to the lakes from the Concepción-Volcán road, turn west onto Calle El Valle (near central Volcán) and follow the signs. No buses go to the lakes, but you can hire a taxi in Volcán to bring you here. If you take your own vehicle, do not leave it unattended; if you must, don't leave anything of value in it. There have been reports of thefts from vehicles here.

BAMBITO

Seven km past Volcán on the road to Cerro Punta, Bambito is barely a town at all. Its only noticeable feature is the large Hotel Bambito. Opposite it, the **Truchas de Bambito** rainbow trout farm is worth a stop; here thousands of trout are raised in outdoor ponds with frigid water from the nearby river. You can buy fresh trout here or hire some tackle and catch your own.

The four-star *Hotel Bambito* (☎ 771-4265, fax 771-4207) offers singles/doubles for US$104/115. It features a swimming pool, sauna, hot tub, tennis courts, horseback riding, mountain bikes, a restaurant, a lounge and more. But for the money, you're much better off at Hotel Los Quetzales in Guadalupe or La Montaña y el Valle in Boquete.

What's That in the River?

Rainbow trout are not native to Panama, but the rivers in Chiriquí Province are filled with them. That's because in 1925, at the suggestion of a US official living in Panama, the Panamanian Bureau of Fisheries cast a few of the cold-water fish into the Río Chiriquí Viejo. The trout didn't flounder in their new home, and the delicious fish made such a splash with area residents that they began introducing trout into other rivers. Today, no matter where you are in Chiriquí Province, you aren't far from a trout stream. ∎

If you can't afford to stay at the Bambito but like the place, you can stop in for a drink in the lounge or a meal in the restaurant and enjoy the lovely views. The food's not cheap here, but it's not as expensive as you might expect; you can get a delicious potato or onion soup (US$4), a pasta dish (US$6.25) and fresh trout (US$8.75), as well as coffee or tea (US$1). On Sunday a big buffet (US$12.50) is served from noon to 3 pm.

Past the trout farm, *Cabañas Kucikas* (☎ 771-4245, fax 269-0623) has 17 spacious A-frame cottages that are set around 36 hectares of parklike grounds with children's play areas, barbecue sites and a river that provides decent trout fishing. Cottages of various sizes, sleeping two to 10 people, have kitchens and hot-water bathrooms. The cost is US$60 for two, but rates are not that much more for up to six people. This is a charming, romantic place.

CERRO PUNTA

At an altitude of 1970m, this town of 6000 people is only a few blocks long, but it's surrounded by beautiful, rich agricultural lands. About 7km north of Bambito, the town offers spectacular views across a fertile valley to the peaks of Parque Internacional La Amistad, a few kilometers away. This is a great place for taking in natural scenery.

Visitors come here primarily during the dry season (November to April) to visit the two nearby parks (Volcán Barú and La Amistad) and to enjoy the beauty of the surroundings. During this time, quetzals are often seen right on the road; though they can be seen here year-round, they tend to live farther up in the mountains during the rainy season.

Things to See & Do

The **Finca Fernández**, five minutes from town, is one of the finest places in Central America to see quetzals. To reach the farm from Cerro Punta, drive about 2km along the road to Guadalupe. When you see a sign – 'Sendero Los Quetzales' – that's opposite a painted bus stop, take the road to the right (it's initially flanked by Honduran pines).

The paved road ends 3km past that turnoff. The Fernández family lives in the house with the blue roof at road's end. For US$10, one of the Fernández brothers will guide you around their forested property. They speak a little English, and if they see your Lonely Planet book they'll know why you're there. Do not leave anything of value in the car.

Other attractions in Cerro Punta include **Fresa Cerro Punta**, where strawberries are grown, and **Panaflores** and **Plantas y Flores**, where flowers are raised for commercial sale; you can visit all these places. Racehorse and prize cattle farms are also here.

The main road continues through Cerro Punta and ends at Guadalupe, 3km farther. Another road takes off to the west, heading for the Las Nubes entrance to Parque Internacional La Amistad, 6.8km away; the turnoff is marked by a large wooden sign

(see the Parque Internacional La Amistad section, later in this chapter, for details on the park).

Places to Stay & Eat

The *Hotel Cerro Punta* (☎ 771-2020), on the main road, has 10 rooms, all past their prime but all with private bathrooms and hot water, for US$22/27 single/double. Also at the hotel is an excellent restaurant that offers several meals daily. Whether you stay here or not, drop by for a blended fruit drink. The local strawberries are the best you'll ever taste, and the strawberry drink is divine, as are the carrot, orange and rhubarb drinks. However, don't drink one right after the other, like someone I know. The pies and jams are homemade and quite good.

Pensión Eterna Primavera (☎ 775-3860) is half a kilometer down the road to Las Nubes, opposite the Delca store. This is a much more basic place, with just five rooms; the two with cold water only cost US$12.50 apiece, and the three with hot water cost US$15.

At either place, it's a good idea to make reservations during the tourist season, from around November to April. The Pensión Eterna Primavera sometimes closes at other times of the year.

Getting There & Away

A bus runs from David to Cerro Punta every 15 minutes from 5:30 am to 6 pm daily (79km, 2¼ hours, US$2.65 each way), stopping at Volcán and Bambito along the way. Cerro Punta is the end of the line for buses from David. If you're coming from Costa Rica, you could catch this bus at the turnoff from the Interamericana at Concepción.

GUADALUPE

Guadalupe is at the end of the road, 3km past Cerro Punta. It's a glorious area where you can walk among meticulously tended farms and gardens and enjoy the climate. Please do respect the signs that read: 'Esteemed Visitor: We are making all Guadalupe a garden – please don't pick the flowers.' The little community is full of flowers, and the agricultural plots curling up the steep hillsides are dreamy.

Sendero Los Quetzales

Two km past Cerro Punta on the road to Guadalupe, a sign points the way to the Sendero Los Quetzales. Keep following the 'Los Quetzales' signs all the way through Guadalupe to reach the trail. One of the most beautiful in Panama, this trail goes 8km to Boquete, crossing back and forth over the Río Caldera. You will want to hire a guide, as you will probably lose the trail should you attempt it on your own. Contact the Hotel Los Quetzales in Guadalupe (see below); alternately, you can hire a guide through hotels in Boquete (try the Hotel Panamonte or La Montaña y el Valle) or through tour operators in Panama City (see the Organized Tours section in the Panama City chapter).

Places to Stay & Eat

In the center of town, the *Hotel Los Quetzales* (☎ 771-2182, fax 771-2226) is a 10-room lodge, new in 1998, with a restaurant, bar/lounge, cafeteria, bakery and pizzeria. Every room features a tall ceiling, cheerful decor and detailed woodwork. The rooms, all with private hot-water bathrooms, cost US$30/35 without/with a bathtub. The Hotel Los Quetzales is operated in conjunction with the Cabañas Los Quetzales (see the Parque Internacional La Amistad section, below), and its rates include free transportation into the international park and free use of ponchos, boots, guides and horses. Not to be overlooked are the romantic spas beside a forest-flanked creek behind the hotel.

There are a couple of other tiny restaurants in town.

Getting There & Away

Buses from David go only as far as Cerro Punta. You can walk to Guadalupe from Cerro Punta, or take a taxi. The 3km, uphill walk takes most people about 40 minutes. The taxi ride takes just a few minutes and generally costs US$2.

PARQUE INTERNACIONAL LA AMISTAD

This 407,000-hectare park, half of which is in Panama and half in Costa Rica, has two Panamanian entrances: one at Las Nubes (near Cerro Punta on the Chiriquí side) and one at Wetzo (near Changuinola on the Bocas del Toro side; see the Bocas del Toro Province chapter for details on the Wetzo entrance and facilities there).

There's a ranger station at Las Nubes where tourists can stay (see below). Permits are required to camp in the park; they're available for US$5 at the ranger station or from INRENARE offices in David or Panama City. Entrance to the park costs US$3. Parking costs an additional US$1.

There are three main trails that originate at the Las Nubes ranger station. One is a 1.4km trail that winds up to the Mirador la Nevera, a lookout point at 2500m. A second trail winds 1.7km to La Cascada, a 45m, high waterfall with a lovely bathing pool. A third trail, named Sendero El Retoño (Rebirth Trail), loops 2.1km through secondary forest.

If you plan to spend much time at Las Nubes, be sure to bring a jacket. This side of the park, at 2280m above sea level, has a cool climate. Temperatures are usually around 75°F in the daytime and drop to about 38°F at night.

Places to Stay

A *ranger station* at Las Nubes has a dormitory room with bunkbeds where tourists can stay for US$5 per night. Due to the popularity of these beds among school groups from Canada and the USA, reservations are well advised. To make them, call the INRENARE office in David (☎ 775-7840/3163). Guests must bring their own bedding.

The same fellow who owns the Hotel Los Quetzales in Guadalupe, Carlos Alfaro, also owns three chalets inside the international park, the *Cabañas Los Quetzales* (☎ 771-2182, fax 771-2226). Carlos and two friends bought the land years before the park was established. The chalets are rustic yet comfortable. Each has a fully equipped

Orchids A-Bloom

About 1km above the Cabañas Los Quetzales (see Places to Stay) lies the Finca Dracula Orchid Sanctuary, one of Latin America's finest and most varied orchid collections, located amid exotic gardens. Comprehensive tours, available by appointment (☎ 771-2070), are led by the prominent Australian orchidologist Ray Thomson, who is also in charge of preserving and reproducing more than 1000 species of orchid, many of them in serious danger of extinction. If you visit the sanctuary, a donation of US$5 is respectfully suggested. ■

kitchen and separate bedrooms, hot water, a fireplace, kerosene lanterns and large terraces. Best of all, they're deep in the rainforest. Here you can stroll the jungle taking in all the sights – or just enjoy complete relaxation. Built in 1996, these chalets are famous all over Panama for their loveliness.

The chalets hold up to five, eight or 14 people. An entire chalet costs US$100 per night; the rate includes transportation to the chalets from the Hotel Los Quetzales, trail guides for exploring the forest, and use of horses, ponchos and boots. It's a great deal.

For a bit extra the hotel can provide you with food (cooked or uncooked). It's a good idea to reserve in advance, especially during the dry season (November to April).

Getting There & Away

Cabañas Los Quetzales is about 20 minutes' drive north of Guadalupe in a 4WD vehicle. You can get a ride to the chalets from Hotel Los Quetzales; due to the poor condition of the road that runs to the chalets, buses and taxis don't make the trip there. If time and money permit, I recommend spending a couple of days at each Quetzales.

RÍO SERENO

At Volcán a paved road turns off and heads west 47km to Río Sereno, on the Costa Rican border. The road winds through lush valleys sprinkled with coffee fields, teak plantations and stands of virgin forest. A sparkling river occasionally appears at roadside, and just as quickly it disappears back into the foliage. Travelers coming from the border crossing at Río Sereno usually have a very favorable first impression of Panama.

See the Costa Rican Border Crossings section of the Getting There & Away chapter for further information on this border town.

Veraguas Province

Panama's third-largest province, near the center of the country, is the only province that has both Caribbean and Pacific coastlines. Veraguas was also the site of the Spaniards' first attempt to obtain a footing on the continental New World; it was here that Christopher Columbus tried to establish a colony, but he abandoned his attempt in the face of an imminent Indian attack. Two later attempts to settle the area were also thwarted, both ending in death by starvation and cannibalism. But Veraguas was then and remains today a land of tremendous natural beauty, with robust rivers and stunning peaks. Nearly 500 years after Columbus' arrival, the area is still one of the least-developed regions on the isthmus.

Veraguas Province is home to 220,000 people, most of whom make their livings farming or ranching. From an airplane, the Caribbean and Pacific slopes of Veraguas look as different from each other as Canada's Rocky Mountains do from Australia's Great Sandy Desert. Heavy rainfall, virgin forest and little evidence of people characterize the Caribbean slope. Most of the Mosquito Coast of Veraguas can only be reached by boat, although there are plans to extend roads from the Carretera Interamericana (Pan-American Hwy) over the Cordillera Central and into the lush forests that still remain here.

The Pacific slope of Veraguas – from the summit of the cordillera to the Pacific Ocean – is an environmentalist's nightmare. Perhaps 5% of the original forest remains. Where vast forests filled with tropical animals and plants once stood, today there are only barren rocks and grassy hills on which graze the livestock for tomorrow's cheeseburgers and pepper steaks. Farther south, the land gives way to farm after farm. Longtime residents say they used to get a lot of rain, but much less falls since the forests were cut down, and water shortages and pesticide pollution are recurring problems. Parque Nacional Cerro Hoya was established in 1984 to save what little remains of the original forest.

Off the Pacific coast but still within the province is Panama's largest island, Isla de Coiba, which is both part of a national park and home to residents of a federal penal colony who live on beaches in huts and eat lots of coconuts. The diving around Coiba and neighboring islands is excellent, and the fishing is world class. Also world class are some of the waves that curl up to nearby Playa Santa Catalina, which is more of a lava field than a beach, at the end of a bad road near the western edge of the mouth of the Golfo de Montijo. Waves that have 5m faces and 150m rides are not uncommon here in April, July and August.

HIGHLIGHTS

- Parque Nacional Isla de Coiba, a national park, a penal colony and home to great dive sites

- Santa Fé, a pleasant, cool mountain town known throughout Panama for its magnificent orchids

- Iglesia San Francisco de Veraguas, one of the Americas' best examples of Baroque art and architecture

- Exploring the forests of Hacia Alto de Piedra on horseback

- Playa Santa Catalina, which attracts some of the world's top surfers

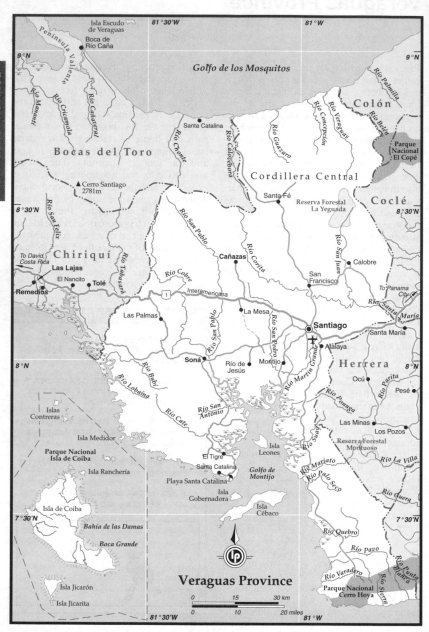

Veraguas Province

History

Columbus' first three voyages westward toward Asia were in search of land; his fourth and final voyage was undertaken to find a water passage to the region of Cathay, which was visited by Marco Polo – a strait that would, by Columbus' miscalculation, pass south of Asia into the Indian Ocean. To the north the admiral had found Cuba, which he believed was part of eastern Asia. To the south he had found South America, which he described in his log book as a 'New World' as yet unknown to Europeans. Columbus believed that the Atlantic Ocean flowed through a strait between them, and he was determined to find it.

For this venture, in which he proposed to sail around the world, Columbus chartered four small vessels. The year was 1502, and the great explorer spent most of it commanding his little worm-eaten fleet up and down the Caribbean coast from Venezuela to Nicaragua. Unable to find a strait, but seeing gold on Indians in the region and hearing from them of rich mines, the admiral cast anchor at the mouth of the Río Belén – the river that today constitutes the boundary between Veraguas and Colón

Provinces. He was determined to not return to Spain empty-handed: If the strait had eluded him, the gold wouldn't.

In February 1503 Columbus gave orders to establish a colony on a hill beside the river's silt-filled mouth. The Quibian, the area's native inhabitants, disapproved. Armed with spears, the Indians massacred an exploratory party that had gone up the Río Belén to investigate signs of Indian hostility. When Spanish corpses came floating down the river, Columbus, fearing an attack, ordered everyone back to their ships, and he set sail for Hispaniola.

Writing in his journal, Columbus said: 'I departed, in the name of the Holy Trinity, on Easter night, with the ships rotten, worn out, and eaten with holes.' Three years later the admiral died in an inn in Valladolid, Spain, of diseases he had acquired during his voyages. He died believing he'd seen Asia, unaware that he'd found instead the second-largest landmass on earth, comprising the two continents of the Western Hemisphere.

A few years after Columbus fled the Río Belén, Diego de Nicuesa led an expedition to the site to accomplish what the admiral couldn't. But even before the expedition

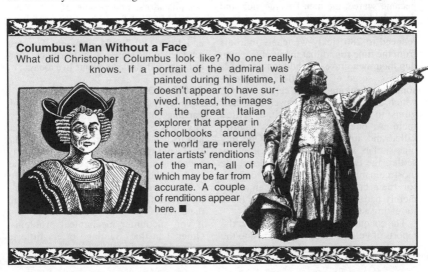

Columbus: Man Without a Face

What did Christopher Columbus look like? No one really knows. If a portrait of the admiral was painted during his lifetime, it doesn't appear to have survived. Instead, the images of the great Italian explorer that appear in schoolbooks around the world are merely later artists' renditions of the man, all of which may be far from accurate. A couple of renditions appear here. ■

had reached shore, four of its members drowned in rough surf. The provisions they brought from Hispaniola had spoiled, and because there was little recognizable food in northern Veraguas, starvation soon set in. One day a foraging party of 30 came upon a dead Indian and devoured the putrescent corpse, which killed every one of them. Living Indians took the lives of other Spaniards. Before Nicuesa called it quits, half of his 400 men had died. Eventually he packed up his ships, and he and his men fled the Río Belén, sailing east to found Nombre de Dios in what is now Colón Province.

In 1535 a third attempt was made to found a colony on the Caribbean coast of Veraguas, along the shore of the aptly named Golfo de los Mosquitos. This time the Spaniards, led by Felipe Gutierrez, landed beside the mouth of the Río Concepción, about 10km west of the Río Belén. As is usual on this coast, it rained almost continuously, damaging their supplies and interfering with planting. Floods came and swept away some settlers and most of their houses. The disasters that had plagued earlier New World colonists also assailed the Gutierrez party: Provisions became scarce, the men became sick and death paid frequent visits.

In little time 400 healthy men were reduced to 280 sickly wretches. Journals from the time report that many of the men dug their own graves. To add to the party's distress, some of the settlers were poisoned by drinking from a certain spring, which caused their lips to swell and their gums to soften, and sometimes killed them. At one point the settlers caught, killed and ate several Indians. One day nine settlers killed and devoured a fellow settler; the two who were considered the most culpable were later burned to death for their crime, while the other seven merely had a 'C' branded into their faces for eating a Christian.

The conquistadors, not ones to forget the reports of gold in Veraguas, returned to the area two decades later and eventually overcame the Indians and the torrential rains of northern Veraguas. They found gold, established mines and, in 1560, at the town of Concepción, 10km west of the Río Belén, they set up a headquarters and a smelter for the mines. African slaves were brought in to extract the gold (most of the blacks who live in Veraguas Province today are their descendants).

Because the heavy rains prevented cultivation of the land, supplies were brought from Hispaniola, Cuba, Jamaica and Nicaragua. From Concepción, it was 40km to the mountain town of Santa Fé, by a road passable only on foot; that same road still exists today, and it is still only passable on foot. Fifty km beyond Santa Fé was Natá in what is now Coclé Province, from whence cattle were brought to furnish the miners with meat. The towns of La Filipina, Los Santos and Parita were created to provide food for the miners.

By 1590 the mines were spent. Many miners left for newfound gold deposits in Colombia. Others escaped or were set free and took to farming throughout Pacific Veraguas and the Península de Azuero. Today the people on the peninsula fall into three main groups: black-skinned descendants of the slaves, fair-skinned descendants of the conquistadors, and people of mixed ancestry. Many of the Indians who had lived on the peninsula died by Spanish swords and from Old World diseases. The rest retreated to the slopes of the Cordillera Central, where their descendants live today.

SANTIAGO

Santiago (population 50,000), 250km from Panama City, is Panama's fourth-largest city. It is bisected by the Interamericana, and its central location – just north of the Península de Azuero and about halfway between Panama City and Costa Rica – has made it a hub of rural commercial activity.

This town is a good place to break up a long drive from the Costa Rican border to the capital or to get your vehicle serviced if you encounter mechanical problems. Other than that, Santiago offers little to the tourist. Most of the town's commerce and services – including stores, banks,

VERAGUAS PROVINCE

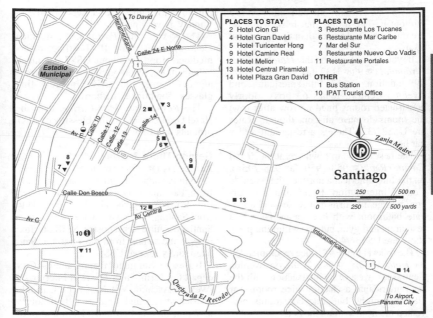

PLACES TO STAY
2 Hotel Cion Gi
4 Hotel Gran David
5 Hotel Turicenter Hong
9 Hotel Camino Real
12 Hotel Melior
13 Hotel Central Piramidal
14 Hotel Plaza Gran David

PLACES TO EAT
3 Restaurante Los Tucanes
6 Restaurante Mar Caribe
7 Mar del Sur
8 Restaurante Nuevo Quo Vadis
11 Restaurante Portales

OTHER
1 Bus Station
10 IPAT Tourist Office

Santiago

gas stations, restaurants and hotels – are along the Interamericana and Avenida Central, which splits off from the highway.

Information

The Instituto Panameño de Turismo (IPAT; ☎ 998-3929, fax 998-0928) has an office on the northern side of Avenida Central a half-kilometer west of its junction with the Interamericana. The office is staffed with three people, one or two of whom speak some English. Maps and brochures are available, but they are not very helpful. The office is closed on weekends.

There's a Migración y Naturalización (Immigration and Naturalization) office in Santiago as well.

Places to Stay

The *Hotel Gran David* (☎ 998-4510, fax 998-1866), on the Interamericana about 500m north of the Avenida Central intersection, is a good value, with clean though dark rooms with decent beds and private hot-water bathrooms for US$12/15 single/double, or US$18/21 with air-con and TV.

The *Hotel Cion Gi* (☎ 998-2756, fax 998-7272), on the highway close to the center of town, has 72 dirty and gloomy rooms ranging from US$15 for one person without air-con to US$23 for two people with air-con. The rooms' only strength is their size; if you're traveling with a large pet – an elephant, for instance – it could stay in your room without cramping your style.

A better value is the *Hotel Plaza Gran David* (☎ 998-3433, fax 998-2553), on the Interamericana on the eastern side of town. It is one of the nicer places around, with singles/doubles with air-con, good beds and private hot-water bathrooms for US$18/29. There's also a swimming pool and a Chinese restaurant on the grounds.

The *Hotel Turicenter Hong* (☎ 998-0671, fax 998-4059), on the Interamericana opposite the Hotel Gran David, is a good find, with 45 clean rooms with TVs, phones and private hot-water bathrooms for US$19/27 with air-con and US$13 without it. The rooms that have windows are much more cheerful than those without them.

If you're in a pinch, the *Hotel Central Piramidal* (☎ 998-3132, fax 998-5411) is at the junction of the Interamericana and Avenida Central. It has 63 boxy, poorly constructed rooms lined up row after row; the rooms do have air-con, though. Rates are US$21/32. There's a restaurant and a bar here.

The best rooms in town are at the *Hotel Camino Real* (☎ 958-7950, fax 958-7954), on the Interamericana north of the Avenida Central intersection. Each room has air-con, a large TV, firm mattresses and a private bathroom with hot water. There's a restaurant and gym, but no swimming pool. Rates are US$36/42.

The folks at the IPAT office recommended the *Hotel Melior* (☎ 998-4158), on Avenida Central just west of its intersection with the Interamericana, as having nice rooms for US$25 a night, but time constraints prevented me from visiting the hotel.

Places to Eat

The *Restaurante Los Tucanes,* on the Interamericana just north of the Hotel Gran David, has excellent food at reasonable prices. The chef salad (US$3), the pollo asado con salsa especial (US$4), the filete a la parmesana (US$6) and the langostinos a la criolla (US$6.50) are delicious. It's open late every day.

For superb Peruvian-style seafood at twice the price, try the *Mar del Sur,* on Calle 10 in front of the Don José Building. This place is owned by the people who own the restaurant of the same name in David, and it's just as good. Main dishes range in price from US$7 to US$14. The ceviche is particularly good and served the Peruvian way – very spicy. It's open for lunch and dinner daily.

Next door at the *Restaurante Nuevo Quo Vadis,* you can enjoy an excellent filet mignon (US$5.50), a tasty shrimp with curry sauce (US$7.50) and the fantasía marinera, an orgy of seafood (US$8.50).

Nuevo Quo Vadis' paella, served only on Sunday, is very popular.

The *Restaurante Portales,* on Avenida Central close to the IPAT office, offers mediocre food for about US$7 per meal. What's more, its margaritas are made from an awful mix and arrive in teeny-tiny glasses. The horror, the horror.

The *Restaurante Mar Caribe,* near the Hotel Gran David, has the blessing of IPAT officials, but I have yet to try it.

Getting There & Away

Aeroperlas (☎ 998-0160 in Santiago; 269-4555 in Panama City) flies to Santiago daily from Panama City (US$33/66 one-way/roundtrip). Aeroperlas also flies twice daily from Santiago to Panama City via Chitré; a Santiago-Chitré ticket costs US$18/36. Taxi fares to the airport from most parts of Santiago rarely exceed US$5.

Buses to Santiago from Panama City depart the Terminal de Buses al Interior, on Avenida Ascañio Villalaz in the Curundu district, at 1, 3 and 4 am; then half-hourly to 7 pm; then at 8, 9 and 11 pm and midnight. The trip takes four hours; the one-way fare is US$6. Santiago's bus station is on Calle 10 near the intersection with Avenida E.

Getting Around

Taxis are *the* way to travel in Santiago. They are easy to hail and they go anywhere in town for US$2 or less.

IGLESIA SAN FRANCISCO DE VERAGUAS

In the small town of San Francisco, 16km north of the Interamericana on the road from Santiago to Santa Fé, is one of the best and oldest examples of Baroque art and architecture in the Americas that was created by Indians using native materials. And unlike most Baroque churches, in which seemingly everything is covered in gold leaf, the altar and interior of this church are colorfully painted.

The highly ornate altar is made of ash and bitter cedar. Carved into the altar and elsewhere around the church are the usual

Old Testament scenes – the crucifixion, the Virgin looking divine, the saints ever so saintly – but also throughout the church are finely carved and well-preserved images of the artisans and prominent Indians. Their faces are cleverly inserted into the religious scenes; some appear atop the bodies of cherubs.

One large carving includes items that had special meaning for the Indians or otherwise impressed them – an eagle piercing its own heart with its beak, three large dice, a Spanish sword, a lantern, a human skull.

The captivating altar (most colonial altars in the Americas were brought over from Europe) and the church were constructed within a few years of each other; the date of completion is estimated to be 1727, but no one is exactly sure of the date because the Spaniards kept tight control over church record books, and when they left they took the books with them.

The steeple, incidentally, is not original. The original bell tower survived until 1942, when it suddenly collapsed without warning. Unfortunately, the new one doesn't even resemble the old one. The original served two purposes, one good, one evil – it was, of course, used for religious purposes, but the Spaniards also used it as a lookout tower to monitor the movements of the Indians and slaves in the community.

Near the church in San Francisco is **El Chorro del Spiritu Santo** (Holy Ghost Waterfall), which has a fine swimming hole. To get to it, follow the road as it winds around the church, and then take the road just behind the church. After a few hundred meters, you'll want to take the first right; after another several hundred meters, that road will bring you to the small cascades.

Getting There & Away

To reach the church, drive 16km north on the San Francisco turnoff from the Interamericana, until you reach the police substation (you'll see a stop sign there, and the station is conspicuously located on the main road). Turn right and proceed less

than 1km, and then turn right again at the Supermercado Juan XXIII de San Francisco. Drive 50m farther; the church is on the left.

A bus leaves the Santiago station for San Francisco every 30 minutes beginning at 7 am; the last one leaves at 6 pm. The ride takes about 25 minutes, and the one-way fare is US$1.

If you're short on time, an alternative is to hire a taxi in Santiago to take you to the church and, if you wish, to Santa Fé. Expect to pay US$12 roundtrip to and from San Francisco, and another US$28 if you hire the taxi to take you all the way to Santa Fé.

SANTA FÉ

This pleasant little town lies in the shadow of the Continental Divide, 52km north of Santiago. Because it's at an altitude of about 1000m, the town is cooler than the lowlands, and it's still very green – much of the forest remains, just as it did when the Spaniards founded the town in 1557. This is a great place for hikers and birders.

Orientation & Information

City planning is not a characteristic of Santa Fé. If you look long enough at a map of the town, you can see spaghetti in octopus sauce. The road that heads north to town from Santiago and the Interamericana, winding through lovely valleys along the way, branches out in three directions at the southern edge of town. The middle 'branch' forks yet again after a few more blocks.

None of the streets in town have names, and that's just fine with Santa Fé's residents; the town has a population of only about 100 families, so everybody here knows where everybody else lives. And the structures in town that aren't homes – the mayor's office, the cooperative, the church and so on – can be counted on two hands.

There's no tourist office, bank, laundry or gas station in town, but there is a post office and an orchid lady whose pet parrot can whistle the entire US Marines fight song – and frequently does.

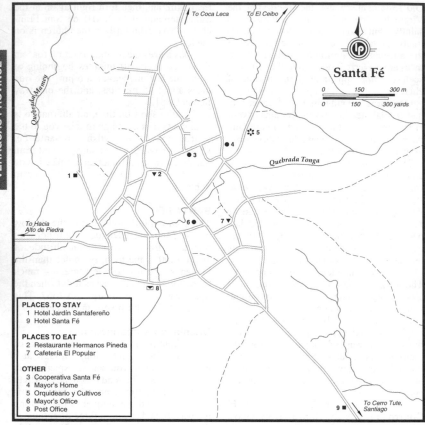

Santa Fé

To Coca Leca
To El Ceibo
To Hacia Alto de Piedra
Quebrada Tonga
Quebrada Mamey
To Cerro Tute, Santiago

0   150   300 m
0   150   300 yards

PLACES TO STAY
1 Hotel Jardín Santafereño
9 Hotel Santa Fé

PLACES TO EAT
2 Restaurante Hermanos Pineda
7 Cafetería El Popular

OTHER
3 Cooperativa Santa Fé
4 Mayor's Home
5 Orquideario y Cultivos
6 Mayor's Office
8 Post Office

Orquideario y Cultivos

Santa Fé is known throughout Panama for its orchids, and in Santa Fé the person to see about these flowers is Bertha de Castrellón, who has an impressive collection of them in her back yard and enjoys showing them to true enthusiasts. Among her orchids are both the largest and the smallest varieties in the world.

Most of the orchids are handsomely displayed in hanging coconut shells. They include a lovely lavender orchid found only in the hills around Santa Fé. Bertha, who speaks some English, is the president of the local orchid society, and she

can tell you a great many things about her plants.

To get to Bertha's house, take the right 'branch' at the point where the Santiago-Santa Fé road forks at the southern edge of town. Then take the second right and proceed 100m or so farther, until you see a driveway flanked by a sign that reads: 'Orquideario y Cultivos Las Fragacias de Santa Fé.' You have arrived.

There are two other things you should know about Bertha: She's the area's top birding guide, offering tours of nearby Cerro Tute, where there's a lovely set of waterfalls and fine bird watching; and, when Bertha claps, her green parrot bobs up and down and whistles US and Panamanian popular songs.

Although Bertha does not charge a fee for showing her orchids, I always insist on giving her US$5 for taking the time to show me her lovely plants. I hope you will too. Remember, you are visiting a home, not an amusement park. Be considerate: Don't show up before 11 am or after 3 pm, and if you call out to her from her gate and there's no answer, assume she's not home. *Don't* open the gate unless she instructs you to do so. There are no residential phones in Santa Fé. If you want to contact Bertha, address your mail to Bertha de Castrellón, Santa Fé de Veraguas, República de Panamá.

Cooperativa Santa Fé

I rarely mention stores, but this is no ordinary store. The Santa Fé Cooperative sells hats made of mountain palm (called *palmilla*) that are much more durable than hats found elsewhere in Panama – and they cost much less (generally from US$16 to US$25). They are not nearly as refined as the lovely hats available in Ocú and Penonomé, but if you're looking for a rugged hat in classic Panama-hat style, you can't do better.

While in the cooperative, you might want to pick up some Café El Tute, the locally grown coffee; it comes in US$1 half-pound bags and convenient 15¢ 28g pouches (you can get four cups of coffee out of one pouch). The Cooperativa Santa Fé is also a good place to stock up on beans, sugar and corn, which sell for half of their Panama City prices – and all the fruit and vegetables sold at the cooperative are locally grown.

The cooperative is open every day.

Cerro Tute & Hacia Alto de Piedra

There are two heavily forested mountainous areas near town that offer some fine birding. Many specialties of eastern Chiriquí and Veraguas Provinces can be found here, including the rufous-winged woodpecker and the crimson-collared tan-

ager. Both areas require a 4WD vehicle, a horse or strong legs.

The turnoff for Cerro Tute is a few kilometers south of town, on the western side of the Santiago-Santa Fé road. There are trails here, but you'd be wise to go with someone who knows the area well, such as Bertha de Castrellón (see above) or with someone she recommends.

Hacia Alto de Piedra, reachable by a road that leaves the western side of town, is an excellent place to explore on horseback. This vast, mountainous and forest-covered area contains many thousands of hectares of pristine wilderness and ranges from the northern edge of Santa Fé to the Caribbean Sea. The entire northern portion of the province – the area where Columbus, Nicuesa and the other Spanish explorers had so much trouble – contains not a single road and is sparsely inhabited. The edge of the awesome forest is only a couple of kilometers from town, and the forest becomes a jungle once you clear the ridge and proceed down the Caribbean slope.

It's possible to rent 4WD vehicles and horses in Santa Fé; see the Getting Around section, below.

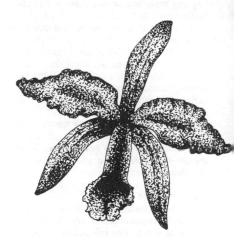

Some of the world's largest and smallest orchid species are grown in Santa Fé.

Special Events

There's an orchid exposition in Santa Fé every August (the exact date varies). Collectors from all over Panama display their finest orchids at this popular event. The IPAT office in Santiago (☎ 998-3929, fax 998-0928) can provide you with the precise date of the exposition.

There is also an agricultural fair in Santa Fé every January 28 to February 2.

Places to Stay & Eat

The *Hotel Santa Fé* (no phone) is on the Santiago-Santa Fé road, just south of Santa Fé and 38km north of the town of San Francisco. The clean and cozy 20-room hotel, on the left side of the road if you're heading north, sits on a bluff and overlooks a gorgeous valley. Six of the rooms have air-con. Some rooms have only one bed; some have two. All have private bathrooms, with cold water only. Rates range from US$18 to US$25. This is a delightful place, with a restaurant and bar. A telephone was due to be installed in mid-1998.

The *Hotel Jardín Santafereño* (☎ 999-5039), on the western edge of town a good walk from the center, is a backpacker's special. It offers four cabañas with worn, sagging beds and private bathrooms (cold water only), and a cheap restaurant. However, it's situated on the highest point in town, nestled in forest and very tranquil. At US$12 per room, this place is quite OK if you don't mind roughing it a little.

In addition to the restaurants at the two hotels, there are two places to eat near the center of town. Neither the *Restaurante Hermanos Pineda* nor the *Cafetería El Popular* will be winning any awards anytime soon, but their prices are attractive. At either place, expect to pay US$2.50 for a plate of chicken, rice and beans, and a soft drink.

Getting There & Away

A bus leaves the Santiago station for Santa Fé hourly, beginning at 7 am; the last one leaves at 4 pm. The ride takes about 1½ hours. The one-way fare is US$1.50. A taxi ride from Santiago costs US$40.

Getting Around

Santa Fé is easily covered on foot, and because of this no taxis operate here on a regular basis.

You can rent 4WD vehicles and horses in Santa Fé. To do this, contact the mayor, Arquimedes Pino, at his office (☎ 954-2155); if that number is busy, call the pay phone just outside his office (☎ 999-5044). He can often be found at his home (see the Santa Fé map), even during business hours. Arquimedes is a very nice guy and will contact people who have jeeps and horses for you. Unfortunately for some people, he speaks only Spanish. A jeep with driver costs US$40 for eight hours, including gas. A horse costs half that.

CERAMICA LA PEÑA

This artisans' market is on the Interamericana, 8km west of Santiago. Here you can find wood carvings and baskets made by the Emberá and Wounaan peoples of the Darién and woven purses and soapstone figurines made by Guaymís living in the area, as well as ceramics from the town of La Arena and masks from the town of Parita, in Herrera Province. There's also a workshop on the premises where you can occasionally see ceramics being made. The market is open 9 am to 4:30 pm weekdays and is closed weekends.

LAS PALMAS

There's nothing of special interest in sleepy Las Palmas, a town 10km south of the Interamericana and 32km northwest of the town of Soná. But if you love waterfalls and have your own wheels, you'll want to know about the nearby cataract and its enticing swimming hole. The scene is set amid light forest, and you'll likely have the place to yourself.

To get to the falls from the Interamericana, take the Las Palmas turnoff and drive 10km. Bypass the first road into town, but turn left at the second (it is just before the town's cemetery). Follow this dirt road for 1km and then take the fork to the right. This much rougher road will take you to the falls after about another 1km. This last kilometer requires a 4WD vehicle. If you aren't driving one, it's best to play it safe and walk the last kilometer to the falls. Be sure to lock up and take your valuables with you.

If you are coming from Soná, drive 32km along the road that leads toward the Interamericana and turn right just beyond the cemetery. Then follow the directions in the preceding paragraph.

Keep in mind that there is no place to stay in Las Palmas, and the few restaurants in town are mediocre at best.

SONÁ

Soná is a very small town in a farming region bisected by the road that links the Interamericana to El Tigre and a host of other small communities on the peninsula that comprises the western shore of the Golfo de Montijo. Soná's chief feature is its bars – about one in every three businesses here is a cantina.

If that sounds good to you, you might like to know that there are two places to stay in Soná. The *Pensión Min* (no phone), on the main road, has 10 basic, fan-on-a-stand rooms with shared cold-water bathroom for US$8 per room, with two single beds in each. The *Hotel Águila* (no phone), near the center of town on a side street a stone's throw from the main road, has slightly better rooms for US$11/14 with fan/air-con.

Buses to Soná from Panama City depart the Terminal de Buses al Interior every two hours from 6 am to 4 pm. The 4½-hour trip costs US$7 each way.

SANTA CATALINA

Sixty-six km south of Soná is Santa Catalina, where 200 people lead simple lives in simple homes near a beach that attracts surfers from around the globe. **Playa Santa Catalina** is a major break, and it's a beach where you can nearly always find a decent wave to ride. At its best it's comparable to Oahu's Sunset Beach on a good day. For more information on the surfing here, see the Surfing section in the Facts for the Visitor chapter.

Places to Stay & Eat

There are three places to stay, all designed for surfer dudes and dudettes who have their own gear (there are no rentals). All three offer easy access to the waves.

A budget place that's very popular with hard-core surfers is *Cabañas Rolo* (no phone), which has six no-frills cabins with three beds each and costs US$6 per person. It's the easiest of the three places to find, at the end of a short, steep driveway in the center of town. To find the driveway, look for a white surfboard beside the main road through town; the hotel's name is scrawled across the board. There are a couple of inexpensive *restaurants* within walking distance of the cabañas.

A major step up in price and comfort is the *Casablanca Surf Resort* (☎/fax 226-3786), at Apartado 6321, Panamá 5, República de Panamá, on a breezy bluff overlooking the ocean. There are nine rooms here, all with fans and shared bathroom. There are also two houses for rent on shore, and a third just offshore on Isla Santa Catalina. Per-person rates range from US$11 to US$40.

Casablanca also offers two meal plans. The basic plan costs an additional US$20 and includes three fine meals daily, prepared by the hotel's very charming Brazilian owners. The deluxe plan costs an additional US$35; its three daily meals are fancier, including such high-ticket items as lobster tails and jumbo shrimp. I like this place a lot.

Surfers' Paradise Camp (☎ 260-9615, fax 441-4859) consists of eight cabins, all with four beds apiece, fans, private cold-water bathrooms and kitchens. This place is an example of unrealized potential. The cabin I stayed in, for example, leaked like crazy when it rained, tap water was only available six hours a day, the window screens didn't keep the bugs out and, after I'd bought groceries, I discovered the stove wasn't hooked up – and wasn't about to be. For whatever reason, the owner has had trouble finishing his cabins. The price of US$35 per person, which includes two meals a day, isn't unreasonable, but expect some peculiarities. The price is a few dollars less if you bring your own food.

To get to the Casablanca Surf Resort and Surfers' Paradise Camp from the main road, turn left just in front of the Jorón Elisa bar. Drive about 1km on this muddy road until it forks, and then take the right branch. Drive another 500m to a sign that reads 'Se Aiquila Cabañas.' Take the right branch here to get to Surfers' Paradise Camp; take the left branch to get to the Casablanca.

Getting There & Away
To reach Santa Catalina from Panama City, first take a bus to Soná (see the Soná section, above, for details). From Soná, two buses serve Santa Catalina daily, leaving at 6:45 and 8:45 am; the one-way fare is US$3. Unless the driver is pushed for time, he will take you to any one of the three hotels that are mentioned above for an additional US$1.

From Santa Catalina, two buses serve Soná daily. They leave at 12:30 pm and 4:30 pm. In Santa Catalina the bus stops at the Jorón Elisa bar. It's only a short walk to the bar from the Cabañas Rolo. The owners of the other two hotels will drive their guests from their places to Jorón Elisa at no extra charge. There are no taxis in town.

PARQUE NACIONAL ISLA DE COIBA
In the Golfo de Chiriquí is Panama's largest island, 493-sq-km Isla de Coiba. The island is both a park and a Devil's Island: In 1991 Coiba – which for decades has been the site of a federal penal colony – became the centerpiece of a 270,000-hectare national park, over 80% of which is oceanic. Today hundreds of murderers, rapists and other convicts live in a large, ominous-looking cellblock known as 'Central' and in huts at 10 beachside prison camps that are scattered around the densely forested island. Also on Isla de Coiba are crocodiles, snakes and the country's last cluster of scarlet macaws.

Due to the presence of the prisoners, tourists cannot simply show up on the island, and their movement and numbers are very restricted. Anyone entering the park's boundaries must first have permission from the INRENARE office in Santiago (☎ 998-4271) and must also check in at the INRENARE ranger station at the northern end of Coiba before engaging in fishing, snorkeling and/or diving.

Because the island is quite far from the mainland (two hours by fast boat), unless you've got your own boat you usually must go through a tour operator to visit this park – and that means money, a rather large amount of it (see Diving, Snorkeling & Fishing, below, for prices). But if you're looking for something completely different, chances are you'll find it in this highly unusual but beautiful national park.

At the time this book went to press, tourists could only count on being allowed to visit one part of Isla de Coiba: the region in the immediate vicinity of the INRENARE ranger station. Within 100m of the station are five cabins with four beds apiece for tourists' use, a small but attractive beach and a lovely cove (the snorkeling here is only so-so, however). Beside the cove is a tiny island that you can snorkel around during high tide; if you choose to do this, be warned that the current on the island's far side is sometimes very strong. If you're a poor swimmer, do not go outside the cove.

Eight to 10 model prisoners are allowed to work at the INRENARE station – preparing meals, washing clothes, even leading tourists on snorkeling jaunts in the cove. Most are murderers who've been on the island for many years and have earned the trust of the guards. They are allowed to roam freely in the vicinity of the station and to chat with guests. They're a pretty nice bunch. One, a Colombian prisoner, will, if asked, accompany you to a swampy area 50m from the station and call out, 'Tito, Tito.' His call always attracts a rather large crocodile who resides in the swamp. The Colombian then usually tosses the croc a little piece of meat. About half the convicts at the station have pets – among them a very friendly deer, a scarlet macaw with a bad wing, and Volvo, a happy black dog

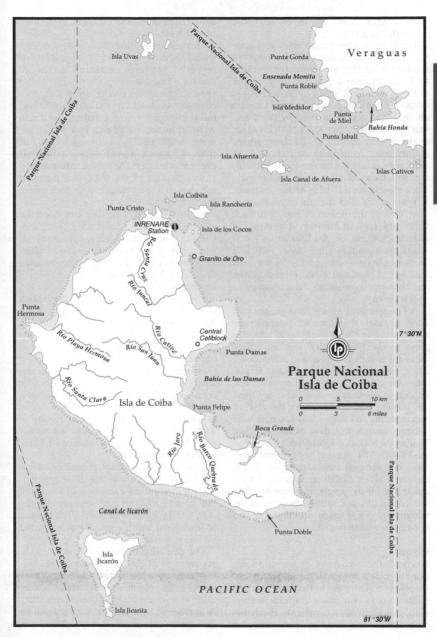

with a white paw whose owner stole Swedish-made cars.

There are two other areas on or very near the island that are occasionally open to tourists: a healthy mangrove forest close to Punta Hermosa and the tiny island of Granito de Oro, where the snorkeling is excellent. Both the mangroves and Granito de Oro can only be reached by boat, and that's only if the chief INRENARE ranger at the station permits it. Because armed guards must accompany tourists to both sites, permission to visit these areas fluctuates with the availability of the guards, who work closely with INRENARE personnel.

Tourists are also sometimes allowed to visit one of the prison camps, but such visits are very uncommon. Central, the huge brick cellblock, has been strictly off-limits to outsiders since 1990, when a human-rights advocate posing as a tourist took lots of photos of the decrepit structure and then led an unsuccessful campaign to shut it down.

A few words of advice: The guards will admit privately that there are escaped prisoners living in Coiba's jungle. If you stay close to the INRENARE station, where there are always guards armed with assault rifles, you are in little danger. But if you take the attitude that nothing bad can happen to you and you wander away from the station, you not only run the risk of encountering an escapee, but you may well become lost. A few days before my last visit to the island, two escapees arrived at the INRENARE station, begging for food. They had escaped from one of the prison camps a week earlier and thought they could live off the jungle. But they had few survival skills, and during their week on the run they had eaten nothing and had become very dehydrated.

History

Isla de Coiba, because of its size and location, was well known in the early days of the Spanish settlement in Panama. The first white man to visit it was Bartolomé Hurtado, a lieutenant of Gaspar de Espinosa, who came to the island in 1516 during an exploration of the coast that lies to the west of the Península de Azuero.

Hurtado, and those who followed him, found on the island Indian inhabitants of powerful physique, speaking a Guaymí dialect. They were armed with heavy spears tipped with sharks' teeth and wore corselets made of layered cotton that was thick enough to turn a bullet, but these were no protection against Hurtado's cannons. Some gold was obtained from the Indians, which probably aided in their eventual undoing. They were exterminated early; the last of the tribe was taken as laborers to work gold mines in the Darién, probably about 1550.

In historic accounts the name of the island is variously recorded as Cabo, Cobaya, Quibo, and Coiba, apparently all variations of the name of the Indian chief in control during the time of the Spanish discovery. There is no record of Spanish settlement of Coiba.

Captain George Shelvocke of the British navy, in his account of his voyage around the world, recorded that he came to Coiba on January 13, 1720. He anchored off the northern point and found three deserted huts that he supposed were used by pearl fishermen, as there were heaps of oyster shells strewn around them. Shelvocke returned to Coiba 15 months later and then recorded a considerable description of it, in which he mentions 'the great variety of birds, which the woods would not permit us to follow,' and the abundance of black monkeys and iguanas.

In time some coconut plantations were established on Coiba, but it seems that there was never any extensive settlement of the island until the 20th century. At the start of the century a pearl fishery was in operation, and a store, a bar and other buildings were present.

The depletion of the oyster beds led the government of Panama to acquire the private holdings, and (according to a plaque on the main guardhouse) the island was set aside as a penal colony in November 1919. A number of work camps were created on the eastern side of the island, and land was cleared for pasture and the planting of food crops adjacent to the camps. Some cattle were later brought to Coiba to add protein to the residents' diet. Today there are more than 2000 head of cattle on the island, providing beef for the convicts and the prison personnel.

The Park

A preliminary study of the marine life in the national park during 1996-97 identified 69 species of fish, although many more likely exist here. Additionally, humpback whales are often seen in the park, as are spotted and bottle-nosed dolphins. Killer, sperm and Cuvier's beaked whales are also present in park waters, but in fewer numbers.

Seventeen species of crocodile, turtle and lizard, as well as 15 species of snake (including the very dangerous fer-de-lance and the coral snake), are found in the park. Although the list is far from complete, to date 147 species of bird (including the Coiba spinetail, a little brown-and-white bird found only on Coiba) have been identified on the island. Scarlet macaws are among the species that nest on Coiba.

Coiba is home to the second-largest eastern Pacific coral reef and arguably the finest diving and snorkeling to be found along the Pacific coast from Colombia to Mexico. The entire island is covered with a heavy virgin forest, except for the prison camps and along the lower courses of the larger streams, where there are swampy woodlands. Rocky headlands project along the coast, and there are sandy beaches broken by mangroves at river mouths.

In addition to Coiba (50,314 hectares), islands within the park include Isla Jicarón (2002 hectares), Isla Brincanco (330 hectares), Isla Uvas (257 hectares), Isla Coibita (242 hectares), Isla Canal de Afuera (240 hectares), Isla Jicarita (125 hectares), Isla Pájaros (45 hectares) and Isla Afuerita (27 hectares).

The Prison

In late 1997 there were more than 850 prisoners on Coiba. At that time INRENARE

rangers on the island voiced their hope that one day soon the penal colony would be shut down and all the prisoners removed from the island. They stated that the national park cannot be fully enjoyed by tourists as long as the prisoners are here. However, overcrowding at all Panamanian prisons and the reluctance of Panama's legislature to allocate funds to build more prisons make it unlikely the penal colony will be closed any time soon. In fact, the island serves as flood control for the country's prison system; when the mainland prisons fill up, as occasionally happens, some of the worst offenders are shipped to Coiba to alleviate overcrowding.

As previously mentioned, some prisoners are held in Central, the cellblock on the eastern side of the island, but most live in beachside camps. At night the camp guards lock themselves inside their rooms with their guns while the much larger population of prisoners roams freely. Each morning roll is taken, and prisoners who fail to respond are considered escapees. First-time escapees face an additional two to three years of imprisonment, while second-time escapees will likely be given life sentences if caught.

About 10% of Coiba's prisoners attempt an escape. Nearly all escapees try to get away on homemade rafts made of balsa wood (the trees can be found all over the island), but nearly all of them are captured, according to guards. Prisoners, however, say that many escapees are never seen again, and it is their belief that some escapees are today living in freedom, while many others were caught and shot by guards and their bodies dumped at sea.

The stories abound: Once a five-log raft holding seven men caught a current that carried the raft all the way to the Galapagos Islands. Only two men were aboard when the raft reached the Galapagos; the others apparently had been forced off the craft or died along the way. Another time, two men pushed off at night, got confused and landed back on Coiba thinking that they'd made it to the mainland; they were captured and their sentences were promptly elongated. Yet another time, a drug kingpin used a prison phone and the next day swam straight out from shore, was met by a yacht, boarded it and was never seen again.

Certainly one of the big attractions on the island *is* the penal colony; if you ask a lot of questions, you'll hear some incredible stories – from prisoners and guards alike, in Spanish and in English. Once the stories start, everyone's a captive audience. According to prisoners who were on the island during the 1980s, the penal colony was once a great place to serve time. Manuel Noriega ran it like a pet project and paid it frequent visits. For a time he and his men vacationed in the cabins that are now used by tourists. During the 1980s, prisoners were allowed to make things to sell, such as wood carvings and jewelry made from the shells of sea turtles. Noriega allowed tourists to visit the cellblock and prison camps and buy souvenirs directly from the convicts. 'Man, that was a great time,' one twice-convicted car thief told me during my only visit to a Coiba prison camp. 'But now we can't make nothing and no tourists can come to visit us. All day long we just sit around doing nothing.'

Diving, Snorkeling & Fishing

At the time of writing, only one tour operator was leading tours into the Parque Nacional Isla de Coiba, and it offered just one weeklong package of scuba diving and snorkeling in the area – you couldn't simply dive or snorkel for a day or two and avoid paying for the entire week. However, the package that Coiba Explorer Panama (☎ 504-871-7181, 800-733-4742, fax 504-871-7150 in Florida; www.coibaexplorer.com) offers is outstanding.

The tour includes dives off the Islas Contreras, where hammerhead sharks, whale sharks, sea turtles, huge snapper, dolphins and billfish are regularly seen; Isla de Coiba, where orcas and humpbacks are fairly common and white-tip sharks are a sure thing; Isla Jicarón, home to purple corals and huge schools of fish; and Isla Montuosa, west of the park, another gorgeous island with drop-dead awesome diving. Although Coiba Explorer's tour is geared to divers, the waters are shallow enough for snorkelers.

With the exception of the first night, which is spent at a hotel in Panama City, all nights are spent aboard a remodeled 30m barge with 'staterooms' (which, honestly, are not all that stately). The cost of the package, which includes your meals and all domestic transportation, is US$2500 per person (the fee is the same whether you're diving or snorkeling). Coiba Explorer Panama also offers weeklong fishing trips in the area, which feature shipboard and beachfront lodging.

Getting There & Away

Unless you have your own boat, you must use a tour operator (see above) to travel to the park. At the time of writing, only Coiba Explorer Panama offered tours to the park. However, Ancon Expeditions and other operators said that they were considering offering tours to the park. If you're interested in visiting Coiba, contact all the tour operators listed in the Getting Around chapter to obtain current information on possible Coiba tours.

PARQUE NACIONAL CERRO HOYA

On the southwestern side of the Península de Azuero, this 32,577-hectare park protects the headwaters of the Ríos Tonosí, Portobelo and Pavo, 30 endemic plant species and fauna that includes the carato parakeet. It contains some of the last remaining forest on a huge peninsula that is one of the most agriculturally devastated regions of Panama. Although the park was created in 1984, much of the forest had been chopped down prior to that time, and it will be a long time before the park really looks like a park.

Anyone thinking of visiting the park should be advised that there are no accommodations for visitors in or near the park (the ranger station is officially open to tourists, but there's nowhere for them to sleep) and that the trails into the park are ill defined.

By far the easiest way to reach the park is by a 100km road that winds along the western edge of the Península de Azuero to within a short hike of the ranger station. Unfortunately, buses don't travel the road.

The only other way to reach the park is by sea, which I don't recommend. The surf along the southern shore of the Península de Azuero is quite rough and the area is frequented by storms.

Herrera Province

The Península de Azuero, long overshadowed by the canal and the cities at its ends, is looked upon by Panamanians as their country's heart and soul. It is here, on plains that more closely resemble the rural USA than the American Tropics, that the Spanish legacy is strongest, in festivals and in faces. On the Azuero, fair complexions, hazel eyes and aquiline features prevail. The people have little Indian ancestry; their descent is nearly pure Spanish.

But human culture on this semiarid peninsula didn't arrive with the Spaniards – it was here centuries before a teenage Italian named Cristóbal Colón got his first sailing lesson. What we know of this culture has been gleaned mainly from archaeology, and perhaps no excavation sites have told us more about the people the conquistadors encountered in Panama than the digs near Parita, in Herrera Province, and those at nearby Sitio Conte, in Coclé Province.

An excavation during the 1940s of tombs within 10km of Parita uncovered some of the most artistic pottery that was ever produced by pre-Columbian Indians. Fanciful bird and reptile designs, in bright colors, adorn the ancient pottery. The bowls often were shaped to resemble king vultures, with finger-long wings flaring from their sides and bulbous heads and stubby tails at their ends.

The remains of a young child with a necklace of hollow gold beads were found in one large painted bowl. In another tomb scientists found long-necked bottles and 40 painted pots in the form of bird effigies. Also found in this tomb were exquisitely carved batons shaped like stylized alligators, made from manatee ribs.

The most amazing find, as far as I'm concerned, was an urn that contained the remains of a single man and a necklace made of 800 human teeth! Nearly all the teeth were front incisors, which means that the teeth of at least 200 people were required to make the jewelry. The circumstances under which the odd necklace was made remain a mystery.

Other sites near Parita have yielded large quantities of ceremonial pottery, mostly vessels mounted on tall pedestal bases. These are of two types: painted globular bowls and other bowls in the form of king vulture effigies, brightly painted with outstretched wings. More than 100 nearly identical red-painted globular jars with short necks were found in one mound.

Tantalizing but far from adequate descriptions of the people who created these objects have been left to us by Gaspar de Espinosa and Gonzalo de Badajoz, who led looting expeditions on the peninsula between 1515 and 1525. According to their writings, at that time the area was controlled by a powerful chief named Parita, of the Guaymí tribe.

Parita's warriors were able to prevent the Spaniards from settling on the Azuero

HIGHLIGHTS

- Extraordinary bird watching at Playa El Aguillito, the Grand Central Station of migratory seabirds

- Pottery factories in La Arena, where artisans produce ceramics that mimic pre-Columbian designs

- Historic Parita, with pridefully maintained buildings dating back to the 16th and 17th centuries

- Watching women braid some of the world's finest Panama hats in Ocú

Herrera Province

HERRERA PROVINCE

for several years, but when Espinosa led a later raid on the peninsula, he found to his pleasant surprise that Parita had recently died. Instead of confronting the chief in combat, the raiders found him lying in state in a room containing 355lbs of gold ornaments. Also found near the dead leader were 20 Indian captives who were lashed to house posts by cords around their necks; these poor souls had been destined to be buried alive with the great chieftain. Also expected to be buried with Parita were his wives and household attendants.

Today very few Indians live near the Parita site. Those Guaymís who could flee went to the jungled mountains in what is now Chiriquí Province. They lived primarily by hunting and by cultivating corn, beans, manioc and bananas. So fearful were they of white people that until only a few decades ago they placed concealed weapons (mainly bows and arrows) along trails where unwary travelers might step into a string and discharge them.

Herrera Province, which is in the center of the Península de Azuero, was lush and only sparsely inhabited during the 16th century, but today the country's smallest province not only contains little forest but also has the third-highest population density of

Panama's nine provinces, with 40 residents per square kilometer. Its 94,000 inhabitants are mostly farmers. The province's chief industries are Panama rum, shoes and detergents, as well as leather products.

Herrera has maintained its Spanish legacy mainly through Spanish festivals. The town of Ocú holds a popular patron saint festival, which begins with religious services and includes the joyous parading of a just-married couple through the streets. Las Minas and Parita are known for their feasts of Corpus Christi (Body of Christ), festivals celebrated 40 days after Easter in honor of the Eucharist. Pesé hosts dramatic public reenactments of the Last Supper, Judas' betrayal and Jesus' imprisonment during the week preceding Easter. And Chitré, a town of 40,000 inhabitants, becomes a city of 80,000 fun-loving souls during Carnaval.

For luxury in Panama, Panama City provides the answers. For verdant forests and excellent bird watching, several national parks in Darién and Panamá Provinces are excellent choices. The deep-blue Pacific waters near Isla de Coiba and Bahía Piña offer world-class sport fishing. But anyone looking for the spirit of Panama would do well to visit Herrera Province.

CHITRÉ

Chitré, the capital of Herrera Province, is the largest city on the Península de Azuero and a convenient base for exploration. It is the site of some of the area's best-known festivals. If you plan to attend any festivals in Chitré, be warned that you will have difficulty finding a place to stay if you arrive without a reservation. This is particularly true during Carnaval, when most of the city's rooms are spoken for more than a year in advance.

In the vicinity of Chitré are the Parque Nacional Sarigua; the Humboldt Ecological Station at Playa El Aguillito; and, a fair walk or short bus ride away, the village of La Arena, 3km west of Chitré, where you can see ceramics being made. All these sites are discussed in this chapter.

Villa de Los Santos, where some of the peninsula's most important festivals take place, is 4km south of Chitré, just inside Los Santos Province (see that chapter for details).

Orientation

The Carretera Interamericana connects with the Carretera Nacional (the National Hwy, also known as the Carretera Central) at the town of Divisa, atop the Península de Azuero, and from there the Carretera Nacional runs southeast 37km to Chitré. From Chitré it runs 31km farther to Las Tablas, in Los Santos Province, and there the highway becomes a loop road that links the coastal and inland towns near the southern edge of the peninsula. Buses travel this circular road in clockwise and counterclockwise directions, with Las Tablas at the noon position.

As the Carretera Nacional winds southeast from Divisa, the first major town it encounters is Chitré. When the highway reaches Chitré, it becomes Paseo Enrique Geenzier; the road changes name again a dozen blocks farther east, becoming Calle Manuel Maria Correa. The Carretera Nacional reemerges at the southern end of town. Changing names like this is something that occurs quite frequently along the Carretera Nacional.

One Name, Many Highways

When you see signs for the Carretera Nacional in Herrera Province, keep in mind that this is also the name given to the loop road that links Chitré, Pesé, Las Minas, Ocú and other Herrera towns that lie at the center and top of the Península de Azuero. Basically, 'Carretera Nacional' doesn't refer to one highway on the peninsula, but to several. This can be a little confusing at times, but if you realize at the outset that there are several highways known as the Carretera Nacional, you'll have a better idea of what's going on when you notice mentions of the seemingly omni-present National Hwy. ∎

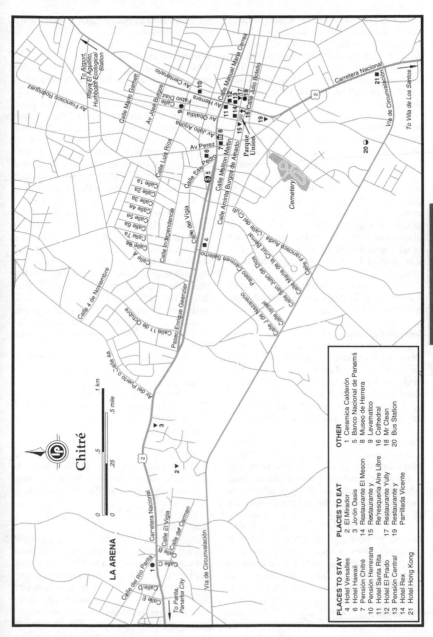

HERRERA PROVINCE

Chitré

LA ARENA

To Airport,
Playa El Aguillo,
Humboldt Ecological
Station

Carretera Nacional

To Villa de Los Santos

Via de Circunvalación

To Partita,
Panama City

Cemetery

Parque
Unión

0   .25   .5
0   .25   .5 mile   1 km

PLACES TO STAY
4 Hotel Versalles
6 Hotel Hawaii
7 Pensión Chitré
10 Pensión Herrerana
11 Hotel Santa Rita
12 Hotel El Prado
13 Pensión Central
14 Hotel Rex
21 Hotel Hong Kong

PLACES TO EAT
2 El Mirador
3 Jorón Oasis
14 Restaurante El Meson
15 Restaurante y
   Re'resquería Aire Libre
17 Restaurante Yully
19 Restaurante y
   Parrillada Vicente

OTHER
1 Ceramica Calderón
5 Banco Nacional de Panamá
9 Museo de Herrera
9 Lavamatico
16 Cathedral
18 Mr Clean
20 Bus Station

To reach Chitré's central square, Parque Union, turn right off Calle Manuel Maria Correa onto either Avenida Obaldía or Avenida Herrera. The town's cathedral and the adjacent Parque Union are one block south of Calle Correa. There are numerous places to stay and eat within a short walk of the square.

Information

Tourist Office In early 1998 the government announced plans to open an Instituto Panameño de Turismo (IPAT) tourist office in Chitré, but a site had yet to be selected at the time this book went to press. If you want to speak with someone at the tourist office, call directory assistance (☎ 102) and ask for IPAT's local phone number; alternately, you can ask a hotel clerk for its location or, if you've just arrived by bus, ask a taxi driver or ticket agent.

There's also a Migración y Naturalización (Immigration and Naturalization) office in Chitré.

Money Because Chitré is a provincial capital, there is no shortage of banks in town. The bank with the most services (including an ATM) is the Banco Nacional de Panamá, on Paseo Enrique Geenzier several short blocks west of the town square. It's open from 9 am to 1 pm Monday to Thursday and Saturday, and 9 am to 3 pm Friday.

Telephone There are many pay phones around town, and you can place an international call from any of them (the same call will cost substantially more if placed from a hotel). There are several pay phones on the town square, on the side that faces the Hotel Rex.

Laundry There are a number of places to get your clothes cleaned in Chitré, but most won't clean undergarments. Lavamatico, on Calle Luis Ríos at Calle Fabio Díaz, does wash underwear and is open from 9 am to noon and 1:30 to 4 pm Monday to Saturday. Mr Clean, at Calle Meliton Martin and Avenida Centenario, is more centrally

located than Lavamatico, but it won't wash *ropas interiores*.

Museo de Herrera

This anthropology and natural history museum, on Paseo Enrique Geenzier at Avenida Julio Arjona, contains many well-preserved pieces of pottery dating from 5000 BC until the time of the Spanish conquest, including some rather elaborate pieces that were used for trading. Some of the pieces that were found at the excavation sites outside Parita are here, although most of those artifacts are on display at the anthropology museum in Panama City.

Also at this museum are replicas of *huacas* found on the peninsula, as well as numerous photographs of archaeologists at work and maps showing where the pottery and huacas were found (see the Shopping section in the Panama City chapter for more details on huacas). Be sure to visit the museum's 2nd floor, where you'll find interesting photos of Azuero residents, authentic folkloric costumes and religious artifacts of the region (including the original bell of Chitré's cathedral, which was cast in 1767).

There is a lot of other interesting stuff in this museum, including photos that were taken during Chitré's Carnavals; if you don't have the good fortune of attending Carnaval here, the Museo de Herrera is an excellent place to check out the zaniness you've missed.

The museum is open 9 am to 12:30 pm and 1:30 to 4 pm Tuesday to Saturday and 9 am to noon Sunday. Admission costs US$1/25¢ adults/children. All of the signage and literature at the museum is in Spanish only.

Cathedral

The cathedral, adjacent to Chitré's central square, dates from the 18th century but was substantially remodeled in 1988. The entire ceiling is made of polished mahogany and the walls are adorned with near-life-size figures of saints. Large, beautifully vivid stained-glass windows depict momentous events in the life of Jesus. The Stations of

Veraguas Province

Top: Surf's up at Playa Santa Catalina, one of Central America's best breaks

Bottom Left: Cascades and swimming hole, Las Palmas

Middle Right: A prisoner and his scaly friend, 'Tito,' Isla de Coiba

Bottom Right: Bertha de Castrellón and her orchid collection, Santa Fé

SCOTT DOGGETT

SCOTT DOGGETT

STUART GR WARNER W

SCOTT DOGGETT

Herrera Province

Top Left: Mask maker Darido Lopez and his colorful creations, Parita

Bottom: Angler returning from a day of fishing, Playa El Rompío

Top Right: The bleak aftermath of deforestation in Parque Nacional Sarigua

Middle Right: Dancing in Ocú at one of the Península de Azuero's vibrant traditional festivals

the Cross are marked by 4m teak crosses and intricately carved figurines. Unlike many cathedrals that impress through their ornateness and overuse of gold, this one is striking for its elegant simplicity and fine balance of gold and wood.

La Arena

Several kilometers to the west of downtown Chitré and bisected by the Carretera Nacional is the village of La Arena, which is known for its ceramics factories. The pottery made here mimics the pre-Columbian designs of the culture that once lived nearby. This is a good place to watch pottery being made – and to try to make some yourself (just ask if you can take a spin at the potter's wheel; if you don't speak Spanish, simply point at yourself and then at the clay and the wheel, and be sure to give a big smile). It's only after you've taken a turn at the wheel – your hands shaping a freaky tornado-resembling thing instead of a lovely vase – that you are able to appreciate the skill involved in this seemingly simple craft.

The best of the several pottery factories is **Ceramica Calderón**, near the intersection of Calle del Río Parita and Carretera Nacional, where you can buy traditional painted ceramics at low cost. These pieces are made on the premises in a workshop directly behind the roadside showroom. All the pottery here is made by hand with the help of a foot-powered potter's wheel. The trick is to make a piece that is not only pleasing to look at, but also has no bubbles (otherwise it will break while baking).

The artisan who makes most of the ceramics sold here is Angel Calderón. In 1997 he told me that he had been making ceramics professionally for 41 of his 52 years. After several minutes of calculation, he estimated that he had made no fewer than 500,000 pieces. Although he owns the factory and has several capable workers, Angel works every day except Christmas and Easter. He said that he works so hard to set a good example for his workers.

If you visit Angel's shop, be sure to take a look at the ovens out back. They are quite impressive.

Other than shopping for pottery and trying your hand at making some, there isn't much for you to do in La Arena – except eat (see Places to Eat) and enjoy the views. There are no hotels in La Arena, but the village makes an excellent day trip from Chitré. A taxi ride from Parque Union costs US$2, but be sure to agree on the price beforehand to avoid a squabble with your driver when you arrive. There's also bus service from Chitré (see Getting There & Away, below).

Special Events

Chitré's Carnaval festivities, held each year on the four days before Ash Wednesday (in February or March), feature parades, folkloric dancing, water fights and lots of drinking. On June 24 Chitré's patron saint festival, the Fiesta de San Juan Bautista, starts with a religious service that's followed by bullfights (the animals are merely teased), cockfights and other popular activities. And on October 19, festivities that celebrate the Founding of the District of Chitré (1848) include parades, historical costumes and much merriment.

Places to Stay

There are several good lodging values in Chitré – the selection ranges from hot and rundown cubicles to spacious, tastefully appointed guestrooms with all the creature comforts. Shown here are tourist-season prices with tax included. Expect to pay at least 50% more for the same room during Carnaval. As stated previously, room reservations for Carnaval must be made at least one year in advance. At the Hotel Hong Kong, the loveliest hotel on the peninsula, reservations must be made three years in advance.

Pensión Herrerana (☎ 996-4356), on Avenida Herrera 2½ blocks north of the cathedral, is a fairly clean but very basic place with some of the cheapest rooms in town. Three rooms have private bathrooms; the rest have shared facilities. There's cold water only. The cost is US$8 per person, but stay here only as a last resort.

The *Pensión Chitré* (☎ 996-1856), on Calle Manuel Maria Correa near Avenida Perez, offers six worn but clean rooms with ceiling fans and private cold-water bathrooms for US$10/12 single/double. Some beds are better than others; ask to see several rooms.

The *Pensión Central* (☎ 996-0059), on Avenida Herrera just a few dozen paces north of the cathedral, offers 12 rooms with air-con (US$16/18) and 10 without (US$12/14). All the rooms have private hot-water bathrooms. These rooms are very worn.

The *Hotel El Prado* (☎ 996-4620/6859) is on Avenida Herrera just to the south of Calle Manuel Maria Correa. It's a clean, well-kept hotel with a 2nd-floor restaurant, sitting area and open balcony overlooking the street, and an off-street car park. The rooms are set back from the street, so they're not too noisy; each has a private bathroom, TV and phone. Rooms with fans cost US$12/18 single/double. Those with air-con cost US$17/26.

The *Hotel Rex* (☎ 996-6660, fax 996-4310), beside the town square, offers 34 rooms, all of which have air-con, color TVs, phones and private hot-water bathrooms. This hotel even accepts credit cards (few do). Ask for room Nos 104 or 106 if you want lots of space. Room Nos 114, 116, 118 and 120 are the next best. Several rooms can handle parties of five. There's a dance club, bar and restaurant. The rate is US$17 per person.

The *Hotel Santa Rita* (☎ 996-4610, fax 996-2404), on the corner of Calle Manuel Maria Correa and Avenida Herrera, is also a good deal. One of the city's first hotels, the Santa Rita offers you 20 rooms, a restaurant/bar and phone and fax service. Rates for the hotel's well-maintained rooms range from US$14 for one person without air-con to US$26 for three people with air-con. All rooms have private hot-water bathrooms.

The *Hotel Hawaii* (☎ 996-3534, fax 996-5330), on Calle San Pedro near Paseo Enrique Geenzier, offers you 33 cheerful rooms, all with air-con, cable TVs, phones

and private hot-water bathrooms. Rates are US$18/31/43 single/double/triple.

As you enter the city from the west, you may notice the *Hotel Versalles* (☎ 996-4422, fax 996-2090) on Paseo Enrique Geenzier. It's quite OK, with a swimming pool, restaurant/bar and guestrooms with air-con, cable TVs, hot-water private bathrooms, phones and writing desks. Rates are US$25/31; suites cost more. The Versalles isn't near the center of town, and in my opinion that is a real drawback.

The *Hotel Hong Kong* (☎ 996-4483, fax 996-5229), on the Carretera Nacional on the way to Villa de Los Santos, is a first-class hotel with absolutely spotless rooms with all the amenities. There are suites with Jacuzzi tubs and kitchenettes. A number of the rooms are wheelchair accessible. There are two swimming pools (one for kids) and a fine restaurant and bar. The service at this family-run hotel is superb. Rates range from US$35/55 for a single/double to US$90 for a suite.

Places to Eat

In Town The *Restaurante El Meson,* at the Hotel Rex, has good, reasonably priced food. Chicken and beef dishes cost US$4 to US$7. The paella (US$5), served only on Sunday, is quite good. The ceviche (US$3.50) here is excellent, but the seafood soup is surprisingly disappointing. The chef will prepare paella for groups of five or more any time, if he's given at least two hours' notice.

There are several Chinese restaurants in town, the best of which is inside the *Hotel Hong Kong.* Breakfasts range from US$2 to US$4. Lunch and dinner items include shrimp chow mein (US$4), Creole-style shrimp (US$4.50), smoked pork chops (US$5) and chicken with cashew nuts (US$5.50). It's open 7 am to 10 pm daily.

Another very good Chinese restaurant is the *Restaurante y Parrillada Vicente,* on Avenida Herrera two blocks south of the cathedral. I've had the chow mein, the chicken with sweet and sour sauce and the roast pork (US$3.75 each) and recommend them all. The grilled octopus (US$6.25), which I've sampled, is delicious. Budget travelers might want to look closely at the menu familiar on the last page of the menu, which lists three set dinners for US$5.50 per person, with a two-person minimum.

The *Restaurante Yully,* on Calle Meliton Martin one block east of the cathedral, is a great place to get cheap food fast. Offered buffet-style are rice (30¢), roast beef (75¢), chicken (US$1.50), ham (US$1.50), steak (US$2), chow mein (US$2) and so on. It's open 6 am to 7 pm daily.

Facing the western end of the plaza is the *Restaurante y Refresqueria Aire Libre,* an open-air café that features lots of beverages. Also available here at low cost (nothing's over US$4) are a variety of rice, chow mein and chicken dishes. You can also find ice cream here. This pleasant café is open 6:30 am to 10 pm daily.

La Arena The highest point within 5km of downtown Chitré is the restaurant *El Mirador* (The Lookout), atop a hill in La Arena. This open-sided restaurant is very casual, with Formica tables, leather-backed chairs and the mandatory TV. The Mirador is popular for its panoramic views and atmosphere (the food is mediocre). All items range from US$3 up to US$7. The Mirador is open from 4 pm to midnight daily.

To find the Mirador from downtown Chitré, head westward on the Carretera Nacional about 2.5km and turn left onto the road that begins just past the large 'Chino Bar' sign. Keep to the right for 400m until you reach the top of the hill. If you don't have wheels, a taxi ride will cost US$2 each way. The restaurant will call a radio taxi for you when you want to leave.

Also in La Arena and quite popular with locals is the *Jorón Oasis,* on the southern side of the Carretera Nacional opposite the Accel gas station. The sopa de carne (meat soup) at this typical roadside open-air restaurant is very good and should be ordered with rice. The local way to eat this combination is to fill your spoon with rice and dip it into the soup. When you're nearly finished with the soup, you'll find a chunk of steer rib in it. Pick up the bone and chew the beef off it. The entire price for this typical regional meal: US$1. Add 75¢ if you want a beer with it.

Getting There & Away

Air Chitré's airport is northeast of town; follow Avenida Herrera north from the town square to reach it. A taxi ride there costs US$2.50.

Aeroperlas (☎ 996-4021 in Chitré; 269-4555 in Panama City) operates daily flights between Panama City and Chitré (US$29/58 one-way/roundtrip). The airline also flies twice daily between Chitré and Santiago (US$18/36).

Bus Chitré is a center for regional bus transportation. Buses arrive at and depart from a central bus station, the Terminal de Transportes de Herrera, 1km south of the center of town. To get from downtown to the station, take a taxi (US$2) or catch a 'Terminal' bus (25¢) at the intersection of Calle Aminta Burgos de Amado and Avenida Herrera. The station has a restaurant that's open 24 hours a day.

Tuasa (☎ 996-5619) buses depart Chitré for Panama City at 1:30, 2:30, 4, 5 and 6 am, and then leave every 45 minutes until the last bus departs at about 6 pm. Transportes Inazun (☎ 996-4177) also has buses to the capital, departing hourly from 6 am to 3 pm. Both companies charge US$6 one way (255km, four hours).

Other service from Chitré includes the following:

Divisa – 37km, 30 minutes, US$1; frequent departures
La Arena – 3km, five minutes, 35¢; frequent departures
Las Minas – 51km, one hour, US$1.50; hourly
Las Tablas – 31km, 30 minutes, US$1; hourly from sunrise to sunset
Ocú – 46km, one hour, US$1.50; hourly from sunrise to sunset
Parita – 10km, five minutes, 50¢; every 45 minutes from sunrise to sunset
Pedasí – 73km, one hour, US$2; hourly from sunrise to sunset
Pesé – 24km, 20 minutes, US$1; hourly from sunrise to sunset

Playa El Aguillito – 7km, 12 minutes, 50¢; hourly from sunrise to sunset

Playas Monagre and El Rompío – 20km, 30 minutes, US$1; hourly from sunrise to sunset

Santiago – 71km, 1¼ hours, US$1.50; hourly from sunrise to sunset

Tonosí – 103km, two hours, US$4; hourly from sunrise to sunset

Villa de Los Santos – 4km, 10 minutes, 50¢; hourly from sunrise to sunset

Buses to Chitré depart Panama City's Terminal de Buses al Interior, on Avenida Ascañio Villalaz in the Curundu district, hourly from 6 am to 11 pm. The trip takes four hours; the one-way fare is US$6.

Getting Around

If you need to travel by vehicle, a taxi is the best way to go. They're so cheap – US$2 is the most you would pay in town, and most fares are US$1 – that it doesn't make any sense to bother with the hot, slow and crowded local buses.

PLAYA EL AGUILLITO

Seven km from Chitré's Parque Union is Playa El Aguillito, which is not so much a sandy beach as it is a mudflat created by silt deposited by two nearby rivers, the Río Parita and the Río La Villa. At low tide the mudflat stretches more than 2km from the high-water mark to the surf, and thousands of birds descend on the mud in search of plankton and small shrimp.

Most of the birds are migratory, flying between Alaska and various South American countries. For reasons that escape scientists – including Francisco Delgado, who heads the nearby **Humboldt Ecological Station** – these birds return year after year to exactly the same beach and to no others in the area. A roseate spoonbill that lands on this beach will never land on Playa El Retén, even though it's only 2km away, and vice versa.

This is rather amazing when you consider how many thousands of kilometers the birds fly during a single season and how many feeding grounds they must fly over. In addition to the spoonbills, other Playa El Aguillito regulars include black-necked stilts,

white-winged doves, yellow-crowned Amazons (which are frequently seen here) and also common ground-doves (which in Panama are found only on this beach).

When the tide is high, these birds congregate around salt ponds to the immediate east of Playa El Aguillito. Few birders know about the beach or the salt ponds, but the bird watching at the ponds during high tide is terrific.

Another reason for birders to visit the beach and ponds is the ecological station, which is the first structure you'll see when you reach Playa El Aguillito. It was established by a group of local environmentalists in 1983. Since then, Francisco and others have banded more than 15,000 birds and monitored them with the help of scientists in other countries. Among the items on display at the station is a map showing the migratory routes of all the bird species that pass through the area.

Francisco, who can speak English and Spanish, knows as much about the birds on the Península de Azuero as anyone. If you have questions about the birds or his work, Francisco usually can be reached at his home (☎ 996-1725) and through the restaurant/bar (☎ 996-1820) beside the beach. The bartender's name is Frederico, and he will pass along messages to Francisco as long as you speak the one language he understands: Spanish.

Getting There & Away

Playa El Aguillito is reached from Chitré via Avenida Herrera (see the Chitré map); it's just past the airport. A bus leaves the Chitré station for the beach hourly from sunrise to sunset. The one-way fare is 50¢. A taxi ride from town costs US$3.

PARQUE NACIONAL SARIGUA

Ten km north of downtown Chitré is this national park, which comprises 8000 hectares of wasteland that INRENARE, Panama's environmental agency, would have you believe is *tropical desert*. The park is not without attractions. The area may be the most important pre-Columbian site in Panama. The Sarigua site has been dated back 11,000 years based on shell mounds and pottery fragments and offers some rich archaeological opportunities. It's a pity that the government isn't allocating any money for excavation of the area. Today all you'll find in the way of artifacts from the site are some arrowheads and a few pieces of pottery on display at the INRENARE station here.

Part of the park actually serves as the waste disposal site for Chitré, Parita and other cities. As a matter of fact, directly behind the INRENARE station (where you pay the US$3 entrance fee), you can see garbage poking up out of the ground – because until recently the very land upon which the station is located was a garbage dump.

The wasteland to which I refer goes far beyond the pockets of actual urban waste buried in this national park, which was created in 1984. Where deciduous forest once stood, the landscape now resembles a desert. Where animals once frolicked amid trees and meadows and creeks, a movie crew could now film a reenactment of man landing on the Moon. And yet the area receives more than 1m of rain each year!

Sarigua is the end product of slash-and-burn agriculture. People moved into the area, cut down all the trees, set fire to the debris, planted crops for a few harvests and then left. Because the forest that had held the thin topsoil in place was removed, the heavy rain that falls here every year carried the topsoil into creeks and thence into rivers and out into the sea. What you see in Sarigua today is the nutrient-deficient rock that had been underneath the topsoil.

Amazingly, despite the example of Sarigua, the Panamanian government wants to open Darién Province and northern Veraguas Province to the same variety of wasteful agriculture.

Getting There & Away

To get here from the Carretera Nacional, take the Puerto Limon turnoff, a couple of kilometers northwest of Parita. After 1km you'll notice a foul smell. It's coming from a pig farm with more than 5000 animals.

After another 1km you'll come to the park turnoff. Follow the signs for 2km, until you come to a house on the left. This is the INRENARE station, and here you must pay the US$3 entrance fee.

Buses do not go to the park. A roundtrip taxi ride to the INRENARE station from Chitré costs about US$20.

PARITA

This beautiful and historic town is 10km northwest of downtown Chitré, just off the Carretera Nacional. It's known to few people outside the Península de Azuero, and there are no hotels here, but the town does offer several pleasant surprises.

Things to See

Parita follows a grid pattern. As you come to intersections near the town's center – which is about 500m from the Carretera Nacional – and glance both ways, you'll see building after building that look much the way they have for centuries. This town was founded in 1558, and most of the structures near its center date from at least the 18th century. They're real beauties, looking very much like Spanish imports. The walls are thick, and the beams are as solid as railroad ties. The roofs are made of red convex tiles, and the fancier structures have arcades on the side facing the street.

The **church** in Parita is the only one in Panama that has its steeple located directly over its entrance rather than over a corner of the structure. This is very unusual, because bell towers are always extremely heavy and therefore are generally built on pillars that rest upon a massive foundation. It is a major curiosity to the old people of Parita that the steeple hasn't collapsed upon the entryway. Although the church was completed in 1723, you'll never see an old Parita resident standing near the entrance.

Two doors down from the southeastern corner of Parita's church is a **workshop** that specializes in the restoration of altars. It is the only such workshop in the country. The artisans working here – Macario José Rodriguez and the twin brothers José Sergio

Lopez and Sergio José Lopez – have been restoring the altars of Panama's colonial churches since the 1970s.

Because at least 15 colonial churches in the republic are in varying states of repair, there's no shortage of work for these three. But don't hesitate to stop by and say hello. All three men speak some English, and they are very friendly. Chances are they'll let you take a look around. I don't recall seeing any electric tools. It takes little stretch of the imagination to imagine that you're in a colonial workshop that's producing altars for the new churches of the New World.

To find the home of the country's top **mask maker**, return to the Carretera Nacional and find the Shell station, not far from the turnoff. Cross the street here and you'll be within 75m of his home; just ask for *'la casa de Darido Lopez,'* and someone will direct you there.

Darido has been making beautiful and yet disturbing masks for folkloric dancers since the 1960s. While he continues to make masks and satin costumes worn by dirty-devil dancers, these days most of his masks are exported to the USA and to Europe. Darido can make a mask in a single day, and he usually asks between US$20 and US$80 for each one. When asked what he likes most about his work, Darido says that he lives for the Corpus Christi celebrations, because it is only then that he can see his work in its best light.

Getting There & Away
Parita makes an excellent day trip from Chitré. Buses for Parita leave the Chitré station every 45 minutes from sunrise to sunset and cost 50¢ each way. A faster way to get here is to take a taxi, which costs about US$4.

REFUGIO DE VIDA SILVESTRE CENEGÓN DEL MANGLE
This wildlife refuge near Parita protects a mangrove forest at the mouth of the Río Santa María, an important wildlife area and nesting ground for herons. Its primary attraction is the birds.

However, several sink-size thermal pools here contain waters that are said to have health-giving properties. Some people come to lift the water out with cups and use it on their skin. I put a finger into each of the four tiny pools and found the water cold to the touch. It did not have a sulfuric odor, as thermal water should. It seemed like rainwater to me.

But if you're a believer, then by all means check out the wells. The refuge is not reachable by bus; it's a 45-minute drive north of Chitré via the Carretera Nacional. Take the turnoff to 'Los Pozos' ('The Wells'; there's a sign on the road). After 7km the road forks at a church in the village of Paris; take the right branch and go 5km farther. You'll see a sign indicating that you are 1km from the wells.

Whether the wells contain thermal water is debatable. Whether the water has any health-giving properties is debatable. However, what is not debatable is the fragility of the earth in the vicinity of the wells. Do not enter the roped-off areas or you could find yourself in over your head.

PESÉ
The town of Pesé, southwest of Chitré, is ringed by sugar-cane plantations and becomes extremely popular on Holy Friday during its annual live representation of the Golgotha drama, a reenactment of Christ's crucifixion. I don't believe that there are any hotels here.

Pesé is home to the country's largest *seco* factory, **Seco Herrerano** (☎ 974-9621, fax 974-9753), established in 1936. It's a rather small factory, with only 45 workers, but its output is impressive: 3000 cases of 1-liter bottles every business day (Monday to Saturday), 12 bottles to a case. The distillery and mill are open for tours.

The part of the process that seems to impress most people is the bottling of the liquor and the labeling of the bottles. There is something peaceful and spellbinding about all the machinery working in unison, and the air in the bottling room is practically intoxicating. Alas, there is no free sampling.

The mill operates only during the harvest season, which lasts from mid-January to mid-March. During this time, you can see tons of sugar cane fed into huge presses, which extract sweet juice. The juice is pumped into huge containers, where it ferments. What's neat about this operation is the speed of the pressing.

If you wish to take a tour, note that the factory requests that you make a reservation at least one week in advance.

Getting There & Away

Pesé is 19km southwest of the Carretera Nacional and about another 5km from downtown Chitré. It can be reached by bus from the Chitré station; buses leave hourly from sunrise to sunset. The ride costs US$1 each way.

Buses to Pesé from Panama City depart the capital's Terminal de Buses al Interior every two hours from 9:30 am to 3:30 pm. The trip takes four hours and costs US$6.

LAS MINAS

Las Minas (The Mines) was founded in 1668 and takes its name from the gold mines in its hills that were worked under Spanish control during the 17th century. Today you can spend hours roaming the cool hills and coffee plantations asking locals to point you in the direction of the mines, but no one will admit knowing anything about the mines. Perhaps they really don't know anything about them. Regardless, this tiny country town with no tourist services is pleasant to tour. Just don't expect to see any gold mines.

Buses leave Chitré for Las Minas hourly; the trip takes about an hour and costs US$1.50. To leave Las Minas, catch any bus heading toward your destination and make transfers as warranted. For example, if your destination is Santiago, you should take a northbound bus to the Interamericana; if the driver heads east (away from Santiago) upon reaching the highway, you should hop off and catch a westbound bus. If your destination is far from the Las Minas area (David or Panama City, for example), you'd be wise to go to

Santiago or Chitré and then transfer there to a nonstop bus.

Bus service to Las Minas from Panama City departs the Terminal de Buses al Interior every 1½ hours from 7 am to 5 pm. The trip takes five hours; the one-way fare is US$6.50.

OCÚ

This sleepy town of 3500 people, 49km by road southeast of bustling Santiago, is distinguished by its hat makers. Not long ago, Ocú – which straddles a loop road that links it and the major Herrera Province towns of Chitré, Pesé, Los Pozos and Las Minas – used to be where Panamanians went to buy the finest Panama-style hats made in their country; now people often go to Penonomé, in Coclé Province.

Be advised that there are no hotels in Ocú. However, there is a Banco Nacional de Panamá, a post office and a couple of decent restaurants.

Hat Makers

Until the 1990s Ocú's many hat makers took their intricately braided merchandise to the town square every morning and sold all they had by noon. Truckers, who were major hat buyers, used to make special trips to Ocú for their headgear. But once good-quality hats became available in Penonomé, which is conveniently located on the Interamericana, the truckers stopped making the special trip, and the hat makers

DAVE G HOUSER

HERRERA PROVINCE

began selling to vendors who resell the hats in Penonomé.

Today there are still 20 to 25 hat makers in Ocú, and if you wish, you can visit some of them and see how a genuine Panama hat is made – with great patience and attention to detail. The finest are so tightly braided that you can turn them over and fill them to their rims with water, and they won't leak so much as a drop. Of course, don't expect to leave a hat maker's home (they all work out of their homes) without a little soft sell. The time needed to make a hat varies from one week to one month. The cost ranges from US$25 to US$150.

The hat makers are always women. If you ask one why, you'll get the same answer every time: Men's fingers are too large and clumsy for the intricate work involved in making superior hats!

If you decide to visit a hat maker, go see Elena Montilla and/or Ezequela Maure. They live only two houses apart at the northern end of town on the main street, Avenida Central. To find their houses, drive or walk about 400m on Avenida Central from the town plaza until you reach a fork in the road. Ezequela's house is on the left side of the street, about four houses south of the fork. Elena's house is two doors down. None of Ocú's hat makers speak English.

Special Events
The Festival del Manito, one of the country's best folklore programs, is held in Ocú, usu-ally during the third week in August (check with IPAT for dates). The three-day festival was established to maintain the region's traditional culture, and during it folklore groups from throughout Herrera Province present their dances in traditional dress. The fiesta's climax is a Sunday-morning church wedding, after which the couple is paraded through the streets on horseback by friends and family.

Ocú is also famous for its patron saint festival, usually held January 20 to 23 (check with IPAT, as the dates are flexible). During this festival, an effigy of St Sebastian is paraded through the streets at night, and devotees walk behind the statue carrying lighted candles. The festival includes folklore programs and an agricultural fair.

Bear in mind that the sun is particularly intense in the Tropics. If you attend one of Ocú's special events and haven't already taken steps to protect your face from sunburn, you might want to pick up a Panama hat at the general store beside the town plaza. These hats are locally made and, as mentioned above, are of very good quality.

Getting There & Away
Buses leave Chitré's station for Ocú hourly; they leave the Santiago station every two hours. The ride from either city takes about an hour and costs US$1.50 each way. Bus service to Ocú from Panama City departs the Terminal de Buses al Interior about every 1½ hours from 7 am to 4:30 pm. The trip takes five hours and costs US$6.

Los Santos Province

This province, covering the southeastern third of the Península de Azuero, is home to cowboys, statuesque people and gorgeous beaches. It was here that Panama's cry for independence from Spain was first uttered. And yet the people of The Saints Province take great pride in its Spanish history, and they show it in folkloric festivals that date back to the first settlers.

The Fiesta de Corpus Christi, in Villa de Los Santos, and the Fiesta de Santa Librada, in the provincial capital of Las Tablas, are marked by exuberant displays of traditional clothing and dances born in Spain during the Middle Ages. The most intricate *polleras* – the national costume that is an elaboration on the dresses worn by Spanish peasants during the 17th and 18th centuries – are made in the village of La Enea and in villages around Las Tablas.

As in Herrera Province, in Los Santos Province many locals look distinctly European. The people are taller, their skin fairer, their features more chiseled than those of people elsewhere on the isthmus. Their eyes are often hazel or blue. Some people have red or blond hair. In Los Santos more than in any other province of Panama, the European bloodline is apparent and the whites want to keep it that way.

Yet for at least the past 100 years, the residents of Los Santos Province have known only racial harmony, and their sense of community pride is so strong that one wonders if it's hereditary. If you meet a black, Indian or white Los Santos native in another part of the country, you'll surely know it – they aren't likely to keep it under wraps.

If you speak any Spanish, you'll notice a few things about the people of Los Santos Province: They often end their sentences with an 'eh' (it rhymes with *hey* and *say*). They also say 'chi' a lot (it rhymes with *lie* and *cry,* and it's short for a common local euphemism). And they tell stories with flair.

VILLA DE LOS SANTOS

The Río La Villa, 4km south of downtown Chitré, marks the boundary between Herrera Province and Los Santos Province, and it is just south of that river that one comes to Villa de Los Santos (often called simply 'Los Santos'), on the Carretera Nacional.

This picturesque town of 7000, replete with many colonial structures, is where Panama's first cry for independence from Spain was heard, on November 10, 1821. The event is honored with a museum and an annual celebration. Also worth a look is the old church. There's a good hotel and a wild bar/dance club in town too.

Information

In early 1998 the Instituto Panameño de Turismo (IPAT) was constructing a tourism

---

HIGHLIGHTS

- The people of Los Santos Province – some of the friendliest and most animated on earth

- Celebrations such as Las Tablas' Carnaval and Villa de Los Santos' Corpus Christi bash

- Isla Caña, whose beaches are visited each year by thousands of sea turtles

- Watching *polleras,* the beautiful national costume, being made in La Enea and Santo Domingo

- Playa Venado, one of Panama's finest surfing beaches and also one of its most beautiful

Los Santos Province

office on the Carretera Nacional, 2km south of Villa de Los Santos, on the way to Las Tablas. Stop by to check if any festivals are scheduled to take place while you are in the area.

There's a Banco Nacional de Panamá and a laundry in town.

Museo de la Nacionalidad

This museum, opposite Parque Simón Bolívar, is in the house where Panama's Declaration of Independence was signed in 1821. In the years that followed, the handsome brick-and-tile residence has served as a jail, a school and a legislature.

It predates the town's church, but no one knows exactly when it was built. Inaugurated as a museum in 1974, it was one of the first specialized museums in the country.

It contains artifacts related to Panama's independence, which was declared in Los Santos 18 days before it was declared by the government, as well as objects from the era of the Spanish conquest. Pre-Columbian ceramics and gold pieces occupy one room. Its hours are from 9 am to 4:30 pm Tuesday to Saturday and 9 am to 1 pm Sunday; admission costs US$1/25¢ adults/children.

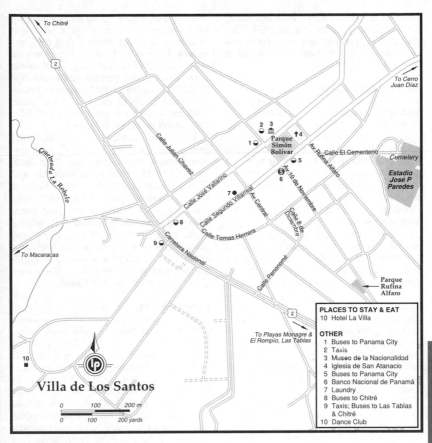

Villa de Los Santos

0   100   200 m
0   100   200 yards

PLACES TO STAY & EAT
10 Hotel La Villa

OTHER
1   Buses to Panama City
2   Taxis
3   Museo de la Nacionalidad
4   Iglesia de San Atanacio
5   Buses to Panama City
6   Banco Nacional de Panamá
7   Laundry
8   Buses to Chitré
9   Taxis; Buses to Las Tablas
    & Chitré
10 Dance Club

Iglesia de San Atanacio

Villa de Los Santos' church, alongside Parque Simón Bolívar, opened its doors to the public in 1782, after nine years of construction. It is a fine example of the Baroque style – lots of intricately carved wood depicting cherubs, saints, Jesus and the Virgin. Almost everything in the church is original, and some of the objects even predate the structure itself. The 12m arch in front of the altar, for example, bears its date of manufacture (1733) and the names of its two creators.

The altar is made of mahogany and rosewood and covered nearly from base to top in gold leaf. Figurines of the Virgin, angels and Jesus adorn it. In a glass sepulcher in front of the altar is a near-life-size wooden statue of Christ that is carried through the streets of Villa de Los Santos on Good Friday, behind a candlelit procession.

In the interior walls of the church are headstones, and behind them are the remains of the church's ministers. Note the black Christ in the altar against the southeastern wall. While inside the church, look above the entrance, where you'll see a balcony; the choir sang from it in years past.

The original church bells have been moved to the Museo de Arte Religioso

Colonial in Panama City; those that are in the steeple today were cast in 1907. This church was granted national monument status by the government in 1938 and is truly a national treasure.

Archaeological Site

The Smithsonian Institution has been conducting an excavation at Cerro Juan Díaz, 3km from Villa de Los Santos, where evidence shows people lived from approximately 300 BC until the time of the Spanish conquest. It's fascinating to watch the archaeologists unearthing pottery, shells and other items. However, this site is not always being worked.

You're welcome to visit the site, and perhaps see the scientists in action, but you may have a hard time finding it on your own. A taxi from the taxi stand northwest of Parque Simón Bolívar can be hired for US$2. Ask the driver to return for you, as there is no other transportation out there.

Special Events

The anniversary of the cry for independence is celebrated in Los Santos each November 10. Other notable festivals include Carnaval (celebrated four days before Ash Wednesday, February/March), Semana Santa (Holy Week, April), the Feria de Azuero (the Azuero Fair, late April/early May) and the Fiesta de Corpus Christi (Thursday to Sunday, 40 days after Easter, May/June).

The Feria de Azuero features folkloric dancing, agricultural attractions and competition among local singers performing regional songs. The Corpus Christi festival, one of the most animated in the country, draws masked and costumed dancers who represent angels, devils, imps and other figures while enacting dramas.

The exact dates of all these events vary from year to year. Contact IPAT or a tour operator for precise dates.

Places to Stay & Eat

The *Hotel La Villa* (☎ 966-9321, fax 966-8201), 500m from the Carretera Nacional in the southwestern section of town, is Villa de Los Santos' only hotel, and it's a bit on the pricey side; if you're on a tight budget, you'll get more value for your money in nearby Chitré. There are 38 rooms at the Villa, including small rooms with air-con and private bathrooms for US$20/27 single/double Monday to Thursday and US$26/32 the rest of the week. Without air-con, the price drops US$3 for one person and US$10 for two.

There are standard rooms (the hotel generously calls them 'suites') with air-con, private bathrooms and firm beds for US$31/38 Monday to Thursday and US$40/47 the rest of the week. The hotel has a swimming pool, a bar and a good restaurant, and there's a very cool dance club next door (see Entertainment, below). If the price for the 'suites' suits you and you're looking for a happening bar/dance scene on a Friday or a Saturday night, I encourage you to stay here. There's no comparable club scene in Chitré.

Entertainment

Adjacent to the Hotel La Villa is a *dance club* that absolutely throbs with color, sound and sexual tension. Amid a sea of Day-Glo paint, black lights and intimate tables are hundreds of wall-mounted photos of Marilyn Monroe that belong to the club's owner, Dr Javier Sarasty. Sarasty has been collecting photos of the blonde sex bomb since the 1970s, and his collection (most of which is on display at area medical clinics) is quite impressive. This club starts hopping weekend nights about 11 pm and doesn't close before dawn. Party animals won't want to miss it. The cover charge rarely exceeds US$2.

Getting There & Away

Chitré-Las Tablas buses stop on the Carretera Nacional. Chitré-Villa de Los Santos buses stop on Calle José Vallarino half a block from the Carretera Nacional. Fares to these destinations or anywhere in the province are usually between 50¢ and US$2.

Buses to Panama City depart from two stops: one is on Calle José Vallarino at Avenida 10 de Noviembre, and the other is a block away on Calle Segundo Villarreal near Avenida 10 de Noviembre.

Buses from Panama City to Villa de Los Santos (stopping in Chitré) depart the Terminal de Buses al Interior, on Avenida Ascañio Villalaz in the Curundu district, hourly from 6 am to 11 pm. The trip takes four hours and costs US$6 each way.

Getting Around
Taxis are the best way to get around Villa de Los Santos and between Villa de Los Santos and Chitré, if you don't feel like walking. The fare won't exceed US$3 if you stay within these cities. Taxis can usually be found near the bus stop on the Carretera Nacional and northwest of Parque Simón Bolívar.

PLAYAS MONAGRE & EL ROMPÍO
Ten km northeast of Villa de Los Santos are the attractive Playas Monagre and El Rompío. Both beaches are popular with fishermen, families and body surfers. It is quite OK to swim at either beach, but beware of possible rip currents (see the Swimming Safety section of the Facts for the Visitor chapter for information on rip currents). El Rompío is less frequented than Monagre and has less litter. Both have a couple of simple, open-sided *restaurants* serving shrimp, corvina and squid.

Every evening, dozens of fishermen beach their brightly painted boats at El Rompío. The scene at this time, with all the boats lined up on the wide beach and fishermen tending to their catches against the backdrop of the Pacific sunset, makes for a lovely photograph.

A bus leaves the Chitré station for Playas Monagre and El Rompío hourly from sunrise to sunset. The 20km ride costs US$1 each way. This bus passes through Villa de Los Santos on the way to the beaches and can be hailed from the Carretera Nacional in town. Look for a bus with 'Monagre' on its windshield. The fare from Villa de Los Santos to either beach is 50¢. A taxi ride from Chitré to either beach costs about US$5; a taxi from Villa de Los Santos costs half that.

ROAD TO LAS TABLAS
The Carretera Nacional from Villa de Los Santos to Las Tablas runs mostly past small farms and cattle ranches. There's no forest in sight. In fact, the men of this province are so proud of their ability to fell trees that during the 1980s many moved to Darién Province, where they now work for lumber companies. Between 1980 and 1990, Los Santos Province saw a 2% decline in its population due to this exodus.

Just south of Villa de Los Santos, on the eastern side of the road, you'll see a small hut flanked by a large pile of coconut husks. The hut is a coconut juice stand that's extremely popular with truckers. The coconuts are kept in a huge fridge, and for 25¢ the vendor will take a machete and hack a quarter-size hole in one for you.

The coconut is still in its thick green husk when it's handed to you, so the fruit is quite large – about the size of a human head. The proper way to drink the semisweet yet raw-tasting juice is to raise the coconut to your lips, tilt your head back and guzzle. Even though the juice is clear, try not to spill any on your clothes; it stains terribly. Coconut juice (or 'milk,' as they call it here) is said to be very good for your kidneys.

As you travel the two-lane Carretera Nacional toward Las Tablas, you'll occasionally see stands with sausages dangling in front of them. The pork sausages made on the Península de Azuero are nationally famous for their delicious taste, but avoid the ones sold at these stands. Who knows how long they've been around or how many flies and filthy hands have been on them? If you like sausages, you might want to get some at one of the grocery stores on the peninsula.

If you're traveling the highway around Carnaval time, you'll also see dozens of smashed-up cars on the roadside. These cars belonged to motorists killed by drunk drivers during Carnaval. The police realize that most of the people on the road during Carnaval are intoxicated. Instead of trying to arrest all the drunk motorists, the police display the old wrecks, hoping the sight will encourage drunks to drive slowly. You should avoid highway travel during Carnaval.

GUARARÉ

The tiny town of Guararé, on the Carretera Nacional between Villa de Los Santos and Las Tablas, offers little of interest to tourists, but it does have some attractions, including a museum, nearby pollera makers and a large annual festival. Keep in mind that there are no hotels or restaurants in town.

Museo Manuel F Zárate

Zárate was a folklorist who was devoted to conserving the traditions and folklore of the Azuero region. The museum, in Zárate's former home, contains polleras, masks, *diablito* (little devil) costumes and other exhibits. It's two blocks behind the not-so-impressive church, about six short blocks from the main road (turn off at the Delta fuel station). It's open 8 am to noon and 12:45 to 4 pm Tuesday to Saturday and 8 am to noon Sunday. Admission costs 75¢/25¢ adults/children.

Polleras

Some of the finest polleras are made in La Enea, a small village northeast of Guararé. The pollera, once nothing more than the daily attire of the lower classes of 17th and 18th-century Spain, has become today an entire national costume of stirring beauty and elegance. Almost every part of the costume is made by hand, from the attractive embroidery on the blouse and skirt to the delicate filigree ornaments tucked around the gold combs in the hair.

The traditional assortment of jewelry worn with a pollera consists of three to seven gold neck chains, two to five combs trimmed with gold and pearls, a dagger-shaped ornament once used to relieve the itching caused by the combs, a bracelet, earrings, four gold buttons on the waistband, buckles on the shoes, small ornaments worn over the temples and 12 pairs of delicate hair ornaments. The jewelry alone can cost US$50,000, and often does.

The glorious national dress of Panama

One of the best-known makers of the national costume lives beside La Enea's plaza, in the green-tiled house next door to the small market with 'Roxana' painted over its door. The dressmaker's name is Ildama Saavedra de Espino, and at the time I visited her she had just been hired to make a pollera for a future Carnaval queen. She estimated that it would take her eight months to make the dress. By convention, the pollera would consist of two basic pieces: a blouse that rests upon the tops of the shoulders and a long skirt divided into two fully gathered tiers.

Each dress requires no less than 10m of fine white linen or cotton cloth. Elaborate needlework in a single color enriches the white background. Flowers, leaves, vines and fruits are the common motifs. Ildama agreed to make the Carnaval queen's dress for US$2000, which is the going price for a fine pollera.

Anyone with a keen interest in needlecraft is welcome to visit Ildama. She is accustomed to strangers stopping by her home to marvel at her handiwork. Be advised that she does not speak English and that her work is motivated chiefly by the pride she takes in seeing her polleras worn by beautiful women during festivals.

If you ask her to make you a dress for even twice the going price, please be polite when she smiles and says no.

If you're looking to buy a pollera, see the Around Las Tablas section in this chapter for other towns where the dresses are available.

Special Events

Like most towns in Los Santos Province, Guararé is not without at least one festival, in this case the Feria de la Mejorana, a combined patron saint and folkloric festival held September 23 to 27. As in all patron saint festivals, a statue of a saint is paraded through the streets.

The folkloric festival, however, is much different than others in Panama. It is the country's largest. Begun by Manuel Zárate in 1950 to stimulate interest and participation in traditional practices, the Feria de la Mejorana has become the best place to see Panama's folklore in all its manifestations. Dance groups from all over the country – and even some from other Latin American countries – attend this annual event. There is even a colorful parade in which participants are hauled through the streets in oxcarts.

Folkloric dances that were once part of other celebrations in other places are today sometimes seen only at this event. For example, this is the only festival in which a dance known as La Pajarita is performed. (The name means 'paper bird.') The dance was once part of the Corpus Christi celebration in Villa de Los Santos, but is no longer. In contrast to the various exuberant devil dances, a calm, religious quality pervades La Pajarita, and the dancers' costumes are simple and unique.

Over dark trousers and a short-sleeved shirt, each dancer wears two tiers of yellow streamers made from palm leaves, one around the neck and the other around the waist. Dancers wear tall hats shaped like bishop's miters, usually made of leather and covered with patches of brightly colored paper. Each dancer carries a maraca (a hollow-gourd rattle containing pebbles or beans) wrapped in a white handkerchief.

A single guitar accompanies the Pajarita, which may involve as many as 10 male dancers. Rhythmic patterns and chord progressions indicate when the dancers should change positions. The men shake their maracas in unison throughout the dance, following the underlying beat of the guitar. Taking their instructions from the music of the guitar, the dancers form two parallel lines and kneel before a cross. The dance is simple and complicated, peculiar and logical. It's one of many performed at this most interesting fair.

Getting There & Away

Guararé is beside the Carretera Nacional, 20km south of Villa de Los Santos. La Enea is to its northeast. You can hop on any bus that travels the highway in the direction of Guararé; you'll be dropped off at the town.

To get to La Enea, I advise taking a taxi. For one thing, there are no hotels in La Enea, and for another the taxi ride will set you back only US$1. Although Guararé has only 4000 inhabitants, it's big enough that there are some taxis around.

LAS TABLAS

Las Tablas, a city of 9000 people and the capital of Los Santos Province, has a fine church and a small but OK museum devoted to former Las Tablas statesman and three-time president Belisario Porras. But the city is really known for its Carnaval, widely regarded as Panama's most authentic. This city is also famous for its combined patron saint/pollera festival – a fun brew of religious ceremony and beauty contest.

Orientation

Las Tablas is 31km southeast of Chitré via the Carretera Nacional and 282km southwest of Panama City via the Carretera Interamericana and the Carretera Nacional. The Carretera Nacional becomes Avenida Laureano Lopez at the northern edge of town and reemerges as the road to Santo Domingo on the southern side of town. Avenida Laureano Lopez runs for nine

Las Tablas

To Guararé, Villa de Los Santos

To El Pausilipo

To Playa El Uverito

To Santo Domingo, Pedasí

PLACES TO STAY
9 Hotel Hospedaje Zafiro
12 Hotel Piamonte

PLACES TO EAT
2 Cafe Union
6 Restaurante Morvel
13 Cafe Monte

OTHER
1 Bus Station
3 Laundry
4 Post Office
5 Banco Nacional de Panamá
7 Taxis
8 Iglesia Santa Librada
10 Museo Belisario Porras
11 Banco del Istmo
14 Taxis

blocks before ending at the Museo Belisario Porras, beside the central plaza.

Almost everything of interest to the tourist is within five blocks of the plaza. This includes one of the finest colonial churches on the peninsula, two banks, a post office, two decent hotels and several restaurants. Out a little farther is a bus station, as well as two taxi stands for the newly arrived.

Information
Stop by the new IPAT office (under construction in early 1998) just south of Villa de Los Santos to check if any festivals are scheduled to take place while you are in the Las Tablas area.

There's a Banco Nacional de Panamá on Avenida Laureano Lopez near Calle 2 and a Banco del Istmo on Calle Belisario Porras. The post office is on Calle 2. The laundry is on Calle Doctor Emilio Castro, at the northern end of town.

Museo Belisario Porras
This museum is in the mud-walled former home of three-time president Belisario Porras, during whose administration the Panama Canal opened. Porras, who is regarded as a national hero, was president

for all but two years from 1912 to 1924. He is credited with establishing Panama's network of public hospitals, creating a national registry for land titles, and constructing scores of bridges and aqueducts.

Among the many artifacts on display are Porras' law school diploma, a post from his canopy bed and his presidential sash. Note that the sash has only seven stars, one for each of Panama's provinces at the time Porras entered office; the country has nine provinces today, because Porras divided two of the original seven to create Herrera and Los Santos.

Incidentally, the huge tomb inside the museum, which bears Porras' name, is empty. Plans to move his remains here from a cemetery in Panama City were never carried out. An interesting aside: All of Porras' male descendants wear their whiskers in his unusual style – a thick, prideful mustache resembling the horns of a Texas longhorn steer.

The museum is open 9 am to 12:30 pm and 1:30 to 4 pm Tuesday to Saturday and 9 am to noon Sunday. Admission costs 50¢/25¢ adults/kids.

Iglesia Santa Librada
This Baroque-style church near the central plaza opened its doors on March 9, 1789, but sustained major damage in 1950 in a fire set off by faulty wiring. The painted faces on the ornate gold-leaf altar are original, but the figurines of Christ, the Virgin and the saints were added after the blaze.

Special Events
Las Tablas is perhaps the best place in Panama to spend Carnaval, which is held during the four days that precede Ash Wednesday. By tradition, the town is divided into two groups, *calle arriba* (high street) and *calle abajo* (low street), which compete intensely with each other in every aspect of the fiesta. Each calle has its own queen, floats and songs. Each day begins with members parading in street clothes, singing songs that poke fun at the rival group. During the parade, jokesters from both sides toss tinted water, blue dye and

shaving cream at the other side. No one, onlookers included, is spared; dress expecting to get creamed.

Both sides take a rest during the heat of the day, and don costumes or put finishing touches on their floats in the late afternoon. Then at dusk, the groups' parades begin on parallel streets, led by floats that are followed by musicians seated in the back of flatbed trucks, who are followed in turn by calle members. Every night, each calle has a different float and different costumes. Crowds pack the sidewalks and fireworks light up the night. The queens make their appearances on Saturday night, dressed at first in gaudily decorated costumes and later in exquisite evening gowns. Their coronation is held on Sunday. Monday is masquerade day, and Tuesday all the women in town who have polleras don them and fill the streets with color and beauty.

Another excellent time to be in Las Tablas is July 21, when the provincial capital hosts two big events: the Fiesta de Santa Librada and the Festival de La Pollera. The highlight of the patron saint festival is the procession through the streets. The sacred event and services inside the church are accompanied by street celebrations that recall a medieval fair – gambling, dancing, singing, bullfights, excessive eating and drinking. It's a strange juxtaposition of the sacred and the profane. The pollera festival is a photographer's delight. Beautiful young women model the national costume as they pass through the streets, all the while being judged on their grace as well as on the artisanship, design and authenticity of their costumes. The scene is like a slice of Spain dropped into Panama, which is the intention.

Places to Stay
A handful of budget lodgings in town are unabashed whorehouses or 'push buttons' (places where married people meet their lovers). Worthwhile hotels open at the time this book was researched are listed below.

The *Hotel Hospedaje Zafiro* (☎ 994-8200), opposite the plaza, is an upstairs hotel – the entrance is around the corner from the plaza, on Calle Belisario Porras. It's clean and cheerful, with an upstairs balcony where guests can look out over the plaza. The nine rooms here, all with private bathrooms, air-con and color TVs, cost US$18/22 single/double. Larger rooms for up to five people are also available.

For twice as much money but not twice the value is the *Hotel Piamonte* (☎ 994-6372), on Calle Belisario Porras two blocks from the plaza. Try this place if Zafiro is full.

Places to Eat

Several little *restaurants* are found in the downtown area, none particularly good but all quite cheap. The restaurant next to the museum, a stone's throw from the church, makes some very OK sandwiches and burgers.

Getting There & Away

Las Tablas' bus station is on Avenida Laureano Lopez at Calle Doctor Emilio Castro. Hourly buses connect Las Tablas with Santo Domingo (5km, 10 minutes, 50¢), Chitré (31km, 30 minutes, US$1), Tonosí (79km, 1½ hours, US$2.50) and other places. There's also daily service to Pedasí (41km, one hour, US$1.50) and Playa Venado (68km, two hours, US$3).

Bus service to Las Tablas from Panama City departs the Terminal de Buses al Interior every 1½ hours from 6 am to 6 pm. The 282km trip takes 4½ hours; the one-way fare is US$6.50.

Getting Around

Las Tablas is a small town and it's easily walked. However, taxis are available for hire. You can find a taxi stand on Calle 1, two blocks north of the central plaza, and another is on Calle Belisario Porras at Calle Estudiante. Fares within town never exceed US$2.

AROUND LAS TABLAS
El Pausílipo

In the countryside a few kilometers from town is El Pausílipo, the former country estate of Belisario Porras. His surname means 'tranquility' in Greek; it's easy to see how the Las Tablas statesman would have treasured the tranquillity here.

The humble residence is located in a parklike setting. The small home has adobe walls covered with a cement sheet that is painted white with a sky-blue trim, just as it was during Porras' lifetime. Most of the rooms are empty today, but one contains handsome leather chairs and a fine table.

The tiny separate structure beside the residence is the original kitchen; kitchens in Porras' day were usually set apart from the living quarters to lessen the likelihood that a kitchen fire would destroy the entire house. A well with a pump was sunk on the property in 1917, and with 60 or 70 vigorous pumps water still rises to the surface.

El Pausílipo and the grounds around it are open 9 am to 4 pm Tuesday to Saturday and 8 am to noon Sunday. Admission is free. The easiest way to get to El Pausílipo is to take a taxi from Las Tablas. For US$5, a taxi driver will take you to the former estate, wait while you take a look around and then return you to the city.

Polleras

If you're in the market for Panama's beautiful national costume, you'll want to know that there are several places besides Guararé where the colorfully embroidered dresses are made. Keep in mind that the polleras may cost US$2000 apiece.

The small town of Santo Domingo, about 10 minutes from Las Tablas by car, is known for its fine polleras, as are the nearby hamlets of La Tiza, El Cocal, El Carate and San José. If you haven't got wheels, your best bet is to hire a taxi. San José, the most remote of the bunch, will set you back US$40 roundtrip. Rides to the other communities won't cost you half as much. San José is also known for its guitars, although they are not particularly good by international standards.

Playa El Uverito

The best beach in the vicinity of Las Tablas is Playa El Uverito. This is a pretty beach, typical of those found all along this section of the coast. It is not reachable by bus. A taxi will take you there from Las Tablas for US$5.

PEDASÍ

This pleasant coastal town of 3000 friendly souls, 41km southeast of Las Tablas, makes a good base for exploration of area beaches. It is also from Pedasí that many people make forays to the Refugio de Vida Silvestre Isla Iguana, a wildlife refuge that offers some fine snorkeling and diving.

Orientation & Information

The Carretera Nacional passes down the western part of Pedasí; it is a low-speed, two-lane road with little traffic as it slices through town. There are some fine beaches (see below) a few kilometers to the east. There are a couple of very comfortable places to stay in town, and there's good food to be had. But there are no banks in Pedasí, nor is there a tourist office or post office, although if you have postage you can leave your letters with your hotel to be picked up by the postal agent. There are several pay phones around town from which you can place domestic or international calls.

Playas El Toro & La Garita

The surf at these beaches (Bull Beach and Gatekeeper's Box Beach, respectively) is usually quite OK for swimming; this is particularly true at La Garita, but El Toro is the more accessible of the two. At El Toro you can actually drive onto the beach if you have a vehicle, but La Garita is flanked by a rocky slope, and a hike of about 100m through light scrub and dirt (mud if there's been any recent rain) is required to reach the beach. Despite their proximity to Pedasí, both beaches are quite isolated and private. However, neither offers an opportunity for snorkeling – the water is simply too murky.

Unfortunately, neither beach is served by buses, and because Pedasí is so small, it isn't served by any taxis. To reach these beaches, you'll need to have your own vehicle, plan on doing some walking, or stand by the road that goes to the beaches and try to coax a lift out of someone heading toward the ocean. To drive to the sand from central Pedasí, turn east off the Carretera Nacional onto the paved street beside the Pensión Moscoso, and drive about 250m to the Cantina Hermanos Cedeño, a bar. Then take the dirt road just past the bar 1km, until the road forks. Follow the signs to the beaches, which are 2km farther along.

Special Events

Pedasí holds its patron saint festival on June 29. It is by no means a spectacular affair, but if you already happen to be south of Chitré at the time, the festival warrants the drive or bus ride to get here.

Places to Stay

There are two places to stay in Pedasí, both of which are good values and easy to find, as they are on the Carretera Nacional.

The *Pensión Moscoso* (☎ 995-2303), near the center of town, is the better of the town's hotels, with lovely rooms with air-con, cable TVs and cold-water private bathrooms for US$20 per room (US$15 without air-con). There is no restaurant on the premises, but there is good food within a short walk.

The *Hotel Residencial Pedasí* (☎ 995-2322), near the northern end of town, has singles/doubles/triples, all with air-con and cold-water private bathrooms, for US$21/26/32. The rooms here are not as spacious as those at the Moscoso. There is a restaurant on the premises.

Places to Eat

Pedasí has some surprises in the culinary category. A very good French restaurant, the *Restaurante Internacional,* is 100m south of the Hotel Residencial Pedasí, on the opposite side of the street. The owner-cook-server was a chef in France and in Canada before he 'retired' in Pedasí. Because this restaurant is a one-person operation, drop by at least several hours before you would like to eat to let him

LOS SANTOS PROVINCE

know you're coming for dinner. The menu varies daily, but typical items and prices include a chicken curry with seafood (US$11), lobster (US$12) and fish of the day (US$15). Wine is available.

If you've got a sweet tooth, be sure to try a slice of cake at the *Dulceria Yely,* across the street from the Pensión Moscoso. Slices of Mrs Dalila Vera de Quintero's delicious cakes sell for 25¢, and they are so good. Her rum cake is glorious, as is her manjar cake (manjar is very similar to caramel in taste and appearance and is a specialty of the region).

Two blocks south of the Dulceria Yely is the colorfully painted *Restaurante Las Delicias,* which is a fine place to have a cheap, hearty breakfast. Three eggs with shredded beef, and two cups of coffee, costs less than US$3. I've not had lunch or dinner at Las Delicias, but I've heard its seafood is particularly good.

Getting There & Away

Pedasí is reachable by bus from Chitré (73km, one hour, US$2) as well as Las Tablas (41km, one hour, US$1.50). Buses leave these provincial capitals for Pedasí several times a day.

REFUGIO DE VIDA SILVESTRE ISLA IGUANA

The Iguana Island Wildlife Refuge is a 55-hectare protected island ringed by coral fields, much of which died in the 1982-83 El Niño. (El Niño is a change in weather patterns that affect ocean currents. Among a great many other horrible things, it starves marine life along the entire eastern Pacific coast.) At the time of writing, El Niño conditions had struck again, and the threat of catastrophic damage to the remaining coral was very real.

Anyone thinking of making a trip to the island would be well advised to contact Iguana Tours (☎ 226-8738, fax 226-4736, iguana@sinfo.net) in Panama City beforehand. Iguana Tours runs frequent snorkeling and diving tours to the island and can give you current information on the state of the coral out there. If the coral

didn't weather the 1997-98 El Niño well, there would be no reason for you to visit the island.

Humpback whales inhabit the waters around Isla Iguana from June to November. These large sea mammals, 15 to 20m long, mate and bear their young here and then teach them to dive. The humpbacks are the famous 'singing whales'; occasionally you can hear their underwater sounds when you're diving here.

The island is supposed to be protected by the Instituto Nacional de Recursos Naturales Renovables (INRENARE), the national environmental agency, but no INRENARE ranger was in sight the last weekend I was there; litter was strewn up and down the main beach and weekend partiers were anchored with no respect for the coral under the water. The island was used for target practice by the US Navy during WWII, and there is still unexploded ordnance here; you really do not want to stray off the beaten paths.

Isla Iguana is reachable by boat from Playa El Arenal, a beach best accessed from Pedasí. However, getting to the beach is a problem, as buses do not go there and there are no taxis in Pedasí. If you have a car, stop by the house of boatman Roberto Peréz (☎ 995-2300), who lives across the street from the Accel station near the northern end of Pedasí. He speaks English and can make your trip to the island and back happen for US$50 for one or two people.

First Roberto picks up a 5-gallon can of gasoline from his storage shed; then you, he and the can drive a few kilometers down a dirt road to the beach. There Roberto puts the gasoline in his boat and takes you to the island, about a 10-minute ride away. You can either get out at the popular beach, which faces a 15-hectare coral field, or you can ask him to take you to a place where he knows there's very good snorkeling.

If you don't have wheels, still check with Roberto, as he might be able to call someone who can take both of you to the beach.

PLAYA LOS DESTILADEROS & PUNTA MALA

Distillers Beach and Bad Point make for fine exploring, but neither is served by bus. To reach them from the center of Pedasí, drive 3.5km south on the Carretera Nacional and then take the El Limon/Los Destiladeros turnoff. Drive 5km down the dirt (mud if it's been raining) road, until it forks at a double tree. If you take the right branch here, you'll come to the beautiful surfer's beach (Playa Los Destiladeros) after another 5km. If you take the left branch, after 6km you'll come to a rocky coast (Punta Mala), a lighthouse with easily accessible steps that you're not supposed to climb, and a former three-story US naval defense viewing building that was used during WWII.

PLAYA VENADO

The Playa Venado (Deer Beach) turnoff is 33km by road southwest of Pedasí. Venado is one of Panama's finest surfing beaches, a real beauty. It's also way off the beaten track, but reachable by bus. There are *cabins* costing US$12 a night during the week, or US$25 for a weekend, but they're very basic. They'll do if you don't mind roughing it, or you can camp out on the beach for free. There's a simple *bar and restaurant* beside the beach that's got a nice, laid-back atmosphere, and almost every night the local men gather around a table here to play dominoes.

A bus operates once a day between Las Tablas and Playa Venado; the 68km trip, initially down the Carretera Nacional and then down a dirt road, takes about two hours. The one-way fare is US$3. Reportedly, the trip will take only 45 minutes if the planned new road is ever constructed.

ISLA CAÑA

At the end of August and all through September, thousands of green sea turtles come ashore at night to lay eggs in the sand on the broad beach of Isla Caña (Cane Island). That the turtles arrive in such numbers is due in large part to the residents of the 10km long island. Locals here let the

---

Rescuing the Tuna

Thirty km southwest of Pedasí, on the southern side of the road, is the entrance to the Laboratorio Achotines, where a group of US marine biologists studies the early life of yellowfin tuna. Their research has played a key role in the implementation of fishing quotas to protect the tuna stock in Pacific Ocean waters from California to Ecuador. Their recommendations to an international regulatory commission on the use of certain types of fishing nets have also played a direct role in reducing the number of dolphins that are killed by tuna fishing in the eastern Pacific, from 500,000 annually to 3000. The research center is not open to the general public. ■

---

turtles do their thing in peace, unlike on the islands of Bocas del Toro and the Comarca de San Blás. This is really a great place to watch the turtles, and getting here is an adventure. Read on!

The turnoff for Isla Caña is easy to miss. It's beside a bus stop on the southern side of the Carretera Nacional, 6.5km west of the turnoff for the town of Cañas; next to the bus stop, there's a fairly large sign that reads 'Piladora.' Put another way, the Isla Caña turnoff is 16km west of the Playa Venado turnoff and 17km by road east of Tonosí. The bus stop is served by Toyota Coaster buses that travel between Chitré and Tonosí hourly from 7 am to 4 pm.

From the turnoff, a 5km drive or hike on a dirt road takes you to the edge of an immense mangrove forest where you can hire a boat to get to nearby Isla Caña. There's usually one or two boatmen here who will take you to the island and bring you back for US$7 – more if you spend over an hour on the island. If there is no boatman in sight when you reach the end of the road, hang tight; one will arrive shortly. If you have a car, honk a few times so that the boatmen know you are there.

If you feel like taking a dip in the black water between the dirt bank and the mangroves, be warned that there are crocodiles in the water and that if you swim into the mangroves and try to stand up, you'll find that the bottoms of mangrove forests are covered with pointy branches and roots. It's best not to think about the snakes at all. Also, because you're doing all this late at night (the turtles only lay their eggs late at night), there's a chance you could get lost.

The 10-minute boat ride to Isla Caña is great fun. The boat sits low in the water and doesn't exactly inspire a sense of security. It's quite normal for people stepping into a small boat at the edge of crocodile-filled mangroves late at night to question their judgment. But don't worry. Soon you're underway, weaving through the mangroves and then crossing open water, and the next thing you know you're on wonderful Isla Caña. It's a short walk to the other side, where the turtles are easy to spot.

Sea turtles are easily frightened, particularly by bright lights (such as flashlights). Unless it's a moonless night, I recommend not using a flashlight at all, at least not on the beach itself. Let your eyes adjust to the moonlight and you'll be able to see well enough – and you won't risk scaring off an expectant mother.

TONOSÍ

This cowboy town, 65km southwest of Pedasí, offers little of interest to the tourist. Its chief attractions are its scenery – the town is in a green valley ringed by tan hills – and its proximity to many isolated surfing beaches.

Tonosí's streets are laid out like a plate of spaghetti. If you arrive from the north, as the vast majority of visitors do, you'll be on the Carretera a El Cacao from the town of El Cacao until you reach the center of Tonosí. Here the highway intersects with Avenida Central, Tonosí's main street, which is flanked on both sides by homes.

A bank, a bar, a pool hall, a couple of restaurants and two hotels are near the intersection of the Carretera a El Cacao and Avenida Central.

Playas Cambutal & Guánico

Cambutal and Guánico are two of the numerous beaches along the southern coast of the Península de Azuero that thrill most surfers. Both are reachable by dirt road from Tonosí, but neither is served by bus. If you don't have your own wheels, go to the INRENARE office, opposite and 50m down from the Restaurante Lindy. There are some helpful rangers there, one of whom speaks some English, and they have an old truck. If you're very friendly and offer to pay US$10 each way, you'll likely get the ride you want. Make sure to arrange a pickup time, of course, or you'll have a long walk back. Guánico is about 16km away from Tonosí, and Cambutal is about 22km away.

Unless you can afford to pay US$20 each day for transportation to and from the surf, plus US$10 for a hotel room, give some thought to camping on the beaches for at least part of the time. You can take some food with you from Restaurante Lindy or a store. You'll likely see some nesting sea turtles if you're on the beaches in late August, September or early October.

Places to Stay & Eat

There are three hotels in town, all of which offer rooms for US$10 with air-con and

US$5 without it. All come with private cold-water bathrooms and squeaky beds.

The best of the lot is *Hospedaje Irtha* (no phone), because it's the quietest and the cleanest. To get to it from the Carretera a El Cacao, take Calle Antonio Degracia one block. The Irtha will be on your right. Calle Antonio Degracia is one street north of Avenida Central; it's opposite the Restaurante Lindy.

Near the intersection of the Carretera a El Cacao and Avenida Central are the *Pensión Boamy* and the *Pensión Rosyini* (no phones). Neither is great, but if you've been camping, the Boamy or the Rosyini will be a treat.

The best place to chow down is the *Restaurante Lindy,* which specializes in – surprise! – rural Panamanian food. There's nothing fancy about this open-sided diner that flies also like a lot, but after a long day of surfing or exploring or just lying on a beach, the food and the ice-cold sodas and beer taste great – and they're cheap. A dockworker's helping of beef stew and two beers will set you back only US$4.

Getting There & Away
Hourly buses link Tonosí and points north all the way to Chitré. They operate only during daylight hours, from 7 am to 4 pm. The most expensive fare on the route, the fare to Chitré, is US$4 each way. The 103km ride can take two hours.

MACARACAS
Little Macaracas (population 1800), 57km northwest of Tonosí and 40km southwest of Chitré, is another small town bisected by a highway. It has nothing to offer the tourist in year-round attractions, but its annual folkloric festival, featuring the drama *The Three Wise Men,* is very popular. The festival is held January 5 to 10.

There are two banks in town, a couple of mediocre restaurants and one hotel, the *Pensión Lorena* (☎ 995-4181), which consists of 11 rooms above a pharmacy. The hotel is on the main road and charges US$12/14 single/double with air-con or US$8/12 without it (expect to pay twice that during the festival, if you're able to get a room at all).

Buses run between Macaracas and Chitré and Macaracas and Tonosí hourly from 7 am to 4 pm. The one-way fare to either destination is US$2, and the journey takes an hour. Bus service to Macaracas departs Panama City's Terminal de Buses al Interior every two hours from 8:30 am to 2:30 pm. The bus ride takes five hours and costs US$7.

Coclé Province

Coclé – land of sugar, salt and presidents. More sugar is refined in this province, more salt is produced here, and more Panamanian presidents have been born in Coclé than in any other province in the country. These are facts in which the people of Coclé take great pride, but the province isn't without a lion's share of tourist attractions as well.

From the traveler's perspective, there are two Coclés: the mountainous and the coastal. The beautiful mountain town of El Valle de Antón (usually known simply as El Valle) is home to a popular Sunday crafts market, lovely nature scenes, a zoo that's a pleasure to stroll through and a thrilling rainforest-canopy ride that uses the suspension equipment of spelunkers and canyon rappelers.

Farther west along the Cordillera Central is an area named Chiguiri Arriba, where peaks jut out of the ground, looking more like the famous karst formations of southern China than the rolling, forested mountains found elsewhere in Panama. Perched atop one such prominence is a lodge from which one can view and explore the dramatic landscape.

Farther west along the mountain range and yet still within the province is Parque Nacional El Copé, which has some of the most beautiful forest in Panama. The road leading up to the park requires a 4WD vehicle with a winch, and it rains seemingly every day, but the bird watching can be tremendous. The park is known for its many species of hummingbird, but birders can expect to see a variety of tanagers, too.

Coastal Coclé is a wonderful area as well. The beach at Santa Clara is idyllic, and there's a variety of lodging in this community, including the nation's only motorhome park. Down the road a little is the village of Farallón, where Manuel Noriega once kept a vacation home. Today you can camp on the wide beach near the home, which no one wants to fix up or occupy out of fear that the general may some day return.

A bit back from the coast and yet not quite into the foothills are Penonomé and Natá. Penonomé, Coclé's bustling provincial capital, is famous for its hats, its anthropology museum and its Carnaval and patron saint festival. Natá is one of the oldest cities in the country, and it is also home to one of the oldest churches in the Americas.

Up the road from Penonomé, toward the mountains, is La Pintada. Few Panamanians have heard of this town, but it's a must-visit for cigar aficionados. Owned and run by a savvy Latina, the Panabanos Cigar Factory here uses only the finest Cuban seeds in the production of its *habanos* (Havana cigars). If you've never

HIGHLIGHTS

- El Valle, home to an exotic Sunday handicrafts market and a wild rainforest-canopy ride

- The artisans' market and fine cigar factory in the foothill town of La Pintada

- The Iglesia de Natá, completed in 1522, with an intricate colonial façade and interior carvings

- Aguadulce's Las Piscinas, three tideland swimming pools that offer an unusual escape from the heat

- Watching sugar being made at the Ingenio de Azúcar Santa Rosa

COCLÉ PROVINCE

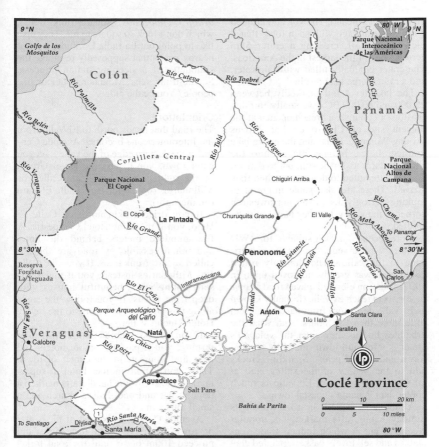

Coclé Province

visited a cigar factory, you'd find a trip to Panabanos educational and fun.

Moving farther southwest on the Carretera Interamericana (the Pan-American Hwy), you'll come to the coastal town of Aguadulce (Sweet Water), which is not without surprises. Among them are three elevated swimming pools built in tideland. When the tide's out, you can walk to them and take a dip; when the tide's in, the pools refill with water. They are nice, particularly on a hot day. And not to disappoint those of you whose breath quickened at the earlier mention of salt and sugar, it *is* possible to tour a huge sugar refinery here, and you

can look out upon salt flats all day, and no one will bother you. After a long day of watching salt crystallize and sugar being refined, you can swim in the pools.

Putting an accent on Coclé are its many festivals. In this province there are no fewer than eight major celebrations, ranging from an aquatic parade on a river in Penonomé to a tomato festival in Natá to patron saint and folkloric festivals in the farming town of Antón.

EL VALLE
This picturesque town, 123km west of Panama City, is nestled in the crater of a

giant extinct volcano. The volcano erupted 3 million years ago with such force that it blew its top off, creating a crater 5km across – one of the largest in the Americas. The crater gradually filled with rainwater, and a rather large lake resulted.

The lake level fell markedly between 25,000 and 10,000 BC. Eventually, through erosion or collapse, a breach opened at the present site of Chorro de Las Mozas (Young Women's Falls) and the entire lake drained. Later, Indians moved into the valley to farm its fertile soil, but to date no one has attempted to determine when they arrived. There are also some impressive-looking petroglyphs in the northwestern corner of the valley, but they have yet to be studied.

More recently, a road suitable for 4WD vehicles was carved from the Interamericana to the valley. That horribly rutted 28km road was greatly improved upon in 1997. Today an elevated, paved road allows motorists to reach El Valle (formally known as El Valle de Antón) from Panama City in little more than two hours. And what the urbanites find as they enter the volcano's crater is a tranquil town ringed by verdant forest and jagged peaks. Sparkling creeks add to the beauty of the valley, and at 1000m above sea level El Valle is much cooler than Panama's coastal towns.

Although El Valle is best known for its Sunday handicrafts market – a popular weekly event at which Indians trade vegetables and sell lovely baskets, painted clay figurines and carved serving trays – the town is also a superb place for walking. Many trails lead into the hills around the valley and, because they are often used by Indians, they are well defined.

Nature lovers, and birders in particular, won't be disappointed. The valley's forests offer very good bird watching (various hummingbirds abound, such as the green hermit, the violet-headed hummingbird and the white-tailed emerald), and El Valle is home to an impressive set of waterfalls and some rare golden frogs.

People who stand to gain from increased tourism to the area like to mention El Valle's *arboles cuadrados* (square-trunk trees), which don't look so square to me. They also like to point out La India Dormida, a set of nearby peaks that supposedly resemble the silhouette of a sleeping Indian princess. Square-trunk trees? Mountains that look like people? You be the judge.

Orientation

The road that heads north to El Valle from the Interamericana becomes Avenida Central at the eastern edge of the valley. As you enter town, you'll pass the Hotel Greco, on the right; just beyond it are Calle Los Millonarios (on the left) and Calle El Hato (on the right).

If you drive 1.5km north on Calle El Hato, you'll reach the Hotel Campestre. A few hundred meters behind the hotel and not accessible by road are the so-called square-trunk trees. If you take Calle Los Millonarios instead, you'll find yourself among some beautiful houses with deep front lawns. If you follow the signs along this street, you'll come to the lovely Hotel Rincón Vallero.

If you stay on Avenida Central instead of turning, you'll pass two more hotels and then find yourself in the center of town. There you'll find another hotel, a supermarket, the site of the handicrafts market, a popular bar and pool hall, a church and a small museum.

Avenida Central ends west of the center of town. Here you can turn right and proceed 100m or so until the road forks. The branch to the left – Calle La Reforma – reaches the Cabañas Potosi after about 800m. The branch to the right – Calle del Macho – reaches the Canopy Adventure, a wild rainforest-canopy ride, and Chorro El Macho (Manly Falls) after 2.2km.

Information

The Instituto Panameño de Turismo (IPAT) had plans to construct a tourist center in El Valle in late 1998 or early 1999, but at the time of writing there wasn't so much as a tourist booth in town.

There aren't any banks in El Valle, but there is a post office and a gas station on the main road through town. A fine zoo is 1km north of downtown El Valle.

Handicrafts Market

More than anything else, El Valle is known for its Sunday handicrafts market to which Indians – mostly Guaymís, but also some Emberá and Wounaan – bring vegetables, fruit and flowers to sell and trade, and a variety of handicrafts to sell to weekend tourists (who mostly come from Panama City).

One of the most traditional items for sale here is the *batea,* a large tray carved from a local hardwood that's heavy as rock when newly cut but surprisingly light once dried. The wood is generally blond, tan or light brown, and most trays use two of these colors side by side. The trays may be polished or unpolished, depending on the maker. Most sell for less than US$10. The Guaymís use them for tossing rice and corn.

Other popular items here, also made by the local Guaymí community, are figurines, typically owls or frogs carved from soapstone and palm-size clay statuettes of Panamanians in common rural settings (such as a *campesino* in a Panama hat seated at a little table with a tiny seco bottle and a glass).

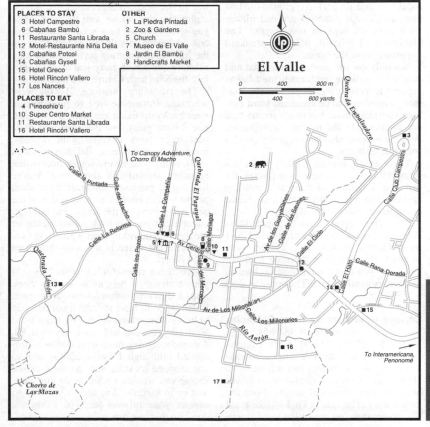

PLACES TO STAY	OTHER
3 Hotel Campestre	1 La Piedra Pintada
6 Cabañas Bambú	2 Zoo & Gardens
11 Restaurante Santa Librada	5 Church
12 Motel-Restaurante Niña Delia	7 Museo de El Valle
13 Cabañas Potosí	8 Jardin El Bambú
14 Cabañas Gysell	9 Handicrafts Market
15 Hotel Greco	
16 Hotel Rincón Vallero	
17 Los Nances	
PLACES TO EAT	
4 Pinocchio's	
10 Super Centro Market	
11 Restaurante Santa Librada	
16 Hotel Rincón Vallero	

El Valle

0   400   800 m

0   400   800 yards

To Canopy Adventure, Chorro El Macho

To Interamericana, Penonomé

Chorro de Las Mozas

Other items for sale include colorful baskets made from palms by the Emberá and Wounaan; gourds painted in brilliant colors, most often depicting animal faces or typical country scenes; *molas* painstakingly stitched by Kuna women; clay flowerpots; Panama hats; and birdcages made of sticks. Few items at the market cost more than US$20, and the posted prices are always negotiable.

The market is open 7 am to 1 pm every Sunday, rain or shine.

Zoo & Gardens
About 1km north of central El Valle is the Hacienda El Nispero (☎ 983-6142), the local zoo and its parklike grounds. Most zoos in Central America are sad places with animals kept in tiny cages. The Hacienda El Nispero offers a pleasant departure from the norm.

Not only are the zoo's grounds vast and lovely for walking, with manicured lawns separating colorful gardens, but the animals' cages tend to be spacious. Most college students share dormitory rooms that are smaller than the macaws' compound. And the toucans also have it pretty good – for caged animals.

There aren't any particularly big creatures at this zoo – no jaguars or pumas, for instance. But most of Panama's monkey species, a variety of large birds and several nocturnal animals are on display.

The zoo is open 7 am to 5 pm daily. Admission costs US$2 for adults and US$1 for children ages three to 12. The best way to reach the zoo from Avenida Central, assuming you don't want to walk 1km to get to it, is to take a taxi. The one-way cost is US$1.50.

Canopy Adventure & Chorro El Macho
The Canopy Adventure (☎ 983-6547 in El Valle; 264-5720, 612-9176 in Panama City; canopy.mit.edu) is a suspended ride that uses cables, pulleys and a harness to allow you to view a rainforest as never before – from dozens of meters above the jungle floor. The ride is kind of like a ski lift, except that you are sitting in a harness

rather than on a bench, and you are descending rather than ascending.

The ride is a little difficult to explain, because it's not really like anything else I've ever experienced. But it works this way: When you arrive, you are fitted for a harness and gloves. You and two assistants then hike through 100m of pristine jungle to a platform where you're shown exactly how the equipment works.

At the first platform you're hooked up to a cable that runs 60m or so from one enormous tree to another. The cable is attached to each tree about three-fourths of the way up its trunk – far above the ground. You ride, suspended from the cable, from one tree to the next. At the second tree there's a platform that allows you to stand while you're hooked up to a second cable, this one connected to a third tree farther down the hill. The adventure involves four long rides, two of which carry you over a waterfall, the 85m high Chorro El Macho.

The rides are thrilling. If you were whizzing from pine tree to pine tree in your backyard using the same equipment, you'd have great fun. But here you glide past huge trees covered with orchids, bromeliads and vines. Brightly colored birds, many with lovely songs, occupy the branches around and above you. You're looking at pristine rainforest from sloth height – high enough to give you a whole new perspective on the jungle, but not high enough that you can look across the top of the forest. And riding over a plunging falls not once but twice is not something you soon forget.

Are these rides for everyone? No. If you're afraid of heights or have a weak grip, I don't recommend this adventure. Riders need to have at least a normal grip to brake themselves. Also, you must be at least 10 years old and not a day over 80. Anyone weighing more than 200lbs is prohibited (although I weigh 220lbs and no one stopped me). Be sure to wear closed shoes; you wouldn't want to do this barefoot or in sandals. And unless you like to expose your private parts to strangers, don't do this in a dress.

Even if you don't want to whiz across the heights of the jungle, you should check out gorgeous Chorro El Macho, particularly if you enjoy rainforest waterfalls. There's a small bathing hole at its base; if it's hot out or if you've been hiking, I can't think of a better way to cool off than taking a dip beneath a jungle-flanked waterfall. Be sure to bring a bathing suit with you.

Admission to the falls costs US$1.50. The Canopy Adventure costs US$40 per person. It's a lot, but the money is used to preserve hundreds of hectares around the falls and to employ local residents who were previously engaged in slash-and-burn agriculture; it's money well spent. A tip is most appreciated but unnecessary. Also, if you would like to go on a guided hike, guides are available for US$10 per person for two hours.

The Canopy Adventure can arrange for you to be driven here from a Panama City hotel and back; call its Panama City numbers, listed above. Transportation, Canopy Adventure rides, a tour of El Valle, a visit to the town's museum and lunch cost US$95 per person. If you go on a Sunday, you'll be able to see El Valle's handicrafts market as well.

La Piedra Pintada

In the northwestern corner of the valley, in a neighborhood known as La Pintada, are some huge boulders extensively adorned with pre-Columbian art. The petroglyphs are Picassoesque, their subjects' features intentionally distorted. Or are they? One can't be sure where one subject ends and another begins here, unlike the subjects of the Spanish painter's works. The lines are all jumbled. Or at least they seemed so to me – and as far as I've been able to learn, no archaeologist has yet taken the time to make sense of it all.

A few subjects resemble the anthropomorphic and zoomorphic images seen in *huacas* and huaca replicas in anthropology museums around Panama, but beyond that it's a giant puzzle. If puzzles or petroglyphs interest you, take a look at these. Their complexity is intriguing.

If you have wheels, drive to the western end of Avenida Central and turn right. The road forks quickly after that; take the right branch, Calle del Macho. After 400m, take Calle la Pintada, which will be on your left. Stay on that road until it ends and then park. Generally the sight of a vehicle will attract some kids, who will be happy to lead you to La Piedra Pintada (Colored Stone) for a few dollars.

If you don't have wheels, hire a taxi in town. The ride, the wait and the return trip will likely cost you US$10. The price varies, depending on what the driver figures you are willing to pay. Be sure to agree on a price beforehand.

Museo de El Valle

On the eastern side of El Valle's conspicuous church is the easily overlooked Museum of El Valle. If you don't have time to visit the museum while you're in town, don't cancel your upcoming trip to Mykonos to return for it. The museum is in need of some interesting exhibits.

There are a few Indian artifacts inside, some information on El Valle's volcano, several examples of colonial art, a dozen shelves of contemporary Indian handicrafts (such as those found down the street every Sunday) and some really bad paintings by local artists.

The museum is open from 10 am to 2 pm daily. A donation of 25¢ is requested.

Places to Stay

Budget travelers will want to check out the four rooms for rent at the *Restaurante Santa Librada* (no phone), on Avenida Central. There's a double and a single bed in each room, plus a TV and fan. The bathrooms provide only cold water, but the guestrooms are very clean. It's an excellent value at US$18 per room per night.

The *Motel-Restaurante Niña Delia* (☎ 983-6110), on Avenida Central five blocks east of the center of things, has six rooms, two with private bathrooms. They cost US$18/23 a single/double on Friday, Saturday and Sunday nights, and US$5 less the rest of the week. The rooms have decent ventilation, but some of the beds are shot and there's no hot water. Because of the motel's location, it's a good value.

On Avenida Central near the eastern end of town are the *Cabañas Gysell* (☎ 983-6507), offering six comfortable rooms with private hot-water bathrooms for US$19 per person. These rooms are some of the better ones around town.

The *Cabañas Potosi* (☎/fax 983-6181 in El Valle; ☎ 231-3811 in Panama City), on Calle La Reforma about 1.5km west of downtown El Valle, are four cabins on park-like grounds. Each cabin has two beds and a hot-water private bathroom and rents for US$33 per night. The views of the craggy ridges ringing the valley seem especially pleasing from here. Meals are available for US$5 apiece. Tent camping, with showers and bathroom available, is an option for US$10. The owners speak English and Spanish and are quite nice.

Smack in the center of town are the *Cabañas Bambú* (☎ 983-6251), which consist of one couple-size cabin for US$33, four cabins for US$55 and one family-size cabin for US$66. Each has an old kitchenette and a cold-water-only private bathroom. The US$33 cabin is a good value, given its location.

A better place, but one located at the edge of town, is the *Hotel Greco* (☎ 998-6149 in El Valle; 261-1870 in Panama City). It has 14 cabins with good beds, clean bathrooms and nice grounds. There are eight rooms with a twin bed in each for US$23, three cabins with a twin bed and a single for US$25, and two cabins with a twin bed and two single beds for US$45. There is also one cabin for US$67 that can accommodate five people. All the cabins have cold-water-only private bathrooms. There's also a restaurant and a bar. This place is quite OK.

Los Nances (☎ 983-6126), a private residence/B&B owned by a retired US Army engineer and his wife, is high above the valley floor and has a lovely panoramic view. The couple rent four of their rooms. Prices range from US$50 to US$70 per room and include a large breakfast. An indoor swimming pool is available to guests. This place is quite popular.

The oldest hotel in town is the *Hotel Campestre* (☎ 983-6146, fax 983-6460), which has 16 rooms in its original 1920s-era two-story lodge for US$60 per room, plus 20 rooms in its recent addition for US$72 apiece. There are also three family-size cabins for US$60 per night. The newer rooms are better than the original ones, but quality varies from room to room. Ask to see several before checking in. The hotel, though old, is not without a certain amount of rustic charm, and it reminds me of a hunting lodge. There's a restaurant and a bar, and horses for rent.

The best place in town is the *Hotel Rincón Vallero* (☎ 983-6175), in a lovely residential neighborhood about 1km south of Avenida Central. Until recently, the hotel was a large family's private home. There are 15 rooms here, each unique but all equipped with private hot-water bathrooms and air-con. Most go for US$70, but there are also two junior suites (US$82) and one suite (US$105). Among the standard rooms, I recommend Nos 2 and 7. Its restaurant's meals are prepared by a chef formerly with the swank Union Club in Panama City. There are two spring-fed swimming pools out back and a small geese pond. Inside, there are cozy sitting areas beside a gently flowing creek. It's wise to reserve a room for weekend nights. The hotel rents four mountain bikes (US$10 per day), plus two 4WD vehicles (US$30 per hour, including gas) and many horses (US$5 per hour).

Places to Eat

The best place to eat in El Valle – the *Restaurante Santa Librada,* on Avenida Central – is also priced right: Lomo de arroz (roast beef with rice) sells for US$2.50, the bistec picado (spicy shredded beef) goes for US$3 and the delicious corvina is offered for US$6. Most sandwiches and breakfasts are priced under US$2. Its excellent sopa de carne (meat soup) costs US$1.

The restaurant at *Hotel Rincón Vallero* is fancier and very good, and it specializes in shrimp with salsa or pepper (US$7), beef with mushrooms and pepper steak (both US$7.50), and corvina (US$9).

Pinocchio's, a pizzeria next to Cabañas Bambú, makes tasty and cheap pizzas. An 11-inch pizza with all the toppings costs US$3.50; a 12-incher costs US$1 more. It opens at 2:30 pm and closes after midnight daily.

Entertainment
The *Jardin El Bambú,* the locals' popular watering hole, is 50m to the west of the conspicuous Super Centro market on Avenida Central. Here standard-size beers go for 50¢; the large bottles cost 85¢. There are pool tables in the back, as well as a very simple restaurant where two tacos cost only 30¢.

Getting There & Away
Buses leave Panama City for El Valle from the Terminal de Buses al Interior, on Avenida Ascañio Villalaz in the Curundu district, hourly from 7 am to 6 pm. The trip takes 2½ hours, and the one-way fare is US$3.50.

To return to the capital from El Valle, you can hop aboard any Panama City-bound bus traveling along Avenida Central. The buses' final destinations are painted on their windshields.

Getting Around
Despite El Valle's small size, taxis ply Avenida Central all day long. You can go anywhere in town for US$2.

SANTA CLARA
The small community of Santa Clara, on the coast approximately 17km southwest of the turnoff for El Valle, offers the tourist a lovely stretch of beach and several cozy places to stay. The area around Santa Clara is arid and sparsely populated, with patches of thin, dry forest. This is a great place to explore on a bicycle (the XS Memories hotel – see Places to Stay & Eat, below – rents bicycles). If you are looking for a place with very pleasing scenery where you can relax and/or go exploring, you'll find it here.

Places to Stay & Eat
There are really two Santa Clara turnoffs from the Interamericana – one is posted for the town and the other is posted for the beach (Playa Santa Clara). The first turnoff you'll see as you come from the east is the turnoff for town. If you go down this road about 1km, you'll see signs for *Cabañas Las Veraneras* and *Las Sirenas.*

Cabañas Las Veraneras (☎ 993-3313, fax 993-3016 in Santa Clara; ☎ 230-1415 in Panama City) has four two-story cabins set upon a knoll 150m from the ocean. The owners are very likable and speak some English. Each cabin has ocean views from its front porch, a loft with a thatch roof, a kitchenette with a fridge, and lots of charm. At US$62 per cabin, Las Veraneras is a very good value. There's also a fifth, larger cabin, set back from the others, that goes for US$110 per night. The owners accommodate tent campers (US$5 per person); it's a great deal. There's a beachside restaurant (the wacho soup, which contains lots of seafood, is a super value at US$2) and a bar as well.

Las Sirenas (☎ 232-5841, fax 232-5842) consists of 11 modern rooms with all the amenities, set on a lush hillside 150m from the surf. Five rooms are particularly attractive, with very tall ceilings. All have kitchenettes and dining areas; there is no restaurant on the premises. Rooms rent for US$85 apiece.

If you stay on the Interamericana, you'll soon come to the *Centro Turístico* (☎ 993-3536), a vast project that has a restaurant, a pool, a small zoo, park and dance club. There's a river that the owner insists is good for swimming, but the water didn't look clean to me. The Centro was still under construction when I saw it, but wasn't too far from completion. I wasn't very taken by what I saw – particularly the jaguars the owner kept in too-small enclosures – but it's worth a look if time permits; the finishing touches may have made a big difference.

Just north of the turnoff for Playa Santa Clara, 100m from the Interamericana, is a hotel that intrigues me. The American owners of the *XS Memories* (☎/fax 993-3096), Sheila and Dennis Parsick, bought a piece of property that once belonged to Noriega's paymaster. In the days after the US invasion, the property was looted and the grounds left in shambles. The Parsicks moved in and they completely rebuilt the place – in style. Today the property contains three fully equipped cabins, each with two double beds and a locked storage container (one has a kitchenette), renting for US$52 per cabin per night; a restaurant that serves breakfast, lunch and dinner (huge burgers cost just $2.50); and 12 water, sewer and electrical hookups for motor homes. There's an area to pitch tents (US$4 per tent per night), and there's even a sports bar that has DirecTV and a slot machine. Did I mention the iguana farm? The ducks? The swimming pool? The fruit trees? The 10- and 12-speed bikes for rent (US$3 a day)? This place, though not romantic nor oceanside like the Cabañas Las Veraneras and Las Sirenas, *is* fun.

Getting There & Away

Santa Clara is easy to get to by bus. From Panama City's bus station, you can take a bus destined for Antón, which is the first good-size town on the Interamericana west of Santa Clara, and tell the driver to drop you at Santa Clara. Or you can take a bus bound for Penonomé, which is northwest of Antón, and tell the driver to drop you in Santa Clara. Buses for both cities leave about every 30 minutes from sunrise to sunset (some buses to Penonomé leave well after dark). A one-way Antón ticket costs US$3; a one-way Penonomé ticket costs US$3.75. If you're coming from Costa Rica, catch any bus that's heading toward Panama City and ask to be dropped at Santa Clara.

Getting Around

Except late at night, there are always taxis parked beside the turnoff for Santa Clara (the town, not the beach). You can take one for US$2 to get to any of the places I've mentioned above.

RÍO HATO & FARALLÓN

About 1km past the Playa Santa Clara turnoff, you'll notice an open area where a wide, paved path stretches straight out from both sides of the Interamericana. It looks like an immense road, but there are no lines painted on it, nor are there any signs indicating that it's a road. That's because it's a runway – or rather it once was. In fact, it was a key runway used by Noriega's forces, and it has some interesting history.

During the days of the Panama Defense Forces (PDF), there was a major army base here, known as Río Hato, to which the runway belonged. There were many barracks, an armory, a clinic – all the stuff you'd expect to find at a major base. And near the end of a 3km road that runs from the Interamericana to the coast, paralleling the runway, was Noriega's vacation home, near the hamlet of Farallón.

At 1 am on December 20, 1989, the 'H-hour' of the US invasion of Panama, two F-117A Stealth fighters swooped undetected out of the night sky and dropped two 2000lb bombs near the Río Hato PDF barracks. The bombing marked the first time that the USA's most sophisticated fighter plane was used in combat.

The US secretary of defense said at the time that the sleek, black, triangular planes performed their missions flawlessly, precisely hitting their intended targets after flying all night from their base in Nevada. Later the Pentagon admitted that the pilots had confused their targets, hitting one out of sequence and badly missing the second. The planes, incidentally, cost US$106 million each.

Río Hato was also where the US Army suffered its highest concentration of casualties during the invasion, but most were not the result of combat. Moments after the bombs exploded, an 850-man contingent of Army Rangers parachuted onto the runway. However, because they jumped from an altitude of only 150m and landed on pavement, many of them sustained serious injuries. More than two dozen members of the elite force were incapacitated by broken legs, torn knee ligaments and other injuries.

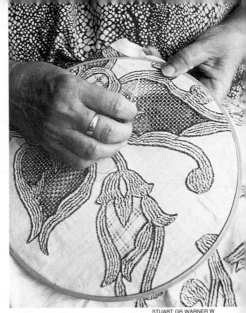

Los Santos Province

Top Left: Celebrant wearing intricate pollera hair ornaments at Las Tablas' Carnaval

Top Right: A pollera in the making, Guararé

Bottom: Making music at Carnaval, Santo Domingo

SCOTT DOGGETT

SCOTT DOGGETT

SCOTT DOGGETT

STUART GR WARNER W

Coclé Province

Top Left: Campesino with trusted friend, Chiguirí Arriba
Bottom: Costumed dancers at festival, Chiguirí Arriba

Top Right: Las Piscinas, near Aguadulce, a cool place
to take a swim on a hot day
Middle Right: Painted gourds for sale at El Valle's
famous handicrafts market

What interests me about all this is not the Army's errors in planning the jump, but that the US military acted with great humanity in its bombing. Strange as that may sound, the targets the Stealths were ordered to hit were empty fields near barracks filled with young Panamanian soldiers, not the barracks themselves. By dropping bombs near the barracks, the US military hoped to scare the soldiers into surrendering and thus avoid unnecessary bloodshed. In fact, hundreds of Panamanian soldiers at Río Hato did surrender immediately. For all the criticism leveled at the USA during and after the invasion, there were many such instances of restraint that went unmentioned.

In early 1998 there were plans to develop Río Hato, and those plans may have been realized by the time you read this. But when I visited the site, the place was profoundly creepy. The camouflaged buildings, 11 in all, stood vacant among tall weeds. Their windows were blown out, their walls pockmarked by bullets. Along one long wall was a wobbly line of holes made by heavy machine-gun fire, most likely .50-caliber rounds unleashed by a helicopter gunship. Small trees grew in rooms where PDF soldiers once carried out their orders. Scattered about were the burned hulks of cars and trucks. If ghosts exist, there must certainly be some here.

One km or so south of the scene of the fighting is the hamlet of Farallón, which is home to a small general store and simple houses containing a few hundred people. A little farther down the road, the houses become increasingly fancy and the walls around them increasingly impenetrable. Many were owned by Noriega's top officers during the 1980s. One – the abandoned two-story house on the right side of the road, pocked from top to bottom with bullet holes – was owned by the general himself.

There's an interesting little war story attached to this residence. One of the reasons US President George Bush ordered the invasion was to arrest Noriega and bring him to trial on drug-trafficking charges. A big story on the third day of the invasion was US General Maxwell Thurman's announcement that US soldiers had found more than 50kg of cocaine in Noriega's Farallón house. It wasn't until a month later, under persistent questioning from reporters, that the Pentagon admitted that the suspicious substance was actually a flourlike powder used to make tamales.

But enough war stories. The road into Farallón eventually reaches a stone gateway to a former PDF compound that is now a police station. Drive in and approach the two-story building to your left, where one or two officers are usually milling about. Tell them you'd like to visit or camp on the beach. If you don't speak Spanish, just smile, point toward the beach and say 'la playa' a couple of times. Most likely one of the officers will escort you there. They're friendly, and they have nothing better to do.

For the latter reason, an officer will probably ask to see your ID, just to make sure you're not in the country illegally. He'll likely jot your name down on a slip of paper (police in Panama occasionally do that; it's no big deal). If for some reason the officer doesn't allow you to camp on the beach, don't do it. Although there's no law against camping on beaches in Panama, antagonizing police is not a wise thing to do.

Getting There & Away
Follow the same Getting There & Away and Getting Around directions given for Santa Clara, above; just tell your taxi driver to take you to Farallón instead of a Santa Clara destination.

ANTÓN
Antón, 15km west of Farallón, is a town of 9000 people in the center of a lush valley that's sprinkled with rice fields and cattle ranches. It has little to offer the tourist in the way of attractions, except for its natural beauty, its annual patron saint festival (from January 14 to 15) and its folkloric festival (October 9). The people of Antón seemingly live for these events. There's a

bank, several restaurants and a couple of gas stations in town.

Places to Stay & Eat

There are two good-value hotels in Antón. The *Pensión Panama* (☎ 239-3163), beside the Interamericana, consists of 10 guestrooms and a restaurant (no items are over US$2.50). The rooms each have a private bathroom, ceiling fan, good bed and good cross-ventilation. The per-room price is US$10 (much more during a festival, if you're even able to get one of these rooms then).

Directly across the street is the *Hotel Rivera* (☎/fax 987-2245), which has 20 rooms with good beds (two beds per room) and private bathrooms. Rooms with ceiling fans cost US$16 per night; rooms with aircon and TVs cost US$20. There's a restaurant and bar on the premises.

Getting There & Away

Buses from Panama City to Antón leave the Terminal de Buses al Interior every 25 minutes from 6 am to 6 pm. The 126km ride takes two hours and costs US$3 each way.

PENONOMÉ

This provincial capital of 48,000 people, 144km west of Panama City and 16km northwest of Antón, is a bustling city with a history. The town was founded in 1581; by 1671 it had become so prominent that it served as the isthmus' capital after the destruction of the first Panama City (now known as Panamá La Vieja), until Nueva Panamá (New Panama) was founded a few years later.

Today the city offers the tourist three principal attractions: its annual festivals, its anthropology museum and its traditional Panama hats.

Orientation

The city straddles the Interamericana. On the eastern side of town, the highway forks around an Esso gas station. One branch, Avenida Juan Demostenes Arosemena, goes to the right, and the other, the Interamericana, goes to the left.

Avenida Juan Demostenes Arosemena is the city's main street. Along it are two banks, a tourism office, a post office and the town church. The avenue actually ends at the church, which faces the central plaza. During Carnaval, the plaza and every street for three blocks around it are packed with people.

The best place to stay, however, isn't near the plaza but at the Hotel Dos Continentes (see Places to Stay), back near the Esso station. Here you're within 100m of three restaurants, a supermarket, a laundry, a bakery, a pharmacy, a bank and the main bus stop. You're also in the area where the best Panama hats are sold.

Information

Tourist Office IPAT has an office (☎ 997-9230, fax 997-7603) on the northern side of Avenida Juan Demostenes Arosemena, two blocks southeast of the church. Some English is spoken here, but don't expect much help. For one thing, the office is closed on weekends and holidays. Its posted hours are from 8:30 am to 4:30 pm weekdays.

Money There's a Banco del Istmo on Avenida Juan Demostenes Arosemena, 50m northwest of the Esso station, and a Banco Nacional de Panamá on the same avenue, about 300m closer to downtown. Both have ATMs and are open 8:30 am to 1 pm Monday to Thursday, 8:30 am to 3 pm Friday and 9 am to noon Saturday.

Post & Communications The post office is in the Palacio Municipal on Avenida Juan Demostenes Arosemena, behind the church. It's open 8 am to 5 pm Monday to Saturday. There are pay phones throughout the city from which you can place domestic and international calls.

Laundry The Lavandería El Sol is on Avenida Juan Demostenes Arosemena, across the street from the Esso gas station. Getting one T-shirt or a pair of blue jeans washed and dried costs 50¢. Having a pair of trousers or a dress shirt cleaned and pressed costs US$1.25. Turnaround time is

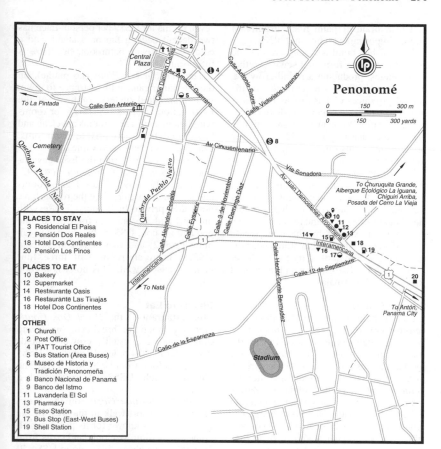

Penonomé

PLACES TO STAY
3 Residencial El Paisa
7 Pensión Dos Reales
18 Hotel Dos Continentes
20 Pensión Los Pinos

PLACES TO EAT
10 Bakery
12 Supermarket
14 Restaurante Oasis
16 Restaurante Las Tinajas
18 Hotel Dos Continentes

OTHER
1 Church
2 Post Office
4 IPAT Tourist Office
5 Bus Station (Area Buses)
6 Museo de Historia y
   Tradición Penonomeña
8 Banco Nacional de Panamá
9 Banco del Istmo
11 Lavandería El Sol
13 Pharmacy
15 Esso Station
17 Bus Stop (East-West Buses)
19 Shell Station

usually three hours. It's open 8 am to 6 pm Monday to Saturday.

Museo de Historia y Tradición Penonomeña

The Penonomé Museum of History and Tradition (☎ 997-8494) is on Calle San Antonio, two blocks south of the central plaza. The museum, which consists of four restored homes, displays some of the finds from Sitio Conte, an excavation site near Natá where Coclé Province yielded much archaeological treasure.

But the museum also displays folkloric masks of the region and colonial religious art. The exhibits range from 10,000 BC to the present and are displayed in chronological order.

The museum is open 9 am to 12:30 pm and 1:30 to 4 pm Tuesday to Saturday and 9:30 am to 1:30 pm Sunday. Admission costs 50¢.

Panama Hats

Penonomé is known throughout Panama as the place to buy the hats that bear the country's name. Unlike the better-known panamas from Ecuador, which are woven from crown to brim in one piece, this kind is made by a braiding process, using a half-inch braid of palm fiber, usually of alternating or mixed white and black.

The finished braid is wound around and around a wooden form and sewn together at the edges, producing a round-crowned, black-striped hat. It's as common in the central provinces of Panama as the wide-brimmed sombrero is in rural Mexico. The highest-quality Penonomé hats are so tightly put together that they can hold water. The price of these hats ranges from US$10 up to US$150.

There's no one place to buy these hats in Penonomé. They are made in outlying towns, such as Ocú, and brought to the city for sale. Many are sold by hat vendors standing outside stores and restaurants near the Esso gas station by the entrance to town. They are also sold in stores near the central plaza. For starters, try the Shell gas station near the Esso station and in front of Restaurante Las Tinajas.

Special Events
Carnaval, held during the four days preceding Ash Wednesday, is a huge happening in Penonomé. In addition to the traditional festivities (the dancing, the masks, the costumes, the queen's coronation and so on), here floats are literally *floated* – down a tributary of the Río Zaratí.

Less popular but still a big crowd pleaser is Penonomé's patron saint festival, generally held from December 8 to 9 (if possible, verify these dates with IPAT, as they are subject to change). Following a special Mass, the city's Catholics carry a statue of a saint through the city's streets. The Mass and procession seem incidental to the celebration that takes place outside the church for two days.

Places to Stay
Three blocks from the central plaza is the *Pensión Dos Reales* (no phone). Features: worn beds; thin, partitioned plywood walls; one exposed light bulb. There is one shower and one toilet for 18 rooms. But the price – US$6 per room – is excellent.

The *Residencial El Paisa* (☎ 997-9242), a half-block from the central plaza, has

seven rooms for US$9 per person. Each has two decent beds, a fan on a stand, and a cold-water private bathroom, but there is little ventilation.

The *Pensión Los Pinos* (no phone), on the Interamericana at the entrance to town, several hundred meters southeast of the Esso station, charges US$13/16 for rooms with fan/air-con. These rooms are clean and have good beds and private bathrooms. This place is a very good value.

Across the street from the Esso gas station, the *Hotel Dos Continentes* (☎ 997-9326, fax 997-9390) has 40 guestrooms and a popular cafeteria. All the rooms have hot-water private bathrooms. Those with one bed and fan only go for US$18; one bed and air-con, US$25; two beds and fan only, US$22; and two beds and air-con, US$29. There are rooms with three, four or five beds as well. This hotel is a good value.

Places to Eat
The restaurant at the *Hotel Dos Continentes* is open for breakfast, lunch and dinner, and it is usually crowded. Sandwiches cost US$4 or less, steaks cost US$5 or less, seafood from US$5 to US$12. The club sandwich (US$3.50) arrives with a fried egg in it.

The *Restaurante Oasis,* on the Interamericana a short walk to the west of the Esso station, is known for its pizza, which comes in medium size only and costs from US$2.75 for a cheese pizza up to US$4.50 for a pizza topped with shrimp. Its sancocho (chicken soup, the national dish) is delicious and cheap (US$1.75).

Opposite the Oasis is the *Restaurante Las Tinajas,* which offers typical Panamanian food buffet-style. Few items cost over US$2. For US$2.75, for example, you get bistec picado (spicy shredded beef) with rice, beans and sweet plantains. For US$3.75, you can really make a pig out of yourself.

Getting There & Away
Buses from Panama City to Penonomé leave the Terminal de Buses al Interior

every 20 minutes from 4:50 am to 9 pm. The 144km ride takes 2½ hours and costs US$3.75 each way.

Buses traveling to and from Penonomé via the Interamericana use a small parking lot opposite the Hotel Dos Continentes as a passenger pick-up and drop-off point. Area buses, such as those to Churuquita Grande, use a station two blocks southeast of the central plaza.

Getting Around

Due to its size and importance, Penonomé has no shortage of taxis. The best place to hail one is by the Esso gas station, near the entrance to town. They can also be seen in numbers near the central plaza. The fare for any destination in town is never more than US$3, and usually it's half that.

LA PINTADA

This small foothill town, which boasts an artisans' market and a cigar factory, is 12km northwest of downtown Penonomé. While I wouldn't recommend either the market or the factory to the general public, I think anyone with a real hankering for handicrafts or a love of cigars would enjoy a visit to La Pintada.

The **Mercado de Artesanias La Pintada** specializes in Penonomé-style Panama hats. The material used in panamas occasionally varies from one town to the next. Here the headgear is made of hat palm and *pitia,* which is related to cactus. There are several pitia plants growing in front of the market, so you can see what they look like.

Other items of particular interest at this store are dolls wearing folkloric costumes and seco bottle covers made from hat palm and pitia. No machines are used in making the dolls' dresses, which sell for around US$15. The bottle covers go for US$5.

There are many other items for sale as well. Take a look at the brooms. These are of the classic variety, such as you might find in a witch's closet. But instead of a clump of sticks at the business end, the maker chose to use slices of palm. I'm told the brooms last for decades. (The people

who told me this are also the people selling the brooms, of course.)

The market is easy to find. As you drive through La Pintada on the main road from Penonomé, you'll come to a very large soccer field on the left side of the road. The market is on the far side of this field.

To get to the **Panabanos Cigar Factory** (☎ 983-0271/0272) from the artisans' market, just drive southeast from the market, straight toward Penonomé. You'll come to Cafe Coclé, on your right; take the descending road just beyond it. Follow this paved road about 1km until you see a barn made entirely of thatch. You've arrived!

The factory's owner, Miriam Padilla, began growing tobacco in La Pintada with three Cubans in 1982. They separated in 1987, when the Cubans went to Honduras to open a cigar factory. Left on her own, Miriam sent samples of her tobacco to tourists and others she'd met in Panama over the years, seeking investors for a factory. One recipient, Julio Chen of Chitré, took the plunge, and the two have been partners ever since.

Today Miriam and Julio employ 34 workers who make a total of 2000 cigars a day. The employees work at rows of desks in a concrete-sided, aluminum-roofed, one-story building the size of a small home, which is the pride of the neighborhood. Outside is the thatch barn, where the tobacco leaves are dried. The day I visited, a shipment of seeds from Cuba had just arrived and was being piled up beside the barn.

In the factory, the workers meticulously roll cigars and put them in form boxes that are placed in a press and squeezed. The press gives the cigars a uniform shape and packs the tobacco just enough to give the smoke that passes through it an even drag. The cigars are packaged in lovely wooden boxes and then shipped to the USA, Holland, France, Australia and the Canary Islands.

A box of 25 naturally flavored cigars costs US$90 in Panama, considerably more outside the country. Panabanos' cigars also come flavored – with a hint of vanilla, whiskey, bitter cedar or Spanish cedar. Premium cigars, which are made from the finest leaves, are available here; a box of 25 will cost you US$300.

Miriam speaks English, and cigars are clearly much more than business to her. If Miriam isn't here when you arrive, ask to speak with her son, Braulio Zurita, who likewise speaks English and knows a great deal about cigars.

ALBERGUE ECOLÓGICO LA IGUANA

This *albergue ecológico* (ecological shelter; ☎ 983-8056), 14km northeast of Penonomé, consists of a lodge, a restaurant and a small private zoo (supposedly illegal in Panama) set on 75 hectares that also contain a modest waterfall and various tree-production projects. There's also a substantial patch of forest on the property that contains iguanas, red-nape tamarins and even a few caimans. Among the 75 species of bird that have been identified here are the white-winged dove (known only in Herrera and Coclé Provinces) and the rare black-and-white hawk-eagle.

The emphasis here is on outdoor recreation. Bicycles and horses are available for rent, and there's a volleyball court and swimming pools for adults and children, but mostly visitors are encouraged to wander the trails through the woods and get in touch with nature. There's an attractive restaurant serving good food at reasonable prices (ceviche for US$3, corvina for US$7, and steak stuffed with shrimp for US$12).

The guestrooms were nearing completion at the time I visited and looked very smartly designed, with a private hot-water bathroom and a cozy loft in each. Room rates are US$55. Camping is available for US$10 per tent.

I'd be more excited about this retreat if the owner, a friendly fellow who speaks English and Spanish, didn't keep many birds and about a dozen mammals in small cages. But the owner insisted that spacious compounds were being constructed and that others were planned, and indeed some large pens were in the works. (See the Endangered Species section in the Facts about Panama chapter for advice on what to do if you see caged animals at Panamanian hotels or businesses.)

Getting There & Away

To reach the Albergue Ecológico La Iguana from the center of Penonomé, take the well-marked turnoff for Churuquita Grande, several hundred meters northwest of the Hotel Dos Continentes (see the Penonomé map). Proceed 13km and begin looking for a sign announcing the retreat on the right side of the road. If you take a taxi from Penonomé, the ride will cost US$10 each way (less if you haggle).

You can also go to Penonomé's area bus station, two blocks southeast of the central plaza, and look for a bus with 'Churuquita Grande' or 'Chiguiri Arriba' on its windshield. Buses to both locations pass by the ecological shelter. Be sure to tell the driver to stop at the shelter's entrance, or he won't. The one-way fare is US$1. The buses run every 30 minutes during daylight hours only. To return to Penonomé, flag down any southbound bus.

POSADA DEL CERRO LA VIEJA

On a paved road in the hilly community of Chiguiri Arriba, 29km to the northeast of Penonomé, is the Posada del Cerro La Vieja (Inn of the Old Mountain; ☎ 983-8088 in Chiguiri Arriba; ☎ 223-4553, fax 264-4960 in Panama City). The inn is atop a summit with sweeping views of forested valleys and imposing peaks intermittently shrouded by clouds. The peaks are reminiscent of the karst formations of Guilin, China.

The main structure, in a gardenlike setting, consists of a lodge with four units: Two have a double and a single bed with a private bathroom, and the other two have two bathrooms and three bedrooms with two beds in each. Other rooms were being added. There is also a restaurant and a bar with panoramic views.

A single log cabin, 50m from the lodge and down many steps, is ringed by gardens and fish-filled ponds and is divided into two separate living quarters. There were bats living in these rooms when I visited, and I found the rooms a bit dark, not half as nice as the rooms in the lodge.

Also on the grounds are a creek-fed swimming pool and an outdoor seating area set aside for people who want to cover themselves in clay (the clay is brought from Chitré and medicinal plants and herbs are added to it). The clay resembles milk chocolate. Guests apply the clay to themselves amid trees and bird calls. Deer stroll the area, nibbling at the ornamental plants. Most people wear the mud for 30 minutes before rinsing.

Prices are per-person and are packaged. For example, a package including one night, four meals, clay treatment and a tour to a waterfall costs US$53. Call or fax the retreat for a current list of packages.

Getting There & Away

To get to Posada del Cerro La Vieja from central Penonomé, take the well-marked turnoff for Churuquita Grande, several hundred meters northwest of the Hotel Dos Continentes (see the Penonomé map). Proceed past Churuquita Grande and follow the signs to Chiguiri Arriba and the inn.

A taxi ride from Penonomé costs US$20 (less if you haggle). Alternately, go to Penonomé's area bus station and look for a bus with 'Chiguiri Arriba' on its windshield. Buses depart at 6, 10 and 11:30 am; noon; and 1, 3 and 5 pm. The one-way fare is US$1.50; the ride takes one hour.

PARQUE NACIONAL EL COPÉ

The turnoff for this nearly inaccessible national park is on the Interamericana, 15km west of Penonomé. From the turnoff, it's another 36km to the park's entrance. The road, paved for the first 28km, winds through rolling countryside dotted with farms and small cattle ranches. The paved road ends at the small town of El Copé. The remaining 8km of the drive to the park are on a dirt road that's so bad that a 4WD vehicle with a very strong motor, a winch and excellent tires is needed. There is no public transportation to the park; visitors must drive.

Partly because the road is so horrible, the forests here are among the most beautiful in Panama and offer superb bird watching. The park starts in montane forest on the Pacific side of the Continental Divide and continues onto the Caribbean side, where the forest is noticeably more humid. Among the rare birds that have been recorded here are the golden-olive woodpecker, red-fronted parrotlet, immaculate antbird, white-throated shrike-tanager and red-headed barbet.

There's an Instituto Nacional de Recursos Naturales Renovables (INRENARE) office in the town of El Copé. It's on a bluff to your left as you enter town. The office is open 8 am to 4 pm weekdays; it is closed weekends. Here you can get a permit (US$3) to enter the park, but you'd be wise to pick it up elsewhere, as this office is often closed during its posted working hours.

There is a *ranger station* in the park that you can stay at if room is available (it usually is, as there are five beds for visitors and few people make it up here). There's no cost to stay at the station, but a tip of US$5 or US$10 is most appreciated.

PARQUE ARQUEOLÓGICO DEL CAÑO

This park is one of only two archaeological sites in the country that are open to the public (the other is Barriles, in Chiriquí Province). It has a museum that contains a few objects that were found nearby. There's an excavation pit in the park as well, which is said to contain the burial site of an Indian chief, but it was in shambles when I visited. According to the gatekeeper, the thatch roof protecting the pit had collapsed a few months earlier and there was no money to construct another. The sacred burial site was calf-deep in rainwater and it was impossible to decipher anything.

The park is open from 9 am to noon and 12:30 to 4 pm Tuesday to Saturday and 9 am to 1 pm Sunday. Admission costs US$1/25¢ adults/children.

The turnoff for the town of El Caño is on the Interamericana, about 8km north of Natá. The park is another 3km from the turnoff. El Caño is not served by bus, but you can take a taxi here from Natá.

NATÁ

In 1515 an Indian chief named Tataracherubi, whose territory covered much of what would later become northern Coclé Province, informed the Spanish conquistadors Alonso Perez de la Rua and Gonzalo de Badajoz of the wealth of his neighbor to the southwest, a chief named Natá. Natá had much gold, but he had few fighting men.

Naturally, the conquistadors went after Natá's gold. Perez and his 30 men arrived first; Badajoz and his 130 men were not far behind. Perhaps a bit overanxious, Perez and his party soon found themselves amid a large Indian settlement. Retreat was impossible, but Perez grabbed the Indian chief and threatened to kill him, and thus forced Natá to tell his warriors to back off.

Then Badajoz and his well-armed soldiers showed up, and Natá was forced to surrender a large quantity of gold. The Christians remained for two months in the village named after the chief before they headed south and plundered more villages. Two years later, the Spaniards, led by Gaspar de Espinosa, returned to Natá and established one of the earliest European settlements on the isthmus.

The Indians, meanwhile, were enslaved. As an incentive to settle in Natá, the ruthless Spanish governor Pedro Arias de Ávila divided the village and its Indians among 60 soldiers who agreed to start a pueblo here.

Today Natá is a sleepy town of 5000 people, most of whom work at the area's sugar refineries, at the salt factory in Aguadulce or in the fields around town. Its church, which was completed in 1522 and is one of the oldest in the country, is its main tourist attraction. There are also a number of well-preserved colonial houses in town.

Iglesia de Natá

The church, which has remained close to its original state all these years, is well worth a visit. It has a fine colonial façade and a remarkable interior. If you look closely at the altar of the Virgin, you'll notice sculpted fruit and leaves and feathered serpents on its two columns – clearly the influence of its Indian artisan.

Notice also the Holy Trinity painting to the right of the altar of the Virgin. The painting was made in 1758 by the Ecuadorian artist José Samaniego. For many years the painting was kept from public view because it represents the Trinity as three people who all look like Christ, which is not in conformity with Church canon.

Special Events

Natá holds its Fiesta de Tomate (Tomato Festival) in mid-April. Dates of the three-day agricultural fair vary each year; check with IPAT in Panama City.

Places to Stay & Eat

There's one place to stay in Natá, the *Pensión David* (☎ 993-5573, fax 993-5478), which is on the main road that leads into town from the Interamericana. Ten of its 12 rooms have air-con; rates are US$16 to US$26. The guesthouse is a good value and often full, so you might want to call ahead. Two doors up, on the Interamericana, the *Café Vega* serves pretty good chow mein (US$3) and decent rice with shrimp (also US$3).

Getting There & Away

Natá can be reached by all the buses that use the stretch of the Interamericana near it, except for the few nonstop buses that cruise between Panama City and Paso Canoas and Panama City and Chiriquí Grande. Tell the driver to drop you at Natá, and he'll let you off beside the Café Vega. Often there's a taxi parked in front of the café. If not, you'll be able to hail one within 30 minutes.

AGUADULCE

Aguadulce's name is a contraction of *agua* and *dulce* (meaning 'sweet water'), and it is said that this bustling city of 15,000 was named by Spaniards who were pleased to come across a freshwater well amid the arid landscape.

Today Aguadulce is known for its sugar, its jumbo shrimp and its salt; there are salt flats south of downtown, and there's a sizable saltworks. The flats provide excellent bird-watching opportunities – you can see marsh and shore birds, particularly the roseate spoonbill and wood stork.

Just outside town are fields and fields of sugar cane. From mid-January to mid-March of each year, the cane is cut and then refined at several large refineries in

the area. One of these mills, the Ingenio de Azúcar Santa Rosa (Santa Rosa Sugar Refinery) offers tours – a must-do if you're in the area during the grinding season. (See details on the refinery at the end of this chapter.)

The sugar and salt industries date back several centuries, and the city's residents, many of whom make their living from these products, celebrate their history with the Museo de la Sal y Azúcar (Museum of Salt and Sugar). The museum, in the heart of the city, is definitely worth a look.

Generally a place in Latin America that acquires a reputation for its crustaceans

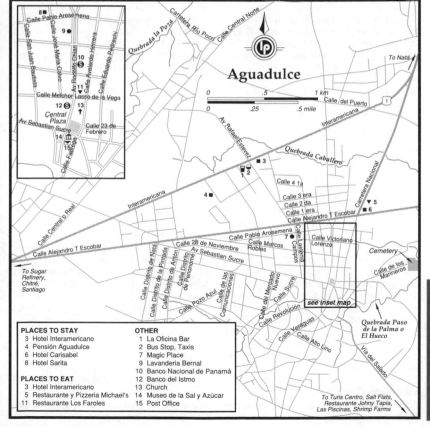

PLACES TO STAY
3 Hotel Interamericano
4 Pensión Aguadulce
6 Hotel Carisabel
8 Hotel Sarita

PLACES TO EAT
3 Hotel Interamericano
5 Restaurante y Pizzeria Michael's
11 Restaurante Los Faroles

OTHER
1 La Oficina Bar
2 Bus Stop, Taxis
7 Magic Place
9 Lavandería Bernal
10 Banco Nacional de Panamá
12 Banco del Istmo
13 Church
14 Museo de la Sal y Azúcar
15 Post Office

COCLÉ PROVINCE

quickly overharvests them and then has none to offer. The Archipiélago de San Blás, for example, was until recently a mecca for lobster aficionados; today the Kuna Indians who inhabit the islands have depleted their stock. But in Aguadulce, which for years has been nationally famous for its jumbo shrimp, restaurants continue to serve them in generous portions.

One of the best places to enjoy shrimp as well as conch is a beachside diner beyond the salt flats called Restaurante Johny Tapia. If the tide's out, I recommend that you feast here and then take a dip in one of three nearby elevated pools. There's nothing fancy about either Johny Tapia or the pools, but they do make for pleasant memories.

There is no tourism office in town, but there are a couple of banks, a post office, a laundry, several hotels and plenty of restaurants. And if you arrive during Carnaval, there's merrymaking everywhere.

Orientation
Aguadulce is in hot, dry country, 10km south of Natá, 185km west of Panama City and 251km east of David. Like so many cities and towns in Panama, Aguadulce is beside the Interamericana. Its downtown, however, is a kilometer or two from the highway.

The main road into town from the Interamericana is Avenida Rafael Estevez. La Oficina Bar is on one side of the intersection of the highway and the avenue; the Hotel Interamericano is on the other side. There are always taxis near La Oficina, and the parking lot next to the bar is also the town's principal bus stop.

To get to Aguadulce's central plaza, drive south on Avenida Rafael Estevez several blocks until it ends at its intersection with Calle Alejandro T Escobar. Turn left here, onto Calle Alejandro T Escobar, drive three and a half blocks to Avenida Rodolfo Chiari and then turn right. The central plaza and church will appear on your left, four blocks later.

Information
Money There are two banks in town, the Banco Nacional de Panamá and the Banco del Istmo. Both are on Avenida Rodolfo Chiari near the central plaza, and both are open from 8:30 am to 1:30 pm Monday to Thursday, 8:30 am to 3 pm on Friday and 9 am to noon on Saturday. Both have outside ATMs.

Post & Communications The post office is near the central plaza, just around the corner from the Museo de la Sal y Azúcar. It's open 8:30 am to 4:30 pm Monday to Saturday. (At the time of writing, there was some talk about moving the post office so that the museum could expand. If the post office has been relocated by the time you read this, the people at the museum should be able to direct you to its new location.)

There are many pay phones in town, and you can place domestic and international calls from any of them. It's much cheaper to place an international call from a pay phone than it is from a hotel.

Laundry At Lavanderia Bernal, on Avenida Rodolfo Chiari three blocks north of the central plaza, you can drop off your clothes to be washed and tumble-dried for US$3 per load. The turnaround time is usually four hours.

Museo de la Sal y Azúcar
This rather unusual museum faces the central plaza, on the side opposite the church. As its name suggests, the museum contains exhibits that document the history of the Aguadulce area's salt and sugar industries. However, the museum also contains artifacts from the Colombian civil war (1899-1903), in which many Panamanians fought. These include guns, uniforms and swords.

Due to its proximity to the Sitio Conte and El Caño archaeological sites, the museum also contains a number of pre-Columbian artifacts. But the majority of exhibits tell how the salt flats were developed, detail the role Aguadulce's salt and sugar have played in Panamanian life, and so on. The museum is open 8 am to 4 pm Tuesday to Sunday. Admission costs US$1/50¢ adults/children.

Turis Centro

This strange place is 4km from downtown Aguadulce, on the road to Restaurante Johny Tapia. Here, in the middle of salt flats and scrub brush, someone decided what was needed was a roller rink with jumps (skates rent for US$1 per day), a BMX track for cross-up bikes (bikes rent for US$2 per hour), paddleboats and kayaks on a small pond, a volleyball court and a restaurant. The place had no appeal for me, but I found myself thinking it might appeal to people in their teens or early 20s. There are also a couple of Ping-Pong and pool tables.

If this place sounds OK to you, the cost to check it out is nothing. A bus shuttles patrons at no cost between Turis Centro and the Restaurante Los Faroles, opposite the church in downtown Aguadulce. The bus leaves at the tourist's request, so there's not a lot of standing around at either end.

Las Piscinas

Las Piscinas (Pools) are 9.5km from downtown Aguadulce, just beyond the salt flats and 250m past Restaurante Johny Tapia. They consist of three crudely built 1.5m high swimming pools that were constructed in tideland about 150m from the high-water mark. If the tide is out, you can walk over the muddy sand that separates the pools from the shore and take a dip in them. The water's murky (it's saltwater, after all), but it's not polluted, as the pools are nearly 10km from town. And it is very refreshing on a hot day, which is every day in Aguadulce. The view from the pools is mostly one of a big, beautiful sky, with distant foothills on one side and the ocean spreading out before you.

The tideland is quite expansive. When the tide is out, you can walk 2km before reaching the ocean. But be careful; once the tide turns, it rises rather quickly. If you've walked a kilometer or so beyond the pools and you're admiring the shore birds out there and notice the tide rising, head inland immediately. How high does the water rise? Sea lions have been seen

swimming near the pools when the tide's in. And if you decide to take some soft drinks out to the pools, please think about those sea lions and take all your litter along when you leave.

The best way to get to the pools is by taxi. Tell the driver to take you to Restaurante Johny Tapia; he'll know the restaurant, although he may know the pools by a name other than Las Piscinas. From Johny Tapia, walk south (away from town). On the left side of the road are mangroves, beginning a little way from the restaurant. After you've walked about 100m, you'll see a clearing in the mangroves perhaps 50m wide, and through the clearing you'll be able to spot the pools (if the tide is out). Don't let the view from the road fool you; the pools are lovely in a funky way. Initially there's no path connecting the road to the pools – there's just muddy sand, but it's not at all deep. After 50m you'll reach some concrete steps that will lead you to the pools.

Special Events

Aguadulce parties hearty three times a year: during Carnaval, held the four days before Ash Wednesday; during its patron saint festival, on July 25; and in honor of the city's founding, on October 18, 19 and 20. The Carnaval festivities are predictably lively. But the founding-day festivities are also great fun. Although the city was officially founded on October 19, the celebration begins at least a day in advance and lasts at least a day afterward. A series of parades, a streetful of floats, Miss Aguadulce ceremonies, and lots of music, dancing and drinking characterize the event.

Places to Stay

Hotel Sarita (☎ 997-4437), on the corner of Calles José Maria Calvo and Pablo Arosemena, has 20 rooms with air-con, hot-water private bathrooms and TVs for US$16/23 single/double, and eight rooms with fans only, cold-water private bathrooms and no TVs for US$10/12. All the rooms are clean. This is a very good value.

The *Hotel Interamericano* (☎ 997-4363, fax 997-4975), on the Interamericana near Avenida Rafael Estevez, is a very good value. All 30 rooms have TVs and hot-water private bathrooms. There's also a swimming pool, a restaurant and a popular bar on the premises. The 15 rooms with air-con cost US$26 apiece; the 15 rooms with fans only cost US$20.

Near the downtown area is the *Hotel Carisabel* (☎ 997-3800, fax 997-3802), on the corner of Calle Alejandro T Escobar and Carretera Nacional. This newer place offers 15 rooms, all with air-con, TVs and hot-water private bathrooms. Nine rooms have double beds; six have single beds. The rates are US$25/29/35 for one/two/three people. There's a pool, a bar and a restaurant as well.

Places to Eat

At the *Restaurante y Pizzeria Michael's,* beside the Hotel Carisabel, there are five ceviches to choose among (US$3 or less). Other offerings at this popular restaurant include chicken and beef dishes (US$3.75 to US$6), seafood (US$3.75 to US$9.50) and pizzas (from US$1.50 for a small cheese to US$9 for a large shrimp).

The *Restaurante Los Faroles,* opposite the church in downtown Aguadulce, offers many items but specializes in pizza. Its Hawaiian pizza has raisins and maraschino cherries in addition to the regular pineapple and ham toppings. Prices range from US$1.50 for a small cheese to US$9.50 for a large shrimp.

The restaurant at the *Hotel Interamericano* offers jumbo shrimp prepared four ways, each for US$8. The restaurant is known for its lunches, especially the ejecutivo (executive lunch; US$2.50). It includes soup, salad, rice, beans, beef and fried plantains.

Just past the salt flats, 9km from downtown Aguadulce, is a basic place named for its ebullient owner-waiter: *Restaurante Johny Tapia.* The black conch ceviche here is superb, the portions and quality of the fish dishes excellent. Typical prices at this restaurant that won my heart include: ceviche, US$1.50; shrimp salad, US$3; fish, US$3; and conch salad, US$3.50.

Entertainment

The hot dance club in town is the *Magic Place,* close to the intersection of Calles Lastenia Campos and Pablo Arosemena. There's live music and an open bar on Thursday, Friday and Saturday nights. Admission is free for women, but men pay as much as US$10 at the door; the price varies with the quality and popularity of the band. The club generally doesn't start hopping before 10 or 11 pm. Closing time is usually around 4 am.

Two km west of Pensión Aguadulce (a place on the Interamericana on the edge of town that's favored by prostitutes and their johns) is the *Mocambo,* possibly the most famous brothel on the international highway between North America and the Darién Gap. This is STD Central. Any guy that would do anything intimate with the prostitutes working here would have to have something wrong with his brain. However, it certainly is an interesting place to have a drink, and there's no cover charge.

Getting There & Away

Buses leave Panama City's main bus station for Aguadulce every 1½ hours from 6 am to 6 pm. The trip takes 4½ hours and costs US$6.50 each way. Buses to Panama City leave about every 45 minutes.

The buses arrive and depart from the small parking lot beside La Oficina Bar, on the Interamericana. A taxi from La Oficina Bar into town costs US$1. Just flag one down if there isn't one parked nearby.

Getting Around

Taxis are the best way to get from one part of Aguadulce to another if you don't feel like walking. Fares rarely exceed US$2, although you can expect to pay a little more at night. Always agree on a price before entering a taxi.

INGENIO DE AZÚCAR SANTA ROSA

The Santa Rosa Sugar Refinery, 15km west of Aguadulce and near the Interamericana, is a must-see if you're in the area when the factory is in operation. That would be from mid-January to mid-March – the grinding season. During these two months, the refinery grinds 6500 tons of sugar cane per day, and the sights at the factory are ones you won't forget. The facility makes for some interesting sightseeing even if you arrive out of season.

In the USA the land is flat and sugar cane can be mechanically harvested, but here the land is hilly and rockier, and thus the tall cane must be harvested by hand. Four thousand people are hired to help with harvesting and production, and they bring the cane in as fast as they can, 24 hours a day, six days a week (the mill is quiet on Monday because the workers are religious and won't cut cane on Sunday). Most of the cane is harvested on company land, but the mill buys about 3% of its cane from campesinos who bring it in on carts pulled by tractors and oxen.

I won't detail the refining process, but it may interest you to know that 135kg of cane enter the mill each second via a huge conveyer belt that's continually fed from trucks coming in from the fields. All this cane is sent through grinders that resemble a stack of studded roller pins – except that each one weighs 20 tons and is about the size of a Buick. They spin quickly, and the cane that passes through them is crushed flat. Things happen really fast and furious here.

Occasionally the machine chokes. A 10-second choke results in a pileup of 1350kg of cane, and jackhammers are required to remove the clog. To give you an idea of the grinders' power: When a choke starts to occur, railroad ties are pushed into the grinders. In the fraction of a second it takes

for the ties to pass through, they are chewed up as if they were breadsticks, but even as they're pulverized, they act as battering rams, punching bunched-up cane through the machines.

Also on the property is a replica of the original house of the mill's first owner, built in 1911. This museum is very nicely done and contains many exhibits; all its furniture and other articles are originals.

Tours are available 7 am to 4 pm weekdays and 7 am to noon on Saturday. The refinery would like at least 24 hours' notice; call Gonzalo Peréz or Christopher Stroud (☎ 987-8101/8102) for a tour. Both men speak English and Spanish.

Getting There & Away

If you're driving from Aguadulce, the turnoff for the mill will be on the right side of the Interamericana. The mill's turnoff is marked by a sign, and there's an Esso station opposite the turnoff (the station is much easier to see than the sign). Take the road half a kilometer, and you'll come to a white guard station with a tiny chapel in front of it. Give your name to the guard and follow instructions.

If you don't have wheels, you can take a taxi from Aguadulce (which could cost US$25 or more if the driver waits for you and takes you back to town), or you can catch any bus headed in the direction of the refinery and tell the driver to drop you at the Ingenio de Azúcar Santa Rosa. Be forewarned that the walk from the guard station to the mill is more than 1km. If there is more than one of you in your party, you're better off taking a taxi.

Colón Province

The history of Colón Province is one of riches – *vast* riches. In the colonial era, gold and silver pilfered from Indians in Panama and Peru were stored at the Caribbean coastal towns of Nombre de Dios and Portobelo, in the northeastern portion of the province, until ships arrived to take the bullion to Spain. For decades these were the wealthiest towns on earth, veritable treasure troves that attracted scores of pirates.

The earliest known history of the province was recorded by Panama's first Spanish settlers. It was here in 1510 that Diego de Nicuesa, the governor of a vast region that included present-day Panama, fled after a failed attempt to settle the Río Belén in what is now Veraguas Province. Leading a small fleet of sick and starving men, Nicuesa looked upon the seemingly fruitful shore near the northernmost point of the isthmus and exclaimed, *'¡Paremos aqui, en nombre de Dios!'* ('Let us stop here, in the name of God!').

His followers, sensing a lucky augury in his words, decided to call the place Nombre de Dios even before they had landed. But Nombre de Dios' humidity and apparent absence of food took a heavy toll on the settlers. They abandoned the site in just a couple of months. It wasn't resettled until 1519 – nine years later.

Supplies from Spain were unloaded at the new Nombre de Dios and sent across the isthmus to the city of Panamá. Moving in the opposite direction were gold and silver taken from Indians on the isthmus and in Peru. Both supplies and stolen bullion traveled along the Sendero Las Cruces (Las Cruces Trail), which consisted of a land route from Panamá to the village of Venta de Cruces and a river route on the Río Chagres from Venta de Cruces to the Caribbean. At the river's mouth, cargo was placed in ships and taken by sea to Nombre de Dios. Eventually a land-only route – the Camino Real (King's Highway) – was also used to transport supplies and ore.

During the 200 years in which Nombre de Dios and, later, Portobelo acted as temporary warehouses for pilfered riches, the ports came under repeated attack from English, French, Dutch and Welsh pirates. Many attacks were successful, as were the assaults on galleons that tried to reach Spain after taking on a king's treasure.

The Spaniards built forts to protect their fortunes, but the forts weren't enough. In 1572 the English privateer Francis Drake easily entered Nombre de Dios – 'the treasure house of the world,' as he called it – and was deciding which riches to plunder when a wound forced his retreat. Drake returned to Nombre de Dios in 1596, and this time his men not only emptied the treasure house but also torched the town.

HIGHLIGHTS

- Historic Portobelo, home to the well-preserved ruins of several colonial forts

- Gatún Locks, the largest of the Panama Canal's three sets of locks

- Fuerte San Lorenzo, built of cut coral and still displaying its old cannons

- Isla Grande, a popular weekend getaway ringed by fine snorkeling and dive sites

- Gatún Dam, once the world's largest earthen dam and still an impressive sight

In 1671 the Welsh buccaneer Sir Henry Morgan took Fuerte San Lorenzo, at the mouth of the Río Chagres, then crossed the isthmus and sacked Panamá. In 1739 Portobelo, which was plundered twice during the 17th century, was destroyed by British Admiral Edward Vernon. After this blow, Spain abandoned the Panama crossing in favor of sailing around Cape Horn to the southern coast of the isthmus.

From then until the mid-19th century, the Caribbean coast of Panama was quiet. That changed in 1848 with the California gold rush, when thousands of people traveled from the East Coast of the USA to the West Coast via Panama. The Panama Railroad was built between 1850 and 1855 to profit from these travelers.

In 1881 a French company began work on a sea-level canal across the isthmus, but it gave up the effort eight years later, after the monetary costs had proved too great and yellow fever and malaria had killed 22,000 workers. Twenty-five years later, the US effort to build a lock-and-lake canal was successful, and the sleepy backwater town of Colón, at the Caribbean terminus of the canal, was transformed into a vibrant provincial capital.

Colón received another big boost in 1948, when a free-trade zone was created within its borders. Today the Zona Libre (Free Zone – as in free of import and export taxes) is the largest free-trade zone in the Americas. It links producers in North America, the Far East and Europe with the Latin American market. As of 1998, 1650 companies and 21 banks were conducting business in the high-walled, 482-hectare compound in the southeastern corner of town, but not much wealth crosses the walls into the city itself.

And the fortified marketplaces of yesteryear in Portobelo, 43km to the northeast? Several still exist, their rusting cannons facing the Bahía de Portobelo as if still on duty. Where Spanish soldiers once stood guard beside the cannons, today little boys cast fishing lines. Where Spanish captains once prayed their galleons would slip undetected past the waiting gauntlet of pirate ships, today yachters share gourmet mustards and drone on about anchorages and trade winds and the weather.

The enormous canal construction project underway

COLÓN PROVINCE

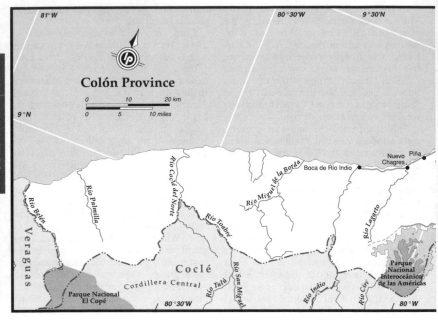

And not 2km away, in a leaden coffin at the bottom of the ocean, lies Drake's body. The English pirate led the sacking of Nombre de Dios in January 1596, but later that month he died of dysentery that he'd acquired in the Tropics. The captain was buried at sea within striking distance of the scenes of his earlier exploits, his descent to the ocean floor accompanied by a thunderous salute fired by his fleet.

In Drake's honor, two of his own ships and his share of the Nombre de Dios treasure were sunk near the spot. A nearby point and a small island were named after him, and a sermon was read aboard Drake's ship, the *Defiance,* with all of the captains of his fleet in attendance. It went like this:

'Where Drake first found, there last he lost his
    name,
And for a tomb left nothing but his fame.
His body's buried beneath some great wave,
The sea that was his glory is his grave.
On whom an epitaph none can truly make,
For who can say, "*Here* lies Sir Francis Drake?"'

COLÓN

The capital of Colón Province occupies a square of land that juts northwest into the Bahía de Limón (Lemon Bay). It is noteworthy mainly for its Zona Libre, a free-trade zone second only to Hong Kong in sales. It is also the northern terminus of the Panama Canal, and it was the northern terminus of the now-defunct Panama Railroad.

The city sits on a former island, which was linked at its southernmost tip to the mainland via landfill in 1852. The unification was part of a US plan, conceived three years earlier, to build a railroad from what had been Isla Manzanillo to Panama City. That railroad – the first transcontinental railroad in the world – was completed on January 27, 1855.

The town that sprang up where Colón stands today was initially called Aspinwall, in honor of William Aspinwall, one of the founders of the Panama Railroad. The government of Colombia changed the

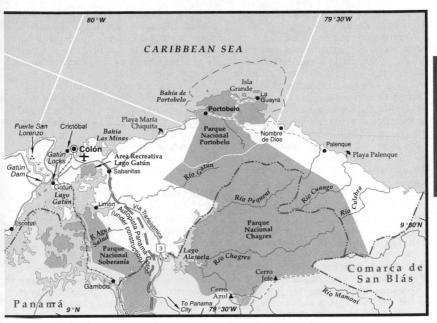

name to Colón in 1890, and the adjacent area, which was inhabited by Americans and inside the Canal Zone, was named Cristóbal. As a result of the 1977 Carter-Torrijos pact, Cristóbal is now in Panamanian hands.

The discovery of gold in California in January 1848 was the impetus behind the railroad's construction. At that time, most of the US public lived on the East Coast of the USA. Traveling out to California via Panama was cheaper, quicker and less dangerous than traveling through the USA's heartland, which was vast and home to many hostile Indians. Would-be millionaires took steamships from the East Coast to the mouth of the Río Chagres and walked the Sendero Las Cruces to the Pacific coast; then they boarded ships that were bound for California. The Panama Railroad made walking the Sendero Las Cruces unnecessary.

From its 1855 completion until the completion of a transcontinental railroad in the USA on May 10, 1869, the Panama Railroad was the only rapid transit across the continental Western Hemisphere. During this time, Colón became a real city, as scores of businesses opened to accommodate the travelers.

When the US transcontinental railroad was established, Colón suddenly became an economically depressed city, and it remained that way up until 1881, when the French began construction of the Interoceanic Canal. The French enterprise brought with it a new batch of laborers and revived the sluggish economy.

The French were four years into their project when a fire, set by a Colombian hoping to spark a revolution, burned nearly every structure in Colón and left 10,000 people homeless. The city was rebuilt in the architectural style popular in France at the time. Many buildings from that era, as well as ones built by Americans between 1904 and 1914 for Panama Canal workers, still exist today. Unfortunately, most are on the verge of collapse, with people still living inside them.

After the completion of the canal, the city's economy began to reel under the weight of thousands of suddenly unemployed canal workers and their families. The Zona Libre was created in 1948 in an attempt to revive the city, but none of the US$10 billion in annual commercial turnover seems to get beyond the walls of the compound. Unfortunately, the Zona Libre is an island of materialism in a sea of unemployment, poverty and crime. (Colón's rates in all three areas are the highest in Panama.) Inside the guarded compound, entrepreneurs cut deals involving the latest technologies and fashions, but outside its walls, children run about in rags and the city's largely black population lives in rotting buildings erected to house the workers who dug the Panama Canal. There are plenty of smugglers in Colón, and with the exception of one seaside residential neighborhood where some fine houses are tucked away behind high walls and security systems, the city is a slum. And if you walk its streets, even in the middle of the day, expect to get mugged. It really is that bad.

Orientation

The city is reached via two major roads on the southern side of town. The roads become Avenida Amador Guerrero and Avenida Bolívar at the entrance of town and run straight up the grid-patterned city, ending near Colón's northern waterfront.

Perpendicular to these avenues are, primarily, numbered streets. Calle 16 is the first of these you'll cross as you enter the city from the south; Calle 1 is located at the northern end of town. As you enter town, you can turn right on Calle 13 and drive about eight blocks to reach the main entrance of the Zona Libre. If you turn left on Calle 13, you'll enter the port of Cristóbal after 200m.

Information

Colón has an Instituto Panameño de Turismo (IPAT) tourist office, a post office, banks and gas stations – most of the services you'd expect to find in a provincial capital. But, again, walking in this city is very dangerous. A white tourist walking out of a bank here will likely be mugged. If you have mail to send, send it from another city.

Many are the reports sent to Lonely Planet by tourists who say they have traveled extensively and were never victimized until they visited Colón. Even representatives of the IPAT headquarters in Panama City, whose job it is to promote the country, encourage tourists to avoid Colón on account of the level of crime here.

Zona Libre

In Colón's sprawling free-trade zone are the showrooms of 1650 companies and the branch offices of 21 banks. Here, as the story goes, you can buy items at wholesale prices and avoid paying taxes. Here, as the story goes, enormous savings await buyers. And that may be the case if you're buying hundreds of refrigerators or 15,000 pairs of designer shoes or placing another large order.

Despite talk you may hear about the bargains that can be found in the Zona Libre, it may be hard to find any. Like many tourists, when I visited the zone I went to the Nikon representative to see what deals the company offered on camera equipment. I found that the prices were no better or only slightly lower than those back home in California; they certainly didn't warrant a trip to Colón.

The Zona Libre, unlike such famous shopping districts as Rodeo Drive in Beverly Hills and the Champs-Élysées in Paris, doesn't even make for very compelling window-shopping. Most items for sale are utilitarian rather than luxurious. And little effort is put into presentation, because the big buyers here know what they want and aren't, like most shoppers, terribly prone to impulse purchases.

Who benefits from the Zona Libre? People who deal in very large numbers, that's who. That's the nature of free-trade zones; buyers and sellers conduct business in terms of hundreds or thousands of units.

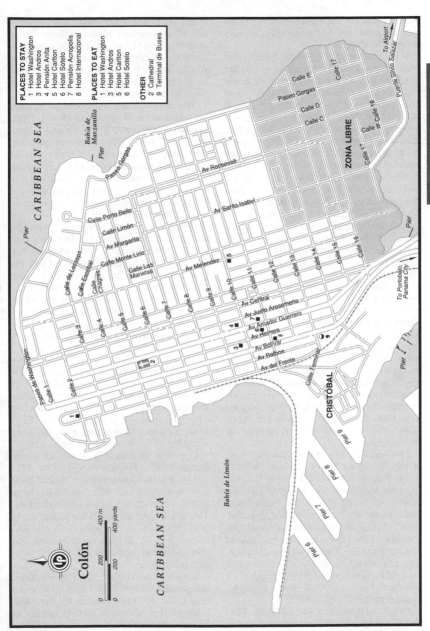

PLACES TO STAY
1 Hotel Washington
3 Hotel Andros
4 Pensión Anita
5 Hotel Carlton
6 Hotel Sotelo
7 Pensión Acropolis
8 Hotel Internacional

PLACES TO EAT
1 Hotel Washington
3 Hotel Andros
5 Hotel Carlton
6 Hotel Sotelo

OTHER
2 Cathedral
9 Terminal de Buses

Colón

CARIBBEAN SEA

Bahía de Manzanillo

CARIBBEAN SEA

Bahía de Limón

ZONA LIBRE

CRISTÓBAL

To Portobelo,
Panama City

To Airport

Puente Silvio Salazar

When dealing in huge quantities, the seller can bring the per-unit cost down, usually below wholesale.

Who else benefits? People from countries where prices for imported goods are terribly high. If the import tax on Japanese watches in your home country is 50%, you will probably find the price of Seikos here to your liking. But if you come from a country such as the USA or Canada, where import taxes are low and competition keeps prices down, you'll be disappointed by the prices you'll encounter in the Zona Libre.

Anyone else benefit? According to US and Panamanian news reports, Colombian drug traffickers do. Not only do they move cocaine from Panama to other countries via cargo ships that frequent the zone, but the narcotraffickers have also been known to set up fictitious companies in the compound in order to avoid revenue-reporting requirements.

The Zona Libre is open during regular business hours.

Places to Stay & Eat

There are quite a few hotels in Colón, and they cover a broad price range. Listed below are all the city's hotels that were in business at the time this book was researched and were not basically fronts for prostitution or otherwise unsavory places. Because the city is so dangerous, anyone who visits should eat at his or her hotel. Also, most of the city's best restaurants are inside hotels.

The best lodgings in town can be found at the four-story *Hotel Carlton* (☎ 441-0111, fax 447-0114), on Calle 10 near Avenida Melendez. This hotel is also the closest one to the Zona Libre. Every room contains at least one good bed, air-con, cable TV, hot-water private bathroom and telephone. The rooms are well maintained and comfortable. There's a popular restaurant, remodeled in 1997, and a conference room. The hotel has an armed guard at its entrance. Rates are US$35/40/45 single/double/triple.

The *Hotel Andros* (☎ 441-0477, fax 441-7921), on Avenida Herrera between Calles

9 and 10, is also a very comfortable place. All of its spacious rooms contain all the amenities you'd find at the Carlton, and the rates are identical. There is also a popular restaurant at the Andros, and no one is able to get to the guestrooms without passing close to the front desk.

The next-best accommodations in town are found at the *Hotel Sotelo* (☎ 441-7702, fax 441-5713), on Avenida Amador Guerrero near Calle 11. All 66 rooms have cable TVs, phones, air-con, hot-water private bathrooms and good beds, and there are ice machines in the halls. At US$30/35 for one/two people, it's little cheaper than the Carlton and Andros. There's a restaurant as well. This place is quite OK.

If you must spend the night in Colón and the Carlton, Andros and Sotelo are packed, the *Hotel Internacional* (☎ 445-2930, fax 441-8870), on Avenida Bolívar at Calle 11, would be an acceptable place to choose. It's beside a 24-hour girlie bar that attracts all kinds of lovely people, but it's otherwise OK. The rooms are a bit worn, but they have air-con, hot-water private bathrooms, phones, TVs and decent beds. Rates are US$30/35/45 single/double/triple.

The *Hotel Washington* (☎ 441-7133, fax 441-7397), on Calle 2 near Avenida del Frente, bills itself as the grand dame of Colón's hotels, but it's only a monstrosity in need of millions of dollars of updating. The pleasure of staying at this 124-room hangover from a long-gone era costs US$55/65/75. There is a restaurant here.

Opposite the Sotelo is one of the city's budget hotels, *Pensión Acropolis* (☎ 441-1456). Its 16 rooms contain decent beds and strong ceiling fans, and they have access to a shared hot-water bathroom. This place is a bit worn, but it's quite tolerable, especially for the price: US$7 for one or two people. There's no restaurant, but you could eat at the Hotel Sotelo, right across the street.

Another budget place, the *Pensión Anita* (no phone), on Avenida Amador Guerrero near Calle 10, offers rooms for the same price as the Acropolis, but its quality is questionable.

There are other budget places in town, including the highly visible *Hotel Oriental,* but I can't recommend them.

Getting There & Away

Air Aeroperlas (☎ 269-4555 in Panama City) offers weekday flights from the capital's Paitilla airport to Colón (US$26/52 one-way/roundtrip).

Bus At the time this book was written, the Autopista Panama-Colón (the new highway connecting Panama City and Colón) had not yet opened, but its completion will definitely affect travel time and bus fares between the two cities. It might even influence where you'd catch a Colón-bound bus in Panama City. If you intend to visit Colón by bus, you'd be wise to confirm the following information with a tour operator or a clerk at your hotel.

Regular bus service for Colón currently departs Panama City from the intersection of Calle P (near Calle 26 Este) and Avenida Central every 20 minutes from around 5 am to 9 pm; after that time, buses leave hourly. The last bus leaves at 1 am. The ride takes 1¾ hours, but once the highway is completed, it probably will take only half as long. Express buses, which have aircon and cost a bit more, depart on the same schedule from a stop on Avenida Perú between Calles 29 and 30 Este.

Colón's Terminal de Buses (☎ 445-6459; English is spoken) is at the intersection of Calle Terminal and Avenida Bolívar. It serves towns throughout Colón Province, including the following:

La Guayra – US$2.25; hourly, 6:30 am to 6 pm
Nombre de Dios – 66km, US$3; hourly, 6:30 am to 6 pm
Portobelo – 43km, US$1.30; hourly, 6:30 am to 6 pm

You should never leave your bags unattended at Colón's bus station.

Getting Around

If you visit Colón, don't walk any farther than you absolutely must. If you arrive by bus, take a taxi from the station to your hotel – even if the hotel is only three blocks away.

AROUND COLÓN

Gatún Locks

The Gatún Locks, 10km south of Colón, raise southbound ships 25.9m from Caribbean waters to the level of Lago Gatún. From there, ships travel 37km to the Pedro Miguel Locks, which lower southbound ships 9.3m to Lago Miraflores, a small body of water that separates the two sets of Pacific locks. The ships are lowered to sea level at the Miraflores Locks.

The lock chambers all have the same dimensions (305m by 33.5m) and were built in pairs, two chambers running side by side in order to accommodate two lanes of traffic. The Gatún Locks consist of three such pairs. There is one pair at Pedro Miguel and two at Miraflores, making six pairs – or 12 chambers – in all.

TOM BOYDEN

A tight fit: Ship squeezing through canal locks

Not only are the Gatún Locks the largest of the three sets, but their size is mind-boggling. In his superlative book *The Path Between the Seas,* David McCullough observes that if stood on its end, a single lock would have been the tallest structure on earth at the time it was built, taller by several meters than even the Eiffel Tower. And each chamber could have accommodated the *Titanic* with plenty of room to spare.

The amount of concrete poured to construct the locks at Gatún – 1,820,000 cubic meters – was record-setting. That amount of concrete is enough to build a wall 2.4m thick, 3.6m high and 213km long. The concrete was brought from a giant mixing plant to the construction site by railroad cars that ran on a circular track. Huge buckets maneuvered by cranes carried the wet concrete from the railroad cars and poured it into enormous steel forms. The forms themselves were moved into place by locomotives.

Concrete is a combination of gravel, sand and cement. The gravel used in the concrete at Gatún came from Portobelo, the sand from the harbor at Nombre de Dios and the cement from New York. It took four years to build the locks. Despite the enormity of the Panama Canal project, they were completed on schedule.

Today you can see the locks in action. From a well-placed viewing stand opposite the control tower, you can watch southbound ships enter the two lower chambers at sea level, rise to the level of Lago Gatún in three steps and then steam onto the lake en route to the Pedro Miguel and Miraflores Locks. While in the chambers, the ships are cabled to locomotives that pull them from one lock to the next.

Just before you reach the viewing stand, you'll see a model of the entire canal and photos of it under construction. Additionally, you will be given a brochure in English or Spanish that provides information about the canal. There is no fee to visit the locks, which are open to the public 9 am to 5 pm daily.

Getting There & Away Buses to the Gatún Locks leave the Terminal de Buses in Colón hourly; the ride costs US$1.25 one way and lasts 20 minutes. It's better to arrive by taxi, however, because you would probably enjoy visiting the Gatún Dam (see below) in addition to the locks; it's only 2km away. A taxi ride from Colón to the locks and dam and back costs US$12, more if the driver is hungry. Agree on a price before leaving.

Gatún Dam

The Gatún Dam, which was constructed to shore up the Río Chagres and to create Lago Gatún, was the world's largest earthen dam until the Fort Peck Dam was built in Montana (USA) in 1940. And until Lake Mead was formed by the 1936 completion of the Hoover Dam on the Nevada-Arizona (USA) border, Lago Gatún was the world's largest artificial body of water. When the Gatún Dam's spillway is open, the sight is quite a rush. The guard at the entrance to the Gatún Locks speaks English and can tell you if the spillway is open.

Power generated by the dam drives all the electrical equipment involved in the operation of the Panama Canal, including the locomotives that tow ships through the locks. Another interesting bit of information: When Lago Gatún was created, it submerged 262 sq km of jungle – an area far greater than that of most capital cities. Also submerged were entire villages and the original tracks of the Panama Railroad.

(The railroad, by the way, which stopped running during the 1980s due to neglect, should return to action by the year 2000. In February 1998 a US company announced it would spend US$60 million to renew service. Plans called for moving 70,000 to 80,000 containers a year initially, and eventually hundreds of thousands annually. There were no plans to provide passenger service.)

For directions on how to reach the dam, see the Getting There & Away section under Gatún Locks, above.

Fuerte San Lorenzo

Fuerte (Fort) San Lorenzo is perched at the mouth of the Río Chagres, on a promontory west of the canal. It was via this river that the pirate Henry Morgan gained access to the interior in 1671, enabling him to sack the first Panama City (the ruins of that destroyed settlement, today known as Panamá La Vieja, are still visible today).

Like the fortresses at Portobelo, this Spanish fort is built of blocks of cut coral and displays rows of old cannons. A British cannon among Spanish ones is evidence of the time when British pirates overcame the fort. Much of San Lorenzo is well preserved, including the moat, the cannons and the arched rooms. The fort commands a wide view of the river and bay far below.

There is no fee to enter this or any of Panama's other forts. You must drive to Fuerte San Lorenzo; taxis do not go there. Drive to the Gatún Locks, continue past the stoplight near the northern entrance to the locks and then follow the signs directing you to the dam, 2km away. Drive over the dam and follow the 'Fort San Lorenzo' signs. These will lead you to the entrance of Fort Sherman, a US military base, where you'll be asked to show ID. Once you've done this, you will be allowed to proceed the remaining 9km to Fuerte San Lorenzo.

At the time this was written, the US Army was scheduled to turn over Fort Sherman to Panama's control on December 31, 1999. However, the US government was negotiating to retain control of the base, because the dense rainforest there lends itself well to jungle training exercises. If you're anxious to see Fuerte San Lorenzo (which is not more impressive than the forts at Portobelo; see below), you'd be wise to contact a tour operator or IPAT to learn about the current accessibility of the site.

WEST OF COLÓN

The many small coastal communities west of Colón (Piña, Nuevo Chagres and Boca de Río Indio, to name a few) are poor, unattractive fishing villages with nothing to offer the tourist. The beaches along this stretch of coast are strewn with litter and the surf contains lots of rip tides. There are no banks, post offices, hotels or restaurants.

PORTOBELO

This bayside town, 99km from Panama City and 43km from Colón, was given the name 'Puerto Bello' (Beautiful Port) by Columbus in 1502 on account of the beauty of its natural harbor. As often happened with Spanish names, this one was abbreviated over time.

Portobelo consisted of not more than 10 houses when it was visited, in 1586, by Juan Bautista Antonelli, who designed many fortresses in the Spanish Indies and was sent to examine the Caribbean ports. After the celebrated Italian engineer noted how well Portobelo's bay lent itself to defensive works, King Félipe II ordered that Nombre de Dios be abandoned and Portobelo colonized.

Despite the order, it wasn't until after Drake's 1596 attack on Nombre de Dios that a slow transfer actually took place. At the time of the transfer, which occurred from 1597 to 1601, two forts were built beside the bay (see Forts, below, for more details). These forts were reinforced and others were constructed in the years that followed. But in spite of these defenses, Portobelo suffered numerous invasions at the hands of buccaneers and the English navy.

However, not all the invasions were the products of superior tactics or numbers. In 1679 the crews of two English ships and one French vessel united in an attack on Portobelo. They landed 200 men at such a distance from the town that it took them three nights of marching to reach it (the pirates hid in the forest during the day). As they neared Portobelo, they were seen by a farmer, who ran ahead to sound the alarm. But the pirates followed so closely behind that the town had no time to prepare. Unaware of how small the buccaneer force was, all the inhabitants fled.

The pirates spent two days and nights in Portobelo, collecting plunder in constant apprehension that the Spaniards would return in great numbers and attack them. However, the buccaneers got back to their ships unmolested and then distributed 160 pieces of eight to each man. At the time,

COLÓN PROVINCE

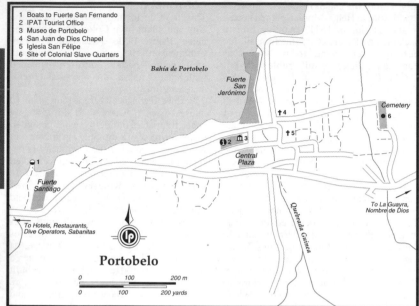

1 Boats to Fuerte San Fernando
2 IPAT Tourist Office
3 Museo de Portobelo
4 San Juan de Dios Chapel
5 Iglesia San Félipe
6 Site of Colonial Slave Quarters

Bahía de Portobelo

Fuerte San Jerónimo

Cemetery
● 6

† 4

🛈 2   🏛 3   † 5

Central Plaza

● 1

Fuerte Santiago

Quebrada Guinea

To La Guayra, Nombre de Dios

To Hotels, Restaurants, Dive Operators, Sabanitas

Portobelo

0   100   200 m
0   100   200 yards

one piece of eight would pay for a night's stay at the best inn in Seville.

Today Portobelo is a sleepy town of fewer than 3000 people who mostly make their living from the sea or tending to crops. Their homes and small businesses (mainly food stands) are situated among the ruins of military buildings, half of which retain some of their original form and appear on the accompanying map. The other half are simply small piles of cut stone or coral, and their origins have been obscured by time.

In addition to the ruins in and about the town, Portobelo is popular for its scuba diving. There are eight major dive sites in the area (including a 110-foot cargo ship and a C-45 twin-engine plane), and their quality ranges from fair to good. There is no exceptional diving in the vicinity of Portobelo, but few people leave here unhappy, because the diving's so relatively cheap. For what you pay, you get a very good value.

There are no places to stay in Portobelo, although there are several hotels on the Sabanitas-Portobelo road. Likewise, while there are some food stands in town, there are no restaurants; there are some very good restaurants, however, along the Sabanitas-Portobelo road.

Orientation

Portobelo consists of about 15 square blocks of mostly rundown homes and businesses beside a well-paved, two-lane road. That road intersects with the Panama City-Colón road at the town of Sabanitas, 33km to the west.

East of Portobelo, the road forks after 9km. The right branch of the road extends 14km farther east to Nombre de Dios; the left branch extends 11km to the hamlet of La Guayra, where visitors can hire boats to take them to Isla Grande, a few minutes' ride away.

Information

There are no banks in Portobelo. At the time of writing, the original *contaduría*

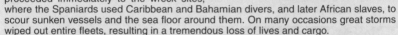

Salvaging Sunken Galleons

During the Spaniards' colonization of the New World in the 16th, 17th and 18th centuries, galleons left Spain carrying goods to the colonies and returned loaded with gold and silver mined in Colombia, Peru and Mexico. Many of these ships sank in the Caribbean Sea, overcome by pirates or hurricanes. During these years, literally thousands of ships – not only Spanish but also English, French, Dutch, pirate and African slave ships – foundered in the green-blue waters of the Caribbean.

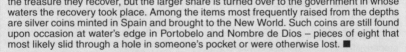

The frequency of shipwrecks spurred the Spaniards to organize operations to recover sunken cargo. By the 17th century, Spain maintained salvage flotillas in the ports of Portobelo, Havana and Veracruz. These fleets awaited news of shipwrecks and then proceeded immediately to the wreck sites, where the Spaniards used Caribbean and Bahamian divers, and later African slaves, to scour sunken vessels and the sea floor around them. On many occasions great storms wiped out entire fleets, resulting in a tremendous loss of lives and cargo.

As early as the 1620s, salvagers were using bronze diving bells to increase the time they could spend underwater. The bell was submerged vertically from a ship and held air in its upper part, allowing divers to enter it to breathe, rest and observe. Over time, such divers became very skilled and the salvaging business very lucrative. So lucrative that the English, who were established in Bermuda and the Bahamas, entered the Caribbean salvage business at the end of the 17th century. And pirates, as you'd expect, were always pleased to come upon a salvage operation.

In recent decades advances in diving and underwater-recovery equipment have led to a boom in Caribbean salvaging efforts. In most cases salvagers get to keep a portion of the treasure they recover, but the larger share is turned over to the government in whose waters the recovery took place. Among the items most frequently raised from the depths are silver coins minted in Spain and brought to the New World. Such coins are still found upon occasion at water's edge in Portobelo and Nombre de Dios – pieces of eight that most likely slid through a hole in someone's pocket or were otherwise lost. ■

(counting house) was being restored and plans called for an IPAT tourist office and a museum to occupy it. The two-story building was originally built in 1630 but has been severely damaged twice – by cannon fire in 1744 and by a strong earthquake in 1882. This is the structure's third major restoration (see the Restoration or Destruction? sidebar on the next page).

Forts

To defend his bullion and galleons from pirates, King Félipe II ordered forts constructed at Portobelo. By 1601 two had been built, both near the mouth of the bay: Fuerte San Félipe was on the northern side, and on the southern side was Fuerte San Diego. In the years that followed, many more fortresses would be erected, some on the sites of earlier, less substantial forts.

Today the remnants of **Fuerte San Jerónimo** and **Fuerte Santiago** can still be seen near town, and the ruins of **Fuerte San Fernando** occupy a grassy flat across the bay from town. Sadly, most of San Fernando was deconstructed by Americans who used its walls to create the breakwater protecting the northern end of the Panama Canal. Boats can be hired at water's edge near Fuerte Santiago for the trip across the bay to this fort. The roundtrip ride costs US$10 per person.

Santiago is the first fort you'll see as you near town from the west. It was built after British Admiral Edward Vernon's 1739 attack and contains many musket ports. Several of its walls are 3m thick, made entirely of cut coral – or 'reef rock,' as the Spaniards called it. Coral was used because it is as tough as granite and yet as light as pumice and can be shaped with a saw. The ruins at Fuerte Santiago include an officers' quarters, an artillery shed, a sentry box, a barracks and batteries.

On a hill overlooking Santiago and much of the bay is a small but well-preserved fort whose name no one can remember. If you're in good health, hike up the grass-covered slope to it. The hike is only a couple of hundred meters long, but the slope is steep at times and the grass can be slippery. A beautiful view awaits those who make it to this fort, which has a dry moat around it and a well in the center.

Fuerte San Jerónimo, closer to the center of town, was the largest fortress ever built to protect the bay. If you're short on time, San Jerónimo is more complete and makes for a better visit than Santiago. Beyond its impressive gateway are the remains of the officers' quarters, a barracks and a guard room. Facing the mouth of the bay are 18 cannon embrasures. Some of the original cannons remain exactly where the Spanish troops left them when they returned home in 1821 – the year Panama declared its independence from Spain.

Diving & Snorkeling

As mentioned above, the diving around Portobelo isn't spectacular, but it is a good value for the money. Competition keeps prices down. There are four dive operators, all within a fairly short distance of one another on the Sabanitas-Portobelo road, west of town. Three are beside the road, and the fourth is within 100m of it. All have English-speakers.

Dive rates vary with the distance traveled and the amount of equipment rented. But people who have their own personal gear, a regulator and a buoyancy control device (BCD) can expect to pay about US$30 for a two-tank dive. People who just want to snorkel and have their own equipment can expect to pay US$10 to US$15 per outing. All the dive operators rent rooms and have meager dining facilities (see Places to Stay, below).

Although Caribbean waters are considerably warmer than what you'll find most anywhere in the Pacific, they can be chilly at times. I recommend at least a Lycra suit; it provides warmth, and you'll be glad you have it on if you bump into a jellyfish. And if you sunburn easily, a Lycra suit will keep the sun's rays off your trunk and limbs.

Restoration or Destruction?

There's an interesting story behind the restoration of Portobelo's old counting house. The large structure, which was where treasure was recorded before it was loaded onto Spanish galleons, was originally built of solid blocks of coral taken from a nearby reef. In the mid-1990s the Spanish government offered to pay for restoration of the historic building, but because it didn't trust the Panamanian government to do the work properly, it insisted on hiring the workers and overseeing the job.

Over the strong objections of environmentalists and others, the Spaniards destroyed most of a coral reef just north of Drake's Island in the process of rebuilding the former counting house. The reef is in the middle of the 35,929-hectare Parque Nacional Portobelo. Restoration of the reef, which can only be performed by nature, will require at least several hundred years. One Panamanian environmentalist, angry that Spain continues to have a role in Panama's affairs, told me: 'The Spanish still think they can dictate to us.' ∎

Scubaportobelo (☎ 461-3841, fax 461-9586) enjoys a solid reputation. It has a wide variety of rental equipment, and on-site tank refill is available. To rent equipment here, you must possess a scuba certification card and leave a cash deposit or signed Visa or MasterCard slip for the equipment's value. A tank, regulator and BCD will typically rent for US$15/20 weekdays/weekends.

Nautilus Dive Club (☎ 448-2035, cellular 613-6557, beeper 263-5044) is very popular, and it's a tad cheaper than the others. Its owner, Javier Freiburghas, probably knows Panama's dive sites as well as anyone; he knows what he's talking about. His company also has a good selection of rental equipment.

Buzo (☎ 448-2175) is owned and operated by a very nice man, Octavio Arango. In addition to its dives, it offers visits to Fuerte San Fernando, lovely Playa Blanca and other comely places for US$10 per person per destination. It's a good deal, and there's something special about seeing this fort-flanked bay as the pirates did – from a boat. As with any operator, before you sign up for a trip, make sure you ask to see proof that this operator's divemasters have received safety training from PADI, NAUI, YMCA or one of the other reputable international scuba-safety organizations.

Divers Haven (☎ 448-2040, ☎/fax 448-2003) is the closest of the operators to town and to the dive sites, which means slightly lower dive rates and less time spent in transit. Another good thing about this operator is that it is possible to make international calls here (you can't do this at the other places). It rents snorkel equipment, but you'll need to see one of the other outfits for dive gear.

If you'd like to be driven from Panama City to one of these operators, that can be arranged. Scubaportobelo is owned by Scubapanama (☎ 261-4064/3841, fax 261-9586), the country's biggest name in scuba diving, and for a reasonable sum Scubaportobelo can arrange for you to be picked up at your hotel in the capital, spend the morning or afternoon diving, and returned to your hotel the same day. Starlite Travel (☎ 232-6401, fax 232-6448), which works with Divers Haven, is a very reputable company, and it offers the same service. Contact it for current rates. English and Spanish are spoken at both Scubapanama and Starlite Travel.

Eight dive sites are frequented by the outfits listed above. You can also often rent boats at Buzo and at Cabañas El Mar (see Places to Stay, below) to visit nearby islands, beaches, mangrove forests and Fuerte San Fernando. You can also snorkel from these boats. The rates are low – usually US$15 per half-day. The cost varies with the distance traveled and the size of the boat, as both factors affect gasoline consumption.

Special Events

The Black Christ Festival is held every October 21 and is a fascinating event to witness. Pilgrims arrive from all over Panama on this day to dance and celebrate in honor of Jesus, many wearing purple (the color of the robe Christ wore). The exact origins of this festival and the black Christ statue it celebrates are a matter of speculation: Many fanciful stories exist (see the Story of the Black Christ sidebar on the next page), but any definitive church records were likely lost in the fire that followed Henry Morgan's sacking of Panamá in 1671. Regardless, on each anniversary of the statue's discovery, it is taken from the Portobelo church and paraded around town. The parade begins promptly at 6 pm, and street festivities follow.

The Congos, a festivity in which black people assume the role of escaped slaves and run around taking 'captives,' is held in Portobelo and sometimes elsewhere in the province during Carnaval, on New Year's Eve and on patron saint days (March 20 in Portobelo). 'The Congos' is both the name of the festivity and the name of the people who maintain this really weird tradition, which is based around a satire of colonial Spaniards.

The tradition dates from the days of Panama's slave trade, when some black

The Story of the Black Christ

Many tales have attempted to explain the origins of the Black Christ statue in Portobelo's church and the festival that honors it. One story has it that a ship bound for Cartagena, Colombia, from Portobelo tried to leave the port five times, but on each occasion a mighty storm appeared and blew the ship back to the town's edge, nearly sinking it in the process. The terrified crew are said to have lightened their vessel by tossing a heavy box overboard. On their sixth attempt to sail out of the bay, no storm appeared and they were able to go on their way unmolested.

According to this tale, several fishermen found the discarded box floating off Portobelo and were shocked to discover a statue of a black Christ inside it. They are said to have placed it in Portobelo's church out of respect. As word got around about the dark wooden statue, which stands 1.5m high, the figure took on a mythic reputation.

A second story claims that the church on Isla Taboga, clear on the other side of the isthmus, ordered a Jesus of Nazareth (a black Christ) statue from a supplier in Spain at about the same time that the Portobelo church ordered an image of Santo Domingo from the same supplier. It is said that the boxes in which the two statues were shipped to Panama were incorrectly labeled, so the church on Isla Taboga received the Santo Domingo statue while the one in Portobelo received the black Christ.

Many efforts were made to swap the figures, according to this tale, but each time something occurred that prevented the black Christ statue from leaving Portobelo. Today the congregation in Portobelo won't allow further attempts because it is convinced the statue is imbued with divine powers and that the Black Christ wishes to remain with the people of Portobelo.

Still another story has it that Portobelo fishermen found a box floating at sea during a cholera epidemic. It contained a black Christ statue that, out of respect, the men placed inside the town church. Almost immediately, so goes this story, the epidemic passed, and people who had been reeling from the terrible disease quickly recovered.

There are other stories. Regardless of the veracity of any of them, the Black Christ Festival on October 21 makes for an interesting time. It begins with the parading of the statue and continues all night, as many people in purple robes – some wearing crowns of thorns and carrying crosses – roam around dancing, gambling and drinking. ■

slaves escaped into the jungle and formed communities there. The satire consists of taking someone prisoner and demanding a huge ransom, but the prisoner is freed when he or she pays a token ransom, perhaps only 50¢. The celebrants are generally dressed in outlandish outfits that include tattered clothes and hats that resemble crowns. Many of them also carry wooden swords. All are so animated that they look like they've just come from an insane asylum.

Los Congos usually perform before audiences that assemble to watch them 'captivate' people, but sometimes a really crazy-looking group of men wielding wooden swords will descend upon a person who's just walking down the street and demand thousands of dollars (but they'll settle for a few coins). Sound bizarre? It is. If you ever find yourself an innocent 'victim' of this tradition, try not to freak out and kill someone. They're just harmless Congos.

Places to Stay

All the dive centers (see Diving & Snorkeling, above) rent rooms and have dining facilities. None of the rooms are particularly nice, but all are fine if you're just looking for a comfortable place to sleep. Expect to pay US$20 to US$30 for a room to yourself, or half that if you're sharing. Because all these places are a good distance from town, plan ahead if you like to end the day with a nightcap; alcohol isn't always available and the selection is usually very limited when it is.

As you approach Portobelo from Sabanitas, the first place you'll see, on the left side of the road, is *Nautilus Dive Club* (☎ 448-2035, cellular 613-6557, beeper 263-5044), which has four rooms, each with air-con, four bunkbeds and access to a shared bathroom with cold water only. The rate is US$10 per person.

As you continue toward Portobelo, the next lodgings are found at *Buzo* (☎ 448-2175), which has six rooms, all with air-con and three beds apiece. There's only a cold-water shared bathroom. The rate is US$25 per room.

The next available lodgings can be found at *Scubaportobelo* (☎ 461-3841, fax 461-9586), which charges US$35 per cabin. Each has air-con and access to a cold-water shared bathroom.

Next in line is the *Cabañas El Mar* (☎ 448-2102), which consists of 12 seaside cabins with good beds, ceiling fans and cold-water private bathrooms. These rooms are too warm for most people's liking. There was talk of maybe installing air-con. Cabins cost US$30 apiece.

Closest to town is *Divers Haven* (☎ 448-2040, ☎/fax 448-2003), which charges US$12 per bed Monday to Thursday and US$17 Friday, Saturday and Sunday. There's only a cold-water shared bathroom. If you've got a tent, you can pitch it here and have access to a shower and toilet for US$7 per tent.

Places to Eat

In addition to the dive centers, all of which have meager dining facilities that aren't always in use, there are three very good restaurants along the Sabanitas-Portobelo road.

As you travel toward Portobelo, the first place you'll come to is *Restaurante Los Cañones,* which is over the water and faces a lovely inlet. The menu includes red snapper, corvina, squid, clams and baby shrimp – all US$6 each – but there's one dish that this restaurant is really known for: octopus, slowly cooked to perfection in a spicy tomato-based sauce and served on a bed of white rice that's been cooked with coconut oil so that it has acquired the fruit's sweet taste. At US$6, it's a sin.

The next restaurant on this road is *Rene's Place,* which serves all the same food you'll find at Los Cañones for the same price, and it's just as delicious. The last time I was at Rene's Place, I was told they'd run out of menus – yet I was the only person in the restaurant. If studying a menu is important to you, you might want to eat elsewhere. Here the friendly waiters usually just tell customers what's available. If you order the octopus (pulpo), you won't go wrong.

Closer to town, on the right side of the road, is *Restaurante La Torre,* which advertises 'cheeseburgers in paradise,' and it delivers the goods. A tasty cheeseburger with fries goes for US$3. English is spoken at this breezy, Colombian-owned restaurant, which displays the day's winning lottery number beside its posted menu. The seafood here is excellent. Typical dishes, which are served with your choice of side order, include half a smoked chicken (US$4.25), grilled beef with fries and a salad (US$4.50), conch in coconut sauce (US$5.75) and whole fried snapper (US$6.50). This place also serves wonderful juices; melon, passion fruit and orange are usually available. Watermelon juice, available three months of the year, is incredibly refreshing.

Getting There & Away

Buses to Portobelo depart Colón's Terminal de Buses hourly from 6:30 am to 6 pm and cost US$1.30 each way. These same buses can be boarded at Sabanitas, the turnoff for Portobelo, and thus you can avoid a trip into Colón.

At the time of writing, regular bus service from Panama City, destined for Colón but stopping at Sabanitas along the way, was departing the capital from the intersection of Calle P (near Calle 26 Este) and Avenida Central every 20 minutes from around 5 am to 9 pm, then hourly until 1 am; express buses were departing on the same schedule from a stop on Avenida Perú between Calles 29 and 30 Este. However, the scheduled summer 1998 completion of the new Panama City-Colón highway may have changed these departure points, so confirm them with a tour operator, hotel clerk or IPAT. And make sure to ask the driver before departing if the bus will stop at Sabanitas.

Getting Around
There are occasional taxis in Portobelo, but not many. The best way to travel the Sabanitas-Portobelo road is to flag down any of the buses headed in the direction you wish to go. No public transportation is available after dark.

ISLA GRANDE
This island, 15km east of Portobelo, is a popular weekend destination for Panama City's party animals. About 300 people of African descent live on the island, most making a living from fishing and coconut production. Seafood and coconut milk are the principal ingredients of the island's food, which includes seafood soups, ceviche, Caribbean king crab, lobster, shrimp, octopus, sea turtle (*tortuga;* please don't eat it), shad and corvina.

There are some lovely beaches on the northern side of the island that can be reached by boat (hire a water taxi at the dock in front of Cabañas Super Jackson) or on foot (there's a water's-edge trail that loops around the 5km long, 1.5km wide island, as well as a slippery and difficult trail that crosses the island). There are also some fine snorkeling and dive sites within a 10-minute boat ride of the island, but there are no dive operators out here (you need to bring all your own equipment). The only surfing waves in the area are in front of Moon Cabins. These short-lived waves break left; from December to April, 2m faces are the norm. The bottom's rocky, so booties are a good idea.

Visitors mainly come here to party and maybe get lucky. Marijuana and cocaine abound, as do plainclothed police officers. Cocaine is readily available here because Colombian narcotraffickers use the nearby waters to drop drug bundles from planes. Traffickers in boats pick the stuff up and take it to Colón, where it's hidden in appliances and shipped to other countries.

Quite a few bundles of coke escape the attention of the boat crews and wash ashore, which is why the drug is so readily available. The helicopters that frequently pass near the island are operated by people hunting drugrunners. Bear in mind that if you're caught with drugs in Panama, you *will* be a much older carbon-based life form before you return to your home country.

A much better high is available here naturally. For US$30 (or US$25 if you're a sweet talker), one of the boatmen in front of Cabañas Super Jackson will take you on a half-day adventure. The possibilities are quite appealing: There are mangroves east of Isla Grande that make for fun exploring, and you could also go snorkeling and take a picnic to a beach on the mainland or a small secluded island.

The French built a lighthouse on the island in 1893, which sent red, green and white light over 100km out to sea. The lighthouse still functions today, but its light is now white, and it is visible for only 70km.

Special Events
San Juan Bautista is celebrated here on June 24 with swimming and canoe races. The Virgen del Carmen is honored on July 16 with a land and sea procession, baptisms and Masses. Carnaval is also celebrated here; the locals dance the conga with ribbons and mirrors in their hair, the women wearing traditional *pollera* dresses and the men in ragged pants tied at the waist with old sea rope. Along with the dancing, there are satirical songs about current events and a lot of joking in the Caribbean calypso tradition.

Places to Stay & Eat
There are numerous places to stay on Isla Grande, and others were being constructed at the time of writing. Those places that

were open for business in early 1998 are mentioned here.

Among the places to stay, the closest to the main pier is the centrally located *Cabañas Super Jackson* (no phone), which has five rooms, each with different features: one bed or two small beds without air-con (US$25), two beds and air-con (US$40), three beds and air-con (US$50), four beds and air-con (US$55). Expect to pay more during holidays. All rooms have private bathrooms and are very clean and cheerful. The hotel is beside a small store selling ice-cold beverages – a major plus on this humid island.

About 150m east of Super Jackson is *Hotel Isla Grande* (no phone), which mostly consists of several multilevel blocks of rooms, each with air-con, private bathroom and an ocean view (US$55 per night). Among the places to stay that you can easily walk to, this is the only one with a sandy beach – and it's quite OK. There's thick jungle at one end of the long beach and a restaurant at the other.

To the west of Super Jackson is *Cabañas Cholita* (no phone), which offers 12 rooms, all with air-con, good mattresses and private cold-water bathrooms. Rates are US$42 for one or two people, US$55 for three or four people and US$75 for five or six people. Restaurant prices range from US$3 for most breakfast dishes to US$18 for 'surf and turf' – lobster and steak.

Farther west is a better deal than the Cholita – *Posada Villa Ensueño* (☎ 269-5819, ☎/fax 235-9917), which has 16 rooms, all more attractive than those at the places mentioned above. There are four rooms with one twin bed in each (US$40 per room), 10 rooms with two beds in each (US$45) and two rooms with three twin beds in each (US$70). There's even a large lawn for campers (US$10 per tent per night, use of showers and toilets included).

Continuing to the west a good way by an occasionally narrow trail, you'll find *Moon Cabins* (☎ 263-2783), a new, very attractive place consisting of numerous hillside cabins that look down upon crashing surf and across at the still-lush peninsula. Each

thatch-roofed cabin is unique, and each was meticulously designed by a Chilean woman architect, with lots of emphasis on carved wood and the use of tile. There's a seaside swimming pool and a restaurant that offers island, international and vegetarian dishes. Rates vary: Cabins with one bed cost US$66 apiece; those with two beds are US$77; those with three beds cost US$125. There's also a surfer's dormitory; beds go for US$25 a night.

The new *Banana Village Resort* (☎ 263-9766, fax 264-7556), on the northern side of the island and best reachable by boat, includes a very tastefully done open-sided restaurant; a gorgeous wraparound bar with a pool table; an hourglass-shaped swimming pool; a long, clean and inviting stretch of beach; and six two-story houses with three guestrooms apiece (two downstairs and one upstairs). All the houses are backed by jungle and fronted by the sea, and all follow the same smart design plan. The houses are placed so that they follow the curve of the island, and none is even partially tucked behind another. Every room is bright and cheerful, spacious and elegant, and all have white wicker furniture, French doors, a safe in a closet and all the amenities you'd find at an upscale big-city hotel. This place is intended for couples; children, while not prohibited, are not desired. Rates, which include meals, are very reasonable: US$85/125 for one/two people.

The pickings are slim at the island's stand-alone restaurants, which seem to specialize in bland, overcooked food. The food at the hotel restaurants is much better. It's particularly good at Banana Village Resort and Moon Cabins.

Getting There & Away

Buses to La Guayra (the coastal hamlet where visitors can hire boats to get to Isla Grande) depart Colón's Terminal de Buses hourly from 6:30 am to 6 pm and cost US$2.25 each way. These buses can be boarded at Sabanitas, the turnoff for Portobelo, La Guayra and Nombre de Dios, and you can thus avoid Colón.

At the time of writing, regular buses from Panama City, destined for Colón but stopping at Sabanitas along the way, were departing the capital from the intersection of Calle P (near Calle 26 Este) and Avenida Central every 20 minutes from around 5 am to 9 pm, then hourly until 1 am; express buses were departing on the same schedule from a stop on Avenida Perú between Calles 29 and 30 Este. As noted earlier in this chapter, the scheduled summer 1998 completion of the new Panama City-Colón highway may have changed these departure points, so you should confirm them with a tour operator, hotel clerk or IPAT. Ask the driver before departing if the bus will stop at Sabanitas.

In La Guayra, there are always skippers hanging about near the water's edge, waiting to take people to the island. The 10-minute boat ride costs US$5 to US$10 per party; the price depends on the skipper and the size of the party.

PLAYA BLANCA

A few kilometers west of Isla Grande is lovely Playa Blanca (☎ 232-4985, fax 272-8181 in Panama City), which consists of a seaside lodge with a spacious and breezy common area, three guestrooms with private bathrooms, and two stand-alone cabins. This relaxing retreat is situated on four hectares on a roadless peninsula and faces a small private cove with an inviting white-sand beach. The site feels more like an island than it does mainland.

The retreat's main attraction is the fine snorkeling that's available in the cove a shell's toss away. There's a pristine coral reef close to shore and another, significantly deeper one about 100m farther out. These may be the least disturbed reefs between Colón and the Archipiélago de San Blás.

The three comfortable guestrooms can each accommodate one couple; the two cabins (with a stove and fridge) can each hold up to three people. Mosquito netting accompanies each bed but usually isn't necessary. The lodge's per-night prices of US$100/150 without/with meals

include boat transportation to and from Portobelo and one daily boat excursion for diving, snorkeling or fishing.

If you must use a hairdryer and aren't complete without a morning cappuccino, this place isn't for you. It's casual without any airs. The available electricity is limited to 12 volts, supplied by solar panels. That voltage is perfect for charging the portable fans guests can place beside their beds, although the nightly dip in temperature generally makes them unnecessary. The water is solar-heated – warm but not steamy.

Meals adhere to traditional Panamanian recipes and consist of whatever is seasonally appropriate. The ingredients used are always fresh and are caught or picked locally. The sauces are prepared by chefs in Panama City. The food's not fancy, but it is delicious and filling. The kitchen is open to those guests who prefer to bring their own food. And yes, there is a bar here.

The retreat, which is owned and run by a couple of retired US military officers, is reached by 'land line,' which is slightly different than your usual telephone line. To place a call directly to the retreat, dial ☎ 441-0672, followed by 4540 after you hear a chime.

NOMBRE DE DIOS

Nombre de Dios, 23km east of Portobelo, has a colorful history but isn't much to look at today. There are no ruins from the Spanish settlement to be found, although people here still occasionally pick up the silver-cross coins used by the Spaniards 400 years ago. There's a salt-and-pepper beach, but it's nothing special.

I can think of only one reason that people want to visit Nombre de Dios: It's possible to hire a boat at Las Cabañas de Chico Marin (see Places to Stay & Eat, below) and spend the entire day fishing and/or snorkeling for only US$20; the fishing and snorkeling sites that Chico and the other local boatmen know are very good. (Beware – the sea can be rough during November, December and January.)

Colón Province

Middle Left: Dancing and singing in 'Los Congos' festival, Portobelo

Bottom Left: Ruins of Fuerte San Lorenzo, which once defended the mouth of the Río Chagres

Top: Bahía de Portobelo, scene of many pirate attacks

Right: Boys fishing from 16th-century fort, Portobelo

SCOTT DOGGETT

DAVE G HOUSER

DAVE G HOUSER

SCOTT DOGGETT

Comarca de San Blás

Top Left: Abandoned smugglers' boat on San Blás reef that has surprised many an unwary skipper

Middle Left: Typical mola, famous textiles of Kuna Indians

Top Right: Kuna woman backed by molas

Bottom: Sunset behind lovely Isla Kuanidup

History

From 1519 to 1598, this settlement was the northern terminus of trade across the isthmus. It was here in 1510 that Nicuesa ordered his small fleet to land after they failed to establish a colony at the mouth of the Río Belén in Veraguas. The little harbor and the beach buttressed by dense vegetation looked promising from the sea, but the area's humid climate and scarcity of food took a heavy toll on the settlers.

About 280 settlers made it to Nombre de Dios (800 men had left Hispaniola with Nicuesa in November 1509), and they used what little strength they had to build a blockhouse and huts. For many weeks the men lived on rotten provisions. On a good day they fed upon an alligator; many lived beside the rivers that drained into the Caribbean, but catching one was never easy. Nicuesa sent a ship to Hispaniola for bacon and other supplies, but the vessel was never heard from again.

One day a scouting party from the Spanish colony at Antigua, in the Darién, stumbled upon Nombre de Dios. By this time only 60 settlers remained; the rest had died of disease or hunger. The survivors told the scouts nasty stories about Nicuesa, who was more concerned about establishing a capital than he was about his men. The scouts returned to Antigua with horror stories about Nombre de Dios and its leader.

Nicuesa and 17 men reached Antigua a few days after the scouts, but they were told not to come ashore. The settlers at Antigua wanted nothing to do with Nicuesa. But the governor was stubborn, and the next day he and his party paddled to shore. The men were seized, placed on the worst vessel in the harbor and forced to sail. The rotting craft left Antigua on March 1, 1511, and the ship and its passengers were never seen again.

It was rumored that the worm-eaten vessel wrecked on the coast of Veraguas, where these words were found carved into a tree: *'Aqui anduvó perdido el desdichado Diego de Nicuesa'* – 'Here wandered lost the wretched Diego de Nicuesa.' Another version has it that, while landing on the coast for water, Nicuesa and his men were captured by Indians, barbecued and eaten. According to yet a third version, a tree was found in Cuba with the words *'Aqui feneció el desdichado Nicuesa'* ('Here died the wretched Nicuesa') carved into it.

The 43 miserable survivors who were barely clinging to life at Nombre de Dios were soon rescued from their hell and taken to Antigua by that colony's leader, Vasco Núñez de Balboa. Eight years later, in 1519, the city of Panamá was founded, and later that year Nombre de Dios was resettled. Nombre de Dios soon became the Caribbean terminus of trade across the isthmus, and so it remained until the late 1590s, when nearby Portobelo took over that role.

But even in its heyday as a trading center, Nombre de Dios was a dreadful place. During the mid-16th century, the town comprised 200 houses, but most of the owners lived here only when Spanish fleets arrived to trade supplies for gold and silver stolen from various tribes on the isthmus and in Peru. During the rest of the year, only about 50 people remained. It rained most days, and the heat was excessive.

According to a 16th-century historian, the town was so unhealthy that Indian women living there became barren, and even the native fruits refused to grow. Strong men are said to have died before their time, and disease always claimed the lives of Spanish children. The town was known as a graveyard for travelers. So many men attached to fleets shuttling between Spain and Panama perished while in Nombre de Dios that the biannual trade fairs, initially lasting 60 days, were shortened to 40. It is fitting that Drake, who spent so much of his life in the Tropics, died of dysentery within days of sacking Nombre de Dios.

The town was attacked not only by pirates but also by bands of runaway slaves. Hundreds of escaped black slaves, whom the Spaniards referred to as Cimarrones, mingled with the equally abused Indians and formed settlements of their own during the mid-16th century. By 1574 the escaped slaves had become such a nuisance to the settlers that the king of Spain granted the Cimarrones their freedom on the condition that they'd keep to themselves.

Following Francis Drake's attack on Nombre de Dios and the rise of Portobelo at the end of the 16th century, the town was all but abandoned, and it remained a backwater hamlet for the next 300 years. At that point it gradually revived to a community of about 2000 people, most of whom were the descendants of slaves. People still died like flies in Nombre de Dios until the beginning of the 20th century, when Americans arrived to dredge sand from the harbor for use in concrete for the Gatún Locks. The Americans built a public hospital, screened houses, dug wells and improved sanitation.

The Americans even rebuilt all the structures in town, but not by design: In April 1910 a spark from a locomotive used in the sand-dredging operations started a fire that leaped from one wooden, thatch-roofed structure to another until all 73 buildings in Nombre de Dios had gone up in flames. The Americans took it upon themselves to rebuild the town. Some of the wooden buildings from those days still exist, but the material of choice today is cinderblock.

Orientation & Information
As you enter the town, you'll pass some hot and very rustic houses on both sides of the road. After perhaps 100m, a short road curves to the left, toward the ocean, where there are more homes and Las Cabañas de Chico Marin, one of the two places to stay in town.

If you stay on the main road, 50m or so past the first turnoff you'll reach a second road that turns toward the ocean. In 75m this road reaches the center of town, marked by a small plaza. Facing the plaza is the other place to stay, the Casa de Huespedes.

There's one pay phone in town, near the plaza. There is no post office or bank.

Places to Stay & Eat
Luxury doesn't spring to mind when you arrive at *Las Cabañas de Chico Marin* (no

phone). The 15 cabins, beside a beach that wears a heavy litter camouflage, are utilitarian with a big 'U,' but they're a great value, all things considered. For US$10 per cabin, you get a light, a mattress, a private water supply in the form of a huge in-room container, and a private toilet and cold-water shower. There's no fan, but a constant breeze blows through. If you've been out fishing and snorkeling all day, your cabin will look good to you at night. There's a simple and cheap restaurant here that'll gladly fry any fish you catch.

Casa de Huespedes (no phone) has nine rooms, each of which contains a stand fan. This no-frills place is clean and a good value. Rooms with private cold-water bathrooms cost US$6. Those rooms that share a bathroom at the end of the hall cost US$5. There is no restaurant here, but there are a couple of simple restaurants nearby. A suggestion: At a small, hot, remote fishing village like this, always order the catch of the day; chicken, beef and/or pork may be available, but the meat may be well beyond its published date of purchase, if you catch my drift.

Entertainment
The formal entertainment centers here consist of a *boxing ring* beside Chico Marin's cabins (Chico used to box professionally and now trains hopefuls), and four one-table pool halls scattered about town. The best of the pool halls is *Chelo's,* a few meters from the plaza. Seven sodas and three games of pool at Chelo's cost US$2.

Getting There & Away
Buses to Nombre de Dios depart Colón's Terminal de Buses hourly from 6:30 am to 6 pm and cost US$3 each way. These same buses can be boarded at Sabanitas, which is the turnoff for Portobelo, La Guayra and Nombre de Dios, so you can avoid Colón.

At the time of writing, regular buses from Panama City, destined for Colón but stopping at Sabanitas, were departing from the intersection of Calle P (near Calle 26 Este) and Avenida Central every 20 minutes from around 5 am to 9 pm, then hourly until 1 am; express buses were departing on an identical schedule from a stop on Avenida Perú between Calles 29 and 30 Este. As noted earlier in this chapter, the scheduled summer 1998 completion of the new Panama City-Colón highway may have changed these departure points, so confirm them with a tour operator, hotel clerk or IPAT. Ask the bus driver before departing if the bus will stop at Sabanitas.

Getting Around
There are no taxis in Nombre de Dios. The only way to get around is by foot. However, this is a very small town. Walking across it takes 20 minutes, tops.

Comarca de San Blás

The Comarca de San Blás is an autonomous region that comprises the Archipiélago de San Blás and a 226km strip of Caribbean coast from Colón Province (to the west) to Colombia (to the east). The southern boundary of the *comarca* (district) consists of two strings of jungle-clad mountains, the Serranía de San Blás and the Serranía del Darién – the highlands of the San Blás and Darién regions.

The Kuna Indians have governed the 2360-sq-km region since the 1920s, when the Panamanian government granted the tribe the right of self-rule following a Kuna uprising that led to the death of 22 Panamanian policemen and 20 Kuna who had befriended them. Today the Kuna not only govern themselves but have two representatives in the Panamanian legislature, as well as the right to vote in Panamanian elections.

Kuna Indians

The Kuna have lived in eastern Panama for at least the last two centuries, but scholars don't agree on their origin. Language similarities with people that once lived several hundred kilometers to the west would indicate that the Kuna migrated eastward. However, oral tradition has it that the tribe emigrated from Colombia after the 16th century, following devastating encounters with Indians armed with poison-dart blowguns.

Some scholars contend the Kuna were well established in eastern Panama at the time the conquistadors arrived, because the Spanish chroniclers indicated that the Indians they met used the Kuna words *ulu* for 'canoe' and *oba* for 'corn.' These scholars also note that many geographic names in eastern Panama during the colonial epoch were Kuna. Nearly all the rivers in Darién Province have Kuna names, for example, although the Emberá and Wounaan Indians live there now.

No matter where the Kuna came from, scholars agree that life on the islands is relatively new for the Indians. Historians at the end of the 18th century wrote that the only people who used the San Blás islands at that time were pirates, Spaniards and the odd explorer.

Today there are an estimated 70,000 Kuna: 40,000 live on the district's islands, 10,000 live on tribal land along the coast and 20,000 live outside the district. So communal are the island Kuna that they inhabit only 40 of the keys; the rest are mostly left to coconut trees, sea turtles and iguanas. On the inhabited islands, so many traditional bamboo-sided, thatch-roofed houses are clustered together that there's scarcely room to maneuver between them.

The Kuna like to say that their archipelago consists of 'one island for every day

HIGHLIGHTS

- The islands, most uninhabited and fit to appear on the covers of travel magazines
- The Kuna, a fiercely independent people who maintain their traditions in a changing world
- Nalunega, home to a simple hotel that's the islands' best lodging value
- Kuanidup, with lots of palm trees, a few lizards and plenty of soft white sand
- Snorkeling at Wreck Reef, which has become a graveyard for many a boat

of the year.' In fact, there are nearly 400 islands in the chain, all small creations of sand and palm rising barely far enough above the blue-green Caribbean to escape complete inundation by breakers during storms. Reefs to the north and east help prevent destructive waves from striking the islands. From the tourist's perspective, there are two kinds of San Blás islands: the white-sand, palm-sprinkled, magazine-cover beauties, and the overcrowded keys where feces and rubbish are found just a few meters from shore.

Few of the islands are more than 10km from the district's mainland, and all the heavily inhabited islands are very close to the coast because the Kuna's agricultural areas and their vital natural resources – such as water, firewood and construction materials – are there. Also on the mainland are the giant trees from which the Indians make their chief mode of transportation – the *cayuco,* a dugout canoe made from a burned and hollowed-out trunk. There are nine towns on the mainland, all within 100m of the sea; there are no restaurants or hotels in these towns.

Visitors to the inhabited islands will find an interesting though at times unfriendly people. The Kuna still adhere to traditions that astonish tourists. For example, a Kuna woman is not given a name until she has had her first menstrual period, at which time a party is held, the young woman's hair is cut short and her parents select a name for her with the help of a medicine man. Until that day the young woman answers to a nickname.

Most Kuna women continue to dress as their ancestors did. Their faces are distinguished by a black line painted from the forehead to the tip of the nose. A gold ring is worn through the nose. A length of colorful printed cloth is wrapped around the waist as a skirt, topped by a short-sleeved blouse covered in brilliantly colored *molas* (traditional Kuna textiles). A printed head scarf and many necklaces, rings and bracelets complete the daily outfit. To make themselves more attractive, the women also wrap their legs, from ankle to knee, in long strands of colorful beads.

The Kuna can appear unfriendly to tourists, and understandably so, because most visitors view them as oddities that must be photographed. Several islands are visited by cruise ships. When the ships arrive, the number of people on an already congested island can triple, leaving barely enough room for anyone to turn around, and yet virtually two-thirds of the populace (the tourists) are trying like crazy to photograph the other third (the Kuna). It's a pretty ugly scene, and it's repeated time and again.

In addition, the behavior of many tourists is appalling to the Kuna. For example, Kuna women dress conservatively, always keeping their cleavages, bellies and most of their legs covered. In their opinion, to do otherwise would be offensive. Yet some foreign women arrive in Kuna villages in bikini tops and short shorts, not only embarrassing themselves in the eyes of the Indians but also showing disrespect for Kuna sensibilities. Likewise, the Kuna tend to limit their drinking of alcohol to celebrations, and they find it very disrespectful when tourists wander around their islands intoxicated or with beers in hand. As a result of repeated violations of their privacy and sensibilities, the Kuna now require that travelers pay visitation fees and fees for photographs taken of them (see Visiting the Comarca de San Blás, below).

Although the island Kuna increasingly want to be paid in US dollars for their goods and services, the district's principal currency remains the coconut. The Kuna grow coconuts like crazy: In a good year they'll harvest more than 30 million of them. They barter away most of these to Colombians, who make the rounds of Kuna towns in old wooden schooners. Each of these low-sitting boats can hold 50,000 to 80,000 coconuts.

In Colombia the coconuts are used in the production of candy, gelatin capsules, cookies, shampoos and other products. Colombia has many processing plants for the fruit, but Panama, oddly, has none. The

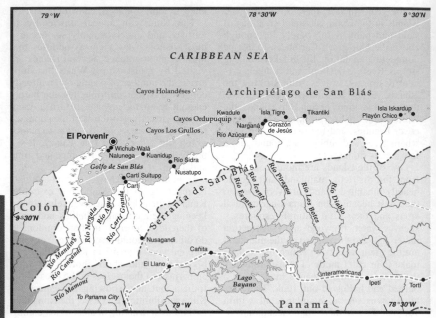

Colombians also sell Kuna coconuts to other South American countries.

In return for the fruit, the Colombians give the Kuna clothing, jars of Nescafé, vinegar, rice, sunglasses, canned milk, batteries, soups and other goods. Colombian products are, by and large, cheaper than Panamanian products. For example, one product the Kuna obtain in exchange for their fruit is bottled coconut oil, which they can get for the equivalent of US$4.50. The same bottle of coconut oil costs US$7 in Panama City. Thus most of the manufactured goods found on San Blás islands come from Colombia.

The Kuna are shrewd businesspeople. Because their economy is based on the sale of coconuts, they protect it by selling the fruit at a predetermined price to prevent their Colombian buyers from playing one Kuna off another to bring down the cost. Every year the tribe's chiefs agree on one price for coconuts (in 1998 the price for a dehusked fruit on any San Blás island was

12¢). If a Kuna is found selling dehusked coconuts at another price, that Indian is punished by the tribe. By price fixing and enforcement, the chiefs prevent price wars among the Kuna. Price wars would hurt the community by lowering the standard of living, and they could even force some Kuna out of business.

In another protectionist move, the chiefs passed a law a few years ago prohibiting outsiders from owning property in the district. Thus they promptly forced out the handful of foreigners living on the islands, and the Kuna burned down their homes. No compensation was paid. As a result of that law, there are less than a dozen places to stay on the islands, because few Kuna have enough money to construct even a very basic hotel. None of the hotels that do exist are fancy.

It's important for visitors to know that the Kuna generally place their own interests before anything else, and thus agreements struck with them aren't always

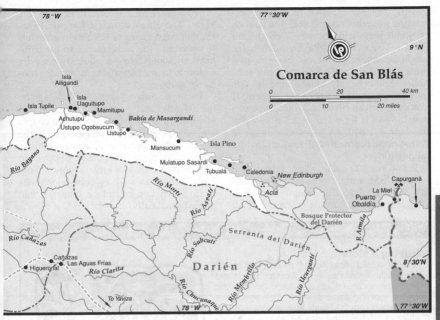

binding. For example, if you hire a Kuna boatman to take you to 10 islands, don't be surprised if he heads home after taking you to only five or six. If asked to explain, he may say that you cannot go to the others because you need special permission (when in fact you don't) or that he must return sooner than agreed because his family is expecting him. Most likely, your boatman has simply had enough of you.

Also, be forewarned that the Kuna engage in some activities that may seem particularly offensive to visitors: for example, they kill endangered sea turtles for meat and eggs, and they don't hesitate to dump garbage into the ocean.

Visiting the Comarca de San Blás

On all the heavily inhabited islands, the Kuna require tourists to register and pay a visitation fee upon arrival. That fee ranges from US$3 to US$5 (the price varies from island to island), and the visitor is expected to pay it regardless of whether he or she

stays a week or only half an hour. For brevity's sake, this fee isn't mentioned again in this chapter, but remember: If you arrive on a populated San Blás island, you're expected to search for and find a small government office where you must present your passport and pay a visitation fee as well.

Visitors must also pay for any photo they take of Kuna. If you want to take someone's photo, be sure to first ask his or her permission and be prepared to pay at least US$1 per subject (some Kuna expect to be paid US$1 per photo).

It's best to visit the San Blás islands with the help of a tour operator (see listings in the Getting Around chapter). If you don't, you should be aware that you'll have a difficult time communicating in the district unless you speak Spanish or Kuna. There probably aren't 10 Kuna on these islands who speak English, although most of the boatmen do speak Spanish in addition to Kuna.

Another thing visitors should know is that all the uninhabited islands are privately owned. You are expected to receive permission from the owner before you land on one, and permission is always contingent upon a visitation fee. Paying such a fee might be amenable to you, but you first must find the owner, and that can take hours. Some largely uninhabited islands may have a single family living on them; if you spot such an island and like it, you can usually visit it for a few hours if you pay the family US$2. Unless you can speak Kuna, your boatman will have to do the talking for you.

If you want to camp on an uninhabited island, US$5 a night per couple will usually do the trick. But camping on such islands isn't wise, because you run the risk of encountering narcotraffickers in the night. The Kuna do not allow the Panamanian coast guard or US antidrug vessels to operate in the archipelago, so the uninhabited islands are occasionally used by Colombian narcotraffickers running cocaine up the coast.

There are only a handful of lodgings on the islands, and none on the mainland. Most of these are basic, although a couple are comfortable. The service at all the hotels is slow, because the Kuna do things at their own pace. Most densely populated islands in the district have a store selling basic items, as well as coin telephones from which you can place domestic and international calls.

Buying a Mola

A mola, a traditional Kuna handicraft, is made of brightly colored squares of cotton fabric laid atop one another. Cuts are made through the layers, forming basic designs. The layers are then sewn together with tiny, evenly spaced stitches to hold the design in place. *Mola* means 'blouse' in Kuna, and Kuna women make molas in thematically matching but never identical pairs. A pair will comprise the front and back of a blouse.

As is true of all art forms, the beauty of a mola is in the eye of the beholder. If you're in the market for a mola, choose one you would like to see on your wall, as a place setting, as part of a dress; don't be swayed by what you think someone else might find attractive.

TOM BOYDEN

Bird mola

I happen to like molas that feature sea turtles, but then I'm a simple fellow.

Regardless of the design, Kuna believe that the very best molas have the following characteristics:

- Stitches closely match the color of the cloth they are set against.
- Stitches are very fine and neatly spaced.
- Stitches are pulled evenly and with enough tension to be barely visible.
- Curves are cut smoothly and the sewing follows the curves of the cut.
- Outline strips are uniform in width, with no frayed edges.

When you're buying molas, it's a good idea to think about how you intend to use them. If you're thinking of making pillows out of them, consider the piece of furniture you'll place the pillows on. On the other hand, if you see a mola you really like, get it and worry about its use later. You can always add a mola to the back of a denim jacket, which gives you a justification for purchasing yet another article of clothing. ■

The poor quality of the islands' food comes as a bit of a surprise to most visitors, and the reasons for it are tragic: The archipelago's waters have been so overfished that the 'catch of the day' at most San Blás lodges is bait fish. The lobster stock is so depleted that they are rarely available or quite small. Same goes for the squid and crab inventories. When Kuna divers want to catch squid, they dump chlorine bleach into the animals' hiding places to force them out. They catch other marine animals the same way, although the chemicals vary. Biologists have found Clorox, agricultural insecticides and other contaminants in San Blás marine life at levels high enough to damage the livers of people who dine on it. If you're particularly health conscious, you may want to consider bringing your own food.

Travelers should also note that the snorkeling in district waters isn't what it should be: In November 1992, marine organisms from the archipelago began to be sold for use in aquariums, sparking a hunt for exotically colored and shaped fish, anemones, soft corals and beautiful clams.

As pretty as the Comarca de San Blás is, it isn't for everyone. The Kuna, who are fearful of losing control of their land, can be difficult, and the islands that are enticing in photographs can disappoint in reality. Travelers who would like to visit a chain of Caribbean islands that has yet to be transformed by wealthy outside developers will find such a chain in the Archipiélago de San Blás. Unfortunately, the Kuna have damaged their environment even without developers' help. For the reasons stated above, I can't recommend the district to people short on vacation time, disposable income or patience. The information in this chapter is intended for people who have plenty of all three.

Getting There & Away

Air Three airlines fly between Panama City's Aeropuerto Paitilla and the Comarca de San Blás: Aereo Taxi (☎ 264-8644 in Panama City), Ansa (☎ 226-7891) and Aviatur (☎ 270-1748).

The airlines fly to 20 San Blás destinations: El Porvenir and Cartí (the towns that are nearest to Panama City), Río Sidra, Río Azúcar, Narganá, Corazón de Jesús, Isla Tigre, Tikantiki, Playón Chico, Isla Tupile, Isla Ailigandí, Achutupu, Mamitupu, Ustupo Ogobsucum, Ustupo, Mansucum, Lulatupu, Tubualá, Caledonia and Puerto Obaldía (which is near the Colombian border).

Aereo Taxi and Ansa serve all the destinations daily except Puerto Obaldía, which is served three days a week. Sample fares on both airlines include US$28/56 one-way/roundtrip for the flight to El Porvenir and US$44/88 to Puerto Obaldía. Fares to other San Blás destinations fall somewhere in between.

Aviatur has morning flights to all 20 San Blás destinations, but it does not offer any flights to the district on Sunday.

Reservations are a must, as the district is served by small aircraft and seats fill up quickly. An airplane flying from Panama City to San Blás may stop at several islands before reaching your destination, so be sure to ask the name of the island you're on before you leave the plane. Likewise, it's probable that the aircraft you board in San Blás to return to Panama City will make several stops before it arrives in the capital.

You can make an airline reservation over the telephone or in person, but you'll want to make two other reservations as well. You'll need to arrange for a boatman to pick you up when you arrive in the district, and you'll also need to make a hotel reservation. For all three reservations, you'd be wise to consult one of the tour operators listed in the Getting Around chapter. Any of them can arrange for you to be picked up at your mainland hotel, driven to the airport, flown to San Blás, met at an airport in the district and then taken to your island hotel.

Car Only one road leads into the district, the rugged El Llano-Cartí road that connects the town of El Llano, on the Carretera Interamericana (the Pan-American Hwy)

COMARCA DE SAN BLÁS

70km east of Panama City, to the San Blás coastal hamlet of Cartí.

The road begins near El Llano at the turnoff for Nusagandi, a forest reserve just inside the Comarca de San Blás. The reserve begins at the southern boundary of the district, 20km north of the Interamericana. A few kilometers north of the district boundary is the very rustic Nusagandi Nature Lodge. (See the Panamá Province chapter for more details on the reserve and the lodge.)

The lodge is reachable only by a 4WD vehicle with a powerful engine, a winch and good off-road tires. Beyond the lodge, the remaining 20km to Cartí is on road that even armored personnel carriers would have difficulty negotiating; it's more of a trail than a road these days. For all practical purposes, the El Llano-Cartí road ends at the lodge.

Getting Around

By far the best way to see the islands is with a guide. If you can afford one, contact one of the tour operators listed in the Getting Around chapter and see the archipelago with someone who knows the islands and their people well. If you don't have a guide and if you don't speak any Spanish or Kuna, you should expect some frustrating moments in the Comarca de San Blás.

Colombian merchant boats travel the Caribbean Sea between Colón and Puerto Obaldía, stopping at inhabited San Blás islands to pick up and drop off people and goods. Other Colombian vessels visit the inhabited islands to take on coconuts. Both fleets are occasionally used for drug trafficking. Travel by these often overloaded boats is neither comfortable nor safe, and it's always very slow going.

A much better way to get around is to pick an area of the archipelago you want to visit, fly as close to it as the nearest airstrip will allow and hire a boatman to take you around. If you speak Spanish or Kuna and have some money, you can usually find someone with a motorized cayuco who will assume the role of boatman. If you don't

speak either language, you could find yourself stranded.

One of the most pleasant sights you'll encounter on a boat trip in the archipelago is the coastline to the south. Behind the generally sandy (although occasionally rocky) shore are jagged peaks that run the length of the district. Initially the verdant hills are covered with a mixture of manioc fields and patches of rainforest, but the farther east you travel the fewer fields there are, and at times the mountains are covered with jungle as far as the eye can see. This is the coast as Columbus saw it – unspoiled, the very darkest of greens and teeming with wildlife. Always making a welcome appearance just above the mountains are cumulus clouds. They may be pure white or gray with rainwater, but they are never tainted by smog. Sunsets are particularly colorful, displaying generous proportions of reds and oranges, violets and lavenders.

EL PORVENIR

El Porvenir, at the northwest end of the district, is the gateway to the San Blás islands. Visitors to the keys tend to fly here, proceed directly to the island's small dock and take a boat elsewhere. That 'elsewhere' is more often than not the Hotel San Blás, on the nearby island of Nalunega, or the Hotel Anai, on the island of Wichub-Walá.

There's a police station and a few homes on El Porvenir, as well as a hotel with a restaurant: *El Porvenir Hotel* (☎ 221-1397; ask for Mrs Bibi), which has 13 rooms. Most contain three twin beds, and each has a toilet, a shower, one light and one power outlet. Electricity is provided from 6 pm 'until all of our guests have gone to bed.' The hotel's walls are concrete and its roof is corrugated tin – nothing fancy – but the place is cool and pleasant. Rates are US$33 per person September to March and half that the rest of the year.

NALUNEGA

This island, with its many traditional Kuna homes close together, is similar to the inhabited San Blás islands found farther south and east in the archipelago. However,

Nalunega is considerably cleaner than the others because the owner of its sole hotel pays several boys to keep the small island free of litter.

The *Hotel San Blás* (☎ 262-5410) is the best-value and most popular hotel in the district. It has 31 rooms, most simple but OK bamboo-and-board adjoining rooms with sandy floors, thatch roofs and shared bathrooms. The guestrooms above the open-sided dining area and the adjacent general store are cooler and cleaner than the others because their floors are not sandy; although the sea is a stone's throw away, the views from these rooms are mostly of thatch roofs. The per-person rate for all these rooms is US$35, which includes three meals daily and boat tours.

Three larger guestrooms were being built at the San Blás at the time of writing, and their rates were not available. The owner, Luis Burgos, speaks English, and the food he provides is the best in the islands. If Luis knows you're coming, he'll arrange for a boatman to meet you on El Porvenir.

WICHUB-WALÁ

This equally small and unusually clean inhabited island, a five-minute boat ride from El Porvenir, contained two hotels in late 1997; construction began on two others in early 1998.

The *Hotel Anai* (☎ 239-3025) has 20 basic rooms, a simple but pleasant dining area and a dirty swimming pool. In each room is a shower stall, a 5-gallon container and a large cup with which to bathe. The cost – US$60 per person – includes three meals daily and boat tours in the morning and afternoon. According to the Anai's elderly owner, Alberto Gonsalez Ieguabi, the hotel's one weakness is that its bamboo walls don't give *wagas* (tourists) enough privacy. 'Tourist women make a lot of noise when they have sex,' he says. 'Kuna women – you can only hear them breathe.'

The *Kuna Kiskua Hotel* (☎ 227-5308; ask for Juan Antonio Martinez) has five basic rooms in a two-story thatch-and-bamboo structure with shared bathrooms 25m away.

Moon Children

Few Kuna marry outside their villages. The result is an inbred people – usually short, large-headed and thick-necked – and the world's highest incidence of albinism. Albinos' eyes are dark pink, their hair yellow-white and their skin pale pink. When seen amid their brown-skinned, black-haired relatives, Kuna albinos are quite captivating.

In some societies albino children are viewed as freaks of nature and ostracized by their peers. Not so in Kuna society. Kuna children are taught that albinos are special people – children of the moon – and that they are destined to be leaders.

As a result, the moon children of the Comarca de San Blás are not only the most popular kids in the tribe, but they are also the most recalcitrant due to their big egos. Kuna children have a lot of confidence as it is, but when you tell some of them that they are particularly gifted – and they surely do look different – they can become very confident indeed.

Unsurprisingly, an unusually high percentage of moon children put their abundant confidence to work for them and actually become community leaders – a fact that further supports the notion that they really are special people. ∎

These rooms, unlike those at the Hotel Anai, are in the middle of the island and do not have ocean views. The year-round rate of US$50 per person includes three meals a day and a snorkeling tour to a nearby island. Some snorkel gear is available for rent at US$5 per day.

CARTÍ SUITUPO

Cartí Suitupo, more commonly known as simply Cartí, is the island closest to the coastal hamlet of Cartí. The hamlet is distinguished by the fact that it is the only town in the district reachable by road, although that road (the El Llano-Cartí road; see the Getting Around section, earlier in this chapter) is really more of a wide, horribly rutted jungle trail. A mere 100m separates the two Cartís. There's an airstrip near the hamlet, and from it you can travel by boat to Cartí Suitupo and thence to other islands.

Cartí Suitupo is very typical of the inhabited islands from here to the Colombian border – it's the size of three football fields, crowded with bamboo houses and terribly polluted. Cartí Suitupo is also one of the San Blás islands that are visited by exploratory boats from cruise ships. Packed with tourists, these boats visit an average of five times a month.

The island has lots of children, as do many San Blás islands these days. The Panamanian government established medical clinics throughout the district in the early 1990s, lowering a sky-high infant mortality rate. Childbirth, once a leading cause of death among Kuna women, has become low risk, increasing the number of women of childbearing age. These factors, combined with the Kuna desire for big families, have sparked a population explosion on the keys.

If you speak Spanish, it's very easy to get from Cartí Suitupo to a pristine, sparsely populated island. Just talk to Tony Adams Harrington, who holds the keys to the Dormitory Cartí Sugdup (see below). To prevent competition and potential animosity, the island's population elected Tony its sole official guide. He will find you shortly after your arrival on Cartí; wagas don't go unnoticed on the inhabited islands for more than a few nanoseconds.

For US$5 per person, Tony can arrange for a boatman to take you to nearby **Isla Aguja** (Needle Island) and pick you up later. The US$5 pays for the boatman, but it would be wise to give Tony a tip as well, just to ensure he'll remind the boatman to pick you up at the specified time. There are only two families living on Isla Aguja, and the beach and swimming there are lovely.

The one hotel on Cartí Suitupo, the *Dormitory Cartí Sugdup* (☎ 228-8917), is a 30 by 20m concrete, bamboo and thatch struc-

ture over the water. The dormitory has five basic rooms with semidecent beds and shared bathroom for US$10 per person. The toilet and shower empty into the sea. There is one light bulb in the hotel, and the guestrooms each contain a lantern. This place is basic, but at least it's inexpensive.

NUSATUPO & RÍO SIDRA

These typically crowded San Blás islands are 15km east of Cartí Suitupo. Only a few minutes' boat ride apart, they are served by the Río Sidra airstrip, which is not on Río Sidra itself but a few kilometers away on the mainland. Nusatupo is the closer of the islands to the airstrip, and there is a hotel on it; Río Sidra, however, has no tourist services at all.

On Nusatupo, *Hotel Kuna Yala* (☎ 229-1920; ask for Manuel Alfaro) has four rooms with a shared bathroom, an over-the-water toilet, concrete floors, a tin roof and no fans; when I stayed there the outside temperature wasn't unusually high but the rooms were hot as Hades. There is a dining area and kitchen, but no electricity. The US$45 per-person rate includes three meals daily and a boat ride to and from several snorkeling sites. Because of its proximity to the keys mentioned below, this place would be a very decent deal if it weren't so uncomfortably hot.

KUANIDUP

This tiny island, 30 minutes by motorized cayuco from the Río Sidra airstrip, is home to a lone cluster of bamboo-and-thatch cabins, lots of palm trees, a few iguanas, soft white sand and little else. It's a beautiful island with a lovely beach for swimming. Hammocks are hung between some trees, and it's awfully easy to fall asleep in one as your mind drifts from the lapping surf to the arcing sea-sky horizon to the swaying palms above you.

Each of the stand-alone cabins at *Cabañas Kuanidup* (☎ 227-0872) has two firm beds, a lantern and sandy floors. A short walk away are pairs of showers, sinks and toilets, and beyond those is a small kitchen and dining area. The per-person rate of US$70 includes three meals daily (be warned that the food here isn't good) and one lengthy snorkeling trip. The friendly owner, who speaks English, also owns a nearby uninhabited island where it's quite OK to sunbathe in the buff. This is a good place to 'get away from it all.'

CAYOS LOS GRULLOS, HOLANDÉSES & ORDUPUQUIP

The dozen or so sparsely inhabited islands known as Cayos Los Grullos are 10km northeast of Río Sidra, at the lower left (southwestern) corner of a triangle of three island groups. Cayos Holandéses (Dutchmen Keys), north of Los Grullos, top the triangle. Cayos Ordupuquip make up the lower right (southeastern) corner of the triangle. These groups, popular with yachters, are 12km from one another, separated by calm blue-green water. There are no tourist facilities on these islands.

All of the islands in these groups are lovely, but the Cayos Holandéses are the tops because they are the closest to a very shallow reef that makes for some interesting snorkeling – not so much for the fish and corals here as for the numerous pieces of wreckage. This ridge of rocks, sand and coral, 100m north of Cayos Holandéses, is called **Wreck Reef**, and it earned its name by snaring all kinds of vessels over the years. The reef's been able to do that because it's pretty far from the closest island, and though the water south of the reef is barely 1m deep, the ocean floor north of the reef plunges 100m in half that distance – or, from a sea captain's perspective, the ocean floor *rises* 100m to a dangerously shallow depth in half that distance. Wreck Reef's distance from the islands and the presence of deep water so close to the reef have fooled many experienced sailors.

Most crafts that smack into the reef these days belong to narcotraffickers and contraband smugglers operating at night. These people are alerted to the presence of the reef by the loud, crunching sound of rock and coral taking a bite out of their hulls. Over time, the surf that crashes against these wrecks breaks them up, and their cargo is tossed into the surrounding sand.

In 1995 a smugglers' boat filled with TV sets slammed into the reef at night, and the crew abandoned ship. The smugglers had hoped to bring the TVs (bought in Colón's Zona Libre) into port at Cartagena, Colombia, without paying any import taxes. The next morning, scores of Kuna in cayucos helped themselves to the TVs. The smugglers were never caught, and today their rusting, looted boat is perched on the reef like a trophy.

Historically, most of the boats claimed by Wreck Reef were the victims of *chocosanos* ('storms that come from the east' in Kuna). Chocosanos are ghastly tempests that whip up monstrous waves that can overrun entire islands. Such waves have swept many San Blás Indians and their homes out to sea. The violent storms are always preceded by a purple-black eastern sky and a lack of breeze and birdsong.

As soon as it's evident that a chocosano is approaching, the Kuna – especially the older ones – combat it by blowing into conch shells. The sound alerts their benevolent god, who tries to disperse the threatening storm. If he fails, as he usually does, the eerie stillness is broken by ground-shaking thunderclaps, howling winds, pounding downpours and a vengeful sea. At the southern end of Wreck Reef is a freighter that lies with its hull fully exposed and its deck flat against the ocean floor – a big vessel that was flipped like a pancake by a mighty chocosano.

RÍO AZÚCAR

This typical, jam-packed island is close to the mainland and has no lodgings or places to eat. But it's known for its festive Carnaval, which is held during the four days preceding Ash Wednesday. It is the only San Blás island that hosts Carnaval festivities, mainly because celebrating in style – and they do celebrate in style here – takes money, and the Kuna have very little of it.

But every year a wealthy and benevolent Panama City lawyer gives generously to the island's Carnaval fund, and the people respond enthusiastically with four days of dancing, singing and costume-wearing. Needless to say, the lawyer never has to pay for his fishing trips when he vacations in the area.

Like most heavily populated islands in the district, Río Azúcar has a public coin-operated telephone from which you can place domestic and international calls. There's also a clinic with a US-trained doctor. There's a very modest store on Río Azúcar, as there is on all the densely populated San Blás islands, that sells batteries, soups and other household products. You can buy sodas at these stores (not diet ones), but bottled water is rarely available.

Also on Río Azúcar is a simple church showing its age, built in 1945 by Italian engineers at the direction of a Spanish priest. The priest is long gone, but the islands have no shortage of *Merki* (American) missionaries who want the Kuna to forget their gods and accept Jesus as their lord.

NARGANÁ & CORAZÓN DE JESÚS

The inhabited islands of Narganá and Corazón de Jesús are 5km northeast of Río Azúcar and reachable by a coastal airstrip. The two islands are linked by an arcing wooden foot bridge perhaps 70m long. At the southwestern end of the bridge is Narganá, home to the district's only courthouse, its only jail and its only bank. There are also a few policemen on the island; if any ask for your passport, you should politely present it – jotting down tourists' names in little books gives them something to do.

The Banco Nacional de Panamá branch office on Narganá is open 8 am to 3 pm weekdays and 9 am to noon Saturday. It is possible to have money wired to this office, but be aware that the service takes 24 hours. It is also possible to cash American Express traveler's checks here, and an ATM was scheduled to go into operation by mid-1998.

At the time of writing, a rundown hotel on Narganá was being rebuilt. The *Hotel Yandup* (no phone) looked like it was going to continue to offer 10 hot, unattractive rooms after the dust settled and the paint dried. A worker seemed pretty certain the daily rate was going to remain US$25 per person, meals excluded.

Corazón de Jesús is the most westernized of the San Blás islands – few Kuna practices are observed here, and most of the structures are made of concrete and tin instead of bamboo and thatch. There are no places to stay on Corazón de Jesús, but you can buy bottled water, canned goods, rope and razor blades here.

KWADULE

On the island of Kwadule, 15 minutes from Narganá by slow cayuco, is the *Kwadule Eco-Resort* (☎ 269-6313), possibly the most comfortable retreat in the archipelago. This 'eco-resort,' which consists of six stand-alone cabins and a large restaurant built over the water, has the small island to itself. Each cabin is quite comfortable, with a good bed, large ceiling fan, hot-water private bathroom, and a large window without glass, facing the sea.

This resort is costly at US$90 per person including meals, and the service in the restaurant is very slow. There's little to see or do on the football-field-size island, which is too small for privacy, although the ocean here is fine for swimming. Six more cabins are planned on the island and will likely be completed by the time you read this.

ISLA TIGRE

This surprisingly clean, traditional Kuna island is 7km east of Narganá. Here Kuna women can be readily seen in their doorways offering molas to passersby; on other islands women often stay out of sight if they know tourists are moving about. On all the inhabited San Blás islands, narrow dirt pathways separate the homes – here, however, the walkways are unusually wide.

There are no lodgings or other tourist facilities on Isla Tigre. Keep in mind that on this island, you will be charged US$50 if you possess a video camera, even if you say that you won't be using it. The Kuna believe that if you have a video camera, you will use it, and thus they require that you pay the fee. (Photos of Kuna cost US$1 here, as elsewhere in the district.)

ISLA ISKARDUP

The *Iskardup Eco-Resort* (☎ 269-6313) fills most of Isla Iskardup (Cayman Island), two hours by slow boat southeast of Isla Tigre and 10 minutes east of Playón Chico (where there's an airstrip).

I couldn't examine the resort at the time of my visit because several Kuna chiefs were inspecting the place and rejected my requests to let me inspect it too. However, a good friend who had toured Iskardup a few weeks earlier told me it consists of 14 wood-floored cabins and an open-sided dining area with sweeping ocean views. He compared Iskardup to Kwadule (in fact, both so-called 'eco-resorts' are owned by the same company), but he said the service at Iskardup is better. He also told me that the food could be improved and that the portions are skimpy. The rate of US$90 per person also applies and is excessive.

The island has a fine beach, and there are a number of uninhabited islands nearby that hotel staff will take you to if you seek. The resort also offers guests the opportunity to go to the mainland for a four-hour jungle trek to a spectacular waterfall.

ISLA TUPILE TO ISLA UAGUITUPO

The ocean can be treacherous along the central part of the archipelago, particularly in the 15km stretch of roiling blue sea from densely populated Isla San Ignacio de Tupile past equally crowded Isla Ailigandí to within 1km of Isla Uaguitupo (Dolphin

Island). Here 3m swells are the norm. If you've been frightened by the sea in the northern part of the archipelago, you can expect to be terrified as you ride these waves. If you plan to travel these waters in a motorized cayuco and have any doubts about your boatman's abilities, you may want to consider hiring another one before attempting this trip.

ISLA UAGUITUPO

Uaguitupo is a pleasant, grassy little isle, 100m from the island of Achutupu (which is served by a coastal airstrip). Taking up most of Uaguitupo is *Dolphin Island Lodge* (☎ 263-3078), which consists of six terribly hot cabins with shared bathrooms. The cabins are slowly being upgraded.

This is a family-run business. The parents speak English, Spanish and Kuna, and the son speaks some English. All are very friendly. The son is usually tasked with taking guests to a nearby island that has lovely beaches and safe places to swim (Isla Uaguitupo itself has no real beach, and the swimming is poor). There's little to do at the lodge itself besides lounging in a hammock. The island has no electricity.

Cabins cost US$170 per person for the first night, including roundtrip airfare from Panama City, and US$72 per person thereafter. Rates include three meals daily and a boat ride to the island with beaches, as well as a trip to the very traditional island of Achutupu, where you can wander among the Kuna. Remember: If you want to take photos of someone on this or any other San Blás island, be sure to ask his or her permission first, and be prepared to pay at least US$1 per subject (some Kuna expect US$1 per photo).

USTUPO OGOBSUCUM

This island, 15km southeast of Uaguitupo, has the largest population of all of the San Blás islands, with 5000 residents. Ustupo Ogobsucum, widely known as simply Ustupo (the same name used by a tiny community on the mainland a short distance away), is crowded and unattractive, and it offers little of interest to the visitor.

Should you decide to visit Ustupo Ogobsucum, you must immediately go to the police station, which is in a two-story structure beside two very tall radio antennae. There you must present your passport and your tourist card or visa, whichever pertains to you (see the Facts for the Visitor chapter). Then you must pay US$5. Next, you must ask permission from the island's chiefs for permission to wander around the island. If you don't speak Spanish or Kuna, you will have a very difficult time explaining yourself, as none of the chiefs speak any English. If they don't like the way you look, your request will be rejected.

Lodgings on Ustupo Ogobsucum consist of the *Motel Awibe Kuna* (no phone). This is a concrete, two-story structure with six partitioned cubicles in one decent-size room. There's a worn mattress on a swaying steel frame in each cubicle and bars on all the windows. There's no fan. The shower consists of a bucket of water in a public area outside the motel, and the toilet is a hole in a board over the ocean with just a little privacy. The price: US$7 a night.

ISLA PINO

Isla Pino (Pine Island), named for the lovely forest that covers most of the island, is 25km southeast of Ustupo Ogobsucum (or 1½ hours by 15-horsepower boat). As you approach the 2km long, 1.5km wide island, you'll note that it looks astonishingly similar to a whale.

There's a sleepy little town on the western side of Isla Pino, and its 300 inhabitants spend most of the day trying to beat the oppressive heat by staying in their hammocks in their thatch houses. When they work, they harvest coconuts and fish.

There are no hotels on the island. In fact, there are no services in town of use to the tourist, except a small *provisions stand* that also serves some snacks, beer and soda – nothing much, but the beverages go down really nicely in this hot place.

If you haven't gotten enough exercise lately and enjoy the occasional walk on the wild side, you can take a trail that winds around the island. It skirts dense jungle

that's home to large boas, wild rabbits and red-naped tamarins, among other creatures you probably don't have at home.

No one on Isla Pino asked me to pay a visitation fee when I visited in 1997, but a plainclothed policeman did ask to see some ID. In general, it's OK to hand over your passport when someone in Panama asks to see it. With few exceptions, the person is a police officer or bouncer who's just doing his or her job.

MULATUPO SASARDÍ

This typical San Blás island, 7km south of Isla Pino, is far removed from the cruise-ship scene, and its 4000 residents actually see very few tourists. The Kuna here are extremely friendly, particularly the children, many of whom will come up to shake your hand and say, 'Hello, mister' or 'Hello, lady' in English (it's about all the English they know).

The place to pay the visitation fee is a two-story building (one of just a few here) facing the island's basketball court. The chiefs usually hang out in this building, and it's important to ask them for permission to see the island. The chiefs, who speak Spanish and Kuna, will give you permission as long as you're not doing something offensive to them, such as going about in a bikini top.

There's a place to stay on the island, the very basic *Isla Herrera Hotel* (☎ 262-5562 in Panama City; ask for the hotel), which costs US$20 per person. You bathe here by dipping a bucket into a big barrel and pouring water over yourself. The barrel is behind a family's home near the hotel, as is the toilet, an over-the-sea contraption.

Also on the island is the *Restaurante Mi Pueblo,* which is run by a Kuna woman who has a smile that could melt a glacier. A delicious chicken, a plate of French fries and a soda will set you back US$3 here.

PUERTO OBALDÍA

Information on Puerto Obaldía, the last significant town in the district before one reaches Colombia, appears in the Getting There & Away chapter.

Aclá & New Edinburgh

In the eastern portion of the Comarca de San Blás are the sites of Aclá and New Edinburgh, which were the settings for dramatic and bloody events in Panama's colonial history. Although jungle has swallowed the ruins of both sites and they are now inaccessible to visitors, the stories of what happened in these settlements still fascinate travelers.

On the coast 40km west of the Colombian border is the historic site of Aclá, long reclaimed by the jungle and all but forgotten. It was here in 1517 that Vasco Núñez de Balboa – the first European to set eyes on the Pacific, a man who was a legend in his time and much adored by the king and queen of Spain he so honorably served – was put to death by the envious and spiteful Spanish governor Pedro Arias de Ávila.

For years Pedrarias, as the governor was widely known, had sought a hero's recognition from the Spanish royalty – recognition he felt was fully deserved. But the spotlight always seemed to be on Balboa, who, among numerous famous deeds, claimed the Pacific Ocean and all territories that bordered it for King Ferdinand and Queen Isabella.

It might be said that Balboa's violent end had its origin in romance – the desire he and another man, Andrés Garabito, felt for a woman. The woman was none other than the beautiful daughter of Careta, chief of the largest Darién tribe. Balboa was smitten with the Indian maiden, and his fondness for her brought about a peaceful alliance between the explorer and the chief. Careta pledged his daughter to Balboa, an action that didn't sit well with Garabito. Garabito and Balboa had been friends, but the men had some fiery words over the Darién beauty, and Garabito slunk away and awaited his opportunity for revenge.

He didn't wait long. Garabito was a crafty fellow and knew of Pedrarias' hatred for Balboa. He also knew that Balboa had been intimate with Pedrarias' daughter. Garabito sent a letter to Pedrarias that stated that Balboa intended to throw off his allegiance to the governor. He also claimed that Balboa never intended to marry Pedrarias' daughter but instead loved only an Indian girl.

In short time Garabito was called before Pedrarias. Garabito was quite pleased to repeat his damning story, which he had spread about in public places. A notary was sent out to gather up evidence against Balboa. Because Garabito had done a good job in spreading his lie, the notary came across quite a few people who said they had heard rumors that Balboa was plotting against Pedrarias. These people would later provide damaging testimony against Balboa.

Balboa was on the Pacific coast with 300 loyal men at the time that the governor and Garabito were plotting their revenge. To lure Balboa to the Caribbean coast and away from his followers, Pedrarias sent him a fatherly letter begging him to come to Aclá to confer with him on a matter of great importance. Balboa fell into the trap, and soon he and his closest aides found themselves in chains facing charges of treason.

A farce of a trial was quickly held and appeals formalities brushed aside. It was clear to all that Balboa and his friends were to be sacrificed. Like sheep, first Balboa and then his four friends were led to the block and beheaded. Pedrarias witnessed the gory spectacle, but still filled with malice, he ordered that Balboa's head be placed on a pole and set in the plaza, where it remained for many days. Balboa was 42 at the time of his death.

Within a few years, the town of Nombre de Dios, to the west, had become the northern terminus of trade across the isthmus, and the residents of Aclá moved there to seek their fortunes. No one was left to stop the advance of the surrounding jungle, and it quickly swallowed up the site.

Aclá's exact location remained a mystery for more than 400 years. In 1985 eight young British explorers, aged 17 to 24, cut a 3m trench through a low artificial mound on what

continued on next page

COMARCA DE SAN BLÁS

they suspected was the western end of the town. This revealed a circular structure made up of coral blocks and bricks thought to be the base of a 16th-century tower. The tower – the earliest European stone building found anywhere in the Americas – was abandoned yet again soon afterward, and has since been reclaimed by the jungle.

Just east of Aclá is the overgrown site of New Edinburgh. No attempt by white people to found a settlement in the Tropics was deadlier or more plagued by disaster than the Scottish effort at this site, on a peninsula at the mouth of a bay just a few kilometers from Aclá.

Today the peninsula is called Punta Escocés, but on Nov-

LIBRARY OF CONGRESS

Balboa's reward

ember 3, 1698, the day the Scots landed and took possession of the site, it was named New Edinburgh. They erected a battery of 16 guns, called Fort St Andrew, to command the harbor. A cut was made through the narrowest part of the peninsula, only 180 paces in width, to let in the sea, thus converting New Edinburgh into an island and strengthening the defenses of the town and fort. A region that encompassed the bay and all the land within several days' walk from it was called Caledonia; today only a small island bears that name.

By April 1699 the Scots, who had never seen so much rain, were suffering badly. Of the 1200 men who had landed, already more than 200 had died of sickness, and the rest were hungry and living in constant fear of attacks by Spaniards, who viewed the Scots as invaders of their territory.

By June the Scots had had enough, and the 900 enfeebled survivors hurriedly evacuated New Edinburgh. The would-be settlers embarked in three ships, the *St Andrew,* the *Unicorn* and the *Caledonia.* Each captain selected his own course to hasten away from the ghastly settlement.

The *St Andrew* reached Jamaica, but not before losing another 100 people to disease. There the Scots continued to die, so there were too few seamen left to sail the ship back to Scotland. The *St Andrew* was deserted, and most of the Scots who had reached Jamaica aboard her never left the island. The *Unicorn* reached New York on August 14,

losing about 150 people on the way. Here the survivors found the *Caledonia,* which had arrived 10 days earlier after losing about the same number.

Of the 900 Scots who left New Edinburgh in June, more than 400 died of disease and were tossed overboard en route to Jamaica and New York. In all, less than 500 of the men who had left Scotland for the New World on July 26, 1698, were alive 13 months later. Few of them ever saw their homeland again.

Unaware of the situation in the Darién, the Scottish company that had financed the first expedition sent 300 more recruits in two vessels, the *Hopeful Binning* and the *Olive Branch,* in May 1699. To their surprise, they found New Edinburgh deserted. Knowing that a third expedition was being assembled, they resolved to await the arrival of that party.

The plan quickly changed a few days later when a careless steward aboard the *Olive Branch* set fire to the ship while pouring a glass of brandy. The ship was entirely consumed, as were most of the provisions, which had been aboard. The *Olive Branch*'s passengers – about 100 people – were taken aboard the *Hopeful Binning.* The ship sailed to Jamaica, where most of the settlers rapidly sickened and died.

The third expedition consisted of 1300 people who sailed from Scotland on September 24, 1699, in four ships. By the time the ships arrived, 160 Scots had already perished. When the survivors arrived, they were hopeful that their luck would change, but the disease and death only increased. Two weeks after their arrival, nine sailors deserted in one of the ship's boats and were never heard from again.

Soon afterward, a plot to seize the leaders and ships and escape from the fateful spot was hatched and discovered. The suspected ringleader was condemned by court-martial and executed in Fort St Andrew.

In February Indians tipped the Scots that the much-feared Spaniards were coming to attack them. Instead of awaiting the assault, 200 Scots and 40 Indians who had befriended the settlers confronted the Spaniards at a site called Yoratuba. There the Scots had a short, sharp engagement with the much-surprised Spaniards, who fled, leaving their dead and dying on the field. Five Spanish survivors were taken prisoner.

The Scots' elation over their successful encounter was short-lived. The very next month a Spanish fleet entered the Bahía de Caledonia and prepared to level the fort and the huts that housed the Scots. Adding to the Scots' desperation, the Spanish located their source of fresh water and took possession of it. The Scots dug a well within the confines of their fort, but it produced only a brackish puddle.

Meanwhile hunger and disease killed the Scots like flies. In a single day 16 people were put in the ground. Spanish musketeers were advancing on the fort and the Scots were preparing to fight and die when the Spanish general offered the Scots a treaty. In return for their promise to leave, the Scots were given 14 days to prepare their departure and allowed to retain their arms. They sailed away with drums beating and colors flying. The Indians who had befriended the Scots were left at the Spaniards' mercy. The Spaniards brutally slaughtered them.

The site was lost to jungle until 1979, when the Panamanian government invited British archaeologists to explore the area. The 30-member team spent three months at the site, clearing and cataloging about half of the fort. They identified remains of Scottish defenses, including a moat, earthen ramparts, bastions, cannon positions and palisades. They also found clay pipes, nails, pottery, various types of glass, and bronze shoe buckles.

Like Aclá, New Edinburgh was again left to the forces of nature and has since been retaken by the jungle. ∎

Darién Province

The Darién is one of the wildest *and* one of the most ravaged areas in the Americas. It is by far the biggest province in Panama (16,671 sq km) and the country's most sparsely inhabited (with fewer than three people per square kilometer). It is home to Panama's most spectacular national park and to its worst scenes of habitat destruction. It is two worlds, really: one with roads and one without – the north and the south, respectively.

The northern Darién has been logged and has suffered serious environmental damage. Southern Darién Province – the vast area south of Yaviza – is the antithesis of the north. Here wildlife abounds and the only 'roads' are jungle-flanked rivers. In fact, most of the southern Darién is within Parque Nacional Darién – 576,000 hectares containing sandy beaches, rocky coasts, mangroves, freshwater marshes, palm forest swamps and four mountain ranges covered with double and triple-canopy jungle.

The park is *the* attraction of the Darién. The bird watching here is among the world's finest. There are places in the park where you can sit back and watch four species of macaw fly by with outstanding frequency. The harpy eagle, the most powerful bird of prey, resides here, as do giant anteaters, jaguars, ocelots, howler monkeys, Baird's tapirs, white-lipped peccaries, caimans and American crocodiles.

The southern Darién is an adventurer's dream. It's the landscape of Indiana Jones movies, offering spectacular opportunities for rainforest exploration by trail or river. It's a place where the primeval meets the present – where the scenery appears much as did a million years ago. It's a place where Indians perfected the use of poison-dart guns and still maintain many of their traditional practices. It's a place for travelers with youthful hearts, intrepid spirits and a yearning for something truly wild. If you've been growing old in a concrete jungle, I highly recommend spending time in this verdant one – even if it's only for a few days. They'll be days you'll never forget.

Emberá & Wounaan Indians

Living within the boundaries of Parque Nacional Darién are the Emberá and the Wounaan peoples – or Chocóes, as they are commonly called. These Indians emigrated here from the Chocó region of Colombia, and they continue to live much the way they have for thousands of years.

Anthropologists place the Chocóes in two linguistic groups: the Emberá and the Wounaan. But with the exception of language, the two peoples' cultural features are virtually identical – no great surprise considering their shared origins and environment.

HIGHLIGHTS

- Parque Nacional Darién, crown jewel of Panama's parks, home to vast jungle, jaguars, crocodiles and Indians

- Lush Cana valley, where macaws abound and jungle trails lead to abandoned mining trains

- Río Sambú, where travelers can take a heart-of-darkness ride through primeval rainforest

- Pirre Station, a superior destination for birders, with unforgettable jungle trails

- Tropic Star Lodge, the world leader in sport-fishing records

The external pressures placed on them (chiefly encroachment by white settlers and habitat destruction by loggers) are virtually identical as well. The tribes, however, prefer to be thought of as two separate peoples.

Some historians contend that the Emberá emigrated from northern Ecuador and southern Colombia beginning in 1830, and that the Wounaan emigrated from the Río San Juan area of Colombia (where the greatest concentration of them lives today) around 1910. Other historians say the tribes arrived much earlier. The Indians themselves aren't entirely sure, as they have no written history.

In Panama, by far the greatest number of Emberá and Wounaan live in the Darién. They reside deep in the rainforest beside rivers, particularly the Ríos Sambú, Jaqué, Chico, Tuquesa, Membrillo, Tuira, Yape and Tucutí. They also live, in far smaller numbers, in Panamá and Colón Provinces. Their total population in Panama is estimated to be around 7000.

The Emberá and Wounaan practice subsistence agriculture, followed by hunting, fishing and poultry raising. To a lesser degree, they also create plantations to grow commercial crops appropriate to the areas in which they live. If a particular area is good for plantains or bananas, for example, the Indians grow those crops to sell. They also commercially cultivate rice and maize, but to a lesser extent.

Increasingly, the Emberá and Wounaan are replacing their traditional attire with western wear. The men, but for a few older individuals, have set aside their loincloths for short pants and now prefer short-sleeved shirts to going around barechested. The women, who traditionally wore only a skirt, increasingly don bras, and some have taken to wearing shirts as well.

All the women used to wear wide silver bracelets and elaborate necklaces made of silver coins, but that practice too is disappearing as tourists offer the Indians more money than they've ever seen to buy their family jewelry. Many Emberá and Wounaan still stain their bodies purplish black with juice from the *jagua* fruit, which is believed to have health-giving properties and to ward off insects.

Emberá and Wounaan homes are well suited to the environment in which the Indians live. Built on stilts 3 to 4m off the ground, the floors consist primarily of thin but amazingly strong strips of palm bark. The homes' stilts protect occupants and food from pesky ground animals and swollen rivers.

To permit breezes to enter, more than half of the typical Indian home is open-sided. The roof is made of thatch, which keeps the rain out and acts as good insulation against the tropical sun. The kitchen occupies one corner and has an oven made of mud. A log with stairs carved into it provides access to the home. Emberá and Wounaan grow medicinal plants and edible vegetables and roots around their homes. Pigs and poultry are often raised in pens beneath the elevated houses.

The government of Panama has erected concrete schoolhouses in many of the Indians' villages. Today most Emberá and Wounaan children spend their mornings in class and their afternoons working the land. For fun, they swim in the rivers.

The Emberá and Wounaan are very good woodcarvers and basket weavers. Traditionally the men carved gorgeous boas, frogs and birds from the dark cocobolo hardwood. More recently they have taken to carving tiny figurines (typically of iguanas, turtles, crocodiles and birds) from the ivory-colored tagua nut. The women are among the world's finest basket makers. (See the Shopping section of the Panama City chapter for more information about Emberá and Wounaan products.)

The Emberá and Wounaan also produce incredibly fine dugout canoes, which they call *piraguas*. The boats have very shallow bottoms, so they can be used during the dry season, when the rivers run low. The Panama Canal Commission (PCC), which has the money to buy any rivercraft it wants, employs Emberá and Wounaan craftsmen to make the piraguas that PCC officials use to reach the higher parts of the

DARIÉN PROVINCE

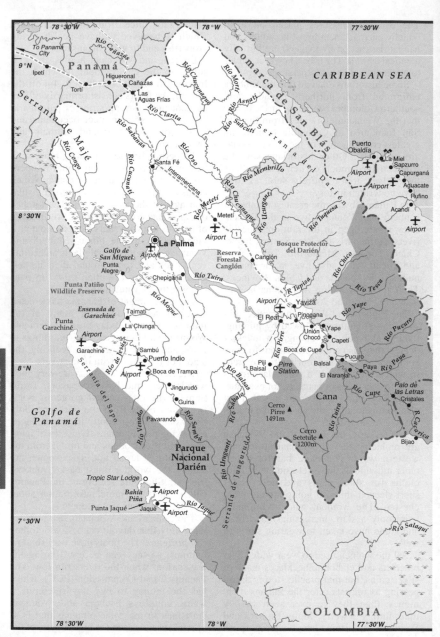

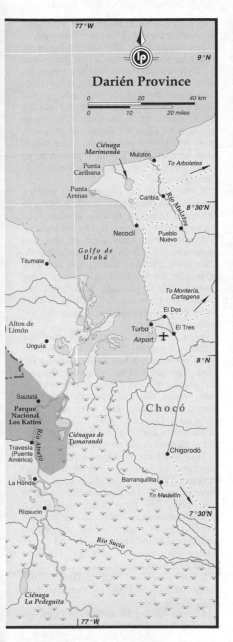

canal's watershed. Most of the Indians' piraguas are powered by paddles, but the PCC piraguas are motorized.

Another powerful organization, the US Air Force, also turns to the Emberá and Wounaan for help, but for an entirely different reason: jungle survival. Because the Indians have the ability to not only survive but to thrive in tropical wilderness, quite a few of them have been added to the corps of instructors that trains US astronauts and Air Force pilots at Fort Sherman, near Colón.

Before the introduction of the gun, the Emberá and Wounaan were expert users of the *boroquera* (blowgun), and they envenomed their darts with lethal toxins from poisonous frogs and bullet ants. Many scholars believe that it was these people who forced the Kuna out of the Darién and into the Caribbean coastal area they now inhabit.

DARIÉN PROVINCE

The Emberá and Wounaan are about the toughest people you'll ever meet, yet their smiles could melt silver. Emberá and Wounaan children are friendly and fun-loving; if you want to score points with them (and their parents), bring along a Polaroid camera and plenty of film. Lots of people take photos in Indian villages, but few ever leave the Indians with pictures of themselves.

Environmental Problems
Today the traditional cultures of the remarkable Emberá and Wounaan tribes appear doomed, because their land is under threat. For many years the Panamanian government was unwilling to construct the last section of the Carretera Interamericana (Pan-American Hwy) and thus close the Darién Gap – a 150km break in the otherwise unbroken 30,600km highway from Alaska to Chile – because it feared that hoof-and-mouth disease would spread from Colombia into Panama. The government was so afraid of the cattle disease that it created Parque Nacional Darién along the border as a buffer zone, and the Colombian government followed suit by establishing adjacent Parque Nacional Los Katíos on its side of the border.

In 1991 US officials monitoring the disease declared that it had been eradicated in Colombia. The governments of Panama and Colombia then revived efforts to close the Darién Gap. The last bit of highway would bisect the Darién and Los Katíos national parks and would open up the forests of the Emberá and Wounaan to loggers, settlers and ranchers. The area's national-park status would not prevent such development.

To glimpse the future of the south, one need only look to the north. The Darién north of Yaviza – the town where the Interamericana presently ends – was covered with virgin forest only three decades ago. But the highway was extended from Chepo to Yaviza 20-some years ago. At first only loggers used the extension, as the new stretch of highway was a dirt road with knee-deep ruts half the year and a mud road with zillions of small pools the rest of the year. Settlers and ranchers followed.

The loggers initially sought big trees within easy reach, felling all the giants near the highway and trampling the young trees with their machinery. Once those trees were gone, the loggers cut roads perpendicular to the highway, which led into the tallest stands of hardwoods. After those stands were chopped down and removed, more roads were cut and yet more stands were leveled. Today even a person using binoculars can't see any Darién forest from the highway.

Right behind the loggers were settlers, thousands of them, poor people looking to eke out a living by turning into cropland the trampled vegetation left by the loggers. With the mature trees gone, all that was required to create cropland was a match; after some crackling and sizzling and a lot of smoke, the would-be subsistence farmers had fields for planting. Panamanian law encourages homesteading, and the settlers were very encouraged; they burned and burned and burned.

As if to punish those who burned the forest, the topsoil that had been held in place by roots washed easily away in the rains. The soil that had underlain the topsoil proved nutrient deficient. After two or three years, the soil couldn't support a decent harvest and little more than grass grew on it. But grass is what cattle eat, so in came ranchers, buying fields that frustrated farmers could no longer use.

This succession of loggers, farmers and ranchers continues in northern Darién Province, although now the loggers must drive far up the side roads they've made to find trees. The farmers are still a step behind the loggers, unintentional nomads employing the slash-and-burn method so widespread in the Third World. And everywhere the settler-farmers go, ranchers move in behind them.

Today nearly all that remains of the forests of northern Darién – complexly layered, fragile and wondrous ecosystems that had been evolving for *millions* of years – is cow pasture. Around these pastures are struggling farmers and loggers closing in on the last trees still standing.

Today the Interamericana is being paved to Yaviza. Gas stations, hotels and restaurants are already in place (see To the Darién Gap, below, for details). The paving will be completed in mid-to-late 1999. For the moment, the only road into the Darién continues to offer travelers an interesting ride, though more for a first-hand look at mass habitat destruction than for anything else.

When will the Gap close? When will construction of the 150km, US$300 million road between Yaviza and Chigorodó, Colombia, commence? No one could say for certain at the time that this book was written. An environmental impact report was being prepared, but in Panama such reports rarely kill projects; if anything, they might cause a section of road to be shifted a little to the right or a little to the left. Knowledgeable people speculated that the report would be finished by the year 2000 and completion of the linking highway would begin 12 months later.

TO THE DARIÉN GAP

The 266km drive from Panama City to Yaviza along the Interamericana presently takes about nine hours. Lodgings and food can be found in several small towns along the way.

The highway passes through Chepo, El Llano, Cañita, Ipetí, Tortí and Higueronal in Panamá Province before crossing into the Darién; see the Panamá Province chapter for details on those towns.

Las Aguas Frías

Near the border of Panamá and Darién Provinces are the towns of Agua Fría Uno and Agua Fría Dos. There's no phone in either town. Agua Fría Dos has a gas station and a place with a sign out front that reads 'Pensión Interiorana,' but its rooms are only rented to longterm tenants.

There is bus service to Las Aguas Frías from Panama City. It departs the Terminal de Buses al Interior, on Avenida Ascañio Villalaz in the Curundu district of the capital,

every 30 minutes from 5 am to 8:30 pm; the one-way fare is US$4.75.

Santa Fé

In this town of 2000 people, which is about 1km from the Interamericana, there is the *Hospeddeía Fuerte* (no phone), which has six very basic rooms with decent beds, ceiling fans and a shared bathroom for US$7/12.

As you continue into Santa Fé, you'll come across a large two-story building on the northern side of the road; *Casa La Esperanza* (no phone) is painted on it in big letters. Upstairs are six very OK rooms that have good beds, wall-mounted fans, TVs and shared bathroom. For US$6 you can sleep in a single bed; for US$4 more you can sleep in a full-size bed. Downstairs at La Esperanza is a bakery and a general store.

Metetí

This town, about 45km from Yaviza, is the headquarters for the border police. There's a gas station here, plus a public phone, a bank and a hotel: *Hotel Felicidad* (no phone), above the Felicidad restaurant, which offers 33 rooms (20 with private bathrooms) for US$10 to US$25 per room. Although there's one other hotel between here and Yaviza, this is the last decent place before the end of the road. There are several restaurants in Metetí; *La Felicidad* is the best of the bunch.

At the time of writing, efforts to pave the Interamericana all the way to Yaviza were underway. This will result in rapid settling all along this portion of the highway. It's quite possible another hotel or two and additional services will be available in Metetí by the time you read this.

Metetí has a small airport. There is also easy access to the Darién river network from here, as the large Río Tuira is close by. It's quite likely that Metetí, because of its access by land, river and air, will soon surpass La Palma (the provincial capital) as the gateway into the Darién.

They Drove the Darién Gap

In 1960 – back when the Carretera Interamericana reached only as far as Chepo, 52km east of Panama City – a group of adventurers sought to become the first people to drive between North and South America. Their destination: Bogotá, Colombia, 433km from Chepo by land – 297km of it through primeval jungle in a region called the Darién. Those 297km then formed the Darién Gap.

The adventurers consisted of a distinguished crew of six men and two women, as well as nine local woodsmen who were hired to cut a path through the jungle for the vehicles – an US-built Jeep and a British Land Rover. Also on board for most of the trip was Kip Ross, a *National Geographic* writer whose fascinating article on the expedition appeared in the society's March 1961 journal.

All told, the entire enterprise took four months and 28 days. The team crossed 180 rivers and streams and was forced to improvise bridges over 125 of them, built mainly from the trunks of palm trees. At times progress was slowed to 5km a day. Although several major vehicular mishaps occurred, no snakebites or serious injuries were sustained.

Among the group were historian Amado Araúz and his wife, Reina, the finest anthropologist Panama has produced. (Amado provided much of the information on the Emberá and Wounaan Indians that appears in this book.) Reina founded nine museums and wrote the definitive books on Panama's tribes before cancer took her life at the age of 48. Their son, Hernán Araúz, is now widely regarded as the country's top nature guide. ■

AMADO ARAÚZ
Pushing through the Gap, 1960

Yaviza

After a nine-hour drive (in the dry season; the trip takes longer during the rainy season and will be much shorter once the road is paved), the Interamericana just kind of fizzles out at the town of Yaviza. No sign announces that you've reached the famous Darién Gap. There's just a stretch of dirt where trucks, buses and a few cars park, and there are lots of people who seem to have nothing but time on their hands.

There are a couple of awful-looking restaurants in this town, which is at the meeting of the Ríos Chucunaque and Chico. There's one hotel, the US$8-a-night *Hotel 3 Americas* (no phone), which has 10 rooms, all with fans, worn beds, stained walls and a common bathroom. There's a loud bar next door, and the town is hot as blazes. Welcome to the end of the road!

Buses for Yaviza depart Panama City's Terminal de Buses al Interior hourly from 5 to 10 am. The ride takes 10 hours (it will

take much less time once the road is paved) and costs US$14 each way.

EL REAL

El Real dates from the days of the early conquistadors. They constructed a fort here, beside the Río Tuira, to prevent pirates from sailing upriver and attacking Santa María. Gold from mines in the valley of Cana, to the south, was brought to Santa María and stored until there was a quantity sufficient to warrant assembling an armada and moving the bullion to Panama City.

Today this hot and humid town of about 3000 souls is one of the largest towns in the Darién, but it is nothing special. It is, however, home to the closest airstrip to the Pirre ranger station, south of town, which offers excellent bird watching (see details under Pirre Station, below). There's an INRENARE office in town where you can get permission to visit Pirre Station. The best way to locate this office is to ask someone to point you toward it, as none of the wide paths in town have names. If you don't speak any Spanish, just repeat 'INRENARE' a few times. See the Pirre Station section for permit requirements.

El Real has no bank, and there's only one hotel, the *El Mazareno* (no phone), with seven mildewy rooms with U-shaped mattresses and shared toilets that don't flush thoroughly. The price is US$8 per person.

Aeroperlas (call ☎ 269-4555 in Panama City) flies from Panama City to El Real daily. On Monday, Wednesday, Friday and Sunday, the flight leaves at 8:45 am. On Tuesday, Thursday and Saturday, the flight leaves at 7:50 am.

Aeroperlas flies from El Real to Panama City at 9:45 am on Monday, Wednesday and Friday, making one stop in Sambú. On Tuesday, Thursday and Saturday, a direct flight leaves at 9:20 am. On Sunday, a direct flight departs at 10:15 am. The fare between El Real and Panama City is US$37/74 one-way/roundtrip.

Aeroperlas also flies between El Real and the provincial capital, La Palma, several times weekly; the fare is US$21/42.

PIRRE STATION

Pirre is an INRENARE ranger station just inside the Parque Nacional Darién, 13km south of El Real as the lemon-spectacled tanager flies. It is of particular interest to birders, although most of the bird species represented here can also be found in Cana, an excellent bird-watching area that lies farther south. Specialties at Pirre include the crimson-bellied woodpecker, white-fronted nunbird and striped woodhaunter.

The station can only be reached by hiking, or by hiking and boating (see Getting There & Away, below). If you intend to visit Pirre Station on your own, without a tour operator's help, you must first get permission from the INRENARE office in Panama City (see contact information in the Panama City chapter). Then you must go to El Real's INRENARE office (see El Real, above) and show the permission to Narciso 'Chicho' Bristan, head of the office. Chicho will sign the document, which you'll show to the rangers at Pirre Station. If you use a tour operator, the company will take care of all the necessary paperwork for you.

The area around Pirre is the most accessible section of the park, and the station's strength is that two good hiking trails originate from it. One trail leads to the Pirre Mountain ridge, which takes most hikers two days to reach. Tents are pretty much a necessity. The other trail winds through beautiful jungle to a series of cascades about an hour's hike away. Neither trail should be attempted without a guide, as they are not well marked and if you get lost out here, you're done for. You can hire a ranger as a guide, or you can contact one of the tour operators listed in the Getting Around chapter.

Fifteen km separate the station and the Cana valley, and between the two there's nothing but virgin rainforest. Unfortunately, no trails link Pirre Station and Cana, although trails lead from both sites to the Pirre Mountain ridge.

At the station itself are barracks with a front room with fold-out cots for visitors, a dining area that consists of two tables and

DARIÉN PROVINCE

four benches beside a very rustic kitchen, a palapa with a few chairs, and one outhouse. Bathing is done in a nearby creek. There is no electricity at the station.

If you plan on eating, you must bring your own food. Remember: This is a ranger station, not a hotel. The rangers will cook for you and provide a cot for a tip (US$10 a day is what I gave them), but you must provide food for yourself, and that includes bottled water. However, if you've got a water-purification system or tablets, the water in the creek should be OK, and there are lots of lemon trees in the vicinity of the station should you want to make lemonade.

Beware: Most of Parque Nacional Darién is prime fer-de-lance territory, and these very deadly snakes have been found near the station. Always wear boots when you're walking in camp at night or entering the forest at any time. This warning should not dissuade you from visiting the station; just be careful. The area surrounding Pirre Station has primeval lowland and premontane rainforest that's gorgeous and shouldn't be missed because of the remote possibility of snakebite.

Be sure to try the *zapote* growing at the station. The fruit's as round as a softball, as hard as a rock and as green as an avocado, but it has a fleshy orange meat with the appearance, taste and texture of mango. It's absolutely addictive.

Getting There & Away

Pirre Station can only be reached via hiking or via a combination of hiking and boating. The hike from El Real takes three hours. You can also take a one-hour canoe ride from El Real to the village of Piji Baisal and then make a one-hour hike from Piji Baisal to Pirre Station.

First, you'll need to get to El Real, which can be reached by plane or boat (see the El Real section, above). Then, if you prefer to hike, take the 'road' connecting El Real and Pirre Station. This road is covered with 2m high lemongrass and won't likely be cleared, as the only people who would clear it are Pirre's rangers, and they do not have vehicles or even enough money for

gas. Hiking this barely discernible road takes about three hours and pretty much requires a guide. The INRENARE station in El Real can help you find a local guide (expect to pay about US$20), and you have to go there anyway to get permission to visit the station.

The alternative is to hire a boatman to take you up the Río Pirre to Piji Baisal. Expect to pay about US$40 plus the cost of gasoline, which will vary depending on the size of your party, the size of the outboard motor and other factors. From Piji Baisal, it's a one-hour hike to the station. Again, you'll need a guide to lead you to the station, as no signs mark the way there.

Ancon Expeditions of Panama (see contact information in the Tour Companies in Panama section of the Getting Around chapter) arranges four-day, three-night guided tours to Pirre Station from Panama City. Rates, which include all domestic transportation and meals, are US$605 per person (for a party of two people), US$420 per person (party of four) and US$360 per person (party of six).

CANA

Cana, a valley nestled in foothills on the eastern slope of Pirre Ridge, is the most isolated place in the Republic of Panama (the nearest town is several days away by foot) and home to some of the world's finest bird watching. About 60 Panamanian bird species can be found only in Parque Nacional Darién, and Cana is at the park's lush heart.

In addition to four species of macaw, Cana is known for its harpy eagles, black-tipped cotingas, red-throated caracaras, dusky-backed jacamars, varied solitaires, rufous-cheeked hummingbirds and golden-headed quetzals. Many bird species can be found much more easily here than elsewhere in Panama. Cana is also home to jaguars, pumas, ocelots, jaguarundis and margays, but you'd be extremely fortunate to see one of these cats. They avoid people and generally prowl at night – when it's cool and when they may cover several kilometers in their search for food.

Although the town of Santa Cruz de Cana, which was founded by Spaniards in the 16th century, has been completely overgrown, the valley is not entirely devoid of human habitations. There's an airstrip at the eastern end of the valley, and a short walk from it there's a border-police station, as well as an INRENARE/Ancon field station (see Places to Stay).

History

A survey of Cana determined that a lake covered most of the valley's floor during prehistoric times. Experts speculate that the lake emptied when an earthquake created a divide that allowed the water to drain; such was the case at El Valle in Coclé Province. As you enter the valley by air, you can still see a marshy area and some ponds – remnants of the prehistoric lake.

During the early 16th century, Spaniards discovered gold in the valley, and in the years that followed they mined the heck out of the place using regional Indians as well as black slaves brought from Africa. Las Minas del Espíritu Santo (Mines of the Holy Spirit), as they were called, at one time filled the valley with 20,000 people. They lived in the town of Santa Cruz de Cana, which has long since been reclaimed by the jungle.

One of the longest rivers in the Darién, the Río Tuira, runs northward past Cana and all the way out to the Pacific Ocean. The Spaniards used to send supplies to the Cana valley via the Tuira, and they sent gold from the valley to Santa María, on the western bank of the river, for safekeeping until boats arrived to transport the precious metal to Panama City.

Naturally, the vast quantities of gold at Santa María attracted pirates, and the town fell many times. In some instances pirates came out of retirement to raid the place. In 1702, for example, a party of retired English buccaneers living in Jamaica sailed to the Darién, where they were joined by former coworkers who had married Indians and settled down. The come-back Kidds and 300 interested Indians drove the Spaniards from the valley and captured 70 black slaves, whom they kept at work for seven days. During that week, the raiders obtained about 36kg of gold from the mines. They set fire to the 900 houses in the valley when they left.

Another group of English pirates, these led by Sir Gregor MacGregor, attempted to take Portobelo in 1819, and the Spaniards managed to capture quite a few of them. Some were shot on the spot, but most were taken to Cana, where they were forced to toil in the mines 'borrowed' by other Englishmen 117 years earlier. A few years later the Spaniards left Panama and the mines were abandoned.

An English outfit visited Cana in the early 20th century and discovered that there was still gold to be found in the hills. They ran train tracks from the valley to Boca de Cupe, 20km away as the toucan flies, and moved men, supplies and gold along them in small locomotives and in freight cars. When these Englishmen cleared out, 20 years later, they left their trains behind. Today you can find several rusting locomotives, numerous freight cars and many mines amid Cana's dense jungle.

Hiking

Three trails begin near the INRENARE/Ancon field station: the **Cituro Trail**, the **Machinery Trail** and the **Stream Trail**. The Cituro Trail begins at the northeastern corner of the station and winds a couple of hundred meters through secondary forest, paralleling some old railroad tracks and passing a rusted-out locomotive with the brand name 'Cituro' forged into it.

The Machinery Trail is a loop trail that begins at the western edge of the station and winds several hundred meters through secondary forest to the remains of another abandoned Cituro locomotive, a very overgrown smelter and other pieces of mining machinery.

The Stream Trail is the most glorious of all on a hot and humid day. It's a short one – only 50m – but it runs from behind the field station to a small creek where you can take a very refreshing dip.

Beside the valley's grass-and-dirt airstrip, which is about 100m from the field station, the mouths of two more trails disappear into the dense rainforest: the **Pirre Mountain Trail** and **Boca de Cupe Trail**.

The Pirre Mountain Trail, starting near the western end of the airstrip, offers a six-hour ridgeline hike to a campsite high above the Cana valley. The campsite is in cloud forest, and it's quite cool and refreshing at night. The trail is arduous in spots, but it offers excellent birding in mostly virgin jungle. If you're traveling to Cana with a tour operator's assistance and want to camp along the ridge, let the operator know in advance so that it can arrange tents for you.

The Boca de Cupe Trail runs north from Cana to the town of Boca de Cupe. A person with good legs can reach Boca de Cupe via the trail in two to three days, depending on the trail's condition. However, because of bandits, guerrillas and paramilitaries in the vicinity of Boca de Cupe, use of this trail is not recommended. Be advised too that the trail crosses the knee-deep Río Cupe six times. It initially passes through secondary and thereafter only virgin jungle.

Please resist the temptation to explore the old mines in the area, even though some people may think it's a good idea to enter a mine that's been abandoned for many years and has who knows how many snakes, jaguars or pumas living in it. At least one tourist who wandered into an old Cana mine developed a life-threatening respiratory illness after inhaling something nasty in the tunnel.

Places to Stay

The valley's *INRENARE/Ancon field station* is a basic wooden structure that was built by gold workers during the 1970s and enlarged in mid-1998 by the wildlife conservation group Ancon. Tourists are welcome to stay at the barrackslike station, at the eastern end of Cana valley, but to do so they must arrange their trips through Ancon Expeditions (see contact information under Tour Companies in Panama in the Getting Around chapter). Although the Cana area is managed by INRENARE, as it's inside a national park, the station is maintained by Ancon (parent to Ancon Expeditions), and thus Ancon does not allow other tour operators to use the facility.

Each room contains two or three beds and a shelf on which to place a candle at night, but nothing more. Food is provided for guests. There's no electricity and it's shared bathrooms only, but the place is quite OK and it's not very hot at night. When you consider the awesome hiking and the bird-watching possibilities in the area, the station is wildly outstanding. See Getting There & Away, below, for rate information.

Getting There & Away

Traveling to Cana is expensive. The only way into the valley is by chartered aircraft, and Ancon Expeditions has a monopoly on the valley's sole lodgings. At the time of writing, Ancon Expeditions offered a three-day, four-night package that included an English-speaking guide, all meals, accommodations (including tent camping along the Pirre Mountain Trail) and transportation to and from Panama City. Rates were US$1330 per person (party of two) and US$965 per person (party of four).

LA PALMA

La Palma is the provincial capital, and with 4500 residents it is also the most populous city in the Darién. La Palma is at the mouth of the Río Tuira, where the wide river meets the Golfo de San Miguel. It was actually the San Miguel gulf, not the much larger Golfo de Panamá, that Balboa saw when he became the first European to set eyes on the Pacific.

Despite its lofty position as capital of the largest province in Panama, La Palma doesn't offer much to see or do. It's pretty much a one-street town, with the street following the sweeping shoreline. Every facility of possible interest to the traveler is on this street, within 300m of the airstrip. A good bit of this hot and muggy community went up in flames a few years back, which is why some of the best pieces of real estate in town have only charred pylons on them.

La Palma is home to the only bank in the Darién, the Banco Nacional de Panamá. There's also a hospital, a port and a police station (if you intend to go anywhere near the Colombian border and speak Spanish, you should speak with the police here first), as well as two hotels, three bars and several food stands. By far the busiest places are the airstrip and the small port. The port is used mainly by people bringing produce out of the jungle via the Río Tuira, and by larger boats that take the produce from the port to Panama City.

Most travelers visit La Palma for one of two reasons: They're here to catch a plane to somewhere else or they're here to take a boat ride to somewhere else. The two most popular boating destinations are the Ancon nature preserve and lodge at Punta Patiño and the Emberá villages along the banks of the Río Sambú; these fine trips are described later in this chapter.

You can visit these destinations on your own; if you speak Spanish, you can usually find someone near the dock who owns a boat and is willing to go on an adventure with you for the right price (US$120 to US$150 per day, gas included, depending on the boat's gas consumption). Most people, however, prefer to make these trips with a guide, so that everything is conveniently prearranged. At the time of writing, only one tour operator, Ancon Expeditions, was organizing boat tours in the area (see contact information in the Getting Around chapter).

Places to Stay

The better of the two hotels in La Palma is the *Hotel Biaquira Bagara* (☎ 299-6224), which also goes by the name of Casa Ramady because the friendly Ramady family lives in a home beneath the 13 rooms they rent. Six rooms have cold-water private bathrooms that contain bathtubs – something rarely found in Panamanian hotels. All the rooms here are clean and fan-cooled, and some have private balconies. This place

is a godsend after a week or two in the jungle. The rates are US$22/26 single/double.

Only 100m from the airstrip is *La Pensión Takela* (☎ 299-6213), which has 11 rooms, three with private bathrooms and old TVs with lousy reception. Each room here has a fan. The hotel, which like the Biaquira Bagara is at river's edge, is not a bad value at US$11/14 with shared bathroom and US$13/15 with private bathroom.

Getting There & Away

Aeroperlas (☎ 269-4555 in Panama City) flies from Panama City's Aeropuerto Paitilla to La Palma at 7:50 am every day but Sunday, when the flight leaves at 8:45 am. The roundtrip fare between Panama City and La Palma is US$75.

Aeroperlas has flights from La Palma to Panama City at 8:45 am on Monday, Wednesday and Friday, with one stop in Garachiné. On Tuesday, Thursday and Saturday, the plane also leaves at 8:45 am but stops in El Real. The Sunday flight departs at 9:40 am and stops at El Real. The fare for the leg between La Palma and El Real is US$21/42 one-way/roundtrip.

Aviatur (☎ 270-1748 in Panama City) flies to La Palma from Aeropuerto Paitilla three times weekly.

PUNTA PATIÑO

Punta Patiño, on the southern shore of the Golfo de San Miguel 25km from La Palma, is known mainly for its 26,315-hectare **wildlife preserve**, which is owned by the conservation group Ancon. The only way to reach the preserve, short of hacking your way through many kilometers of trailless jungle, is by boat (see details in the Getting There & Away section, below).

The boat ride is definitely part of the Punta Patiño experience. The ride begins at La Palma and takes you into the gulf but not too far from shore. You'll pass shrimp boats and fishermen in dugouts using nets. If you've never been on a shrimp boat and would like to see what they're all about, this is a good place to do it. If you speak some Spanish, just pull up beside a shrimper and

TOM BOYDEN
The elusive jaguar makes its home
in Darién Province.

ask if you can come aboard for a look. Unless you catch the shrimpers in a bad mood, they will usually welcome you. Shrimpers tend to view tourists as oddities, so the request won't surprise or alarm them. If you are traveling with a guide, ask the guide to make the request.

After about 45 minutes, if you're traveling in a fairly fast boat, you'll pass the mouth of the Río Mogué, which is flanked primarily by virgin forest. There's an **Emberá village** on the bank of the Mogué, about 30 minutes upriver by boat. The village is home to about 400 people and remains fairly traditional. There are no other settlements on the river. The mouth of the Río Mogué is lined with black mangroves, which are interesting to look at and can make for intriguing and artistic photographs.

About 10 minutes after you leave the mouth of the Mogué and head south along the coast, you'll pass the small black community of **Punta Alegre**. *Alegre* means 'happy,' and this does seem to be a pretty content community despite the poverty in which the 500 or so inhabitants live. Most of the adults make their living fishing from dugout canoes in the gulf. Their music, which relies heavily on bongo drums, is pure West African. If you're lucky, some of the men and women here will bring out their guitars and drums. It doesn't take much to put these people in a festive mood. Take a look at the simple boatyard near the center of town. Here you can see dugouts, called piraguas in the southern Darién, being mended.

There are no places to stay in Punta Alegre, but there are a couple of simple *restaurants*. Punta Alegre's food, which typically consists of fresh fish and prawns, is quite tasty.

A handful of Emberá families live at the southern end of Punta Alegre. Some of the Indians usually offer to paint visiting tourists with jagua-fruit juice, in the same manner that the Emberá paint themselves. The juice stains the skin for about a week and looks much like a tattoo. I recommend getting painted if you're only days from going home and there's someone you'd like to surprise.

Continuing south another 20 minutes, you'll reach an expansive beach. A 400m long dirt road winds from the beach to the restaurant and cabins near the center of the Punta Patiño Ancon preserve, passing a swamp with several crocodiles and a meadow frequented by capybaras, the world's largest rodents.

The preserve contains lots of species-rich primary forest, but the jungle is a fair walk from the cabins. The panorama of the gulf from the dining and viewing area, which is perched atop a ridge near the cabins, is spellbinding, particularly at daybreak. The cabins, all of which have private bathrooms, are quite comfortable. There's no good place to go swimming nearby, however.

Visitors to the preserve are treated to guided night and morning nature hikes. During the day, they can explore by boat the red and black mangroves lining the gulf, chat with fishermen at work (all are friendly but none speak English) or drop by Punta Alegre.

Getting There & Away

If you prefer, you can get to Ancon's preserve on your own – without booking a guided tour through Ancon Expeditions,

SCOTT DOGGETT

STUART GR WARNER W

ALFREDO MAIQUEZ

Darién Province

Top: Daybreak on the Río Sambú, Darién Province
Bottom Left: Wounaan baskets are known throughout
Panama for their beauty and artisanship.

Bottom Right: Emberá girl in Cana, Darién Province

Darién Province

Top Left: Deforestation, the scourge of the Darién's lush jungles

Top Right: Man and his harvest of plantains, Yaviza, Darién Province

Bottom: Valley floor at Cana

the organization's for-profit arm – but you must notify Ancon Expeditions in advance so that it can reserve a cabin for you (see contact information in the Getting Around chapter). If you visit without Ancon Expeditions' help, lodging and three daily meals will cost you US$90 per person per day. You can hire boats in La Palma to reach Punta Patiño; expect to pay your boatman about US$120 to US$150 per day.

Ancon Expeditions offers a package tour to Punta Patiño that includes roundtrip airfare between Panama City and La Palma, a boat ride up the Río Mogué to the Emberá village, a visit to Punta Alegre, hikes in the preserve, guide service and all meals. The three-day, two-night adventure costs you US$585 per person (party of two), US$481 per person (party of four) or US$446 per person (party of six).

RÍO SAMBÚ

The mouth of the wide, brown Río Sambú is 1½ hours by fast boat south of Punta Patiño. Traveling it is a heart-of-darkness experience: You pass through spectacular jungle inhabited by jaguars and mountain lions and Indians who until recently did most of their hunting with blowguns. The river meanders for many kilometers toward the Colombian border, passing Emberá villages along the way. The farther you go up the river, the more traditional are these Indian villages.

Boats and boatmen can be hired in La Palma, or you can travel with a guide (see Getting There & Away, below). When you reach the Río Sambú, you will need to hire a dugout canoe to get farther upriver. During the rainy season, the river is navigable by dugout all the way to Pavarandó, the most inland of the eight Emberá communities on the Sambú.

Prior to 1990 or 1991, the indigenous people living beside the river led traditional Emberá lives – they grew corn, rice, plantains and other crops; they fished the river and went about dressed in the manner of their ancestors (the women bare-breasted and wearing colorful knee-length skirts, the men wearing only loincloths).

Today the Sambú continues to provide the Emberá with fish, traditional methods of agriculture are still practiced, and the Emberá still reside mainly in open-sided thatch-roof houses atop stilts. But western attire is replacing traditional dress, outboard motors are increasingly seen on the Indians' dugouts and Christianity brought by missionaries is replacing traditional Emberá religious practices.

At night, you can make camp where you please if you have a tent. However, unless you've brought a tent for your boatman, he will prefer an alternative – making a deal to sleep on the floor of an Emberá family's home. If you can speak Spanish, finding a family to move in with for the night isn't difficult, and even getting a hot meal is easy. Money talks, and it talks loudly in these Emberá villages. Expect to pay US$10 per person for shelter and US$5 for food.

Before you go to sleep, spray insect repellent liberally to avoid waking up with hundreds of bites. It's hard to say which are more annoying: the mosquitoes, chiggers or fleas. The trouble with chiggers is that they nestle before they bite – they burrow under your skin and hang out there, taking little nibbles of your flesh, for three or four days until they leave your body. Trying to remove them only makes them dig deeper.

Be forewarned: A trip far up the Río Sambú is not everyone's cup of tea. Even before you reach the river, you will be on a boat rather a long time under a broiling tropical sun. And if riding in a boat that's loaded down with leaking gasoline cans bothers you, you should probably pass on the Sambú: You'll need to bring several large containers of gasoline along from La Palma to fuel the canoe that you'll hire upriver. There are no pumping stations on the Sambú.

There are other minor hardships, like the lack of showers and toilets. But the Sambú offers you true adventure, something that may not even be possible anywhere in the Tropics 50 years from now. Even if you travel deep into the Amazon, you'd be hard-pressed to find such wilderness and such people these days.

Getting There & Away

If you speak Spanish, you can travel up the Sambú without the assistance of a tour operator. But if you or your traveling companions don't speak the language, you'll want to hire a guide. You will need to do this because the boat you'll hire in La Palma to reach the Sambú will sit too low in the water to navigate the upper portions of the river. To get any farther upriver, you must negotiate the use of a shallow dugout in one of the Emberá villages. If you don't speak fluent Spanish, these negotiations could prove futile. Be advised that when you rent a boat anywhere in Panama, you're also hiring its owner to operate the vessel. Remember too that you must bring enough gasoline from La Palma to fuel your dugout.

As for guides, only one name jumps to mind when the destination is the Darién: Hernán Araúz. Hernán is widely regarded as *the* guide for Panama's wild eastern province. I've traveled with him here several times and was very impressed with his knowledge of the rivers, the Indians and especially the birds. He's a big guy who packs at least one big gun (legally), but he doesn't take unnecessary risks – even when you push him, as I often did. He's about as levelheaded a person as you're ever likely to meet. Contact information for him appears in the Guides section of the Getting Around chapter.

TROPIC STAR LODGE

Overlooking Bahía Piña, near the southern tip of the Darién, is one of Panama's legendary institutions: Tropic Star Lodge (☎ 264-1165, fax 264-5903 in Panama City; ☎ 800-682-3424, 407-423-9931, fax 407-839-3637 in the USA; www .tropicstar.com). It is the only lodge that serves Bahía Piña, and more International Game Fish Association (IGFA) world records have been broken in the bay than anywhere else – more than 170. At the time of writing, the lodge held 54 world records,

most of them for black, blue and striped marlin and Pacific sailfish.

The facilities include stand-alone cabins, a wing of adjacent rooms, a pool, a restaurant, a bar and porch with lovely bay views, an impressive tackle room and even a so-called 'palace' that was built by a Texas oil tycoon as his home away from home in 1961. The facilities are on a manicured hillside overlooking the protected bay and the lodge's fleet of 31-foot Bertrams, the Ferraris of sport-fishing boats.

Tropic Star's owners and operators, Terri Kittredge Andrews and her husband, Mike Andrews, boast of 85% repeat client business, and I don't doubt it. Everything here is done just right. The multicourse dinners, for example, are a feast; offerings include baked Alaska, cherries jubilee, black bean soup, freshly baked pies and bread, ceviche and always the catch of the day. The mood here is festive, and there's a great sense of camaraderie among the guests, most of whom are millionaires and quite a number of whom are celebrities. (Tropic Star was one of John Wayne's getaways.)

The Andrews' property covers more than 7000 hectares, most of it virgin rainforest. The birding is excellent, and there are also some lovely waterfalls with swimming pools on the grounds. There is a totally secluded white-sand beach a 45-minute hike away, and the bay lends itself well to sea kayaks, which the Andrews have purchased and brought to the lodge. There's even a healthy coral reef for snorkeling.

Tropic Star is only open from mid-December to July, in accordance with the fishing seasons. The prime black marlin season runs from mid-December to April. Pacific sailfish move in from April to July. Striped marlin season is mid-March to May. All species of billfish and nonbillfish can be caught year-round.

At the time this was written, the Andrews were considering keeping their place open the remainder of the year to appeal to ecotourists. They seemed pretty serious about it, and if they follow through on their idea, I'd consider Tropic Star one of Panama's top nature retreats. Because Tropic Star is easily accessed from Panama City – there are regular flights between the capital and the lodge, which has its own airstrip – you might want to contact the Andrews to find out if they decided to stay open year-round. Although the Tropic Star Lodge is quite remote, it's a short trip from the capital by air. And the destination more than makes up for the inconvenience of having to take a plane to get there.

Note that reservations for fishing need to be made an entire year in advance. Per guests' requests, there are no phones at the lodge, nor are there TVs or radios.

Weekly and half-weekly packages are available; both options include the use of a boat with a captain and mate, all meals, and fishing tackle and leaders. Weekly per-person rates include seven nights of lodging and six days of fishing, and they vary with the number of people in a boat: US$5500 (one person in one boat), US$3300 (two people in a boat), US$2650 (three people in a boat) and US$2250 (four people in a boat). Half-weekly rates include four nights of lodging, along with three days of fishing: US$2475 (one person in a boat), US$1485 (two people in a boat), US$1192 (three people in a boat) and US$1012 (four people in a boat). Discounts are available for stays of more than a week. Rates for people who don't want to fish are also available.

Getting There & Away

Aeroperlas (☎ 269-4555 in Panama City) flies from the capital to the Bahía Piña airstrip, which was built by Tropic Star, at 9:30 am every Tuesday, Thursday and Saturday. Planes that land here also stop at the town of Jaqué, 8km away. Which airstrip the plane lands at first seems to depend on the pilot's mood, so be sure to ask if you have arrived at Bahía Piña or Jaqué before you leave the aircraft. A short dirt road links the Bahía Piña airstrip to the Tropic Star Lodge.

The plane that brings you into the area also takes you back out, leaving Bahía Piña at 10:25 am and Jaqué at 10:45 am on Tuesday, Thursday and Saturday; it stops at La Palma. The fare is US$42/84 one-way/

roundtrip. Be sure to make a reservation at least a day in advance.

Aviatur (☎ 270-1748 in Panama City) flies to Bahía Piña and Jaqué three times weekly.

Note: At these and other remote airstrips, it's common for a police officer to ask to see your passport and tourist card (if applicable). It may seem Big-Brotherly, but in the unlikely event that you disappear, it would be very helpful for searchers to know that on the date in question a police officer recorded that, for instance, you were in Jaqué and appeared to be headed for the Colombian border on a tricycle.

RÍO JAQUÉ

If you can spend time on only one river in Panama, I advise making a trip up the Río Jaqué, which empties into the Golfo de Panamá south of Bahía Piña. It's not nearly as jungly or rapidy as other rivers discussed in this book (such as the Ríos Chiriquí, Teribe and Sambú), but it's still a very pleasant way to spend a day.

The small town of **Jaqué**, near the river's mouth, has an airstrip, and travelers can hire boats here. There's one ugly hotel in Jaqué, which wasn't out of business but wasn't open, either, when I passed through town in late 1997.

There are several Emberá villages along the river. I've visited the first village and the next three and found them all fairly westernized. However, few tourists go farther than the first village, so the last three are more pleasant to visit; the kids in one village, for example, had never seen a video recorder and were astonished to see themselves on its built-in monitor when I set the machine on playback for a few minutes.

Unless you look intimidating to the Indians, you should be able to negotiate food and a place to sleep in any of the Emberá villages.

If you make the trip, be sure to bring a bag of candy, which you can buy at the Jaqué market. Emberá – adults as well as children – love candy, so handing some out when you arrive is a very nice way to greet

DARIÉN PROVINCE

them. Keep in mind too that the Emberá would probably close their villages to outsiders if tourists were to frequently pass through without giving anything or buying anything, but only taking photos and invading the Indians' privacy. As noted earlier in this chapter, bringing a Polaroid camera and presenting the Indians with photos of themselves is another great way to score points with these very tolerant people.

Be alert to the fact that the upper portion of the Jaqué runs pretty close to the Colombian border. There may not be any guerrillas in the area, but there almost certainly are Colombian bandits and cocaine labs here. If you stick to the river and the riverside villages, you shouldn't have any run-ins with such people. But please don't go exploring in the jungle, or you may discover something someone wishes you hadn't.

Getting There & Away
If you speak Spanish, you can make the trip up the Río Jaqué without a guide. Simply fly to Jaqué (see flight information under Tropic Star Lodge, above) and start asking around for a boatman. Check first at the ticket office near the airstrip, as the ticket agents are helpful people.

Be sure to tell the boatman at the very outset that you want to go far up the river, to several villages; otherwise he'll assume you want to go only as far as the first village and he won't carry enough gasoline. For a lengthy trip on the river, you'll need to bring several containers of gas, and you'll need to switch to a piragua at some point. Expect to pay US$100 to US$150 for a day on the river, including gas; this price is per party, not per person. Your boatman will acquire the gas.

If you don't speak Spanish, you'll need to find someone who does. This means either calling on a tour operator (see the Tour Companies in Panama section of the Getting Around chapter) or finding a tourist who speaks Spanish and convincing that person to make the trip with you. If you contact a tour operator, emphasize that you want to visit at least three and probably four villages on the river. The idea is to go where most travelers don't, to 'take the road less traveled.' And believe me, very few people take a piragua far up the jungle-flanked Río Jaqué.

Glossary

Note: For food and drink terms, see the Facts for the Visitor chapter. For additional terms and information on the Spanish language, see the Spanish for Travelers section.

Ancon – National Association for the Conservation of Nature, Panama's leading private environmental organization
apartado – post office box (as in mailing addresses)
ATM – automated teller machine

bahía – bay
balboa – the basic unit of Panamanian currency
boroquera – blowgun once used by the Emberá and Wounaan Indians
bote – motorized canoe

cabaña – cabin
cacique – Kuna tribal leader
campesino/a – rural resident, peasant
Carretera Interamericana – the Pan-American Hwy, the nearly continuous highway running from Alaska to Chile (it breaks at the Darién Gap)
cayuco – dugout canoe
cerro – hill
chitra – sand fly
chocosano – violent storm, in Kuna
cine – cinema
comarca – district
cordillera – mountain range
cuatro por cuatro – 4WD vehicle

edificio – building

finca – farm
fuerte – fort

Gali-Gali – the distinct Creole language of Bocas del Toro Province that combines English, Spanish and Guaymí
gringo/a – tourist, especially a North American tourist

habano – Havana cigar
huacas – golden objects made on the Panamanian isthmus in the pre-Columbian era and buried with Indians

iglesia – church
INAC – Panama's National Institute of Culture
INRENARE – National Institute of Renewable Natural Resources, Panama's national environmental agency
IPAT – Panamanian Tourism Institute, the national tourism board
isla – island

lago – lake
lavamático – laundromat
lavandería – dry cleaner

mestizo/a – person of mixed indigenous and Spanish ancestry
metate – flat stone platform used for grinding corn by Panama's pre-Columbian Indians
Migración y Naturalización – Immigration and Naturalization office
mirador – lookout point
molas – colorful hand-stitched appliqué textiles made by Kuna women
muelle – pier
museo – museum

palmilla – mountain palm, sometimes used in hat making
PDF – the Panama Defense Forces, the national army under Manuel Noriega
piragua – canoe carved from a tree trunk
playa – beach
pollera – the intricate, lacy, Spanish-influenced dress of the Península de Azuero; the national dress of Panama for festive occasions
pozos – springs
punta – point

río – river

sendero – trail
serranía – mountain range
STD – sexually transmitted disease

taxi marino – water taxi
típico – Panamanian folkloric music

tortuga – sea turtle
trucha – trout

volcán – volcano

waga – tourist, in Kuna

Spanish for Travelers

Pronunciation

Pronunciation of Spanish is not difficult, given that many Spanish sounds are similar to their English counterparts, and there is a clear and consistent relationship between the pronunciation and the spelling. Unless otherwise indicated, the English words used below to approximate Spanish sounds take standard American pronunciation.

Vowels Spanish has five vowels: **a**, **e**, **i**, **o** and **u**. They are pronounced something like the highlighted letters of the following English words:

a as in 'f**a**ther'
e as in 'm**e**t'
i as in 'f**ee**t'
o as in the British 'h**o**t'
u as in 'b**oo**t'

Diphthongs A diphthong is one syllable made of two vowels, each of which conserves its own sound. Here are some diphthongs in Spanish and their approximate English pronunciations:

ai as in 'h**i**de'
au as in 'h**ow**'
ei as in 'h**ay**'
ia as in '**ya**rd'
ie as in '**ye**s'
oi as in 'b**oy**'
ua as in '**wa**sh'
ue as in '**we**ll'

Consonants Many consonants are pronounced much as they are in English, but there are some exceptions:

c is pronounced like 's' in 'sit' when before 'e' or 'i'; elsewhere, it is like 'k'
ch as in 'choose'
g as the 'g' in 'gate' before 'a,' 'o' and 'u'; before 'e' or 'i', this is a harsh, breathy sound like the 'h' in 'hit.' Note that when 'g' is followed by 'ue' or 'ui,' the 'u' is silent, unless it has a dieresis (ü), in which case it functions much like the English 'w':
    guerra 'GEH-rra'
    güero 'GWEH-ro'
h always silent
j a harsh, guttural sound similar to the 'ch' in Scottish 'loch'

ll as the 'y' in 'yellow'
ñ a nasal sound like the 'ny' in 'canyon'
q as the 'k' in 'kick'; always followed by a silent 'u'
r is a very short rolled 'r'
rr is a longer rolled 'r'
x is like the English 'h' when it follows 'e' or 'i' – otherwise it is like the English 'x' as in 'taxi'; in many Indian words, 'x' is pronounced like the English 'sh'
z is the same as the English 's'; under no circumstances should 's' or 'z' be pronounced like the English 'z' – that sound does not exist in Spanish

There are a few other minor pronunciation differences, but the longer you stay in Panama, the easier they will become. The letter **ñ** is considered a separate letter of the alphabet and follows 'n' in alphabetically organized lists and books, such as dictionaries and phone books.

Stress There are three general rules regarding stress:

- In words ending in a vowel, 'n' or 's,' the stress goes on the penultimate (next-to-last) syllable:

    naranja na-RAHN-ha   *joven* HO-ven   *zapatos* sa-PA-tos

- In words ending in a consonant other than 'n' or 's,' the stress is on the final syllable:

    estoy es-TOY   *ciudad* syoo-DAHD   *catedral* ka-teh-DRAL

- Any deviation from these rules is indicated by an accent:

    México MEH-hee-ko   *mudéjar* moo-DEH-har   *Cortés* cor-TESS

Gender

Nouns in Spanish are either masculine or feminine. Nouns ending in 'o,' 'e' or 'ma' are usually masculine. Nouns ending in 'a,' 'ión' or 'dad' are usually feminine. Some nouns take either a masculine or feminine form, depending on the ending; for example, *viajero* is a male traveler and *viajera* is a female traveler. An adjective usually follows the noun it modifies and must take the same gender as the noun.

Greetings & Civilities

Hello/Hi.	*Hola.*
Good morning/Good day.	*Buenos días.*
Good afternoon.	*Buenas tardes.*
Good evening/Good night.	*Buenas noches.*
See you.	*Hasta luego.*
Goodbye.	*Adiós.*
Pleased to meet you.	*Mucho gusto.*
How are you? (to one person)	*¿Cómo está?*
How are you? (to more than one person)	*¿Cómo están?*
I am fine.	*Estoy bien.*
Please.	*Por favor.*
Thank you.	*Gracias.*
You're welcome.	*De nada.*
Excuse me.	*Perdóneme.*

People

I	*yo*	my wife	*mi esposa*
you (familiar)	*tú*	my husband	*mi esposo, mi marido*
you (formal)	*usted*	my sister	*mi hermana*
you (plural formal)	*ustedes*	my brother	*mi hermano*
he/it	*él*	friend	*pasiero(a)*
she/it	*ella*	Sir/Mr	*Señor*
we	*nosotros*	Madam/Mrs	*Señora*
they (m)	*ellos*	Miss	*Señorita*
they (f)	*ellas*		

Useful Words & Phrases

For words pertaining to food and restaurants, see the Food section in the Facts for the Visitor chapter.

Yes.	*Sí.*	I am . . .	*Estoy . . .*
No.	*No.*	(location or temporary condition)	
What did you say?	*¿Mande?* (colloq)	here	*aquí*
	¿Cómo?	tired (m/f)	*cansado/a*
good/OK	*bueno*	sick/ill (m/f)	*enfermo/a*
bad	*malo*		
better	*mejor*	I am . . .	*Soy . . .*
best	*lo mejor*	(permanent state)	
more	*más*	a worker	*trabajador*
less	*menos*	married	*casado*
very little	*poco* or *poquito*		

Shopping

How much?	*¿Cuánto?*
How much does it cost?	*¿Cuánto cuesta esto?* or *¿Cuánto se cobra?*
How much is it worth?	*¿Cuánto vale?*
I want . . .	*Quiero . . .*
I do not want . . .	*No quiero . . .*
I would like . . .	*Quisiera . . .*
Give me . . .	*Deme . . .*
What do you want?	*¿Qué quiere?*
Do you have . . . ?	*¿Tiene . . . ?*
Is/are there . . . ?	*¿Hay . . . ?*
market	*mercado*
convenience store (usually owned by a Chinese person in Panama)	*tiendita*

Nationalities

American (m/f)	*(norte)americano/a*	English (m/f)	*inglés/inglesa*
Australian (m/f)	*australiano/a*	French (m/f)	*francés/francesa*
British (m/f)	*británico/a*	German (m/f)	*alemán/alemana*
Canadian (m & f)	*canadiense*		

Languages

I speak . . .	*Yo hablo . . .*
I do not speak . . .	*No hablo .*
Do you speak . . . ?	*¿Habla usted . . . ?*
Spanish	*español*
English	*inglés*
German	*alemán*
French	*francés*
I understand.	*Entiendo.*
I do not understand.	*No entiendo.*
Do you understand?	*¿Entiende usted?*
Please speak slowly.	*Por favor hable despacio.*

Crossing the Border

birth certificate	*certificado de nacimiento*
border (frontier)	*la frontera*
car-owner's title	*título de propiedad*
car registration	*registración*
customs	*aduana*
driver's license	*licencia de manejar*
exit permit	*permiso de salida*
identification	*identificación*
immigration	*immigración*
insurance	*seguro*
passport	*pasaporte*
tourist card	*tarjeta de turista*
tourist extension form	*prórroga de turista*
vehicle control certificate	*tarjeta de circulación*
visa	*visado*

Getting Around

avenue	*avenida*	forward, ahead	*adelante*
block	*cuadra*	straight ahead	*todo recto* or *derecho*
boulevard	*bulevar, boulevard*	this way	*por aquí*
corner (of)	*esquina (de)*	that way	*por allí*
corner/bend	*vuelta*	north	*norte (Nte)*
highway	*carretera* or *autopista*	south	*sur*
road	*camino*	east	*este*
street	*calle* or *vía*	east (in an address)	*oriente (Ote)*
to the left	*a la izquierda*	west	*oeste*
to the right	*a la derecha*	west (in an address)	*poniente (Pte)*

Where is . . . ?	*¿Dónde está . . . ?*
the airport	*el aeropuerto*
the bus station	*el terminal de autobuses/central camionera*
the bus station for the interior of the country	*la piquera*
the train station	*la estación del ferrocarril*
a long-distance phone	*un teléfono de larga distancia*
the post office	*el correo*

bus	*camión* or *autobús*
minibus	*colectivo*
city bus stop	*parada*
taxi	*taxi*
train	*tren*
ticket sales counter	*taquilla*
waiting room	*sala de espera*
luggage check-in	*(recibo de) equipaje*
toilet	*sanitario* or *baño*
departure	*salida*
arrival	*llegada*
platform	*andén*
left-luggage room/checkroom	*(guardería* or *guarda) de equipaje*

How far is . . . ?	¿A qué distancia está . . . ?
How long? (How much time?)	¿Cuánto tiempo?
short route	vía corta
a ride (as in hitchhiking)	un bote

Driving

gasoline	gasolina		full	lleno
fuel station	gasolinera		oil	aceite
unleaded	sin plomo		tire	llanta
regular/leaded	regular/con plomo		puncture	agujero
fill the tank	llene el tanque; llenarlo			

How much is a liter of gasoline?	¿Cuánto cuesta el litro de gasolina?
My car has broken down.	Se me ha descompuesto el carro.
I need a tow truck.	Necesito un remolque.
Is there a garage near here?	¿Hay un garaje cerca de aquí?

Accommodations

hotel	hotel		shower	ducha or regadera
guesthouse	casa de huéspedes		hot water	agua caliente
	or pensión		air-conditioning	aire acondicionado
inn	posada		blanket	manta
room	cuarto, habitación		towel	toalla
room with one bed	cuarto sencillo		soap	jabón
room with two beds	cuarto doble		toilet paper	papel higiénico
room for one person	cuarto para una		the check (bill)	la cuenta
	persona			
room for two people	cuarto para dos		What is the price?	¿Cuál es el precio?
	personas		Does that include taxes?	
double bed	cama matrimonial		¿Están incluidos los impuestos?	
twin beds	camas gemelas		Does that include service?	
with bathroom	con baño		¿Está incluido el servicio?	

Money

money	dinero
traveler's checks	cheques de viajero
bank	banco
exchange bureau	casa de cambio
credit card	tarjeta de crédito
exchange rate	tipo de cambio
I want/would like to change some money.	Quiero/quisiera cambiar dinero.
Is there a commission?	¿Hay comisión?

Telephones

telephone	teléfono
telephone call	llamada
telephone number	número telefónico
area code	clave
prefix for long-distance call	prefijo
local call	llamada local
long-distance call	llamada de larga distancia

long-distance telephone	*teléfono de larga distancia*	
coin-operated telephone	*teléfono de monedas*	
long-distance telephone office	*caseta de larga distancia*	
tone	*tono*	
operator	*operador(a)*	
collect (reverse charges)	*por cobrar*	
Dial the number.	*Marque el número.*	
Please wait.	*Favor de esperar.*	
busy	*ocupado*	
toll/cost (of call)	*cuota/costo*	
time and charges	*tiempo y costo*	
Don't hang up.	*No cuelgue.*	

Times & Dates

Monday	*lunes*		tomorrow	*mañana*
Tuesday	*martes*		right now	*horita, ahorita*
Wednesday	*miércoles*		already	*ya*
Thursday	*jueves*		morning	*mañana*
Friday	*viernes*		tomorrow morning	*mañana por la*
Saturday	*sábado*			*mañana*
Sunday	*domingo*		afternoon	*tarde*
yesterday	*ayer*		night	*noche*
today	*hoy*		What time is it?	*¿Qué hora es?*

Numbers

0	*cero*	14	*catorce*	60	*sesenta*	
1	*uno* (m), *una* (f)	15	*quince*	70	*setenta*	
2	*dos*	16	*dieciséis*	80	*ochenta*	
3	*tres*	17	*diecisiete*	90	*noventa*	
4	*cuatro*	18	*dieciocho*	100	*cien*	
5	*cinco*	19	*diecinueve*	101	*ciento uno*	
6	*seis*	20	*veinte*	143	*ciento cuarenta y tres*	
7	*siete*	21	*veintiuno*	200	*doscientos*	
8	*ocho*	22	*veintidós*	500	*quinientos*	
9	*nueve*	30	*treinta*	900	*novecientos*	
10	*diez*	31	*treinta y uno*	1000	*mil*	
11	*once*	32	*treinta y dos*	2000	*dos mil*	
12	*doce*	40	*cuarenta*			
13	*trece*	50	*cincuenta*			

Panamanian Slang & Other Expressions

Think you know enough Spanish? Here's a quick rundown on some of the expressions and colorful colloquialisms you may hear while traveling:

¡Bien cuidado!	literally, 'Well taken care of!'; used by a street person when asking a tip for taking care of your car, normally in parking lots at restaurants, cinemas, bars, etc
salve	street slang for *propina*, or tip
tongo	street slang for cop
chota	street slang for police car
diablo rojo	literally, 'red devil'; refers to public buses

rabiblanco/a	literally, 'white ass'; pejorative reference to a member of the socioeconomic elite
mangajo/a	someone who is filthy
chombo/a	an acceptable reference to black people of Antillean descent
mala leche	literally, 'bad milk'; means bad luck
buena leche	good luck
salado/a	literally, 'salty'; refers to someone with bad luck
ladilla	literally, 'crab louse'; refers to an annoying person
Eso está bien pretty.	refers to something nice
¡Eso está pretty pretty!	refers to something super-nice
¡Entonces laopé!	Hey, dude!
¡Hey, gringo!	Hey, white person! (friendly)
¡Juega vivo!	Be alert, look out for your best interests!
Voy por fuera.	I am leaving right now.
Me estoy comiendo un cable.	literally, 'I am eating a cable'; I'm down on my luck
¡Ayala bestia!	Holy cow!
Chuleta!	common expression similar to 'Holy cow!'
pelao or *pelaito*	common expression for a child
Pa' lante.	Let's go now.
enantes	just now
Eres un comemierda.	refers to someone pretentious
¡Pifioso!	a showoff, or something that looks cool
¿Ven acá tú crees que yo soy un guevón?	Hey man, you think I'm an idiot ?
Tas buena, mami.	You're looking good, mama.
Nos pillamos.	We'll see each other later.
una pinta or *una fría*	a beer
Dame una fría.	Give me a cold one (a beer).
guaro	hard liquor
nueve letras	literally, 'nine letters'; refers to Seco Herrerano (the second word has nine letters)
vuelve loco con vaca	literally, 'makes crazy with cow'; refers to drinking seco and milk
chupata	an all-out drinking party

Index

MAPS

TEXT

SIDEBARS

Int. calling code
  011+ 507+ desired #

<u>In Bocas</u>:
We're staying at <u>La Veranda</u> 757-9211
  [Heather is propriator $16.50/night]
> shared Bath (we're expected around 5:Pm.)
  Fri night ⟶ Sun. night

  <u>Pension Max</u> : 757-?

  Tony Pension _____ : 757-9122

  Jose's cell phone - 614-7811

<u>Bastemientos</u>: RED FROG BEACH
  Bolas - Barnabute ($5/pp
SNORKELING @ HOSPITAL POINT (WATER TAXI = $1/pp)
  HOUSE ABOVE LIVES CLAUDIO & ANGELA.

1ST   2ND RED FROG BEACH
              BLU'S (HERMIT)
                $$/FOOD
                CAMPING
↓   ↓   ↓   ↓
TOWN

Places to stay:
Finca verde (up by Bluff Beach) $40 Is. Colon

LONELY PLANET JOURNEYS

JOURNEYS is a unique collection of travel writing – published by the company that understands travel better than anyone else. It is a series for anyone who has ever experienced – or dreamed of – the magical moment when they encountered a strange culture or saw a place for the first time. They are tales to read while you're planning a trip, while you're on the road or while you're in an armchair, in front of a fire.

JOURNEYS books catch the spirit of a place, illuminate a culture, recount a crazy adventure, or introduce a fascinating way of life. They will always entertain, and always enrich the experience of travel.

'Idiosyncratic, entertainingly diverse and unexpected . . . from an international writership'
– The Australian

'Books which offer a closer look at the people and culture of a destination, and enrich travel experiences'
– American Bookseller

FULL CIRCLE
A South American Journey
Luis Sepúlveda

(translated by Chris Andrews)

Full Circle invites us to accompany Chilean writer Luis Sepúlveda on 'a journey without a fixed itinerary'. Whatever his subject - brutalities suffered under Pinochet's dictatorship, sleepy tropical towns visited in exile, or the landscapes of legendary Patagonia - Sepúlveda is an unflinchingly honest yet lyrical storyteller. Extravagant characters and extraordinary situations are memorably evoked: gauchos organizing a tournament of lies, a scheming heiress on the lookout for a husband, a pilot with a corpse on board his plane . . . Part autobiography, part travel memoir, *Full Circle* brings us the distinctive voice of one of South America's most compelling writers.

Luis Sepúlveda was born in Chile in 1949. Imprisoned by the Pinochet dictatorship for his socialist beliefs, he was for many years a political exile. He has written novels, short stories, plays and essays. His work has attracted many awards and has been translated into numerous languages.

'Detachment, humor and vibrant prose' **– El País**

'an absolute cracker' **– The Bookseller**

This project has been assisted by the Commonwealth Government through the Australian Council, its arts funding and advisory body.

LONELY PLANET PHRASEBOOKS

Building bridges,
Breaking barriers,
Beyond babble-on

Listen for the gems

Speak your own words

Ask your own questions

Master of your own image

- handy pocket-sized books

- easy to understand Pronunciation chapter

- clear and comprehensive Grammar chapter

- romanization alongside script to allow ease of pronunciation

- script throughout so users can point to phrases

- extensive vocabulary sections, words and phrases for every situation

- full of cultural information and tips for the traveler

'... vital for a real DIY spirit and attitude in language learning.' – Backpacker

'the phrasebooks have good cultural backgrounders and offer solid advice for challenging situations in remote locations'
– San Francisco Examiner

'... they are unbeatable for their coverage of the world's more obscure languages'
– The Geographical Magazine

Arabic (Egyptian)
Arabic (Moroccan)
Australian
  *Australian English,
  Aboriginal and Torres Strait
  languages*
Baltic States
  *Estonian, Latvian,
  Lithuanian*
Bengali
Brazilian
Burmese
Cantonese
Central Asian
Central Europe
  *Czech, French, German,
  Hungarian, Italian and Slovak*
Eastern Europe
Ethiopian Amharic
Fijian
French
German
Greek

Hindi/Urdu
Indonesian
Italian
Japanese
Korean
Lao
Latin American Spanish
Malay
Mandarin
Mediterranean Europe
  *Albanian, Croatian, Greek,
  Italian, Macedonian, Maltese,
  Serbian, Slovene*
Mongolian
Nepali
Pidgin (Papua New Guinea)
Pilipino (Tagalog)
Quechua
Russian
Scandinavian Europe
  *Danish, Finnish, Icelandic,
  Norwegian and Swedish*

South East Asia
  *Burmese, Indonesian, Khmer,
  Lao, Malay, Tagalog (Pilipino),
  Thai and Vietnamese*
Spanish (Castilian)
  Basque, Catalan and Galician
Sri Lanka
Swahili
Thai
Thai Hill Tribes
Tibetan
Turkish
Ukrainian
USA
  *US English, Vernacular,
  Native American languages
  and Hawaiian*
Vietnamese
Western Europe
  *Basque, Catalan, Dutch,
  French, German, Irish, Italian,
  Portuguese, Scottish, Gaelic,
  Spanish (Castilian) and Welsh*

LONELY PLANET TRAVEL ATLASES

Lonely Planet has long been famous for the number and quality of its guidebook maps. Now we've gone one step further and produced a handy companion series: Lonely Planet travel atlases–maps of a country produced in book form.

Unlike other maps, which look good but lead travelers astray, our travel atlases have been researched on the road by Lonely Planet's experienced team of writers. All details are carefully checked to ensure the atlas corresponds with the equivalent Lonely Planet guidebook.

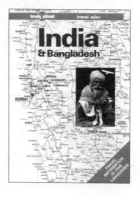

The handy atlas format means no holes, wrinkles, torn sections or constant folding and unfolding. These atlases can survive long periods on the road, unlike cumbersome fold-out maps. The comprehensive index ensures easy reference.

- full-color throughout
- maps researched and checked by Lonely Planet authors
- place names correspond with Lonely Planet guidebooks – no confusing spelling differences
- legend and traveling information in English, French, German, Japanese and Spanish
- size: 230 x 160 mm

Available now:
Chile & Easter Island • Egypt • India & Bangladesh • Israel & the Palestinian Territories • Jordan, Syria & Lebanon • Kenya • Laos • Portugal • South Africa, Lesotho & Swaziland • Thailand • Turkey • Vietnam • Zimbabwe, Botswana & Namibia

LONELY PLANET TV SERIES & VIDEOS

Lonely Planet travel guides have been brought to life on television screens around the world. Like our guides, the programs are based on the joy of independent travel, and look honestly at some of the most exciting, picturesque and frustrating places in the world. Each show is presented by one of three travelers from Australia, England or the USA and combines an innovative mixture of video, Super-8 film, atmospheric soundscapes and original music.

Videos of each episode–containing additional footage not shown on television–are available from good book and video shops, but the availability of individual videos varies with regional screening schedules.

Video destinations include: Alaska • American Rockies • Australia (Southeast) • Baja California • Brazil • Central Asia • Chile & Easter Island • Corsica, Sicily & Sardinia • East Africa, Tanzania & Zanzibar • Ecuador & the Galápagos Islands • France • Greenland & Iceland • Indonesia • Israel & the Sinai Desert • Jamaica • Japan • La Ruta Maya • Morocco • New York City • North India (Varanasi to the Himalayas) • Pacific Islands • South India • Southwest China • Turkey • Vietnam • West Africa • Zimbabwe, Botswana & Namibia

The Lonely Planet TV series is produced by:
Pilot Productions
The Old Studio
18 Middle Row
London W10 5AT UK

For video availability and ordering information, contact your nearest Lonely Planet office.

Music from the TV series is available on CD & cassette.

PLANET TALK

Lonely Planet's FREE quarterly newsletter

We love hearing from you and think you'd like to hear from us.
When... is the right time to see reindeer in Finland?
Where... can you hear the best palm-wine music in Ghana?
How... do you get from Asunción to Areguá by steam train?
What... is the best way to see India?

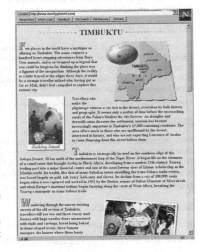

For the answer to these and many other questions, read PLANET TALK.

Every issue is packed with up-to-date travel news and advice including:

- a letter from Lonely Planet founders Tony and Maureen Wheeler
- travel diary from a Lonely Planet author–find out what it's really like out on the road
- feature article on an important and topical travel issue
- a selection of recent letters from our readers
- the latest travel news from all over the world
- details on Lonely Planet's new and forthcoming releases

To join our mailing list, contact any Lonely Planet office.

Also available: Lonely Planet T-shirts. 100% heavyweight cotton (S, M, L, XL)

LONELY PLANET ONLINE

Get the latest travel information before you leave or while you're on the road

Whether you've just begun planning your next trip or you're chasing down specific info on currency regulations or visa requirements, check out Lonely Planet Online for up-to-the-minute travel information.

As well as travel profiles of your favorite destinations (including maps and photos), you'll find current reports from our researchers and other travelers, updates on health and visas, travel advisories, and discussion of the ecological and political issues you need to be aware of as you travel.

There's also an online travelers' forum where you can share your experience of life on the road, meet travel companions and ask other travelers for their recommendations and advice. We also have plenty of links to other online sites useful to independent travelers.

And of course we have a complete and up-to-date list of all Lonely Planet travel products, including guides, phrasebooks, atlases, Journeys and videos and a simple online ordering facility if you can't find the book you want elsewhere.

www.lonelyplanet.com or AOL keyword: lp

LONELY PLANET PRODUCTS

Lonely Planet is known worldwide for publishing practical, reliable and no-nonsense travel information in our guides and on our web site. The Lonely Planet list covers just about every accessible part of the world. Currently there are nine series: *travel guides, shoestring guides, walking guides, city guides, phrasebooks, audio packs, travel atlases, Journeys*–a unique collection of travel writing–and *Pisces Books* (diving and snorkeling guides).

EUROPE

Amsterdam • Austria • Baltic States & Kaliningrad • Baltic States phrasebook • Britain • Central Europe on a shoestring • Central Europe phrasebook • Czech & Slovak Republics • Denmark • Dublin • Eastern Europe on a shoestring • Eastern Europe phrasebook • Finland • France • French phrasebook • Germany • German phrasebook • Greece • Greek phrasebook • Hungary • Iceland, Greenland & the Faroe Islands • Ireland • Italy • Italian phrasebook • Lisbon • London • Mediterranean Europe on a shoestring • Mediterranean Europe phrasebook • Paris • Poland • Portugal • Portugal travel atlas • Prague • Romania & Moldova • Russia, Ukraine & Belarus • Russian phrasebook • Scandinavian & Baltic Europe on a shoestring • Scandinavian Europe phrasebook • Slovenia • Spain • Spanish phrasebook • St Petersburg • Switzerland • Trekking in Greece • Trekking in Spain • Ukrainian phrasebook • Vienna • Walking in Britain • Walking in Italy • Walking in Switzerland • Western Europe on a shoestring • Western Europe phrasebook

NORTH AMERICA

Alaska • Backpacking in Alaska • Baja California • Bermuda • California & Nevada • Canada • Chicago • Deep South • Florida • Hawaii • Honolulu • Los Angeles • Mexico • Mexico City • Miami • New England • New Orleans • New York City • New York, New Jersey & Pennsylvania • Pacific Northwest USA • Rocky Mountains USA • San Francisco • Seattle • Southwest USA • USA phrasebook • Washington, DC & The Capital Region

CENTRAL AMERICA & THE CARIBBEAN

Bahamas, Turks & Caicos • Central America on a shoestring • Costa Rica • Cuba • Eastern Caribbean • Guatemala, Belize & Yucatán: La Ruta Maya • Jamaica • Panama

SOUTH AMERICA

Argentina, Uruguay & Paraguay • Bolivia • Brazil • Brazilian phrasebook • Buenos Aires • Chile & Easter Island • Chile travel atlas • Colombia • Ecuador & the Galápagos Islands • Latin American Spanish phrasebook • Peru • Quechua phrasebook • Rio de Janeiro • South America on a shoestring • Trekking in the Patagonian Andes • Venezuela

Travel Literature: Full Circle: A South American Journey

AFRICA

Arabic (Moroccan) phrasebook • Africa on a shoestring • Africa–The South • Cape Town • Cairo • Central Africa • East Africa • Egypt & the Sudan • Egypt travel atlas • Ethiopian (Amharic) phrasebook • Kenya • Kenya travel atlas • Malawi, Mozambique & Zambia • Morocco • North Africa • South Africa, Lesotho & Swaziland • South Africa travel atlas • Swahili phrasebook • Trekking in East Africa • Tunisia • West Africa • Zimbabwe, Botswana & Namibia • Zimbabwe, Botswana & Namibia travel atlas

Travel Literature: The Rainbird: A Central African Journey • Songs to an African Sunset: A Zimbabwean Story

ISLANDS OF THE INDIAN OCEAN

Madagascar & Comoros • Maldives & Islands of the East Indian Ocean • Mauritius, Réunion & Seychelles

Also Available: Brief Encounters • Travel with Children • Traveller's Tales

MAIL ORDER

Lonely Planet products are distributed worldwide. They are also available by mail order from Lonely Planet, so if you have difficulty finding a title please write to us. North American and South American residents should write to 150 Linden St, Oakland CA 94607, USA; European and African residents should write to 10A Spring Place, London NW5 3BH, UK; and residents of other countries to PO Box 617, Hawthorn, Victoria 3122, Australia.

NORTH-EAST ASIA

Beijing • Cantonese phrasebook • China • Hong Kong • Hong Kong, Macau & Canton • Japan • Japanese phrasebook • Japanese audio pack • Korea • Korean phrasebook • Mandarin phrasebook • Mongolia • Mongolian phrasebook • North-East Asia on a shoestring • Seoul • Taiwan • Tibet • Tibet phrasebook • Tokyo

Travel Literature: Lost Japan

MIDDLE EAST & CENTRAL ASIA

Arab Gulf States • Arabic (Egyptian) phrasebook • Cairo • Central Asia • Central Asia phrasebook • Iran • Israel & the Palestinian Territories • Israel & the Palestinian Territories travel atlas • Istanbul • Jerusalem • Jordan & Syria • Jordan, Syria & Lebanon travel atlas • Lebanon • Middle East • Turkey • Turkey travel atlas • Turkish phrasebook • Trekking in Turkey • Yemen

Travel Literature: The Gates of Damascus • Kingdom of the Film Stars: Journey into Jordan

INDIAN SUBCONTINENT

Bengali phrasebook • Bangladesh • Delhi • Goa • Hindi/Urdu phrasebook • India • India & Bangladesh travel atlas • Indian Himalaya • Karakoram Highway • Nepal • Nepali phrasebook • Pakistan • Rajasthan • Sri Lanka • Sri Lanka phrasebook • Trekking in the Indian Himalaya • Trekking in the Karakoram & Hindukush • Trekking in the Nepal Himalaya

Travel Literature: In Rajasthan • Shopping for Buddhas

SOUTH-EAST ASIA

Bali & Lombok • Bangkok • Burmese phrasebook • Cambodia • Ho Chi Minh • Indonesia • Indonesian phrasebook • Indonesian audio pack • Jakarta • Java • Laos • Lao phrasebook • Laos travel atlas • Malay phrasebook • Malaysia, Singapore & Brunei • Myanmar (Burma) • Philippines • Pilipino phrasebook • Singapore • South-East Asia on a shoestring • Thailand • Thailand's Islands & Beaches • Thai phrasebook • Thailand travel atlas • Thai audio pack • Thai Hill Tribes phrasebook • Vietnam • Vietnamese phrasebook • Vietnam travel atlas

ANTARCTICA

Antarctica

AUSTRALIA & THE PACIFIC

Australia • Australian phrasebook • Bushwalking in Australia • Bushwalking in Papua New Guinea • Fiji • Fijian phrasebook • Islands of Australia's Great Barrier Reef • Melbourne • Micronesia • New Caledonia • New South Wales & the ACT • New Zealand • Northern Territory • Outback Australia • Papua New Guinea • Papua New Guinea phrasebook • Queensland • Rarotonga & the Cook Islands • Samoa • Solomon Islands • South Australia • Sydney • Tahiti & French Polynesia • Tasmania • Tonga • Tramping in New Zealand • Vanuatu • Victoria • Western Australia

Travel Literature: Islands in the Clouds • Sean & David's Long Drive

THE LONELY PLANET STORY

Lonely Planet published its first book in 1973 in response to the numerous 'How did you do it?' questions Maureen and Tony Wheeler were asked after driving, bussing, hitching, sailing and railing their way from England to Australia.

Written at a kitchen table and hand collated, trimmed and stapled, *Across Asia on the Cheap* became an instant local best seller, inspiring thoughts of another book.

Eighteen months in South-East Asia resulted in their second guide, *South-East Asia on a shoestring*, which they put together in a backstreet Chinese hotel in Singapore in 1975. The 'yellow bible', as it quickly became known to backpackers around the world, soon became the guide to the region. It has sold well over half a million copies and is now in its 9th edition, still retaining its familiar yellow cover.

Today there are 240 titles, including travel guides, walking guides, language kits & phrasebooks, travel atlases, diving guides and travel literature. The company is the largest independent travel publisher in the world. Although Lonely Planet initially specialized in guides to Asia, today there are few corners of the globe that have not been covered.

The emphasis continues to be on travel for independent travelers. Tony and Maureen still travel for several months of each year and play an active part in the writing, updating and quality control of Lonely Planet's guides.

They have been joined by over 70 authors and 170 staff at our offices in Melbourne (Australia), Oakland (USA), London (UK) and Paris (France). Travelers themselves also make a valuable contribution to the guides through the feedback we receive in thousands of letters each year and on our website.

The people at Lonely Planet strongly believe that travelers can make a positive contribution to the countries they visit, both through their appreciation of the countries' culture, wildlife and natural features, and through the money they spend. In addition, the company makes a direct contribution to the countries and regions it covers. Since 1986 a percentage of the income from each book has been donated to ventures such as famine relief in Africa; aid projects in India; agricultural projects in Central America; Greenpeace's efforts to halt French nuclear testing in the Pacific; and Amnesty International.

'I hope we send people out with the right attitude about travel. You realize when you travel that there are so many different perspectives about the world, so we hope these books will make people more interested in what they see. Guidebooks can't really guide people. All you can do is point them in the right direction.'

– Tony Wheeler

LONELY PLANET PUBLICATIONS

Australia
PO Box 617, Hawthorn 3122, Victoria
☎ (03) 9819 1877 fax (03) 9819 6459
e-mail talk2us@lonelyplanet.com.au

USA
150 Linden Street
Oakland, California 94607
☎ (510) 893 8555, TOLL FREE (800) 275 8555
fax (510) 893 8572
e-mail info@lonelyplanet.com

UK
10A Spring Place, London NW5 3BH, UK
☎ (0171) 428 4800 fax (0171) 428 4828
e-mail go@lonelyplanet.co

France
1 rue du Dahomey, 75011 Paris
☎ 01 55 25 33 00 fax 01 55 25 33 01
e-mail bip@lonelyplanet.fr

World Wide Web: www.lonelyplanet.com or *AOL keyword: lp*